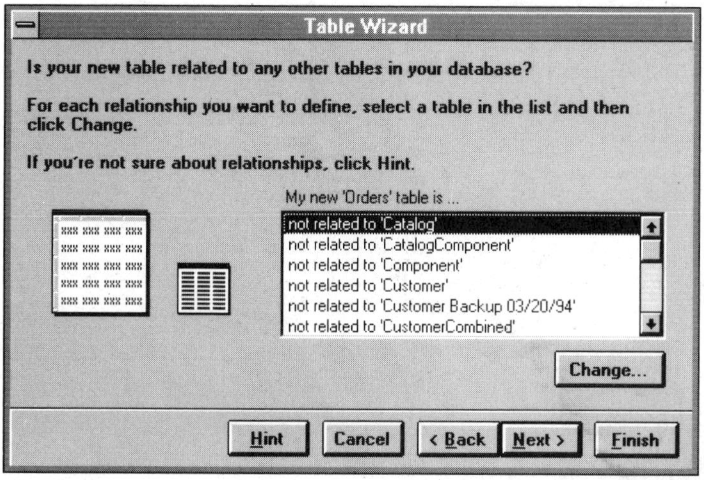
Table Wizard
Is your new table related to any other tables in your database?
For each relationship you want to define, select a table in the list and then click Change.
If you're not sure about relationships, click Hint.
My new 'Orders' table is ...
not related to 'Catalog'
not related to 'CatalogComponent'
not related to 'Component'
not related to 'Customer'
not related to 'Customer Backup 03/20/94'
not related to 'CustomerCombined'
Change...
Hint
Cancel
< Back
Next >
Finish

Step 3:

Confirm how your new table is related to other tables.

Step 4:

Tell the Wizard whether you want to make additional design changes, or begin editing the data.

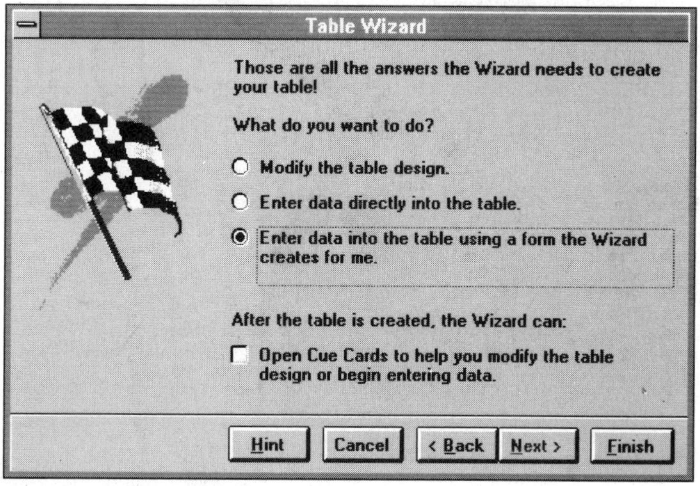
Table Wizard
Those are all the answers the Wizard needs to create your table!
What do you want to do?
Modify the table design.
Enter data directly into the table.
Enter data into the table using a form the Wizard creates for me.
After the table is created, the Wizard can:
Open Cue Cards to help you modify the table design or begin entering data.
Hint
Cancel
< Back
Next >
Finish

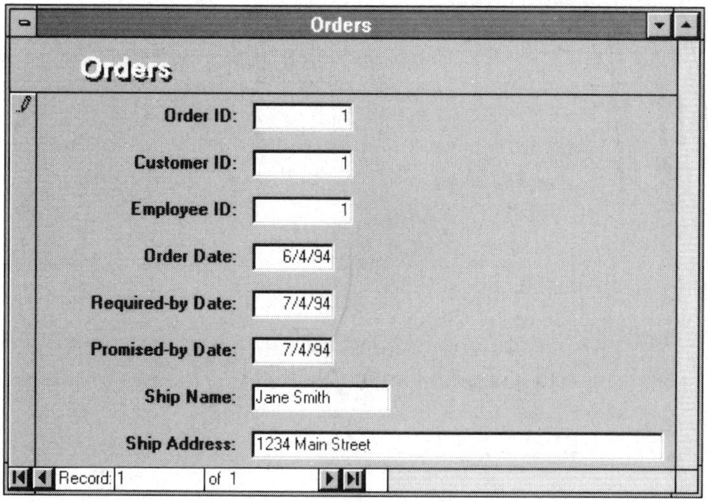
Orders
Orders
Order ID: 1
Customer ID: 1
Employee ID: 1
Order Date: 6/4/94
Required-by Date: 7/4/94
Promised-by Date: 7/4/94
Ship Name: Jane Smith
Ship Address: 1234 Main Street
Record: 1 of 1

Step 5:

Presto! You can begin working with your table.

RUNNING Microsoft ACCESS® 2 FOR WINDOWS™

Microsoft PRESS

JOHN L. VIESCAS

PUBLISHED BY
Microsoft Press
A Division of Microsoft Corporation
One Microsoft Way
Redmond, Washington 98052-6399

Library of Congress Cataloging-in-Publication Data
Viescas, John L., 1947–
Running Microsoft Access 2 : for Windows
John L. Viescas.
p. cm.
Includes index.
ISBN 1-55615-592-1
1. Data base management. 2. Microsoft Access. I. Title.
QA76.9.D3V555 1994
005.75'65--dc20 93-48486
CIP

Printed and bound in the United States of America.

4 5 6 7 8 9 AG-M 9 8 7 6 5

Distributed to the book trade in Canada by Macmillan of Canada, a division of Canada Publishing Corporation.

A CIP catalogue record for this book is available from the British Library.

Microsoft Press books are available through booksellers and distributors worldwide. For further information about international editions, contact your local Microsoft Corporation office. Or contact Microsoft Press International directly at fax (206) 936-7329.

Acquisitions Editor: Dean Holmes
Project Editor: Jack Litewka
Technical Editor: Jim Fuchs

Acknowledgments

Many thanks, for the second time around, to Steve Alboucq and his incredible support team, who monitor the forums on CompuServe. These folks did a magnificent job running the beta test forum for Microsoft Access version 2 while also keeping up with the huge volume of messages on the "regular" forum every day. Without their support on CompuServe, folks like me who write books about new software would have a heck of a time sorting out the bugs from just plain goofs. Special thanks to Scott Fallon, the Microsoft product manager responsible for spearheading the version 2 effort, and to Michael Mee, who helped us all understand the intricacies of the new data access objects.

This book wouldn't have happened without the tireless efforts of Jack Litewka, my manuscript and project editor, and Jim Fuchs, technical editor par excellence. Somehow, Jack manages to take my writing and make it crystal clear without hampering my style. And I'm not sure I know when Jim found time to eat or sleep during the final weeks of this intense project. There are also lots of other folks working behind the scenes at Microsoft Press to ensure the high quality of every book they produce—thanks to all of them.

Thanks go to Dave Rygmyr and Craig Parsons of Prompt Computer Solutions, Inc., who again allowed me to use their small business application as the core example throughout this book. Thanks also to Peter Raulerson of ParaTechnology, Inc., for allowing me to use his information database as one of the examples in this book.

Finally, special thanks to my entire family, who put up with my work schedule over the holidays and let me hide out in my upstairs office so that I could finish crucial chapters on time. And thanks to Halibut, my "fur person," who curled up under the lamp on my desk every day to keep me company. Now, if I could just teach him how to design a database....

John Viescas

Chapters at a Glance

Table of Contents

Using the Companion Disk

Bound into the back of this book is a 3.5-inch 1.44-megabyte companion disk. The companion disk contains PROMPT.MDB, a fully functional database that illustrates the examples in the book. Also included are four additional sample databases that show you efficient table designs for common applications.

Backing Up the Companion Disk

You should back up the companion disk before you install the disk's files. To do so, use a blank 3.5-inch 1.44-MB disk and follow this procedure:

1. Start Windows File Manager.
2. Place the companion disk in your 3.5-inch floppy-disk drive.
3. Choose the Copy Disk command from the Copy menu.
4. Select the source and the destination drive, and then click OK.
5. Respond to the on-screen prompts.

When you've finished, put the original companion disk in a safe place and use the copy to install the sample databases.

Installing the Companion Disk

To install the files found on the companion disk, place the copy of the disk in your 3.5-inch floppy-disk drive and type

```
A:\INSTALL
```

at the command prompt. (Type *B:\INSTALL* if your 3.5-inch floppy-disk drive is drive B.) Follow the on-screen instructions.

Every effort has been made to ensure the accuracy of the book and this disk. If you encounter a problem, please contact Microsoft Press at the following address:

Microsoft Press
Attn: Running Microsoft Access Editor
One Microsoft Way
Redmond, WA 98052-6399

No telephone calls, please.

Introduction

In 1993, Microsoft Access arguably became the most popular database software ever introduced. Thanks in part to a shrewd "introductory" price of only $99 in the United States, the product can claim an incredibly large user base—more than 1,000,000 copies sold. The vast majority of Microsoft Access users have discovered that Access is far more valuable than its introductory price might have implied. I've seen overflowing Access sessions at Microsoft's Tech*Ed conferences; I've taught oversold seminars on the product, from introductory to advanced levels; and I've seen everyone from novice end users to developers of advanced database applications making productive use of the product. The high volume of activity on the MSACCESS forum on CompuServe is another testament to the success of the product.

Microsoft Access is really just one part of Microsoft Corporation's overall data management product strategy. Microsoft Access is not just a database; it also complements other database products because it has several powerful features. Microsoft Access <u>does</u> have a data storage system, and like all good relational databases, it allows you to link related information easily—for example, customer and order data that you enter. One of the real strengths of Microsoft Access, as its name implies, is that it can work with data from other sources, including many popular PC database programs (such as dBASE, Paradox, FoxPro, and Btrieve) and many SQL (structured query language) databases on servers, minicomputers, and mainframes. With the implementation of advanced OLE 2 (Object Linking and Embedding) in version 2, Access now fully integrates with the other applications in the Microsoft Office package: Microsoft Word 6, Microsoft Excel 5, PowerPoint 3, and Microsoft Mail.

Microsoft Access also has a very sophisticated application development system for the Microsoft Windows operating system, which makes extensive use of information about your data—whatever the data source—to help you build applications quickly. In fact, you can build simple applications by defining (literally drawing on the screen) forms and reports based on your data and linking them together with a few simple macros or a few Microsoft Access Basic statements; there's no need to write any complex code in the classical programming sense.

For small businesses (and for consultants creating applications for small businesses), Microsoft Access is all that's required to store and manage the data used to run the business. Microsoft Access coupled with Microsoft SQL Server is an ideal way for many medium-sized companies to build new applications for Windows very quickly and inexpensively. For large corporations having both a big investment in mainframe relational database applications and a proliferation of desktop applications that rely on PC databases, Microsoft Access provides the tools to easily link host and PC data in a single Windows-based application.

About This Book

If you're developing a database application, this book gives you a thorough understanding of "programming without pain" using Microsoft Access. The book provides a solid foundation for designing databases, forms, and reports and getting them all to work together. You'll discover you can quickly create complex applications by linking design elements with Microsoft Access's powerful macro facilities or with easy-to-understand Microsoft Access Basic language. Even if someone else has built most of the application for you, you'll find this book useful for understanding how to use an Access application and for extending that application to suit your changing needs.

Running Microsoft Access 2 is divided into six major parts:

Part 1 gives you a thorough overview of Microsoft Access. Chapter 1 describes how Microsoft Access fits into the world of personal computer database systems; Chapter 2 describes how you might use Microsoft Access; and Chapter 3 takes you on a tour of Microsoft Access, introducing you to the basic concepts and terminology. Chapter 3 also provides summaries of all the new features in version 2.0.

Part 2 tells you how to design, define, and modify database definitions in Microsoft Access. Starting with a good design is the key to building easy-to-use applications. Chapter 4 explains a fairly simple, yet methodical, technique that you can use to design a good relational database application with little effort. Even old pros might appreciate this technique.

Part 3 focuses on working with data. Here you'll learn not only how to add, update, delete, or replace data in a Microsoft Access database but also how to design queries to work with data from multiple tables, calculate values, or update many records with one command. The heart of the book is perhaps Chapter 10, "Importing, Attaching, and Exporting Data." Here you'll learn how Microsoft Access can connect you to many other popular databases, spreadsheets, and even text data. Chapter 11 in this new edition includes a comprehensive look at the SQL database language that Access uses to manage and update its data.

Part 4 is all about forms. Chapter 12 introduces you to forms—what they look like and how they work. The remaining chapters provide you with an extensive tutorial on designing, building, and implementing simple and complex forms, including use of the Form Wizard feature.

Part 5 gives you detailed information about reports. The first chapter in this part leads you on a guided tour of reports and explains the major features that you can use. The following chapters teach you how to design, build, and implement both simple and complex reports in your application.

Part 6 shows you how to bring together tables, queries, forms, and reports. You'll learn how to use the programming facilities in Microsoft Access—macros and Microsoft Access Basic—to make your database application "come alive." First, you'll learn how to create Microsoft Access macros and how to use them to link forms and reports in an application. Chapter 21 introduces you to Access Basic, and the last two chapters show you how to use the powerful new Code Behind Forms feature to create really robust production applications.

Throughout this book you'll see examples that explain how to build major portions of a Microsoft Access application for a small computer company (Prompt Computer Solutions, Inc.). You can find this sample database

(PROMPT), as well as databases that provide the table designs for several other types of common applications, on the companion disk provided with this book. (See page xxiv, "Using the Companion Disk," for details.) Please note that the companies, names, and data used in the PROMPT database are fictitious.

Running Microsoft Access 2 also contains two appendixes. Appendix A provides instructions for installing Access over a network, shows you how to define and manage connections using Open Database Connectivity, and explains how to convert a version 1.0 or 1.1 database to version 2.0. Appendix B provides the definitions for all the tables used in the PROMPT sample database; it also provides four other sample database schemas.

Conventions Used in This Book

The following conventions are used throughout this book to represent keystroke and mouse operations:

Convention	Meaning
Alt-F	Press and hold down the Alt key, and then, while holding down Alt, press the F key.
Alt,F	Press the Alt key, release it, and then press the F key.
Choose	Pick and execute an item on a menu or in an option group.
Select	Highlight a field in a table or an item in a list.
Click	Move the mouse pointer to the named item, and press the left mouse button once.
Double-click	Move the mouse pointer to the named item, and press the left mouse button twice in rapid succession.
Drag	Move the mouse pointer to the named item, press the left mouse button, and then move the mouse pointer while holding down the left mouse button.
Enter	Type in a value, as in "Enter a name for the file in the File Name text box."
Press	Press the named key on your keyboard, as in "Select the file you want to open, and then press the Enter key."

PART 1

Understanding Microsoft Access

1

Microsoft Access Is a Database and More

If you're a serious user of a personal computer, you've probably been using word processing or spreadsheet applications to help you solve problems. You might have started a number of years ago with character-based products running under MS-DOS but have since upgraded to software that runs under the Microsoft Windows operating system. You might also own some database software, either as part of an integrated package such as Microsoft Works or as a separate program.

Database programs have been available for personal computers for a long time. Unfortunately, these programs have been either simple data storage managers that really aren't suitable for building applications or so complex and difficult to use that even many computer-literate people have avoided database systems unless handed a complete, custom-built database application. Microsoft Access, however, represents a significant turnaround in ease of use, and many people are drawn to create their own useful databases and full database applications.

Now that Microsoft Access is in its second release and has become an even more robust product, perhaps it's time to take another look at how you work with your personal computer to get the job done. If you've previously shied away from personal computer database software because you felt you needed programming skills or because it would take you too much time to get the job done, you'll be pleasantly surprised at how easy it is to work with Access. But how do you decide whether you're ready to move up to a database system such as Access? To help you decide, let's take a look at the advantages of using database application development software such as Microsoft Access.

What Is a Database?

In the simplest sense, a *database* is a collection of records and files that are organized for a particular purpose. On your computer system, you might keep the names and addresses of all your friends or customers. Perhaps you collect all the letters you write and organize them by recipient. You might have another set of files in which you keep all your financial data—accounts payable and accounts receivable or your checkbook entries and balances. The word processor documents that you organize by topic are one type of database. The spreadsheet files that you organize according to their uses are another type of database.

If you're very organized, you can probably manage several hundred spreadsheets by using directories and subdirectories. When you do this, you're the database manager. But what do you do when the problems you're trying to solve get too big? How can you easily collect information about all customers and their orders when the data might be stored in several document and spreadsheet files? How can you maintain linkages between the files when you enter new information? How do you ensure that data is being entered correctly? What if you need to share your information with many people but don't want two people to try updating the same data at the same time? Faced with these challenges, you need a *database management system (DBMS).*

Relational Databases

Nearly all modern database management systems store and handle information using the *relational* database management model. The name *relational* stems from the fact that each record in the database contains information *related* to a single subject and only that subject. Also, data about two classes of information (such as customers and orders) can be manipulated as a single entity based on *related* data values. For example, it would be redundant to store customer name and address information with every order that the customer placed. So, in a relational system, the information about orders contains a data field that stores data, such as a customer number, that can be used to connect each order with customer information.

In a relational database management system, sometimes called an *RDBMS,* the system manages all data in tables. Tables store information about a subject (such as customers) and have columns that contain the different kinds of information about the subject (for example, customers' addresses) and rows that describe all the attributes of a single instance of the subject (for example, data on a specific customer). Even when you use one of the DBMS facilities to fetch information from one or more tables (often called a *query*), the result is always something that looks like another table. In fact, you can execute one query that uses the results of another query.

Some Relational Database Terminology

- *Relation*—Information about a single subject such as customers or orders or employees. A relation is usually stored as a *table* in a relational database management system.
- *Attribute*—A specific piece of information about a subject, such as the address for a customer or the salary for an employee. An attribute is normally stored as a data *column* or *field* in a *table*.
- *Relationship*—The way information in one *relation* is related to information in another *relation*. For example, customers have a *one-to-many relationship* with orders because one customer can place many orders, but any order belongs to only one customer.
- *Join*—The process of linking tables or queries on tables via their related data values. For example, customers might be joined to orders on matching customer ID.

See Chapter 4, "Designing Your Database Application," for more details.

You can also *join* information from multiple tables or queries on *related* values. For example, you can connect customer information with order information to find out which customers placed which orders. You can connect employee information with order information to find out which salesperson handled the order.

Database Capabilities

A database management system gives you complete control over how you define your data, work with it, and share it with others. The system also provides you with sophisticated features that make it easy to catalog and manage large amounts of data in many tables. A database manager has three main types of capabilities: data definition, data manipulation, and data control.

All this functionality is contained in the powerful features of Microsoft Access. Let's take a look at how Access implements these capabilities and compare them to what you can do with spreadsheet or word processing programs.

Microsoft Access as an RDBMS

Microsoft Access is a fully functional relational database management system (RDBMS). It provides all the data definition, data manipulation, and data control features you need to manage large volumes of data.

Main Functions of a Database

- *Data definition*—You can define what data will be stored in your database, the type of data (for example, numbers or characters), and how the data is related. In some cases, you can also define how the data should be formatted and how the data should be validated.
- *Data manipulation*—You can work with the data in many ways. You can select which data fields you want, filter the data, and sort it. You can join data with other related information and summarize (total) the data.
- *Data control*—You can define who is allowed to read, update, or insert data. In many cases, you can also define how data can be shared and updated by multiple users.

Data Definition and Storage

While you're working with a document or a spreadsheet, you generally have complete freedom to define the contents of the document or each cell in the sheet. Within a given page in a document, you might include paragraphs of text, a table, a chart, or multiple columns of data displayed with multiple fonts. Within a given column on a spreadsheet, you might have text data at the top to define column headers for printing or display, and you might have various numeric formats within the column, depending on the function of the row. You need this flexibility because your word processing document must be able to convey your message within the context of a printed page, and your spreadsheet must store the data you're analyzing as well as provide for calculation and presentation of the desired result.

This flexibility is great for solving relatively small, well-defined business problems. But a spreadsheet becomes difficult to manage when it contains more than a few hundred rows of information, and documents become unwieldy when they extend beyond a few dozen pages. As the amount of data grows, you might also find that you exceed the data storage limits of your spreadsheet or word processing program or of your computer system. If you design a document or spreadsheet to be used by others, it's difficult (if not impossible) to control how they will use the data or enter new data. For example, on a spreadsheet, even though one cell might need a date and another a currency value to make sense, the user might easily enter character data in error.

Some spreadsheet programs allow you to define a "database" area within a spreadsheet to help you manage the information you need to produce the desired result. However, you are still constrained by the basic storage limitations of the spreadsheet program, and you still don't have much control over what's entered in the rows and columns of the "database" area. Also, if you need to handle more than number and character data, you might find that your spreadsheet doesn't understand such things as pictures or sounds.

A DBMS allows you to define the kind of data you have and how the data should be stored. You can also usually define rules that the DBMS can use to ensure the integrity of your data. In its simplest form, a *validation rule* might ensure that you can't accidentally store alphabetic characters in a field that should contain a number. Other rules might define valid values or ranges of values for your data. In the most sophisticated systems, you can define the relationship between collections of data (usually called tables or files) and ask the DBMS to ensure that your data remains consistent. For example, you could have the system automatically check to ensure that every order is entered for a valid customer.

With Microsoft Access, you have complete flexibility to define your data (as text, numbers, dates, times, currency, pictures, sounds, documents, spreadsheets), to define how Access stores your data (string length, number precision, date/time precision), and to define what the data looks like when you display or print it. You can define simple or complex validation rules to ensure that only accurate values exist in your database. You can request that Access check for valid relationships between files or tables in your database.

Because Microsoft Access is a state-of-the-art application for Microsoft Windows, you can use all the facilities of *Dynamic Data Exchange (DDE)* and *Object Linking and Embedding (OLE)*. DDE lets you execute functions and send data between Microsoft Access and any other Windows-based application that supports DDE. You can also make DDE connections to other applications using macros or Access Basic. OLE is an advanced Windows capability that allows you to link objects to or embed objects in your Microsoft Access database. Objects include pictures, graphs, spreadsheets, or documents from other applications for Windows that also support OLE. Figure 1-1 shows you a display of data from the sample Northwind Traders (NWIND) database that Microsoft ships with Microsoft Access. You can see an employee record that not only has the typical name and address information but also has a picture and biographical text.

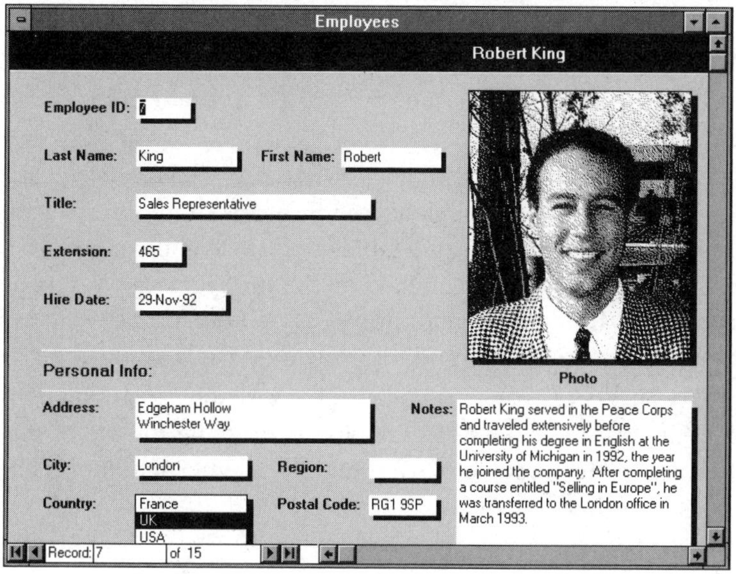

FIGURE 1-1.
An employee record form in Microsoft Access.

Microsoft Access also has the capability of understanding and using a wide variety of other data formats, including many other database management system file structures. You can import and export data from word processing files or spreadsheets. Microsoft Access can directly access and update Paradox, dBASE III, dBASE IV, Btrieve, FoxPro, and other files. You can also import data from these files into a Microsoft Access table. In addition, Access can work with most popular databases that support the *Open Database Connectivity (ODBC) standard*, including Microsoft SQL Server, Oracle, DB2, and Rdb.

Data Manipulation

Working with data in a word processing or spreadsheet program is very different from working with data in a database. In a word processing document, you can include tabular data and perform a limited set of functions on the data in the document. You can also search for text strings in the original document and, with Object Linking and Embedding, include tables, charts, or pictures from other applications. In a spreadsheet, some cells contain functions that determine the desired result, and you enter in other cells the data that provides the source information for the functions. The data in a given spreadsheet serves one particular purpose, and it's cumbersome to use the same data to solve a different problem. You can link to data in another spreadsheet to solve a new problem, or you can use limited search capabilities to copy a selected subset of the data in one spreadsheet to use in problem-solving in another spreadsheet.

A DBMS provides you with many ways to work with your data. You can, for example, search a single table for information or request a complex search across several related tables or files. You can update a single field or many records with a single command. You can write programs that use DBMS facilities to read and update your data. Many systems provide you with data entry and report generation facilities.

Microsoft Access uses the powerful *SQL* database language to process data in your tables. Using SQL, you can define the set of information that you need to solve a particular problem, including data from perhaps many tables. But Access simplifies data manipulation tasks. You don't even have to understand SQL to get Access to work for you. Microsoft Access uses the relationship definitions you provide to automatically link the tables you need. You can concentrate on how to solve information problems without having to worry about building a complex navigational system linking all the data structures in your database. Microsoft Access also has an extremely simple yet powerful graphical query definition facility (called *graphical query by example*, or *QBE*) that you can use to specify the data you need to solve a problem. Using point and click, drag and drop, and a few keyboard strokes, you can build a complex query in a matter of seconds.

Figure 1-2 shows you a complex query under construction in Microsoft Access. Access displays field lists from selected tables in the top of the window, and the lines between field lists indicate the automatic links that Access will use to solve the query. To create the query, you simply select the fields you want from the top of the window and drag them to the QBE grid in the bottom of the window. Select a few options, type in any criteria, and you're ready to have Microsoft Access select the information you want.

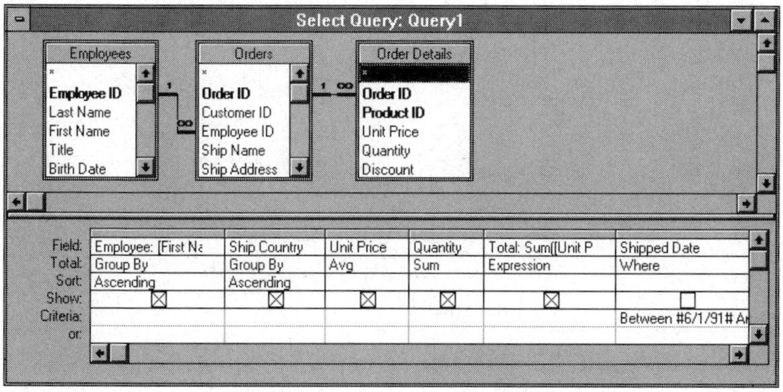

FIGURE 1-2.
A Query window in Microsoft Access.

Figure 1-3, on the next page, shows you an example of an SQL statement that Microsoft Access automatically creates from your specifications in the QBE grid. Figure 1-4, also on the next page, shows you the result of running the query.

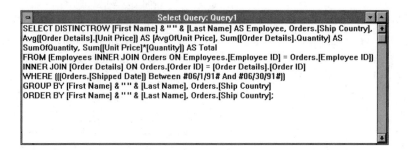

FIGURE 1-3. The SQL text generated by the query in Figure 1-2 on the previous page.

Select Query: Query1

```
SELECT DISTINCTROW [First Name] & " " & [Last Name] AS Employee, Orders.[Ship Country],
Avg([Order Details].[Unit Price]) AS [AvgOfUnit Price], Sum([Order Details].Quantity) AS
SumOfQuantity, Sum([Unit Price]*[Quantity]) AS Total
FROM (Employees INNER JOIN Orders ON Employees.[Employee ID] = Orders.[Employee ID])
INNER JOIN [Order Details] ON Orders.[Order ID] = [Order Details].[Order ID]
WHERE (((Orders.[Shipped Date]) Between #06/1/91# And #06/30/91#))
GROUP BY [First Name] & " " & [Last Name], Orders.[Ship Country]
ORDER BY [First Name] & " " & [Last Name], Orders.[Ship Country];
```

FIGURE 1-4. The results of running the query in Figure 1-3: total amounts sold by each employee in each country for the month of June 1991.

Select Query: Query1

Employee	Ship Country	AvgOfUnit Price	SumOfQuantity	Total
Andrew Fuller	France	$20.00	24	$448.00
Janet Leverling	Germany	$11.43	33	$371.00
Janet Leverling	Switzerland	$19.45	57	$560.40
Margaret Peacock	France	$12.20	100	$1,148.00
Margaret Peacock	Germany	$26.53	54	$1,405.00
Margaret Peacock	USA	$25.00	97	$2,409.30
Margaret Peacock	Venezuela	$24.85	7	$192.10
Michael Suyama	Austria	$8.38	145	$1,423.50
Michael Suyama	Brazil	$21.13	37	$753.40
Michael Suyama	Italy	$5.40	20	$108.00
Michael Suyama	Venezuela	$10.40	109	$1,057.60
Steven Buchanan	Germany	$8.70	2	$17.40

Record: 1 of 12

Data Control

Spreadsheets and documents are great for solving single-user problems but are difficult to use when more than one person needs to share the data. Spreadsheets are also useful to provide a template for simple data entry, but they don't do the job well if you need to perform complex data validation. For example, a spreadsheet works well as a template for an invoice in a small business with a single proprietor. But when the business expands so that a number of salespeople are entering orders, you need a database. Likewise, a spreadsheet can work to assist employees with expense reports in a large business, but the data eventually must be captured and placed in a database for corporate accounting.

When you need to share your information with others, true database management systems allow you to make your information secure so that only authorized users can read or update your data. A DBMS that is designed to allow data sharing also provides features to ensure that no two people try to change the same data at the same time. The best systems also allow you to group changes (a series of changes is sometimes called a *transaction*) so that either all of the changes or none of the changes appear in your data. For example, while entering a new order for a customer, you probably would like to know that all items are recorded or, if you encounter an error, that none of the changes are saved. You would also like to be sure that no one else can view any part of the order until you have entered all of it.

Microsoft Access is designed to be used either as a stand-alone DBMS on a single workstation or in a shared client-server mode across a network. Because you can share your Access data with other users, Access has excellent data security and data integrity features. You can define which users or groups of users can have access to objects (tables, forms, queries) in your database. Microsoft Access automatically provides locking mechanisms to ensure that no two people can update an object at the same time. Access also understands and honors the locking mechanisms of other database structures (such as Paradox, dBASE, and SQL databases) that you attach to your database.

Microsoft Access as Something More

Being able to define exactly what data you need, how it should be stored, and how you want to access it solves the data management part of the problem. However, you also need a simple way to automate all the most common tasks you want to perform. For example, each time you need to enter a new order, you don't want to have to run a query to search the Customers table, execute a command to open the Orders table, create a new record, and enter the data for the order. And what about scanning the table that contains all your products to verify sizes, colors, and prices?

Advanced word processing software lets you define templates and macros to automate document creation, but it's not designed to handle complex transaction processing. In a spreadsheet, you enter formulas that define what automatic calculations you want performed. If you're an advanced spreadsheet user, you might also create macros to help automate entering and validating data. If you're working with a lot of data, you've probably figured out how to use one spreadsheet as a "database" container, and you use references to selected portions of this data in your calculations.

Developing Application Logic

Although you can build a fairly complex "application" using spreadsheets, you really don't have the debugging and application management tools you need to be able to easily construct, say, a complete order entry and inventory control system. On the other hand, database systems are specifically designed for application development. They give you the data management and control tools you need and provide facilities to catalog the various parts of your application and manage their interrelationships. You also get a full programming language and debugging tools with a database.

So, you need a powerful relational database management system and an *application development system* to help you automate your tasks. Virtually all database systems include application development facilities to allow programmers or users of the system to define the procedures needed to automate the creation and manipulation of data. Unfortunately, many database application development systems require knowledge of a programming language, such as C or Xbase, to define procedures. Although these languages are very rich and powerful, they require experience before they can be used properly. To really take advantage of some database systems, you must learn programming or hire a programmer or buy a ready-made database application (which might not exactly suit your needs) from a programming company.

Fortunately, Microsoft Access makes it easy to design and construct database applications without requiring you to know a programming language. Although you begin in Access by defining the relational tables and the fields in those tables that will contain your data, you will quickly branch out to defining actions on the data via forms, reports, and macros.

You can use forms and reports to define how you want the data displayed and what additional calculations you want performed—very much like spreadsheets. In this case, the format and calculation instructions (in the forms and reports) are separate from the data (in the tables), so you have complete flexibility to use your data in different ways without affecting the data. Just define another form or report using the same data. When you want to automate some of the actions, Microsoft Access provides a macro definition facility to make it easy to respond to events (such as changing data in a field on a form) or to link forms and reports together. If you want to do more sophisticated things, such as making calls to Windows routines, you can code an Access Basic procedure.

Microsoft Access provides advanced database application development facilities to process not only data in its own database structures but also information stored in many other popular database formats. Perhaps Access's greatest strength is its ability to handle data from spreadsheets, text files, dBASE files, Paradox, Btrieve, and FoxPro databases, and any SQL database supporting the ODBC standard. This means you can use Access to create an application for Windows that can process data from a network SQL server or from a mainframe SQL database.

Deciding to Move to Database Software

When you use a spreadsheet or a document to solve a problem, you define both the data and the calculations or functions you need at the same time. For simple problems with a limited set of data, this is an ideal solution. But when you start collecting lots of data, it becomes difficult to manage in many separate spreadsheet or document files. Adding one more transaction (another order or a new investment in your portfolio) might push you over the limit of manageability. It might even exceed the memory limits of your system or the data storage limits of your software program. Because most spreadsheet programs must be able to load an entire spreadsheet file into memory, running out of memory will probably be the first thing that forces you to consider switching to a database.

If you need to change a formula or the way certain data is formatted, you might find you have to make a change in many places. When you want to define new calculations on existing data, you might have to copy and modify an existing document or create complex linkages to the files that contain the data. If you make a copy, how do you keep the data in the two copies synchronized?

Before you can use a database such as Microsoft Access to solve problems that require a lot of data or that have complex and changing requirements, you must change the way you think about solving problems with document or spreadsheet programs. In Access, you store a single copy of the data in the tables you design. Perhaps one of the hardest concepts to grasp is that you store only your basic data in database tables. For example, in a database you would store the quantity of items ordered and the price of the items, but you would not store the extended cost (a calculated value). You use a form or report to define the quantity-times-price calculation.

You can use the query facility to examine and extract the data in many ways. This allows you to keep only one copy of the basic data yet use it over and over to solve different problems. In an order-entry database, you might create one form to display individual orders and the calculated total for each order. You could use a report defined on the same data to graph the sum of orders over specified time periods. You don't need a separate copy of the data to do this, and you can change either the form or the report independently, without destroying the structure of your database. You can also add new order information easily without having to worry about the impact on any of your forms or reports. You can do this because the data (tables) and the routines you define to operate on the data (queries, forms, reports, macros, or modules) are completely independent of each other. Any change you make to the data via one form is immediately reflected by Microsoft Access in any other form or query that uses the same data.

If you're wondering how you'll make the transition from spreadsheets and documents to Microsoft Access, you'll be pleased to find features in Access to help you out. You can use the import facilities of Microsoft Access to copy the data from your existing spreadsheet or text files. You'll find that Access supports most of the same functions you have used in your spreadsheets, so defining calculations in a form or report will seem very familiar. Within the Help facility, there are Cue Cards to walk you through key tasks you need to learn to begin working with a database. In addition, Microsoft Access provides you with powerful Wizard facilities to give you a jump-start on moving your spreadsheet to the Access database by automating form and report definition.

Take a long look at the kind of work you're doing today. The box on this page summarizes some of the key reasons why you might need to move to Microsoft Access. Is the number of files starting to overwhelm you? Do you find yourself creating copies of old files when you need to answer new questions? Are there others who need to share and update the data with you? Do you find yourself exceeding the limits of your current software or the memory on your system? If the answer to any of these is *yes*, then you should be solving your problem with a database like Microsoft Access.

Reasons to Switch to a Database

Reason 1: You have too many separate files or too much data in individual files. This makes it difficult to manage the data. Also, the data might exceed the limits of the software or the capacity of the system memory.

Reason 2: You have multiple uses for the data—detail transactions (e.g., invoices), summary analysis (e.g., quarterly sales summary), and "what if" scenarios. Therefore you need to be able to look at the data in many different ways, and you find it difficult to create a "view" of data.

Reason 3: You need to share data. For example, numerous people are entering/updating data and analyzing data. Whereas only one person can update a spreadsheet or a word processing document, many people can share and update a database table. Also, databases ensure that people reading data see only committed updates.

Reason 4: You must control the data because different users access the data, because the data is used to run your business, and because the data is related (e.g., customers and orders). This means you must secure access to data, control data values, and ensure data consistency.

In the next chapter, "The Uses of Microsoft Access," you'll read about some uses of the Microsoft Access application development system in different professional settings. Then, in Chapter 3, "Touring Microsoft Access," you'll open the sample application distributed with the product (Northwind Traders, the NWIND database) to explore some of the many features and functions of Access.

2

The Uses of Microsoft Access

Microsoft Access has all the features of a classic database management system—and more. Access is not only a powerful, flexible, and easy-to-use DBMS but also a complete database application development facility. You can use Access to create and run under the Microsoft Windows operating system an application tailored to your data management needs. You can limit, select, and total your data using queries. You can create forms for viewing and changing your data. You can also use Access to create simple or complex reports. Both forms and reports "inherit" the properties of the underlying table or query, so in most cases you need to define such things as formats and validation rules only once. Among the most powerful features of Access are the Wizards that you can use to create tables and queries and to customize a wide variety of forms and reports simply by selecting from options with your mouse. Access makes it easy for you to link data to forms and reports using macros to fully automate your application. You can build most applications without ever having to write anything that looks remotely like computer program code. But if you need to get really sophisticated, there's also a comprehensive programming language, Microsoft Access Basic, that you can use to add complexity to your applications.

Finally, you get all of these development facilities not only for working with the Access database but also to attach to and work with data stored in many other popular formats. You can build an Access application to work directly with dBASE files; with Paradox, Btrieve, and FoxPro databases; and with any SQL database that supports the Open Database Connectivity (ODBC) standard. You can also easily import and export data as text, word processing files, or spreadsheet files.

This chapter describes four scenarios in which Microsoft Access is used to meet the database and application development needs of the owners of a small business, a PC application developer or consultant, a management information systems (MIS) coordinator in a large corporation, and a home computer user.

In a Small Business

If you're the owner of a small business, you can use the simple yet powerful capabilities of Microsoft Access to manage the data you need to run your business. In addition, you will soon find dozens of Access-based applications available that will add to your productivity and make running your business much simpler. Because Access's application design facilities are so simple to use, you can be confident in creating your own applications or customizing applications provided by others for your specific needs.

Throughout much of the rest of this book, you'll read about the progressive design and creation of a portion of a database application for a small computer business called Prompt Computer Solutions, Inc. This business is real and is owned by two friends of mine.

Prompt Computer Solutions is like many small businesses. The two partners got started a few years ago custom-assembling personal computer systems and local area networks for their friends and other small businesses. Even though they understood computers very well, most of their business was run out of a filing cabinet. They did use tools such as Microsoft Excel and Microsoft Word to automate some of their information and to produce price lists and fliers for their customers. They had taken the time to build templates in Excel that they used to prepare invoices for customers—one template for each major type of computer system that they built. When assembling a price quote, they would cut and paste or enter by hand the add-on items to their base computer systems.

Ultimately, each order spreadsheet became a build record and a customer invoice. They were pretty smart about creating subdirectories on their hard disks and using naming conventions to manage their files. Nonetheless, they practically had to shut down for two weeks every March to gather information for their accountant so that they could file their tax return. Things became a bit more complex when they added some rental business. The situation had been pretty simple when they took an order, recorded it in a Microsoft Excel file, built the computer system, and recorded the payment. But now they had to produce monthly invoices for their rental customers and keep track of computer system serial numbers and ongoing payments.

When it was suggested that maybe it was time for them to buy an application or a database system to simplify their lives, their reaction was swift: "Forget it. We don't have the time to go searching for an application that would work for us, and we can't afford to hire a consultant to custom-build an application from scratch. Most databases we've looked at would take us years to learn to use, and even if we knew a database, it would take us too much time to write something that could help us out."

Enter Microsoft Access. It took almost no time to lay out the tables they needed to keep track of everything for their business. They were even able to import some of their old data directly from Microsoft Excel. In just a few days they created several forms, a couple of reports, and some macros to link them together, and they had solved a big piece of their data management problem. Figure 2-1 shows their Order Entry/-Review form.

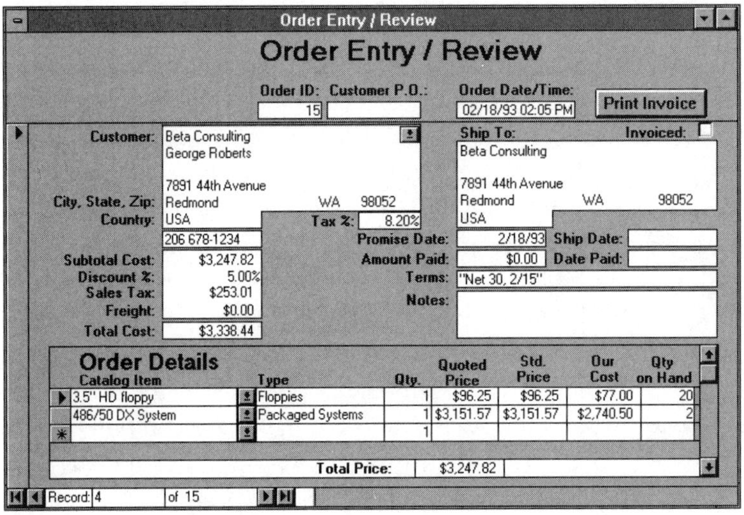

FIGURE 2-1. The Order Entry/-Review form in the database application for Prompt Computer Solutions.

The bottom line? Yes, the folks at Prompt Computer Solutions are pretty comfortable working with computers. But you'll notice that before Microsoft Access, they didn't dream they'd ever be able (or have the time) to tackle a PC database system. Now they have the database they need for their growing business. If you're a small business owner who understands that computers should be able to do more than spreadsheets and word processing programs can do, perhaps Access is for you too. You'll find a lot of computer consultants ready and able to put together a Microsoft Access application for you in record time and at low cost. Even if someone has constructed your database for you, you'll want to know more about Access so that you can take advantage of its native features.

In Contract Work

In today's highly competitive consulting marketplace, the developer who can deliver custom applications quickly and inexpensively will win the lion's share of the business. If you're a PC application developer or consultant, you will find that the forms, reports, and macro facilities of Microsoft Access allow you to create complete applications for your clients in record time. You can also take advantage of Microsoft Access Basic to satisfy unique requirements and produce truly custom applications. If you've worked with products such as Microsoft Visual Basic for Windows, you'll find the Access application development features very familiar, with the added benefit of a full-function relational database management system.

If you're a consultant building applications for a vertical market, you'll especially appreciate how Access makes it easy to build your core application and modify the application for each client's needs. You can create optional add-on features that you can price separately. Whether you're building a custom application from scratch or modifying an existing one, your clients will appreciate the fact that you can sit down with them and use Access to prototype the finished application so that they can see exactly what they'll be getting.

You can scale your application to your client's needs by taking advantage of the fact that Microsoft Access can connect to and work with other database management systems. For smaller clients, you'll find the native Access database system more than adequate. For larger clients, you can connect your application to Microsoft SQL Server or other host databases without having to change any of the forms, reports, macros, or modules in your application.

Imagine a local bookstore chain that has personal computers in each store for use by customers to locate a book by title, subject, or author. Suppose the database system was built by you several years ago using an xBase product. The bookstore chain would like to upgrade by converting the system to run under the Microsoft Windows operating system. The chain would also like to connect the database system to the current inventory information that is kept in an SQL Server database. Your client wants the new database system to tell customers whether a book is in stock. If a book is in stock, the new system should tell customers, by means of an on-screen map, where they can find the book in the bookstore.

Sounds like Microsoft Access might be a perfect solution. You can use the existing xBase data or convert it easily to Microsoft Access format. You can also connect the new application to the existing SQL Server inventory data. Adding a map of the store is easy—and you can even include location indicators that show the customers where they are and where they have to go to find the book they want. Figure 2-2 shows such an application for a bookstore.

FIGURE 2-2.

A bookstore application containing traditional information plus a map showing the book's location.

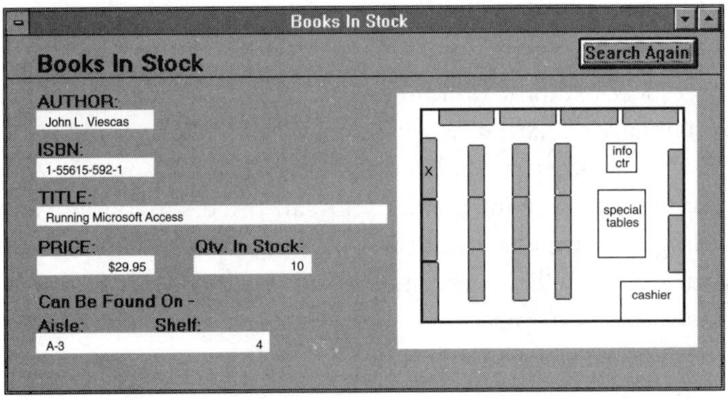

In a Large Corporation

All companies today recognize that one of the ways to remain competitive is to use computer-stored data for more than just the day-to-day operation of the company. Creative managers are constantly looking for ways to "turn data into information." As a result, companies no longer have "data processing" units; they have vast MIS departments charged with the care and feeding of the company's valuable computer-stored information.

Nearly all corporations start by building operational data processing systems. These systems collect and process the individual transactional data required to run the business on a day-to-day basis. Examples of transactional data include the following:

- Checks cleared and money withdrawn and deposited in a banking demand deposit system

- Incoming inventory and items sold in a retail system
- Raw materials ordered and received and finished goods shipped in a manufacturing system
- Energy consumed, raw product delivered, and service-connected or service-disconnected data in a utility system

These systems are relatively simple to design and implement in terms of the data input, the processes required on this data, and the data output. They are also easy to cost-justify because they can reduce clerical tasks, handle rapidly growing volumes (imagine trying to post 10 million checking accounts manually), or achieve efficiency.

After operational systems are in place and management begins to become aware of the vast amounts of data being collected, management often begins to examine the data to gain a better understanding of how the business interacts with its customers, suppliers, and competitors—to learn how to become more efficient and more competitive. Information processing in most MIS departments usually begins quite innocently as an extension of operational systems. In fact, some information processing almost always gets defined as part of an operational application system design. While interviewing users of a system during the systems analysis phase, the system designer usually hears requests such as "When the monthly invoices are produced, I'd also like to see a report that tells me which accounts are more than 90 days past due." Printing the invoices is <u>not</u> information processing. Producing the report <u>is</u> information processing.

On the surface, it would seem simple to answer a question about delinquent accounts, given the data about all accounts receivable. However, the operational system might require only 30 days of "current" data to get the job done. The first information request almost always begins to put demands on the data processing systems, and these demands far exceed the data and processing power needed to merely run the business. At some point, the MIS organization decides consciously to reserve additional data storage and processing capability to meet the growing need for information. However, managing the transition of data collected in operational systems into the data required to support information systems is complex indeed. While operational systems are well understood in terms of the inputs available, the outputs required, and the processes necessary to go from input to output, information systems are defined only by the next question that might be asked.

This growing thirst for information has led companies to build vast networks of departmental systems, which are in turn linked to desktop systems on employees' desks. As more and more data spreads down through the corporation, the data becomes more difficult to manage, locate, and access, as Figure 2-3 makes clear. Multiple copies of the same data proliferate, and it becomes hard to figure out who has the most current and accurate data.

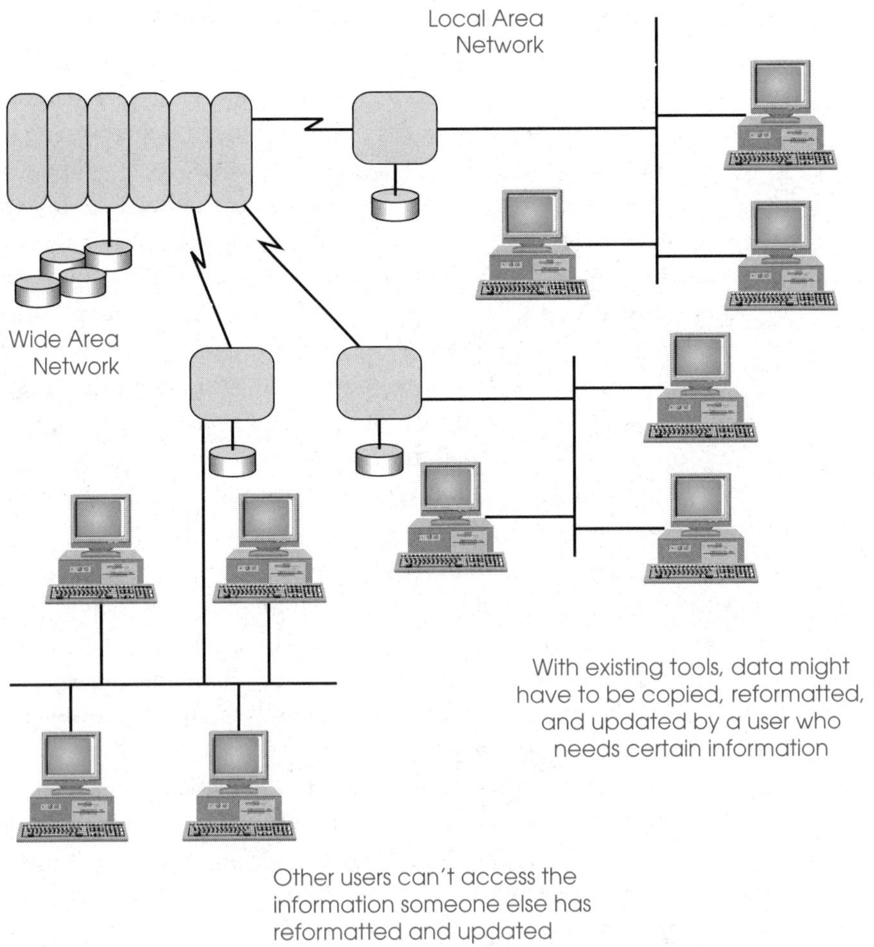

FIGURE 2-3. The typical corporate computing environment, in which data can spread and become difficult to manage, locate, and access.

Why do so many copies exist? Many copies of data exist because the vast majority of existing tools aren't designed to work with data in more than one format or to connect to data from multiple sources. Employees must resort to obtaining a copy of the data they want and then converting it to the format understood by their tool of choice.

The main strength of Microsoft Access in a corporate environment is its ability to link to a variety of database formats on the workstation, on database servers, or on host computers. A manager trying to solve a problem no longer has to figure out how to get copies of data from several different sources to plug into a spreadsheet-based graph for analysis. Using Access, the manager can connect directly to the source data, build a query to extract the necessary information, and create a report with an embedded graph—all with one tool.

Workgroup Applications

Large corporations will find Microsoft Access especially well suited for creating the workstation portion of client-server applications. Unlike many other Windows-based client application development systems, Access uses its knowledge of the application data and structure to simplify the creation of forms and reports. Applications developed using Access can be made available to users at all levels of the corporation. And with Access it's easy to design truly "user-friendly" applications that fully utilize the investment in employee workstations.

Because Microsoft Access can link to and share data in many different database formats, it's ideal for creating workgroup applications that maintain data on local departmental servers yet need to periodically tap data from applications in other departments or upload data to corporate servers. For smaller workgroup applications, local data can be stored and shared across the workgroup using native Access database files. For larger applications, a true database server such as SQL Server can be used to store the data, with Access as the workstation client. When data must be shared with other workgroups or corporate servers, the Access application can use the Open Database Connectivity (ODBC) standard to execute queries that read or update data that is stored in any of several database formats.

See Also: See Chapter 10, "Importing, Attaching, and Exporting Data," for more details about ODBC.

Information Processing Systems

Perhaps a more common use for Microsoft Access in a corporate environment is as the front-end tool for information processing systems. Knowledgeable executives can use Microsoft Access to create their own "drill down" queries, graphs, and reports. MIS departments also find that Access is a great tool for creating the end-user interface for information processing applications.

For example, the marketing department at Microsoft Corporation provides its marketing representatives with a Microsoft Access database containing information about leading systems and network integrators around the country. When the representatives are working with a customer, they can use this tool to quickly search for local companies that might be available to help implement a new system. The marketing representatives can also use the information to provide integrators in their area with information about upcoming products or seminars.

Figure 2-4 (on the facing page) shows the main search criteria screen of an information database that I helped design and build. The left column shows available search criteria, and the combo boxes provide alphabetic lists of all valid values in the database. It's easy for users of this system to choose criteria to build the search list shown in the boxes on the right. When they have the search list they want, they click the "Go Scout!" button to build a list of qualifying companies. From this list, they can "drill down" to detailed descriptive information—a list of company managers, financial data, current clients, and technology specialties. They can also choose a subset of companies from the found list and specify what data they want to print.

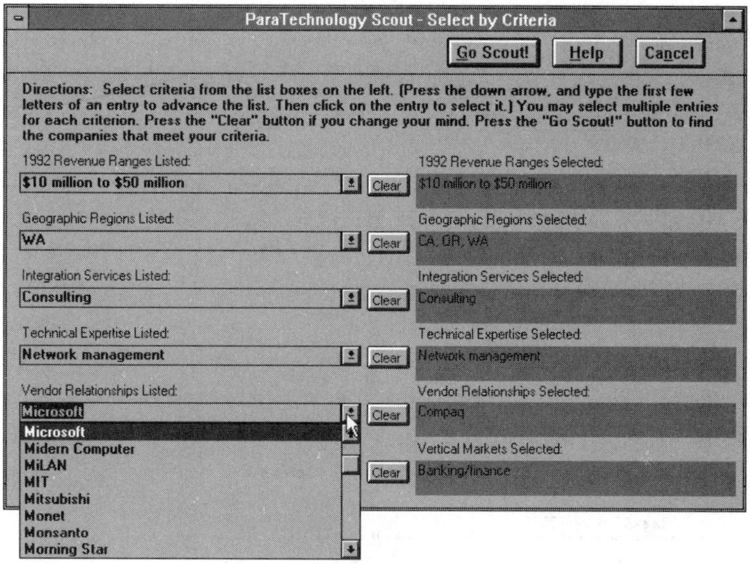

FIGURE 2-4. The main search panel for the ParaTechnology Systems and Network Integrators database.

As a Personal DBMS

Last, but certainly not least, Microsoft Access is a great tool for managing personal information on your home computer. If you're one of the millions of PC users who has a home computer system that can run Microsoft Windows, you can use Access to help make you more productive.

You might want to build a database application to manage your investment portfolio. You could create a directory containing the addresses, birthdays, and anniversaries of all your friends. If you like to cook, a recipe database could be useful. Perhaps you'd like to keep track of your collection of movies or books. I have a friend who uses Access to keep track of his athletic training.

When one of our daughters got married last year, I created a small Access application to keep track of the wedding guest list. You can see the form that I designed for this purpose in Figure 2-5 on the next page.

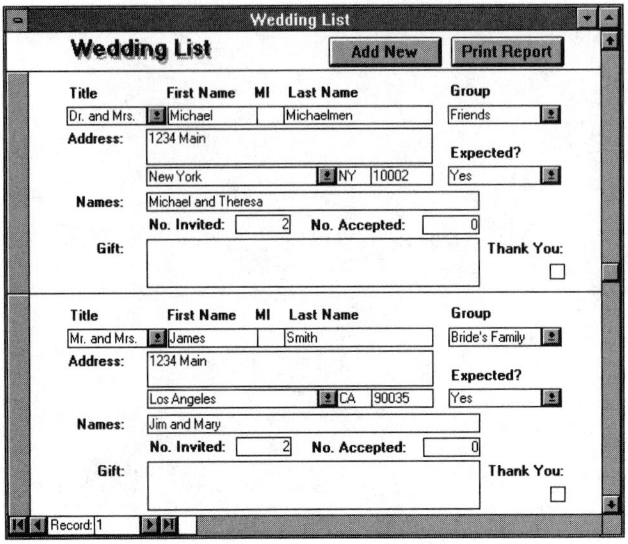

FIGURE 2-5. Keeping track of wedding guests and gifts.

We also used the database to keep track of who had accepted. It was a snap to produce a summary report by groom's family, bride's family, or friends. After the wedding, we used the form to keep track of the gifts received and thank-you notes written.

Because Microsoft Access makes it so easy to create forms and reports and link them together with macros or with Microsoft Access Basic, you can create small personal applications in a jiffy. Access also supports the Object Linking and Embedding (OLE) Version 2 standard, so you can get very creative with your applications. Imagine embedding sound snippets from your favorite albums in the database you use to catalog your compact disc collection. The possibilities are endless.

Uses for Microsoft Access

Small Business:

- Accounting
- Order entry
- Customer tracking
- Contact management

Consulting:

- Vertical markets
- Cross-industry applications

Large Corporations:

- Workgroup applications
- Information processing systems

Personal Use:

- Address book
- Investment management
- Cookbook
- Collections—records, books, movies

In the next chapter, you'll learn more about Microsoft Access's many features as I take you on a quick tour of the product.

3

Touring Microsoft Access

Before you explore the many facets of Microsoft Access, it's worth spending a little time looking it over and "kicking the tires." This chapter helps you understand the relationships between the main components in Access and shows you how to move around within the product.

Windows Features

Microsoft Access takes advantage of the many easy-to-use features of the Microsoft Windows operating system. If you've used other Windows-based products, such as Microsoft Excel or Microsoft Word for Windows, you'll be right at home with Access's menus, toolbars, and drop-down lists. Even if you're new to the Windows operating system, you'll discover that all the techniques you quickly learned in the first chapter of the *Microsoft Windows User's Guide* apply just as easily to Access. When working with data, you'll find familiar cut/copy/paste capabilities for moving and copying data and objects within Access. In addition, Access supports useful *drag and drop* capabilities to assist you in designing queries, forms, reports, and macros. For example, you can select a field in a table and then drag the field, dropping it where you want that data to appear in a report.

NEW!

New General Features in Version 2

- New "tabular" look to database window
- Menus more compatible with other Microsoft Office products
- Ability to customize toolbars
- Ability to create custom toolbars
- New shortcut menus activated by right mouse click
- Detailed reports about the design of any object in the database
- Improved output to Microsoft Excel worksheets (XLS), Rich Text Format (RTF), and text (TXT) files
- Direct output available to Microsoft Mail

Access uses the Multiple Document Interface (MDI) of Microsoft Windows to allow you to work on multiple objects at one time. This means that you can be working with multiple tables, forms, reports, macros, or modules at the same time. If you've used some of the other products in the Microsoft Office package, you already know how to open multiple Microsoft Word documents, Microsoft Excel spreadsheets, macros, or graphs, or Microsoft PowerPoint slide presentations within a single application window. As an example, Figure 3-1 shows you a Microsoft Access session with the Customers form and the Order Review form in the NWIND sample database open at the same time.

FIGURE 3-1.
Viewing two forms at the same time in the Multiple Document Interface of Microsoft Access.

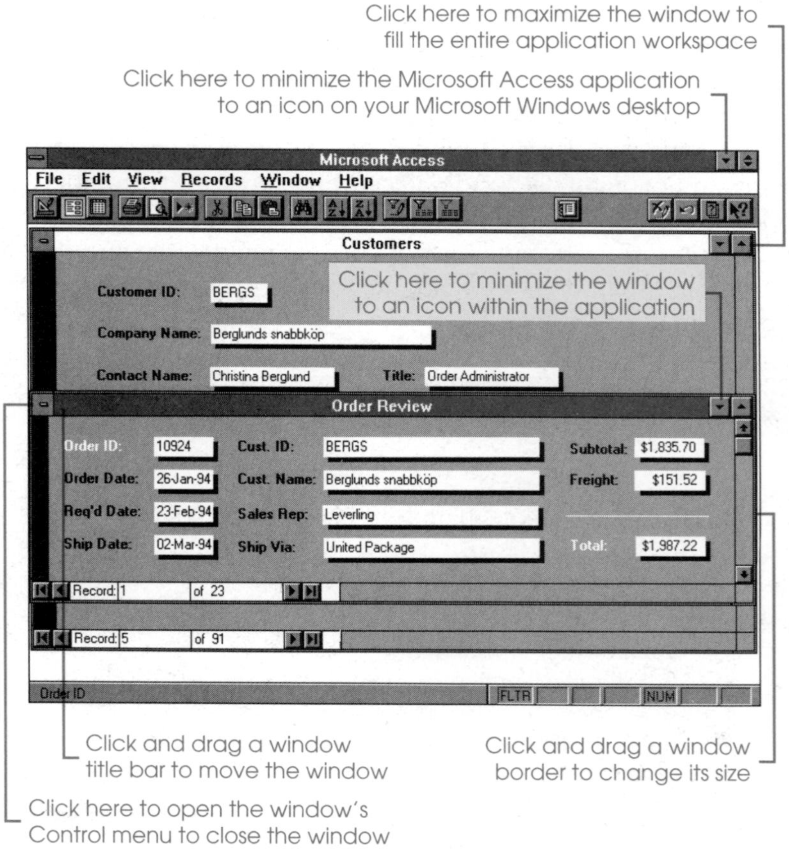

Microsoft Access also supports the Object Linking and Embedding (OLE) standard version 2. This means you can embed (in your tables, queries, forms, and reports) objects from other applications, such as pictures, word processing documents, spreadsheets, graphs, sounds, and more. You'll learn how to use OLE objects in a Microsoft Access database later in this book.

The Architecture of Microsoft Access

Microsoft Access calls anything that can have a name an *object*. Within an Access database, the main objects are tables, queries, forms, reports, macros, and modules.

If you have used other database systems on desktop computers, you might have seen the term *database* used to refer to only those files in which you store data. In Microsoft Access, a database also includes all the major objects related to the stored data, including those objects you define to automate the use of your data. Here are the major objects inside a Microsoft Access database:

Table	An object you define and use to store data. Each table contains information about a particular subject, such as customers. Tables contain *fields* that store the different kinds of data, such as a customer name or address, and *records* (also known as *rows*) that collect all the information about a particular instance of the subject, such as all the information about a customer named Jane Smith. You can define a *primary key* (one or more fields that have a unique value for each record) and one or more *indexes* on each table to help speed access to your data.
Query	An object that provides a custom view of data from one or more tables. In Microsoft Access, you can use the graphical query by example (QBE) facility or you can write SQL statements to create your queries. You can define queries to select, update, insert, or delete data. You can also define queries that create new tables from data in one or more existing tables.
Form	An object designed primarily for data input or display, or control of application execution. You use forms to completely customize the presentation of data that is extracted from queries or tables. You can also print forms. You can design a form to run a *macro* or *module* (see below) in

(continued)

response to any of a number of events—for example, to run a macro when the value of data is changed.

Report — An object designed for formatting, calculating, printing, and summarizing selected data. You can view a report on your screen before you print it.

Macro — An object that is a structured definition of one or more actions that you want Access to perform in response to a defined event. For example, you might design a macro that opens a second form in response to the selection of an item on a main form. You might have another macro that validates the contents of a field whenever the value in the field changes. You can include simple conditions in macros to specify when one or more actions in the macro should be performed or skipped. You can use macros to open and execute queries, open tables, or print or view reports. You can also run other macros or module functions from within a macro.

Module — An object that contains custom procedures you code using Microsoft Access Basic, a variant of the Microsoft Basic language that is designed to work with Access. Modules provide a more discrete flow of actions and allow you to trap errors, something you can't do with macros. Modules can be stand-alone objects containing functions that can be called from anywhere in your application, or they can be directly associated with forms or reports to respond to events on the associated form or report. Modules associated with forms and reports are new in version 2.

NEW!

Figure 3-2 shows you a conceptual overview of how objects in Microsoft Access are related. Tables store the data that you can extract with queries and display in reports or that you can display and update in forms. Notice that forms and reports can use data directly from tables or from a filtered "view" of the data using queries. Queries can use Access Basic functions to provide customized calculations on data in your database. Access also has many "built-in" functions that allow you to summarize and format your data in queries.

Events on forms and reports can "trigger" either macros or Microsoft Access Basic functions or subroutines. What is an "event"? An *event* is any change in state of a Microsoft Access object. For example, on forms you can write macros or Access Basic routines to respond to opening the form, closing the form, entering a new row on the form, or data changing either in the current record or in an individual *control* (an object on a form or report containing data). You can even respond to the user pressing individual keys on the keyboard when entering data!

> **See Also:** For a complete list of events on forms and reports, see Chapter 18, "Advanced Report Design."

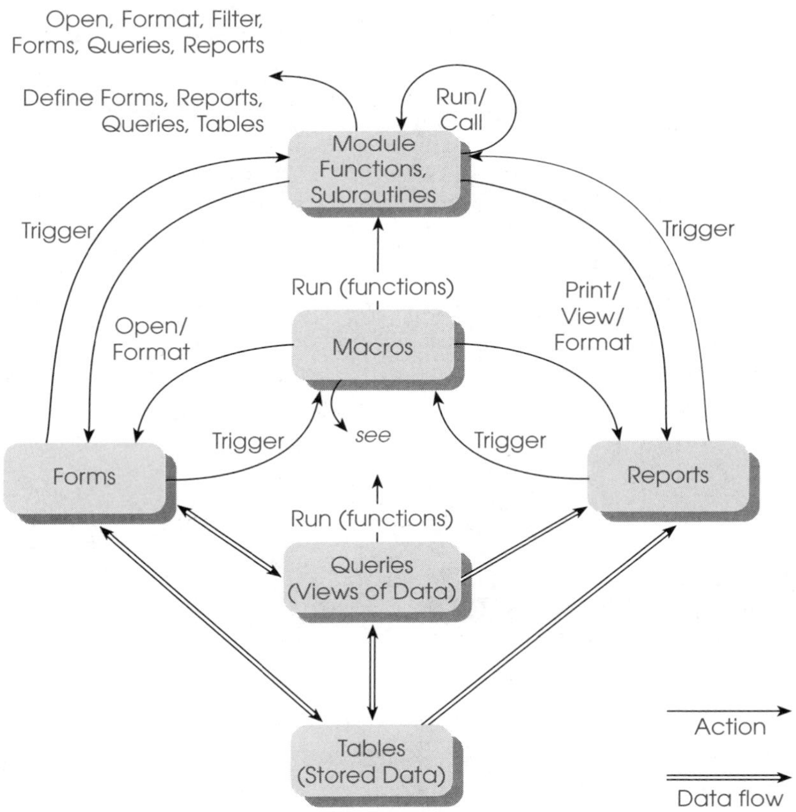

FIGURE 3-2. Main objects and their relationships in Microsoft Access.

From macros and modules you can change the flow of your application; open, filter, and change data in forms and reports; run queries; and build new tables. In Access Basic, you can create, modify, and delete any Access object, manipulate data in your database row by row or column by column, and handle exceptional conditions. From module code you can even call Microsoft Windows Application Programming Interface (API) routines to extend your application beyond the built-in capabilities of Access.

See Also: Chapter 21, "Microsoft Access Basic Fundamentals," and Chapter 22, "Automating Your Application with Access Basic," contain more information about using Microsoft Access modules.

Exploring the NWIND Database

Now that you know a little bit about the major objects that make up a Microsoft Access database, a good next step is to spend some time exploring the extensive Northwind Traders (NWIND) sample database application that you received with the product. Start Access, open the File menu, and choose the Open Database command, shown highlighted in Figure 3-3. In the Open Database dialog box, shown in Figure 3-4, select the file NWIND.MDB in the *sampapps* subdirectory of your Microsoft Access directory. You'll see the *Database window* for the NWIND database, as shown in Figure 3-5.

FIGURE 3-3.
The File menu.

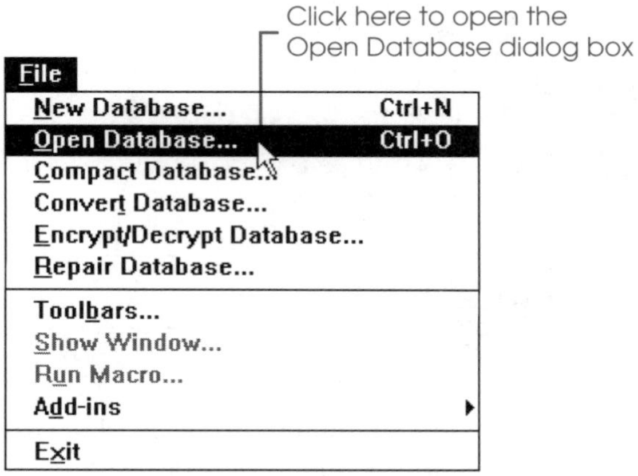

TIP: You can also open the Open Database dialog box by pressing Alt-F,O or Ctrl-O.

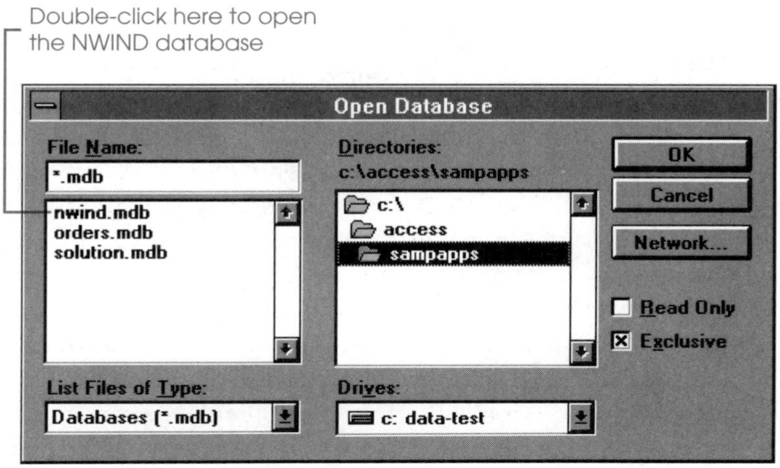

FIGURE 3-4.
The Open Database dialog box.

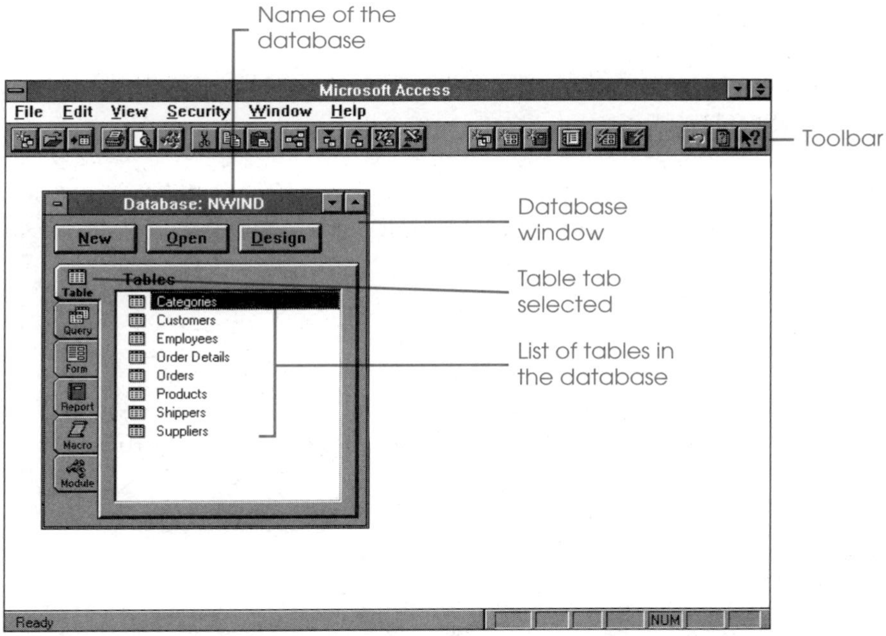

FIGURE 3-5.
The Database window.

The Database window shown in Figure 3-4 always opens toward the upper left corner of the Access workspace. The title bar shows you the name of the database that you have open. Although you can have only one Access database open at any one time, you can connect that open database (and its forms, reports, macros, and modules) to tables in other Access databases, to data in Paradox, dBASE, or Btrieve databases, or to data in SQL Server databases on a network.

NEW! NEW! Notice that in Figure 3-5 Access displays a few additional buttons on the toolbar after you open a Database window. As you explore Microsoft Access, you'll see that Access provides you with more than a dozen built-in toolbars. Normally, Access shows you the toolbar that has buttons most appropriate for the work you're currently doing. However, you can control which toolbars are active, and you can customize which buttons appear on which toolbars. You can even define custom toolbars that you display all the time or open and close from macros or modules. If you want a short descriptive tip that tells you what a particular toolbar button does, place your mouse cursor over the button, but don't click it. In about a half-second, Access pops up a "tool tip" that describes the button.

Down the left side of the Database window are tabs that allow you to choose one of the six major object types: tables, queries, forms, reports, macros, or modules.

Tables

When you first open the Database window, Microsoft Access selects the Table tab and shows you the list of available tables in this database, as shown in Figure 3-5. Across the top of the window, just under the title bar, you can see three command buttons. One allows you to create a new table, and the other two allow you to open one of two available views of existing tables:

Lets you define a new table.

Lets you view and update the data in the selected table from the table list. Clicking this button opens a Table window in Datasheet view.

Lets you view and modify the selected table's definition. Clicking this button opens a Table window in Design view.

When the Database window is active, you can select any of these command buttons from the keyboard by pressing the first letter of the command button name while holding down the Alt key. You can also open a table in Datasheet view by double-clicking the table name in the Database window with your left mouse button, or you can open the table in Design view by holding down the Ctrl key and double-clicking the table name using your left mouse button. If you click once with your right mouse button on a table name, Access pops up a *shortcut menu* that lets you perform a number of handy operations on the item you selected, as shown in Figure 3-6. Simply click on one of the options in the menu, or click anywhere else in the Access window to dismiss the menu.

New Table Features in Version 2

- Table Wizard to help define tables
- Graphical definition of relationships
- Field input masks to automatically add formatting characters to data such as phone numbers, social security numbers, or zip codes
- Ability to store blank as well as Null fields in the database
- Validation rules for fields enforced at the table level
- Table validation rules to validate one field against another
- Separate editor for indexes

FIGURE 3-6. A shortcut menu in the Database window.

Table Window in Design View

When you want to change the *definition* of a table (the structure or design of a table, as opposed to the data in a table), you must open the Table window in Design view. With the NWIND database open, hold down the Ctrl key and double-click the table named Customers with your left mouse button; this opens the Customers table in Design view, shown in Figure 3-7. Notice that the NWIND Database window appears behind the active Table window. You can click in any part of the Database window to make it active and bring it to the front. You can also use the F11 key to make the Database window active (or use Alt-F1 on keyboards with 10 or fewer function keys).

Notice that in Design view each row in the top portion of the Table window defines a different field in the table. You can use your mouse to select any field that you want to modify. You can also use the Tab key to move left to right across the screen from column to column. Use Shift-Tab to move right to left across the screen from column to column. Use the up and down arrow keys to move from row to row in the field list. As you select a different row in the field list in the top portion of the window, you can see the property settings for the selected field in the bottom portion of the Table window. Use the F6 key to move between the top (the field list) and bottom (the property settings) portions of the Table window in Design view.

Microsoft Access has many convenient features. Wherever you can choose from a limited list of valid values, Access provides a drop-down

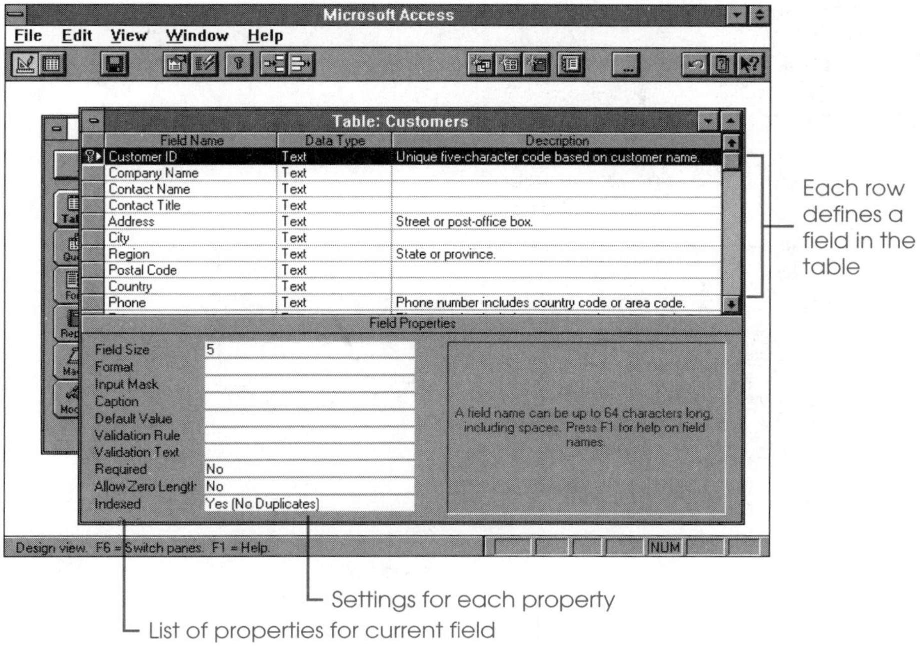

FIGURE 3-7.
A Table window in Design view.

list box to assist you in selecting the proper value. For example, when you tab to an area in the Data Type column, you should notice that a small, gray down arrow button appears at the far right of the column. Click the arrow or press Alt-down arrow to see the list of available valid data types, shown in Figure 3-8 on the next page. When you begin designing a new table, Microsoft Access provides a *Table Wizard* to make it easy to create tables for many common applications.

NEW!

You can open as many as 254 tables (fewer if limited by your computer's memory). You can also minimize any of the windows to an icon by clicking the down arrow in the upper right corner of the window, or you can maximize the window to fill the Access workspace by clicking the up arrow in that same corner. If you don't see a window you want, you can use a list of active windows in the Window menu to bring the window to the front. You can use the Hide command in this menu to make selected windows temporarily disappear or use the Show command to make visible any windows that you've previously hidden. Figure 3-9 on the next page shows an example of multiple open windows. Choose the Close command from the File menu or the window's Control menu to close any window.

See Also: You'll learn about creating table definitions in Chapter 5.

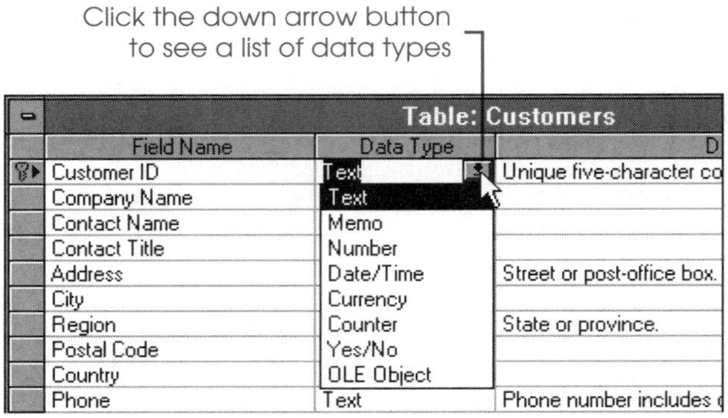

FIGURE 3-8. The Data Type drop-down list box.

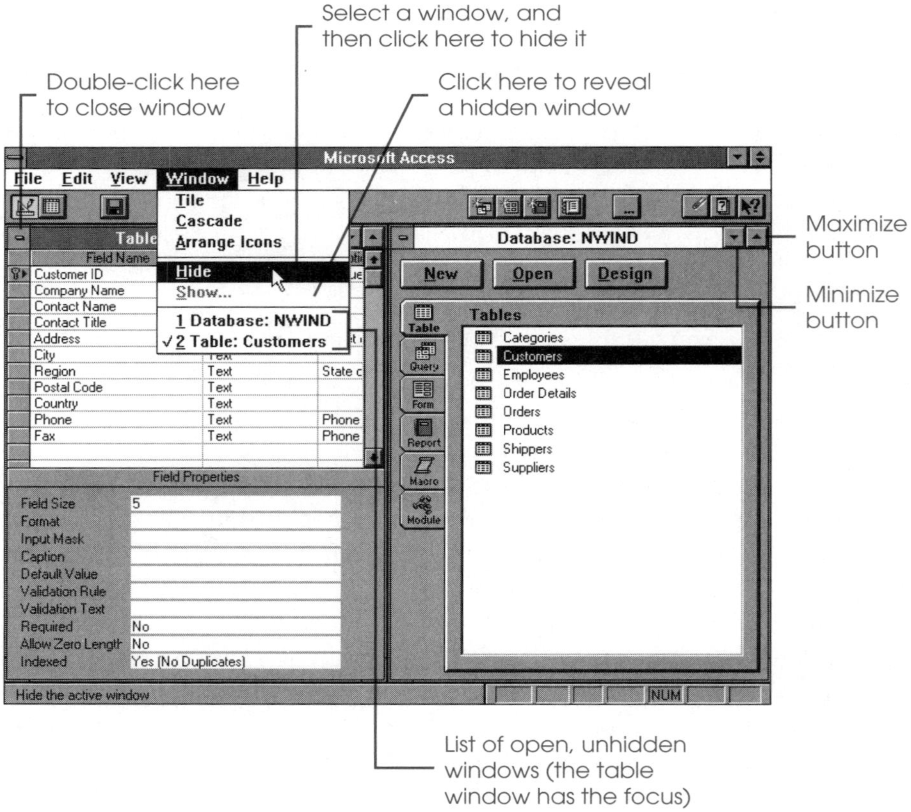

FIGURE 3-9. Working with multiple windows in Microsoft Access.

Table Window in Datasheet View

To view, change, insert, or delete data in a table, you can use the table's Datasheet view. A datasheet is a simple way to look at your data in rows and columns without any special formatting. You can open a table's Datasheet view by selecting the name of the table you want in the Database window and clicking the Open button. When you open a table in Design view, such as the Customers table in Figure 3-7, you can also go directly to the Datasheet view of this table (shown in Figure 3-10) by clicking the Datasheet button on the toolbar.

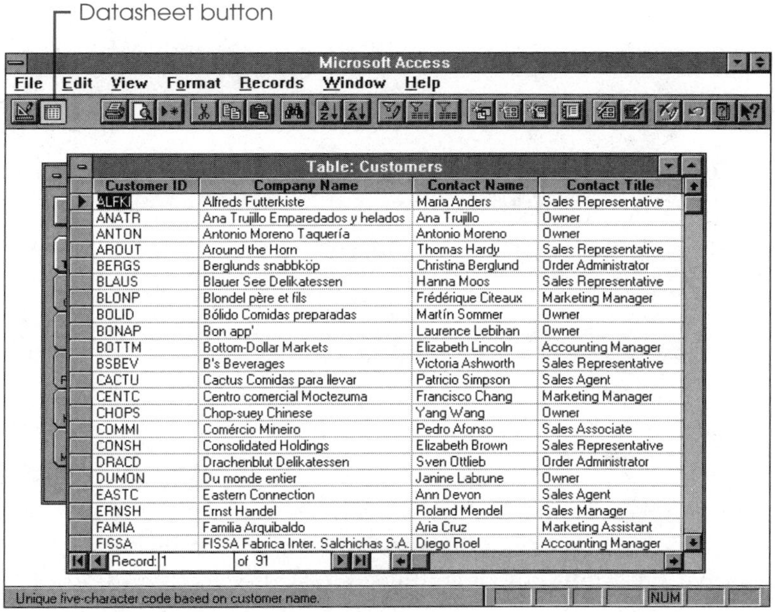

FIGURE 3-10.
A Table window in Datasheet view.

As in the Table window in Design view, in Datasheet view you can move from field to field with the Tab key and move up and down the records with the arrow keys. You can also use the scroll bars at the bottom and on the right side to move around in the datasheet. To the left of the bottom scroll bar, Access shows you the current record number and the total number of records in the currently selected set of data. You can select the record number with your mouse (or press the F5 key), type a new number, and press Enter to go to that new record number. As shown in Figure 3-11, you can use the arrows on either side of this record number box to move up or down one record or to move to the first or last record in the table.

See Also: You'll read more about working with data in Datasheet view in Chapter 7, "Using Datasheets."

Close the Customers table now by double-clicking the window's Control-menu box or by choosing the Close command from the File menu. You should now be back in the Database window for NWIND.

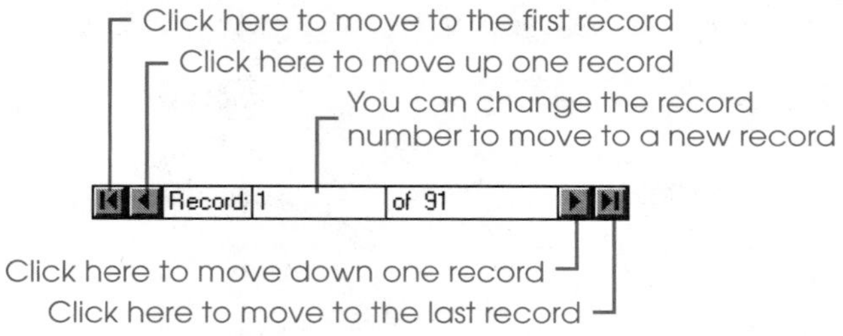
Click here to move to the first record
Click here to move up one record
You can change the record number to move to a new record
Record: 1
of 91
Click here to move down one record
Click here to move to the last record

FIGURE 3-11. Using the record number box to move to a different record in Datasheet view.

Queries

You probably noticed that the Datasheet view of the Customers table gave you all the fields and all the records in the table. What if you want to see just the customer names and addresses? Or maybe you'd like to see information about customers and all of their outstanding orders in one view. To solve these problems, you can create a *query*. Click the Query tab in the Database window to see the list of queries available in NWIND, shown in Figure 3-12.

NEW!

New Query Features in Version 2

- "Rushmore" query optimization (from FoxPro)
- Query Wizard to help design queries
- Output column properties (format, decimal places, input mask, and so forth)
- Ability to save query datasheet layout
- Query builders available in many areas (such as form combo box controls)
- Improved automatic join definition
- Support for UNION and subqueries (in SQL)
- Improved SQL editing window
- Native support for passthrough queries (using the SQL syntax of the target database)
- More fields in joined queries now updatable

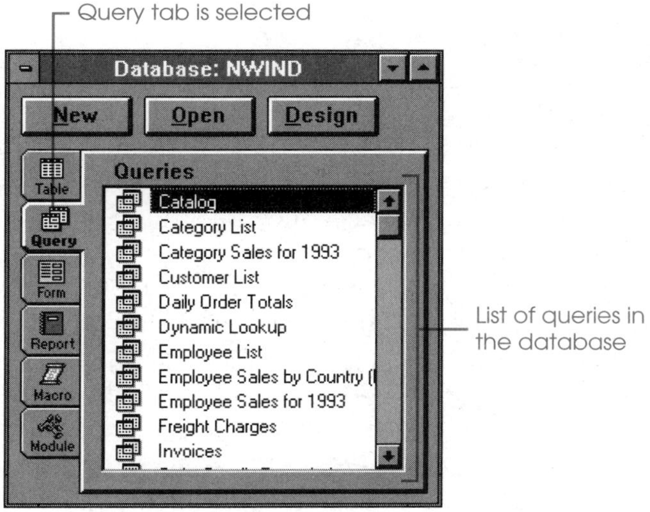

FIGURE 3-12.
A Queries list in the Database window.

Across the top of the Database window, just under the title bar, you can see three command buttons:

Lets you define a new query.

Lets you view and possibly update the data gathered by the query selected in the query list. (You might not be able to update all data in a query.) Clicking this button opens a Query window in Datasheet view. If the query is an action query, this button runs the query.

Lets you view and modify the definition of the selected query. Clicking this button opens a Query window in Design view.

When the Database window is active, you can select any of these command buttons from the keyboard by pressing the first letter of the command button name while holding down the Alt key. You can also open a query in Datasheet view by double-clicking the query name in the window using your left mouse button, or you can open the query in Design view by holding down the Ctrl key and double-clicking the query name using your left mouse button.

Query Window in Design View

When you want to change the definition of a query (the structure or design, as opposed to the data represented in the query), you must open the Design view of the query. Take a look at one of the more complex queries in the NWIND query list by scrolling to the Order Review query. Hold down the Ctrl key and double-click the Order Review query with your left mouse button to see the query in Design view, shown in Figure 3-13. You can also select the query name with your mouse and then click the Design button at the top of the Database window.

At the top of a Query window in Design view, you can see the field lists of the tables or other queries that this query uses. The lines connecting the field lists show you how Microsoft Access links the tables to solve your query. If you define relationships between tables in your database design, Access draws these lines automatically. (See Chapter 5, "Building Your Database in Microsoft Access," for details.) You can also define relationships when you build the query by dragging a field from one field list and dropping it on another field list.

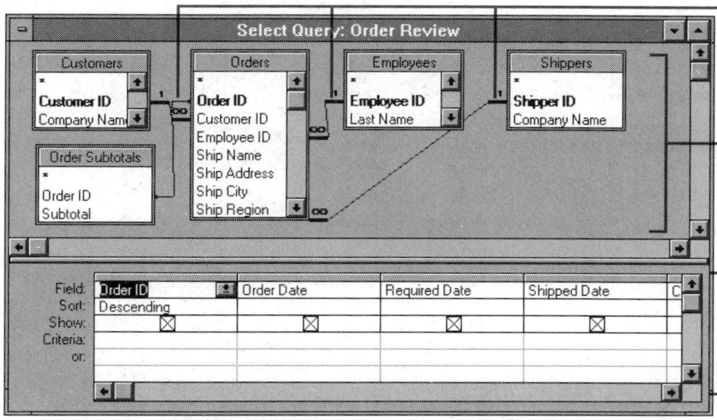

FIGURE 3-13. A Query window in Design view, showing five field lists.

At the bottom of the Query window, you can see the fields that Access uses in this query, the tables or queries from which the fields come (when the Table Names command is selected on the View menu), any sorting criteria, whether fields show up in the result, and any selection criteria for the fields. You can use the bottom scroll bar to bring other fields in this query into view. As in the Design view of tables, you can use the F6 key to move between the top and bottom portions of the Query window.

See Also: Chapters 8, 9, and 11 contain details about creating queries.

Query Window in Datasheet View

Click the Datasheet button on the toolbar to run the query and see the query results in Datasheet view, shown in Figure 3-14 on the next page.

The Query window in Datasheet view is similar to a Table window in Datasheet view. Even though the fields in the query datasheet in Figure 3-14 are from five different tables, you can work with the fields as though they were in a single table. If you're designing an Access application for another person, you can use queries to hide much of the complexity of the database and make the application much simpler to use. Depending on how you designed the query, you might also be able to update some of the data in the underlying tables simply by typing in new values as you would in a Table window in Datasheet view.

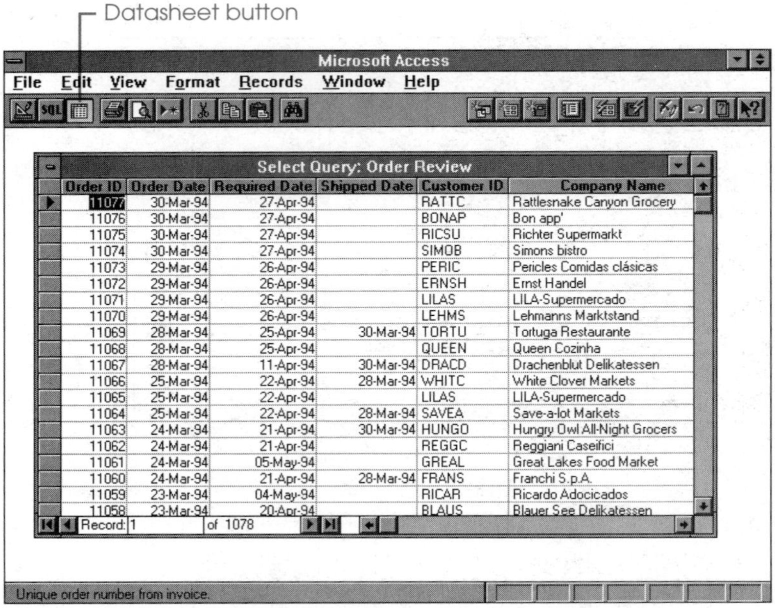

FIGURE 3-14.
A Query window in Datasheet view.

Close the Query window to see only the Database window.

Forms

Datasheets are useful for looking at and changing data in your database, but they're not particularly attractive or simple to use. If you want to format your data in a special way or automate how your data is used and updated, you need to use a *form*. Forms provide several key capabilities:

- You can control and enhance the way your data looks on the screen. For example, you can add color and shading or add number formats. You can add controls such as a drop-down list box or a check box. You can display OLE objects such as pictures and graphs directly on the form. And you can calculate and display values based on data in a table or a query.
- You can perform extensive editing of data using a form with macros or modules.
- You can link multiple forms or reports together with macros or modules that are run from buttons on a form. You can also customize the menu bar using macros associated with your form.

Click the Form tab in the Database window to see the list of available forms, shown in Figure 3-15.

NEW!

New Form Features in Version 2

- Auto forms to automatically build a form for a table or query with a single command
- Control Wizards for command buttons, combo boxes, and list boxes
- Ability to set many additional properties (such as color) at runtime from macros or Microsoft Access Basic
- Many additional form events, such as mouse movement and keypress, more closely matching the Visual Basic model
- Forms that can contain local Microsoft Access Basic code (called *code behind forms*) to respond to form events
- Property builders to help you create entries such as complex expressions and SQL statements

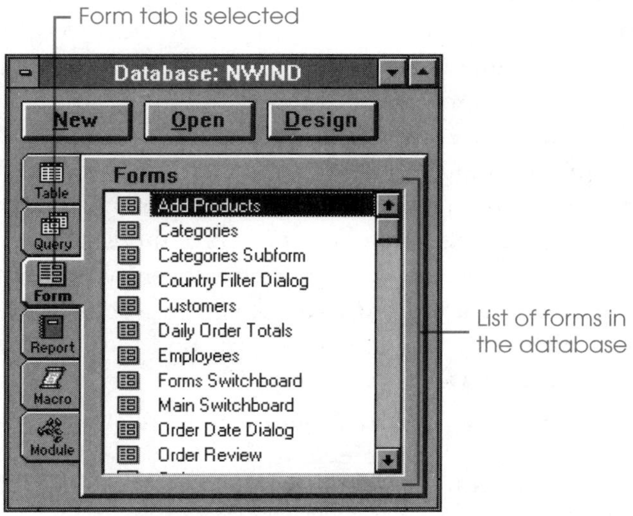

FIGURE 3-15.
A Forms list in the Database window.

Across the top of the Database window, immediately under the title bar, you can see three command buttons:

Lets you define a new form.

Lets you view and update your data through the form you have selected in the form list. Clicking this button opens a Form window in Form view.

Lets you view and modify the definition of the form you have selected in the form list. Clicking this button opens a Form window in Design view.

When the Database window is active, you can select any of these command buttons from the keyboard by pressing the first letter of the command button name while holding down the Alt key. You can also open a form in Form view by double-clicking the form name in the window using your left mouse button, or you can open the form in Design view by holding down the Ctrl key and double-clicking the form name using your left mouse button.

Form Window in Design View

When you want to change the definition of a form (the structure or design, as opposed to the data represented in the form), you must open the form in Design view. Take a look at the Order Review form in the NWIND database; it's designed to display the data from the Order Review query just discussed. Scroll down through the list of forms in the Database window, hold down the Ctrl key and double-click the Order Review form with your left mouse button to see the design for the form, shown in Figure 3-16. You can also select the form name with your mouse and then click the Design button at the top of the Database window. (Don't worry if what you see on your screen doesn't exactly match Figure 3-16. In this figure a few things have been moved around and several options have been selected so that you can see all the main features of the Form window in Design view.)

When you first open this form in Design view, you should see the toolbox in the lower left area of the screen. If you don't see the toolbox, select the Toolbox command from the View menu or click the Toolbox button (crossed pick and wrench symbol) on the toolbar. This is the action center of form design; you'll use the tools here to add to your form the controls you want, to display data, and to trigger macros or modules.

See Also: You'll learn more about form design in Chapter 12, "Form Basics," and Chapter 13, "Building a Form."

In the lower right of the window shown in Figure 3-16 on the next page, you can see a field list labeled Order Review. This is the query you looked at earlier in this chapter. You might see the field list near the top of the Form window when you first open the form. If you don't see the field list, choose the Field List command from the View menu or click the Field List button (the mini-datasheet symbol) on the toolbar. You can move the field list by dragging the title bar. When you read about form design in Chapter 11, you'll see that you can pick a tool from the toolbox and then drag and drop a field from the field list to place a field-display control on the form.

After you place all the controls on a form, you might want to customize some of them. You'll do this by opening the property sheet, which you can see in the lower left of Figure 3-16. To see this window, select the Properties command from the View menu or click the Properties button (a datasheet with a finger pointing symbol) on the toolbar. The property sheet always shows the property values for the currently selected control in the Form window. You can use the combo box at the top of the property window to choose all properties or to choose only properties for data, layout, or events. In the example shown in Figure 3-16, the text box called Freight has been selected, toward the right side of the form. Looking at the property sheet, you can see that Access displays the Freight field from the query in a Currency format. The designer specified a validation rule and a validation message to be displayed if the validation rule fails. The designer could have named a macro or a module to perform a more complex data validation. If you scroll down the list of other properties in this text box, you can see the wide range of conditions for which you can specify a macro or initiate a Microsoft Access Basic module. NEW!

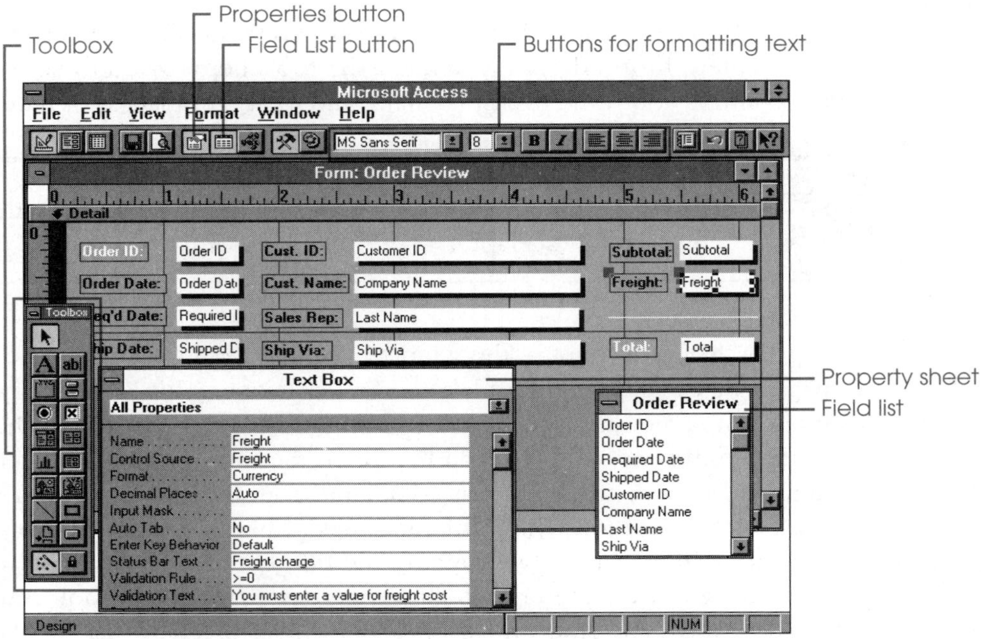

FIGURE 3-16. A Form window in Design view.

You might have noticed that Access made available some additional boxes and buttons on the toolbar when you selected the Freight control. When you select a text box on a form in Design view, Access shows you drop-down list boxes to make it easy to select a font and font size, and Access shows you two buttons to let you set the Bold and Italic properties. To the right of these are three buttons to set text alignment: Left, Center, or Right.

If all of this looks just a bit too complex, don't worry! Building a simple form is really quite easy. In addition, Access provides you with a *Form Wizard* that you can use to automatically generate a number of standard form layouts based on the table or query you choose. You'll find it simple to customize a form to your needs once the Form Wizard has done most of the hard work.

See Also: In Chapter 14, "Customizing Forms," you'll learn to customize a form.

Form Window in Form View

To view, change, insert, or delete data via a form, you can use the form's Form view. Depending on how you've designed the form, not only can you work with your data in an attractive, clear context, but you can also have the form validate the information you enter or you can use it to trigger other forms or reports based on actions you decide to perform. You can open a form by selecting the form's name in the Database window and clicking the Open button. Because you have the Order Review form open in Design view, you can go directly to the Form view by clicking the Form View button on the toolbar. (See Figure 3-17.)

This is actually a fairly simple form that brings together information from four tables into a display that's easy to use and understand. This form includes all the fields from the Order Review query. In addition, the form calculates a total that didn't exist in the query. You can tab or use the arrow keys to move through the fields. You'll discover, however, that the form is designed so that the user cannot accidentally enter data.

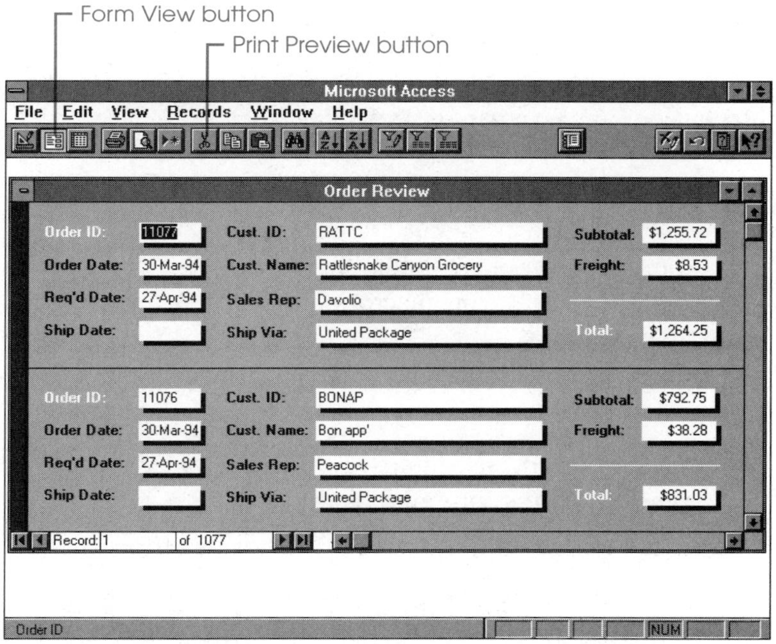

FIGURE 3-17.
A Form window in Form view.

There are two other ways to look at a form: in the Datasheet view and in the Print Preview. You can use the Datasheet View button on the toolbar to see all the fields on the form arranged in a datasheet—similar to a datasheet for a table or a query. You can click the Print Preview button on the toolbar to view on your screen what the form will look like on a printed page. You'll read more about Print Preview in the next section on reports. For now, close the Order Review window so that only the Database window is visible on your computer screen.

Reports

Although you can print information in a datasheet or form, neither of those formats provides the flexibility you need to produce complex printed output (such as invoices or summaries) that might include many calculations and subtotals. Formatting in datasheets is limited to sizing the rows and columns and specifying fonts. You can do a lot of formatting in a form, but because forms are designed primarily for viewing and entering data on your screen, they are not suited for extensive calculations, grouping of data, or multiple totals and subtotals in print.

NEW!

New Report Features in Version 2

- Auto reports to automatically build a report for a table or query with a single command
- Ability to set many additional properties (such as color) at runtime from macros or Microsoft Access Basic
- Reports that can contain local Access Basic code (called *code behind reports*) to respond to report events
- Property builders to help you create entries such as complex expressions and SQL statements
- Ability to save output in BIFF, RTF, or text formats
- New "Pages" property for total number of pages at runtime

If your primary need is to print data, you should use a report. Click the Report tab to see the list of reports available in NWIND, shown in Figure 3-18.

Across the top of the Database window, just under the title bar, you can see three command buttons:

Lets you define a new report.

Lets you see how the report you selected will look on a printed page. Clicking this button initiates the Print Preview command.

Lets you view and modify the definition of the report you selected. Clicking this button opens a Report window in Design view.

When the Database window is active, you can select any of these command buttons from the keyboard by pressing the first letter of the command button name while holding down the Alt key. You can also look at the report in Print Preview by double-clicking the report name in the window using your left mouse button, or you can open the report in Design view by holding down the Ctrl key and double-clicking the report name using your left mouse button.

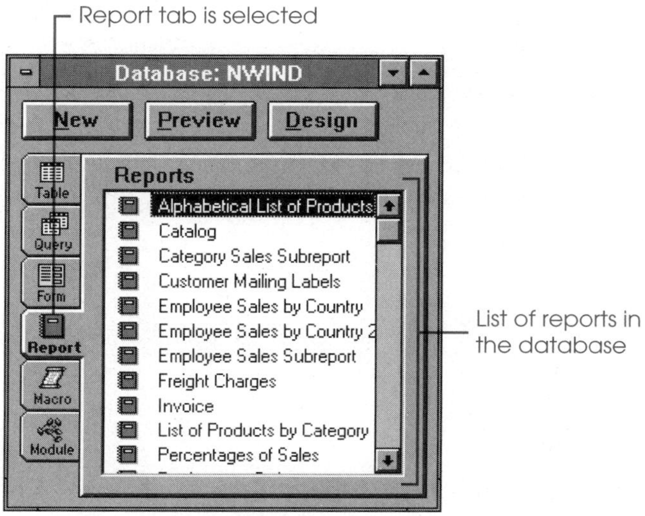

FIGURE 3-18.
A Reports list in the Database window.

Report Window in Design View

When you want to change the definition of a report, you must open the report in Design view. In the report list for NWIND, hold down the Ctrl key and double-click the Alphabetical List Of Products report with your left mouse button to see the design for the report, shown in Figure 3-19. You can also select the report name with your mouse and then click the Design button at the top of the Database window. Don't worry if what you see on your screen doesn't exactly match Figure 3-19. A few things were moved around and several options were selected so that you could see all the main features of the Report window in Design view.

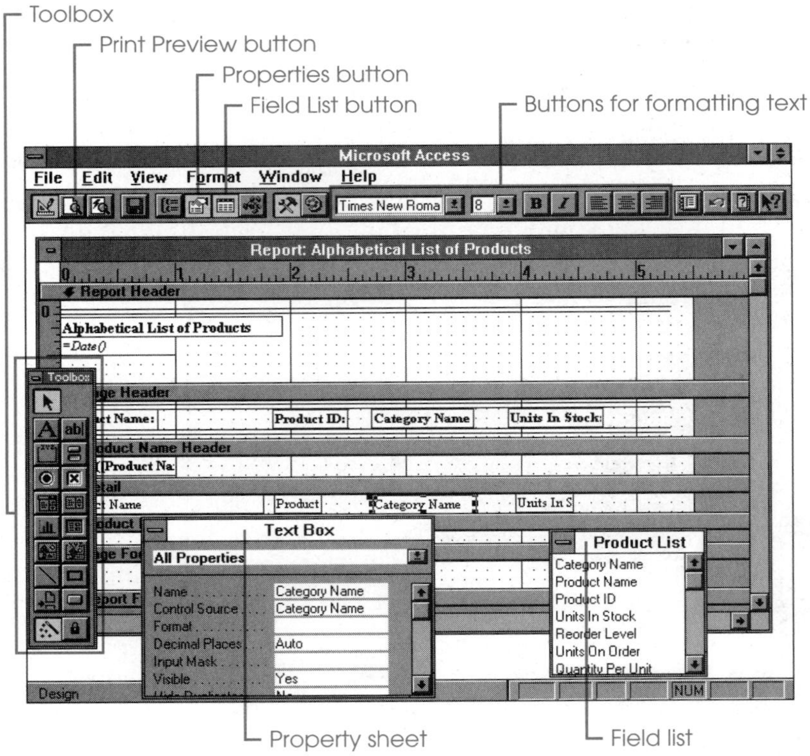

FIGURE 3-19.
A Report window in Design view.

You can see that the Design view for reports is similar to the Design view for forms. (Refer to Figure 3-16.) Reports provide additional flexibility, allowing you to group items and to total them (either across or down). You can also define header and footer information for the entire report, for each page, and for each subgroup.

When you first open this report in Design view, you should see the toolbox in the lower left area of the screen. If you don't see the toolbox, select the Toolbox command from the View menu or click the Toolbox button on the toolbar.

In the lower right of Figure 3-19 you can see a window titled Product List. This is a field list containing all the fields from the Product List query that provides the data for this report. You might see this list near the top of the report's Design view when you first open it. If you don't see the field list, select the Field List command from the View menu or click the Field List button on the toolbar. You can move the field list by dragging the title bar.

See Also: When you read about report design in Chapter 16, "Report Basics," you'll see that you can pick a tool from the toolbox and then drag and drop a field from the field list to place the field-display control on the form.

After you place all the controls on a report, you might want to customize some of them. You'll do this by opening the property sheet, which you can see in the lower center of Figure 3-19. To see this window, select the Properties command from the View menu or click the Properties button on the toolbar. The property sheet always shows the property settings for the currently selected control in the Report window. In the example shown in Figure 3-19, the text box called Category Name is selected. You can see that Access displays the Category Name field from the query as the input data for this control. You can also specify complex formulas that calculate additional data for report controls.

You might have noticed that Access made available some additional list boxes and buttons on the toolbar when you selected the Category Name control. When you select a text box in a report in Design view, Access shows you drop-down list boxes to make it easy to select a font and font size, and Access displays two buttons—Bold and Italic—to let you set the values for a property. To the right of these are three buttons to set text alignment: Left, Center, and Right.

NOTE: In version 1 of Microsoft Access, the text format controls didn't appear until you picked a control. In version 2, they're there all the time, but they're grayed out (disabled) if you haven't picked a text control. Ditto for forms.

Reports can be even more complex than forms, but building a simple report is really quite easy. As with forms, Access provides you with a *Report Wizard* that you can use to automatically generate a number of standard report layouts based on the table or query you choose. You'll find it simple to customize a report to suit your needs after the Report Wizard has done most of the hard work.

See Also: You'll learn how to customize a report in Chapter 17, "Constructing a Report," and in Chapter 18, "Advanced Report Design."

Report Window in Print Preview

Reports do not have a Datasheet view. To see what the finished report looks like, click the Print Preview button (shown in Figure 3-19) on the toolbar when you're in the Report window in Design view. From the Database window, you can also select the report name and then click the Preview button. Figure 3-20 shows you a Report window in Print Preview.

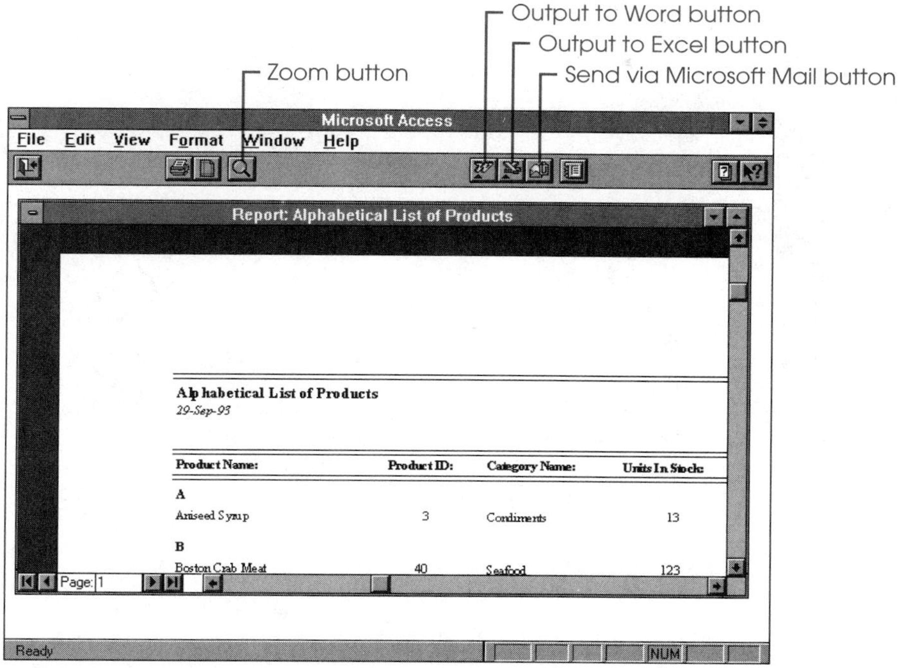

FIGURE 3-20.
A Report window in Print Preview.

Microsoft Access initially shows you the upper left corner of the report. To see the report centered in full-page view in Print Preview, click the Zoom button on the toolbar. The full-page view is a reduced picture, shown in Figure 3-21 on the next page, which gives you an overall idea of how Access arranges major areas of data on the report; but unless you have a large monitor, you won't be able to read the data. When you move the mouse pointer over the window, the mouse pointer changes into a magnifying glass icon. To zoom in, place this icon in an area that you want to see more closely, and click. You can also click the Zoom button on the toolbar to again see a close-up view of the upper left corner of the report and then use the scroll bars to move around in the magnified report. Access also provides buttons on the standard print preview toolbar to let you output the report to Microsoft Word for Windows or Microsoft Excel or to send the report to other people via Microsoft Mail.

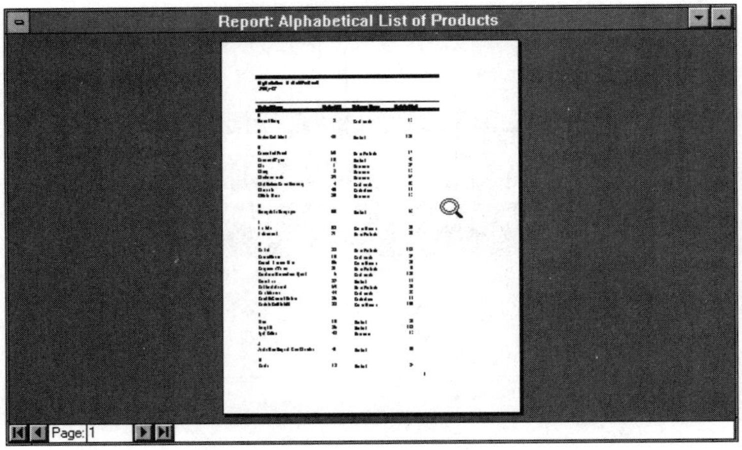

FIGURE 3-21.
A "zoomed" (full-page view) report in Print Preview.

Close the Report window to return to the Database window.

Macros

You can make working with your data much easier within forms and reports by triggering a macro action. Microsoft Access provides more than 40 actions that you can include in a macro. They perform tasks such as opening tables and forms, running queries, running other macros, selecting options from menus, and sizing open windows. You can even start other applications that support Dynamic Data Exchange (DDE), such as Microsoft Excel, and exchange data from your database with that application. You can group multiple actions in a macro and specify conditions that determine when each set of actions will or will not be executed by Access.

NEW!

New Macro Features in Version 2

- Five new macro actions to enhance usability
- A Menu Builder
- Support for submenus
- Expression builders to help you create complex expressions and SQL statements

In the Database window, click the Macro tab to see the list of available macros in the NWIND database, shown in Figure 3-22.

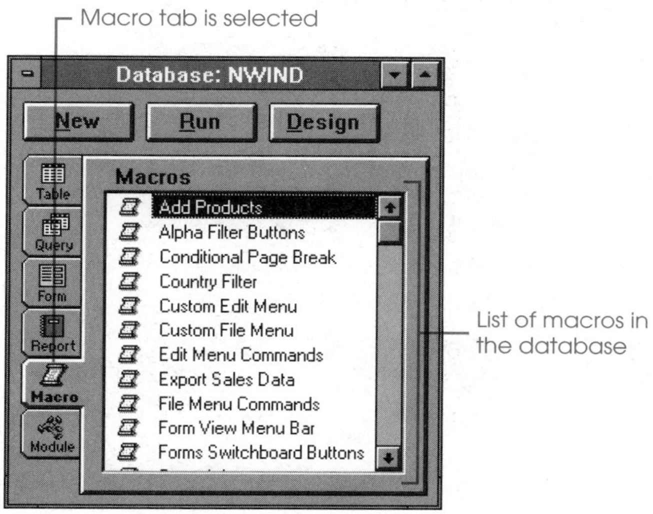

FIGURE 3-22.
A Macros list in the Database window.

Across the top of the Database window, just under the title bar, you can see three command buttons:

Lets you define a new macro.

Lets you execute the actions in the macro you have selected in the Database window. A macro file can consist of a single set of commands or multiple named sets. If you select a macro file from the Macros list and then click the Run button, Access runs the first macro in the file.

Lets you view and modify the definition of the macro you have selected in the Database window. Clicking this button opens a Macro window in Design view.

When the Database window is active, you can select any of these command buttons from the keyboard by pressing the first letter of the command button name while holding down the Alt key. You can also run a macro by double-clicking the macro name in the window using your left mouse button, or you can open the Macro window in Design view by holding down the Ctrl key and double-clicking the macro name using your left mouse button.

One of the most useful things you can do with a macro is to validate data entered on a form. You can even check the value in one control based on the value of another control. For example, take a look at the Validate Postal Codes macro in the NWIND database. Scroll down in the Database window until you see this macro name, select it, and click the Design button. You'll see a window similar to the one shown in Figure 3-23.

FIGURE 3-23.
A field-validation macro.

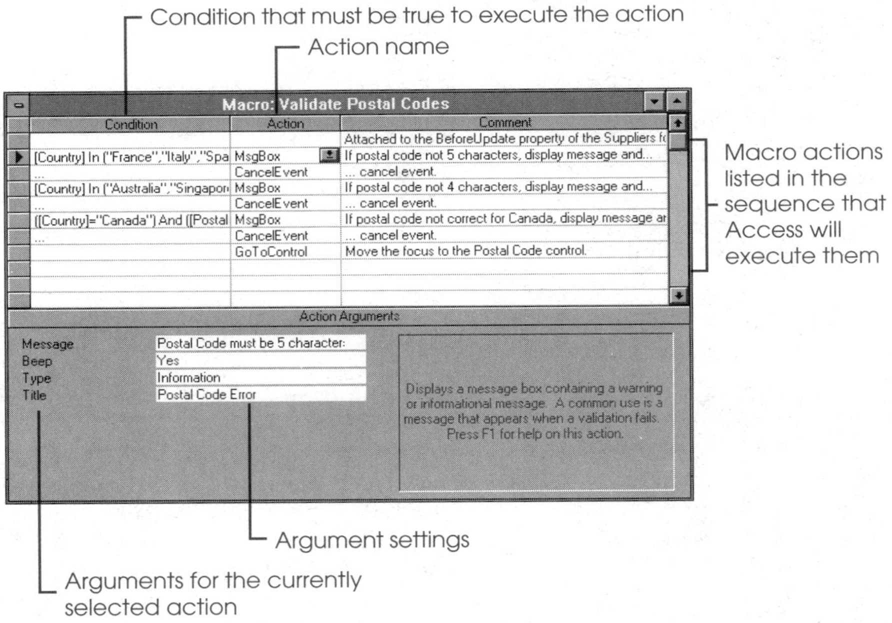

This macro is designed to validate the length of the postal code when a postal code is entered along with the country in a form. In France, Italy, and Spain, the postal code must be five characters long. In Australia and Singapore, the postal code is only four characters long. The postal codes in Canada consist of a letter-number-letter combination, a space, and a number-letter-number combination. In the Validate

Postal Codes macro shown in Figure 3-23, when any condition is not true, the MsgBox action opens a window and displays an appropriate error message. The CancelEvent action prevents the record update and returns you to the erroneous field. You can just begin to imagine some of the possibilities with macros. Close the Macro window to return to the Database window.

See Also: Chapter 19, "Adding Power with Macros," provides a detailed discussion of macros.

Modules

You might find that you keep coding the same complex formula over and over in some of your forms or reports. Although you can easily build a complete Microsoft Access application using only forms, reports, and macros, you might find there are some actions that are difficult or impossible to define in a macro. You can create a procedure that performs a series of calculations, and then you can use that procedure as a function in a form or report.

If your application is complex enough to need to deal with errors (such as two users trying to update the same record at the same time), you must use Access Basic. Since the Microsoft Access Basic language is a complete programming language with complex logic and the ability to link to other applications and files, you can solve unusual or difficult programming problems with a module.

NEW!

As of version 2, you can also code Access Basic routines in special modules attached directly to the forms and reports that they support. You can create these routines from Design view for forms or reports by requesting the code builder in any event property. You can also edit this "code behind forms" by choosing Code from the View menu in Design view for forms and reports. (See Chapters 21 and 22 for details.)

NEW!

New Access Basic Features in Version 2

- Ability to directly write code behind forms and reports to handle events
- Direct access to form or report event code via the property setting
- Manipulation of all database object definitions, including tables, queries, forms, reports, fields, indexes, relationships, and controls
- Improved error handling
- Improved debugging facilities
- Enhanced event model similar to Visual Basic
- Support for OLE 2.0
- Ability to create custom Wizards and expression builders

Click the Module tab in the Database window to display the list of available modules, shown in Figure 3-24. The complete NWIND database application does not require any modules. However, Microsoft Access includes a sample module in NWIND called Utility Functions, which helps you understand the programming examples in the manuals.

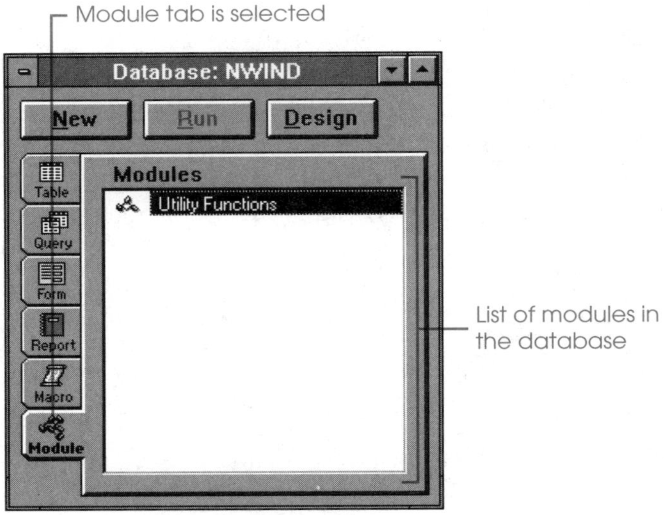

FIGURE 3-24. A Modules list in the Database window.

From the Database window you can either start a new module with the New button or open the design of an existing module with the Design button. You can run a module function from a macro, a form, or a report. You can also use functions in expressions in queries and as validation functions from a table or a form.

Select the Utility Functions module and click the Design button to open a window containing the Microsoft Access Basic code in the module. Use the Procedure drop-down list box on the toolbar or choose the Procedures command from the View menu to look at the procedure names available in the sample. One of the functions in this module, called *IsLoaded*, checks all forms open in the current Microsoft Access session to see if the form name passed as a parameter is one of the open forms. This function is useful in macros or other modules to direct the flow of an application based on which forms the user has opened. You can see this function in Figure 3-25.

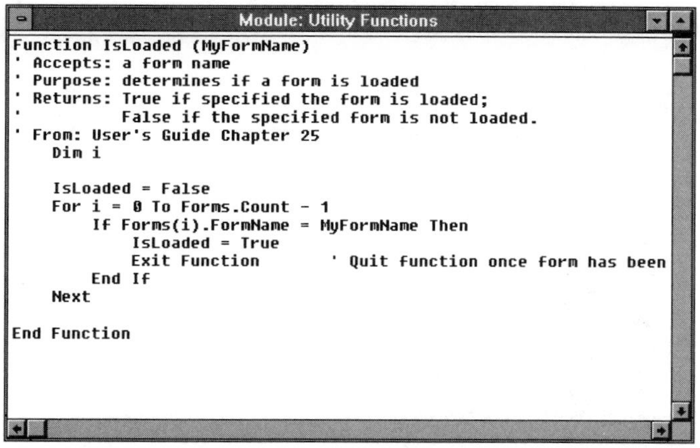
Module: Utility Functions
Function IsLoaded (MyFormName)
' Accepts: a form name
' Purpose: determines if a form is loaded
' Returns: True if specified the form is loaded;
'   False if the specified form is not loaded.
' From: User's Guide Chapter 25
Dim i
IsLoaded = False
For i = 0 To Forms.Count - 1
If Forms(i).FormName = MyFormName Then
IsLoaded = True
Exit Function   ' Quit function once form has been
End If
Next
End Function

FIGURE 3-25.
A Microsoft Access Basic module.

You will find that you can perform many tasks you need without modules, using only forms, reports, and macros.

See Also: Chapter 21, "Microsoft Access Basic Fundamentals," and Chapter 22, "Automating Your Application with Access Basic," introduce coding with modules.

Now that you've had a chance to look at the major objects in the NWIND sample database, you should be getting comfortable with how you will go about working with Access. Perhaps the most important aspect of building an application is designing the database that will support your application. The next chapter describes how you should design your application data structures. Building a solid foundation makes creating the forms and reports for your application easy.

PART 2

Building a Database

4

Designing Your Database Application

You could begin building a database in Microsoft Access much as you might begin creating a simple single-sheet problem in a spreadsheet application such as Microsoft Excel—just start organizing your data into rows and columns and throw in calculation formulas where you need them. If you've ever worked extensively with a database or spreadsheet application, you already know that this unplanned technique will work for only the most trivial situations. Solving real problems takes some planning, or you end up rebuilding your application over and over again. One of the beauties of a relational database such as Access is that it's much easier to make midcourse corrections; however, it's well worth your while in the long run to spend time up front designing the tasks you want to perform, the data structures you need to support those tasks, and the flow of tasks within your database application.

You don't have to go deeply into application and database design theory to build a solid foundation for your database project. You'll read about application design fundamentals in the next section, and then you'll apply those fundamentals in the following sections, "Determining Application Tasks" and "Data Analysis." The section titled "Database Design Concepts" teaches you a basic method for designing the tables you'll need for your application and for defining the relationships between those tables.

Application Design Fundamentals

Methodologies for good computer application design were first devised in the 1960s by recognized industry consultants such as James Martin, Edward Yourdon, and Larry Constantine. At the dawn of computing, building an application or fixing a broken one was so expensive that the experts often advised spending 60 percent or more of your total project time getting the design right before penning a single line of code.

Today's application development technologies make building an application incredibly inexpensive and fast. An experienced user can sit down with Microsoft Access and build in an afternoon on a PC what used to take months to create (if it was even possible) on the early mainframe systems. It's also a lot easier than ever to go back and fix mistakes or "redesign on the fly."

But today's technologies also give you the power to build very complex applications. Also, the pace of computing is several orders of magnitude faster than it was even a decade ago. Despite powerful tools, creating a database application (particularly a moderately complex one) without first spending some time determining what the application should do and how it should operate is inviting lots of expensive rework time. If your application design is not well thought out, it will also be very expensive and time-consuming later to track down any problems or to add new functionality.

The following is a brief overview of the steps involved in building any database application.

Step 1: Task Analysis

Before you start building an application, you probably have some idea of what you want it to do for you. It will be well worth your while to spend some time making a list of *all* the major tasks you want to accomplish with the application—including those that you might not need right away but might want to implement in the future. By "major" tasks, I mean application functions that will ultimately be represented in a form or a report in your Microsoft Access database. So "Enter customer orders" is a major task that you would accomplish through a form for that purpose, but "Calculate extended price" is most likely a subtask of "Enter customer orders" that would be accomplished on the same form. (See details later in this chapter for suggestions about ways to document your tasks.)

Step 2: Task Flow Layout

So that your application operates smoothly and logically, you should lay out your major tasks in topic groups and then order those tasks within groups based on the sequence in which the tasks must be performed. For example, you'll probably want to separate employee-related tasks from sales-related ones. Within sales, entering an order into the system must be completed before you can print invoices or examine sales totals.

You might discover that some tasks are related to more than one group or that a task in one group is a prerequisite to a task in another group. Grouping and charting the flow of tasks helps you discover a "natural" flow to your tasks that you can ultimately reflect in the way your forms and reports link together in your finished application. Later in this chapter, you can see how I laid out the tasks demonstrated in the sample application used in this book.

Step 3: Data Analysis

After you've developed your task list, perhaps the most important design step is to list for each task all the bits and pieces of data that you'll need to perform that task. You'll need some pieces of information as input to the task (for example, a price to calculate an extended amount owed on an order), but you won't update them. You'll examine some data in performing the task and then update the data when you complete the task. You might delete some data items (remove invoices paid, for example) or add new ones (insert new order details). Finally, you'll calculate some data and display it as part of the task, but you won't save it anywhere in the database.

Step 4: Data Design

After you've determined all the data elements you need for your application, you must organize the data by subject and map subjects into tables and queries in your database. For a relational database system such as Microsoft Access, you'll use a process called *normalization* to help you design the most efficient and flexible way to store your data. (See "Database Design Concepts," later in this chapter, for a simple method of creating a normalized design.)

Step 5: Prototyping, User Interface Design

After you've built the table structures you need to support your application, Microsoft Access makes it very easy to mock up the application flow in forms and to tie the forms together using simple macros. You can build the actual forms and reports you'll need in your application "on screen," switching to Form view or Print Preview periodically to check your progress. If you're building the application to be used by someone else, you can easily demonstrate and get approval for the "look and feel" of your application before you've written any complex code that you might need to actually accomplish your tasks. Parts 4 and 5 of this book show you how to design and construct forms and reports. Part 6 shows you how to use macros and Access Basic code to link forms and reports together to form an application.

Step 6: Application Construction

For very simple applications, you might find that the prototype is the application. Most applications, however, will require that you write code to fully automate all the tasks you identified in your design. You'll probably also need to create certain linking forms that facilitate moving from one task to another. For example, you might need to construct *switchboard* forms that provide the navigational roadmap to your application. You might also need to build parameter input dialogs to allow users to easily filter the data they want to use in a particular task. You might also want to build custom menus for most, if not all, forms.

Step 7: Testing, Reviewing, Refining

As you complete various components of your application, you should test each option that you have provided. As you'll learn in Part 6 of this book, you can test macros by stepping through the commands you've written, one line at a time. If you automate your application using Access Basic, you'll have many debugging tools at your disposal to verify application execution and to identify and fix errors.

If at all possible, you should provide completed portions of your application to users so they can help you test your code and provide feedback about the flow of the application. Despite your best efforts beforehand to identify tasks and lay out a smooth task flow, users will invariably think of new and better ways to approach a particular task after they've seen your application in action. Users often discover that some features they told you were very important to include are not important at all when it comes time to actually put your application to use. A required change discovered early in the implementation stage can save you lots of rework time.

Putting your application "in production" doesn't necessarily mean that the refinement and revision process stops. Most software developers recognize that after they've finished one "release," they often must begin again designing and building enhancements to their software. For major revisions, you should start over at Step 1 to assess the overall impact of the desired changes so that you can smoothly integrate enhancements to your earlier work.

Typical Application Development Steps

- Task analysis
- Task flow layout
- Data analysis
- Data design
- Prototyping, user interface design
- Application construction
- Testing, reviewing, refining

Determining Application Tasks

Throughout the rest of the book, I will use a Prompt Computer Solutions sample application as an example, and you will build pieces of the application as you explore the architecture and features of Microsoft Access. This sample application, PROMPT, is somewhat more complex than the Northwind Traders sample (NWIND) provided with the product. The PROMPT application employs some techniques not found in the product documentation. The PROMPT database is described in Appendix B. The companion disk that comes with this book contains all the tables, queries, forms, reports, macros, and modules of the PROMPT database. (See "Using the Companion Disk" on page xxiv for details.)

The two major schools of thought, when it comes to designing databases, are *process-driven design* (also known as *top-down design*), which focuses on the functions or tasks you need to perform, and *data-driven design* (also known as *bottom-up design*), which concentrates on identifying and organizing all the bits of data you need. The method used here incorporates ideas from both philosophies.

This book begins by having you identify and group tasks to help you decide whether you need only one or more than one database. (This is a top-down approach.) As explained previously, databases should be organized around a group of related tasks or functions. For each task, you choose the individual pieces of data you need. Next, you gather all the data fields for all related tasks and begin organizing them into subjects. (This is a bottom-up approach.) Each subject forms the foundation for the individual tables in your database. Finally, you apply the rules you will learn in the "Database Design Concepts" section of this chapter to create your tables.

Identifying Tasks

Assume you've been given an assignment to act as a Microsoft Access database consultant to a small company, Prompt Computer Solutions, Incorporated. This company custom-builds and resells personal computer systems, software, and components. The owners of the company need a better way to keep track of customers, of the computer systems and components they order, and of the many suppliers from which Prompt Computer Solutions obtains the parts, boards, software, and peripherals that the company resells. The owners need to do the following:

- Record customer orders
- Schedule customer order fulfillment
- Calculate charges (probably as part of generating an order)
- Bill customers
- Record customer payments
- Manage inventory
- Order parts and components from suppliers
- Keep track of money owed to suppliers
- Pay supplier bills
- Prepare monthly income statements
- Analyze quarterly sales
- Produce a sales catalog
- Track profit margins

To start, this chapter will introduce you to an application design worksheet that you would fill out for each task. A blank worksheet is shown in Figure 4-1.

Consider the first task—recording customer orders. For this task, you provide a list of available company products so that the ordered items can be entered on an order form (and in the database) when a customer calls in or sends in an order. The list of related tasks probably

FIGURE 4-1. An application design worksheet for use in describing tasks.

APPLICATION DESIGN WORKSHEET #1 - TASKS

Task Name:

Brief Description:

Related Tasks:

Data Name	Usage	Description	Subject

includes fulfilling orders, calculating charges, billing customers, and recording payments. You would fill out one task worksheet for each related task, and then you would be ready to start working on the data you need.

Selecting the Information You Need

After you've identified all tasks, you must list for each task the data items you need to do that task. On the task worksheet, you enter a name for each data item, how the data item will be used, and a brief description. The Usage column on the form has five codes—I, O, U, D, and C—which stand for Input, Output, Update, Delete, and Calculate. In the Subject column, you enter the name of the Microsoft Access object to which you think each data item belongs. For example, an address might belong to a Customer table. A completed application design worksheet for the Record Customer Orders task might look like the one that is shown in Figure 4-2 on the next page.

Organizing Tasks

You should now use your task sheets as a guide in laying out an initial structure for your application. Part of the planning you did on the task worksheets was to consider usage—whether a piece of information might be needed as input, for update, or as output of a given task. Wherever you have something that is required as input, you should have a *precedent* task that creates that data item as output.

For example, in the Record Customer Orders task worksheet shown in Figure 4-2, you clearly must create catalog items to be able to sell to a customer before you can record customer orders. Similarly, you need the customer information created in some other task before you can use that information (or update it) in this task. So you should have a task for creating catalog items and a task for creating customer lists. You'll find when you look at catalog items that some of them might be made up of several components. So, even before defining catalog items, you need a task to create components.

You might also be able to combine some tasks. In the example in Figure 4-2, you can see a reference to the Calculate Charges task that might well be handled within the Record Customer Orders task. You can also see tasks on the worksheet that are subordinate to Record Customer

FIGURE 4-2. A completed application design worksheet for the Record Customer Orders task.

APPLICATION DESIGN WORKSHEET #1 - TASKS

Task Name:	Record Customer Orders
Brief Description:	Capture customer orders when they call in Help customer choose items Inform customer of total price
Related Tasks:	Schedule customer order fulfillment Record customer payments Calculate charges Bill customer

Data Name	Usage	Description	Subject
Company Name	I	Name of the company	Customer
Customer Name	I	Name of the person ordering	Customer
Address	I, U	Customer's address	Customer
City	I, U		Customer
State/Province	I, U		Customer
Postal Code	I, U	Zip or postal code	Customer
Country	I, U		Customer
Phone Number	I, U	Customer's phone #	Customer
Fax Number	I, U	Customer's fax #	Customer
Credit Limit	I	Credit we're willing to extend	Customer
Item Name	I	Description of item	Items
Item Description	I	Name of item we're selling	Items
Cost	I	Our cost	Items
Quantity on Hand	I	In-stock amount	Items
Sales Representative	O	Person who quoted/entered order	Order
Quantity Ordered	O	Amount customer wants	Order detail
Price Quoted	O	Price charged this customer	Order detail
Discount	O	Discount we're offering on total order	Order
Sales tax	C	Tax we have to charge	Order
Shipping Charge	C	Cost to send the item(s)	Order
Total Cost	C	Total for the order	Order

Orders: Bill Customers (print an invoice), Schedule Customer Order Fulfillment, and Record Customer Payments. It's useful to lay out all your defined tasks in a relationship diagram. The relationships of the tasks in the Prompt Computer Solutions database are shown in Figure 4-3.

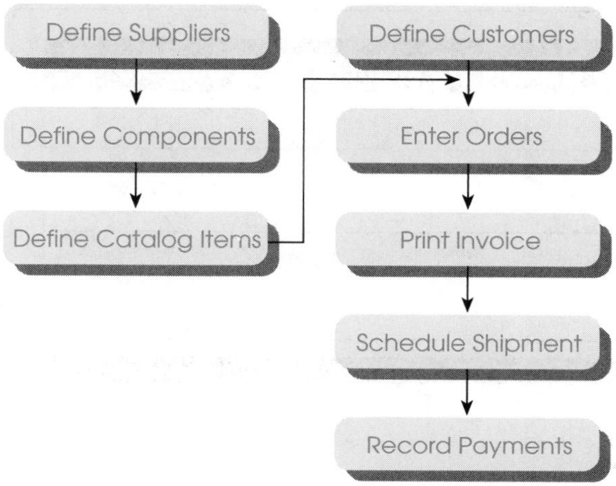

FIGURE 4-3. The relationships between the tasks in the Prompt Computer Solutions database.

Data Analysis

Now you're ready to begin a more thorough analysis of your data and organization of the individual items into data subjects. These subjects become candidates for tables in your database design.

Choosing the Database Subjects

If you've been careful in identifying the subject for each data item you need, your next step is very easy. You would create another set of worksheets, each worksheet similar to the one shown in Figure 4-4 on the next page, to help you collect all the data items that belong to each subject. At the top of the form for each subject, you would list the related subjects that appear in any given task. Under the Relationship column, you would enter the kind of relationship (one-to-many or one-to-one). For example, the Customer subject might have "many" Orders. A completed application design worksheet for the Customer subject is shown in Figure 4-5 on page 87.

As you copy each data item to the subject worksheet, you decide the data type (text, number, currency, memo, and so on) and how large the stored data needs to be. The data item description is a short descriptive phrase that you can enter into the design for your table. Access will

FIGURE 4-4.
An application design worksheet for use with subjects.

APPLICATION DESIGN WORKSHEET #2 - SUBJECTS

Subject Name:

Brief Description:

Related Subjects: **Name** **Relationship**

Data Name	Data Type	Description	Validation Rule

use the description as the default information that will be displayed in the status bar at the bottom of the screen whenever the field is selected on a datasheet, form, or report.

Finally, you might make a note of any validation rules that should always apply to the data field. Later, you can define these rules in Microsoft Access, and Access will check each time you create new data to ensure that you haven't violated any of the rules. Validating data can

APPLICATION DESIGN WORKSHEET #2 - SUBJECTS

Subject Name:	Customer
Brief Description:	Information about customers

Related Subjects:

Name	Relationship
Orders	Many
Sales Reps	One
Sales History	Many

Data Name	Data Type	Description	Validation Rule
Company Name	Text (25)	Customer company name	Required
Customer Name	Text (25)	Name of company contact	
Address	Text (30)	Street address	Required
City	Text (20)	City	Required
State/Province	Text (2)	State or province	Required
Postal Code	Text (12)	Zip or postal zone code	Required
			USA: *nnnnn-nnnn*
			Canada: *xnx nxn*
Country	Text (6)	Country name	Canada, USA
Phone Number	Number (10)	Phone number	*(nnn) nnn-nnnn*
			2nd digit 0 or 1
Fax Number	Number (10)	Fax machine phone number	(same as Phone)
Credit Limit	Currency	Maximum credit allowed	<50,000

FIGURE 4-5. A completed application design worksheet for the Customer subject.

be especially important when you create a database application for other people to use.

Mapping Subjects to Your Database

After you fill out all of your subject sheets, each sheet becomes a candidate to be a table in your database design. For each table you must confirm that all the data you need is included. You should also be sure you don't have any unnecessary data.

For example, if any customers need more than one line for an address, you can add a second data field. If you regularly have more than one contact person within a company, you might need to create a separate Contact table that contains records for each name and phone number. The next section in this chapter shows you how to use four simple rules to create a flexible and logical set of tables from your subject worksheets.

Database Design Concepts

In a relational database system such as Microsoft Access, you should begin by designing each database around a specific set of tasks or functions. For example, you might have one database designed for order processing, and this database would contain information about customers, orders, the items each customer ordered, how the orders were shipped, how much the customers owed for each order, who supplied the items you sold, and so forth. The NWIND sample database is this sort of database. The sample application we'll build in the remaining chapters of this book is also designed for order processing. You might have another database that handles your company's human resources tasks and contains all the relevant information about your employees—their names, job titles, employment history, dependents, insurance coverage, and the like. (You can find an example of a design for a human resources database in Appendix B and on the companion disk.)

At this point you face your biggest design challenge: How do you organize information within each task-oriented database so that you take advantage of the relational capabilities of the tool and avoid inefficiency and waste? If you've followed the steps outlined earlier in this chapter for analyzing application tasks and identifying database subjects, you're well on the way to creating a logical, flexible, and usable database design. But what if you've just "dived in" and started to lay out your data tables without first analyzing tasks and subjects? The rest of this chapter shows you how to apply some rules to avoid problems.

Waste Is the Problem

You use a table within your database to store the information you need for the tasks you want to perform. A table is made up of columns, or *fields,* each of which contains a specific kind of information (such as customer name or item price) and rows, or *records,* that collect all the information about a particular person, place, or thing. You can see this organization in the NWIND database's Customers table, as shown in Figure 4-6.

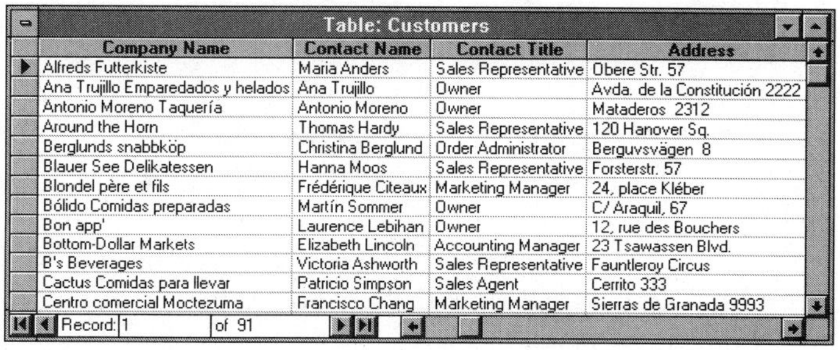
Table: Customers

Company Name	Contact Name	Contact Title	Address
Alfreds Futterkiste	Maria Anders	Sales Representative	Obere Str. 57
Ana Trujillo Emparedados y helados	Ana Trujillo	Owner	Avda. de la Constitución 2222
Antonio Moreno Taquería	Antonio Moreno	Owner	Mataderos 2312
Around the Horn	Thomas Hardy	Sales Representative	120 Hanover Sq.
Berglunds snabbköp	Christina Berglund	Order Administrator	Berguvsvägen 8
Blauer See Delikatessen	Hanna Moos	Sales Representative	Forsterstr. 57
Blondel père et fils	Frédérique Citeaux	Marketing Manager	24, place Kléber
Bólido Comidas preparadas	Martín Sommer	Owner	C/ Araquil, 67
Bon app'	Laurence Lebihan	Owner	12, rue des Bouchers
Bottom-Dollar Markets	Elizabeth Lincoln	Accounting Manager	23 Tsawassen Blvd.
B's Beverages	Victoria Ashworth	Sales Representative	Fauntleroy Circus
Cactus Comidas para llevar	Patricio Simpson	Sales Agent	Cerrito 333
Centro comercial Moctezuma	Francisco Chang	Marketing Manager	Sierras de Granada 9993

Record: 1 of 91

FIGURE 4-6. The NWIND database's Customers table in Datasheet view.

For the purposes of this design exercise, assume you want to build a brand-new database (named PROMPT) for order processing for Prompt Computer Solutions without the benefit of first analyzing the tasks and subjects you'll need. You might be tempted to put all the information about the task you want to do—processing orders—in a single Orders table whose fields are represented in Figure 4-7.

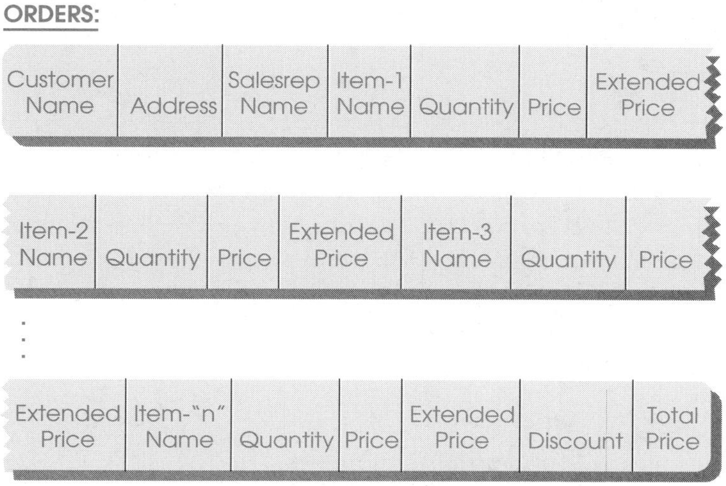

FIGURE 4-7. The design for the PROMPT database's order processing, which uses a single table.

Basically, three things are wrong with this technique:

1. Every time the same customer places another order, you have to duplicate the CustomerName and Address fields in another record for the new order. Storing the same name and address over and over in your database wastes a lot of space—and you can easily make a mistake if you have to enter basic information about a customer more than once.
2. You have no way of predicting how many items a customer might order at one time. If you try to keep track of each item the customer orders in one record, you have to guess what the largest number of items in an order might be and leave space for Item-1, Item-2, Item-3, Item-4, and more, all the way up to the maximum number. Again, you're wasting valuable space in your database. If you guess wrong, you'll have to change your design just to accommodate an order that has too many items. Also, if you later want to find out which customers ordered what products, you'll have to search each Item field in every record.
3. You have to waste space in the database storing data that can easily be calculated when it's time to print a report or produce an invoice. For example, you certainly want to keep track of how many items were ordered and the unit price that was quoted to the customer, but you do not need to calculate and keep the total amount owed in a TotalPrice field.

Normalization Is the Solution

To minimize the kinds of problems noted above (although it might not always be absolutely desirable to eliminate all duplicate values), you'll use a process called *normalization* to organize data fields into a group of tables. The mathematical theory behind normalization is rigorous and complex; the tests you can apply to determine whether you have a design that makes sense and is easy to use are quite simple—and can be stated as rules.

Rule 1: Field Uniqueness

The first test is a rule about field uniqueness.

Rule 1: Each field in a table should contain a unique type of information.

This rule means that you should get rid of the repeating Item fields in the PROMPT database's Orders table. You can do this by creating a row in this table for each item ordered and inserting an OrderLine-Number field to uniquely identify the individual rows in each order. One possible result is shown in Figure 4-8.

ORDERS:

Customer Name	Address	Salesrep Name	Order Line Number	Item Name	Quantity	Price	Extended Price	Discount	Total Price

FIGURE 4-8.
A design for the PROMPT database's order processing that eliminates repeating item fields.

This table is much simpler because it's now easy to process one record per item ordered—whether you're pulling items from inventory to ship or creating a detailed bill for the customer. Also, you don't have to worry about having enough "buckets" in your records to hold large orders. And if you want to find out who has ordered a particular item, you need to look in only one place in each record.

However, the duplicate data problem is now somewhat worse because you are repeating the CustomerName, Address, SalesrepName, TotalPrice, and DateShipped fields in each and every record. You can solve that problem by assigning a unique code number to each order and moving the information about items out to another table. The result is represented in Figure 4-9.

ORDERS:

Order Number	Customer Name	Address	Salesrep Name	Date Shipped	Total Price

ORDERITEM:

Order Number	Order Line Number	Item Name	Quantity	Price	Extended Price

FIGURE 4-9.
A design for the PROMPT database's order processing that includes a separate table for item information.

Although it appears that you've created duplicate data with the OrderNumber field in each table, you've actually significantly reduced the total amount of data stored. The customer name and address information is stored only once in the Orders table for each order and not for each and every item ordered. You've duplicated only a small piece of information, the OrderNumber field, which allows you to *relate* the OrderItem data to the appropriate Orders data. Relational databases are especially equipped to support this design technique by giving you powerful tools to bring related information back together easily. (You'll take a first look at some of these tools in Chapter 8, "Adding Power with Select Queries.")

But you still have the customer name information stored in each and every order. You're also repeating the item name information in each and every order item. To eliminate this situation, you need to understand a few additional rules about relational tables.

Rule 2: Primary Keys

To qualify as a good relational database design, each record in any table must be unique. That is, there must be no two rows in a table that can possibly be identical. For example, it doesn't make sense to keep two records that both describe the same customer.

Rule 2: Each table must have a unique identifier, or primary key, that is made up of one or more fields in the table.

In the Orders table, the OrderNumber field is probably unique in the PROMPT database's order-processing system, so the OrderNumber field could well be the primary key of that table, as shown in Figure 4-10.

FIGURE 4-10. The primary key for the PROMPT database's Orders table.

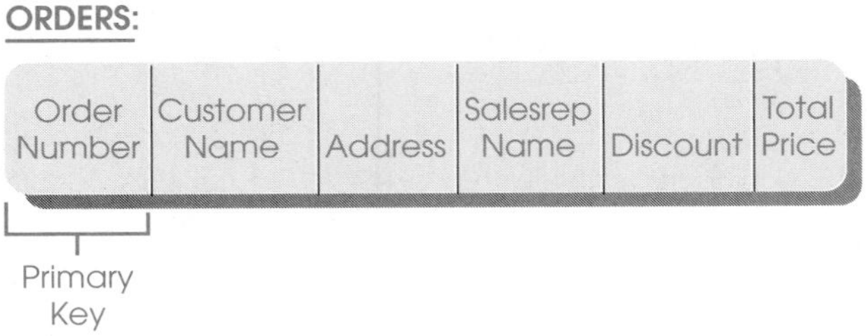

In the PROMPT OrderItem table, the order number might be repeated many times—once for each line item in the order. The order line number is also not unique—every order has a line number 1. However, the combination of order number and order line number is unique and can serve as the primary key for this table, as shown in Figure 4-11.

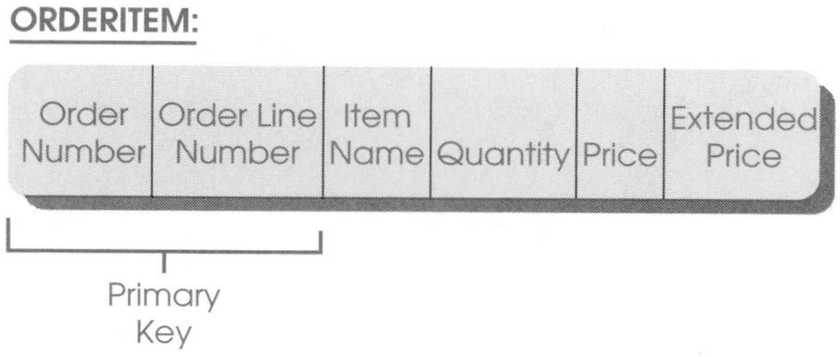

FIGURE 4-11. The primary key for the PROMPT database's Order-Item table.

Whenever you build a table in a Microsoft Access database, Access always recommends that you define a primary key for a table. You can let Access build an artificial primary key, in which case Access adds a counter field to each record; Access increments that counter by 1 each time you add a new record.

Rule 3: Functional Dependence

Once you have a primary key in each table, you can check to see whether you have included all the information relevant to the subject of the table. In terms of relational database design theory, you should check to see whether each field is *functionally dependent* on the primary key.

Rule 3: For each unique primary key value there must be one and only one value in any of the data columns, and that value must be relevant to the subject of the table.

This rule works in two ways. First, you shouldn't have any data in a table that is not relevant to the subject (as defined by the primary key) of the table. For example, you don't need an employee salary in your Orders table. Second, the information in the table should completely describe the subject. For example, if some of your customers have both a billing and a shipping address, one address field in the Orders table will not be sufficient. Or perhaps your sales representatives work in teams; then one SalesrepName field is not enough. Fortunately, the information in the PROMPT Orders table is all relevant.

If you need a more complete address, simply changing "Address" to "Billing Address" and then adding another address field ("Shipping Address") might work, as shown in Figure 4-12.

FIGURE 4-12. A single "Address" field replaced by a "Billing Address" field and a "Shipping Address" field in the PROMPT database's Orders table.

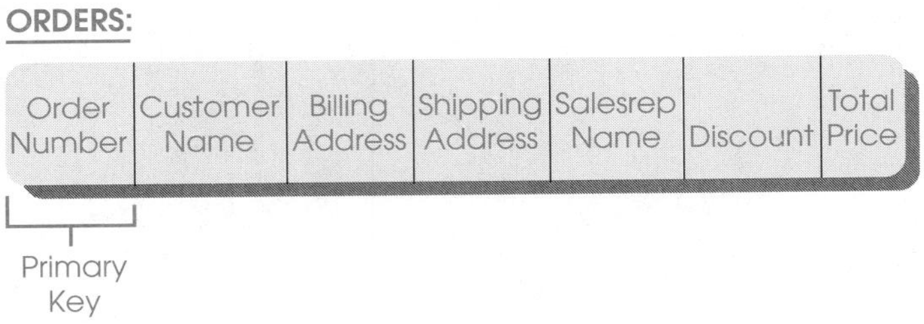

In the second example of missing information (multiple sales rep names), you should probably create another table to hold the information about the members of each sales team, as shown in Figure 4-13.

You might be tempted to create the SalesTeams table with a single SalesTeamID field and multiple columns to contain the SalesrepName fields. If you do that, you are violating Rule 1, which calls for unique information in each field. However, if all of your sales teams are made up of exactly two or exactly three people, it is acceptable to do this. Notice that in this design there's a TeamMemberNumber field as part of the primary key to accommodate sales teams of any size.

FIGURE 4-13. A SalesTeams table added to the PROMPT database.

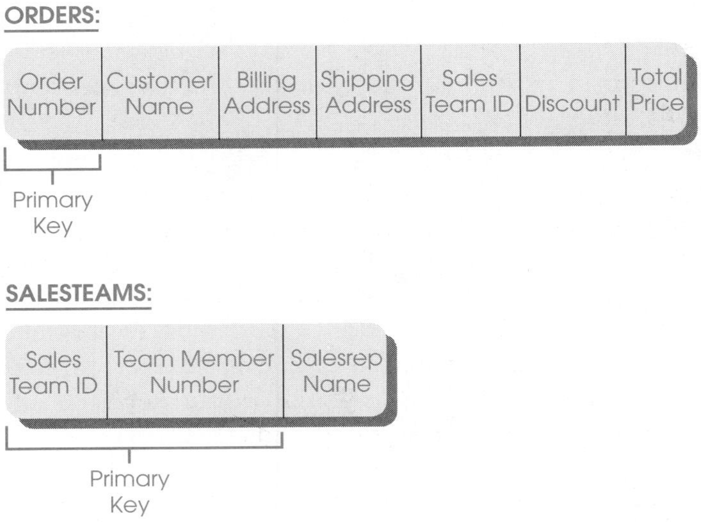

Rule 4: Field Independence

The last rule checks to see whether you'll have any problems when you make changes to the data in your tables.

Rule 4: You must be able to make a change to any field (other than fields in the primary key) without affecting any other field.

Take a look again at the Orders table in Figure 4-13. The first field outside the primary key is CustomerName. If you need to correct the spelling of a name, you can do so without affecting any other fields in this record. If you got the customer wrong (the order is really for Jameson Labs on Main Street, not James Company on First Street), you can't change a customer name without also fixing the billing address and shipping address information. The CustomerName, BillingAddress, and ShippingAddress fields are not independent of one another. In fact, BillingAddress and ShippingAddress are functionally dependent on CustomerName. (See Rule 3, above.) CustomerName describes another subject, different from the subject of orders. When you have this situation, it calls for another table in your design. You need a separate Customers table, as shown in Figure 4-14.

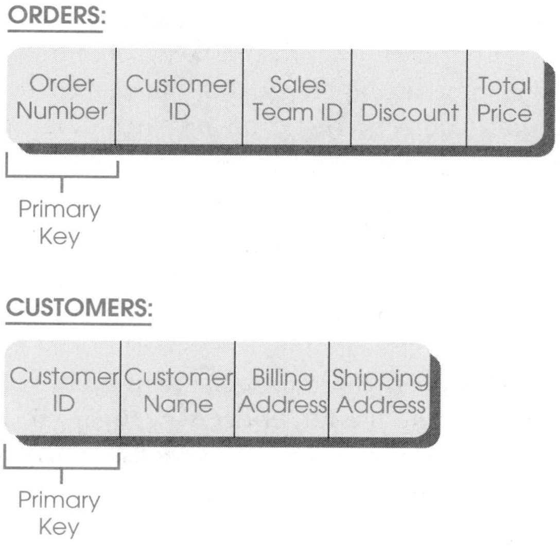

FIGURE 4-14. A Customers table added to PROMPT's database that is separate from Orders.

Now, if you've spelled the name incorrectly, you just change the customer name in the Customers table. Note that instead of using CustomerName (which might be 40 or 50 characters long) as the primary key of the Customers table, you create a shorter CustomerID field (perhaps a five-digit number) to minimize the size of the relational data you need in the Orders table.

Another (although less rigorous) way you can check for this condition of field independence is to see whether you have the same information repeated over and over in your records. In the previous design, you would soon notice that whenever a customer had placed more than one order, you had had to enter the customer's name and the addresses in multiple order records. Now that you have a separate Customers table, if you need to correct the spelling or change an address, you have to make the change only in one field of one record in the Customers table. If you find you have the wrong customer, you have to change only the customer ID information in the Orders table to fix the problem.

What about the other fields in the Orders table? You can make a change to sales team ID or discount independently of the other information. You can also change the total price information without affecting other information in this record; but TotalPrice is related to two fields, Quantity and Price, in the Order Items records. In fact, TotalPrice is one of those calculated fields (the sum of the quantity-times-price for all items in the order) that you would be better off not including in your table.

The only reason to keep a calculated field in your table is to improve performance. For example, if you frequently produce a report that lists outstanding orders and the amounts owed and if you never need to show the details of the items ordered, then keeping the calculated total in the Orders table saves searching the OrderItem table each time you want that report. However, you must be sure to build your application so that you always update the total price whenever you add a new item to the order or change the quantity or price in OrderItems. You'll learn how to do this in Chapters 20 and 22 of this book.

One additional design note: After examining the way that customers ask to have orders shipped, Prompt Computer Solutions decided to include a ShippingAddress field in the Orders table as well as in the Customers table. For many customers, the shipping address remains constant. However, several customers frequently request that their orders be shipped to a different location. So the Customers table contains the usual shipping address, while the Orders table has fields to reflect where a particular order is to be sent.

See Also: In Chapter 22, "Automating Your Application with Access Basic," you'll learn how to design the order entry form to automatically copy the usual shipping address but allow the person entering the order to change it for a particular order.

If you look at the OrderItem table in Figure 4-11, you can see that the ItemName and Price fields probably also belong in another table. Be careful that the price you charge a customer is always the latest price in the new Items table. If you have a policy of charging the price quoted at the time of the order or if you have different discounts that you give to each customer, you might need to keep a QuotedPrice field in the OrderItem table that is different from the Price field in the Items table, as shown in Figure 4-15.

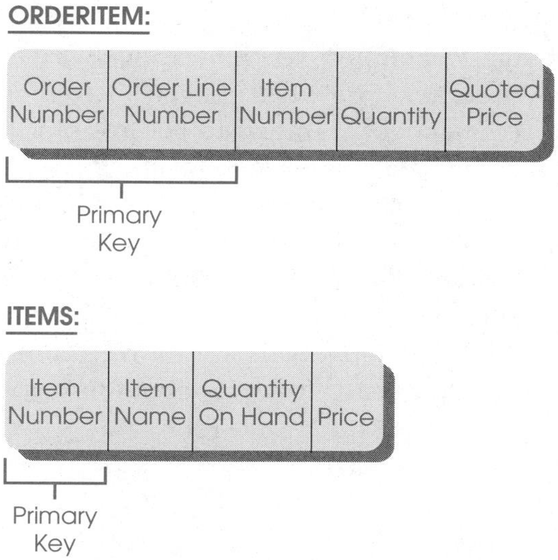

FIGURE 4-15.
A new Items table, which is separate from OrderItem.

After applying all the rules, the database design includes five tables, which are all shown in Microsoft Access in the query in Figure 4-16. Notice that additional fields were created in each table to fully describe the subject of each table. For example, Customers have a second-line address field, Orders have an OrderDate and a ShipDate field, and sales representatives have an EmailName field.

The Four Rules for Good Table Design

Rule 1: Each field in a table should contain a unique type of information.

Rule 2: Each table must have a unique identifier, or primary key, that is made up of one or more fields in the table.

Rule 3: For each unique primary key value there must be one and only one value in any of the data columns, and that value must be relevant to the subject of the table.

Rule 4: You must be able to make a change to any field (other than fields in the primary key) without affecting any other field.

Efficient Relationships Are the Result

When you apply good design techniques, you end up with a database that efficiently links your data. You probably noticed that when you normalize your data as recommended, you tend to get lots of separate tables as a result. Before relational databases were invented, you had to either compromise your design or manually keep track of the relationships between files or tables. For example, you had to put customer information in your Orders table or write your program to first open and read a record from the Orders table and then search for the matching record in the Customers table. Relational databases solve those problems. With a good design you don't have to worry about how to bring the data together when you need it.

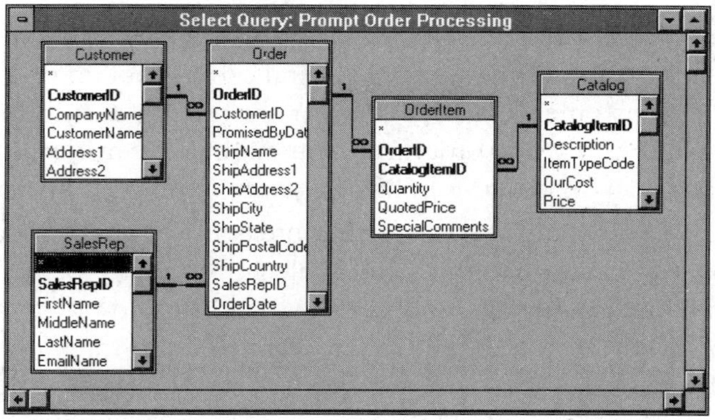

FIGURE 4-16. The PROMPT database's order processing tables shown in a Microsoft Access query.

Foreign Keys

You probably noticed as you followed along in the PROMPT example above that each time you created a new table, you left behind a small piece of information that could link you to the new table—CustomerID and SalesrepID fields in the Orders table and an ItemNumber (CatalogItemID) field in the Order Items table. These "linking" fields are called *foreign keys.*

In a well-designed database, foreign keys result in efficiency. You keep track of related foreign keys as you lay out your database design. When you define your tables in Microsoft Access, you link primary keys to foreign keys to tell Access how to join the data when you need to get information from more than one table. To improve performance, you also instruct Access to build indexes on your foreign keys.

See Also: For details on defining indexes, see the section in Chapter 5 titled "Adding Indexes."

One-to-Many and One-to-One Relationships

In most cases, the efficient relationship between any two tables is one-to-many. That is, for any one record in the first table, there are many related records in the second table, but for any record in the second table, there is exactly one matching record in the first table. You saw many instances of this pattern of relationship in the PROMPT design. For example, each customer might have several orders, but an order applies to only one customer. An order has many order items, but each order item is a part of only one order. An item might appear in many different order items, but an order item has only one item.

Occasionally, you might want to further break down a table because you use some of the information in the table infrequently or because some of the data in the table is highly sensitive and should not be available to everyone. For example, you might want to keep track of some descriptive information about each of your customers for marketing purposes, but you don't need that information all the time. Or you might have data such as credit rating or amount of credit that should only be accessible to authorized people in your company. In either case, you can create a separate table that also has a primary key of CustomerID. The relationship between the original Customers table and the CustomerInfo or CustomerCredit tables is one-to-one. That is, for each record in the first table, there is exactly one record in the second table. Like the one-to-many relationship, the one-to-one relationship of tables is an efficient design.

Creating Table Links

The last step in designing your database is to create the links between each of your tables. For each subject, look at the subjects for which you wrote *Many* in the Relationship column of the worksheet. Be sure that the corresponding relationship for the other table is *One*. If you find *Many* in both Relationship columns, you must create a separate *intersection* table to handle the relationship. In this example of the Record Customer Order task, one order can contain "many" items, and any given item can appear in "many" orders. The OrderItem table is an intersection table that clears up this many-to-many relationship between the Order and Item tables. OrderItem works as an intersection table because it is in a one-to-many relationship with both Order and Item.

After you've straightened out the many-to-many relationships, you need to create the links between tables. To complete the links, place a copy of the primary key from the "one" tables into the "many" tables. For example, by looking at the worksheet for Customers shown in Figure 4-5 on page 87, you can surmise that the primary key for the Customers table (probably a field called CustomerID) also needs to be in the Orders table (a "many") and in the SalesHistory table (a "many"). On the other hand, the primary key from the SalesReps table (a "one") should appear in the Customers table.

Now that you understand the fundamentals of good database design, you're ready to do something a little more fun with Access—actually building a database. The next chapter, "Building Your Database in Microsoft Access," shows you how to create a new database and tables; and Chapter 6, "Modifying Your Database Design," shows you how to make changes later if you discover you need to modify your design.

In the following chapters, you'll learn about the mechanics of defining queries, forms, and reports using Microsoft Access. You'll find that you're building some pieces of the database to satisfy the tasks shown in Figure 4-3 on page 85. In the final part of the book, you'll learn about macros and how to link together the queries, forms, and reports that you've built to create a working application.

5

Building Your Database in Microsoft Access

After you've designed the tables for your database, defining them in Microsoft Access is incredibly easy. This chapter shows you how it's done. Continuing with the exercise of building a database for Prompt Computer Solutions, Inc. (begun in Chapter 4, "Designing Your Database Application"), this chapter shows you how to create a new database, define the Customers table, define the Orders table using a Table Wizard, and relate these tables to other tables.

See Also: For a complete description of the PROMPT database, refer to Appendix B, "Sample Database Schemas."

Creating a New Database

When you first start Microsoft Access, you see only the File and Help menus on the menu bar. On the toolbar are more than a dozen buttons, but only the two buttons at the far left (New Database and Open Database) and the two buttons at the far right (Cue Cards and Help) are immediately available. The remaining buttons become enabled as soon as you open or create a database. (The full description of the buttons begins on page 107.) For now, open the File menu to see the commands shown in Figure 5-1. If you've previously opened other databases, such as the NWIND sample, you'll also see a "most recently used" list of up to four numbered database selections just above the Exit command.

FIGURE 5-1.
The File menu.

To begin creating a new database, simply choose the New Database command from the File menu. This command opens the dialog box shown in Figure 5-2. Select the drive you want from the Drives drop-down list box, and select a directory from the Directories list box. The drive and directory will be the location for the new database. In this example, the *sampapps* subdirectory of the *access* directory is selected on the C drive. Finally, go to the File Name text box and type the name of your new database. Access appends an MDB extension to the filename for you. Access uses a file with an MDB extension to store all your database objects, including tables, queries, forms, reports, macros, and modules. If you're creating a database for Prompt Computer Solutions, you might choose to name the database PROMPT.MDB. If you've installed the PROMPT database from the companion disk included with this book, you might name your new database MYPROMPT.MDB. (See page xxiv for instructions on using the companion disk.) Click the OK button to create your database.

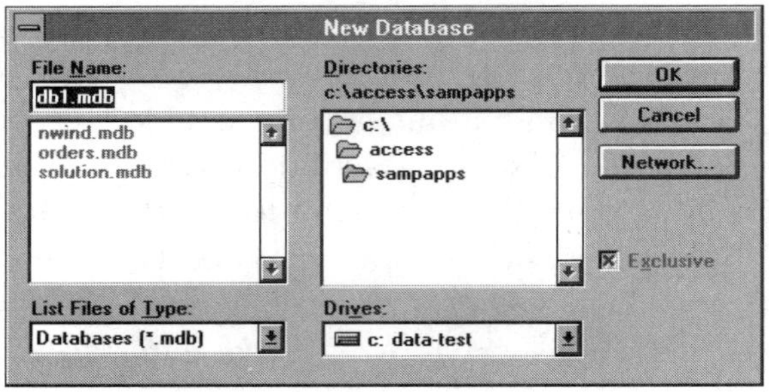

FIGURE 5-2.
The New Database dialog box.

> **TIP:** You can create a new database either by choosing the New Database command from the File menu or by clicking the New Database button on the toolbar. The New Database button is the first button at the left end of the toolbar when you start Microsoft Access.

Microsoft Access takes a few moments to create the system files in which it keeps all the information about the tables, queries, forms, reports, macros, and modules that you might create. When Access has completed this process, you see the Database window for your new database displayed in the upper left corner of your Access workspace, as shown in Figure 5-3.

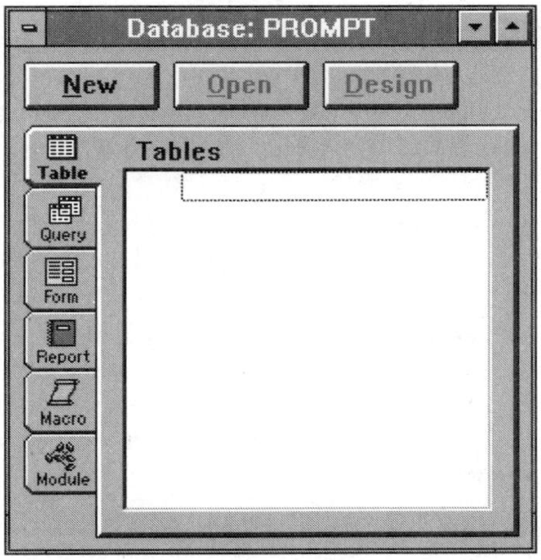

FIGURE 5-3.
The Database window for a new database.

When you open any database, Access selects the Table tab and shows you the available tables in the Database window. Because this is a new database, no tables exist yet and the Database window is empty.

The Built-In Toolbar for the Database Window

Before you get right down to defining tables in your new database, it's worth spending a few moments to look at the Database toolbar that Microsoft Access displays when the Database window is active. The buttons, from left to right, are as follows:

New Database button. Click this button to create a new database.

Open Database button. Click this button to open an existing database. If you already have a database open, Microsoft Access closes it before opening another database.

(continued)

(continued)

Attach Table button. Click this button to attach a table from another Microsoft Access or SQL database or a Paradox, FoxPro, dBASE, or Btrieve file to this database. (See Chapter 10, "Importing, Attaching, and Exporting Data," for details.)

Print button. Select any table, query, form, report, or module, and click this button to print your selected object. This prints the Datasheet view for tables and queries, the Form view for forms, the Report view for reports, and a listing of the code in modules.

Print Preview button. Select a table, query, form, or report, and click this button to see what the selected item will look like in printed form in the Print Preview window.

Code button. Select a form or report, and click this button to view and edit any Microsoft Access Basic code stored with the form or report. (See Chapter 21, "Microsoft Access Basic Fundamentals," and Chapter 22, "Automating Your Application with Access Basic," for details.)

Cut button. Select an object in the Database window, and click this button to delete the object from the database and place a copy of the object on the Clipboard.

Copy button. Select an object in the Database window, and click this button to copy the object to the Clipboard.

Paste button. Click this button to paste an object saved on the Clipboard into the database. Access prompts you for a new name for the object.

Relationships button. Click this button to view and edit the definition of relationships between tables and queries. (See "Defining Relationships," later in this chapter, for details.)

Import button. Click this button to import an object from another Microsoft Access database; to import data from text, spreadsheet, Paradox, FoxPro, dBASE, or Btrieve database files; or to import data in tables in another SQL database. (See Chapter 10, "Importing, Attaching, and Exporting Data," for details.)

Export button. Click this button to export an object to another Microsoft Access database; to export data from a table or query to a text, spreadsheet, Microsoft Word for Windows, Paradox, FoxPro, dBASE, or Btrieve file; or to export a table from another SQL database. (See Chapter 10 for details.)

Merge It button. Select a table or query in the Database window, and click this button to start the Microsoft Word Mail Merge Wizard. You can use this Wizard to merge data from your tables or queries into a new or an existing Microsoft Word document.

Analyze It With MS Excel button. Choose a table, query, form, or report in the Database window, and click this button to output the data to a Microsoft Excel spreadsheet file and start Excel with that file open. If you choose a form, Access writes the data from the form's Datasheet view to the file. If you choose a report, Access writes the data from all text box controls on the report to the file.

New Query button. Click this button to start designing a new query. If you've selected a table or a query in the Database window, Access starts you off with the selected table or query as the basis for your new query. (See Chapter 8, "Adding Power with Select Queries," for details on building a query.)

New Form button. Click this button to start designing a new form. (See Chapter 13, "Building a Form," for details on creating forms.)

New Report button. Click this button to start designing a new report. (See Chapter 17, "Constructing a Report," for details on basic report design.)

Database Window button. Click this button to place the focus on the Database window. This button also unhides the window if you've hidden it and restores the window if you've minimized it.

AutoForm button. Select a table or a query in the Database window, and click this button to have Microsoft Access build a simple single view form for you. (See Chapter 12, "Form Basics," for details on building a simple form.)

AutoReport button. Select a table or a query in the Database window, and click this button to have Microsoft Access build a simple report and display it in Print Preview. (See Chapter 16, "Report Basics," for details on constructing a simple report.)

Undo button. Click this button to undo your last action. Undo has the same effect as the Undo command on the Edit menu or Ctrl-Z. The button is disabled when there are no changes that can be undone.

(continued)

(continued)

Cue Cards button. Click this button to open the main menu of the Cue Cards facility. The Cue Cards facility leads you through step-by-step instructions for most common tasks.

Help button. Click this button to add a question mark to your mouse pointer. Click with this pointer on any displayed object to receive context-sensitive help about that object.

TIP: You can see a short description of any toolbar button by placing your mouse pointer over the button (but don't click the button) and waiting for a second. Access displays a small label (called a *ToolTip*), below the button, which contains the name of the button. If you can't see ToolTips, choose the Toolbars command from the View menu when you have a database open and be sure the Show ToolTips box is checked in the Toolbars dialog box.

More About Microsoft Access Help

In addition to the Help button on the Database window toolbar, there are several other ways of opening Microsoft Access Help. You can use the commands on the Help menu. The Contents command opens the Contents screen for Help, shown in Figure 5-4.

You can also access Cue Cards, go to the topics on Technical Support, or request a search dialog box to look for a topic by keyword directly from the Help menu. You can bring up context-sensitive help by pressing the F1 key. Whenever you press F1, a Help window opens with information about the active window or the currently highlighted keyword. To obtain context-sensitive help on a button or another screen control, press Shift-F1 or click the Help button on the toolbar. A special mouse pointer appears, which you use to click the screen element about which you have a question. The Help window then opens with the information about the screen element you clicked.

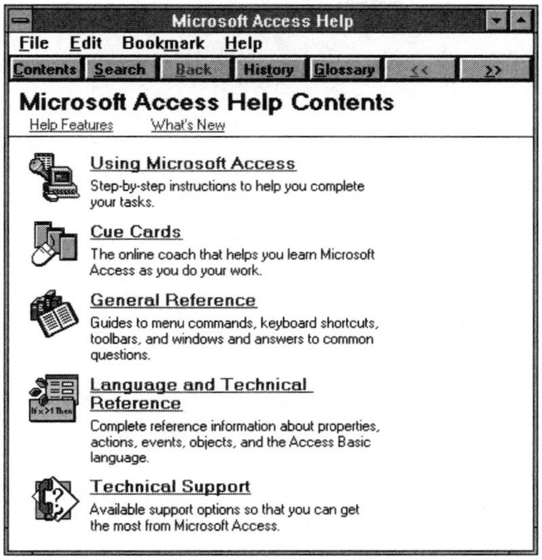

FIGURE 5-4.
The Contents screen in Microsoft Access Help.

On the Contents screen for Help, you can see an underlined topic called Cue Cards, which you can click. Cue Cards is a special area in Microsoft Access help that uses pop-up windows linked to the main window to walk you through the individual steps required to perform any common task. Figure 5-5 on the next page shows the primary menu in Cue Cards. From this menu, you can choose one of seven major topic areas: general information about databases (a tutorial), building databases and tables, working with data in a table in Datasheet view, designing and running queries, creating forms, designing reports, and writing macros.

Within each major Cue Cards area, Microsoft Access asks you what you want to do next. If you decide to try a task that requires a database to be open, Cue Cards prompts you to open or create a database if one isn't already open. Simply follow the steps displayed for each task. The Cue Cards window stays open on top of the Access workspace to provide an instant reference for each step. As you complete each step, simply click the Next button to go on to the next step. Use the Back button at the top of the window to go back one step. Click the Menu button to go back to the previous list of options. Use the Search button to find specific topics that interest you.

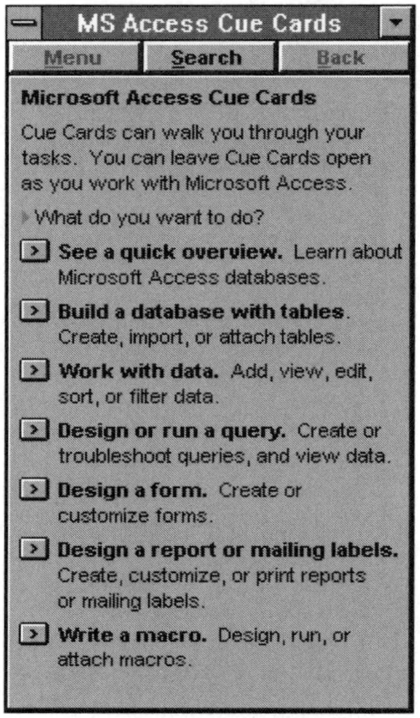

FIGURE 5-5. The Cue Cards list in Microsoft Access Help.

Defining Tables

If you want to define a new table in a database, the Database window (shown in Figure 5-3 on page 107) must be active. Click the Table tab (the top tab on the left side of the Database window), and then click the New button at the top of the Database window. The dialog box shown in Figure 5-6 opens and asks whether you want to use the Table Wizard or build the table on your own. For now, click the New Table button; Access displays a blank Table window in Design view, as shown in Figure 5-7. You'll use a Table Wizard later in this chapter to build a second table.

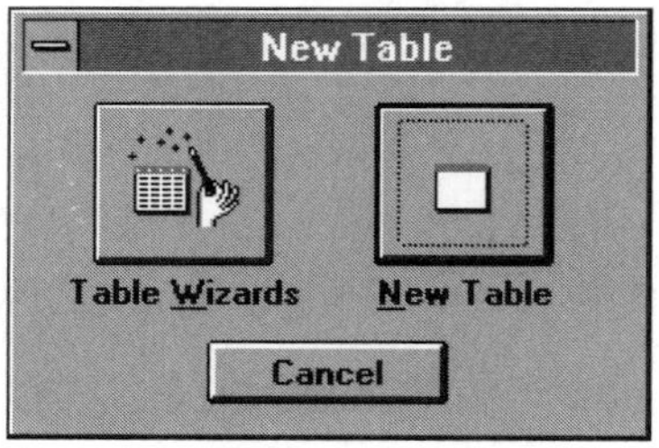

FIGURE 5-6. The New Table options dialog box.

> **TIP:** You can use the New Table button on the toolbar to start designing a new table instead of going to the Database window, choosing the Table tab, and clicking the New button.

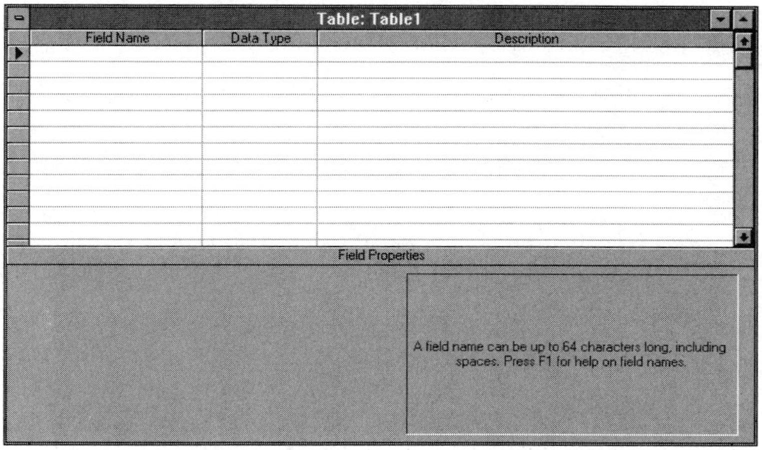

FIGURE 5-7. A blank Table window in Design view.

At the top of the Table window in Design view are columns in which you can enter each field name, the data type for the field, and a description of the field. After you select a data type for a field, Access allows you to set field properties in the lower left corner of the Table window. In the lower right corner of the Table window is a box in which Access displays informative messages about fields or properties. The contents of this box changes as you move your cursor from one location to another within the Table window.

The Built-In Toolbar for the Table Window in Design View

When you open a Table window in Design view, the toolbar changes. The buttons, from left to right, are as follows:

Design View button. This button initially appears activated, indicating that you are in Design view. Click this button to return to Design view from Datasheet view.

Datasheet View button. After you have finished designing your table and have saved the design, you can use this button to enter Datasheet view so that you can begin entering data in your table. (See Chapter 7, "Using Datasheets," for more details on Datasheet view.)

NEW!

Save button. Click this button to save any changes.

Table Properties button. Click this button to open the Table Properties window.

NEW!

Indexes button. Click this button to open the Indexes window for this table. (See later in this chapter for more information about defining indexes.)

Set Primary Key button. Click this button to define a selected field or fields as the primary key for this table.

NEW!

Insert Row button. Click this button to insert an empty row above the current row. You must place the cursor on a line in the top half of the Table window in Design view to use this button.

NEW!

Delete Row button. Click this button to delete the current row. You must place the cursor on a line in the top half of the Table window in Design view to use this button.

NEW!

Build button. Click in the Field Name column, and click this button to start the Field Builder Wizard to insert a field definition from one of dozens of sample tables provided with Microsoft Access. Click in a field property box that can accept a complex expression, and then click this button to start the Expression Builder. (See the section titled "Using the Expression Builder" in Chapter 8 for an example.)

Defining Fields

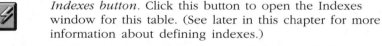

Now you're ready to begin defining the fields for the Customers table. Be sure the cursor is in the first position of the Field Name column, and then type the name of the first field, *CustomerID.* Press the Tab key once to move to the Data Type column. A little gray button with a down arrow appears on the right side of the box in the Data Type column. Here and elsewhere in Microsoft Access, this type of button signifies the presence of a drop-down list. Click the down arrow or press Alt-down arrow to open the list of data type options, shown in Figure 5-8 on the next page. In the Data Type column, you can either type a valid value or select from the list of values in the drop-down list box. The data type values are explained later in this chapter, in the section titled "Field Data Types."

> **NOTE:** Although you can use spaces anywhere in names in Microsoft Access, you should lean toward creating field names and table names without embedded spaces. Most SQL databases to which Microsoft Access can attach do not support spaces in names. Should you ever want to move your application into a true client-server environment and store your data in an SQL database such as Microsoft SQL Server or Oracle, you'll have to change every name in your database tables that has an embedded blank. As you'll learn later in this book, table field names propagate into the queries, forms, and reports that you design using these tables. So any name you decide to change later in a table must also be changed in all your queries, forms, and reports.

After you've selected a data type, Access displays some property boxes in the Field Properties area at the bottom of the window. These boxes allow you to set properties and thereby customize a field. Access shows you different boxes, depending on the data type selected; when the boxes appear, they have some default properties in place, as shown in Figure 5-8. The various property settings for each property box are explained a little later in this chapter in the "Field Properties" section.

In the Description column for each field (in the upper right corner of the Table window), you have the option of entering a descriptive phrase for each field. Microsoft Access displays this description in the status bar (at the bottom of the Access window) whenever you select this field in a query in Datasheet view or in a form in Form view or Datasheet view.

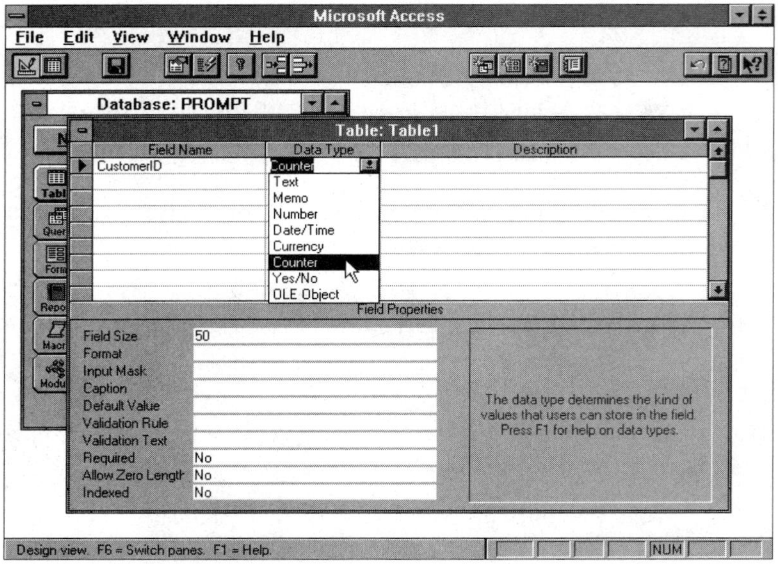

FIGURE 5-8.
The open list of data type options.

Field Data Types

Microsoft Access supports eight types of data, each with a specific purpose. These data types are described in Figure 5-9. Choose the data type for each field in your tables that is most appropriate for how you will use that field's data. For character data, you should normally choose the Text data type. You can control the maximum length of a Text field by using a field property, as explained below. Use the Memo data type only for long text that might exceed 255 characters or that might contain formatting characters such as tabs or carriage returns.

When you choose the Number data type, you'll need to think carefully about what you enter as the Field Size property because these choices will affect precision as well as length. (For example, integer numbers do not have decimals.) Always use the Currency data type for storing money. Currency has the precision of integers, but with a fixed number of decimal places. The Date/Time data type is useful for calendar or clock data and has the added benefit of allowing calculations in

Data Type	Usage	Size
Text	Alphanumeric data	Up to 255 bytes
Memo	Alphanumeric data—sentences and paragraphs	Up to 64,000 bytes
Number	Numeric data	1, 2, 4, or 8 bytes
Date/Time	Dates and times	8 bytes
Currency	Monetary data, stored with 4 decimal places of precision	8 bytes
Counter	Unique long integer generated by Access for each new record	4 bytes
Yes/No	Boolean data	1 bit
OLE Object	Pictures, graphs, or other OLE objects from another application for Windows	Up to about 1 gigabyte

FIGURE 5-9.
Microsoft Access data types.

minutes, seconds, hours, days, months, or years. For example, you can find out the difference in days between two Date/Time values. The Counter data type is a special kind of integer specifically designed for automatic generation of primary key values. You can include only one field using the Counter data type in any table.

Use the Yes/No data type to hold Boolean (true or false) values. This data type is particularly useful for flagging accounts paid or not paid or tests passed or not passed. Finally, the OLE Object data type allows you to store complex data, such as pictures, graphs, or sounds, that can be maintained by a dynamic link to another application for the Microsoft Windows operating system. For example, Access can store and allow you to edit a Microsoft Word document, a Microsoft Excel spreadsheet, a Microsoft PowerPoint presentation slide, a WAV sound file, an AVI video file, or pictures created using the Paintbrush or Draw application.

Field Properties

You can customize each field with specific properties you set. These properties vary according to the data type you choose. Here are the properties for a field in a table:

Field Size

You can specify the length of Text and Number data types. Text can be from 1 through 255 characters long, with a default length of 50 characters. For Number, the field sizes are as follows:

Byte	A single-byte integer containing values from 0 through 255
Integer	A 2-byte integer containing values from –32,768 through +32,767
Long Integer	A 4-byte integer containing values from –2,147,483,648 through +2,147,483,647
Single	A 4-byte floating-point number containing values from -3.4×10^{38} through $+3.4 \times 10^{38}$
Double	An 8-byte floating-point number containing values from -1.797×10^{308} through $+1.797 \times 10^{308}$

Format

You can control how your data is displayed or printed. The format options vary by data type.

For Text and Memo data types, you can specify a custom format that controls how Access displays the data. For details on custom formats, see the section "Setting Control Properties" in Chapter 14 or the Format Property—Text and Memo Data Types topic in Access Help.

For Number, Currency, and Counter, the standard format options are as follows:

General Number	The default (no commas or currency symbols; decimal places shown depend on the precision of the data)
Currency	Currency symbols and two decimal places
Fixed	At least one digit and two decimal places
Standard	Two decimal places and separator commas
Percent	Percentage
Scientific	Scientific notation (as in 1.05×10^3)

For the Date/Time data type, the format options follow the patterns of the examples below:

General Date	The default 04/15/94 05:30:10 PM (US) 15/04/94 17:30:10 (UK)
Long Date	Wednesday, April 15, 1994 (US) 15 April 1994 (UK)
Medium Date	15-Apr-94
Short Date	4/15/94
Long Time	5:30:10 PM
Medium Time	5:30 PM
Short Time	17:30

For the Yes/No data type, the options are as follows:

Yes/No	The default
True/False	
On/Off	

Decimal Places	For Number and Currency data types, you can specify the number of decimal places that Access displays. The default specification is Auto, which causes Access to display two decimal places for Currency, Fixed, Standard, and Percent format and the number of decimal places necessary to show the current precision of the numeric value for General Number format. You can also request a fixed display of decimal places, ranging from 0 through 15.
Input Mask	NEW! For Text, Number, Currency, and Date/Time data types, you can specify an editing mask that the user sees when entering data in the field. For example, you can have Access provide the delimiters in a date field: (__/__/__). Or you can have Access format a U.S. phone number: (###) 000-0000. See later in this chapter for details.
Caption	You can enter a more fully descriptive field name that Access displays on form labels and in report headings. (Note: If you create field names with no embedded spaces, you can use the Caption property to specify a name that includes spaces for Access to use in labels and headers associated with this field in queries, forms, and reports.)
Default Value	You can specify a default value for all data types except Counter, Memo, and OLE Object. For numbers,

(continued)

(continued)

	the default value is 0. Access provides a Null default value for Text and Memo data types.
Validation Rule	You can supply an expression that must be true whenever you enter or change data in this field. For example, *<100* specifies that a number must be less than 100. You can also check for one of a series of values. For example, you can have Access check for a list of valid cities by specifying *"Chicago" Or "New York" Or "San Francisco"*. In addition, you can specify a complex expression that includes any of the Microsoft Access built-in functions. (See the section "Defining Simple Field Validation Rules," later in this chapter, for details.)
Validation Text	You can have Microsoft Access display text whenever the data entered does not pass your validation rule.
Required	If you don't allow a Null value in this field, set this property to Yes.
NEW! Allow Zero Length	For Text and Memo fields, you can set the field equal to a zero length string (" "). (See the sidebar below, "Nulls and Zero Length Strings," for more information.)
NEW! Indexed	You can ask that an index be built to speed access to data values for Text, Number, Date/Time, Currency, and Counter data types. You can also require that the values in the indexed field always be unique for the entire table. (See the section titled "Adding Indexes," later in this chapter, for details.)

Nulls and Zero Length Strings

Relational databases support a special value in table fields, called a *Null,* which indicates an unknown value. Nulls have special properties. A Null value cannot be equal to any other value, not even to another Null. This means that you cannot join (link) two tables on Null values. Also, the test "A = B", when A or B or both contain a Null value, yields a False result. Finally, Null values do not participate in aggregate calculations involving such functions as *Sum* or *Avg* (average). However, you can test for the existence of a Null value by comparing it to the special keyword NULL or by using the *IsNull* built-in function.

(continued)

continued

Nulls and Zero Length Strings

In contrast, you can set text or memo fields equal to a *zero length string* to indicate that the value of a field is known but the field is empty. You can join tables on zero length strings, and two zero length strings will compare to be equal. However, for text and memo fields, you must set the Allow Zero Length property to Yes to allow users to enter zero length strings. If you do not do this, Microsoft Access converts any zero length or all-blank string entered by the user to a Null before storing the value in the database. If you also set the Required property of the text field to Yes, Access stores a zero length string if the user enters either " " or blanks in the field.

Why is it important to differentiate Nulls from zero length strings? Here's an example: Suppose you have a database that stores the result of a survey about automobile preferences. For questionnaires that have no response to a color-preference question, it would be appropriate to store a Null value. You wouldn't want to match responses based on an "unknown" response, and you wouldn't want to include the row in calculating totals or averages. On the other hand, some people might have responded "I don't care" for a color preference. In this case, you have a known "nothing" answer, and a zero length string is appropriate. You can match all "I don't care" responses and include the responses in totals and averages.

Another example might be fax machine numbers in your customer database. If you store a Null, it means that you don't know whether the customer has a fax number. If you store a zero length string, you know the customer does not have a fax number. Access gives you the flexibility to deal with both types of "empty" values.

Completing the Fields in Your First Table

You now know enough about field data types and properties to enable you to finish designing the Customers table for the PROMPT database example. The table you create now will be changed in Chapter 6, "Modifying Your Database Design," so that it is more like the final PROMPT Customers table. (To build the entire PROMPT database, you can use the first database schema in Appendix B. You can also install the complete PROMPT database from the companion disk included with this book; see "Using the Companion Disk" on page xxiv.) Use the information listed in Figure 5-10 to define the table shown in Figure 5-11.

Field Name	Data Type	Description	Field Size
CustomerID	Counter	Customer identifier	–
CompanyName	Text	Customer company name	30
CustomerName	Text	Name of company contact	25
Address	Text	Street address line 1	30
City	Text	City	20
State	Text	State or province	12
PostalCode	Text	Zip or postal zone code	10
Country	Text	Country name	6
PhoneNumber	Text	Phone number	20
FaxNumber	Text	Fax machine number	20
CreditLimit	Currency	Maximum credit allowed	–
AmountOwed	Currency	Total amount owed	–
LastPayDate	Date/Time	Date of last payment	–

FIGURE 5-10.
The field definitions for the Customers table.

Defining Simple Field Validation Rules

To define a simple check on the values that you allow in a field, enter an expression in the Validation Rule property box for the field. Microsoft Access won't allow you to enter a field value that violates this rule. Access performs this validation for data entered via the Table window in Datasheet view, an updatable query, or a form. You can specify a more restrictive validation rule in a form, but you cannot override the rule in the table by specifying a different rule in a form.

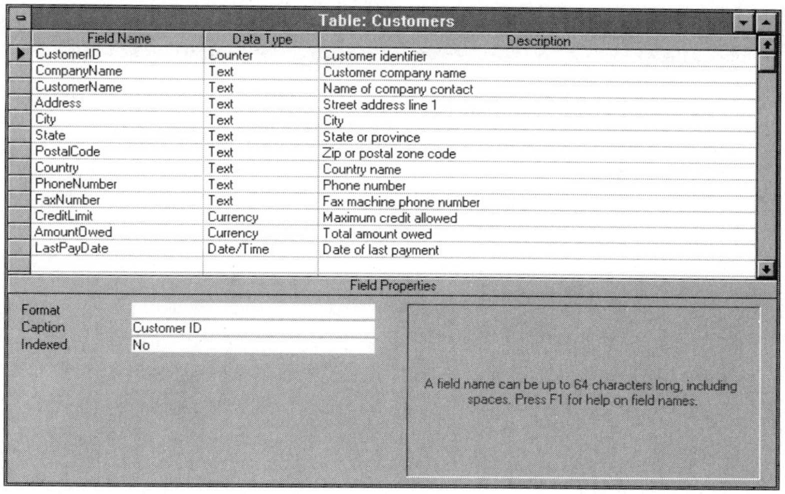

FIGURE 5-11.
The fields in the Customers table.

In general, a field validation expression consists of an operator (see Figure 5-12 on the next page) and a comparison value. If you do not include an operator, Access assumes you want an "equals" (=) comparison. You can specify multiple comparisons separated by the Boolean operators OR and AND. For example, in Figure 5-13 on the next page, you can see a validation rule for the Country field that tests for values *"USA" Or "Canada"*. If one of your values is a text string containing blanks or special characters, be sure to enclose the entire string in quotes. For example, you might enter a validation rule for states surrounding our nation's capital as *"Maryland" Or "Virginia"*. If you are comparing date values, you must enclose date constants in pound sign (#) characters, as in *#01/15/94#*.

You can use the comparison symbols to compare the value in the field to a value or values in your validation rule. For example, you might want to check that a numeric value is always less than 1000. To do this, enter *<1000*. You can use one or more pairs of comparisons to check that the value falls within certain ranges. For example, if you want to verify that a number is in the range from 50 through 100, enter either *>50 And <100* or *BETWEEN 50 And 100*.

Another way to test for a match in a list of values is to use the IN comparison operator. For example, another way to test for states surrounding the U.S. capital is to enter *IN ("Virginia", "Maryland")*.

Operator	Meaning
<	Less than
<=	Less than or equal to
>	Greater than
>=	Greater than or equal to
=	Equal to
<>	Not equal to
IN	Test for "equal to" any member in a list; comparison value must be a list enclosed in parentheses
BETWEEN	Test for a range of values; comparison value must be two values (a low and a high value) separated by the keyword AND
LIKE	Test a text or memo field to match a pattern string

FIGURE 5-12.
Some comparison symbols that can be used in validation rules.

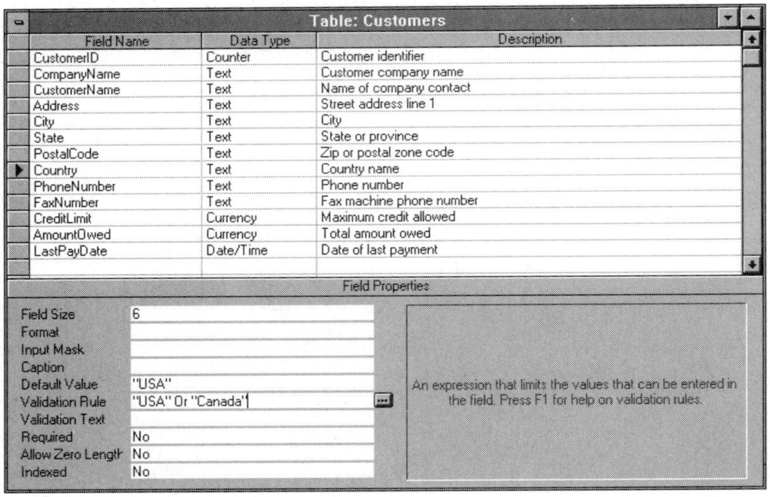

FIGURE 5-13.
A validation rule for the Country field.

If you need to validate a text or memo field against a matching pattern (for example, a zip code or a phone number), you can use the LIKE comparison operator. You provide a text string as a comparison value that defines which characters are valid in which positions. Access understands a number of *wildcard* characters, which you can use to define positions that can contain any single character, zero or more characters, or any single number. These characters are shown in Figure 5-14.

Wildcard Character	Meaning
?	Any single character
*	Zero or more characters; used to define leading, trailing, or embedded strings that don't have to match any of the pattern characters
#	Any single number

FIGURE 5-14.
LIKE wildcard characters.

You can also specify that any particular position in the text or memo field can contain only characters from a list that you provide. To define a list of valid characters, enclose the list in left and right brackets ([ ]). You can specify a range of characters within a list by entering the low value character, a hyphen, and the high value character, as in *[A-Z]* or *[3-7]*. If you want to test a position for any characters <u>except</u> those in a list, start the list with an exclamation point (!). Some examples of validation rules using LIKE are shown in Figure 5-15 on the next page.

Defining Input Masks

NEW!

To assist you in entering formatted data, Microsoft Access allows you to define an *input mask* for any type of field except Memo, OLE Object, and Counter data types. You can use an input mask to do something as simple as forcing all letters entered to be uppercase or as complex as adding parentheses and dashes to phone numbers. You create an input mask by using the special mask definition characters shown in Figure 5-16 on the next page. You can also embed strings of characters that you want displayed for formatting or stored in the data field.

Validation Rule	Tests For
LIKE "#####" or LIKE "#####-####"	A U.S. zip code
LIKE "[A-Z]#[A-Z]#[A-Z]#"	A Canadian postal code
LIKE "Smith*"	A string beginning with *"Smith"*
LIKE "*smith##*"	A string with *"smith"* followed by two numbers anywhere in the string
LIKE "??00####"	An eight-character string that has any first two characters followed by exactly two zeros and then any four numbers
LIKE "[!0-9BMQ]*####"	A string that has any character other than a number or the letter *B, M,* or *Q* in the first position and ends with exactly four numbers

FIGURE 5-15.
Some validation rules that use the LIKE comparison operator.

Mask Character	Meaning
0	A number must be entered in this position. Plus (+) and minus (-) signs are not allowed.
9	A number or a space can be entered in this position. Plus and minus signs are not allowed. If the user skips this position by moving the cursor past the position without entering anything, Microsoft Access stores nothing.
#	A number, space, or plus or minus sign can be entered in this position. If the user skips this position by moving the cursor past the position without entering anything, Access stores a space.
L	A letter must be entered in this position.

FIGURE 5-16. *(continued)*
Input mask definition characters used to create an input mask.

FIGURE 5-16. *continued*

Mask Character	Meaning
?	A letter can be entered in this position. If the user skips this position by moving the cursor past the position without entering anything, Access stores nothing.
A	A letter or number must be entered in this position.
a	A letter or number can be entered in this position. If the user skips this position by moving the cursor past the position without entering anything, Access stores nothing.
&	A character or a space must be entered in this position.
C	Any character or a space can be entered in this position. If the user skips this position by moving the cursor past the position without entering anything, Access stores nothing.
.	Decimal placeholder (depends on the settings in the International section of Windows Control Panel).
,	Thousand separator (depends on the settings in the International section of Windows Control Panel).
: ; - /	Date and time separators (depends on the settings in the International section of Windows Control Panel).
<	Converts all characters that follow to lowercase.
>	Converts all characters that follow to uppercase.
!	Causes the mask to fill from right to left when you define optional characters on the left end of the mask. You can place this character anywhere in the mask.
\	Causes the character immediately following to be displayed as a literal character rather than as a mask character.
"literal"	You can also enclose any literal string in double quotation marks rather than using the \ character repeatedly.

An input mask consists of three parts separated by semicolons. The first part defines the mask string using mask definition characters and embedded fixed data. The optional second part is an indicator to tell

Access whether you want the formatting characters stored in the field in the database. Set this second part to 0 to store the characters or to 1 to store only the data entered. In the optional third part, you can define the single character that Access uses as a placeholder character to indicate positions where data can be entered. The default placeholder character is an underscore (_).

Perhaps the best way to learn to use input masks is to take advantage of the Input Mask Wizard. In the Customers table in PROMPT, for example, the PhoneNumber and FaxNumber fields could benefit from the use of an input mask. Click on the PhoneNumber field in the top of the Table window in Design view, and then click anywhere in the Input Mask property in the lower part of the window. You should see a small button with three dots on it (called a *Build* button) appear at the right of the property, as shown in Figure 5-17.

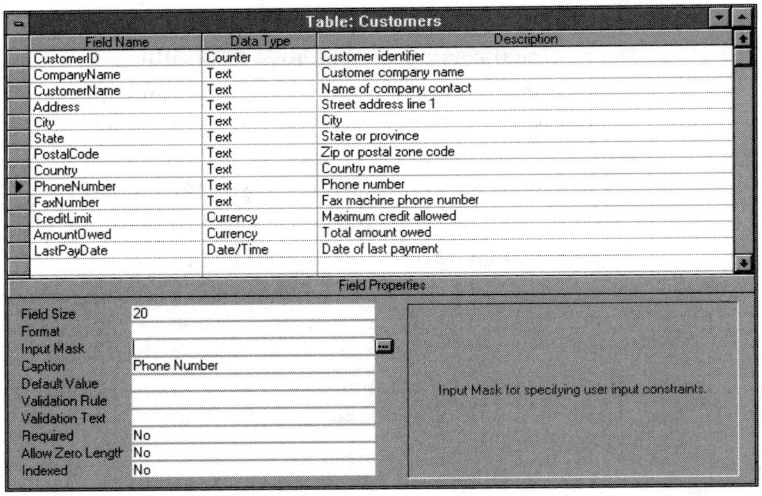

FIGURE 5-17.
The Build button available on the Input Mask property.

Click the Build button to activate the Input Mask Wizard. On the first screen, the Wizard gives you a number of choices for "standard" input masks that the Wizard can generate for you. In this case, click the first one in the list—Phone Number. Your screen should look like the one shown in Figure 5-18. Note that you can click in the test box below the input mask selection box to try out the mask.

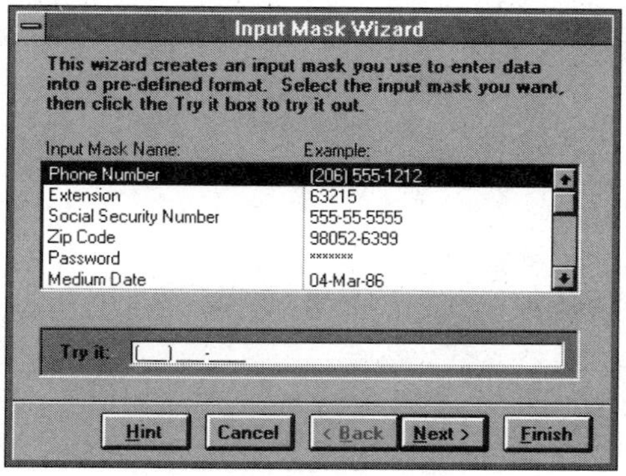

FIGURE 5-18.
Selecting an input mask in the Input Mask Wizard.

Click the Next button to go to the next screen. On this screen, shown in Figure 5-19, you can see the mask name, the proposed mask string, a selection box to pick the placeholder character, and another test box. The default underscore character (_) works well for phone numbers. Click Next to go to the next screen, where you can choose whether you want the data stored without the formatting characters (the default) or stored in the field to include the parentheses, spaces, and dash separator. In Figure 5-20 on the next page, the data is being saved with the formatting characters. Click Next to go to the final screen, and then click the Finish button on that screen to store the mask in the property setting. Figure 5-21 on page 131 shows you the mask entered in the PhoneNumber field. You should define this same mask for the FaxNumber field.

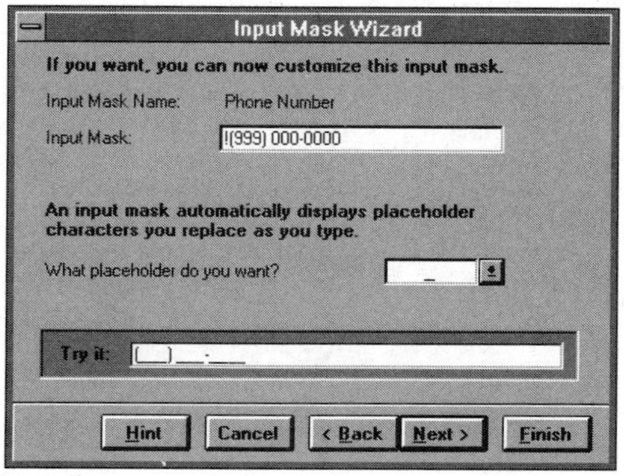

FIGURE 5-19.
Choosing the placeholder character in the Input Mask Wizard.

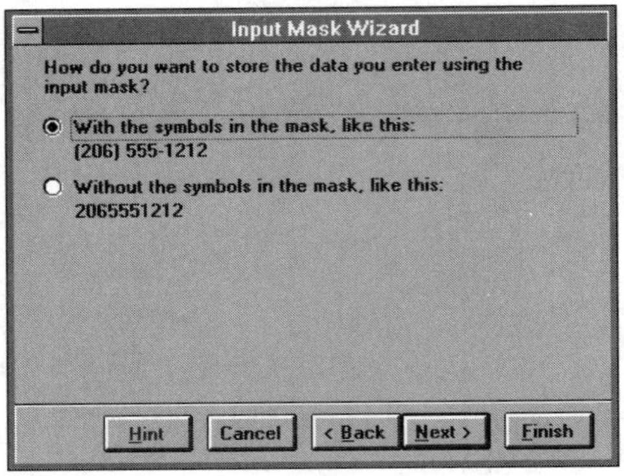

FIGURE 5-20. Opting to store formatting characters.

Defining a Primary Key

Every table in a relational database should have a primary key. If you used the procedure outlined in Chapter 4, "Designing Your Database Application," you should know what fields must make up the primary key for each of your tables.

Telling Microsoft Access how to define the primary key is quite simple. Select the first field in the primary key by clicking the selector button to the left of that field's name in the Table window in Design view. If you need to select multiple fields for your primary key, hold down the Ctrl key and click the button of each additional field you need.

When you've selected all the fields you want for the primary key, click the Primary Key button on the toolbar, or choose the Set Primary Key command from the Edit menu. Access displays a key symbol to the left of the selected fields to acknowledge your definition of the primary key. (To eliminate all primary key designations, see the section "Adding Indexes," later in this chapter.) When you've finished creating the Customers table for Prompt Computer Solutions, the primary key should be the CustomerID field, as shown in Figure 5-21.

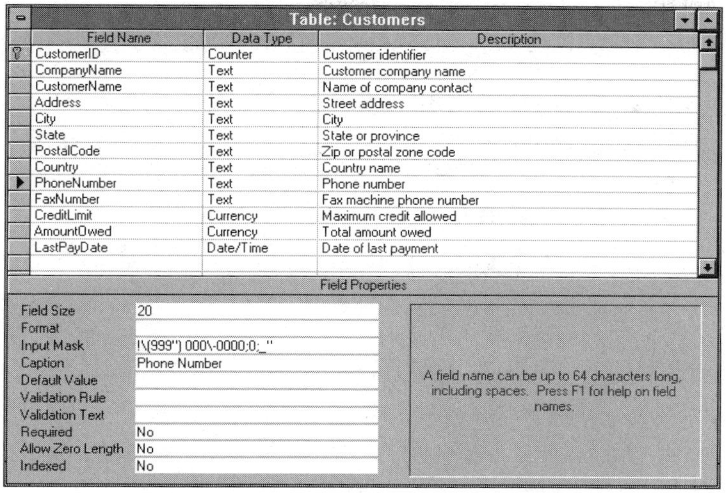

FIGURE 5-21.
The Customers table with a primary key and phone number input mask defined.

Defining a Table Validation Rule

The last detail you might want to define is any validation rule that you want Microsoft Access to check for each row you save in the table. Although field validation rules get checked as you enter each new value, Access checks the table validation rule only when you save or add a row. To define the table validation rule, click the Table Properties button on the toolbar or choose the Table Properties command from the View menu to open the Table Properties window, shown in Figure 5-22.

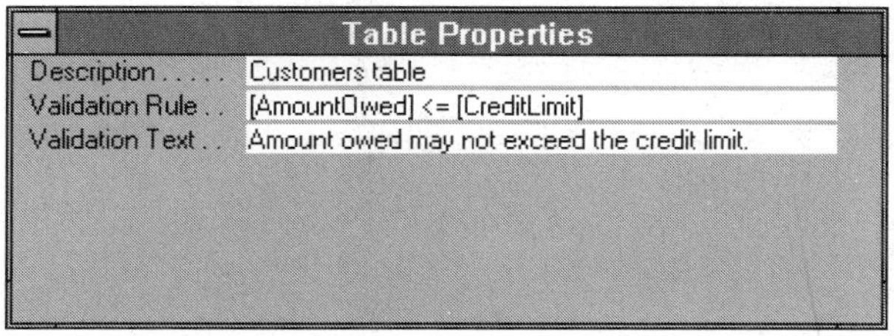

FIGURE 5-22.
Entering a table validation rule in the Table Properties window.

In the Table Properties window, you can enter a description of the table on the first line. On the second line, you can enter any valid comparison expression. Note that here you can compare the contents of one field to the contents of another. In this case, it might be a good idea to ensure that the amount owed by this customer does not exceed the credit limit established. When you want to refer to a field name, enclose the name in left and right brackets ([ ]), as shown in the example. You'll use this technique whenever you refer to the name of an object anywhere in an expression. On the third line in the Table Properties window, enter the text that you want Access to display whenever the table validation rule is violated.

Saving a New Table and Entering Data

The last step you need to perform for a new table is to save it. From the File menu choose the Save command or the Save As command. Microsoft Access will open the table Save As dialog box, as shown in Figure 5-23. Type the name of your table, *Customers*, and click OK to save the table.

FIGURE 5-23. The Save As dialog box appears when a table is being renamed.

NOTE: In the PROMPT sample database provided on the companion disk, most tables, queries, forms, and reports have singular names (for example, *Customer*). All exercises in this book use plural names (for example, *Customers*) so that you can work directly with examples you create based on the sample database—without altering the original database.

Now you're ready to enter some data in your table. Click the Datasheet button on the toolbar, or choose the Datasheet command from the View menu. Then enter the data shown in Figures 5-24 and 5-25 for Alpha Products, Beta Consulting, and Condor Leasing. You'll notice that these figures do not show the CustomerID field. Microsoft Access will automatically enter unique numbers for the CustomerID field because it is set to the Counter data type.

Table: Customers

	Company Name	Customer Name	Address 1	City	State	Postal Code
▶	Alpha Products	Jim Smith	1234 Main Street	Bellevue	WA	98004
	Beta Consulting	George Roberts	7891 44th Avenue	Redmond	WA	98052
	Condor Leasing	Marjorie Lovell	901 E. Maple	Vancouver	BC	V6C 2R7
*						

Record: 1 of 3

FIGURE 5-24.
The data in some fields of the Customers table.

Table: Customers

	Country	Phone Number	Fax Number	Credit Limit	Amount Owed	Last Pay Date
▶	USA	(206) 551-6363	(206) 551-6364	$10,000.00	$1,197.00	2/25/94
	USA	(206) 678-1234		$15,000.00	$1,462.00	3/10/94
	Canada	(604) 589-1100	(604) 589-1159	$13,000.00	$270.00	3/8/94
*	USA			$10,000.00	$0.00	

Record: 1 of 3

FIGURE 5-25.
The data in the remaining fields of the Customers table.

Using the Table Wizard

NEW!

The full PROMPT sample database contains 10 main tables (and a few tables used to store intermediate results). If you had to create every table "by hand," it could turn out to be quite a tedious process. Fortunately, Microsoft Access comes with a *Table Wizard* to help you build most common tables.

To build a table using the Table Wizard, go to the Database window, click the Table tab, and click the New button. In the resulting dialog box, click the Table Wizard button at the left. You'll see the opening screen for the Wizard, shown in Figure 5-26 on the next page.

> **TIP:** You can make the Database window active at any time by pressing the F11 function key.

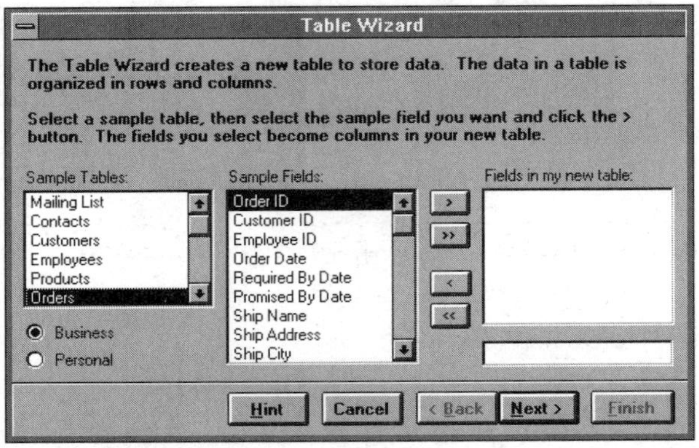

FIGURE 5-26. The first Table Wizard screen.

Toward the bottom of the left side of the screen, you can see two option buttons—Business (to select business-oriented tables) and Personal (to select personal tables). Because Prompt Computer Solutions is a business, you're most likely to find suitable tables in the business samples. You need a table to store order information for the PROMPT database, so scroll down until you can see Orders in the left list box. When you select it, the Wizard displays all the fields in the sample table in the middle list box.

To choose a field, select it in the middle list box and click the single right arrow (>) button to move it to the list box on the far right. (You can also choose a field by double-clicking in it.) You define the sequence of fields in your table based on the sequence in which you choose them from the sample list. If you choose a field that you decide you don't want, select it in the far right list box and click the single left arrow (<) button to remove it. If you want to start over, you can remove all fields by clicking the double left arrow (<<) button.

Almost all the fields in the sample Orders table are fields you'll need in the Orders table for PROMPT, so choose them all by clicking the double right arrow (>>) button. Click the Next button to see the screen shown in Figure 5-27. In this screen, you can choose a new name for your table. Because the sample table in PROMPT is Order, accept the default name here. You can also choose to let the Wizard build a primary key for you, or you can define your own. In most cases, the Wizard chooses the most logical field or fields to be the primary key and uses the Counter data type wherever possible. Because the primary key in the PROMPT Order table is a single field called OrderID, which is a Counter, you can let the Wizard build the default.

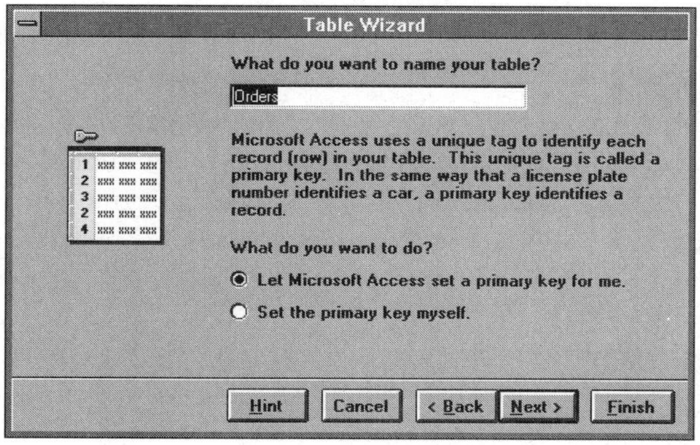
Table Wizard
What do you want to name your table?
Orders
Microsoft Access uses a unique tag to identify each record (row) in your table. This unique tag is called a primary key. In the same way that a license plate number identifies a car, a primary key identifies a record.
What do you want to do?
Let Microsoft Access set a primary key for me.
Set the primary key myself.
Hint
Cancel
< Back
Next >
Finish

FIGURE 5-27. Selecting a table name and primary key option in the Table Wizard.

Click the Next button to define the relationships between existing tables and this new table, as shown in Figure 5-28. Because the Orders table created by the Wizard has a CustomerID field that matches the primary key of your Customers table, the Wizard assumes that the Customers table is related one-to-many to the Orders table. (One customer can have many orders.) For now, click the Change button and choose The Tables Aren't Related so that you can learn to define this relationship in the next section.

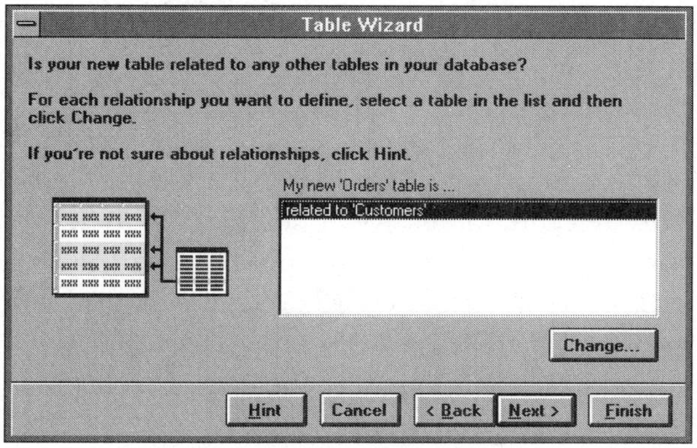
Table Wizard
Is your new table related to any other tables in your database?
For each relationship you want to define, select a table in the list and then click Change.
If you're not sure about relationships, click Hint.
My new 'Orders' table is ...
related to 'Customers'
Change...
Hint
Cancel
< Back
Next >
Finish

FIGURE 5-28. Defining the relationship between the Customers table and the Orders table.

Click the Next button to go to the final screen, which has three options: Modify The Table Design, Enter Data Directly Into The Table, and Enter Data Directly Into The Table Using A Form The Wizard Creates For Me. Enter Data Directly Into The Table opens the table in Datasheet view; Enter Data Directly Into The Table Using A Form The Wizard Creates For Me builds a form for you based on the table and opens it in Form view;

and Modify The Table Design opens the table in Design view, allowing you to make a few adjustments to your new table.

The Orders table built by the Table Wizard is shown in Figure 5-29. You'll need to change a couple of the fields and add a few more fields to get to the final table design needed in PROMPT, which you'll learn how to do in the next chapter, "Modifying Your Database Design." For now, close the table so that you can work on defining some relationships.

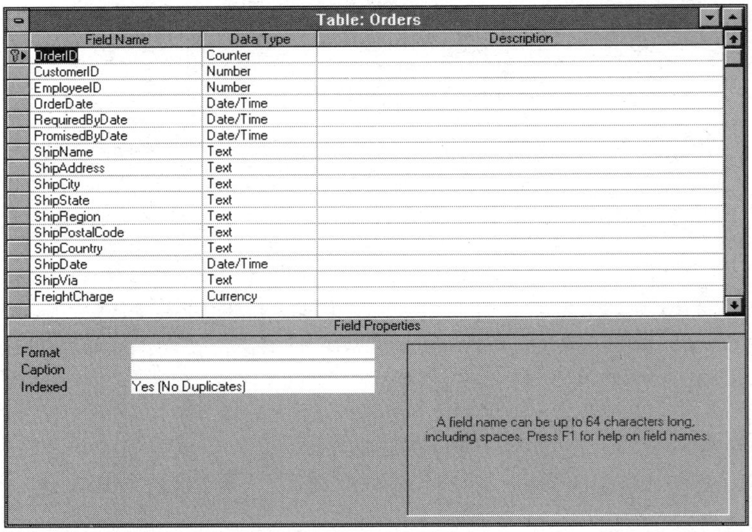

FIGURE 5-29. The Orders table built by the Table Wizard.

If you would like to practice with the Table Wizard, you can build skeletons for several of the other tables you'll need for PROMPT. For the Catalogs and Components tables, select the fields from the Products sample. For the OrderItems table, use the Order Details sample. You can extract the fields you need for the SalesReps table from the Employees sample. And you can build the Suppliers and the Types tables using the Suppliers and the Category samples.

Defining Relationships

After you have defined two or more related tables, you should tell Microsoft Access how the tables are related. If you do this, Access will know how to link all your tables when you need to use them later in queries, forms, or reports.

To define relationships, you need to return to the Database window by closing any Table windows that are open and by clicking in the Database window to make it active. Then choose the Relationships command from the Edit menu. If this is the first time you have defined relationships in this database, Access opens a blank Relationships window and opens the Add Table dialog box shown in Figure 5-30.

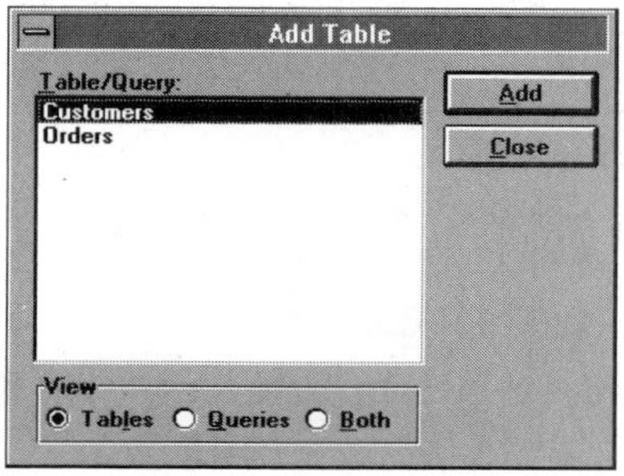

FIGURE 5-30. Adding tables to the Relationships window.

For now, select the Customers table and click the Add button; then select the Orders table and click the Add button. Click Close to dismiss the Add Table dialog box. Your Relationships window should now look like the one shown in Figure 5-31.

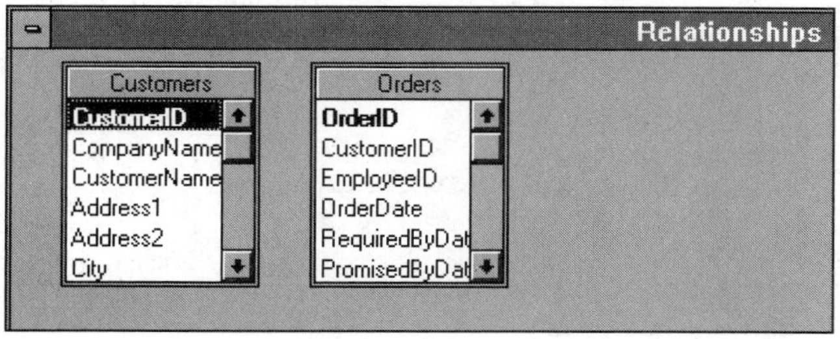

FIGURE 5-31. The Customers and Orders tables in the Relationships window.

The Built-In Toolbar for the Relationships Window

Before you define your first relationship, it's worth spending a few moments to look at the Relationships toolbar that Microsoft Access displays when the Relationships window is active. Here are descriptions of the buttons unique to this toolbar:

Add Table button. Click this button to open the Add Table dialog box shown in Figure 5-30 on the previous page.

Show Direct Relationships button. After you've defined many relationships, you can delete some tables from the display to simplify what you see. (This does not delete the relationships.) You can click on any remaining table and then click this button to make all tables to which the selected table is related reappear.

Show All Relationships button. After you've defined many relationships, you can delete some tables from the display to simplify what you see. (This does not delete the relationships.) You can click this button to cause all undisplayed tables and their relationships to reappear.

Defining Your First Relationship

If you remember the design work you did in Chapter 4, you know that a customer can have several orders, but any order is for one and only one customer. This means that customers are related to orders one-to-many. You can see that for the CustomerID primary key in the Customers table, there's a matching CustomerID foreign key in the Orders table. To create the relationship you need, click on the CustomerID field in the Customers table and drag and drop it onto CustomerID in the Orders table, as shown in Figure 5-32.

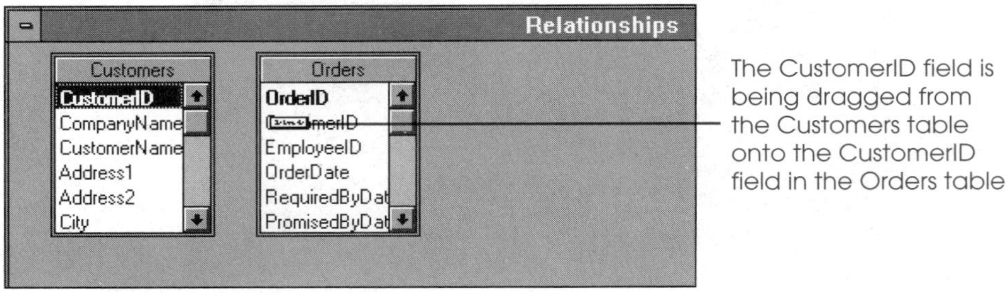

FIGURE 5-32. Dragging the linking field from the "one" table to the "many" table.

When you release the mouse, Microsoft Access opens the Relationships dialog box, shown in Figure 5-33.

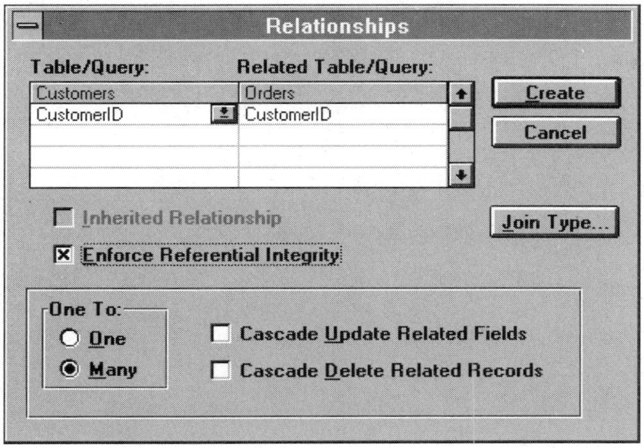

FIGURE 5-33.
The Relationships dialog box.

Notice that Access filled in the field names for you. If you need to define a relationship between two tables that involve multiple fields, you can use the additional blank lines to define those fields. Because you probably don't want any orders lying around for nonexistent customers, click the Enforce Referential Integrity check box. When you do this, Access ensures that you can't add an order for an invalid customer ID. Also, Access won't let you delete any customer records that have orders outstanding.

Note that after you click the Enforce Referential Integrity check box, Access makes two additional options available: Cascade Update Related Fields and Cascade Delete Related Records. If you choose Cascade Update Related Fields, Access updates all the foreign key values in "child" tables (the "many" table in a one-to-many relationship) if you change a primary key value in a "parent" table (the "one" table in a one-to-many relationship). If you choose Cascade Delete Related Records, Access deletes child rows (the related rows in the "many" table of a one-to-many relationship) when you delete a parent row (the related row in the "one" table of a one-to-many relationship). In this application, you'll create some Microsoft Access Basic routines (see Chapter 22) to verify the deletion of orders (child rows) if you delete a customer (parent row), so don't choose either of these options.

You probably noticed that the Add Table dialog box gives you the option to include queries as well as tables. Sometimes you might want to define relationships between tables and queries or between queries so that Access knows how to join them properly. You can also define what's known as an *outer join* by choosing the Join Type button in the Relationships dialog box. With an outer join, you can find out, for example, which customers have no orders outstanding.

See Also: For details on *outer joins*, see Chapter 8, "Adding Power with Select Queries."

After you click the Create button to finish your relationship definition, Access draws a line between the two tables to indicate the relationship. Notice that when you ask Access to enforce referential integrity, Access displays a 1 at the end of the relationship line, next to the "one" table, and an infinity symbol (∞) next to the "many" table. If you want to delete the relationship, click on the line and press the Del key. If you want to edit or change the relationship, double-click on the line to open the Relationships dialog box again. Figure 5-34 shows you the Relationships window for all the main tables in the PROMPT database.

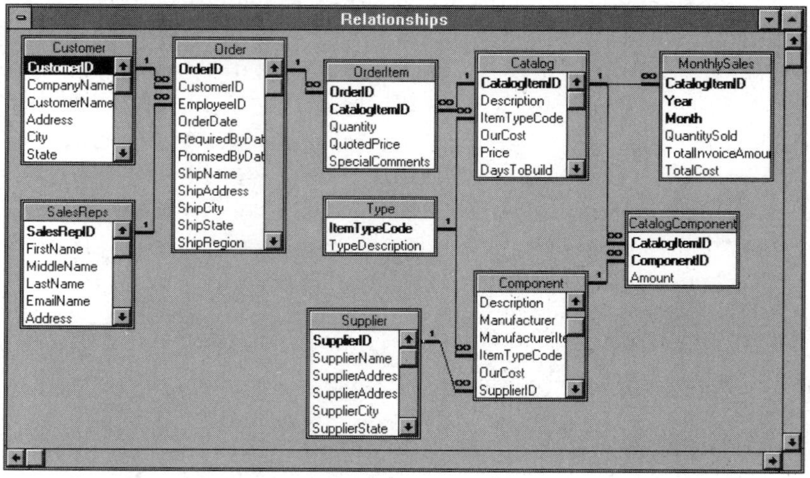

FIGURE 5-34. The Relationships window showing all the main tables in the PROMPT database.

When you close the Relationships window, Access asks whether you want to save your changes. Click Yes to make your changes permanent. That's all there is to it. Later, when you use multiple tables in a query in Chapter 8, "Adding Power with Select Queries," you'll see that Access builds the relationships between tables based on the relationships you've defined.

Adding Indexes

The more data you have in your tables, the more you need indexes to help Microsoft Access search your data efficiently. An index is simply an internal table that contains two columns: the value in the field or fields being indexed and the location of each record in your table that contains that value. Let's assume that you often search your Customers table by state. Without an index, when you ask Access to find all the customers in the state of Utah, Access has to search every record in your table. This search is fast if you have only a dozen or so customers but very slow if you have hundreds or thousands of customers. If you create an index on the State field, Access can use the index to directly find the records for the customers in the state you specify.

Single Field Indexes

Most of the indexes you need to define will probably contain the values from only a single field. Access uses this type of index to help narrow the number of records it has to search whenever you provide search criteria on the field—for example, *State = WA* or *ItemTypeCode = 005*. If you have defined indexes on multiple fields and provided search criteria for more than one of the fields, Access uses the index that is most likely to yield the fewest records to search. For example, if you have indexes on State and City and you ask for *State = CA* and *City = San Francisco*, Access uses the City index because there are likely to be fewer entries for the city of San Francisco than for the entire state of California. If you request *State = IL* and *City = Springfield,* Access might use the State index because there are at least 21 cities in the U.S. named Springfield, so there actually might be fewer records for the state of Illinois.

Creating an index on a single field in a table is easy. Open the table in Design view, and select the field for which you want an index. Click the Indexed property box in the bottom half of the Table window to drop down the list of choices, as shown in Figure 5-35.

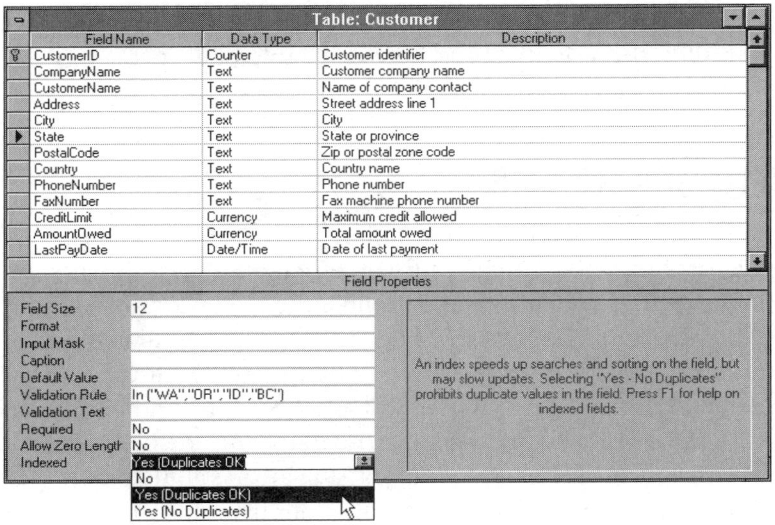

FIGURE 5-35.
Using the Indexed property box to set an index on a single field.

The default indexed property setting for all fields except the primary key is *No*. If you want to set an index for a field, there are two *Yes* choices. In most cases, a given field will have multiple records with the same value—perhaps multiple customers in the state of Texas or multiple products that come in red. You should select Yes (Duplicates OK) to create an index on this type of field. Note that you can use Microsoft Access to enforce unique values in any field by creating an index that doesn't allow duplicates: Yes (No Duplicates). Access performs this check automatically for the primary key index.

Multiple Field Indexes

If you often provide multiple criteria in searches against large tables, you might want to consider creating a few multiple field indexes to help Microsoft Access narrow the search quickly. For example, suppose you often perform a search for customers who live in a specific state and city and who work for a particular company. If you create an index that has all three of these fields, Access can satisfy your query very rapidly.

To create a multiple field index, you must open the Table window in Design view and open the Indexes window (shown in Figure 5-36) by clicking the Indexes button on the toolbar or by choosing the Indexes command from the View menu. You can see the primary key index and the index that you defined on State in the previous section. Each of these indexes is made up of exactly one field.

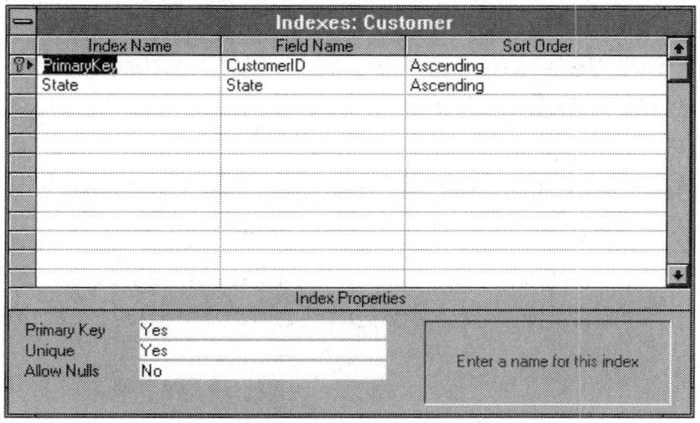

FIGURE 5-36.
A single field index is defined in the Indexes window.

To create a multiple field index, move the cursor down to an empty row in the Indexes window and type a unique name. In this example, you want a multiple field index using State, City, and CompanyName fields, so *StateCityCo* might be a reasonable index name. Select the State field in the field name column of this row. To add other fields, simply skip down to the next row and select another field without typing a new index name. When you're done, your Indexes window should look like the one shown in Figure 5-37.

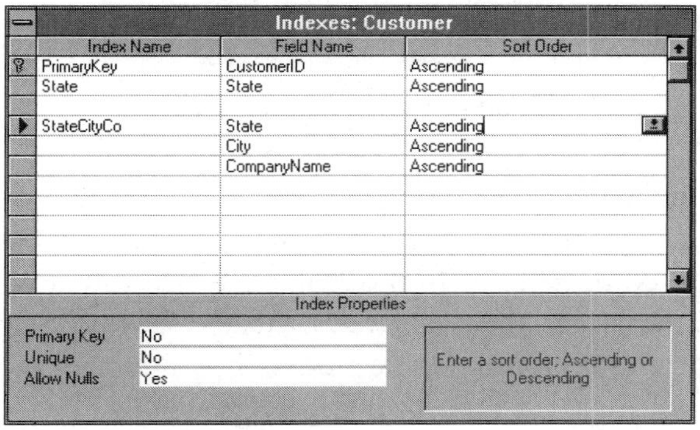

FIGURE 5-37.
The result of defining a multiple field index.

NOTE: You can remove an existing index by simply highlighting the row (by clicking the selector buttons) that defines the index and then pressing the Del key. Any indexes you define, change, or delete are saved when you save the table definition.

Access will use a multiple field index in a search even if you don't provide search values for all the fields. Access can use a multiple field index as long as you provide search criteria for consecutive fields starting with the first field. Therefore, in the multiple field index shown in Figure 5-37 on the previous page, you can search for state, or state and city, or state and city and company name. There's one additional limitation on multiple field indexes: Only the last search criterion can be an inequality, such as >, >=, <, or <=. In other words, Access can use the index shown in Figure 5-37 when you specify searches such as this:

```
State = CA
State > CA
State = CA And City = Los Angeles
State = CA And City >= San
State = CA And City = San Francisco And Company→
 Name > Ma
```

But Access cannot use the index shown in Figure 5-37 if you ask for

```
State = CA And Company Name = Marble Industries (Can't→
 skip a field, in this case City)
State > CA And City > San (Only the last field you→
 search can be an inequality, in this case City)
City = San Diego (Must include the first field, in→
 this case State)
```

Printing a Table Definition

After you've created several tables, you might want to print out their definitions to provide a permanent paper record. You can do this by selecting the table you want to print in the Database window and then choosing Print Definition from the File menu. Access displays several choices in the Table Printing Options dialog box, shown in Figure 5-38.

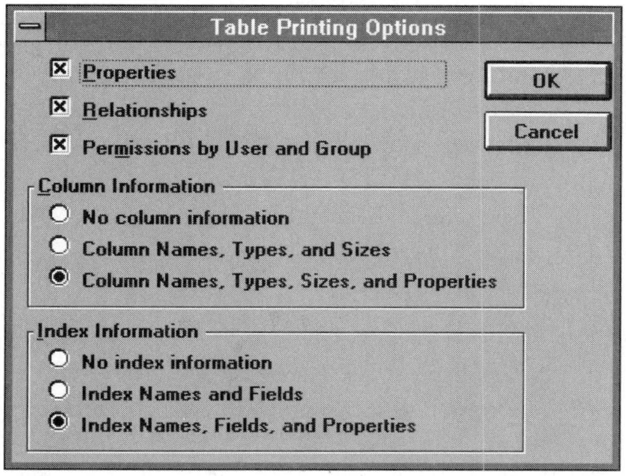

FIGURE 5-38.
Table definition printing options.

As you can see in the above figure, you can choose to print several different types of information about the table, the columns in the table, and the indexes. Click OK to view the report in a Print Preview window. You can print the report or output it to a document or text file. When you've finished, close the table and save it.

Database Limitations

As you design your database, you should keep in mind the following limitations:

- A table can have up to 255 fields.
- A table can have up to 32 indexes.
- A multiple field index can have up to 10 columns. The sum of the lengths of the columns cannot exceed 255 bytes.
- A row in a table, excluding memo fields and OLE objects, can be no longer than approximately 2 kilobytes.
- A memo field can store up to 64,000 bytes.
- An OLE object can be up to 1 gigabyte in size.

- There is no limit on the number of records in a table, but a Microsoft Access database cannot be larger than 1 gigabyte. If you have several large tables, you might need to define each one in a separate Microsoft Access database and then attach them to the database that contains the forms, reports, macros, and modules for your applications. See Chapter 10, "Importing, Attaching, and Exporting Data," for details.

Now that you've started building PROMPT, you can read the next chapter to learn how to make modifications to an existing database.

6

Modifying Your Database Design

No matter how carefully you design your database, you can be sure that you'll need to change it at some later date. Here are some of the reasons you might need to change your database:

- You have some tables that you don't need any longer.
- You want to be able to perform some new tasks that require not only creating some new tables but also inserting some linking fields in existing tables.
- You've discovered that you use some fields in a table much more frequently than others, so it would be easier if those fields appeared first in the table design.
- You thought you would need to keep track of a certain kind of data when you first designed your database, but you've discovered that you don't need that data after all.
- You want to add some new fields that are very similar to fields that already exist.
- You've discovered that some data you defined would be better stored as a different data type—for example, a field that you originally designed to be all numbers (such as a U.S. zip code) must now contain some letters (as in a Canadian postal code).
- You have a number field that needs to hold larger values or have a different number of decimal places than originally planned.
- You find you could improve your database design by splitting an existing table into two tables or by joining two tables into a single table.
- You discover that the field you defined as a primary key isn't always unique, so you need to change your key definition.
- You find that some of your queries take too long and might run better if you added an index to your table.

This chapter takes a look at how you can make these changes easily and relatively painlessly with Microsoft Access. If you want to follow along with the examples in this chapter, you should create the Customers table and the Orders table as described in Chapter 5, "Building Your Database in Microsoft Access."

NOTE: You might have noticed that the Customers table you defined for Prompt Computer Solutions in the previous chapter is different from the Customer table in the PROMPT database as defined in Appendix B, "Sample Database Schemas" (and as located on the companion disk that comes with the book). In this chapter, you'll modify the Customers table so that it is more like the Customer table. You'll also learn how to modify the standard Orders table created by the Table Wizard to match the Order table in the PROMPT design.

Before You Get Started

Microsoft Access makes it easy for you to change the design of your database, even when you already have data in your tables. You should, however, understand the potential impact of any changes you plan and take steps to ensure that you can recover if you make a mistake. Here are some things to consider before you make changes:

- Microsoft Access does not automatically propagate changes you make in tables to any queries, forms, reports, macros, or modules. You must make changes to dependent objects yourself.

TIP: You can find out which other objects use the tables or fields you plan to change by using the Print Definition facilities of Microsoft Access.

- You cannot change the data type of a field that is part of a relationship definition between tables. You must first delete the relationship definition.
- You cannot change the definition of any table that you have open in a query, form, or report. You must first close any other objects that refer to the table you want to change before you open that table in Design view. If you allow other users on a network access to your database, you must be sure no one has your table open before you try to change it.

> **TIP:** One helpful feature of Access is that it always prompts you for confirmation before committing any changes that permanently alter or delete data in your database. If any changes would result in losing any data, Access informs you and gives you a chance to cancel the operation.

Making a Backup Copy

The safest way to make changes to your database design is to make a backup copy of the database before you begin. If you plan to make extensive changes to several tables in your database, you should make a copy of the MDB file, which contains your database, using a utility such as File Manager in the Microsoft Windows operating system. If you created the PROMPT database for use as you work through examples in this book, now would be a good time to make a backup copy of the PROMPT.MDB file.

If you want to change a single table, you can easily make a backup copy of that table right in your database. Use the following procedure to copy any table structure (the contents of the Table window in Design view), table data (the contents of the Table window in Datasheet view), or structure and data together:

1. Open the database containing the table you want to copy. If the database is already open, click the Table tab in the Database window.
2. Select the table you want to copy by clicking on it in the Database window. The table name will be highlighted.
3. Choose the Copy command from the Edit menu, or click the Copy button on the toolbar. (See Figure 6-1 on the next page.) This operation copies the entire table (structure and data) to the Clipboard.
4. Choose the Paste command from the Edit menu, or click the Paste button on the toolbar. Access opens the Paste Table As dialog box, shown in Figure 6-2 on the next page. Type in the new name for your table. (When making a backup copy, you can add *Backup* and the date to the original table name, as shown in Figure 6-2.) The default option is to copy both the structure and the data. You also have the option of copying only the table's structure or of appending the data to another table.

FIGURE 6-1. The Copy command will copy a table from the Tables list.

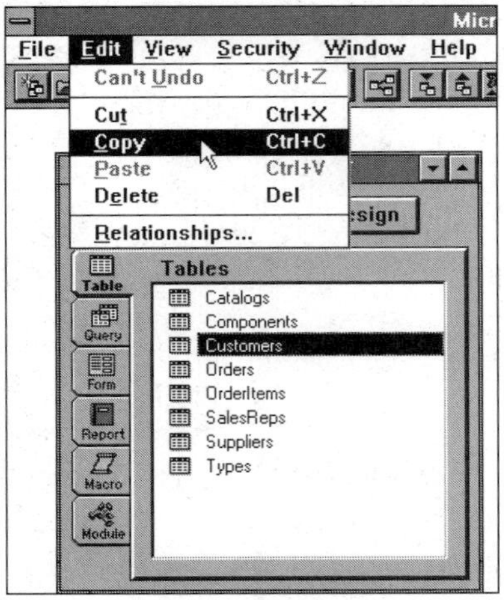

FIGURE 6-2. This dialog box appears when you paste a table into your database.

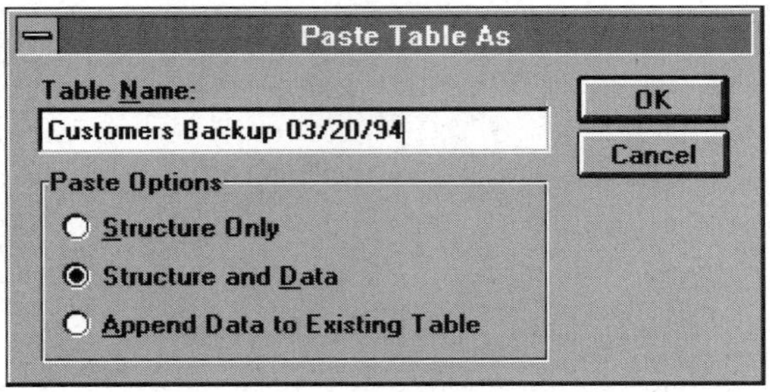

Reversing Changes

If you make several changes and then decide you don't want any of them, you can close the Table window without saving it. When you do that, Access opens the dialog box shown in Figure 6-3. Simply click the No button to abort all of your changes. Click the Cancel button to return to the Table window without saving or aborting your changes.

FIGURE 6-3. This dialog box gives you the option of aborting the unsaved changes to a table.

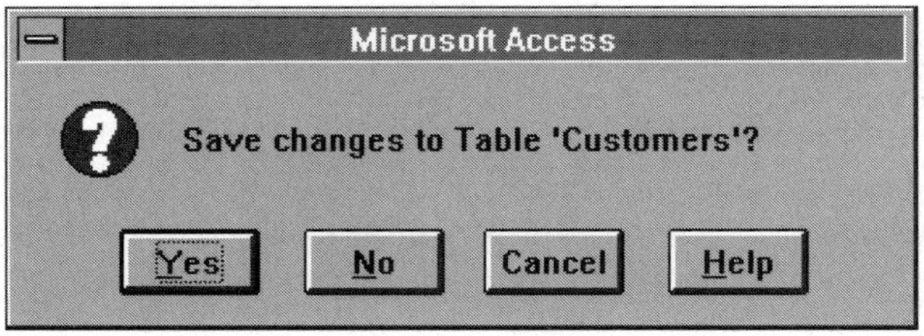

> **TIP:** You can always reverse the last change you made by choosing the Undo command from the Edit menu.

Deleting Tables

You probably won't want to delete an entire table very often. However, if you set up your application to collect historical information—for example, to collect sales history in tables by month—you'll eventually want to delete old information that you no longer need. You also might want to delete a table if you've made extensive changes that are incorrect and you decide it would be easier to delete your work and restore the table from a backup.

To delete a table, select it in the Database window and press the Del key or choose the Delete command from the Edit menu. Access opens the dialog box shown in Figure 6-4 to give you a chance to confirm or cancel the delete operation. Even if you mistakenly confirm the deletion, you can immediately select the Undo command from the Edit menu to get your table back.

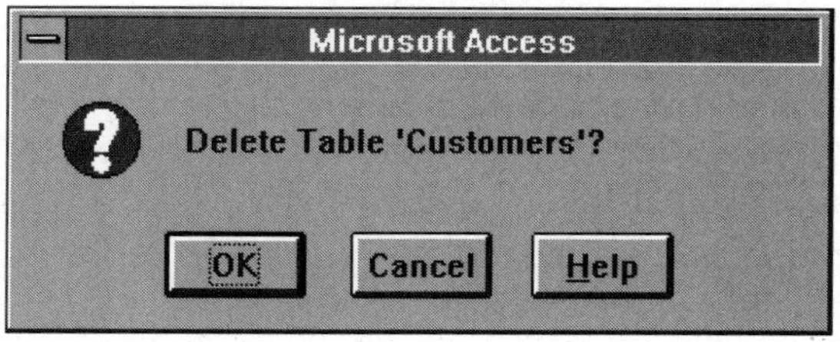

FIGURE 6-4.
This dialog box gives you the option of canceling the deletion of a table.

> **TIP:** You can use the Cut command on the Edit menu or the Cut button on the toolbar to delete a table. Both of these methods place a copy of the table on the Clipboard. After you close the database in which you've been working, you can open another database and paste the table that's on the Clipboard.

Renaming Tables

If you keep transaction data (such as receipts, deposits, or checks written), you might want to save that data at the end of each month in a table with a unique name. One way to save your data is to rename the existing table (perhaps by adding a date to the name). You can then create a new table (perhaps by making a copy of the backup table's structure) to start collecting information for the next month.

> **TIP:** It's wise to rename a table when you want to restore a table from a backup copy.

To rename a table, select it in the Database window and choose the Rename command from the File menu. Microsoft Access prompts you with the Rename dialog box, shown in Figure 6-5. Type in the new name, and click OK to rename the table.

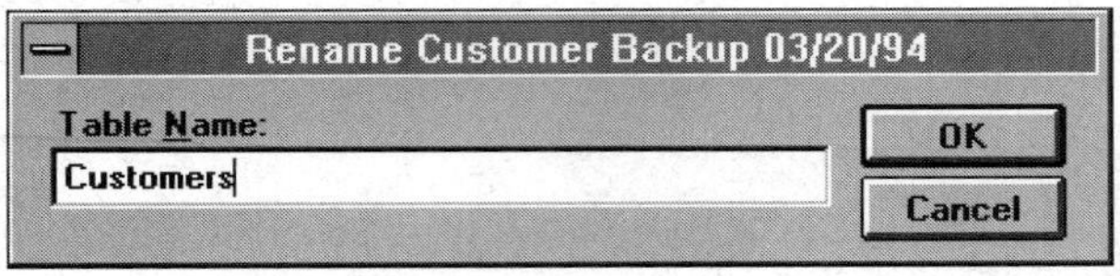

FIGURE 6-5.
The Rename dialog box allows you to rename a table.

If you enter the name of a table that already exists, Access asks you whether you want to replace the existing table. If you click the OK button, Access deletes the old table before performing the rename operation. Even if you replace an existing table, you can undo the rename operation by immediately choosing the Undo command from the Edit menu.

Changing Field Names

Perhaps you misspelled a field name when you first created one of your tables. Or perhaps you decide that one of your field names isn't quite descriptive enough. You won't want the hassle of giving the field a new name every time it appears in a query, form, or report. Fortunately, Microsoft Access makes it easy to change a field name in a table—even if you already have data in the table.

Assume that you're maintaining the PROMPT database for Prompt Computer Solutions and that you've run into some customer addresses that need a mail stop or suite number right after the company name line. The current Address field in the Customers table contains a street address, so the new address line should go after the company name but before the existing Address field. As the first step, you decide to rename the Address field and call it *Address2*. This will have the effect of moving all existing one-line addresses to the second line. (You'll insert a new field for the first line of the address a bit later in this chapter.)

Open the Customers table in Design view, move the cursor to the Address field, and at the end of the name type a *2*. Next, change the Description field. Update this line to read *Street Address Line 2,* as shown in Figure 6-6.

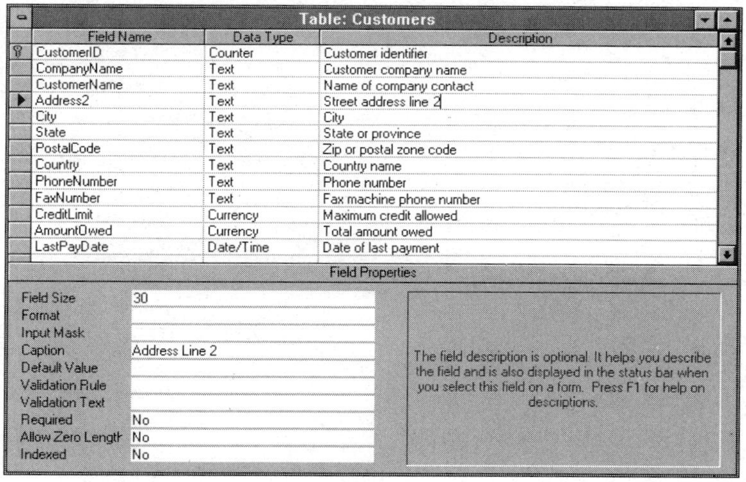
Table: Customers
Field Name
Data Type
Description
CustomerID
Counter
Customer identifier
CompanyName
Text
Customer company name
CustomerName
Text
Name of company contact
Address2
Text
Street address line 2
City
Text
City
State
Text
State or province
PostalCode
Text
Zip or postal zone code
Country
Text
Country name
PhoneNumber
Text
Phone number
FaxNumber
Text
Fax machine phone number
CreditLimit
Currency
Maximum credit allowed
AmountOwed
Currency
Total amount owed
LastPayDate
Date/Time
Date of last payment
Field Properties
Field Size
30
Format
Input Mask
Caption
Address Line 2
Default Value
Validation Rule
Validation Text
Required
No
Allow Zero Length
No
Indexed
No
The field description is optional. It helps you describe the field and is also displayed in the status bar when you select this field on a form. Press F1 for help on descriptions.

FIGURE 6-6.
You change a field name by simply typing in a new name.

CAUTION: If you have defined any queries, forms, reports, modules, or macros that use a field whose name you have changed, you must also change the field name in those other objects. You can find out which other objects use this field by running Print Definition reports for your forms, reports, and queries. If you save the reports in files, you can use the search capabilities of most text editors to find references to the name you changed.

If you created the Orders table using the Table Wizard in Chapter 5, you should rename several fields to match the PROMPT design. Open the Orders table in Design view, and then change ShipAddress to *Ship-Address2* and EmployeeID to *SalesRepID*. Now would be a good time to add descriptive comments and captions to the other fields. Your result should look like Figure 6-7.

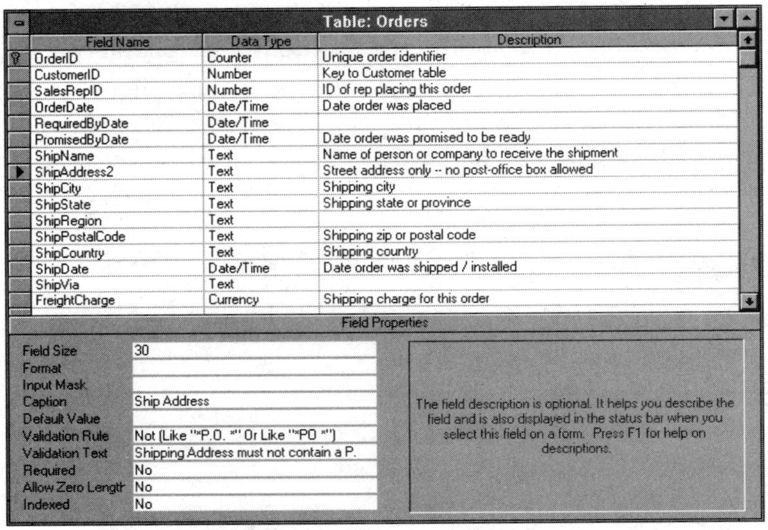

FIGURE 6-7. Changing field names in the Orders table created by the Table Wizard.

You can see that a few fields are missing, and you won't need some of the fields to match the PROMPT design. You'll learn how to fix these problems in the following sections.

Inserting Fields

Perhaps one of the most common changes you'll make to your database is to insert a new field into a table. In the preceding exercise, you changed the field name Address in the Customers table to Address2 and the field name ShipAddress in the Orders table to ShipAddress2 so that you could have two separate address fields in each table. Now you're ready to insert a field for the new first line of the address into both tables. To begin, open the Customers table in Design view.

First, you must select the row or move your cursor to the row that defines the field <u>after</u> the point where you want to insert the new field. In this case, if you want to insert a new row between CustomerName and Address2, you should place your cursor anywhere in the row that defines the Address2 field or select that row. Using the arrow keys or your mouse, move the cursor anywhere in the Address2 row. Next, choose the Insert Row command from the Edit menu (as shown in Figure 6-8), or press the Insert Row button on the toolbar.

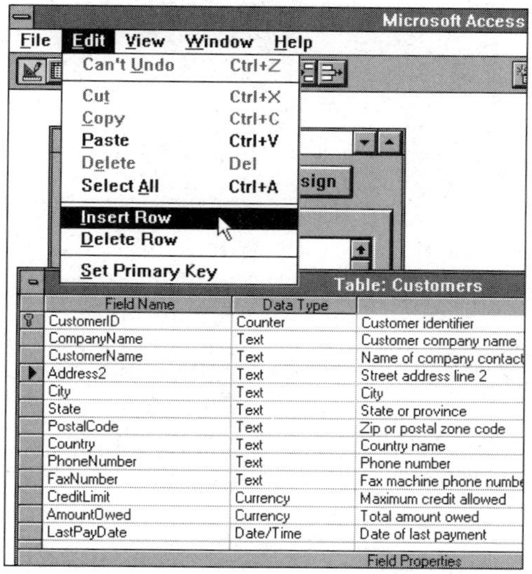

FIGURE 6-8.
The Insert Row command will insert a new row above a selected row.

Microsoft Access gives you a new blank row that you can use to define your new field. Type in the definition for the Address1 field. When you've finished, your Table window in Design view should look like the one shown in Figure 6-9 on the next page. Don't worry about setting properties just yet.

> **TIP:** You can move the cursor between the top half and the bottom half of any Table or Query window in Design view by pressing the F6 key.

FIGURE 6-9.
You create a new field by inserting a blank row and typing a field definition.

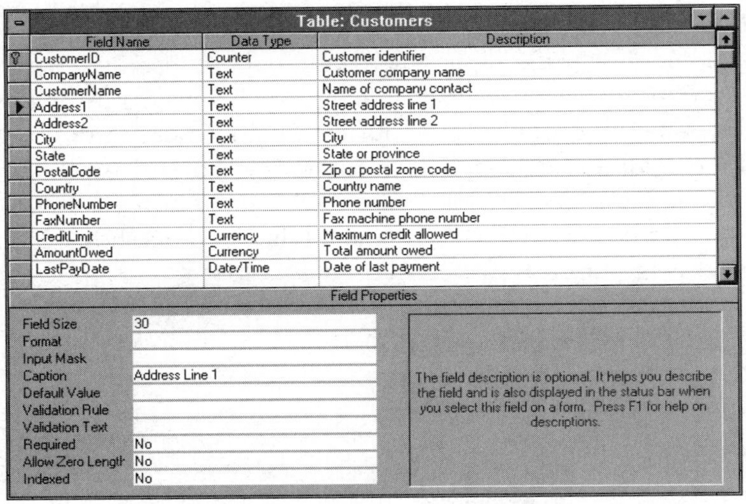

In the Orders table, you'll need several new fields to match the design of the PROMPT database. These fields are shown in this table:

Field Name	Data Type	Description	Field Size
SubtotalCost	Currency	Cost of items in the order	–
Discount	Number	Discount % on this order	Double
SalesTaxPercent	Number	Tax percent for this order	Double
SalesTax	Currency	Total sales tax for this order	–
CustomerPO	Text	Customer purchase order number (if any)	15
Terms	Text	Payment terms	20
Invoiced	Yes/No	Flag to indicate whether order has been invoiced	–
AmountPaid	Currency	Amount paid to date	–
DatePaid	Date/Time	Date of last payment	–
Notes	Memo	Special notes about this order	–

When you've finished inserting these fields into the Orders table, your result should look like Figure 6-10. (Note that the figure doesn't show you all the fields from the beginning of the table.)

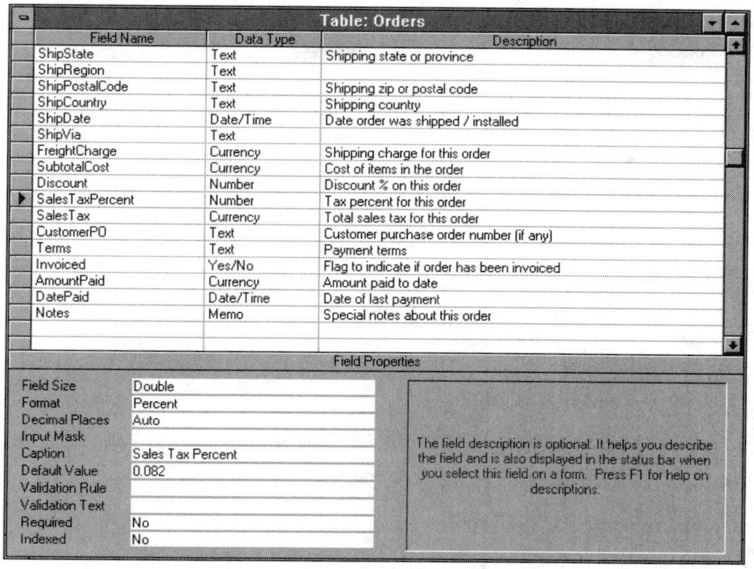

FIGURE 6-10.
The Orders table with all the PROMPT database fields added.

Copying Fields

As you create table definitions, you might find that several field definitions in your table are similar. Rather than enter each field definition separately, you can enter one field definition and copy it as many times as necessary.

You might have noticed that we haven't yet defined the ShipAddress1 field for the Orders table, as listed in Appendix B. You could insert a blank row and then type in the data. ShipAddress1 is, however, nearly identical to the ShipAddress2 field you've already defined.

Select the entire row containing the field definition that you want to copy by clicking the row selector or by moving the cursor to that row with an arrow key and pressing Shift-Spacebar. Next, choose the Copy command from the Edit menu to copy the row, as shown in Figure 6-11 on the next page. Move the cursor to the row that should follow your new inserted row. (In this case, you're already in the ShipAddress2 field, which should follow your new field.) Insert a new blank row by choosing Insert Row from the Edit menu or by clicking the Insert Row button on the toolbar. Select the new row by clicking the row selector at the far left end of the row or by pressing Shift-Spacebar while in the row.

Choose the Paste command from the Edit menu to insert the copied row, as shown in Figure 6-12. You can use the Paste command repeatedly to insert the row more than once. Remember to change the name of the copied field to ShipAddress1 before you save the modified table definition.

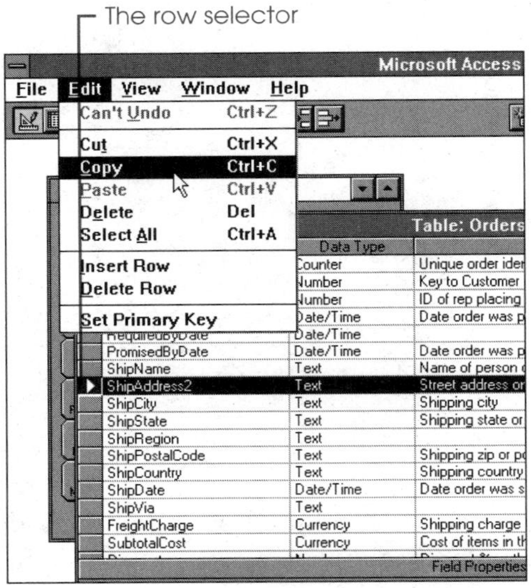

FIGURE 6-11. The ShipAddress2 field is selected and copied.

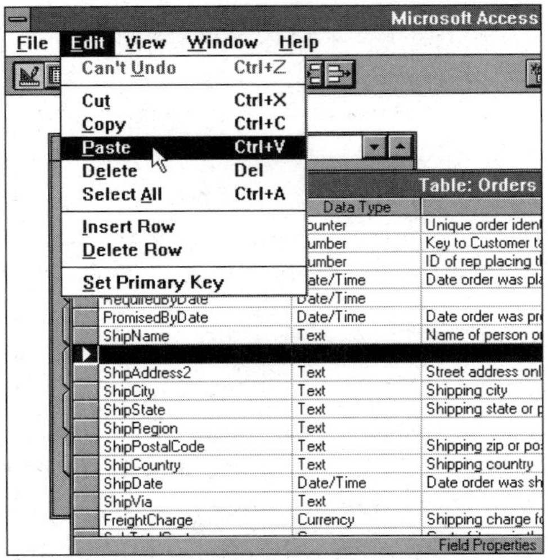

FIGURE 6-12. The field copied in Figure 6-11 can be inserted into a new blank row.

NOTE: If the Paste command is chosen when a row containing data is selected, the copied row will replace the selected row. Should you make this replacement in error, you can choose the Undo command from the Edit menu to restore the original row.

After you've pasted the copied row, it's a simple matter to change the name of the copied row from ShipAddress2 to ShipAddress1. Note that this procedure also has the benefit of copying forward any formatting, default value, or validation rule information.

Deleting Fields

Removing unwanted fields is easy. With the Table window open in Design view, select the field definition that you want to delete by clicking the row selector. You can extend the selection to multiple fields by holding down the Shift key while you extend the selection using the up and down arrows. You can also select multiple contiguous rows by clicking the row selector of the first row and, without releasing the mouse button, dragging the selection up or down to include all the rows you want.

If you chose all the fields from the Orders table in the Table Wizard to build the Orders table for the PROMPT database, you don't need three fields: RequiredByDate, ShipVia, and ShipRegion. You can click on the row selector for these fields one at a time and press the Del key to remove them. Your result should look like that shown in Figure 6-13 on the next page.

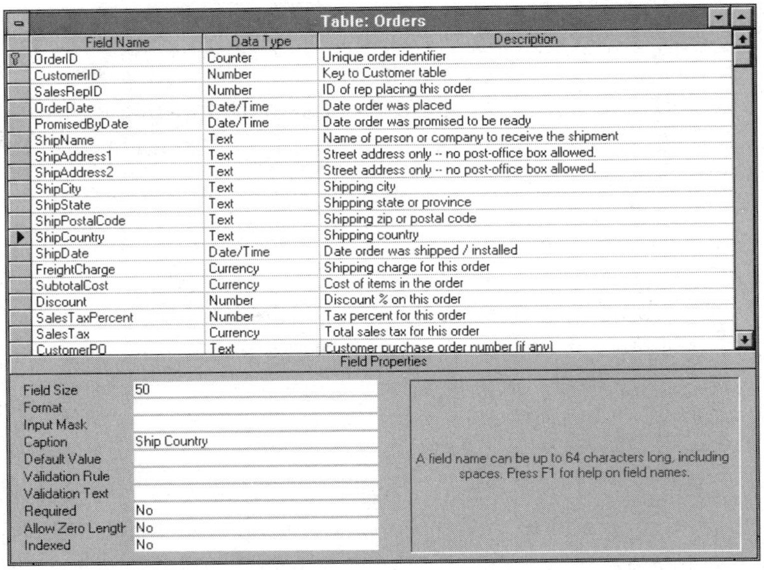

FIGURE 6-13. The Orders table with three fields (RequiredByDate, ShipVia, and ShipRegion) deleted.

If a table contains one or more rows of data (in Datasheet view), Access prompts you when you delete field definitions in Design view, as shown in Figure 6-14. Click the OK button to complete the deletion of the fields and the data in those fields. Click the Cancel button if you think you made a mistake.

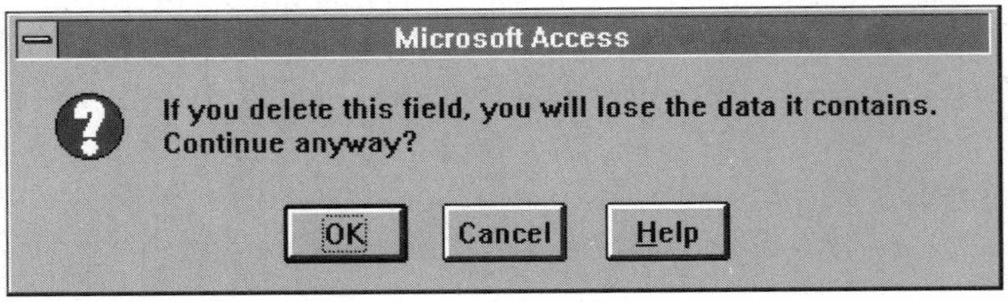

FIGURE 6-14. This dialog box allows you to confirm a field deletion.

Moving Fields

You might want to move a row in a table definition for a number of reasons. Perhaps you made an error as you entered or changed the information in a table. Or perhaps you discover that you're using some fields you defined at the end of a table quite frequently in forms or reports, in which case it would be easier to find and work with those fields if they were nearer the beginning of your table definition.

You can use your keyboard or your mouse to move one or more rows that define the fields. To use your keyboard, do the following:

1. Open the table you want to change in Design view.
2. Use F6 (if necessary) to move your cursor to the top half of the Table window.
3. Use the arrow keys or the Tab key to move the cursor anywhere in the row that defines the first field you want to move.
4. Press Shift-Spacebar to select the entire row.
5. If you want to move a group of rows, hold down the Shift key and extend the selection using the arrow keys.
6. Press Ctrl-F8 to turn on Move mode. You will see MOV appear on the status bar to show you that you've activated this mode.
7. Use the up and down arrow keys to move the selected fields up and down until you've placed them where you want them. Press Esc to turn off Move mode.

Using a mouse can be quicker but requires a sure eye. To select a field definition you want to move, first click the row selector for the row. If you want to move multiple consecutive fields, click the row selector for the first row in the group and scroll until you can see the last row in the group. Hold down the Shift key and click the row selector for the last row in the group. The first and last rows and all the rows in between will be selected. Release the Shift key, click any of the row selectors in the highlighted rows, and drag the field definitions to a new location. A small shaded box attaches to the bottom of the mouse pointer while you're dragging field definitions, and you'll see a highlighted line appear, indicating the position to which the rows will move when you release the mouse button.

In the design for the Orders table in PROMPT, SalesRepID and OrderDate come after the ShipCountry field. Also, FreightCharge appears after SalesTax. You can select the SalesRepID and OrderDate fields by clicking on the row selector for SalesRepID and dragging down with your mouse pointer until Microsoft Access also highlights the OrderDate row. You can click the row selector for either field again and drag both of them down past ShipCountry. In Figure 6-15 on the next page, you can see that the mouse pointer has changed and that the line between the ShipCountry field and the ShipDate field is highlighted just before you release the mouse button.

FIGURE 6-15. The SalesRepID and OrderDate fields have been selected and are being dragged (with the row selector) to their new position between the ShipCountry and ShipDate fields.

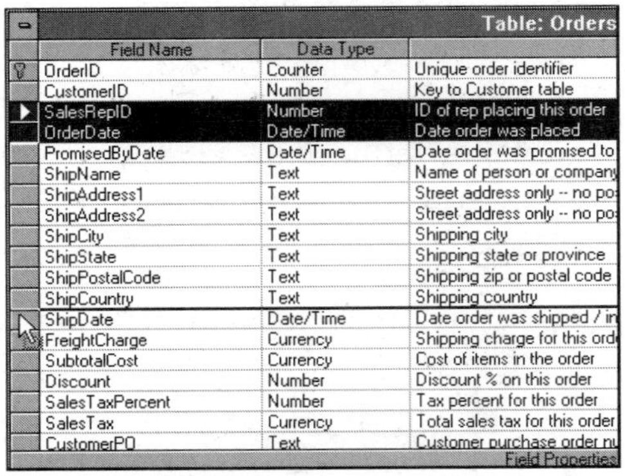

You need to move the FreightCharge field in a similar way. In Figure 6-16, the rows are positioned correctly.

FIGURE 6-16. The SalesRepID and OrderDate fields, shown selected and about to be moved in Figure 6-15, are now correctly placed.

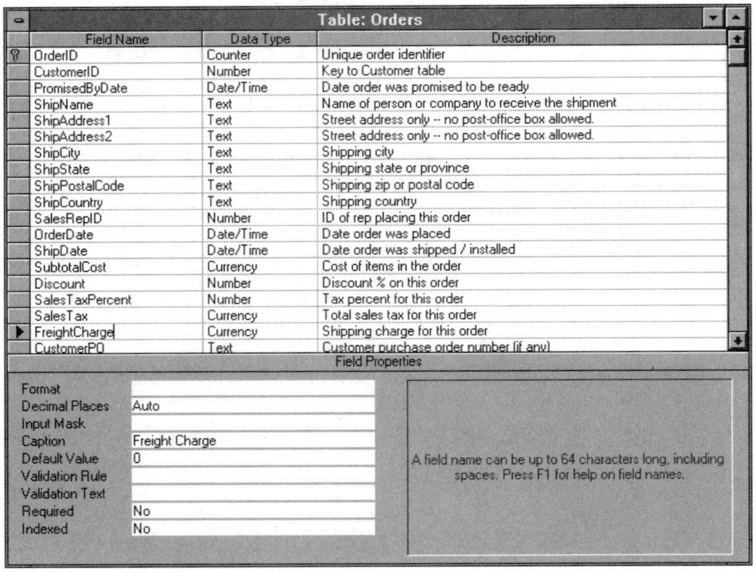

> **TIP:** When it comes to moving fields, you might find a combination of mouse and keyboard methods a bit easier. Use your mouse to select the row or rows you want to move. Then activate Move mode by pressing Ctrl-F8, and use the arrow keys to position the rows. As you experiment with Access, you'll discover more than one way to perform many tasks, and you can choose the techniques that are easiest for you.

Changing Data Attributes

As you learned in the previous chapter, Microsoft Access provides you with a number of different data types. These different data types help Access work more efficiently with your data and also provide a base level of data validation; for example, you can enter only numbers in a Number or Currency field.

When you initially design your database, you should match the data type and length of each field to its intended use. You might discover, however, that a field you thought would contain only numbers (such as a U.S. zip code) must now contain some letters (perhaps because you've started doing business in Canada). You might find that one or more number fields need to hold larger values or a different number of decimal places. Access allows you to change the data type and length of many fields, even after you've entered data in them.

Changing Data Types

Changing the data type of a field in a table is simple. Open the table in Design view, click in the data type column of the field definition you want to change, click the down arrow button at the right to see the available choices, and choose a new data type. The only data type that you cannot convert to another data type is OLE Object. With a few limitations, Access can successfully convert every other data type to any other data type. Figure 6-17, on the next page, shows you the possible conversions and potential limitations.

Convert From	Convert To	Limitations
Text	Memo	Access deletes indexes that include the text field
	Number	Text must contain only numbers and valid separators
	Date/Time	Text must contain a recognizable date and/or time, such as 11-Nov-92 5:15 PM
	Currency	Text must contain only numbers and valid separators
	Counter	Not possible if table contains data
	Yes/No	Text must contain only one of the following values: Yes, True, On, No, False, or Off
Memo	Text	Access truncates text longer than 255 characters
	Number	Memo must contain only numbers and valid separators
	Date/Time	Memo must contain a recognizable date and/or time, such as 11-Nov-92 5:15 PM
	Currency	Memo must contain only numbers and valid separators
	Counter	Not possible if table contains data
	Yes/No	Memo must contain only one of the following values: Yes, True, On, No, False, or Off
Number	Text	No limitations
	Memo	No limitations
	Date/Time	Number must be between –657,434 and 2,958,465.99998843
	Currency	No limitations
	Counter	Not possible if table contains data
	Yes/No	Zero or Null = No; any other value = Yes

FIGURE 6-17. *(continued)*

The data type conversion limitations.

FIGURE 6-17. *continued*

Convert From	Convert To	Limitations
	Number (different precision)	Number must not be larger or smaller than can be contained in the new precision
Date/Time	Text	No limitations
	Memo	No limitations
	Number	No limitations
	Currency	No limitations, but value might be rounded
	Counter	Not possible if table contains data
	Yes/No	12:00:00 AM or Null = No; any other value = Yes
Currency	Text	No limitations
	Memo	No limitations
	Number	Number must not be larger or smaller than can be contained in the data type
	Date/Time	Number must be between –$657,434 and $2,958,465.99
	Counter	Not possible if table contains data
	Yes/No	Zero or Null = No; any other value = Yes
Counter	Text	No limitations
	Memo	No limitations
	Number	No limitations
	Date/Time	Value must be less than 2,958,466
	Currency	No limitations
	Yes/No	All values evaluate to Yes
Yes/No	Text	Converts to text "Yes" or "No"
	Memo	Converts to text "Yes" or "No"
	Number	No = 0; Yes = –1
	Date/Time	No = 12:00:00 AM; Yes = 12/29/1899
	Currency	No = 0; Yes = –$1
	Counter	Not possible

Changing Length

For text and number fields, you can define the maximum length of the data that can be stored in the field. Although a text field can be up to 255 characters long, you can restrict the length to as little as 1 character. If you don't specify a length for text, Access assigns a default length of 50 characters. Access won't let you enter in a text field data longer than the defined length. If you find you need more space in a text field, you can increase the length at any time; but if you try to redefine the length of a text field so that it's shorter, you might get a warning that Access will truncate a number of the data fields when you try to save your change.

Sizes for numbers can vary from a single byte (that can contain a value from 0 through 255) through 8 bytes (necessary to hold very large floating-point or currency numbers). You can change the size of numbers at any time, but you might get errors if you make the size smaller. Access also rounds and truncates numbers when converting from floating-point data types (Single or Double) to Integer or Currency values.

Conversion Errors

When you try to save a changed table definition, Microsoft Access always warns you if any changes in data type or length will cause conversion errors. For example, if you change the Field Size property of a Number field from Integer to Byte, Access warns you if any of the records contain a number larger than 255. You'll see a dialog box (similar to the one shown in Figure 6-18) warning you about fields that Access will set to a Null value if you proceed with your changes. Click the OK button to complete the changes. You'll have to examine your data to correct any conversion errors.

If you click the Cancel button when the dialog box warns you of conversion errors, Access shows you the dialog box in Figure 6-19. If you deleted any fields or indexes, added any fields, or renamed any fields, Access will save those changes. Otherwise, the database will be unchanged. You can correct any data type or length changes you made and try to save the table definition again.

FIGURE 6-18.
This dialog box informs you of conversion errors.

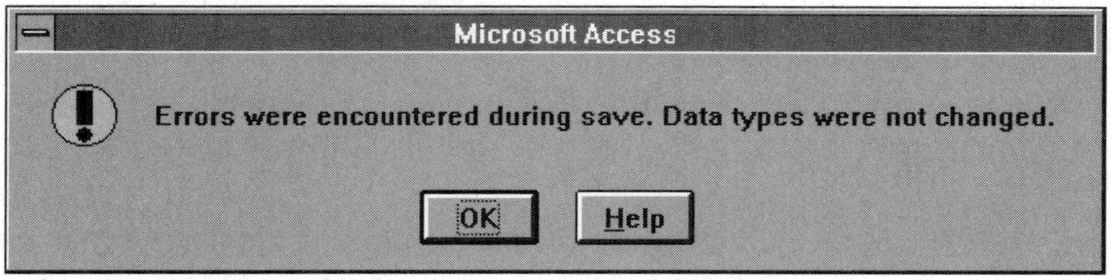

FIGURE 6-19.
This dialog box appears when you decide not to save a changed table definition because of conversion errors.

Splitting a Table

After you've worked with your application for a while, you might discover one or more tables that have an excessive number of fields. If most of your queries or forms use data from only a part of a table and rarely from the whole table, you might get better performance if you split your table into two or more tables.

Another reason to split a table is that some of the fields contain sensitive information you don't want all users of your application to see. Examples of sensitive information include employee salaries and customer credit ratings. Although you can create views and secure your table so that only authorized people can access certain data, it's easier to control sensitive information if it's placed in a separate table.

In the Prompt Computer Solutions, Inc. database, you might want to separate the credit limit information about a customer from less-sensitive data such as address and phone numbers. Start by backing up your entire database just in case you ever need the combined Customers table again. Simply close the database, switch to File Manager, and make a copy of the PROMPT.MDB file.

The easiest way to split the Customers table is to create two copies of the original, including all the data. Use the same copy-and-paste procedure that you read about earlier in this chapter to make two backup copies of the Customers table. Name one copy *CustomerInfo* and the other copy *CustomerCredit.*

In the CustomerInfo table, select the CreditLimit, AmountOwed, and LastPayDate fields and delete them. Microsoft Access warns you if you are about to permanently delete data, but that's OK. Also open the Table Properties window, and delete the table validation rule that references CreditLimit and AmountOwed. If you try now to save the table with this rule defined, you'll get an error because you've deleted these fields. Save your changes.

In the CustomerCredit table, open the Indexes window and delete the indexes on State, City, and CompanyName. Because those fields no longer exist, you'll get an error when you try to delete them. Select the name, address, and phone number fields in the CustomerInfo table in Design view and delete them. Be sure to keep the CustomerID field in both the CustomerInfo and the CustomerCredit tables; that's how you'll link them together. You can check the Table Properties window to ensure that this table has the validation rule you want for CreditLimit and AmountOwed. Save your changes.

Having created two new tables, you might want to create a backup of just the definition of the old combined Customers table for future reference. From the Database window, select the Customers table and then choose the Copy command from the Edit menu. Choose the Paste command from the Edit menu, and the Paste Table As dialog box will open. Type in a name such as *Old Customer Structure*, click the Structure Only option button, and then click OK.

Now you need to remove all relationships that you've defined in the Customers table and define the relationships for your two new tables. To do this, follow these steps:

1. Select the Database window, and then choose Relationships from the Edit menu or click the Relationships button on the toolbar to see the Relationships window.
2. To ensure that you can see all relationships, click the Show All Relationships button on the toolbar, shown in Figure 6-20. (Note that Figure 6-20 shows only the relationships between the tables in the PROMPT sample database, not the tables you created in Chapter 5.)

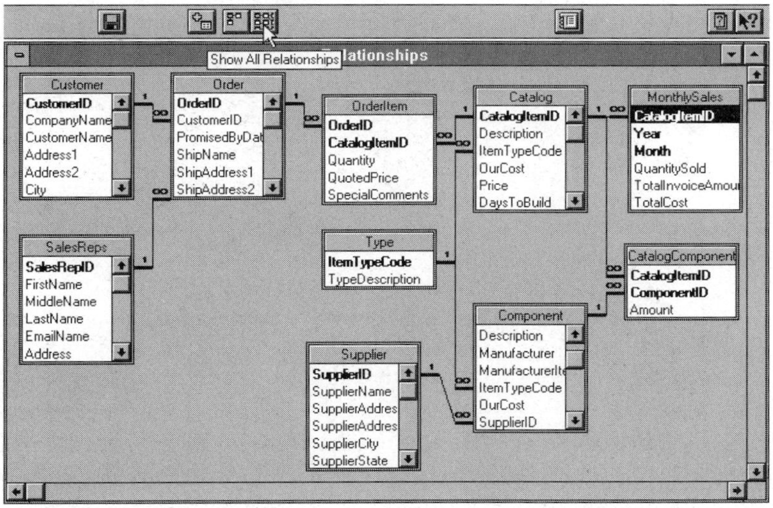

FIGURE 6-20.
Click the Show All Relationships button to ensure that you can see all relationships in the Relationships window.

3. Click on the relationship line between Customers and Orders, and press the Del key to remove the relationship.
4. Click on the Customers table, and press the Del key to remove it from the relationship display.
5. Choose Add Table from the Relationships window or click the Add Table button on the toolbar to open the Add Table dialog box.
6. Choose the CustomerInfo and CustomerCredit tables, and click the Add button to add them to the Relationships diagram. Click Close to dismiss the dialog box.

7. Drag the CustomerID field from the CustomerInfo table to the CustomerID field in the Orders table. Define a one-to-many relationship, as described in Chapter 5.
8. Drag the CustomerID field from CustomerInfo to the CustomerID field in CustomerCredit. Your result should look similar to that shown in Figure 6-21.

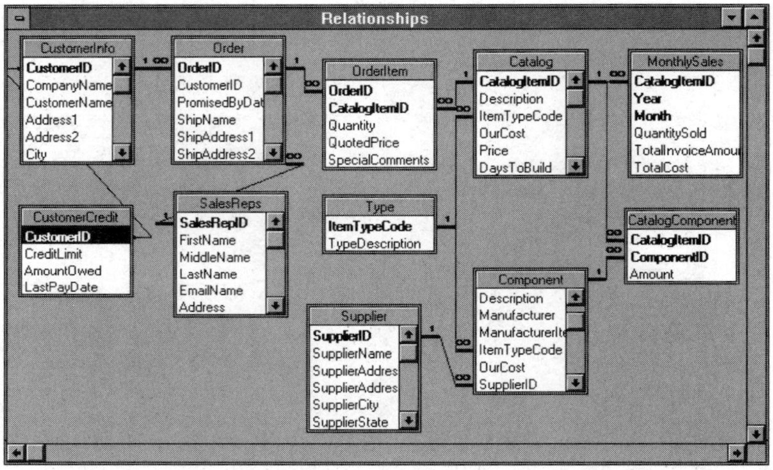

FIGURE 6-21. The Relationships window shows you the new relationship between the CustomerInfo table and the CustomerCredit table.

You can now delete the Customers table from the PROMPT sample database if you want. (You'll re-create this table later in this chapter.)

NOTE: You can ask Access to control the integrity between two tables that are linked one-to-one, such as CustomerInfo and CustomerCredit in this example. However, you will have to be sure to define a query that allows you to add a row to both tables at the same time, or you won't be able to add customers. (See Chapter 8, "Adding Power with Select Queries," for details.)

Combining Tables

As you discovered in Chapter 4, "Designing Your Database Application," you use a process called *normalization* to come up with a good relational database design. If you follow all the rules rigorously, it's possible to end up with lots of little tables—known as an *over-normalized database*. That's not a serious problem in Microsoft Access because Access has an excellent query capability that allows you to easily work with data from many tables in a single view. Whenever Access has to join multiple tables, however, performance is likely to be slower than if Access were working with data in a single table.

One way to detect whether you have over-normalized your database is to check whether you're always using two or more tables together and very rarely separately. If you are, and especially if one of the tables has a lot of data, you can probably improve performance by combining tables. For example, you might have items for sale that you normally group into a number of categories—such as the Components table and the Types table in the PROMPT database.

However, if you have thousands of products and only a dozen or fewer categories and if you always retrieve the category name with the product, you might want to sacrifice disk storage space in exchange for speed by eliminating the join with the Category table and putting the full category name in the Products table. Even if you decide to place the full category name in the Products table, you'll probably still want to keep the Category table as a "master list" of all valid categories that might be used to classify a product. Such a table is called a *code table* and can be very useful for simplifying data entry on forms by providing a short predefined list. (See Chapter 13, "Building a Form," for details.)

Whatever your reason for combining two tables, it's a fairly simple procedure when you use a query and save the result as a physical table. In the following example, you can put the CustomerInfo table and the CustomerCredit table in the PROMPT database back together.

See Also: For the full details on creating and using queries, see Chapter 8, "Adding Power with Select Queries."

Begin by opening the PROMPT database and highlighting the CustomerInfo table in the Database window. Click the New Query button on the toolbar. You don't need a Query Wizard for this problem, so click the New Query button in the New Query dialog box to open the

Query window in Design view. Access places the field list from the table you selected in the top half of the window. By default, you are creating a select query, but you really want to make a new table with the results of this query. To do that, choose the Make Table command from the Query menu, as shown in Figure 6-22.

FIGURE 6-22.
The Make Table command is used to combine tables using a query.

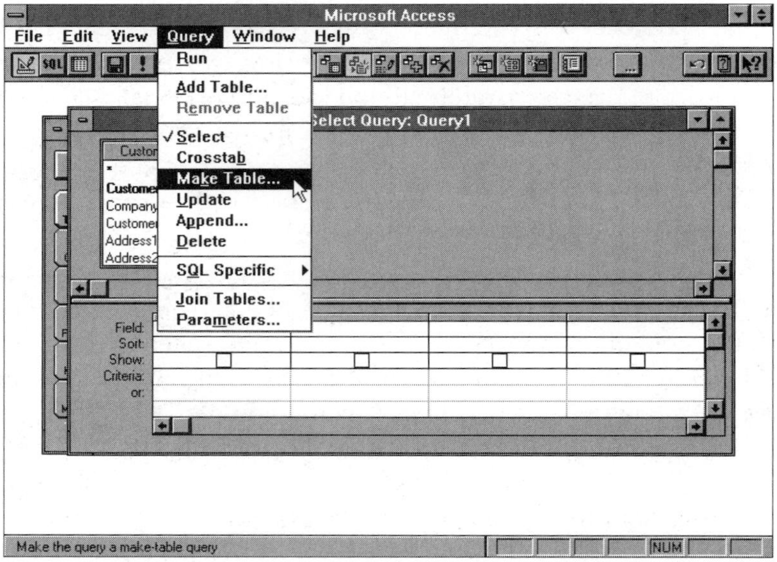

When you use a Make Table command on a query, Access asks you for the name of the table you want to build. You're creating a combined customer table from two tables, so enter *Customers* for the table name, as shown in Figure 6-23. Click the OK button to save the name.

FIGURE 6-23.
The Query Properties dialog box is used to name a new table.

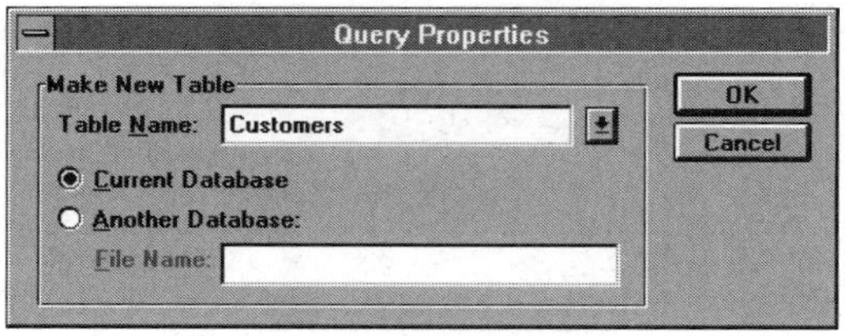

Next you need to add the second table to the query. Drag the title bar of the Query window in Design view aside until you can see the Database window, or choose the Tile command from the Window menu to line up the two windows side by side, as shown in Figure 6-24. Use your mouse to drag the name of the CustomerCredit table from the table list in the Database window to the top part of the Query window in Design view. If you created the relationship between the two tables properly, you should see a line connecting the CustomerID field in the CustomerInfo field list to the CustomerID field in the CustomerCredit field list. This connection must exist for the query to execute properly. If the line is not there, you can create the relationship now by dragging the CustomerID field from one field list and dropping it on the CustomerID field in the other field list.

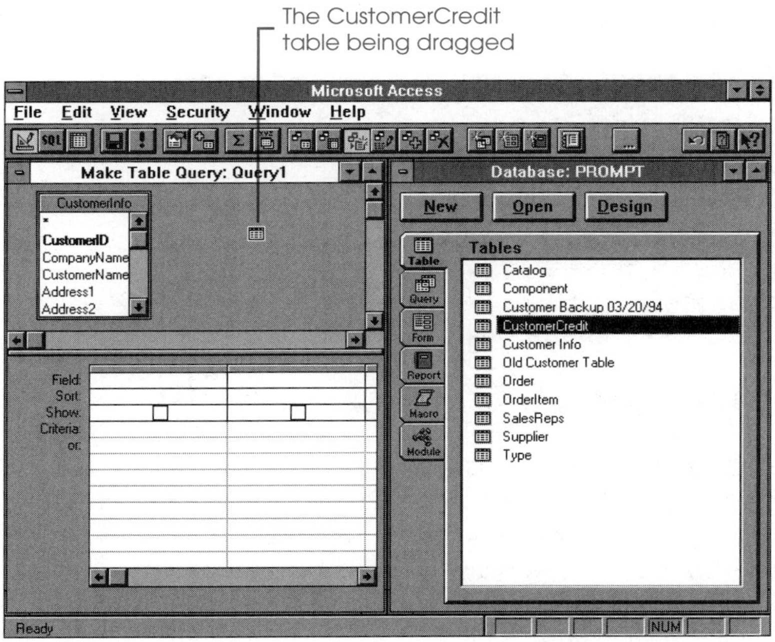

FIGURE 6-24.
A second table is dragged to the Query window in Design view as the next step in making a combined table.

Choose Cascade from the Window menu to place the Query window back in the center of your workspace. Now you need to tell Microsoft Access which fields you want in the resulting table. You want all the fields from both tables, except that you want only one CustomerID field. At the top of the field list for each table there is an asterisk that is shorthand for "give me all the fields in this table." Use your mouse to drag the asterisk from the CustomerInfo field list to the first field box in the QBE (query by example) grid at the bottom half of the Query window in Design view. Access displays CustomerInfo.* in this field, as shown in Figure 6-25. You could have typed this yourself, but dragging and dropping is much quicker and easier. Now you need all the fields from the CustomerCredit field list except CustomerID. Click the Credit-Limit field in the CustomerCredit field list, and then hold down the Shift key and click the LastPayDate field in the CustomerCredit field list to highlight all the fields from CreditLimit to LastPayDate. Drag the highlighted fields to the second field box in the QBE grid at the bottom half of the Query window. Your mouse pointer changes to show that you've grabbed a set of fields. When you release the mouse button, Access fills in all the field names you selected from the CustomerCredit table. Your completed query should look like Figure 6-25.

FIGURE 6-25. The fields from two tables are dragged to the grid in a Query window in order to make a combined table.

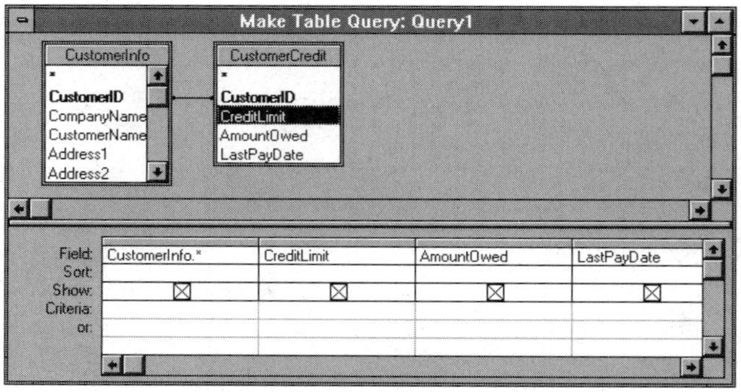

Now you're ready to create the new table with data combined from the two old tables. Simply click the Run button (the exclamation point) on the toolbar to run your query. Access retrieves the data you asked for and then shows you how many rows you're creating in the new table, as shown in Figure 6-26. Click the OK button to finish creating the table. If you didn't delete the old table, Access also prompts you to confirm whether you want to replace the existing Customers table.

FIGURE 6-26. A dialog box asks you to confirm the Make Table query.

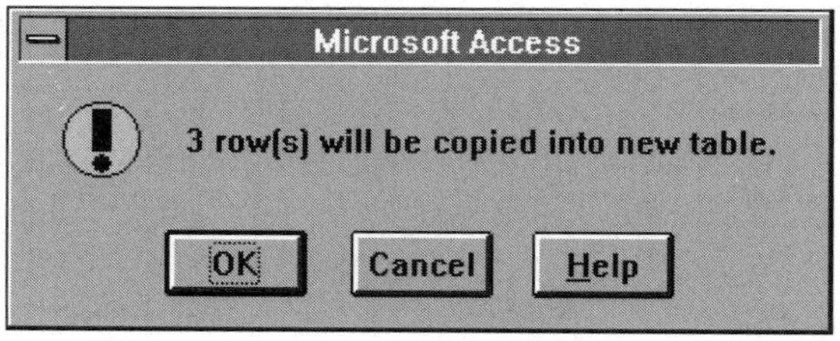

The rest of this book deals with the single Customers table, so you might want to go back to the Relationships window, remove the split tables, and put the Customer table back. Be sure to define a one-to-many relationship between the Customers table and the Orders table.

Changing the Primary Key

Chapter 4, "Designing Your Database Application," discusses the need to have one or more fields that provide a unique value to every row in your table. This field with unique values is identified as the *primary key*. If a table doesn't have a primary key, you can't define a relationship between it and other tables, and Microsoft Access has to guess to automatically link tables for you. Even when you choose a primary key in your initial design, you might discover later that it doesn't really contain unique values. In that case, you might have to define a new field or fields to be the primary key.

Suppose that in designing the Components table in the PROMPT database, you used the item code from each manufacturer as a unique key for items in the table, as shown in Figure 6-27. Later you discover that some of the item codes from a couple of the manufacturers are the same. You decide to insert a new Counter field that will serve as the primary key.

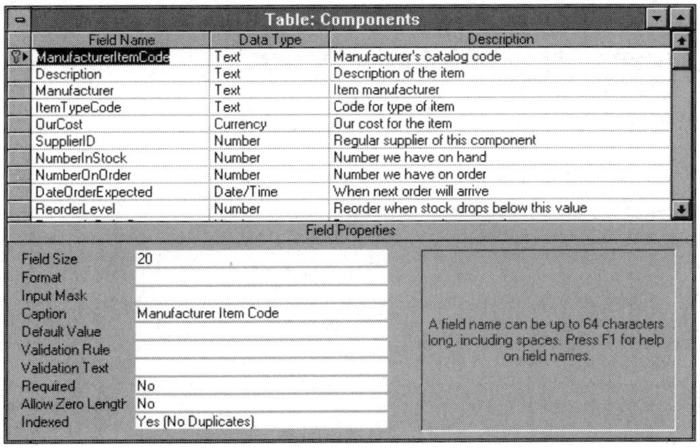
Table: Components
Field Name | Data Type | Description
ManufacturerItemCode | Text | Manufacturer's catalog code
Description | Text | Description of the item
Manufacturer | Text | Item manufacturer
ItemTypeCode | Text | Code for type of item
OurCost | Currency | Our cost for the item
SupplierID | Number | Regular supplier of this component
NumberInStock | Number | Number we have on hand
NumberOnOrder | Number | Number we have on order
DateOrderExpected | Date/Time | When next order will arrive
ReorderLevel | Number | Reorder when stock drops below this value
Field Properties
Field Size 20
Format
Input Mask
Caption Manufacturer Item Code
Default Value
Validation Rule
Validation Text
Required No
Allow Zero Length No
Indexed Yes (No Duplicates)
A field name can be up to 64 characters long, including spaces. Press F1 for help on field names.

FIGURE 6-27.
The Components table with ManufacturerItemCode as the primary key.

First, you need to remove the primary key definition on ManufacturerItemCode—but not remove the field. To remove the existing primary key, open the Indexes window by clicking the Indexes button on the toolbar or by choosing Indexes from the View menu. Click on the primary key row, as shown in Figure 6-28, and press the Del key to remove the index.

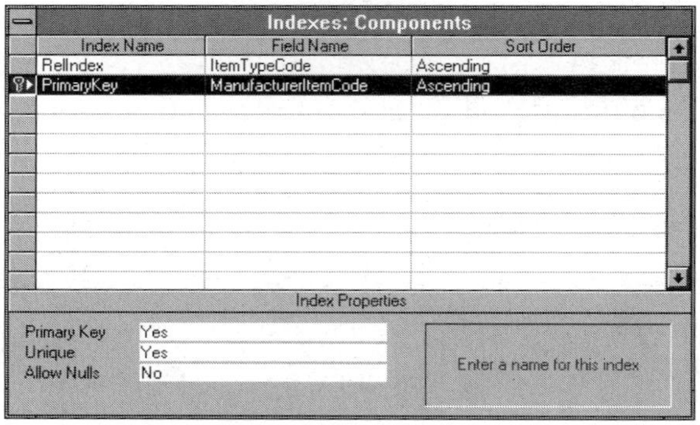

FIGURE 6-28.
A primary key designation is removed in the Indexes window when you click the primary key and then press the Del key.

Next, insert a new field—*ComponentID*—at the beginning of the table. Be sure your new field is a Counter. Select the new field and click the Primary Key button on the toolbar to make the field the primary key. When you save the table, Microsoft Access will create new unique counter values in all existing rows for the new primary key.

Compacting Your Database

Microsoft Access reuses as much space as possible within the space allocated to the file that contains your database. Whenever you change a definition, Access saves the new definition and deletes the old one. If you delete records or object definitions, Access can use that space again later for new records or object definitions. Over time, however, the file allocated to your database can grow larger than it needs to be to store all your definitions and data.

To regain unused space, you should compact your database periodically. No database can be open when you run the compact utility. Also, no other users should be accessing the database you intend to compact. To execute the compact utility, open the File menu in the

Microsoft Access window after all databases have been closed. Choose the Compact Database command. Access opens the dialog box shown in Figure 6-29.

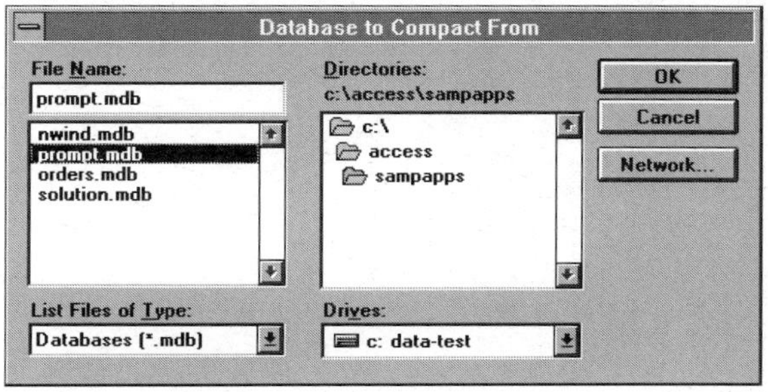

FIGURE 6-29.
The dialog box for specifying a database to compact.

Select the database you want to compact, and then click OK. Access asks you for a database name for the compacted database, as shown in Figure 6-30. You can create a compacted copy of your database under another name, or you can enter the same name as the database you are compacting. (Access warns you if you choose the same name.) When you choose the same name, Access compacts your database into a temporary file. When compaction is successfully completed, Access deletes your old database and automatically gives its name to the new compacted copy.

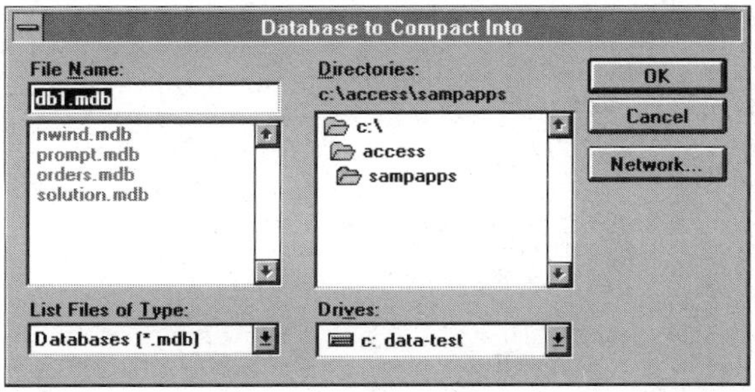

FIGURE 6-30.
The dialog box in which you name a compacted database.

You now have all the information you need to modify and maintain your database table definitions. In the next chapter, you'll explore working with the data in your tables.

PART 3

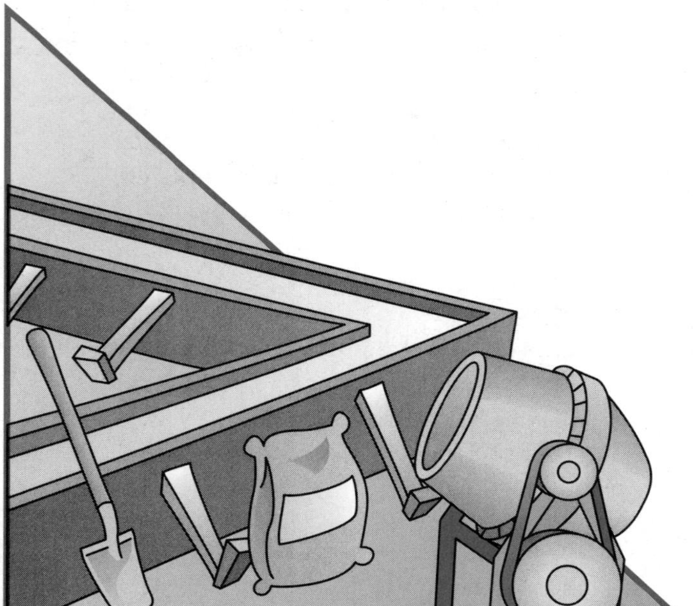

Working with Data

7

Using Datasheets

The simplest way to look at your data is to open a table in Datasheet view. When you build your application, you'll probably work with your data mostly through forms that you design. Studying datasheets is useful, however, because it improves your understanding of basic concepts such as viewing, updating, inserting, and deleting data. Microsoft Access performs these functions in the same way regardless of whether you're using a datasheet or a specially designed form to work with your data. On some forms, you might decide to embed a Datasheet view to make it easy to look at several rows and columns of data at once. Even after you've built an application to work with your data, you'll find that Datasheet view is often useful to verify data at the basic table level. Throughout this chapter, you'll look at examples of operations using the Customer table in the PROMPT database that you designed using Appendix B—or that you installed from the companion disk included with this book. Take a moment now to copy the Customer table. The copy procedure is described in Chapter 6, "Modifying Your Database Design." Name your copy *CustomerBackup*. Figure 7-1 shows the table in Datasheet view and explains some key terms.

FIGURE 7-1.
A table in Datasheet view consists of fields (columns) and records (rows).

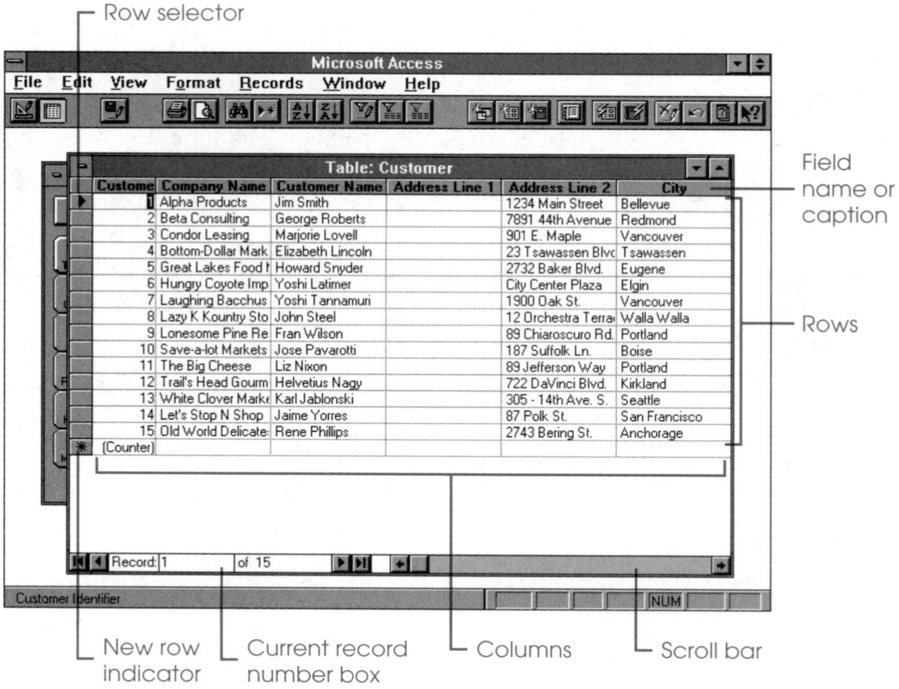

The Built-In Toolbar in Datasheet View

Before you go exploring datasheets, it's useful to take a moment to look at the toolbar that Microsoft Access displays when you open any table in Datasheet view. From left to right, the buttons are as follows (see page 108 for a description of the Cut, Copy, and Paste buttons):

Design View button. Click this button to see the Table window in Design view.

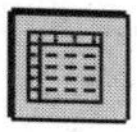

Datasheet View button. This button appears pressed when you're looking at a Table window in Datasheet view.

Print button. Click this button to print the data on the datasheet.

Print Preview button. Click this button to see a preview of the printed page.

New button. Click this button to jump to the empty row at the end of the table to insert a new record.

Find button. Click this button to initiate a search for particular values in the table.

Sort Ascending button. Click anywhere in a column you want to sort, and then click this button to order the rows in the table based on ascending values in the selected column. NEW!

Sort Descending button. Click anywhere in a column you want to sort, and then click this button to order the rows in the table based on descending values in the selected column. NEW!

Edit Filter/Sort button. You can restrict and sort the data you see in the table. Click this button to create or edit a filter or sorting criteria. NEW!

Apply Filter/Sort button. Click this button to apply any filter or sorting criteria you have created. NEW!

Show All Records button. Click this button to remove any filter and display all records in the table. NEW!

New Query button. Click this button to begin designing a new query based on the current table. (See Chapter 8, "Adding Power with Select Queries," for details.)

(continued)

(continued)

New Form button. Click this button to begin designing a new form based on the current table. (See Chapter 13, "Building a Form," for details.)

New Report button. Click this button to begin designing a new report based on the current table. (See Chapter 17, "Constructing a Report," for details.)

Database Window button. Click this button to place the focus on the database window. This button also un-hides the window if you've hidden it and restores the window if you've minimized it.

NEW!

AutoForm button. Click this button to have Microsoft Access build a simple single view form for you using the current table. (See Chapter 12, "Form Basics," for details on building a form.)

NEW!

AutoReport button. Click this button to have Microsoft Access build a simple report using the current table and display it in Print Preview. (See Chapter 16, "Report Basics," for details on constructing a report.)

Undo Current Field/Record button. Click this button to undo all changes to any field in the current record. The button is disabled when there are no changes that can be undone.

Undo button. Click this button to undo your last change. Undo has the same effect as Ctrl-Z or the Undo command on the Edit menu. The button is disabled when there are no changes that can be undone.

Cue Cards button. Click this button to open the main menu of the Cue Cards facility. The Cue Cards facility leads you through step-by-step instructions for most common tasks.

Help button. Click this button to add a question mark to your mouse pointer. Click with this pointer on any displayed object to receive context-sensitive help about that object.

Viewing Data

To look at data in one of your tables in Datasheet view, do the following:

1. Open your database. By default, Microsoft Access will display the list of tables in the database within the Database window.
2. Double-click on the name of the table you want. If you want to use the keyboard, press the up or down arrow key to move the highlight to the table you want, and then press Enter or Alt-O.

Figure 7-2 shows you the Datasheet view of the Customer table from the PROMPT database on your companion disk. Open this table on your computer now. If you like, you can make the datasheet fill the workspace by clicking the Maximize button in the upper right corner of the window. Or you can press Alt- - (hyphen) to open the Control menu and then press *X* to choose the Maximize command.

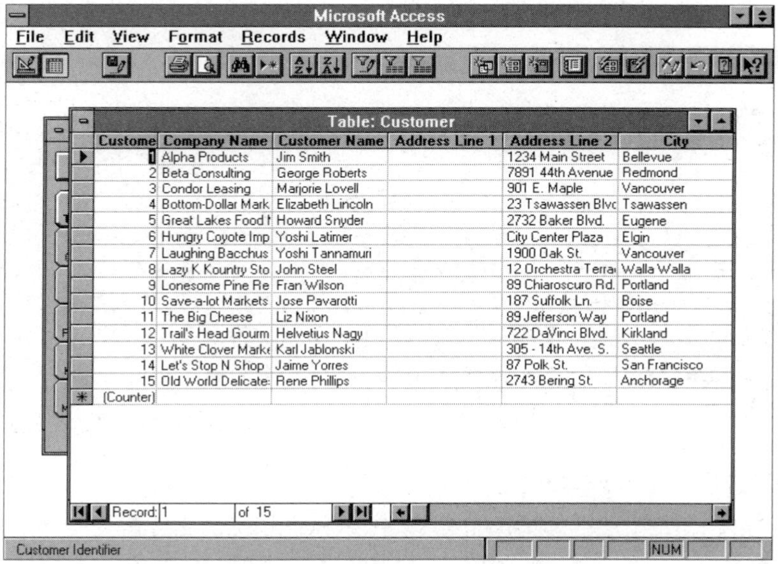

FIGURE 7-2.
The Datasheet view of the PROMPT Customer table.

Moving Around

Changing the display to show you different records or fields is very simple. You can use the horizontal scroll bar, shown in Figure 7-3, or the vertical scroll bar.

FIGURE 7-3.
The scroll bars can be used to change the display of records and fields in a window.

In the lower left corner of the table in Datasheet view, you can see a record number box, as shown in Figure 7-4 on the next page. The record number box shows you the *relative record number* of the current record (meaning the number of the record where the cursor is located or where some data is selected). Note that you might not see the current record in the window if you've scrolled the display. The record number box also shows the total number of records available in the current display. If you've applied a filter against the table (see the section titled "Searching for and Filtering Data," later in this chapter), the number might be less than the total number of records in the table.

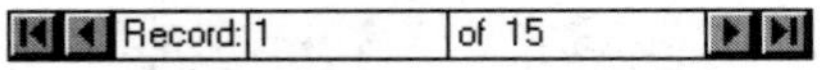

FIGURE 7-4.
The record number box is at the bottom left of a table in Datasheet view.

You can use the record number box to quickly move to the record you want. As you'll read a bit later, you'll usually select some data in a record in order to change it. You can also choose the Go To command from the Records menu to move to the first, last, next, previous, or a new record. You can also make any record current by clicking anywhere in its row, and the number in the record number box will change to indicate the new row you've selected.

Keyboard Shortcuts

You might find it easier to use the keyboard rather than the mouse to move around on the datasheet, especially if you've been typing in new data. Some keyboard shortcuts for scrolling in a datasheet are listed in Figure 7-5 and for selecting data on a datasheet in Figure 7-6.

Keys	Scrolling Action
PgUp	Up one page
PgDn	Down one page
Ctrl-PgUp	Left one page
Ctrl-PgDn	Right one page

FIGURE 7-5.
The keyboard shortcuts for scrolling in a datasheet.

Keys	Selecting Action
Tab	Next field
Shift-Tab	Previous field
Home	First field, current record
End	Last field, current record
Up arrow	Current field, previous record
Down arrow	Current field, next record
Ctrl-up arrow	Current field, first record
Ctrl-down arrow	Current field, last record
Ctrl-Home	First field, first record
Ctrl-End	Last field, last record
F5	Record number box

FIGURE 7-6.
The keyboard shortcuts for selecting data on a datasheet.

Modifying the Datasheet Format

You can make a number of changes to the appearance of your datasheet. You can change the height of rows or the width of columns. You can rearrange or hide columns. You can set the display or printing font and decide whether you want to see gridlines. You can make most of these changes from the Format menu, shown in Figure 7-7.

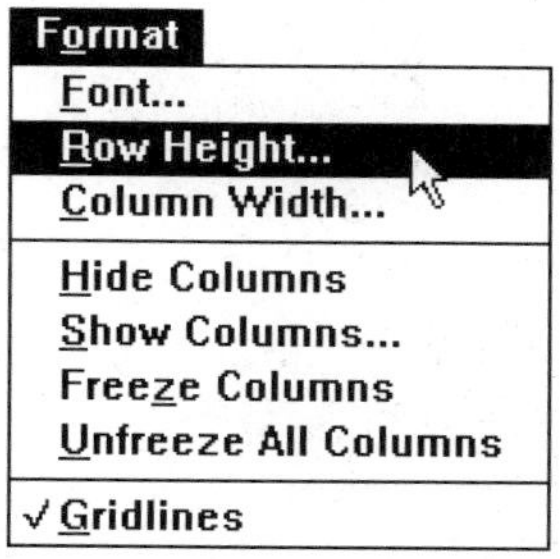

FIGURE 7-7.
The Format menu in Datasheet view.

Changing Row Height and Column Width

Microsoft Access initially displays all the columns and rows using a default width and height. The standard width is probably wider than it needs to be for columns that contain a small amount of data, but it's not wide enough for other columns with a large amount of data. For example, the first column in the PROMPT Customer table is wider than it needs to be to display the CustomerID field. The second column, however, is not wide enough to display the typical CompanyName entry.

One way to fix the column width is to select any value in the column that you want to change and then choose the Column Width command from the Format menu. You'll see a dialog box similar to the one shown in Figure 7-8. You can type in a new width value in number of characters. The "standard" width is approximately 1 inch when printed, based on the current font selection. If you click the Best Fit button, Access sets the column width to accommodate the longest displayed data value in this column in the table.

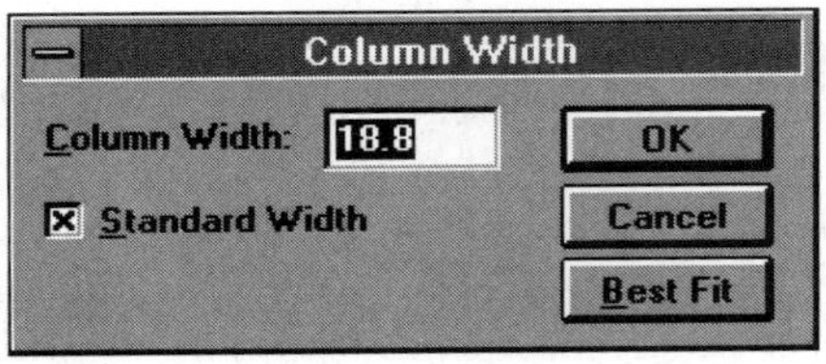

FIGURE 7-8.
The Column Width dialog box.

You can also modify the column widths directly on the screen by placing the mouse pointer on the gray line between the column names at the top of the Table window. (See Figure 7-9.) When you do this, the mouse pointer changes into a vertical bar with arrows pointing to the left and right. By dragging the column boundary, you can adjust the size of the column.

If you plan to print your datasheet, you might want to increase the height of the rows to create some space between records on the report. Choose the Row Height command from the Format menu to see a dialog box similar to the one shown in Figure 7-10. The row height is measured in points—units of approximately 1/72 inch (1/28 centimeter). To allow space between rows, Access calculates a standard height that is approximately 30 percent taller than the current font's point size. You can enter a new height in the text box. If you choose a number that is shorter than the font size, your rows will overlap when printed. You can also change the row height by dragging the row boundary from within the record selector on the left, in the same way you changed the column width with the mouse. (See Figure 7-9.)

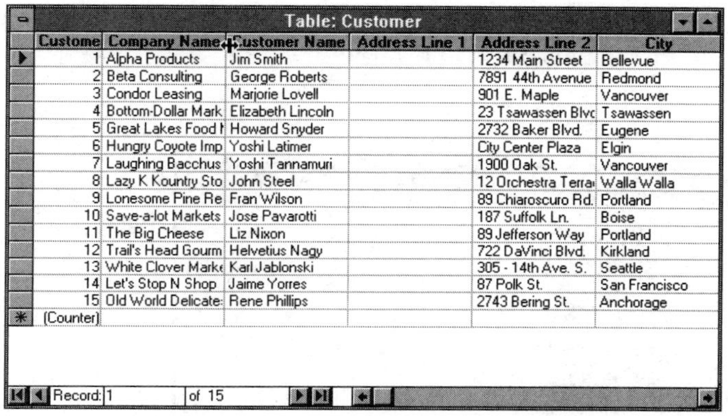

Custome	Company Name	Customer Name	Address Line 1	Address Line 2	City
1	Alpha Products	Jim Smith		1234 Main Street	Bellevue
2	Beta Consulting	George Roberts		7891 44th Avenue	Redmond
3	Condor Leasing	Marjorie Lovell		901 E. Maple	Vancouver
4	Bottom-Dollar Mark	Elizabeth Lincoln		23 Tsawassen Blvc	Tsawassen
5	Great Lakes Food I	Howard Snyder		2732 Baker Blvd.	Eugene
6	Hungry Coyote Imp	Yoshi Latimer		City Center Plaza	Elgin
7	Laughing Bacchus	Yoshi Tannamuri		1900 Oak St.	Vancouver
8	Lazy K Kountry Sto	John Steel		12 Orchestra Terra	Walla Walla
9	Lonesome Pine Re	Fran Wilson		89 Chiaroscuro Rd.	Portland
10	Save-a-lot Markets	Jose Pavarotti		187 Suffolk Ln.	Boise
11	The Big Cheese	Liz Nixon		89 Jefferson Way	Portland
12	Trail's Head Gourm	Helvetius Nagy		722 DaVinci Blvd.	Kirkland
13	White Clover Mark	Karl Jablonski		305 - 14th Ave. S.	Seattle
14	Let's Stop N Shop	Jaime Yorres		87 Polk St.	San Francisco
15	Old World Delicate	Rene Phillips		2743 Bering St.	Anchorage
(Counter)					

FIGURE 7-9.
You can use the mouse to adjust the column width. The mouse pointer, when placed on the gray line between columns, becomes a vertical bar with arrows pointing left and right, allowing you to drag the column boundary.

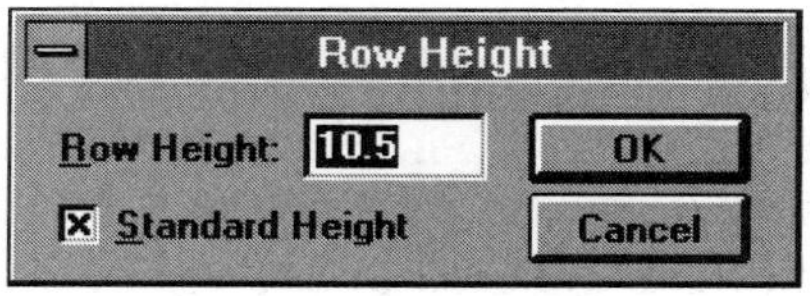

FIGURE 7-10.
The Row Height dialog box.

Arranging Columns

The default order of fields from left to right in Datasheet view is the order in which the fields were defined in the table. You can easily change the column order for viewing or printing. Select the column you want by clicking the field selector (the field name bar at the top of the column). Microsoft Access highlights the entire column. You can select multiple columns by dragging across several columns in either direction before you release the mouse button. You can also click a field selector and extend the selection by holding down the Shift key while using the left or right arrow key to expand the highlighted area.

To move the selected columns, drag a field selector to the desired new location. (See Figure 7-11.) To move the columns using the keyboard, press Ctrl-F8 to turn on Move mode. Access displays *MOV* in one of the areas on the status bar. Shift the columns to the left or right using the arrow keys. Press Esc to turn off Move mode.

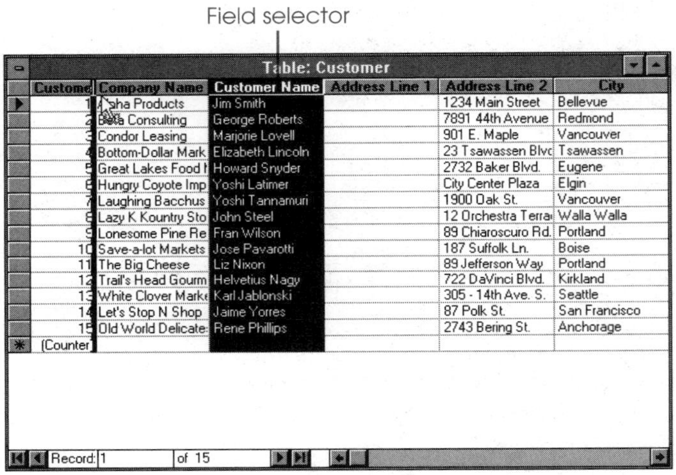

FIGURE 7-11.
You move a column by first selecting it and then dragging the field selector.

Hiding and Showing Columns

By default, Microsoft Access displays all of the columns in the table in Datasheet view, although you might have to scroll to see some of them. If you're not interested in looking at or printing all these fields, you can hide some of them. One way to hide a column is to drag the right column boundary to the left (from within the field selector) until the column disappears. You can also select one or more columns and choose the Hide Columns command from the Format menu.

You can use the Show Columns dialog box (available from the Format menu) to reveal hidden columns or to hide additional ones. (See Figure 7-12.) Select a column from the list, and then click the appropriate option button. The checked columns are already showing. You can select multiple contiguous fields by clicking one field, scrolling up or down in the dialog box until you see the first or last field in the range you want, and then clicking that field while holding down the Shift key.

You can select multiple noncontiguous fields by clicking each one while holding down the Ctrl key. Click Close to close the dialog box.

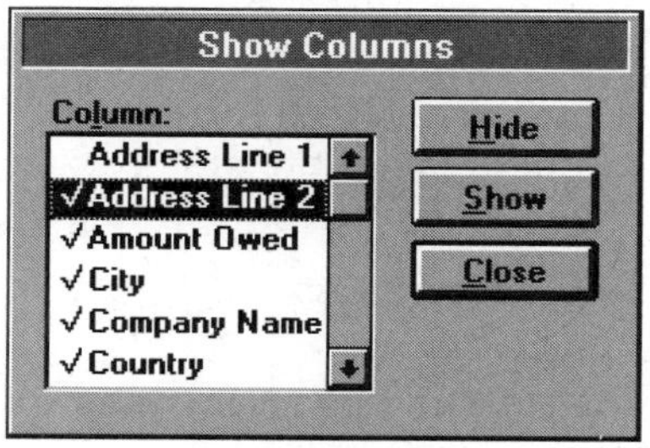

FIGURE 7-12. The Show Columns dialog box, with options for revealing hidden columns and for hiding columns.

Freezing Columns

Sometimes while viewing data, you might want to keep one column on the screen while scrolling left or right through the other columns. For example, you might want to keep the Customer Name column on the screen as you scroll all the way to the right to see the phone numbers. You can freeze one or more columns by selecting them (as a group of contiguous selected columns or one column at a time) and then choosing the Freeze Columns command from the Format menu. Access moves the selected columns to the far left and "freezes" them there. Those fields do not scroll off the left of the window when you scroll right. To release frozen columns, choose the Unfreeze All Columns command from the Format menu. Figure 7-13 shows the Company Name column frozen to the left with the rest of the display scrolled right to show the postal code, country, and phone numbers.

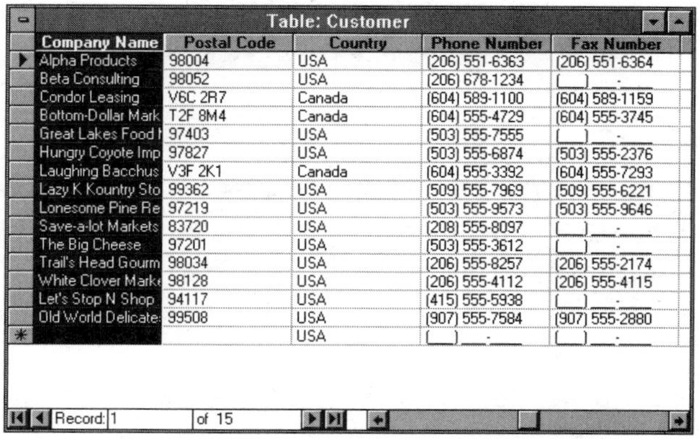
Table: Customer
Company Name | Postal Code | Country | Phone Number | Fax Number
Alpha Products | 98004 | USA | (206) 551-6363 | (206) 551-6364
Beta Consulting | 98052 | USA | (206) 678-1234 |
Condor Leasing | V6C 2R7 | Canada | (604) 589-1100 | (604) 589-1159
Bottom-Dollar Mark | T2F 8M4 | Canada | (604) 555-4729 | (604) 555-3745
Great Lakes Food | 97403 | USA | (503) 555-7555 |
Hungry Coyote Imp | 97827 | USA | (503) 555-6874 | (503) 555-2376
Laughing Bacchus | V3F 2K1 | Canada | (604) 555-3392 | (604) 555-7293
Lazy K Kountry Sto | 99362 | USA | (509) 555-7969 | (509) 555-6221
Lonesome Pine Re | 97219 | USA | (503) 555-9573 | (503) 555-9646
Save-a-lot Markets | 83720 | USA | (208) 555-8097 |
The Big Cheese | 97201 | USA | (503) 555-3612 |
Trail's Head Gourm | 98034 | USA | (206) 555-8257 | (206) 555-2174
White Clover Mark | 98128 | USA | (206) 555-4112 | (206) 555-4115
Let's Stop N Shop | 94117 | USA | (415) 555-5938 |
Old World Delicate | 99508 | USA | (907) 555-7584 | (907) 555-2880
USA
Record: 1 of 15

FIGURE 7-13. A datasheet with a frozen column (Company Name).

Removing Gridlines

The Datasheet view normally has gridlines between the columns and rows. Microsoft Access also includes these gridlines if you print the datasheet. You can easily remove the gridlines by choosing the Gridlines command from the Format menu. Choose it again to turn the gridlines back on. Figure 7-14 shows you the datasheet from Figure 7-13, but without the gridlines. Notice that a line is present to indicate that the Company Name column is "frozen." Access includes this line if you decide to print a report with frozen columns.

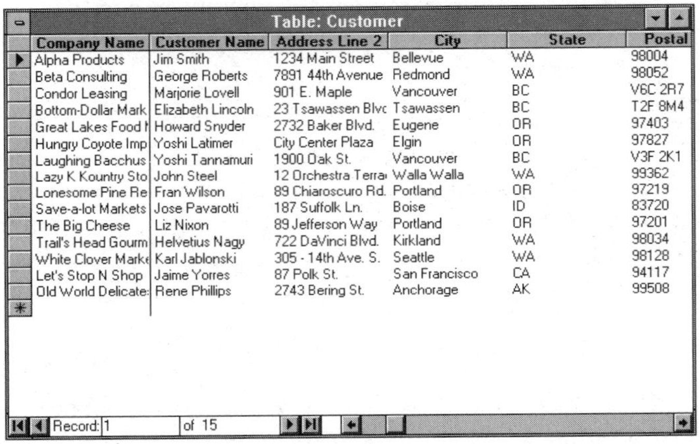

Company Name	Customer Name	Address Line 2	City	State	Postal
Alpha Products	Jim Smith	1234 Main Street	Bellevue	WA	98004
Beta Consulting	George Roberts	7891 44th Avenue	Redmond	WA	98052
Condor Leasing	Marjorie Lovell	901 E. Maple	Vancouver	BC	V6C 2R7
Bottom-Dollar Mark	Elizabeth Lincoln	23 Tsawassen Blvc	Tsawassen	BC	T2F 8M4
Great Lakes Food M	Howard Snyder	2732 Baker Blvd.	Eugene	OR	97403
Hungry Coyote Imp	Yoshi Latimer	City Center Plaza	Elgin	OR	97827
Laughing Bacchus	Yoshi Tannamuri	1900 Oak St.	Vancouver	BC	V3F 2K1
Lazy K Kountry Sto	John Steel	12 Orchestra Terra	Walla Walla	WA	99362
Lonesome Pine Re	Fran Wilson	89 Chiaroscuro Rd.	Portland	OR	97219
Save-a-lot Markets	Jose Pavarotti	187 Suffolk Ln.	Boise	ID	83720
The Big Cheese	Liz Nixon	89 Jefferson Way	Portland	OR	97201
Trail's Head Gourm	Helvetius Nagy	722 DaVinci Blvd.	Kirkland	WA	98034
White Clover Marke	Karl Jablonski	305 - 14th Ave. S.	Seattle	WA	98128
Let's Stop N Shop	Jaime Yorres	87 Polk St.	San Francisco	CA	94117
Old World Delicate	Rene Phillips	2743 Bering St.	Anchorage	AK	99508

FIGURE 7-14. A datasheet without gridlines. The line to the right of the Company Name column indicates that this column is "frozen."

> **TIP:** To print the datasheet without the line, choose the Unfreeze All Columns command from the Format menu before printing the datasheet.

Selecting Fonts

The last thing you can do to customize the look of a datasheet is to select a different font. Choose the Font command from the Format menu to see the dialog box shown in Figure 7-15.

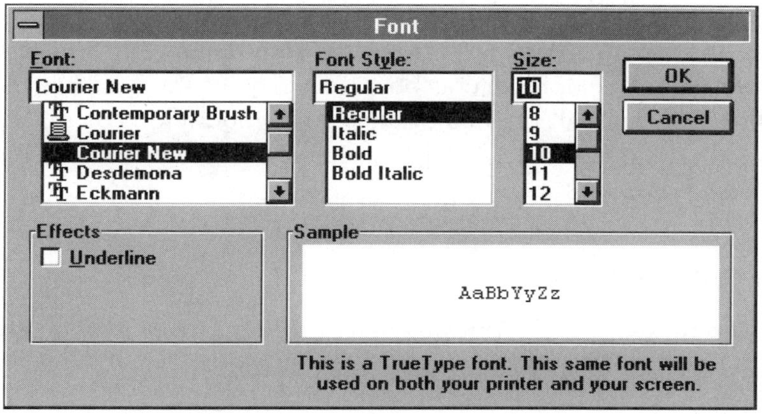

FIGURE 7-15. The Font dialog box.

In the Font list box at the upper left of the dialog box, you can see all the fonts that are installed in your Windows operating system. You can scroll down through the list box and select the font name you want.

The icon to the left of the font name indicates whether the font is a screen font (blank), a printer font (printer icon), or a TrueType font (TT icon) that you can use for both screen display and printing. If you select a printer font, Access uses the closest matching screen or TrueType font to display the datasheet on your screen. If you choose a screen font, Access uses the closest matching printer or TrueType font when you print. In either case, your printed result might look different from the image on your screen.

When you select a font, Access shows you a sample of the font in the Sample box. Depending on the font you choose, you might also see a wide range of font styles (such as italic or bold) and font sizes. Click the Underline check box at the lower left if you want all the characters underlined. Click OK to set the new font for the entire datasheet. Click Cancel to dismiss the dialog box without changing the font.

Saving the Datasheet Layout and Setting Defaults

After you have the datasheet formatted the way you want it, you don't have to lose your work when you close the table. Choose the Save Table command from the File menu to keep the format. Microsoft Access also asks whether you want to save a new layout when you try to close a table that's been changed.

You can also reset the default font for all datasheets. To do this, choose the Options command from the View menu. In the Datasheet category in the Options dialog box, you can set the font name, size, weight (light, normal, or bold), italics, and underline. You'll also find options here to reset the default column width and the display of gridlines.

Changing Data

Not only can you view and format data in a datasheet, you can also insert new records, change data, and delete records.

Record Indicators

You might have noticed as you moved around the datasheet that occasionally icons were displayed on the record selector at the far left of each row. (See Figure 7-1 on page 184.) These *indicators* and their meanings are listed below.

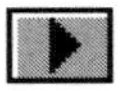
Indicates that this is the current row.

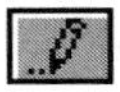
Indicates that you have made a change to one or more entries in this row. Microsoft Access saves the changes when you move to another row. Before moving to a new row, you can press Esc once to undo the change to the current value or press Esc twice to undo all changes in the row. If you're updating a database that is shared on a network with other users, Access locks this record when you save the change so that no one else can update it until you're finished. (See the last indicator below.)

Indicates the blank row at the end of the table that you can use to create a new record.

Indicates that another user might be changing this record. You'll see this icon only when you're accessing a database that is shared by other users on a network. You should wait until this indicator disappears before attempting to make changes to this record.

Adding a New Record

As you are building your application, you might find it useful to place some data in your tables so that you can test the forms and reports that you design. You might also find it convenient from time to time to add data directly to your tables by using Datasheet view rather than by opening a form. If your table is empty, Microsoft Access shows you a single blank row when you open Datasheet view. If you have data in your table, Access shows a blank row beneath the last record. You can jump to the blank row to begin adding a new record either by selecting the Go To command from the Records menu and then choosing New, by clicking the New button on the toolbar or by pressing Ctrl-+. Access places the cursor in the first column when you start a new record. As soon as you begin typing, Access changes the indicator to the pencil icon to show that updates are in progress. You can press Tab to move to the next column.

If the data you enter in a column violates a validation rule, Access notifies you as soon as you attempt to leave the column. You must provide a correct value before you can move to another column. Press Esc, choose Undo Current Field from the Edit menu, or click the Undo button on the toolbar to remove your changes in the current field.

Press Shift-Enter at any place in the record or press Tab in the last column in the record to commit your new record to the database. You can also choose the Save Record command from the File menu. If the changes in your record violate the validation rule for the table, Access tells you when you try to save the record. You must correct the problem before you can save your changes. If you want to cancel adding the record, press Esc twice or click the Undo Current Record button on the toolbar. If you want to use the Edit menu to undo the current record, you have to choose Undo Current Field from the Edit menu first if you are in a field that contains changes; Access then changes the available Edit menu item to Undo Current Record, so you can undo all changes. NEW!

Access provides several keyboard shortcuts to assist you as you enter new data, as shown in Figure 7-16 on the next page.

Keys	Data Action
Ctrl-; (semicolon)	Enters the current date
Ctrl-: (colon)	Enters the current time
Ctrl-Alt-Spacebar	Enters the default value for the field
Ctrl-' (single quotation mark) or Ctrl-" (double quotation mark)	Enters the value from the same field in the previous record
Ctrl-Enter	Inserts a carriage return in a memo or text field
Ctrl-+ (plus sign)	Adds a new record
Ctrl- - (minus sign)	Deletes the current record

FIGURE 7-16.

The keyboard shortcuts for entering data in a datasheet.

Selecting and Changing Data

After you have data in your table, you can easily change the data by editing it in Datasheet view. You must select data before you can change it, and you can do this in several ways:

- Click inside the box containing the data you want to change, just to the left of the first character you want to change, and then drag the highlight to include all the characters you want to change.
- Double-click on any word in a box to select the entire word.
- Click at the lower left corner of a box in the grid (that is, when the mouse pointer turns into an arrow pointing up and to the right). Access selects the entire contents of the box.

Any data you type replaces the old, selected data. In Figure 7-17, the address value for Bottom-Dollar Markets in the PROMPT Customer table has been selected. In Figure 7-18, that value has been changed before the record was saved. Microsoft Access also selects the entire entry if you tab into the box on the datasheet grid. If you want to change only part of the data (for example, to correct the spelling of a street name), you can shift to single-character mode by pressing F2 or by clicking the location at which you want to start your change. Use the Backspace key

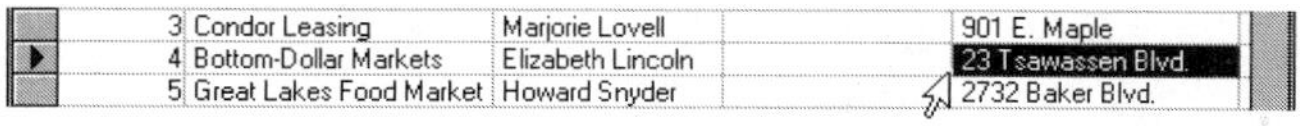
3 Condor Leasing | Marjorie Lovell | 901 E. Maple
4 Bottom-Dollar Markets | Elizabeth Lincoln | 23 Tsawassen Blvd.
5 Great Lakes Food Market | Howard Snyder | 2732 Baker Blvd.

FIGURE 7-17.

The old data is selected.

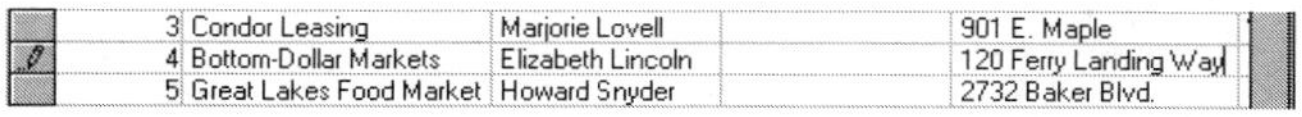
3 Condor Leasing | Marjorie Lovell | 901 E. Maple
4 Bottom-Dollar Markets | Elizabeth Lincoln | 120 Ferry Landing Way
5 Great Lakes Food Market | Howard Snyder | 2732 Baker Blvd.

FIGURE 7-18.

The new data is typed in, replacing the old.

to erase characters to the left of the cursor and the Del key to remove characters to the right of the cursor. Hold down Shift and press the right or left arrow key to select multiple characters to replace. You can press F2 again to select the entire entry. A useful keyboard shortcut for changing data is to press Ctrl-Alt-Spacebar to restore the data to the default value you specified in the table definition.

You can set two options to control how the arrow keys and the Enter key work as you move from entry to entry. Choose the Options command from the View menu, and select the Keyboard category in the Options dialog box, as shown in Figure 7-19 on the next page. To control what happens inside an entry by using the right or left arrow key, you can set the Arrow Key Behavior item to Next Field (selection moves to the next field in the record) or Next Character (cursor moves over one character). I like to set my Arrow Key Behavior to Next Character because this allows me to always use the arrow keys to move one character at a time while reserving the Tab key for moving a field at a time.

If you set the Move After Enter item to Next Field, pressing the Enter key completes the update of the current field in the record and tabs to the next field. If you set the Move After Enter item to Next Record, pressing Enter moves you to the next row on the datasheet. If you set the Move After Enter item to No, pressing Enter selects the current entry.

You can set Cursor Stops At First/Last Field to Yes to prevent the arrow keys from causing you to leave the current record. If you leave this option set to No, you'll move to the first field in the next row when you press right arrow while you're at the last character in the row, and you'll move to the last field in the previous row when you press left arrow while you're at the first character in the row.

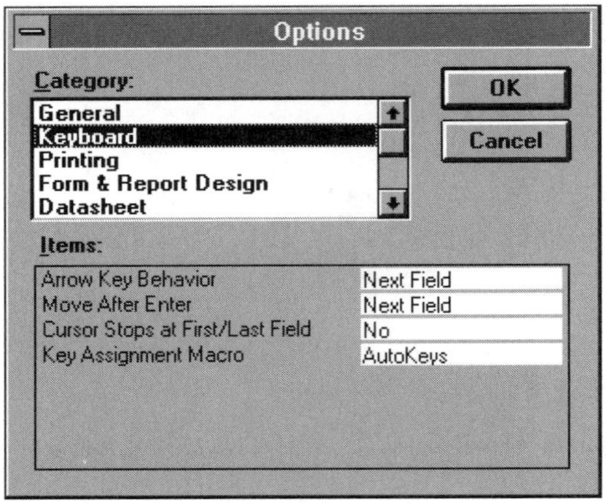

FIGURE 7-19. The Options dialog box with the Keyboard category selected.

Replacing Data

What if you need to make the same change in more than one record? Microsoft Access has a way to make that kind of change too. Select any entry in the column whose values you want to change (select the entry in the first row if you want to start at the beginning of the table), and then choose the Replace command from the Edit menu or press Shift-F7 to see the dialog box shown in Figure 7-20. For example, to fix the spelling of *Seatle* in the City field in the PROMPT table, select the City field in the first row, choose the Replace command, and type *Seattle* in the Replace With field, as shown in Figure 7-20. Click the Find Next button to search for the next occurrence of the text in the Find What text box. Click the Replace button to change data selectively, or click the Replace All button to change all the entries that match the Find What text. Notice that you have the option to search all fields, to exactly match the case for text searches (because searches in Access are normally case-insensitive) and to select an entry only if the Find What text matches the entire entry in the field.

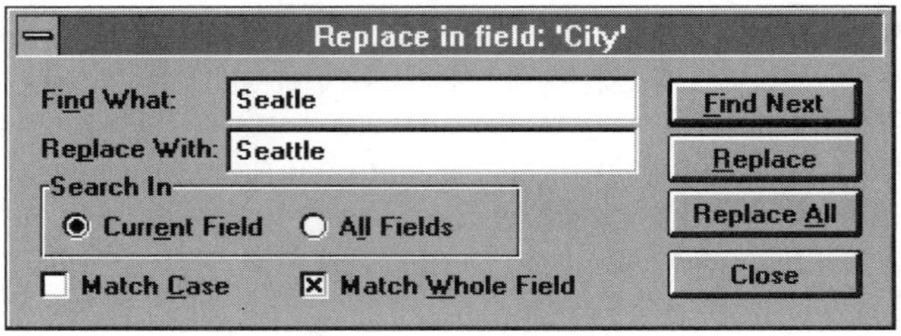

FIGURE 7-20. The Replace dialog box.

Copying and Pasting Data

You can copy or cut any selected data to the Clipboard in the Windows operating system. In Access this data can be pasted into another field or record. To copy data, tab to the entry or click at the lower left corner of the box on the datasheet grid to select it. Choose the Copy command from the Edit menu, or press Ctrl-C. You can also choose the Cut command from the Edit menu or press Ctrl-X to delete (cut) the data you have selected. To insert the data at another location, select the data you want to replace in that location and choose the Paste command from the Edit menu or press Ctrl-V. If the new location is blank, move the cursor to the new location before choosing the Paste command.

To select an entire record to be copied or cut, click the record selector at the far left of the row. You can also move to any entry in the row with the Tab key or arrow keys and then select the entire row by pressing Shift-Spacebar. If you happen to click the wrong record selector, you can use the up and down arrow keys to move the selection highlight. You can drag through the record selectors or press Shift-up arrow or Shift-down arrow to extend the selection to multiple rows. Choose the Copy command from the Edit menu or press Ctrl-C to copy the contents of multiple rows to the Clipboard. You can open another table and paste the copied rows into the table, or you can use the Paste Append command on the Edit menu to paste the rows at the end of the same table. You can paste copies of records into the same table only if the table has no primary key or if the primary key is a Counter data type. When the primary key is a Counter, Access automatically generates new counter values for you.

Be aware that cutting the rows from the table is the same as deleting them. (See the next section.) Using the Cut command, however, is handy for moving data you don't want in an active table to a backup table. You can have the other table open in Datasheet view at the same time. Simply switch to that window, and paste the cut rows using the Paste Append command.

Whenever you paste rows into a table, Microsoft Access warns you about the paste operation. (See Figure 7-21 on the next page.) Click the OK button to proceed, or click Cancel if you decide to abort the operation.

FIGURE 7-21.
The dialog box warns you that a paste operation can't be undone.

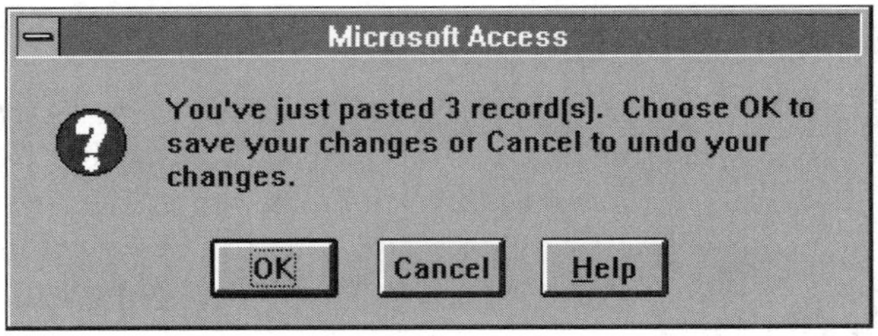

NOTE: You can't change the physical sequence of rows in a relational database by cutting rows from one location and pasting them in another location. Microsoft Access always pastes new rows at the end of the current display. If you close the datasheet after pasting new rows and then open it again, Access displays the rows in sequence by the primary key you have defined. If you want to see rows in some other sequence, see "Sorting and Searching for Data," later in this chapter.

Deleting Rows

To delete one or more rows, select the rows using the record selectors at the left of the rows and then delete. For details on selecting multiple rows, see the previous discussion on copying and pasting data. You can also use Ctrl- - (hyphen) to delete just the current row. When you delete rows, Access gives you a chance to change your mind if you made a mistake. (See Figure 7-22.) Choose OK in the dialog box to delete the rows, or click Cancel to abort the deletion.

FIGURE 7-22.
The dialog box that appears when you delete a row.

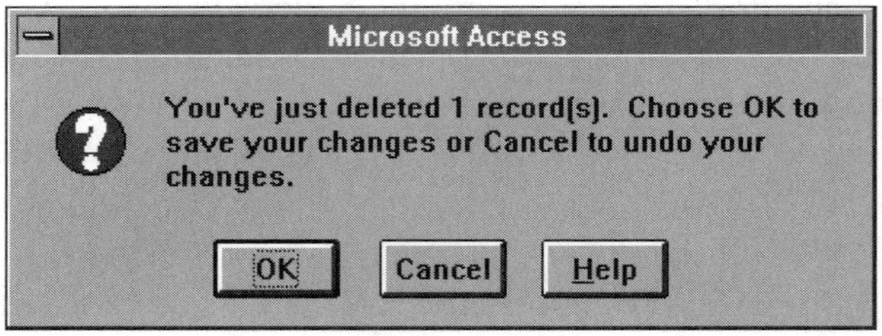

WARNING: After you choose OK, you cannot restore the deleted rows. You'll have to reenter them or copy them from a backup.

Sorting and Searching for Data

When you open a table in Datasheet view, Microsoft Access shows you all the rows sorted in sequence by the primary key you defined for the table. If you didn't define a primary key, you'll see the rows in the sequence in which you entered them in the table. If you want to see the rows in a different sequence or search for specific data, Access provides you with tools to do that.

Sorting Data

NEW!

Version 2.0 lets you sort data in table Datasheet view. As you might have noticed earlier (in the discussion of the built-in toolbar), two handy buttons allow you to quickly sort the rows in the table in ascending or descending order, based on the values in a single column. To see how this works, open the Customer table, click anywhere in the Company Name column, and click the Sort Ascending button on the toolbar. You'll see that Access sorts the display to show you the rows ordered alphabetically by company name, as in Figure 7-23.

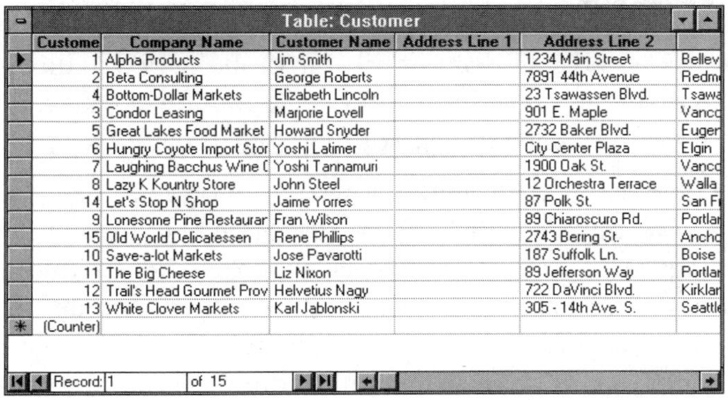

Table: Customer

Custome	Company Name	Customer Name	Address Line 1	Address Line 2	
1	Alpha Products	Jim Smith		1234 Main Street	Bellev
2	Beta Consulting	George Roberts		7891 44th Avenue	Redm
4	Bottom-Dollar Markets	Elizabeth Lincoln		23 Tsawassen Blvd.	Tsawa
3	Condor Leasing	Marjorie Lovell		901 E. Maple	Vanco
5	Great Lakes Food Market	Howard Snyder		2732 Baker Blvd.	Eugen
6	Hungry Coyote Import Stor	Yoshi Latimer		City Center Plaza	Elgin
7	Laughing Bacchus Wine C	Yoshi Tannamuri		1900 Oak St.	Vanco
8	Lazy K Kountry Store	John Steel		12 Orchestra Terrace	Walla
14	Let's Stop N Shop	Jaime Yorres		87 Polk St.	San F
9	Lonesome Pine Restaurar	Fran Wilson		89 Chiaroscuro Rd.	Portlan
15	Old World Delicatessen	Rene Phillips		2743 Bering St.	Ancho
10	Save-a-lot Markets	Jose Pavarotti		187 Suffolk Ln.	Boise
11	The Big Cheese	Liz Nixon		89 Jefferson Way	Portlan
12	Trail's Head Gourmet Prov	Helvetius Nagy		722 DaVinci Blvd.	Kirklan
13	White Clover Markets	Karl Jablonski		305 - 14th Ave. S.	Seattle
(Counter)					

Record: 1 of 15

FIGURE 7-23. The PROMPT Customer table sorted by company name.

You can use the Sort Descending button to sort the rows in descending sequence. It might be useful, for example, to sort all the rows based on the amount each customer owes. You'll see the customers who owe the most at the top of the list.

If you want to sort more than one field, you must use the filtering and sorting feature. Let's assume you want to sort by State, then by City within State, and then by Customer Name. Here's what you should do:

1. Click the Edit Filter/Sort button, or choose Edit Filter/Sort from the Records menu. You can see the Filter/Sort design grid, shown in Figure 7-24, with a list of fields in the Customer table shown in the top portion.

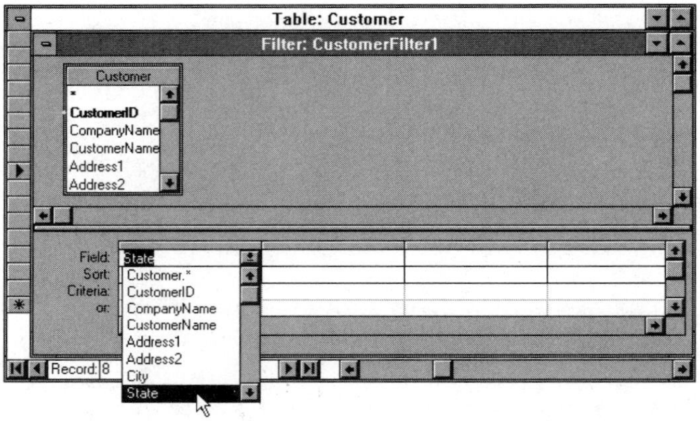

FIGURE 7-24. Entering the State field on the table Filter/Sort design grid.

2. Microsoft Access normally places the cursor in the box in the first row of the first column of the Field row in the lower part of the window. If you can't see the cursor there, click that box.
3. Open the field list by clicking the down arrow or by pressing Alt-down arrow on the keyboard. Choose the State field in the list, as shown in Figure 7-24. You can also place the State field in this first column by finding State on the list of fields in the Customer field list in the top half of the window and dragging and dropping it onto the Field row in the first column of the design grid.
4. Click in the Sort row, immediately below the State field, and choose Ascending from the drop-down list.

5. Add the City and CompanyName fields to the next two columns, and choose Ascending in the Sort row for both. Your result should look like Figure 7-25.

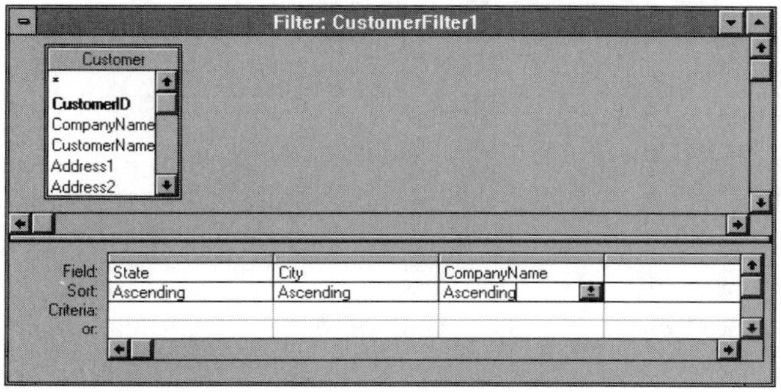

FIGURE 7-25. Sort criteria defined for State, City, and CompanyName fields.

6. Click the Apply Filter/Sort button or choose Apply Filter/Sort from the Records menu to see the result in Figure 7-26.

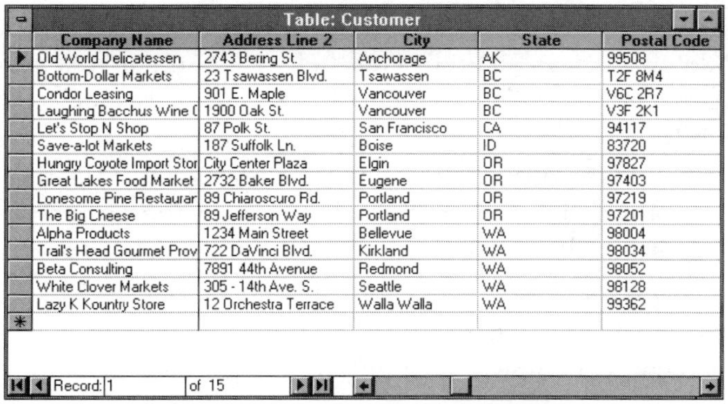

Table: Customer

Company Name	Address Line 2	City	State	Postal Code
Old World Delicatessen	2743 Bering St.	Anchorage	AK	99508
Bottom-Dollar Markets	23 Tsawassen Blvd.	Tsawassen	BC	T2F 8M4
Condor Leasing	901 E. Maple	Vancouver	BC	V6C 2R7
Laughing Bacchus Wine (	1900 Oak St.	Vancouver	BC	V3F 2K1
Let's Stop N Shop	87 Polk St.	San Francisco	CA	94117
Save-a-lot Markets	187 Suffolk Ln.	Boise	ID	83720
Hungry Coyote Import Stor	City Center Plaza	Elgin	OR	97827
Great Lakes Food Market	2732 Baker Blvd.	Eugene	OR	97403
Lonesome Pine Restaurar	89 Chiaroscuro Rd.	Portland	OR	97219
The Big Cheese	89 Jefferson Way	Portland	OR	97201
Alpha Products	1234 Main Street	Bellevue	WA	98004
Trail's Head Gourmet Prov	722 DaVinci Blvd.	Kirkland	WA	98034
Beta Consulting	7891 44th Avenue	Redmond	WA	98052
White Clover Markets	305 - 14th Ave. S.	Seattle	WA	98128
Lazy K Kountry Store	12 Orchestra Terrace	Walla Walla	WA	99362

Record: 1 of 15

FIGURE 7-26. PROMPT Customer records sorted by State, City, and then CompanyName.

Searching for and Filtering Data

If you want to look for data anywhere in your table, Microsoft Access provides you with powerful searching and filtering capability. To perform a simple search on a single field, select that field first. Open the Find dialog box shown in Figure 7-27 on the next page by choosing the Find command from the Edit menu or by pressing F7 or by clicking the Find button on the toolbar.

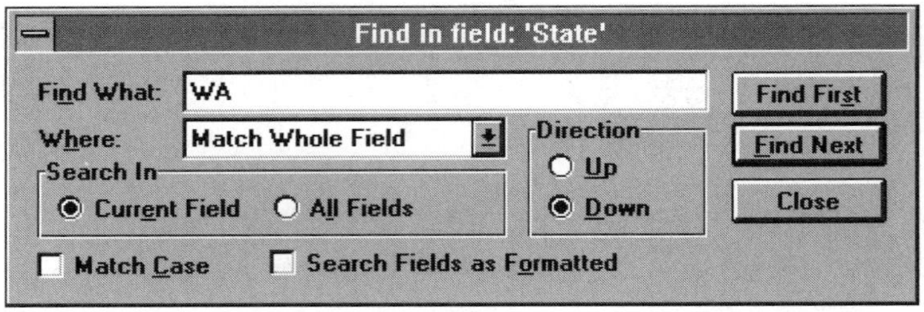

FIGURE 7-27. The Find dialog box.

In the Find What text box within the Find dialog box, you can type the data that you want Access to find. You can include wildcard characters to perform a generic search similar to that of the LIKE comparison operator you learned about in the section "Defining Simple Field Validation Rules," in Chapter 5. Use an asterisk (*) to indicate a string of unknown characters of any length, and use a question mark (?) to indicate exactly one unknown character. For example, "*AB??DE*" matches "Aberdeen" and "Tab idea" but not "Lab department." If you're searching a date field for dates in January, you can specify **-Jan-** provided that you click the Search Fields As Formatted check box and provided that you chose the Medium Date format when you designed the table.

By default, Access searches the field your cursor was in before you opened the Find dialog box. To check the entire table, click All Fields in the Search In group box. Access searches down from the current record position unless you choose the up direction. Click the Match Case check box if you want to find text that exactly matches the uppercase and lowercase letters you typed. By default, Access is case-insensitive unless you click this check box.

Click the Search Fields As Formatted check box if you need to search the data as it is displayed rather than as it is stored by Access. Although searching this way is slower, you probably should click this check box any time you are searching a Date/Time field. You might also want to use "as formatted" when searching a Yes/No field for Yes because any value except 0 is a valid indicator of Yes.

Click the Find First button to start the search from the beginning of the table. Click Find Next to start searching from the current record. After you've established search criteria, you can press Shift-F4 to execute the search from the current record without having to open the Find dialog box again.

To search on multiple fields or to limit the display to include only fields that meet your search criteria, you can use the Filter/Sort design window that you saw in Figure 7-24. Let's say you want to sort by State, City, and CompanyName fields, but you also want only customers in the states of Washington and Oregon and only those with a credit limit greater than $10,000. To do that, follow these steps:

1. Open the Customer table, and then open the Filter/Sort design grid again by clicking the Edit Filter/Sort button or by choosing Edit Filter/Sort from the Records menu.
2. Enter the sorting criteria as you did in the previous exercise.
3. Enter *"WA" Or "OR"* in the Criteria row under the State field.
4. Add the CreditLimit field to the design grid. You don't have to choose any sorting criteria for this field.
5. Enter *>10000* in the Criteria row under CreditLimit. Your result should look like Figure 7-28.

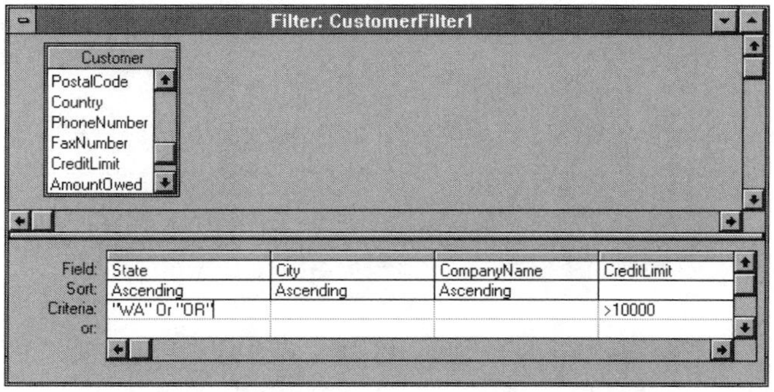

FIGURE 7-28.
The filter/sort criteria to choose and sort customers in Washington and Oregon with credit limits above $10,000.

6. Click the Apply Filter/Sort button to see the result shown in Figure 7-29.

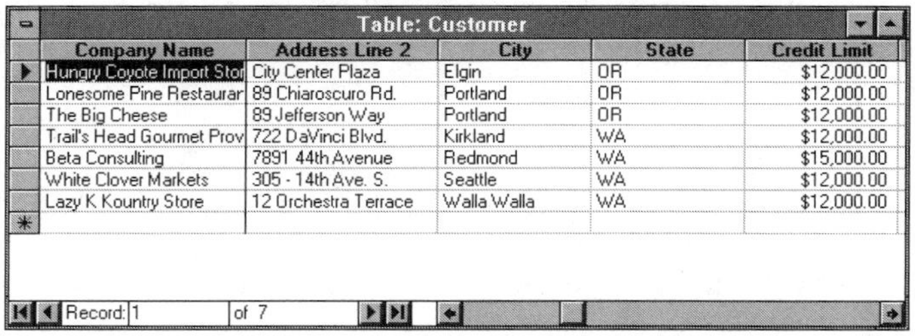

Table: Customer

Company Name	Address Line 2	City	State	Credit Limit
Hungry Coyote Import Stor	City Center Plaza	Elgin	OR	$12,000.00
Lonesome Pine Restaurar	89 Chiaroscuro Rd.	Portland	OR	$12,000.00
The Big Cheese	89 Jefferson Way	Portland	OR	$12,000.00
Trail's Head Gourmet Prov	722 DaVinci Blvd.	Kirkland	WA	$12,000.00
Beta Consulting	7891 44th Avenue	Redmond	WA	$15,000.00
White Clover Markets	305 - 14th Ave. S.	Seattle	WA	$12,000.00
Lazy K Kountry Store	12 Orchestra Terrace	Walla Walla	WA	$12,000.00

Record: 1 of 7

FIGURE 7-29.
The result of filtering and sorting the PROMPT Customer table.

TIP: You might notice that each time you close the table datasheet, Microsoft Access discards any filtering or sorting criteria you have defined. If you want to save your filter/sort definition, click the Edit Filter/Sort button on the toolbar, define your criteria, and choose Save As Query from the File menu and give your criteria a name. The next time you open the table, open the Edit Filter/Sort window, and then choose Load From Query from the File menu to find the criteria you saved and reuse them.

You can actually define very complex filtering criteria using expressions and the Or: row in the Filter/Sort window. In fact, the Filter/Sort window uses the query capabilities of Microsoft Access to accomplish the result you want, so you can use all the same filtering capabilities you'll find for queries in the table in Datasheet view.

See Also: Chapter 8, "Adding Power with Select Queries," provides details about building complex filtering criteria.

Printing from the Datasheet

NEW!

You can use Datasheet view to print information from your table. If you have applied filter/sort criteria, you can limit which records Microsoft Access prints and can define the print sequence. You also can control which fields are printed. (You cannot perform any calculations; you need to create a query form or report to do that.) As you discovered earlier in this chapter, you can format the fields you want to print, including setting the font and adjusting the spacing between columns and the spacing between rows. If you use the Caption property when defining fields in Design view, you can also customize the column headings.

To produce the datasheet layout shown in Figure 7-30 for the PROMPT Customer table, you can hide all but the columns shown, select a 10-point serif font (such as Bookman Old Style or Times New Roman), and size the columns so that you can see all the information. You also should eliminate the gridlines by being sure that the Gridlines command is unchecked in the Format menu. It's a good idea to maximize the window in Datasheet view so that you can see as many columns as possible.

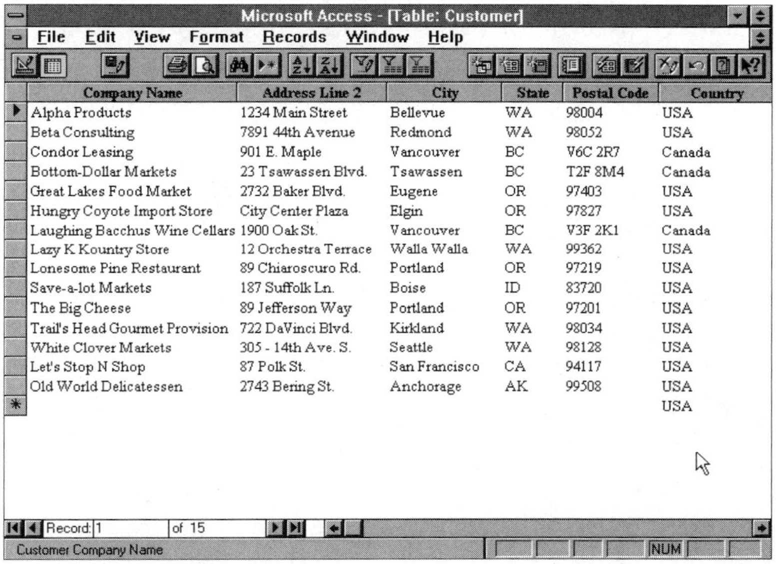

Company Name	Address Line 2	City	State	Postal Code	Country
Alpha Products	1234 Main Street	Bellevue	WA	98004	USA
Beta Consulting	7891 44th Avenue	Redmond	WA	98052	USA
Condor Leasing	901 E. Maple	Vancouver	BC	V6C 2R7	Canada
Bottom-Dollar Markets	23 Tsawassen Blvd.	Tsawassen	BC	T2F 8M4	Canada
Great Lakes Food Market	2732 Baker Blvd.	Eugene	OR	97403	USA
Hungry Coyote Import Store	City Center Plaza	Elgin	OR	97827	USA
Laughing Bacchus Wine Cellars	1900 Oak St.	Vancouver	BC	V3F 2K1	Canada
Lazy K Kountry Store	12 Orchestra Terrace	Walla Walla	WA	99362	USA
Lonesome Pine Restaurant	89 Chiaroscuro Rd.	Portland	OR	97219	USA
Save-a-lot Markets	187 Suffolk Ln.	Boise	ID	83720	USA
The Big Cheese	89 Jefferson Way	Portland	OR	97201	USA
Trail's Head Gourmet Provision	722 DaVinci Blvd.	Kirkland	WA	98034	USA
White Clover Markets	305 - 14th Ave. S.	Seattle	WA	98128	USA
Let's Stop N Shop	87 Polk St.	San Francisco	CA	94117	USA
Old World Delicatessen	2743 Bering St.	Anchorage	AK	99508	USA
					USA

FIGURE 7-30.
A datasheet that's ready to print.

Print Preview

After you've formatted a datasheet the way you want, you can activate Print Preview to verify that the data you want fits on a printed page. Choose the Print Preview command from the File menu, or click the Print Preview button on the toolbar, to see the display shown in Figure 7-31 on the next page. Notice that the mouse pointer changes to a small magnifying glass. You can move the mouse pointer to any part of the report and click to zoom in and see the data up close. You can also click the Zoom button on the toolbar (the magnifying glass icon) to magnify the report and display the upper left corner of the current page. While zoomed in, you can use the arrow keys to move around the displayed page in small increments. Press the PgUp or PgDn key to move around in larger increments. You can press Ctrl-down arrow to move to the bottom of the page, Ctrl-up arrow to move to the top, Ctrl-right arrow to move to the right margin, and Ctrl-left arrow to move to the left margin.

Ctrl-Home puts you back in the upper left corner, and Ctrl-End moves the display to the lower right corner. Click the Zoom button again or click the left mouse button to zoom out.

If your printed output has multiple pages, you can use the PgUp and PgDn keys while zoomed out to move between pages. Click the Close button (the door exit icon on the far left) to exit Print Preview without printing. Click the Print button (printer icon) to send your formatted datasheet to a printer. Click the Page Setup button (next to the printer icon) to specify printer setup options, as explained in the next section. You can also see buttons to export the report to Microsoft Word or Microsoft Excel or to send it via Microsoft Mail (if you have these products installed).

NEW!

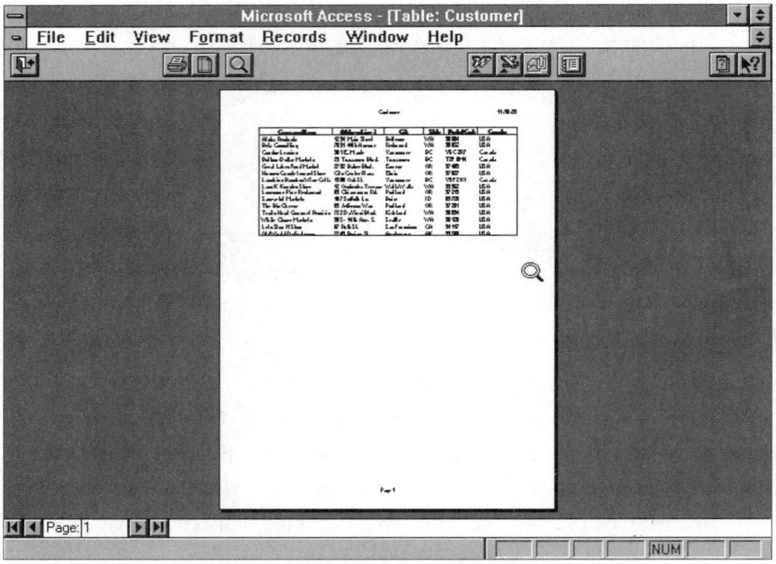

FIGURE 7-31. The datasheet in Print Preview. Here the mouse pointer has become a magnifying glass that, when you click over the data, zooms in to provide an enlarged view.

Print Setup

Using the Print Setup command can be difficult, particularly if your system is connected to more than one printer. When you click the Print Setup button on the toolbar from Print Preview or when you choose the Print Setup command from the File menu, Microsoft Access opens the dialog box shown in Figure 7-32.

Access initially chooses your default printer in the Printer group box. If you have more than one printer, you can select the one you want to use from the Specific Printer drop-down list. Other options in this dialog box let you choose the paper size and tray source (if your printer supports multiple trays), the margins, and the orientation—Portrait or Landscape.

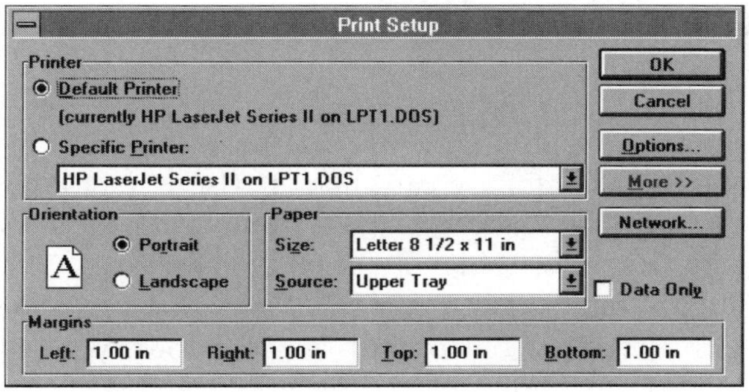

FIGURE 7-32.
The Print Setup dialog box.

If you have a PostScript printer and you click the Options button, Access displays the dialog box shown in Figure 7-33 on the next page. When printing in PostScript mode, you can send your output directly to the printer or you can create a file that you can print later. If the data you chose doesn't fill the full page, you can specify a scale larger than 100 percent to use more of each page. If the printed data is too wide or too long, you can scale it down to fit on one page. However, you won't be able to see the results in the Print Preview window. Later, when you design forms using color, you can click the Color check box in this dialog box in order to print colors on your form (if you have a color printer). Although it might take a bit longer to start printing each report, it's a good idea to always send the PostScript header to ensure that your printer is set up properly.

If you click the Advanced button in the PostScript Options dialog box, you will see the dialog box shown in Figure 7-34 on the next page. You can send output to a PostScript printer as either Adobe or Bitmap. If your documents are printing correctly when they include graphics or if your documents include only text (as should be the case when you're printing a datasheet), use Adobe to print faster. If all the TrueType fonts

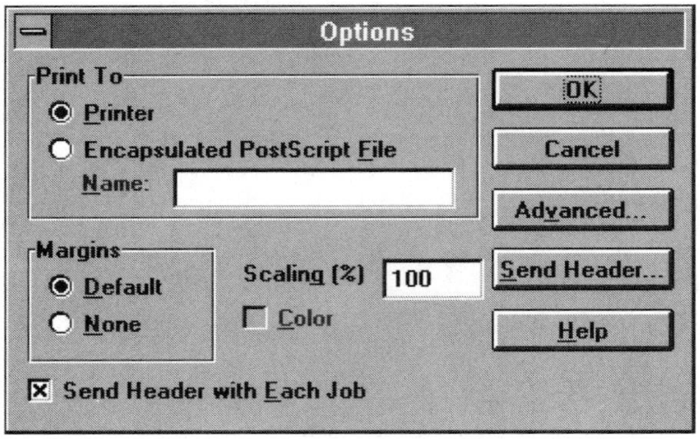

FIGURE 7-33. The PostScript options for printer setup.

you use have printer equivalents, you can click the Use Printer Fonts For All TrueType Fonts check box. Otherwise, you should click the Use Substitution Table check box in order to map fonts for printing. Click the Edit Substitution Table button to scan your available fonts and change the mapping from TrueType to your printer. You can force your printer driver to download a soft font specification (a set of characters of a particular style and size and stored on disk and sent to a printer's memory when needed) for all TrueType fonts, but this will cause your documents to print more slowly. In general, Setup establishes good font mapping when you install Windows, so you shouldn't need to change these settings unless you're having problems.

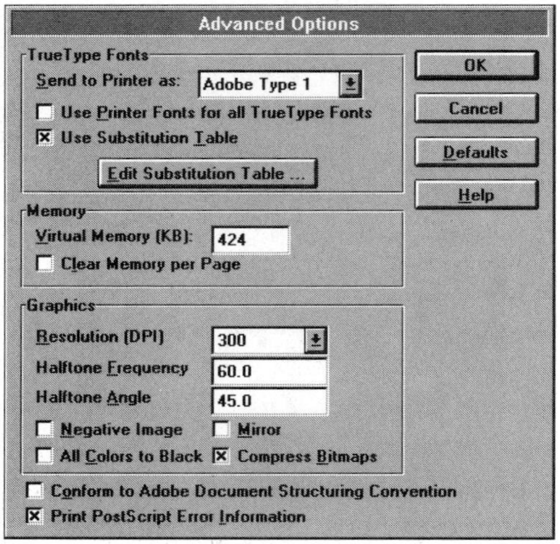

FIGURE 7-34. The Advanced Options dialog box for PostScript printer setup.

In the Memory section, you can enter the value for how much memory you have installed on your printer. If your printer has more memory than shown, you can improve performance by increasing this number. If you're having problems printing documents with multiple fonts, try clicking the Clear Memory Per Page check box.

In the Graphics section, you can select a coarse or fine printer resolution. (Most PostScript printers can handle a full 300 dots per inch, or more, easily.) You can also select halftone frequency (density) and angle if you have pictures in your documents. Click the Negative Image check box to reverse black and white in your document. Click the Mirror check box to click the print image from left to right. Click the All Colors To Black check box if images with multiple colors are not being printed properly. Click the Compress Bitmaps check box to speed the printing of graphics. Then click the OK button to save changes or click the Cancel button to abort any changes or click the Defaults button to restore all settings to the default.

If you have a Hewlett-Packard LaserJet or compatible printer, the Options dialog box is a bit less daunting, as Figure 7-35 makes clear. For colored pictures, you can set the level of dithering to control the relative gray variation between colors. Choose the None option to print colors in black. Choose the Line Art option to print only the outline of colored areas. You can also control graphics printing by adjusting the Intensity Control. Choose this option for forms and reports if you print white characters on a black or colored background. At the bottom of the window, you can see a check box titled Print TrueType As Graphics. Normally, the LaserJet printer driver maps TrueType fonts to available printer fonts. If you click this check box, you'll see TrueType font text printed as you actually see it on the screen, but printing will be slower.

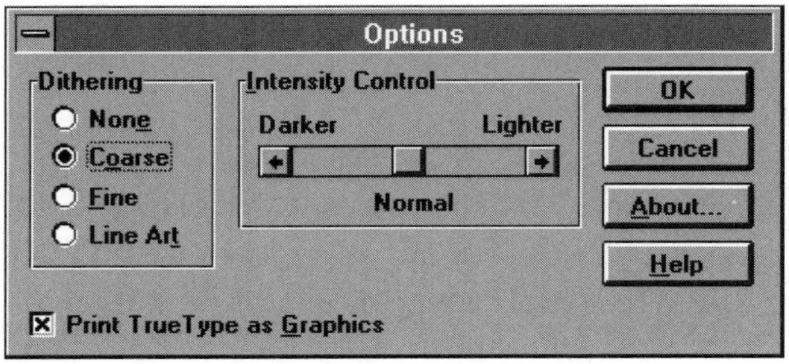

FIGURE 7-35.
The Hewlett-Packard LaserJet printer setup options.

Printing

To send the datasheet to your printer, click the Print button on the Print Preview toolbar. You can also print a datasheet directly from the Database window by selecting the table you want and choosing the Print command from the File menu. Microsoft Access shows you a Print dialog box similar to the one shown in Figure 7-36. (This dialog box varies depending on your printer.)

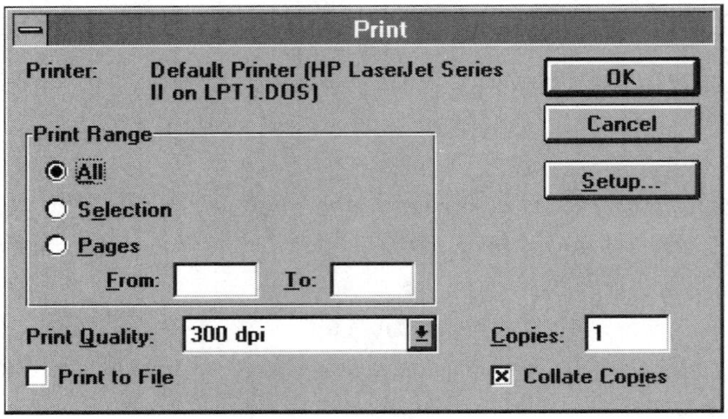

FIGURE 7-36. The Print dialog box.

In all Print dialog boxes, you can choose to print multiple copies. You can also choose to print all pages or a range of pages. If you ask Access to collate multiple copies, Access prints the first through last pages in sequence and repeats for each set of pages. If you deselect the Collate Copies check box, Access prints the number of copies you requested for the first page, then the number of copies you requested for the second page, and so on. You can also tell Access to send your output to a file that you can copy to your printer later.

When you tell Access to send the output to a printer, Access formats and sends the pages to the Windows operating system Print Manager, if you've selected the Use Print Manager check box in the Control Panel's Printers option. You will see a printing progress report in a dialog box, as shown in Figure 7-37. After all pages are sent to Print Manager, you can generally continue with other activities in Access while your pages are printing.

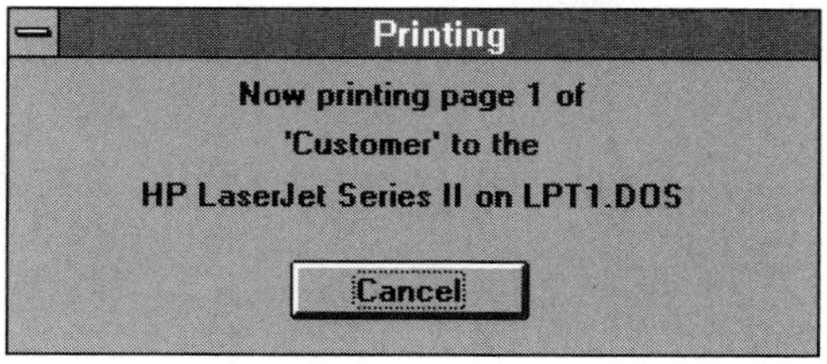

FIGURE 7-37.
The Printing dialog box, which shows the printing status.

Now that you've worked with data directly out of tables by using datasheets, it's time to deal with data from multiple tables and to update many rows in a table in one operation. To handle these operations, you need the power of queries, as explained in the next chapter.

8

Adding Power with Select Queries

In the previous chapter, you learned about working with the data in your tables in Datasheet view. Although you can do a lot with datasheets—including browsing, sorting, filtering, updating, and printing your data—you'll find that many times you need to perform calculations on the data in your tables or retrieve related data from multiple tables. To select a set of data to work with, you use queries.

When you define and run a *select query* (which selects information from the tables and queries in your database, as opposed to an *action query,* which inserts, updates, or deletes data), Microsoft Access creates a *recordset* of the selected data. In most cases, you can work with a recordset in the same way you work with a table: You can browse through it, select information from it, print it, and even update the data in it. But, unlike a real table, a recordset doesn't actually exist in your database. Access creates a recordset from the data that exists in your tables and queries at the time you run the query. When you update data in a recordset, Access reflects your changes in the tables underlying your query.

As you learn to design forms and reports later in this book, you'll find that queries are the best way to focus in on only the data you need for the task at hand. When you get into advanced form design, you'll find that queries are also useful for providing choices for list boxes, which will make entering data in your database much easier.

NOTE: This chapter assumes that you're working with the tables and data from the PROMPT sample database on the companion disk included with this book. (See "Using the Companion Disk" on page xxiv.) Your results will be different if you're using different tables.

To open a new Query window in Design view, click the Query tab in the Database window, and then click the New button above the Queries list. You'll see a dialog box open that lets you either choose a Query Wizard or simply open a New Query. (You'll learn about Query Wizards later in this chapter.) To open an existing query in Design view, click the Query tab in the Database window (which displays the Queries list of the complete PROMPT database shown in Figure 8-1), select the query you want, and click the Design button.

FIGURE 8-1.

The Database window is used to open the Query window in Design view.

Figure 8-2 shows an existing query whose window has been opened in Design view. The Query window contains field lists and a query by example (QBE) grid.

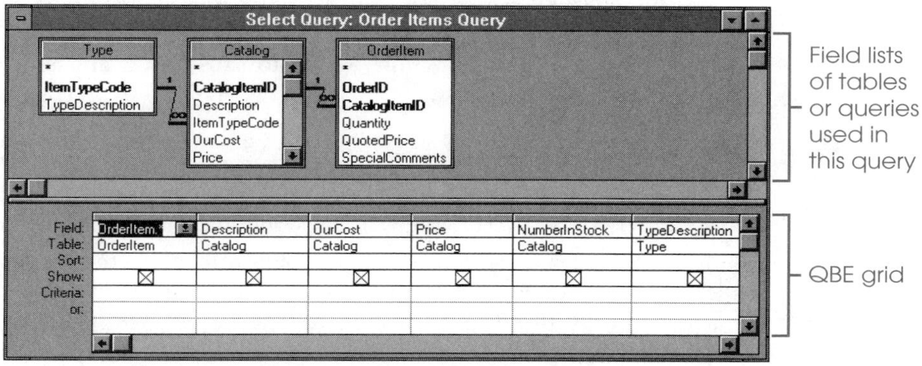

FIGURE 8-2.

An existing query opened in Design view.

All the examples in this chapter, including the query that is shown in Figure 8-2, use data from the Prompt Computer Solutions database (PROMPT) that you can copy from the companion disk that comes with this book.

The Built-In Toolbar for the Query Window in Design View

Microsoft Access provides many useful actions on the built-in toolbar for the Query window in Design view. You can see the following action buttons from left to right on the toolbar:

Design View button. This button initially appears pressed, indicating that you're in Design view. Click this button to return to Design view from Datasheet view or from SQL view.

NEW!

SQL View button. Microsoft Access uses the SQL database language to define all queries. Click this button to view and edit the SQL statement for this query. You must use SQL statements to define certain advanced queries. (See Chapter 11, "Advanced Query Design—SQL," for details.)

NEW!

Datasheet View button. After you've finished designing your query, you can use this button to enter Datasheet view to see the recordset created by this query. For action queries, you'll see the data that Access will act upon. (See Chapter 7, "Using Datasheets," for more details on Datasheet view. For information about action queries, see Chapter 9, "Modifying Data with Action Queries.")

Save button. Click this button to save any changes.

Run button. For select queries (as described in this chapter), this button does the same thing as the Datasheet View button—it displays the recordset. For action queries (as described in Chapter 9), click this button to run the query.

Properties button. Click this button to open the property sheet. You can change various query and field properties in the property sheet, depending on the type of query you are designing.

Add Table button. Click this button to open the Add Table dialog box. This dialog box lets you easily add other tables or queries to the query you are designing.

Totals button. Click this button to open the Total row in the query by example (QBE) grid. You can create a query to calculate totals across groups of data. (See the section "Totals Queries" later in this chapter for more information.) This button is not available for action queries (which are described in Chapter 9).

Table Names button. Click this button to see the row of table names in the QBE grid. This can be very useful when you're working with fields from several tables.

Select Query button. By default, all new queries are select queries. You'll see this button pressed when you first open a new query. If you've clicked one of the next five buttons to change query type, you can click this button to convert your query back to a select query.

Crosstab Query button. Click this button to create a special type of totals query that allows you to see calculated values in a spreadsheetlike format. (See the section "Crosstab Queries" later in this chapter for details.)

Make Table Query button. Click this button to select data from one or more tables and use the output to create a new table. (See Chapter 9, "Modifying Data with Action Queries," for details.)

Update Query button. Click this button to create a query that will update one or more of the fields in all the rows in the selected data. (See Chapter 9 for details.)

Append Query button. Click this button to create a query that selects rows from one or more tables and appends them to another table. (See Chapter 9 for details.)

Delete Query button. Click this button to create a query that deletes a group of rows from a table. (See Chapter 9 for details.)

New Query button. Click this button to design a new query based on the current table or query. You must save the current table or query before you can design another query based on it.

New Form button. Click this button to design a new form based on the current table or query. You must save the current table or query before you can design a new form based on it. (See Chapter 13, "Building a Form," for details.)

New Report button. Click this button to design a new report based on the current table or query. You must save the current table or query before you can design a new report based on it. (See Chapter 17, "Constructing a Report," for details.)

Database Window button. Click this button to place the focus on the Database window. This button also un-hides the Database window if you have hidden it and restores the window if you have minimized it.

(continued)

NEW!

(continued)

Build button. Microsoft Access provides a sophisticated Expression Builder to assist you in defining entries in the Field and Criteria rows. Click in a field or criteria box in which you want to use a complex expression, and then click this button to start the Expression Builder.

Undo button. Click this button to undo your last change. Undo has the same effect as Ctrl-Z or as the Undo command on the Edit menu. The button is disabled when there are no changes that can be undone.

Cue Cards button. Click this button to open Cue Cards for query design. The Cue Cards facility leads you through step-by-step instructions for building a query.

Help button. Click this button to add a question mark to your mouse pointer. Click with this pointer on any displayed object to receive context-sensitive help about that object.

> **TIP:** It's a good idea to click the Table Names button whenever your query includes more than one table. Because you might have the same field name in more than one of the tables, showing table names on the query by example (QBE) grid helps ensure that you're referring to the field you want.

Selecting Data from a Single Table

One advantage of using queries is that they allow you to find data in multiple related tables easily. You'll also find queries useful for sifting through the data in a single table. And all the techniques you use for working with a single table apply equally to more complex multiple table queries. So this chapter begins by using queries to select data from a single table.

The easiest way to start building a query on a table is to open the Database window, select the table you want, and click the New Query button on the toolbar. Do that now with the Customer table in the PROMPT database, and then choose New Query in the resulting dialog box and click the Table Names button. You'll see the window shown in Figure 8-3.

The Query window in Design view has two main sections. In the top section, you can see field lists with the fields for the tables or queries you've chosen for this query. The bottom section of the window is the QBE grid, in which you'll do all your design work. Each column in the grid represents one field that you'll be working with in this query. As you'll see later, a field can be a simple field from one of the tables, a calculated field based on several fields in the tables, or a totals field using one of the functions provided by Microsoft Access.

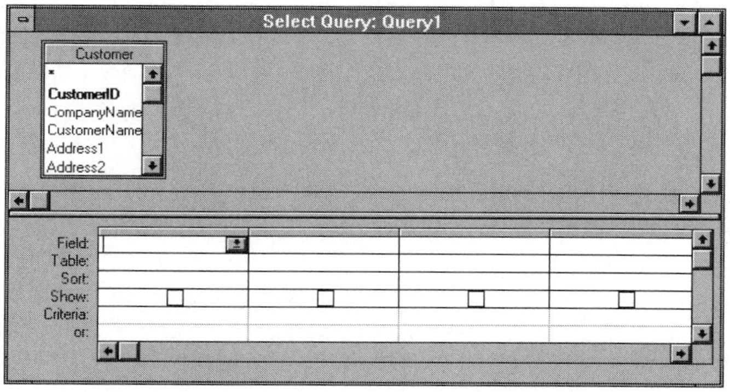

FIGURE 8-3.
The Query window in Design view.

You'll use the first row on the QBE grid to select fields: the fields you want in the resulting recordset, the fields you want to sort, and the fields you want to test for values. As you'll learn later, you can also generate custom field names (for display in the resulting recordset), and you can use complex expressions or calculations to generate a calculated field.

Because the Show Table Names button was clicked, Access displays the table name (which is the source of the selected field) in the second row of the QBE grid. In the next row, you can specify whether Access should sort the selected or calculated field in ascending or in descending order.

In the Show row, you can use the check boxes to specify the fields that will be shown in the recordset. By default, Access shows all the fields you've selected on the QBE grid. Sometimes you want to include a field in the query to allow you to select the records you want (such as the customers or shippers in a certain state), but you don't need that field in the recordset. You can add that field to the QBE grid so that you can define criteria, but you should deselect the Show box underneath to exclude the field from the recordset.

Finally, you can use the Criteria row and the rows labeled *or* to enter the criteria you want to use as filters. Once you understand how it's done, you'll find it easy to specify exactly the fields and records you want.

Specifying Fields

The first step in building a query is to choose the fields you want in the recordset. You can select the fields you want in several ways. Using the keyboard, you can tab to an available column on the QBE grid and press Alt-down arrow to open the list of available fields. (If you need to move the cursor to the QBE grid, press the F6 key.) Use the up and down arrow keys to move the highlight to the field you want, and press Enter to select the field.

Another way to select a field is to drag it from one of the field lists in the top of the window to one of the columns on the QBE grid. In Figure 8-4, the CreditLimit field is being dragged to the QBE grid. When you drag a field, the mouse pointer turns into a small rectangle.

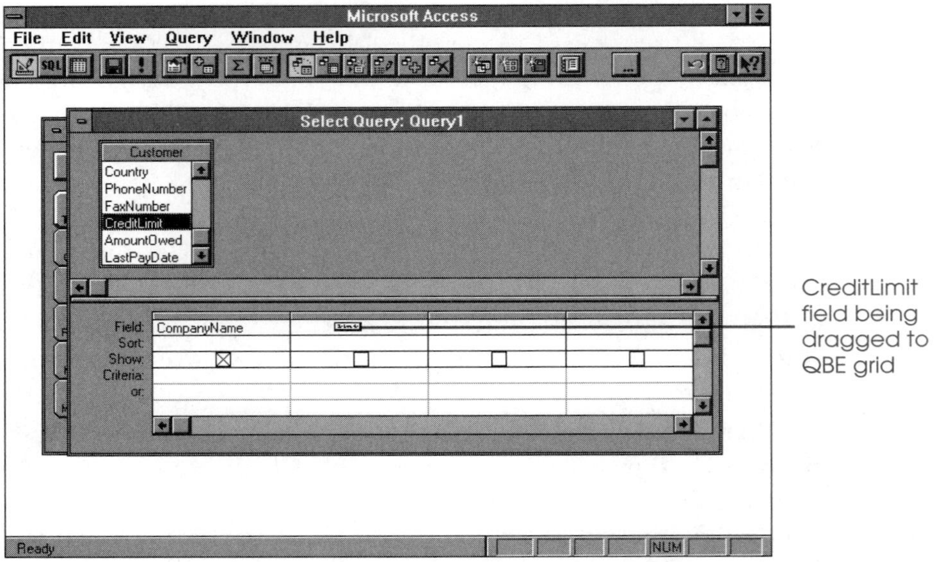

FIGURE 8-4. A field being dragged to a column in the query by example (QBE) grid.

At the top of each field list in the top section of the Query window (and also next to the first entry in the Field drop-down list on the QBE grid) is a special asterisk (*) symbol. This symbol is shorthand for "all fields in the table or query." Whenever you want to include all the fields in the table or query, you don't have to define each one individually on the QBE grid (unless you also want to define some sorting or selection criteria for specific fields). You can simply add the asterisk to the QBE grid to include all the fields from a list. Note that you can add individual fields to the grid in addition to the asterisk in order to define criteria for those fields, but you should deselect the Show box for the individual fields so that you don't see them twice in the recordset.

TIP: Another way to easily select all the fields in a table is to double-click the title bar of the list field in the top section of the query by example (QBE) grid. This highlights all the fields. Simply click in any of the highlighted fields and drag to the field row on the QBE grid. You'll notice that your mouse pointer changes to a multiple rectangle icon, indicating that you're dragging multiple fields. When you release the mouse pointer, you'll see that Microsoft Access has copied all the fields for you.

In this exercise, select CompanyName, State, CreditLimit, and AmountOwed from the PROMPT Customer table. If you switch the Query window to Datasheet view at this point, you'll see only the fields you selected from all the records in the underlying table.

Setting Field Properties

NEW!

In general, fields output by a query inherit the properties defined for the field in the table. You can define a different Description property (the information that is displayed on the status bar when you select that field in the query datasheet), Format property (how the data is displayed), Decimal Places property (for numeric data), Input Mask property, and

Caption property (the column heading). When you learn to define calculated fields later in this chapter, you'll see that it's a good idea to define the properties for these fields.

To set the properties of a field, click on any row of the field's column on the lower part of the QBE grid and then click the Properties button on the toolbar or choose Properties from the View menu. The new property settings for the CreditLimit field are shown in Figure 8-5. If you make these changes and switch to Datasheet view, you'll see a result similar to that shown in Figure 8-6. Notice that the column heading is now "Maximum Credit," that no decimal places are displayed, and that the text on the status bar is different.

FIGURE 8-5.
Setting field properties.

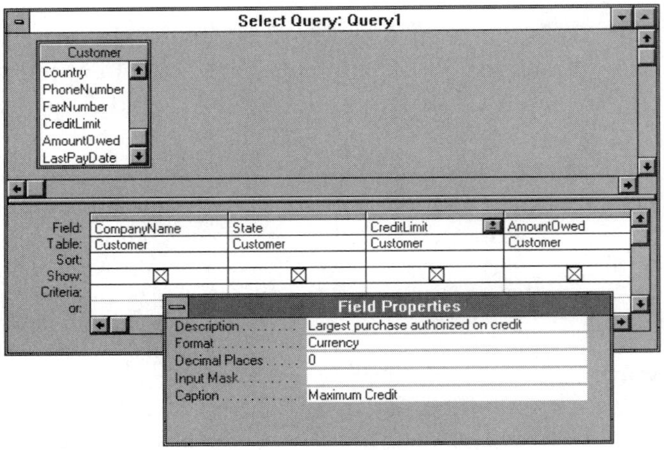

TIP: You'll notice that in Datasheet view the queries built using the PROMPT Customer table have no gridlines and use a serif font. These attributes are inherited from the table settings that you saw in the previous chapter, "Using Datasheets." While in a query's Datasheet view, you can set the display format exactly like table datasheets by using the commands on the Format menu. (See Chapter 7, "Using Datasheets," for details.)

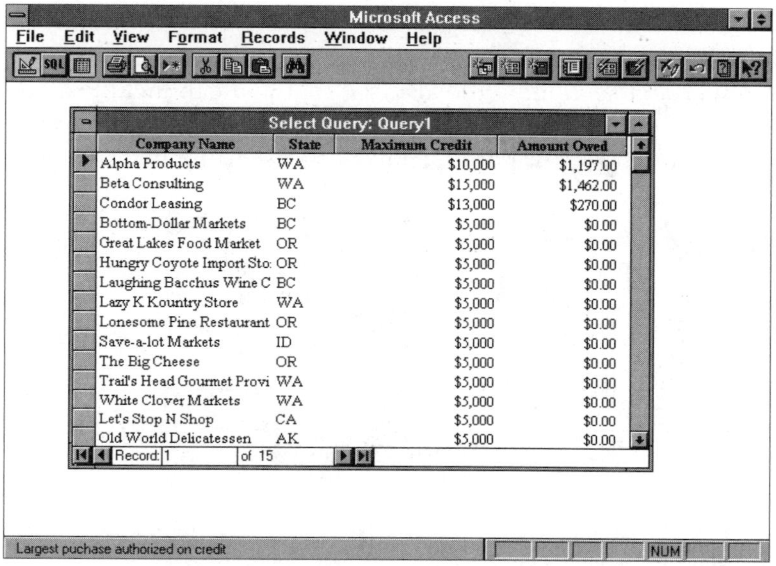

FIGURE 8-6.
The CreditLimit field displayed with new properties.

Entering Selection Criteria

The next step is to further refine the values in the fields you want. In the example shown in Figure 8-7 on the next page, you focus on customers in the state of Washington.

Entering selection criteria in a query is similar to entering a validation rule for a field, which you learned about in Chapter 5. To look for a single value, simply type it in the Criteria row below the field you want to test. If the field you're testing is a text field and the value you're looking for has any blanks in the middle, you must enclose each value in quotation marks. Note that Access adds quotes for you around single text values. (In Figure 8-7, *WA* was typed, but the field shows *"WA"* after Enter was pressed.)

If you want to test for the existence of any of several values, simply enter each of them in the Criteria row, separated by the word *Or*. For example, specifying *"WA" Or "CA"* searches for records for either of the two states. You can also test for any of several values by entering each one in a separate Criteria or Or row under the field you want to test. For example, enter *CA* in the Criteria row, *WA* in the next row (the first Or row), and so on—but you have to be careful if you're also specifying criteria in other fields, as explained below.

In the next section, you'll also see that you can include a comparison operator in the Criteria row to look for values less than (<), greater than or equal to (>=), or not equal to (< >) the value that you specify.

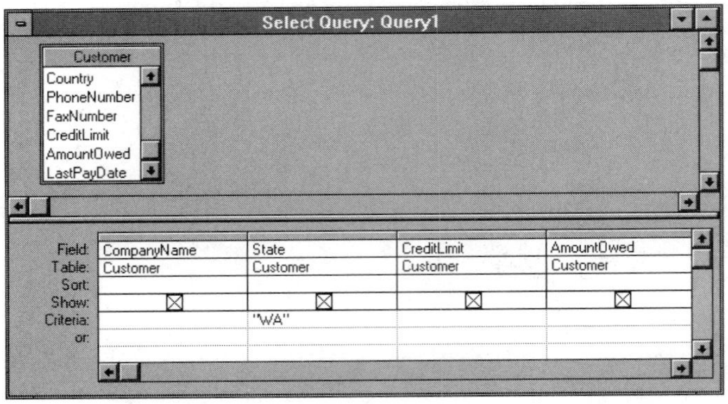

FIGURE 8-7. A query by example (QBE) grid that specifies *"WA"* as a selection criterion.

AND vs. OR

When you enter criteria under several fields, all the tests in a single Criteria row or Or row must be true for a record to be included in the recordset. That is, Microsoft Access performs a logical AND operation between multiple criteria in the same row. So, if you enter *WA* under State and *>10000* under CreditLimit, the record must be for the state of Washington and have a credit limit greater than $10,000 in order to be selected. If you enter *"WA" or "CA"* under State and *>=10000 And<=15000* under CreditLimit, the record must be for the state of Washington or California, and the credit limit must be between $10,000 and $15,000 inclusive.

Figure 8-8 shows the result of applying a logical AND operator between any two tests. As you can see, both tests must be true for the result of the AND to be true and the record to be selected.

When you specify multiple criteria for a field separated by a logical OR operator, only one of the criteria must be true for the record to be selected. You can specify several OR criteria for a field, either by entering them all in a single Criteria row separated by the logical OR opera-

AND	True	False
True	Selected	Rejected
False	Rejected	Rejected

FIGURE 8-8.
The result of applying the logical AND operator between two tests.

tor, as shown earlier, or by entering each of the criteria in a separate Or row. When you use multiple Or rows, all the criteria in only one of the Or rows must be true for a record to be selected. If, for example, you enter criteria in three rows on the QBE grid (call them A, B, and C), you have asked Access to include a record in the recordset whenever all the criteria in row A are true or all the criteria in row B are true or all the criteria in row C are true. Figure 8-9 shows the result of applying a logical OR operation between any two criteria or sets of criteria. As you can see, only one of the tests must be true for the result of the OR to be true and the record selected.

OR	True	False
True	Selected	Selected
False	Selected	Rejected

FIGURE 8-9.
The result of applying the logical OR operator between two tests.

Look at a specific example. In Figure 8-10 on the next page, you specify *WA* in the first Criteria row of the State field. In the next row (the first Or row), you specify *CA* in the State field and *>10000* in the corresponding Or row of the CreditLimit field. When you run this query, you'll get all the records for the state of Washington. You'll also get any records for the state of California in which the credit limit is more than $10,000.

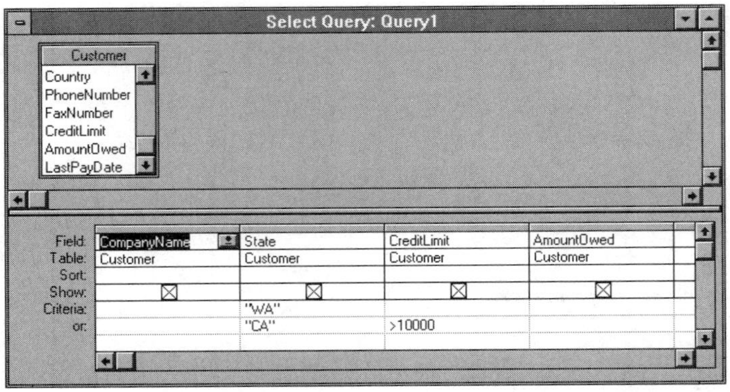

FIGURE 8-10. A query by example (QBE) grid that specifies multiple AND and OR selection criteria.

In Figure 8-11, you can see the recordset that results from running this query (the Datasheet view).

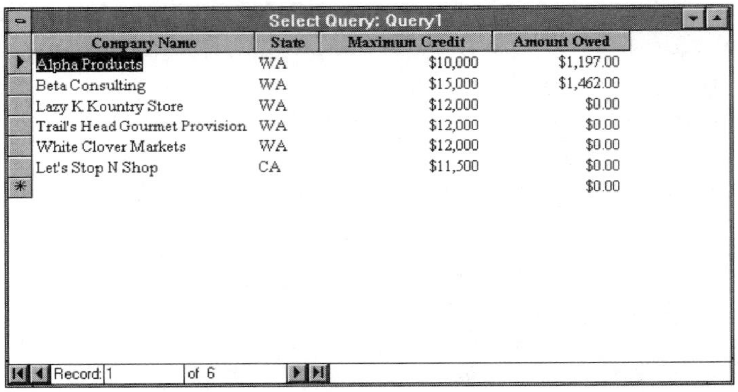
Select Query: Query1

Company Name	State	Maximum Credit	Amount Owed
Alpha Products	WA	$10,000	$1,197.00
Beta Consulting	WA	$15,000	$1,462.00
Lazy K Kountry Store	WA	$12,000	$0.00
Trail's Head Gourmet Provision	WA	$12,000	$0.00
White Clover Markets	WA	$12,000	$0.00
Let's Stop N Shop	CA	$11,500	$0.00
			$0.00

Record: 1 of 6

FIGURE 8-11. The recordset of the query shown in Figure 8-10.

BETWEEN, IN, and LIKE

In addition to comparison operators, Microsoft Access provides you with three special predicate clauses that are useful for specifying the data you want in the recordset:

BETWEEN — Useful for specifying a range of values. The clause *Between 10 And 20* is the same as specifying *>=10 And <=20*.

IN — Useful for specifying a list of values, any one of which can match the field being searched. The clause *In ("WA", "CA", "ID")* is the same as *"WA" Or "CA" Or "ID"*.

LIKE	Useful for searching for patterns in text fields. You can include special characters and range values in the Like comparison string to define the character pattern you want. Use *?* to indicate any single character in that position. Use * to indicate zero or more characters in that position. The character # specifies a single numeric digit in that position. Include a range in brackets to test for a particular range of characters in a position, and use *!* to indicate exceptions. The range [0–9] tests for numbers, [a–z] tests for letters, and [!0–9] tests for any characters except 0 through 9. As an example, a phrase such as *Like "?[a–k]d[0–9]*"* tests for any single character in the first position, any character from *a* through *k* in the second position, the letter *d* in the third position, any character from *0* through *9* in the fourth position, and any number of characters after that.

Suppose that in your Customer table you want to find all companies in Washington or Idaho whose names begin with *L* and who have a credit limit greater than or equal to $10,000 but less than or equal to $15,000. Figure 8-12 shows how you would enter these criteria. And Figure 8-13 shows the recordset of this query.

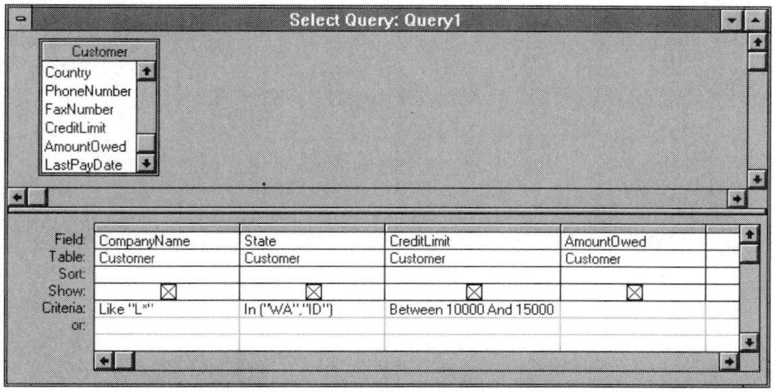

FIGURE 8-12.
A query by example (QBE) grid that uses BETWEEN, IN, and LIKE.

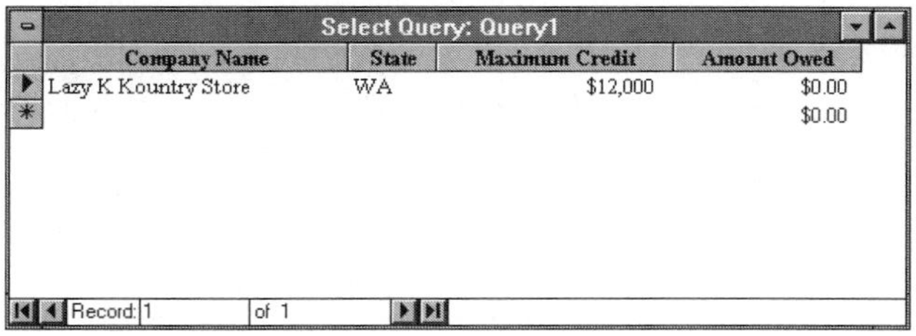

FIGURE 8-13.
The recordset of the query shown in Figure 8-12.

See Also: For additional examples using the BETWEEN, IN, and LIKE comparison operators, see the section "Defining Simple Field Validation Rules" in Chapter 5 and the "Predicate" sections in Chapter 11.

Working with Dates and Times in Criteria

Microsoft Access stores dates and times as double-precision floating-point numbers. The value to the left of the decimal point represents the day, and the fractional part of the number stores the time as a fraction of a day. Fortunately, you don't have to worry about converting internal numbers to specify a test for a particular date value because Access handles date and time entries in several formats.

You must always surround date and time values with the pound-sign character (#) to tell Access that you're entering a date or time. To test for a specific date, use the date notation that is most comfortable for you. For example, *#April 15, 1994#*, *#4/15/94#*, and *#15-Apr-1994#* are all recognized as the same date by Access when you set Country to U.S. in the International section of the Control Panel of Microsoft Windows. Also, *#5:30 PM#* and *#17:30#* both specify 5:30 in the evening.

Access has several useful functions to assist you in testing date and time values. These are explained below with examples that use the LastPayDate field in the PROMPT database:

Day(date)	Returns a value from 1 through 31 for the day of the month. For example, if you want to select records with LastPayDate values after the 10th of any month, enter *Day([LastPayDate])* as a calculated field, and enter *>10* in the criteria for that field.
Month(date)	Returns a value from 1 through 12 for the month of the year. For example, if you want to find all records that have a LastPayDate value of June, enter *Month([LastPayDate])* as a calculated field, and enter *6* in the criteria for that field.

Year(date)	Returns a value from 100 through 9999 for the year. If you want to find a LastPayDate value in 1993, enter *Year([LastPayDate])* as a calculated field, and enter *1993* in the criteria for that field.
Weekday(date)	As a default, returns from 1 (Sunday) through 7 (Saturday) for the day of the week. To find business day dates, enter *Weekday([LastPayDate])* as a calculated field, and enter *Between 2 And 6* in the criteria for that field.
Hour(date)	Returns the hour (0 through 23). To find a payment made before noon, enter *Hour([LastPayDate])* as a calculated field, and enter *<12* in the criteria for that field.
Datepart(interval,date)	Returns a portion of the date or time, depending on the interval code you supply. Useful interval codes are *"q"* for quarter of the year (1 through 4) and *"ww"* for week of the year (1 through 53). For example, to select dates in the second quarter, enter *Datepart("q",[LastPayDate])* as a calculated field, and enter *2* in the criteria for that field.
Date( )	Returns the current system date. To select dates more than 30 days ago, enter *<Date( ) – 30* in the criteria for that field.

NOTE: If you would like the first day of a week (for the *Weekday* and other week-related functions) to fall on a day other than Sunday (the default), choose Options from the View menu and set the First Weekday property.

Calculating Values

You can specify a calculation on any of the fields in your table and make that calculation a new field in the recordset. You can use any of the many built-in functions that Microsoft Access provides. (You can see examples of some of the date and time functions in the previous section.) You can also create a field in a query by using arithmetic operators on fields in the underlying table to calculate a value. In an OrderItem record, for example, you might have a Quantity field and a Price field, but not the extended price (quantity times price). You can include that value in your recordset by typing in the calculation in the field of an empty column in the QBE grid using the Quantity field, the multiplication operator (*), and the Price field.

You can also create a new text (string) field by concatenating either fields containing text or string constants. You create a string constant by enclosing the text you want in double or single quotation marks. Use the ampersand character (&) between text fields or strings to indicate that you want to concatenate them. For example, you might want to create an output field that concatenates the LastName field, a comma and a blank (", "), and then the FirstName field.

The operators you can use in expressions include the following:

+	Adds two numeric expressions.
–	Subtracts two numeric expressions.
*	Multiplies two numeric expressions.
/	Divides the first numeric expression by the second numeric expression.
\	Rounds both numeric expressions to integers and divides the first number by the second number. The result is rounded to an integer.
^	Raises the first numeric expression to the power indicated by the second numeric expression.
MOD	Rounds both numeric expressions to integers, divides the first number by the second number, and returns the remainder.
&	Creates an extended text string by concatenating the first text string to the second text string. If either expression is a number, Microsoft Access converts it to a text string before concatenating.

Try creating a query using the SalesReps table in PROMPT that shows a single field containing the last name, a comma, the first name, a space, and the middle name. Your expression should look like

```
[LastName] & ", " & [FirstName] & " " & [MiddleName]
```

The Query window in Design view for this example is shown in Figure 8-14.

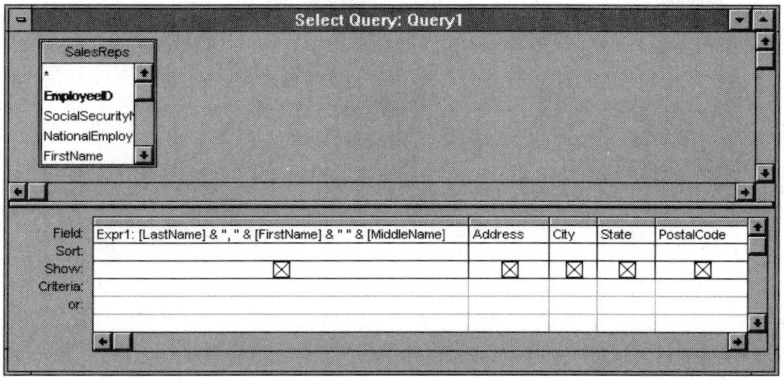

FIGURE 8-14.
The Query window in Design view.

When you look at the result in Datasheet view, you should see something like the query result shown in Figure 8-15.

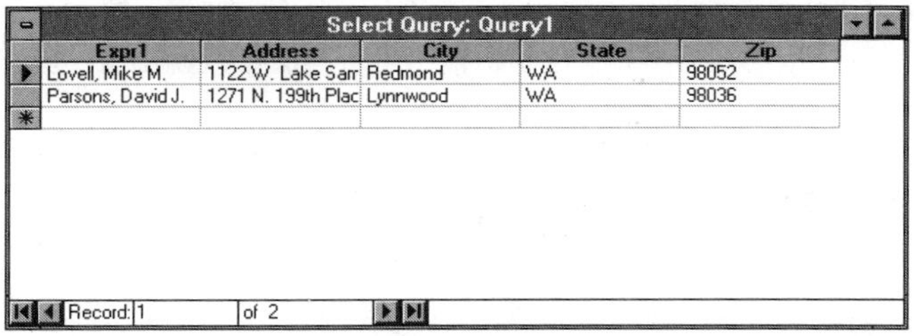

FIGURE 8-15.
A query result with a concatenated text field.

Using the Expression Builder

For more complex expressions, Microsoft Access provides a utility called the Expression Builder. Let's say you want to calculate the total amount owed for an order in the PROMPT database. There are several fields that you'll have to work with to get this done: SubtotalCost, Discount, SalesTax, and FreightCharge. To use the Expression Builder, start a new query on the Order table. Click in an empty field on the QBE grid, and then click the Build button on the toolbar. Microsoft Access opens the Expression Builder window shown in Figure 8-16 on the next page.

At the top of the window is a blank text box in which you can build an expression. You can type the expression yourself, but it's much easier to use the various Expression operator buttons just below the text box to help you out. At the bottom are three list boxes you can use to find field names and function names that you need to build your

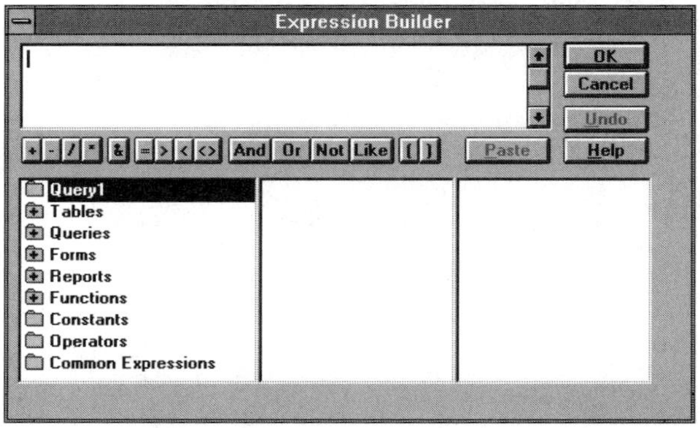

FIGURE 8-16. The Expression Builder window.

expression. Because you need fields from the Order table, double-click on the Tables folder in the far left list box to expand the list to show you all the table names. Scroll down or drag the bottom of the Expression Builder window down until you can see the Order table. Click on the Order table to see the list of fields in the table in the middle list box, shown in Figure 8-17.

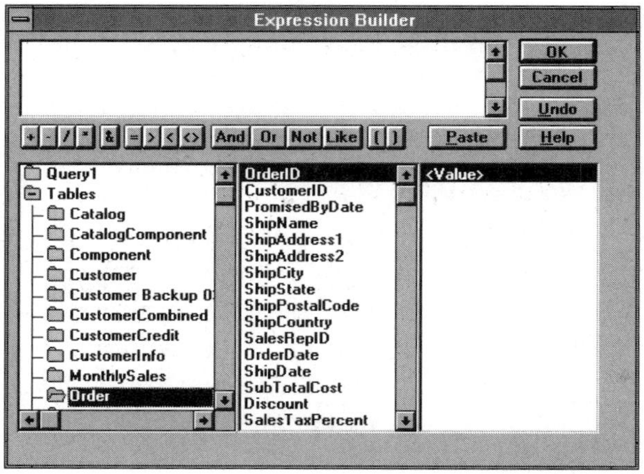

FIGURE 8-17. Choosing from a table field list in the Expression Builder window.

To get the total amount owed for the order, you need to start with SubtotalCost. Click in that field, and then click the Paste button to move the field to the expression area. You'll notice that Microsoft Access pastes *[Order]![SubtotalCost]* into the expression area. First, all names of objects in Access should be enclosed in left and right brackets ([]). If you designed the name without any blanks, you can leave out the brackets, but it's always best to include them. Second, the Expression Builder doesn't know whether you might include other tables in this query and whether some of those tables might also have field names that match the ones you're choosing now. The way to avoid conflicts is to <u>fully qualify</u> the field names by preceding them with the table name. When using names that you created, separate the parts of the name with an exclamation point (!). As you'll learn later in form and report design, sometimes you'll use a period (.) to separate names created by Microsoft Access.

Next, you need to subtract any discount. You calculate the discount by multiplying the subtotal cost by the discount percentage. Click the Minus Sign button to add it to the expression. If you make a mistake, you can always click the Undo button to erase your last entry. Because you want to subtract the result of another calculation, click the Left Parenthesis button (to begin enclosing the calculation), choose the SubtotalCost field again, click the Multiplication Sign button, choose the Discount field, and finally click the Right Parenthesis button. To finish the expression, click the Plus Sign button, choose the SalesTax field, click the Plus Sign button again, and finally choose the FreightCharge field. Your result should look like that shown in Figure 8-18.

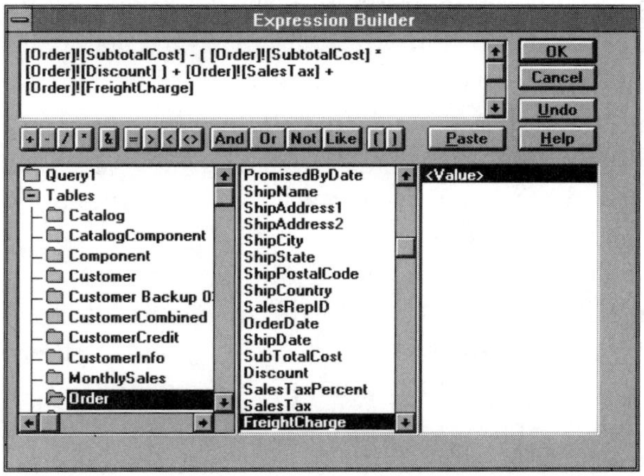

FIGURE 8-18.
The completed order cost expression.

TIP: A quick way to choose a field in the Expression Builder window is to double-click on the field's name.

Click OK to paste your result onto the QBE grid. You might want to include the ShipName field and all the fields used in the calculation in your query as well. When you open your query in Datasheet view, it should look something like the one shown in Figure 8-19.

FIGURE 8-19. A query with a calculated field.

Select Query: Query1

Ship Name	Subtotal Cost	Discount	Sales Tax	Freight Charge	Expr1
Beta Consulting	$10,410.00	5.00%	$810.94	$37.50	$10,737.94
Condor Leasing	$3,615.50	0.00%	$296.47	$0.00	$3,911.97
Old World Delicate:	$434.63	0.00%	$0.00	$0.00	$434.63
Beta Consulting	$1,399.00	0.00%	$114.72	$0.00	$1,513.72
White Clover Mark	$1,599.00	0.00%	$131.12	$0.00	$1,730.12
Beta Consulting	$3,072.75	0.00%	$251.97	$0.00	$3,324.72
Old World Delicate:	$471.25	0.00%	$40.06	$8.29	$519.60
The Big Cheese	$2,289.00	0.00%	$0.00	$0.00	$2,289.00
Bottom-Dollar Mark	$3,020.50	0.00%	$223.52	$62.50	$3,306.52
Hungry Coyote Imp	$1,771.50	0.00%	$0.00	$0.00	$1,771.50
Bottom-Dollar Mark	$6,308.00	0.00%	$466.79	$0.00	$6,774.79
White Clover Mark	$2,009.00	0.00%	$164.74	$0.00	$2,173.74
Hungry Coyote Imp	$7,725.50	2.00%	$0.00	$0.00	$7,570.99
Condor Leasing	$4,058.00	5.00%	$316.12	$0.00	$4,171.22
Condor Leasing	$3,247.82	5.00%	$253.01	$0.00	$3,338.44
*	$0.00	0.00%	$0.00	$0.00	

Record: 1 of 15

Specifying Field Names

You learned earlier that you can change the *caption* (column heading) for a field in a query by using the property sheet. You might have noticed that when you created any expression in the field row of the QBE grid, Microsoft Access prefixed what you entered with a name such as *Expr1* followed by a colon. Every field in a query must have a name. By default, the name for a field in a table is the name of the field. Likewise, the default caption for the field is the field name.

You can change or assign field names that will appear in the recordset of a query. This feature is particularly useful when you've calculated a value in the query that you'll use in a form, a report, or another query. In the queries in Figures 8-15 and 8-19, you calculated a value and Access assigned a temporary field name. You can replace this name with something more meaningful. For example, in the first query you might want to use something like *FullName:*. In the second query, *TotalOrderCost:* could be appropriate. Figure 8-20 shows you the second query with the field name changed.

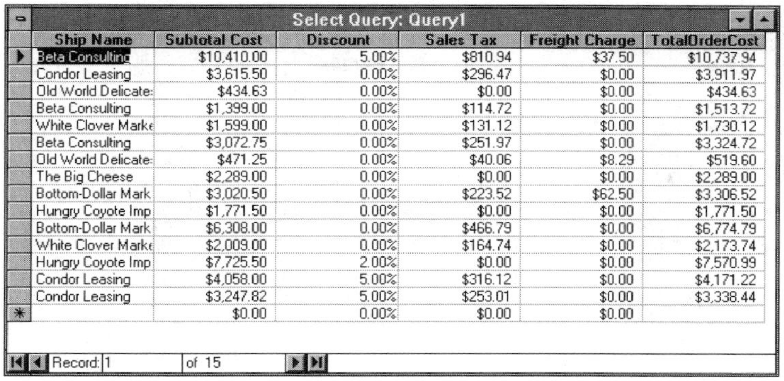

Select Query: Query1

Ship Name	Subtotal Cost	Discount	Sales Tax	Freight Charge	TotalOrderCost
Beta Consulting	$10,410.00	5.00%	$810.94	$37.50	$10,737.94
Condor Leasing	$3,615.50	0.00%	$296.47	$0.00	$3,911.97
Old World Delicate:	$434.63	0.00%	$0.00	$0.00	$434.63
Beta Consulting	$1,399.00	0.00%	$114.72	$0.00	$1,513.72
White Clover Mark	$1,599.00	0.00%	$131.12	$0.00	$1,730.12
Beta Consulting	$3,072.75	0.00%	$251.97	$0.00	$3,324.72
Old World Delicate:	$471.25	0.00%	$40.06	$8.29	$519.60
The Big Cheese	$2,289.00	0.00%	$0.00	$0.00	$2,289.00
Bottom-Dollar Mark	$3,020.50	0.00%	$223.52	$62.50	$3,306.52
Hungry Coyote Imp	$1,771.50	0.00%	$0.00	$0.00	$1,771.50
Bottom-Dollar Mark	$6,308.00	0.00%	$466.79	$0.00	$6,774.79
White Clover Mark	$2,009.00	0.00%	$164.74	$0.00	$2,173.74
Hungry Coyote Imp	$7,725.50	2.00%	$0.00	$0.00	$7,570.99
Condor Leasing	$4,058.00	5.00%	$316.12	$0.00	$4,171.22
Condor Leasing	$3,247.82	5.00%	$253.01	$0.00	$3,338.44
*	$0.00	0.00%	$0.00	$0.00	

Record: 1 of 15

FIGURE 8-20. The result of changing the Expr1 column heading shown in Figure 8-19.

Sorting Data

Normally, Microsoft Access presents the rows in your recordset in the order in which they're retrieved from the database. You can add sorting information to determine the sequence of the data in a query exactly as you did for table datasheets in the previous chapter. Click in the Sort row under the field you want to sort, and choose Ascending or Descending from the drop-down list. In the example, shown in Figure 8-21, the query results are to be sorted in descending sequence based on the calculated TotalOrderCost field. The recordset will list the largest orders first. You can see the resulting Datasheet view in Figure 8-22 on the next page.

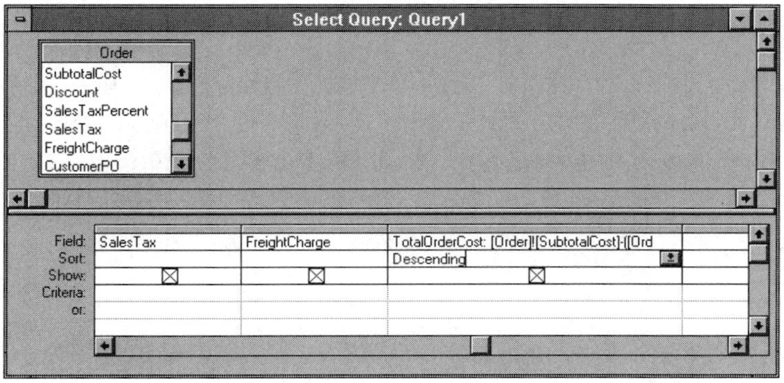

FIGURE 8-21. A query with sorting criteria added.

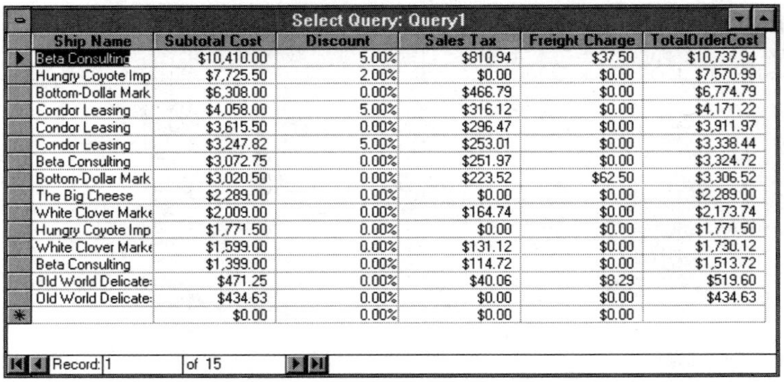
Select Query: Query1

Ship Name	Subtotal Cost	Discount	Sales Tax	Freight Charge	TotalOrderCost
Beta Consulting	$10,410.00	5.00%	$810.94	$37.50	$10,737.94
Hungry Coyote Imp	$7,725.50	2.00%	$0.00	$0.00	$7,570.99
Bottom-Dollar Mark	$6,308.00	0.00%	$466.79	$0.00	$6,774.79
Condor Leasing	$4,058.00	5.00%	$316.12	$0.00	$4,171.22
Condor Leasing	$3,615.50	0.00%	$296.47	$0.00	$3,911.97
Condor Leasing	$3,247.82	5.00%	$253.01	$0.00	$3,338.44
Beta Consulting	$3,072.75	0.00%	$251.97	$0.00	$3,324.72
Bottom-Dollar Mark	$3,020.50	0.00%	$223.52	$62.50	$3,306.52
The Big Cheese	$2,289.00	0.00%	$0.00	$0.00	$2,289.00
White Clover Marke	$2,009.00	0.00%	$164.74	$0.00	$2,173.74
Hungry Coyote Imp	$1,771.50	0.00%	$0.00	$0.00	$1,771.50
White Clover Marke	$1,599.00	0.00%	$131.12	$0.00	$1,730.12
Beta Consulting	$1,399.00	0.00%	$114.72	$0.00	$1,513.72
Old World Delicate:	$471.25	0.00%	$40.06	$8.29	$519.60
Old World Delicate:	$434.63	0.00%	$0.00	$0.00	$434.63
*	$0.00	0.00%	$0.00	$0.00	

Record: 1 of 15

FIGURE 8-22. The recordset of the query shown in Figure 8-21, but in Datasheet view.

You can also sort on multiple fields. Access honors your sorting criteria from left to right in the query's QBE grid. If, for example, you want to sort by State and then by TotalOrderCost, you should include the State field to the left of the TotalOrderCost field. If the additional field you want to sort is already on the QBE grid but in the wrong location, you can click the selector box above the field to select the entire column. You can then click the selector box again and drag the field to its new location.

Totals Queries

Sometimes you aren't interested in each and every row in your table. You'd rather see totals of different groups of data. For example, you might want the total sales to all customers in a particular state. Or you might want to know the average of all sales for each month in the last year. To get these answers, you need a *totals query.* To calculate totals within any query, click the Totals button on the toolbar in Design view to open the Total row on the QBE grid, as shown in Figure 8-23.

Totals Within Groups

When you first click the Totals button on the toolbar, Microsoft Access displays *Group By* in the Total row for any fields you already have on the QBE grid. At this point the records in each field are grouped but not totaled. If you were to run the query now, you'd get one row in the recordset for each set of unique values—but no totals. You can create totals by replacing Group By with some *totals functions* in the Total row.

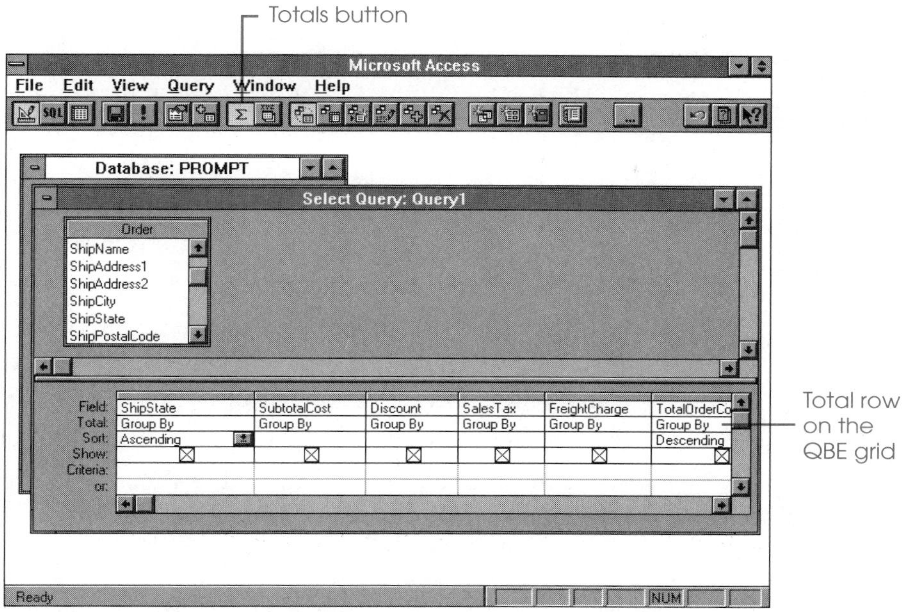

FIGURE 8-23.
The Totals button and the Total row on the QBE grid.

Access provides nine totals functions for your use. You can choose the one you want by typing its name in the Total row on the QBE grid or by selecting it from the drop-down list. The available functions are as follows:

Sum	Calculates the sum of all the values for this field in each group. You can specify this function only with number or currency fields.
Avg	Calculates the arithmetic average of all the values for this field in each group. You can specify this function only with number or currency fields. Microsoft Access does not include any Null values in the calculation.
Min	Returns the lowest value found in this field within each group. For numbers, returns the smallest value. For text, returns the lowest in collating sequence, without regard for case. Access ignores Null values.
Max	Returns the highest value found in this field within each group. For numbers, returns the largest value. For text, returns the highest in collating sequence, without regard for case. Access ignores Null values.

(continued)

(continued)

Count	Returns the count of the rows in which the specified field is not a Null value. You can also enter the special expression COUNT(*) in the Field row to count all rows in each group, regardless of the existence of Null values.
StDev	Calculates the statistical standard deviation of all the values for this field in each group. You can specify this function only with number or currency fields. If the group does not contain at least two rows, Access returns a Null value.
Var	Calculates the statistical variance of all the values for this field in each group. You can specify this function only with number or currency fields. If the group does not contain at least two rows, Access returns a Null value.
First	Returns the first value in this field.
Last	Returns the last value in this field.

Try working with a totals query now by first changing the ShipName field from the query in Figure 8-21 on page 239 to *ShipState* and then clicking the Totals button on the toolbar. Then, in order to group the totals you create by state, keep Group By in the Total row for the ShipState field. Next, choose totals functions for the remaining fields, as follows: the *Avg* function for the SubtotalCost, SalesTax, and FreightCharge fields; the *Max* function for the Discount field; and the *Sum* function for the calculated TotalOrderCost field. Change the name of the TotalOrderCost field by preceding it with the word *Grand*. Remove all criteria from the Criteria row. Figure 8-24 shows these changes on the QBE grid. Figure 8-25 shows the results when you run the query.

In the drop-down list for the Total row on the QBE grid, you can also find an Expression setting. Choose this when you want to create an

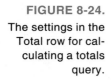

FIGURE 8-24. The settings in the Total row for calculating a totals query.

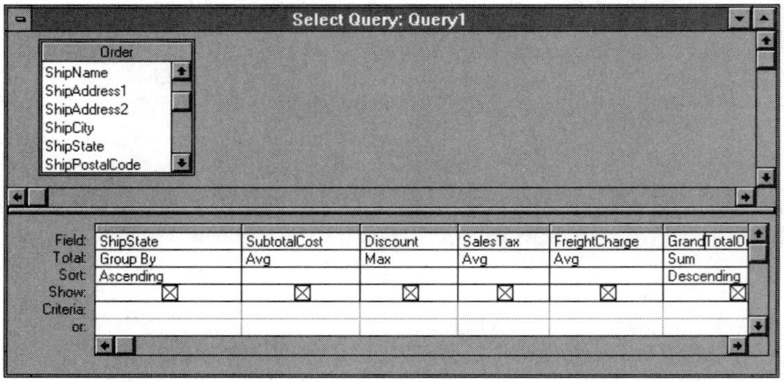

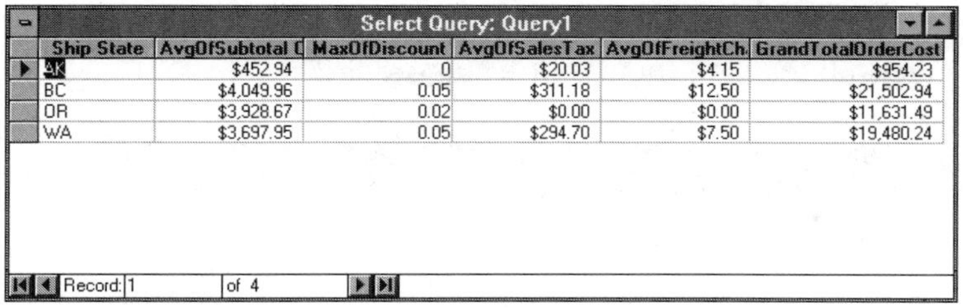

FIGURE 8-25. The recordset of the query shown in Figure 8-24.

expression in the Field row that uses one or more of the totals functions listed above. For example, you might want to calculate a value that reflects the range of values in the group, as in the following:

Max([Discount]) – Min([Discount])

Selecting Records to Form Groups

You might not want to include some records in the groups that form your totals query. To filter out certain records from groups, you can add to the QBE grid the field or fields you want to use as filters. To do so, choose the Where setting in the Total row, deselect that field's Show check box, and enter criteria that tell Access which records to exclude. In the Order table in PROMPT, for example, you can narrow the selection to records of customers in the U.S. by dragging the ShipCountry field to the QBE grid and then choosing the Where setting in the Total row and deselecting the Show check box. (In version 2, Access automatically un-checks the Show check box when you choose Where.) Finally, you must enter *USA* in the Criteria row. This example is shown in Figure 8-26.

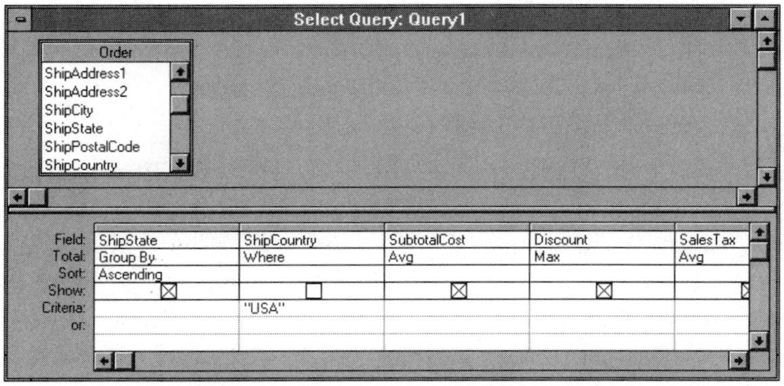

FIGURE 8-26. The ShipCountry field is used to select the rows that will be included in groups.

Now, when you run the query, you get totals only for customers in the United States. See the result in Figure 8-27.

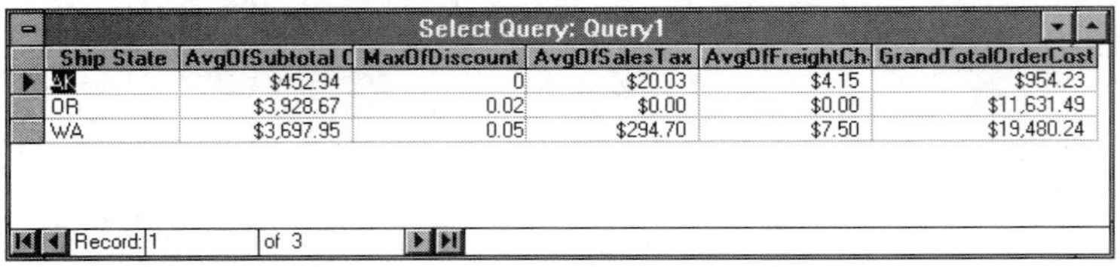

Ship State	AvgOfSubtotal C	MaxOfDiscount	AvgOfSalesTax	AvgOfFreightCh	GrandTotalOrderCost
AK	$452.94	0	$20.03	$4.15	$954.23
OR	$3,928.67	0.02	$0.00	$0.00	$11,631.49
WA	$3,697.95	0.05	$294.70	$7.50	$19,480.24

FIGURE 8-27. The recordset of the query shown in Figure 8-26.

Selecting Specific Groups

You can also filter out groups of totals. To do that, enter criteria for any field that has a Group By setting in the Total row, one of the nine Access totals functions, or an Expression using the totals functions. For example, you might want to find out which states have more than $10,000 in total orders. To find that out, you would use the settings shown in Figure 8-26 on the previous page and enter a criterion of *>10000* for the GrandTotalOrderCost field, as shown in Figure 8-28.

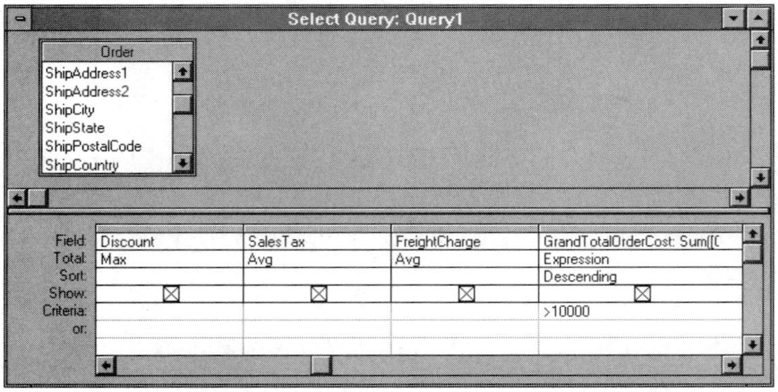

FIGURE 8-28. A criteria setting for the GrandTotal-OrderCost field.

Using Query Parameters

Thus far you've been entering selection criteria directly onto the QBE grid of the Query window in Design view. However, you don't have to decide at the time you design the query exactly what value you want Microsoft Access to search for. Instead, you can include a parameter in the query, and Access will prompt you for the criteria before the query is run.

To set a parameter, you enter a name or phrase enclosed in brackets ([ ]) instead of entering a value in the Criteria row. What you enclose in brackets becomes the name by which Access knows your parameter. Access displays this name in a dialog box when you run the query, so it's a good idea to enter a phrase that describes what you want. You can enter several parameters in a single query, so each parameter name needs to be unique and informative.

You can adapt the query in Figure 8-26 so that Access will prompt for the state name criteria each time the query is run. In the State field, add the *[Sum Orders in State:]* parameter in the Criteria row, as shown in Figure 8-29.

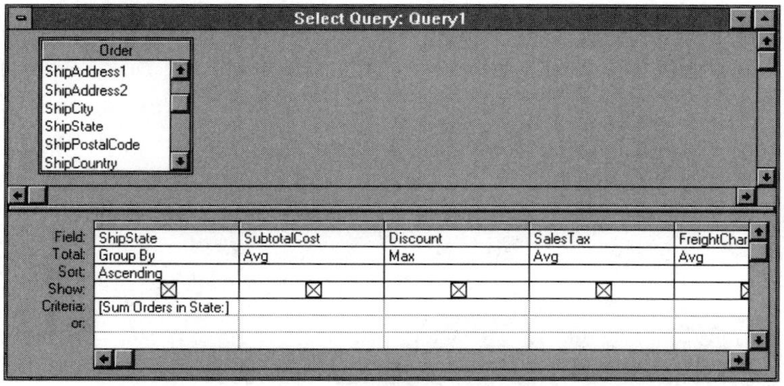

FIGURE 8-29.
A query parameter is set for the ShipState field.

For each parameter in a query, you can tell Access what data type to expect. Access uses this information to validate the value entered. For example, if you define a parameter as a number, Access won't accept alphabetic characters in the parameter value. By default, Access assigns the text data type to query parameters, which is fine for our example. If you need to change a parameter's data type, choose the Parameters command from the Query menu; Access displays the Query Parameters dialog box, shown in Figure 8-30 on the next page.

In this dialog box, enter each parameter name whose data type you want to specify in the Parameter column, exactly as you entered it on the QBE grid but without the brackets. In the Data Type column, select the appropriate data type from the drop-down list. Click the OK button when you've finished defining all your parameters.

FIGURE 8-30. The Query Parameters dialog box.

When you run the query, Access prompts you for an appropriate value for each parameter, one at a time, with a dialog box such as the one shown in Figure 8-31. Because Access displays the "name" of the parameter that you provided on the QBE grid, you can see why naming the parameter with a phrase can help you enter the correct value later. In this case, *WA* is typed in the Enter Parameter Value dialog box, and the recordset is shown in Figure 8-32.

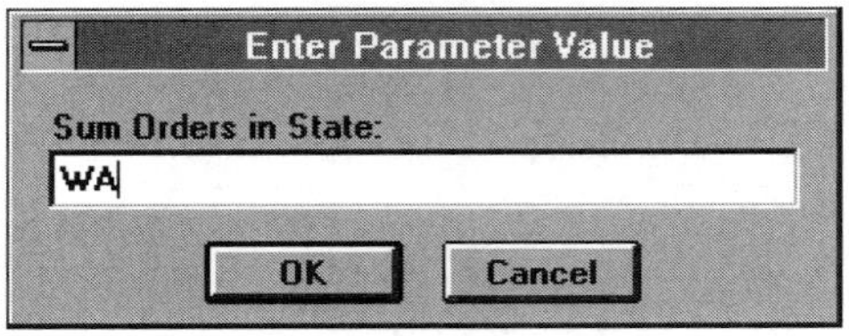

FIGURE 8-31. The Enter Parameter Value dialog box.

FIGURE 8-32. The recordset of the query shown in Figure 8-29, when *WA* is typed in the Enter Parameter Value dialog box.

Crosstab Queries

Microsoft Access supports a special type of totals query called a *crosstab query* that allows you to see calculated values in a spreadsheetlike format. For example, you can use this type of query to see total sales by month (in columns across) for each type of item (rows down) in the PROMPT MonthlySales table.

To build a crosstab query, first select the table you want in the Database window and click the New Query button on the toolbar. Choose New Query in the New Query dialog box. Then choose the Crosstab command from the Query menu. Access adds a Crosstab row to the QBE grid, as shown in Figure 8-33. Each field in a crosstab query can have one of four crosstab settings: *Row Heading, Column Heading, Value* (calculated in the crosstab grid), or *Not Shown*. For a crosstab query to work, you must specify at least one field to be a row heading, one field to be a column heading, and one field to be a value in your query. Each row heading and column heading must have Group By as the setting in the Total row. You must choose one of the available totals functions or enter an expression that uses a totals function for the field that contains the Value setting on your QBE grid.

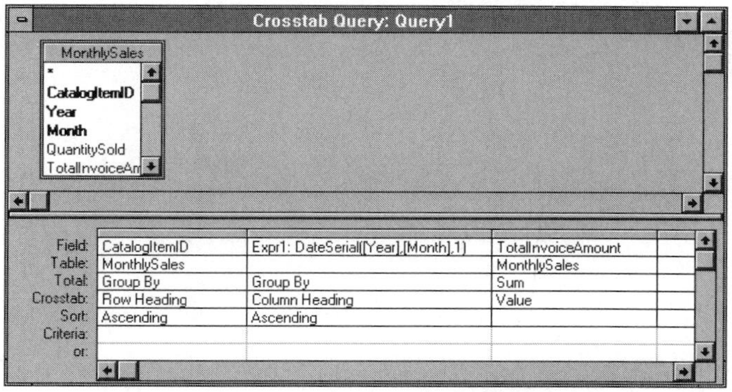

FIGURE 8-33.
A crosstab query in Design view.

As in other types of totals queries, you can include other fields to filter out values from the result. For these fields you should select the Where setting in the Total row and the Not Shown setting in the Crosstab row and then enter your criteria. You can also enter criteria for any heading columns, and you can sort any of the fields.

To build the example crosstab query referred to above, one that shows total sales by month for each type of item, start by selecting the MonthlySales table in the PROMPT Database window. Click the New Query button on the toolbar. Then choose the Crosstab command from the Query menu. Drag the CatalogItemID field from the field list to the first field on the QBE grid. Fill in the column as shown in Figure 8-33 (with the Group By, Row Heading, and Ascending settings).

To generate output in the form of columns of monthly sales, you can create an expression that uses one of the Access functions. Because the MonthlySales table has integer values for Year and Month, you'll need to convert these to a date/time value for grouping. In the second field of the QBE grid, type

```
Expr1: DateSerial([Year],[Month],1)
```

The *DateSerial* function in this expression creates a date/time value for the first day of the month. This is your column heading. Fill out the second column of your QBE grid, as shown in Figure 8-33 (with the Group By, Column Heading, and Ascending settings).

Finally, drag the TotalInvoiceAmount field to the third column on the QBE grid. This field will generate the values for the crosstab query. Use the Sum and Value settings.

Figure 8-34 shows the recordset of the query shown in Figure 8-33. Notice that the *DateSerial* function has returned a short date format for the column headings.

FIGURE 8-34. The recordset of the query shown in Figure 8-33.

Crosstab Query: Query1

Catalog Item ID	12/1/92	1/1/93	2/1/93	3/1/93	4/1/93
1	$542.85	$616.88	$987.00	$493.50	$370.13
2		$442.50	$885.00	$1,548.75	$221.25
3		$367.50	$735.00	$2,205.00	$735.00
6		$1,151.25	$1,918.75	$767.50	
7		$9,337.50	$7,781.25	$11,205.00	$6,847.50
10	$4,261.25				
11		$4,523.75	$5,757.50	$3,701.25	$6,991.25
15		$2,145.00	$3,412.50	$2,437.50	$3,705.00
16					
17	$2,568.75				
22	$1,732.50	$3,272.50	$2,695.00	$4,235.00	$3,561.25
24		$450.00		$630.00	
25	$180.00				
26		$2,465.00	$3,262.50	$1,957.50	$2,755.00
29	$6,270.00	$6,270.00	$3,420.00	$4,275.00	$5,415.00
31		$1,173.75	$782.50	$1,956.25	$1,173.75
32		$7,068.75	$4,241.25	$5,183.75	$3,298.75
35		$15,725.00	$10,175.00	$12,950.00	$18,037.50

Record: 1 of 27

You might prefer to see only the month name and year in the column headings. Because you converted Year and Month to a date value, you can now use another Access function—the *Format* function—to display the short month name and year. You enclose the *DateSerial* function within the *Format* function by typing

```
Expr1: Format(DateSerial([Year],[Month],1), "mmm yy")
```

Figure 8-35 shows you the required *Format* function. Notice that you originally asked for the dates in ascending order. That works when Access is using the actual date values in the records but not after you've reformatted them. If you run the query as is, you'll get Apr first, followed by Aug, and so on—the collating sequence of the displayed names, not the actual dates.

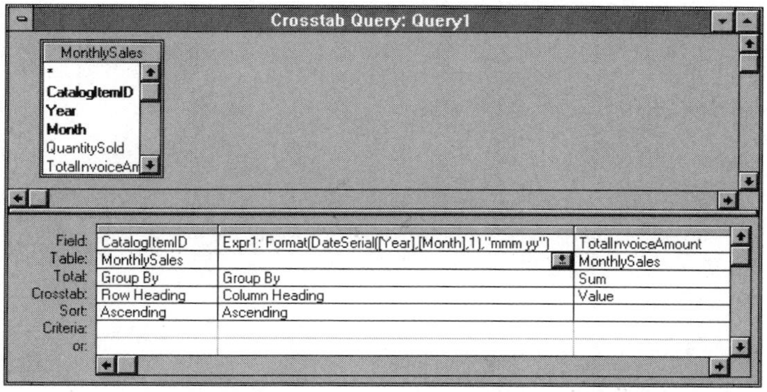

FIGURE 8-35.
A crosstab query with a customized heading.

Access provides a solution for that too. You can specifically define the order of columns for any crosstab query by using the property sheet. Click in the top section of the Query window in Design view, and then click the Properties button on the toolbar to see the property sheet, shown in Figure 8-36.

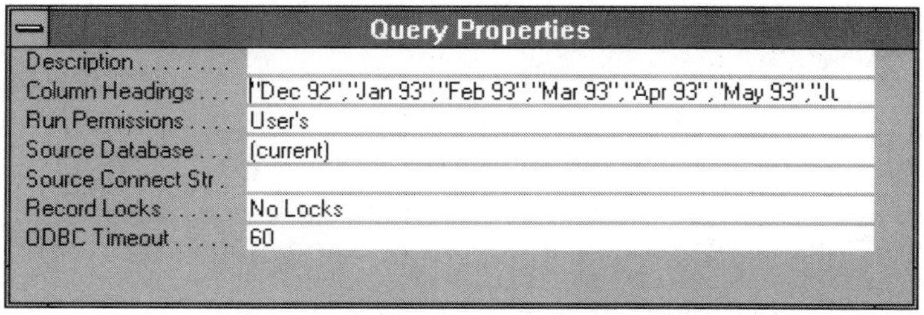

FIGURE 8-36.
The entries in the property sheet that fix the order of column headings for the query in Figure 8-35.

To control the order of columns displayed, enter the headings exactly as they are formatted and in the order you want in the Column Headings property sheet. Be careful that you include all the column headings that match the result of the query. If you omit (or misspell) a column heading, Access won't show that column. When you run the query again with formatted column headings, you see the recordset shown in Figure 8-37.

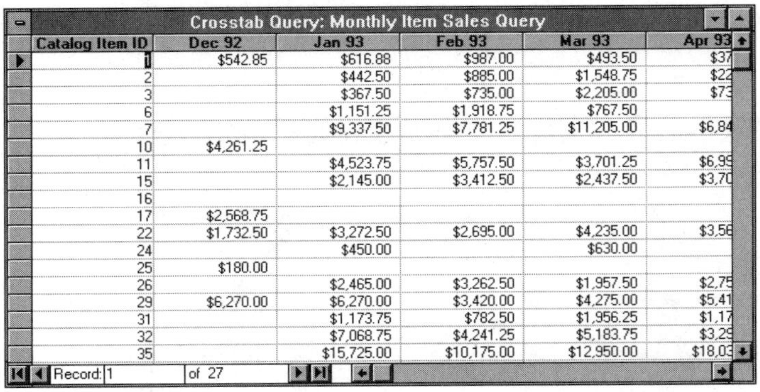

Crosstab Query: Monthly Item Sales Query

Catalog Item ID	Dec 92	Jan 93	Feb 93	Mar 93	Apr 93
1	$542.85	$616.88	$987.00	$493.50	$37
2		$442.50	$885.00	$1,548.75	$22
3		$367.50	$735.00	$2,205.00	$73
6		$1,151.25	$1,918.75	$767.50	
7		$9,337.50	$7,781.25	$11,205.00	$6,84
10	$4,261.25				
11		$4,523.75	$5,757.50	$3,701.25	$6,99
15		$2,145.00	$3,412.50	$2,437.50	$3,70
16					
17	$2,568.75				
22	$1,732.50	$3,272.50	$2,695.00	$4,235.00	$3,56
24		$450.00		$630.00	
25	$180.00				
26		$2,465.00	$3,262.50	$1,957.50	$2,75
29	$6,270.00	$6,270.00	$3,420.00	$4,275.00	$5,41
31		$1,173.75	$782.50	$1,956.25	$1,17
32		$7,068.75	$4,241.25	$5,183.75	$3,29
35		$15,725.00	$10,175.00	$12,950.00	$18,03

Record: 1 of 27

FIGURE 8-37. A crosstab query recordset with custom headings, as defined in Figures 8-35 and 8-36.

Save this query as *Monthly Item Sales Query*. You'll use it later in this chapter.

Searching Multiple Tables

At this point, you've been through all the variations on a single theme—queries on a single table. It's easy to build on this knowledge to retrieve related information from many tables and to place that information in a single view. You'll find this ability to select data from multiple tables most useful in designing forms and reports later in this book.

Try the following example, in which you combine information about an order and about the customer who placed it. Start by bringing the PROMPT Database window to the front. Click the Query tab on the left side of the Database window, and then click the New button and select New Query in the New Query dialog box to open a new Query window in Design view. Access immediately opens the Add Table dialog box. This dialog box enables you to select tables and queries from which you can design a new query. Select the Customer and Order tables and then close the dialog box.

If you defined the relationships between your tables correctly, the top section of the Query window in Design view should look like the one shown in Figure 8-38. Access links multiple tables in a query based on the relationship information you provided when you designed each table. Access shows you the links between tables as a line drawn from the primary key in one table to its matching field in the other table. If you didn't define relationships between tables, Access makes a best guess by linking fields that have the same name and matching data type.

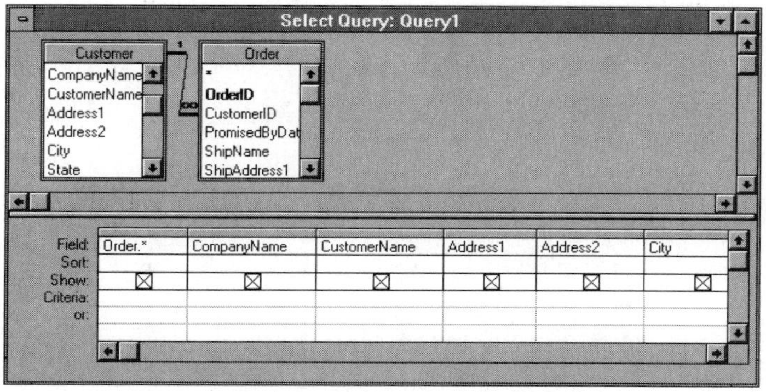

FIGURE 8-38.
A query that selects information from the Customer and Order tables.

In this example, you want all of the information from the Order table and some of the information (company name, customer name, and address) from the Customer table. Click the asterisk (the special indicator for "all fields") at the top of the Order table and drag it to the QBE grid. Find the CompanyName, CustomerName, Address1, Address2, City, and State fields in the Customer table and drag them individually to the QBE grid.

When you run your query, you see the recordset shown in Figure 8-39 on the next page. The fields from the Order table appear first, left to right. You can scroll to the right to see the fields you added from the Customer table.

As mentioned earlier, you can do many of the things with Query windows in Datasheet view that you can do with Table windows in Datasheet view. To see customer information alongside order information, you can move the OrderID, CustomerID, and SubtotalCost fields together, select them, and then choose the Freeze command from the Layout menu. This action will lock those fields at the left of the datasheet. You can then scroll to the right to bring the company name into view, as shown in Figure 8-40 on the next page.

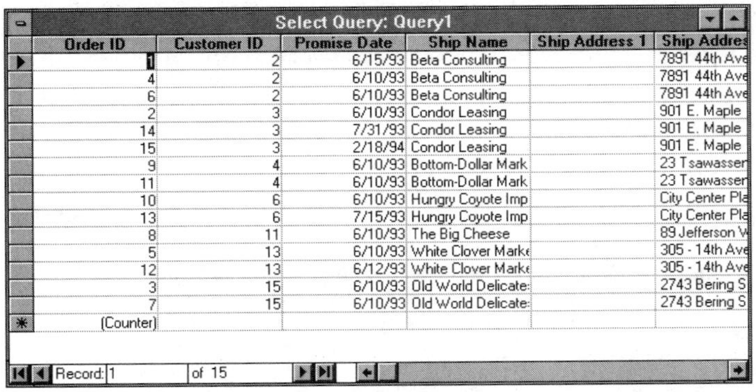

Select Query: Query1

Order ID	Customer ID	Promise Date	Ship Name	Ship Address 1	Ship Addres
1	2	6/15/93	Beta Consulting		7891 44th Ave
4	2	6/10/93	Beta Consulting		7891 44th Ave
6	2	6/10/93	Beta Consulting		7891 44th Ave
2	3	6/10/93	Condor Leasing		901 E. Maple
14	3	7/31/93	Condor Leasing		901 E. Maple
15	3	2/18/94	Condor Leasing		901 E. Maple
9	4	6/10/93	Bottom-Dollar Mark		23 Tsawasser
11	4	6/10/93	Bottom-Dollar Mark		23 Tsawasser
10	6	6/10/93	Hungry Coyote Imp		City Center Pla
13	6	7/15/93	Hungry Coyote Imp		City Center Pla
8	11	6/10/93	The Big Cheese		89 Jefferson W
5	13	6/10/93	White Clover Marke		305 - 14th Ave
12	13	6/12/93	White Clover Marke		305 - 14th Ave
3	15	6/10/93	Old World Delicate		2743 Bering S
7	15	6/10/93	Old World Delicate		2743 Bering S
(Counter)					

Record: 1 of 15

FIGURE 8-39. The recordset of the query shown in Figure 8-38.

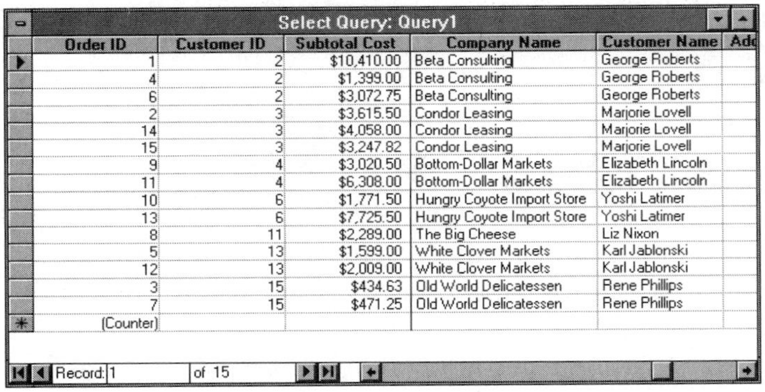

Select Query: Query1

Order ID	Customer ID	Subtotal Cost	Company Name	Customer Name	Add
1	2	$10,410.00	Beta Consulting	George Roberts	
4	2	$1,399.00	Beta Consulting	George Roberts	
6	2	$3,072.75	Beta Consulting	George Roberts	
2	3	$3,615.50	Condor Leasing	Marjorie Lovell	
14	3	$4,058.00	Condor Leasing	Marjorie Lovell	
15	3	$3,247.82	Condor Leasing	Marjorie Lovell	
9	4	$3,020.50	Bottom-Dollar Markets	Elizabeth Lincoln	
11	4	$6,308.00	Bottom-Dollar Markets	Elizabeth Lincoln	
10	6	$1,771.50	Hungry Coyote Import Store	Yoshi Latimer	
13	6	$7,725.50	Hungry Coyote Import Store	Yoshi Latimer	
8	11	$2,289.00	The Big Cheese	Liz Nixon	
5	13	$1,599.00	White Clover Markets	Karl Jablonski	
12	13	$2,009.00	White Clover Markets	Karl Jablonski	
3	15	$434.63	Old World Delicatessen	Rene Phillips	
7	15	$471.25	Old World Delicatessen	Rene Phillips	
(Counter)					

Record: 1 of 15

FIGURE 8-40. The OrderID, CustomerID, and SubtotalCost fields are frozen at the left of this Query window in Datasheet view.

Save this query and name it *Orders Query*. You will use this query in Chapter 22, "Automating Your Application with Access Basic," to design a form. (You'll find this query already defined in the PROMPT sample database.)

Outer Joins

Most queries that you create to request information from multiple tables will show results based on matching data in one or more tables. For example, the Query window in Datasheet view shown in Figure 8-39 will contain the names of customers who have orders in the Order table—and will not contain the names of customers who don't. This type of query is called an *equi-join*. What if you want to see customers and orders and want to include customers who don't have any outstanding orders? You can get the information you need by creating an *outer join*.

To create an outer join, you must modify the join properties. Look at the Design view of the Orders Query you created in the previous section in the PROMPT sample database. Double-click on the join line between the two tables in the top section of the Query window in Design view, as shown in Figure 8-41, to see the Join Properties dialog box, shown in Figure 8-42.

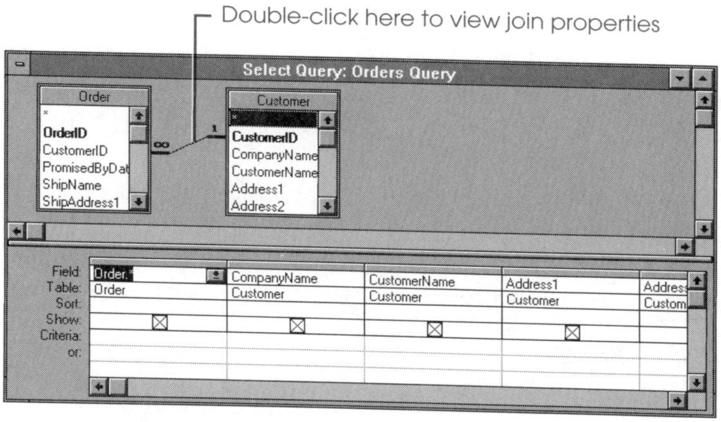

FIGURE 8-41.
The join line between two tables in a query can be double-clicked to open the Join Properties dialog box. (The field lists have been separated to make the join line more visible.)

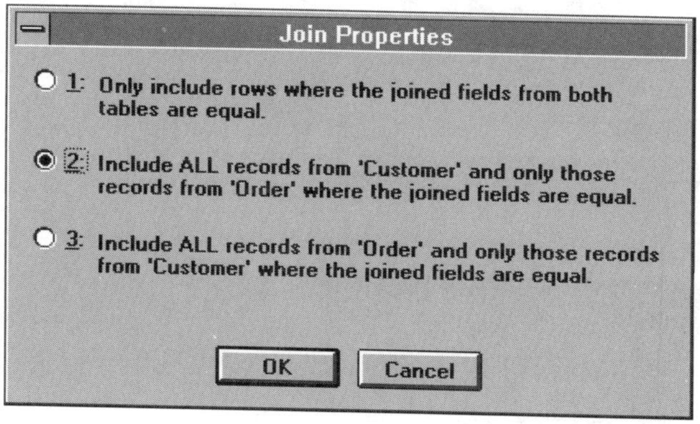

FIGURE 8-42.
The Join Properties dialog box with the second option selected.

The default setting in the Join Properties dialog box is option number 1—to include rows only where a match can be found in both tables. You can see that you have two additional options for this query: to see all customers and any orders that match or to see all orders and any customers that match. If you have been entering data correctly, you shouldn't have orders for nonexistent customers. If you asked Microsoft Access to enforce referential integrity (discussed in Chapter 5) when you defined the relationship between the Customer table and the Orders table, Access won't let you create any orders for nonexistent customers.

Click option number 2 and then click the OK button in the dialog box. You should now see an arrow on the join line pointing from the Customer field list to the Order field list, indicating that you have asked for an outer join with all records from Customer regardless of match, as shown in Figure 8-43. When you run this query, you should see a result similar to Figure 8-44. With the OrderID, CustomerID, and SubtotalCost fields still frozen at the left of the Query window in Datasheet view, you can scroll until you can compare this data with the CompanyName field. You can see that only a few customers have outstanding orders.

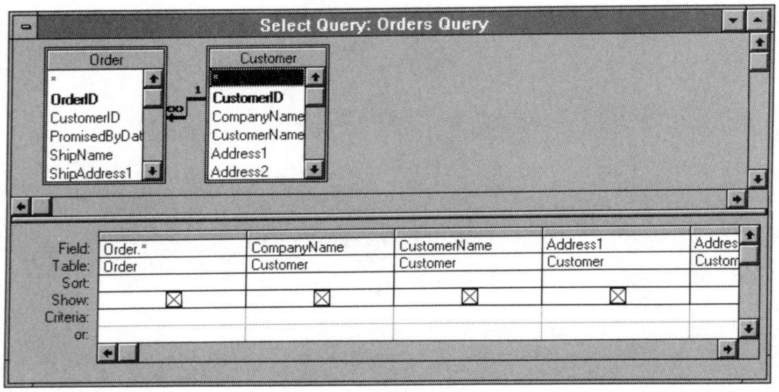

FIGURE 8-43. The join line reflects an outer join that includes all records from the Customer table.

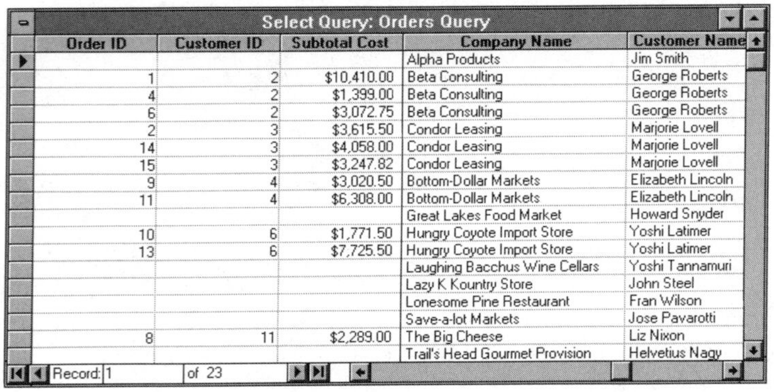

Order ID	Customer ID	Subtotal Cost	Company Name	Customer Name
			Alpha Products	Jim Smith
1	2	$10,410.00	Beta Consulting	George Roberts
4	2	$1,399.00	Beta Consulting	George Roberts
6	2	$3,072.75	Beta Consulting	George Roberts
2	3	$3,615.50	Condor Leasing	Marjorie Lovell
14	3	$4,058.00	Condor Leasing	Marjorie Lovell
15	3	$3,247.82	Condor Leasing	Marjorie Lovell
9	4	$3,020.50	Bottom-Dollar Markets	Elizabeth Lincoln
11	4	$6,308.00	Bottom-Dollar Markets	Elizabeth Lincoln
			Great Lakes Food Market	Howard Snyder
10	6	$1,771.50	Hungry Coyote Import Store	Yoshi Latimer
13	6	$7,725.50	Hungry Coyote Import Store	Yoshi Latimer
			Laughing Bacchus Wine Cellars	Yoshi Tannamuri
			Lazy K Kountry Store	John Steel
			Lonesome Pine Restaurant	Fran Wilson
			Save-a-lot Markets	Jose Pavarotti
8	11	$2,289.00	The Big Cheese	Liz Nixon
			Trail's Head Gourmet Provision	Helvetius Nagy

FIGURE 8-44. The recordset shows customers who have no orders (the fields from the Order table are blank) in the Order table.

Using Multiple Tables in Totals Queries

As you might suspect, you can also use multiple tables in a totals or a crosstab query. In Figures 8-35 and 8-36 on page 249, you built a crosstab query that you named Monthly Item Sales Query. The query showed total sales grouped by catalog item ID and month. However, catalog item ID isn't very informative—particularly if you want to use this query as the source for a report. The item description would be much more informative, but the item description is in another table.

Figure 8-45 shows you the crosstab query with the Catalog table added. Instead of using Catalog Item ID for the row heading, you can now use the Description field from the Catalog table instead. The settings in the field remain the same (Group By, Row Heading, and Ascending). Figure 8-46 shows you the recordset of the query, with item descriptions instead of the catalog item ID. You should save this updated query because you'll use it in a later chapter to create a report with a graph.

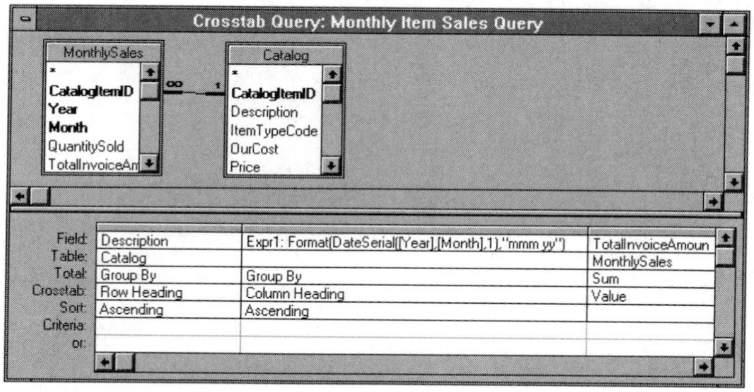

FIGURE 8-45.
A crosstab query that uses multiple tables.

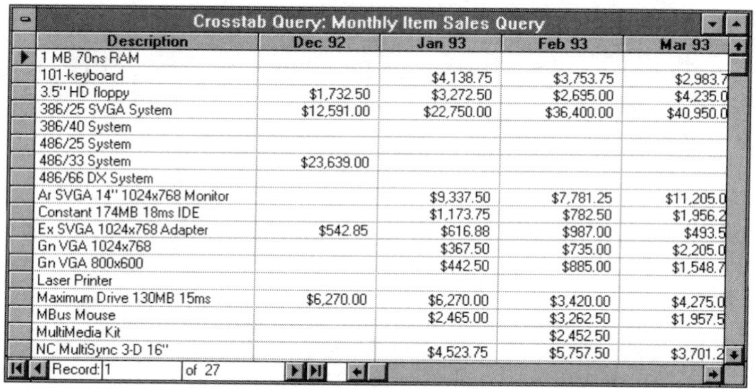

Crosstab Query: Monthly Item Sales Query

Description	Dec 92	Jan 93	Feb 93	Mar 93
1 MB 70ns RAM				
101-keyboard		$4,138.75	$3,753.75	$2,983.7
3.5" HD floppy	$1,732.50	$3,272.50	$2,695.00	$4,235.0
386/25 SVGA System	$12,591.00	$22,750.00	$36,400.00	$40,950.0
386/40 System				
486/25 System				
486/33 System	$23,639.00			
486/66 DX System				
Ar SVGA 14" 1024x768 Monitor		$9,337.50	$7,781.25	$11,205.0
Constant 174MB 18ms IDE		$1,173.75	$782.50	$1,956.2
Ex SVGA 1024x768 Adapter	$542.85	$616.88	$987.00	$493.5
Gn VGA 1024x768		$367.50	$735.00	$2,205.0
Gn VGA 800x600		$442.50	$885.00	$1,548.7
Laser Printer				
Maximum Drive 130MB 15ms	$6,270.00	$6,270.00	$3,420.00	$4,275.0
MBus Mouse		$2,465.00	$3,262.50	$1,957.5
MultiMedia Kit			$2,452.50	
NC MultiSync 3-D 16"		$4,523.75	$5,757.50	$3,701.2

Record: 1 of 27

FIGURE 8-46.
The recordset of the crosstab query shown in Figure 8-45.

NEW!

Using a Query Wizard

All through this chapter, you've seen the tantalizing button in the New Query dialog box labeled *Query Wizards*. You can use the Query Wizards to help you build certain types of "tricky" queries such as crosstab queries and queries to find duplicate rows or unmatched rows. For example, you could have used the Query Wizards to build the query shown in Figure 8-44 to locate customers who have no outstanding orders.

To try this, click the Query tab in the Database window, and then click the New button. This time, click the Query Wizards button in the New Query dialog box. Microsoft Access shows you the Wizard options, as in Figure 8-47.

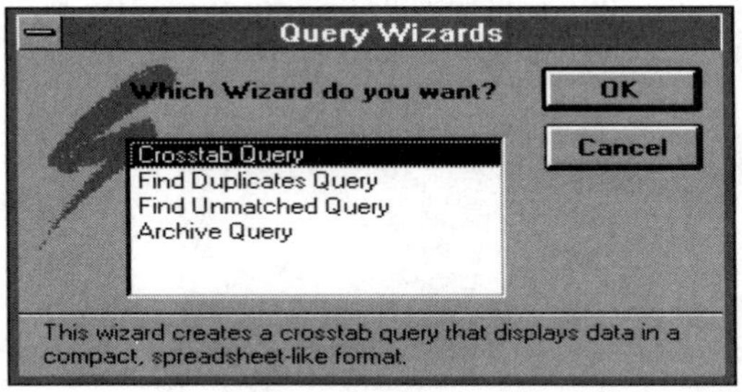

FIGURE 8-47.
Choices of Query Wizards.

Choose the Find Unmatched Query option. In the next dialog box, shown in Figure 8-48, the Query Wizards show a list of tables from which to choose the result rows. If you want to search in an existing query, click the Queries option. If you want to look at all queries and tables, click the Both option. In this case, you're looking for customers who have no outstanding orders, so click on the Customer table and then click the Next button.

In the next dialog box, shown in Figure 8-49, choose the table that contains the related information you expect to be unmatched.

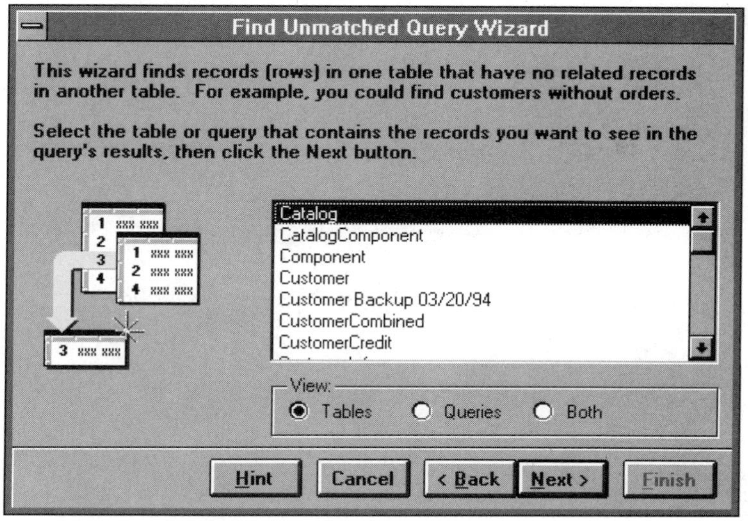

FIGURE 8-48.
The second dialog box in the Find Unmatched Query Wizard.

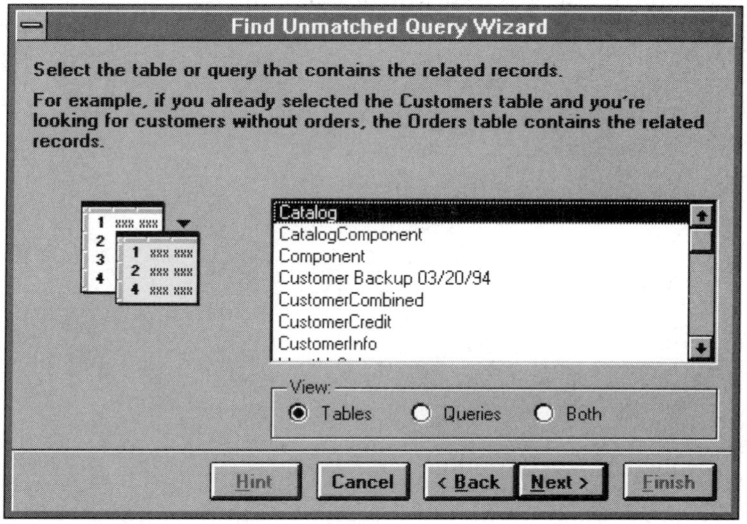

FIGURE 8-49.
The dialog box in which you select the table that contains records related to the table you chose in Figure 8-48.

For this query, you're looking for customers who have no orders outstanding, so click on the Order table and then click the Next button to go to the next dialog box, shown in Figure 8-50 on the next page.

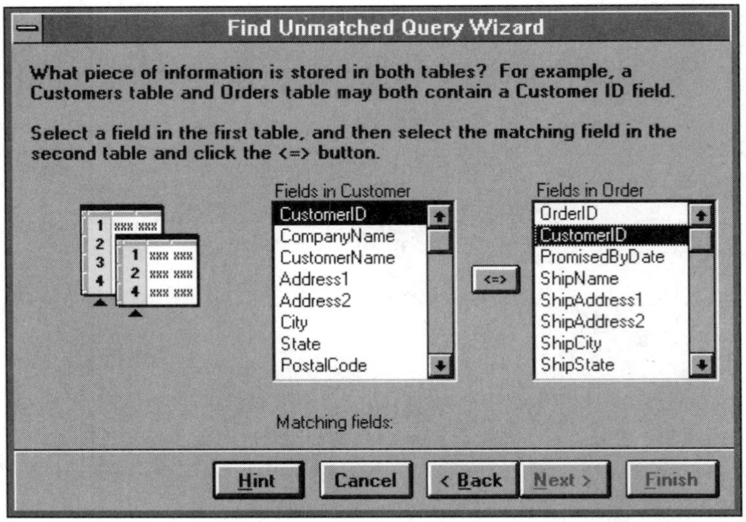

FIGURE 8-50. Defining the unmatched link.

Next, the Wizard needs to know the linking fields between the two tables. If you've defined relationships properly, the Wizard should select the related fields correctly. If you haven't, click the linking field in the first table (Customer) in the left list box, click the linking field for the second table (Order) in the right list box, and then click the <=> button in the center to define the link. Click Next to go on, and the dialog box shown in Figure 8-51 appears.

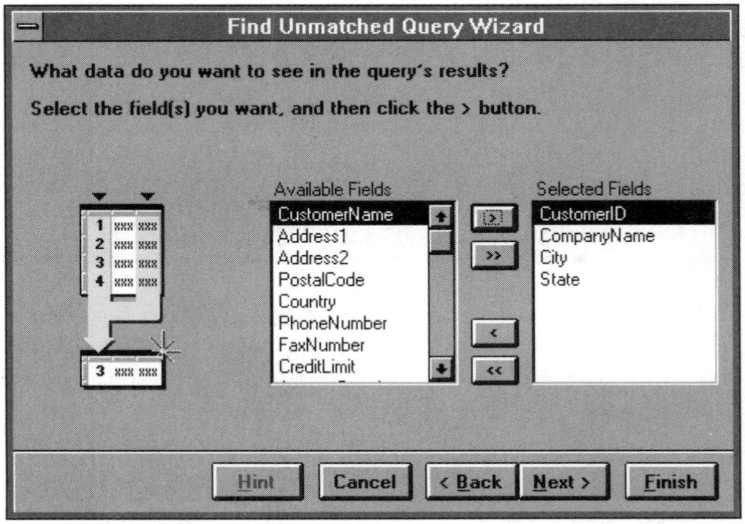

FIGURE 8-51. The dialog box in which you select the fields to be displayed in a query.

Finally, choose the fields you want to display and then tell the Wizard whether you want to open the Query window in Datasheet view or in Design view. Figure 8-52 shows you the query you'll need to find customers who have no orders.

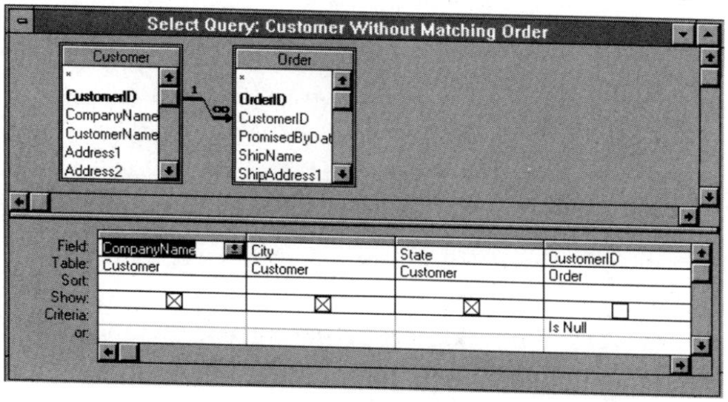

FIGURE 8-52.
A query to find customers who have no orders.

Limitations on Using Select Queries to Update Data

The recordset that Microsoft Access creates when you run a query looks and acts pretty much like a real table containing data. In fact, in most cases you can insert rows, delete rows, and update the information in a recordset, and Access will make the necessary changes to the underlying table or tables for you.

In some cases, however, Access won't be able to figure out what needs to be changed. Consider, for example, any calculated field. If you try to increase the amount in a Total field whose value is a result of multiplying data in the Quantity field by data in the Price field, Access can't know whether you mean to update the Quantity field or the Price field. You can, however, change either the Price field or the Quantity field and then immediately see the change reflected in the calculated Total field.

In addition, Access won't accept any change that might potentially affect many rows in the underlying table. For that reason, you can't change any of the data in a totals query or a crosstab query. Access can't update data in a field that has a Sum or Avg setting when the result might be based on the values in many records.

When working with a recordset that is the result of a join, Access lets you update all fields from the "many" side of a join, but only the nonkey fields on the "one" side. For example, one customer can have many orders. In a recordset that is the result of a join between the Customer and Order tables, you can update any fields that come from the Order table, but you can't update any fields that form the primary key of the Customer table (in this case, the CustomerID field). Access does let you change other fields in the Customer table, such as CustomerName or the address fields.

This ability to update fields on the "one" side of a query could produce unwanted results if you aren't careful. For example, you could intend to assign an order to a different customer. If you change the customer name, you'll be changing that name for all orders related to the current customer ID. What you really need to do is change the customer ID in the Order table, not the customer name in the Customer table. You'll learn techniques later in form design to prevent the inadvertent update of fields in queries.

Customizing Query Properties

Microsoft Access provides a number of properties associated with queries that you can use to control how a query runs. It's worth spending a moment to examine these properties before going on to the next chapter. Figure 8-53 shows the property sheet for select queries.

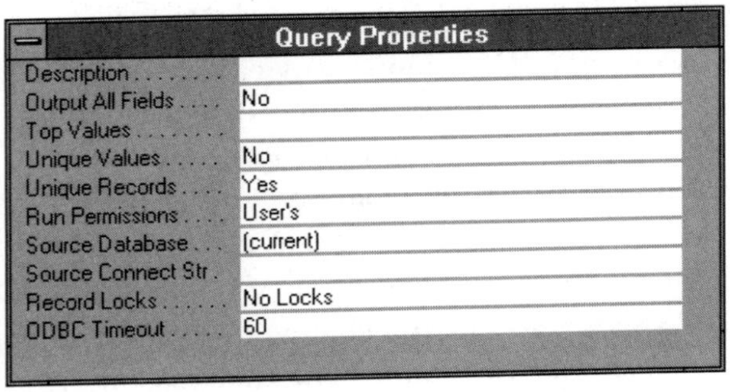

FIGURE 8-53. The property sheet for select queries.

You'll normally select only specific fields that you want returned in the recordset when you run a select query. However, if you're designing the query to be used in a form and you want all fields from all tables in the query available to the form, set the Output All Fields property to Yes. It's a good idea to keep the default setting of No and change this option only on specific queries.

> **TIP:** To open the property sheet for queries, click on the top section of a Query window in Design view outside of the field lists, and then click the Properties button.

When a query is very complex, Access might need several seconds (or perhaps minutes) to find all the rows and begin to display information. If you're interested in only the "first" or "top" rows returned by a query, you can use the Top Values property to tell Access that you want to see information as soon as Access has found the first *n* rows or the first *x*% of rows. If you enter an integer value, Access displays the result when the number of rows specified has been found. If you enter a decimal value of less than 1, Access displays the result when approximately that percentage of rows has been found.

When you're running a query, it's often possible that Microsoft Access can find duplicate rows in the recordset. The default in Access is to return unique records. This means that the identifier for each row (the primary key of the table in a single-table query or the concatenated primary keys of a multiple-table query) is unique. If you don't ask for unique values, Access returns only rows that are different from each other. If you want to see all possible data (including duplicate rows), set both the Unique Values property and the Unique Records property to No. You cannot update fields in a query that has its Unique Records property set to No.

If you have designed your database to be shared by multiple users across a network, you might want to secure the tables and grant access to other users only through queries. The owner of the table always has full access to any table. You can deny access to the tables to everyone and still let authorized users see certain data in the tables. You accomplish this by setting the Run Permissions property to User's. If you want to allow users of this query to "inherit" the owner's permission to access tables when they use this query, set Run Permissions to Owner's.

Use the Record Locks property to control the level of editing integrity when this query is designed to access data that is shared across a network. The default is to not lock any records when the user opens the query. Access applies a lock only when it needs to write a row back to the source table. Choose the Edited Record setting to lock a row as soon as the user begins to enter any changes in that row. The most restrictive locking, All Records, locks every record retrieved by the query as long as the user has the query open. Use this setting only when the query must perform multiple updates to a table and others should not access any data in the table until the query is finished.

The remaining three properties—Source Database, Source Connect Str, and ODBC Timeout—apply to attached tables. See Chapter 10, "Importing, Attaching, and Exporting Data," for details.

Now that you understand the fundamentals of building select queries with Microsoft Access, you're ready to move on to updating sets of data with action queries in the next chapter.

9

Modifying Data with Action Queries

In Chapter 7, "Using Datasheets," you learned how to insert, update, and delete single rows of data within a datasheet. In Chapter 8, "Adding Power with Select Queries," you discovered that you can precisely select the data you want—even from multiple tables—using queries. Now you can take the concept of queries one step further and use *action queries* to quickly change, insert, create, or delete sets of data in your database.

NOTE: This chapter assumes that you're using the tables and data from the PROMPT sample database included on the companion disk that comes with this book.

Updating Groups of Rows

It's easy enough to use a table or a query in Datasheet view to find a single record in your database and change one value. But what if you want to change lots of similar records in the same way? Making changes to one record at a time could be very tedious.

Suppose that, in the Prompt Computer Solutions example, you've just found out that your major competitor is raising its prices on video adapter cards by 12 percent. This sounds like a great opportunity to increase your profit margin, yet remain more than competitive, by raising your prices 10 percent.

It turns out that there are only six video cards in the sample database, but imagine the size of the problem if there were dozens of different ones and you had to calculate the 10 percent addition to price for each item and enter the new values one at a time. Why not let Microsoft Access do them all for you with a single query?

Testing with a Select Query

Before you create and run a query to update lots of records in your database, it's a good idea to create a select query first, using criteria that select the records you want to update. You'll see below that it's easy to convert this select query to an update query or other type of action query, after you're sure Access will be processing the records you want.

It turns out that all video cards in the sample database are listed in the Catalog table and have an ItemTypeCode of 008. You can use that code to select the rows you want to update. You can also include the Type table in the query and add the TypeDescription field to the query to be sure you're getting just the "Video boards." Figure 9-1 shows a select query that includes the Description field (to be doubly sure you have the rows you want), the ItemTypeCode field with a criterion setting of 008, the TypeDescription field, and the Price field that you want to update. (See Chapter 8 if you need to review the process for creating select queries.)

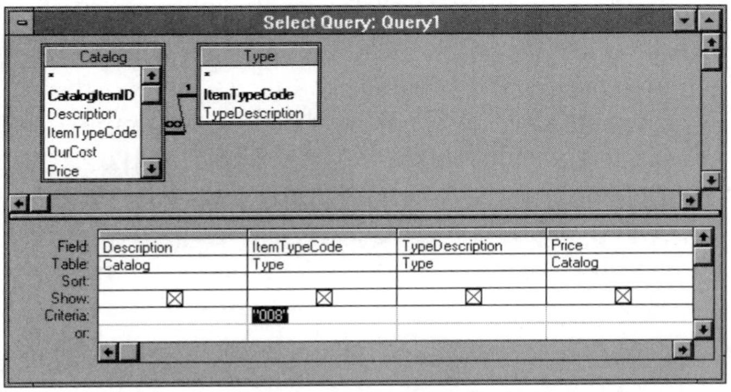

FIGURE 9-1.
A select query to show video card listings and prices.

When you run the query, you'll see the video card records that you want to change, as shown in Figure 9-2.

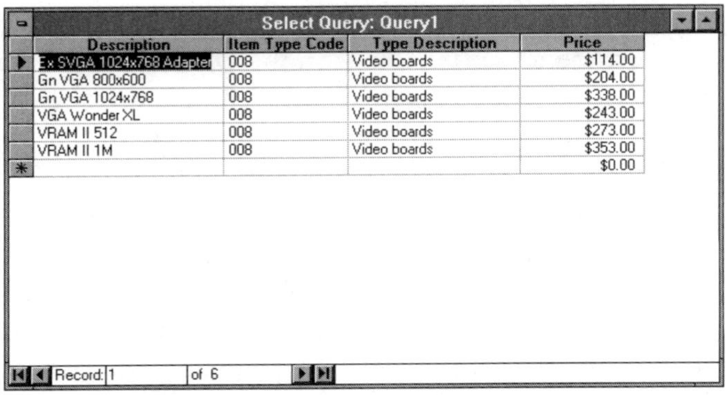

Select Query: Query1

Description	Item Type Code	Type Description	Price
Ex SVGA 1024x768 Adapter	008	Video boards	$114.00
Gn VGA 800x600	008	Video boards	$204.00
Gn VGA 1024x768	008	Video boards	$338.00
VGA Wonder XL	008	Video boards	$243.00
VRAM II 512	008	Video boards	$273.00
VRAM II 1M	008	Video boards	$353.00
			$0.00

Record: 1 of 6

FIGURE 9-2.
The recordset of the select query in Figure 9-1.

TIP: You might have noticed that the query in Figure 9-1 uses the ItemTypeCode field from the Type table instead of the Catalog table. Whenever you want to include an equals search criterion for a field that is used to join two tables, your query will run much faster if you apply the criterion to the field from the "one" side of the join. This is particularly true when you have defined an index on the field in the "one" table. If you ask Microsoft Access to match on the field in the "many" table, Access will generally have to search many more records to find what you want. In addition, it will do a "reverse join" back to the "one" table for each row it finds in the "many" table. This can cause Access to read the same row in the "one" table many times. If you apply the criterion to the "one" table, Access might need to read the row from the "one" side only once (which is exactly the case in this example) and then use available indexes to efficiently link to the rows in the "many" table.

Converting a Select Query to an Update Query

Now you're ready to change the query so that it will update the table. When you first create a query, Microsoft Access creates a select query by default. You can find commands for the four types of action queries—make table, update, append, and delete—on the Query menu when the query is in Design view, as shown in Figure 9-3. Choose the Update command from this menu to convert the test select query to an update query. You can also click the Update Query button on the toolbar.

When you convert your select query to an update query, Access changes the title bar of your Query window in Design view and adds an Update To row in the QBE (query by example) grid. You use this new row to specify how you want your data changed. In this case, you want to add 10 percent to the current price values, so enter *[Price]*1.1* in the Update To row under the Price field, as shown in Figure 9-4. (The *1* equals 100 percent of the current price, and the *.1* equals the 10 percent price increase.)

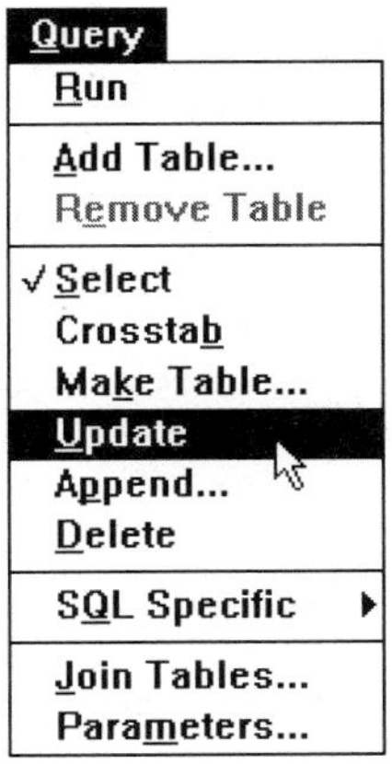

FIGURE 9-3.
The Query menu when the query is in Design view.

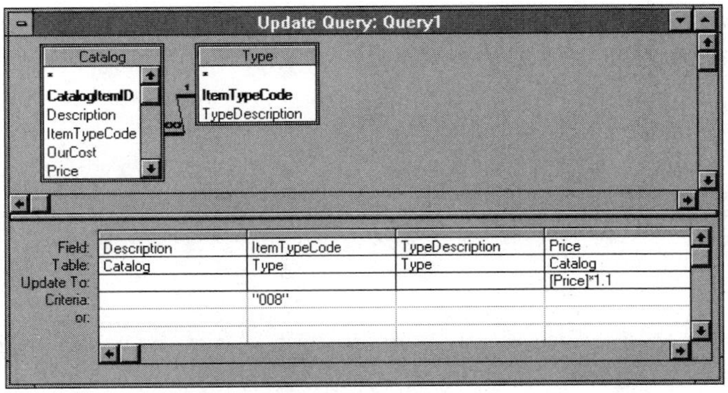

FIGURE 9-4.
An update query with its Update To setting.

Running Your Update Query

If you want to be completely safe, you should make a backup copy of your table before you run your update query. To do that, go to the Database window, select the table you're about to update, and choose the Copy command from the Edit menu. Then choose the Paste command from the Edit menu, and give the copy of your table a different name when Microsoft Access prompts you with a dialog box. Now you're ready to run your update query.

To run your query, choose the Run command from the Query menu or click the Run button on the toolbar. Access first scans your table to determine how many rows will change based on your selection criteria and then displays a dialog box like the one shown in Figure 9-5 on the next page.

You already know that there are six records for video cards in the sample table, so this dialog box suggests that your update query is OK.

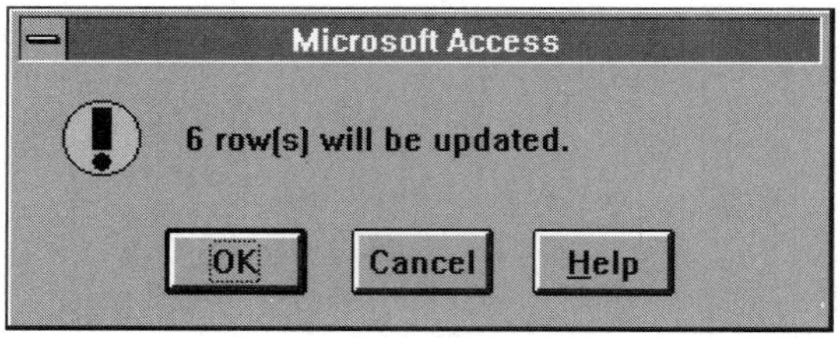

FIGURE 9-5. The dialog box that reports the number of rows to be changed in an update to a table.

To perform the updates, click the OK button in the dialog box. If you don't see the number of rows that you expect or if you're not sure that Access will be updating the correct records or fields, click the Cancel button to stop the query without updating. After the update query runs, you can check the table to confirm that Access made the changes you wanted. Figure 9-6 shows the result—new prices that are 10 percent higher for video cards.

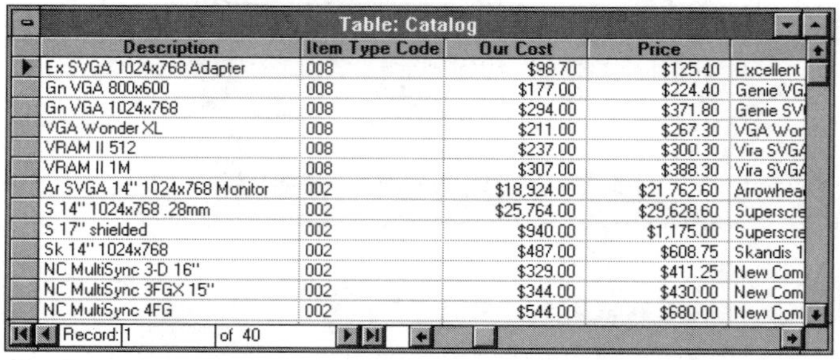

Table: Catalog

Description	Item Type Code	Our Cost	Price	
Ex SVGA 1024x768 Adapter	008	$98.70	$125.40	Excellent
Gn VGA 800x600	008	$177.00	$224.40	Genie VG
Gn VGA 1024x768	008	$294.00	$371.80	Genie SV
VGA Wonder XL	008	$211.00	$267.30	VGA Wor
VRAM II 512	008	$237.00	$300.30	Vira SVGA
VRAM II 1M	008	$307.00	$388.30	Vira SVGA
Ar SVGA 14" 1024x768 Monitor	002	$18,924.00	$21,762.60	Arrowhea
S 14" 1024x768 .28mm	002	$25,764.00	$29,628.60	Superscre
S 17" shielded	002	$940.00	$1,175.00	Superscre
Sk 14" 1024x768	002	$487.00	$608.75	Skandis 1
NC MultiSync 3-D 16"	002	$329.00	$411.25	New Com
NC MultiSync 3FGX 15"	002	$344.00	$430.00	New Com
NC MultiSync 4FG	002	$544.00	$680.00	New Com

Record: 1 of 40

FIGURE 9-6. The updated data in the Catalog table.

If you think you might want to perform this update again, you can save your query and give it a name. In the Database window, Access distinguishes action queries from select queries by displaying a special icon, followed by an exclamation point, before action query names. For example, Access displays a writing pencil and an exclamation point next to the new update query that you've just created. To run your action query again, select it in the Database window and click the Open button. When you run an action query from the Database window, Access displays the action query confirmation dialog box shown in Figure 9-7. Click the OK button to complete the update. If you want to disable this extra confirmation, choose the Options command from the View menu and, in the General category, set Confirm Action Queries to No.

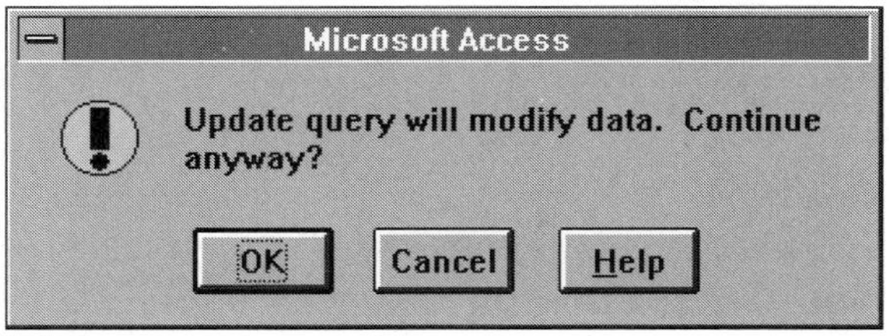

FIGURE 9-7.
The dialog box that confirms action queries.

Updating Multiple Fields

When you create an update query, you aren't limited to changing a single field at a time. You can ask Microsoft Access to update any or all of the fields in the record by including them on the QBE grid and by specifying an update formula. You can also update one field by using a formula that is based on a different field in the record.

When Access is about to update a record in your underlying table or query, it first makes a copy of the original record. Access applies the formulas you specify to the values in the original and places the result in the copy. It then updates your database by writing the updated copy to your table. Because updates are made to the copy from the original, you can, if you want, swap the values in a field named *A* and a field named *B* by specifying an Update To setting of [B] in the A field and an Update To setting of [A] in the B field. If Access were making changes directly to the original copy, you'd need a third field to swap values to because the first assignment of B to A would destroy the original value of A.

If you followed along in Chapters 5 and 6, you built a Customers table in Chapter 5 and entered three rows of data. In Chapter 6, you renamed the Address field *Address2* and created a new Address1 field that could hold a suite number or a company mail stop. You might have later corrected some of the rows to add first-line address information, as shown in Figure 9-8 on the next page.

After you finished this, you might decide that you want the street address information in the Address1 field if there is no special first-line address information. You could open the table in Datasheet view and cut and paste Address2 to Address1 in each row where Address1 is empty.

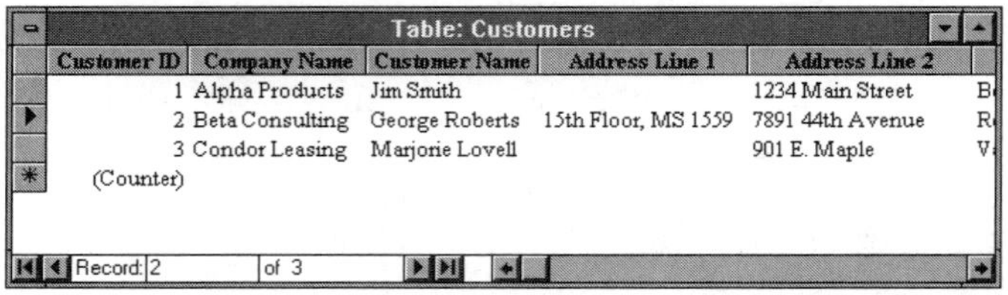

FIGURE 9-8.
A customer (Beta Consulting) with a two-line address.

In this example, with only three rows of data, this process would be quite easy. But if you have several hundred customers, that's a lot of work. Is there an easier way? Yes. An update query to test and update the two fields will do the trick.

To solve this problem, you need to begin designing a new update query based on the Customers table. Drag the Address1 and Address2 fields to the QBE grid. Under Address1, specify Is Null to test for an empty field. When the field is empty, you need the Update To field under Address1 set to [Address2] to copy the data. (You need to place brackets around the field name to let Access know that you're entering a field name and not a literal value.) You also need a value of Null under Address2 to blank out that field. Your query should look something like the one shown in Figure 9-9. After you run the query, your table should look like the one shown in Figure 9-10.

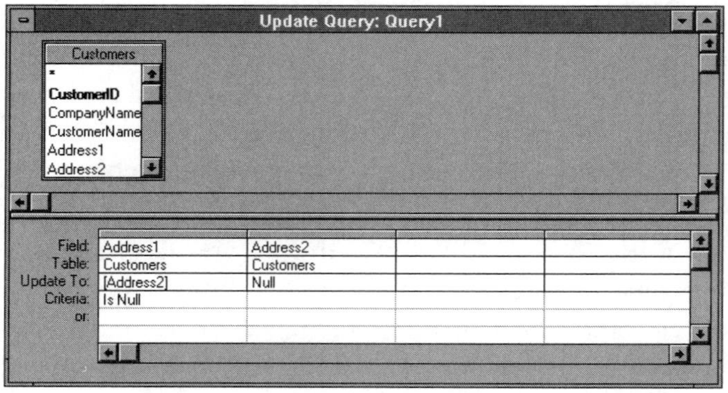

FIGURE 9-9.
A query to update multiple fields.

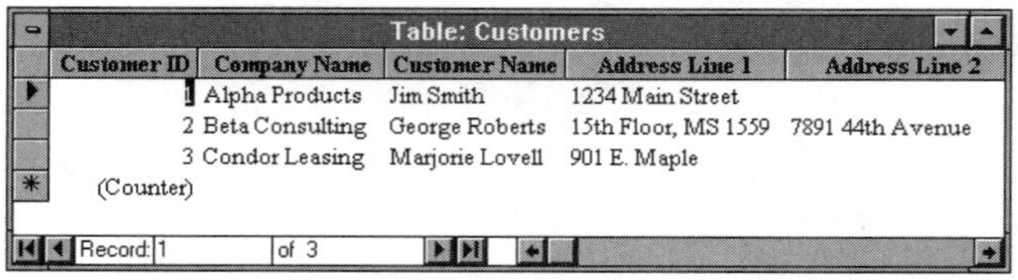

FIGURE 9-10.
The Customers table in Datasheet view after you've run the update query shown in Figure 9-9.

Deleting Groups of Rows

You're not likely to keep forever all the data you collect in your database. You'll probably summarize some of your detailed information as time goes by and then delete the data you no longer need. You can remove sets of records from your database with a type of action query called a *delete query*.

Testing with a Select Query and Parameters

The PROMPT database contains a MonthlySales table. (At the end of this chapter, you'll learn how to summarize sales details into a monthly sales history at the end of each month.) The owners of Prompt Computer Solutions decided that they want to keep information about sales in the database for only a couple of years. So they need a query to selectively delete old data from this table.

This is clearly the kind of query that will be used over and over again. You can design the query to automatically calculate which records to delete based on the current system date and the year and month fields in the records. The query can also be designed with parameters so that a user can specify which data to delete at the time the query is run. Microsoft Access makes it unnecessary to change the query design at each use.

As with an update query, it's a good idea to test which rows will be affected by a delete query by first building a select query to isolate these records. Make a copy of the PROMPT MonthlySales table, and name it *MonthlySalesChap9*. Select the MonthlySalesChap9 table in the PROMPT Database window, and open a new Query window in Design view.

You need only the Year and Month fields on the QBE grid to perform the deletion, but it's useful to include the CatalogItemID field and the QuantitySold field in this select version of the query in order to check out the rows you'll delete. To request that Access prompt you for Year and Month values, add parameters to the Criteria row on the QBE grid, as shown in Figure 9-11 on the next page.

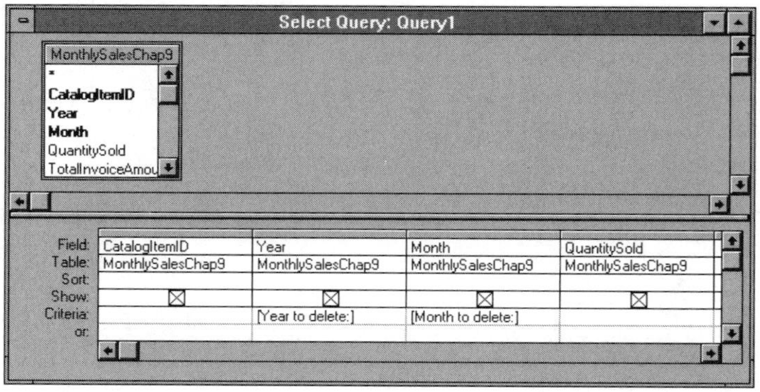

FIGURE 9-11. A query to select monthly sales data to delete. The Criteria row contains parameters that prompt for the year and date. (See Figure 9-12 for the resulting dialog boxes.)

When you run this query, Access prompts you first for the year and then for the month, as shown in Figure 9-12. The entries in the dialog boxes in Figure 9-12 will test the query using December 1992.

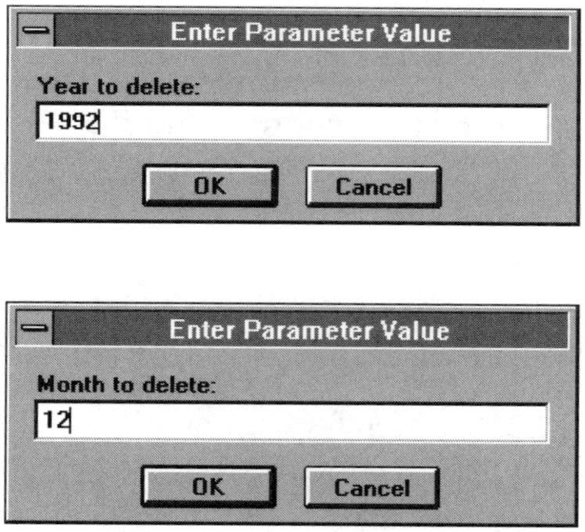

FIGURE 9-12. The two Enter Parameter Value dialog boxes for the query shown in Figure 9-11, with entries that select records for December 1992.

Using the parameter values you entered in Figure 9-12, Access creates the recordset shown in Figure 9-13. Because the recordset shows the rows you want to remove, you can now convert the select query to a delete query and run it to remove these rows.

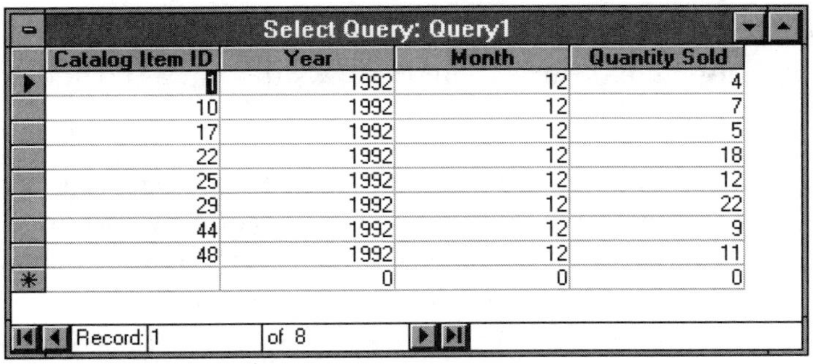

Select Query: Query1

Catalog Item ID	Year	Month	Quantity Sold
1	1992	12	4
10	1992	12	7
17	1992	12	5
22	1992	12	18
25	1992	12	12
29	1992	12	22
44	1992	12	9
48	1992	12	11
	0	0	0

Record: 1 of 8

FIGURE 9-13. The recordset of the select query shown in Figure 9-11 for December 1992.

Running Your Delete Query

Because you won't be able to retrieve any deleted rows, it's a good idea to make a backup copy of your table, especially if this is the first time that you've ever run this delete query. Use the procedure described previously in the section "Running Your Update Query" to make a copy of your table.

You can create a delete query from a select query by choosing the Delete command from the Query menu when your query is in Design view. (See Figure 9-3 on page 267.) You don't have to make any further changes to choose the rows to delete. Simply choose Run from the Query menu or click the Run button on the toolbar to ask Access to delete the rows you've specified. Because you included parameters in this query, you'll need to respond to the two dialog boxes shown in Figure 9-12. Access selects the rows to be deleted and displays the confirmation dialog box shown in Figure 9-14.

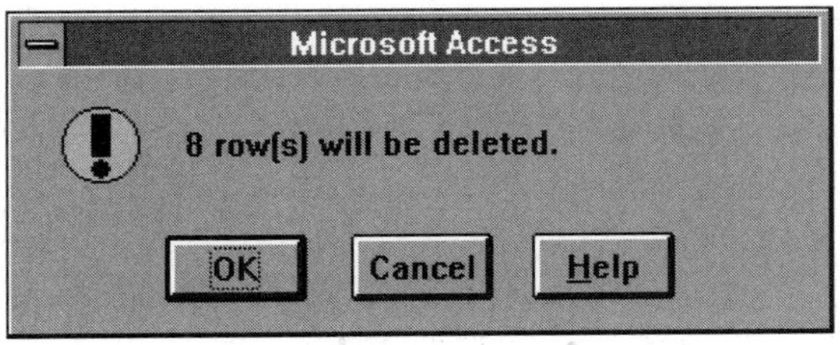

FIGURE 9-14. A dialog box that confirms a deletion.

Click the OK button to complete the deletion of the rows. Click the Cancel button if you're unsure about the rows that Access will delete.

> **TIP:** You can see what rows a delete query will delete by converting the query into a select query and running it. To do so, open the query in Design view and choose the Select command from the Query menu.

Inserting Data from Another Table

Using an append query, you can copy a selected set of information and insert it into another table. (You'll learn how to insert accumulated sales data into a MonthlySalesHistory table in the example at the end of this chapter.) You can also use an append query to bring data from another source into your database—for example, a list of names and addresses purchased from a mailing list company—and then edit the data and insert it into an existing table. In Chapter 10, you'll learn how to import data from external sources.

Creating an Append Query

In Chapter 6, you began creating a Customers table for the PROMPT database. You entered just three records in the Customers table at that time. Earlier in this chapter, you used an update query to modify the two address fields. Suppose you want to expand the PROMPT database to include some of the customer information from the sample NWIND database. You can append the NWIND data to the PROMPT Customers table easily. (You should make a backup copy of the PROMPT Customers table before you start this procedure.)

First, open the NWIND database and select the Customers table in the Database window. Click the New Query button on the toolbar, choose New Query in the New Query dialog box, and choose the Append command from the Query menu (or click the Append Query button on the toolbar). In the Query Properties dialog box, Access prompts you for the name of the table to which you want to append the data, as shown in Figure 9-15. Click the Another Database option, and type the full pathname to your *PROMPT.MDB* file in the File Name box. Click the down arrow next to the Table Name box, and choose Customers from the drop-down list of PROMPT tables. Click OK to close the dialog box.

The QBE grid for the append query is partially shown in Figure 9-16 on the next page. Notice that Access shows you an Append To row. If all the fields in NWIND's Customers table exactly matched those in the PROMPT Customers table, you could simply move the shortcut asterisk field to the grid to indicate that you want to copy all the fields. Because many of the fields don't match, you have to move the ones you want one at a time.

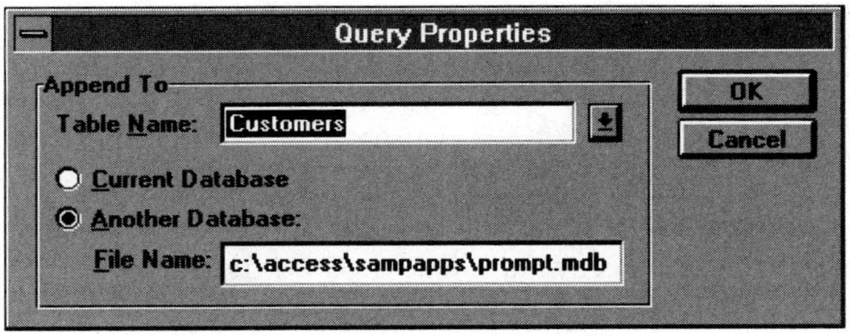

FIGURE 9-15.
The Query Properties dialog box that appears when you choose the Append command.

You don't need the Customer ID field from NWIND's Customers table because the CustomerID in the PROMPT Customers table is a Counter field. Access generates the next value for a Counter field as it inserts new records into the table. When you move the Company Name field, you'll have to enter *CompanyName* in the Append To row or choose it from the drop-down list that appears when you click on the right side of that box on the QBE grid. Likewise, you'll have to map the Contact Name field from NWIND's Customers table to the CustomerName field in PROMPT's Customers table and the Address field from NWIND to the Address1 field in PROMPT. Notice that when you move the City field to the QBE grid, Access guesses that you want to move it to the field with the matching name in the PROMPT Customers table and fills that in for you in the Append To row.

FIGURE 9-16.
An append query in Design view.

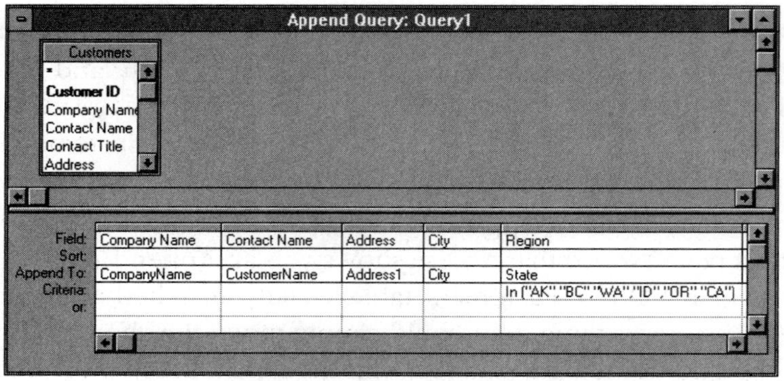

Other fields that you'll need to map from NWIND to PROMPT include Region to State, Postal Code to PostalCode, Phone to PhoneNumber, and Fax to FaxNumber. For fields that exist in PROMPT but not in NWIND, Microsoft Access will store the default value (if defined) for each of those fields as it copies new records into PROMPT. Although the default CreditLimit in the PROMPT Customers table is $10,000, you might want to assign a different limit, depending on the source of your customer list. For example, you can set the credit limit for these new customers to $5,000 by selecting a blank field on the query grid, typing in the value *5000,* and entering *[CreditLimit]* in the Append To row.

You can also specify selection criteria on the QBE grid. Because Prompt Computer Solutions is a small company with customers only on the west coast of the United States and Canada, you should add a criterion under the Region field to choose rows from "AK", "BC", "WA", "ID", "OR", and "CA", as shown in Figure 9-16.

Running an Append Query

As with other action queries, you can run an append query as a select query first to be sure you will be copying the rows you want. However, Access doesn't retain the name mappings when you switch to a select query and back; you'll have to rebuild the mappings of field names between the two tables if you run the query as a select query before you run it as an append query. Although you can find and delete rows you append in error, you can save time if you make a backup of the receiving table first.

To run your completed append query, simply choose the Run command from the Query menu or click the Run button on the toolbar. Access displays a count of the new records, as shown in the dialog box in Figure 9-17.

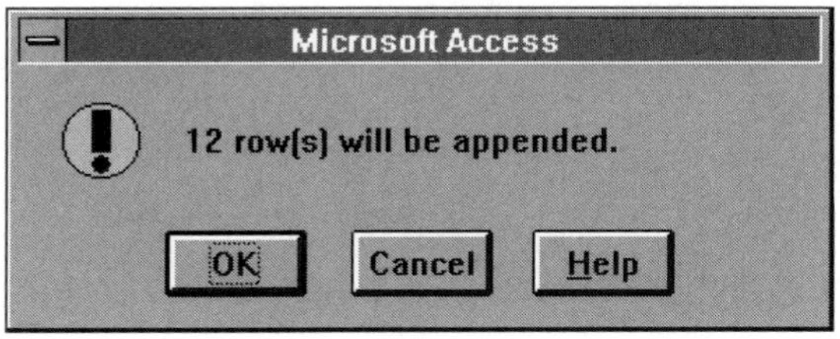

FIGURE 9-17. The dialog box that informs you of the results of an append query.

Click the OK button to append the new rows. Click the Cancel button if you're not sure you want Access to finish appending the new rows.

After you run this append query, open the Customers table in the PROMPT database in Datasheet view. You should see a display similar to the one shown in Figure 9-18. The sample here includes rows that were originally in the PROMPT Customers table, followed by the customer information from the Customers table in NWIND.

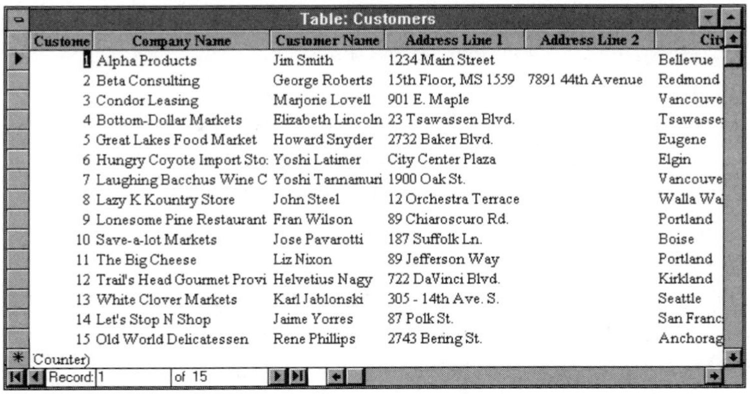

Table: Customers

Custome	Company Name	Customer Name	Address Line 1	Address Line 2	City
1	Alpha Products	Jim Smith	1234 Main Street		Bellevue
2	Beta Consulting	George Roberts	15th Floor, MS 1559	7891 44th Avenue	Redmond
3	Condor Leasing	Marjorie Lovell	901 E. Maple		Vancouve
4	Bottom-Dollar Markets	Elizabeth Lincoln	23 Tsawassen Blvd.		Tsawasse
5	Great Lakes Food Market	Howard Snyder	2732 Baker Blvd.		Eugene
6	Hungry Coyote Import Sto	Yoshi Latimer	City Center Plaza		Elgin
7	Laughing Bacchus Wine C	Yoshi Tannamuri	1900 Oak St.		Vancouve
8	Lazy K Kountry Store	John Steel	12 Orchestra Terrace		Walla Wa
9	Lonesome Pine Restaurant	Fran Wilson	89 Chiaroscuro Rd.		Portland
10	Save-a-lot Markets	Jose Pavarotti	187 Suffolk Ln.		Boise
11	The Big Cheese	Liz Nixon	89 Jefferson Way		Portland
12	Trail's Head Gourmet Provi	Helvetius Nagy	722 DaVinci Blvd.		Kirkland
13	White Clover Markets	Karl Jablonski	305 - 14th Ave. S.		Seattle
14	Let's Stop N Shop	Jaime Yorres	87 Polk St.		San Franc
15	Old World Delicatessen	Rene Phillips	2743 Bering St.		Anchorag
(Counter)					

Record: 1 of 15

FIGURE 9-18. The PROMPT Customers table (rows 1–3) with customer information appended from NWIND (rows 4–15).

Creating a New Table with a Query

Sometimes you might like to save as a real table the data that you extract with a select query. If you find that you keep executing the same query over and over against data that isn't changing, it can be faster to access the data from a real table rather than from the query, particularly if the query must join several tables. Saving a query as a table is also useful for gathering summary information that you intend to keep long after you delete the detailed data on which the query is based.

Creating a Make Table Query

Assume that at the end of each year, you want to create and save a table for Prompt Computer Solutions that summarizes the sales for the year. The MonthlySales table contains the totals by month that must be calculated and saved in this summary. Just to make it interesting, you also need to pick up the Description field from the Catalog table. This is a good idea because you might want to keep the table of annual totals for a long time. Two or three years from now, Prompt Computer Solutions might no longer carry a particular item, and the description will have disappeared from the current Catalog table. A later query on this annual summary won't be able to retrieve a meaningful description unless you save the Description field now.

Start by creating the following query for the MonthlySales and Catalog tables. (See Chapter 8 if you need to review the process for creating a query.) Click the Totals button on the toolbar or choose the Totals command from the View menu in order to total the information for an entire year. Drag the CatalogItemID field from the MonthlySales table; the Description field from the Catalog table; and then the Year field, the QuantitySold field, the TotalInvoiceAmount field, and the TotalCost field from the MonthlySales table to the QBE grid. Change the Total row under the QuantitySold, the TotalInvoiceAmount, and the TotalCost fields to *Sum*. (See Figure 9-19.) You should also give these total fields a new name; otherwise, Access will name them SumOfQuantitySold, SumOfTotal, InvoiceAmount, and SumOfTotalCost in the resulting table. Enter the year you want to summarize in the Criteria row for the Year field. You can also create a parameter so that Access will prompt you for the year value when you run the query. (See Figures 9-11 and 9-12 on page 272 for an example of how to do this.)

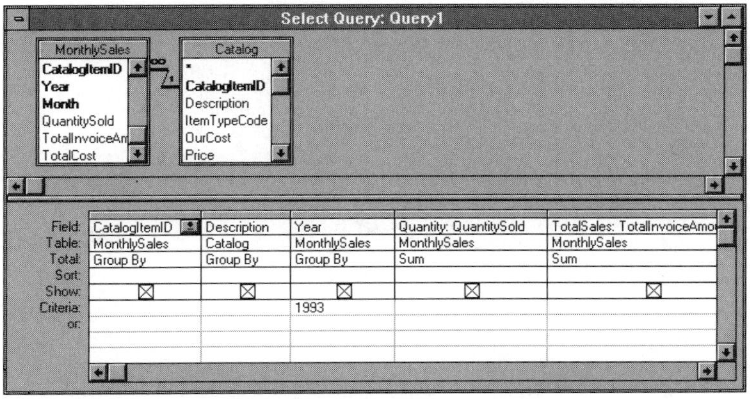

FIGURE 9-19.
The query that can be used to make a table of 1993 sales.

If you like, you can run this query to verify that you'll get the rows you want. To convert this select query to a make table query, choose the Make Table command from the Query menu. Access displays the Query Properties dialog box shown in Figure 9-20. Type an appropriate name for the summary table you are creating, and click OK to close the dialog box.

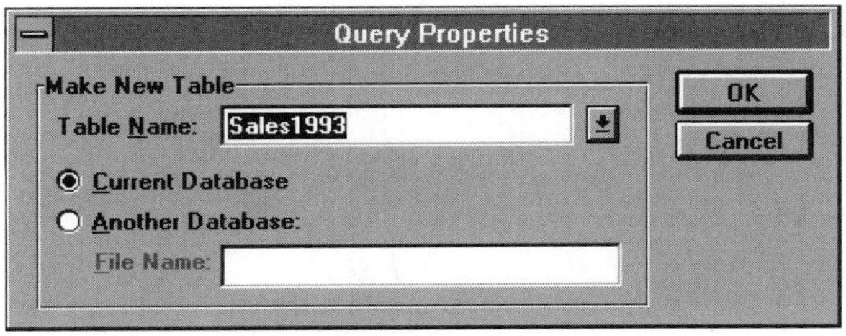

FIGURE 9-20.
The Query Properties dialog box for the Make Table command.

You can reopen this dialog box to change the name of the table you want to create. Choose the Query Properties command from the View menu whenever the query is in Design view.

Running a Make Table Query

After you have set up your make table query, you can run it by choosing Run from the Query menu or by clicking the Run button on the toolbar.

Access creates the records that will be inserted in the new table and displays a dialog box, as shown in Figure 9-21, to inform you of how many rows you'll be creating in the new table.

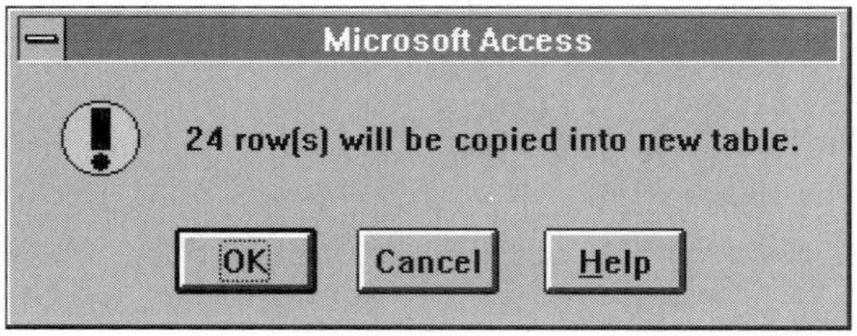

FIGURE 9-21. The dialog box that confirms the results of a make table query.

Click the OK button to create your new table and insert the rows. Switch to the Database window and click the Table tab to bring up the table list, and you should see your new table. Open the new table in Datasheet view to verify the information, shown in Figure 9-22. You might want to switch to Design view to correct field names or define formatting information. Microsoft Access copies only basic field attributes when creating your new table.

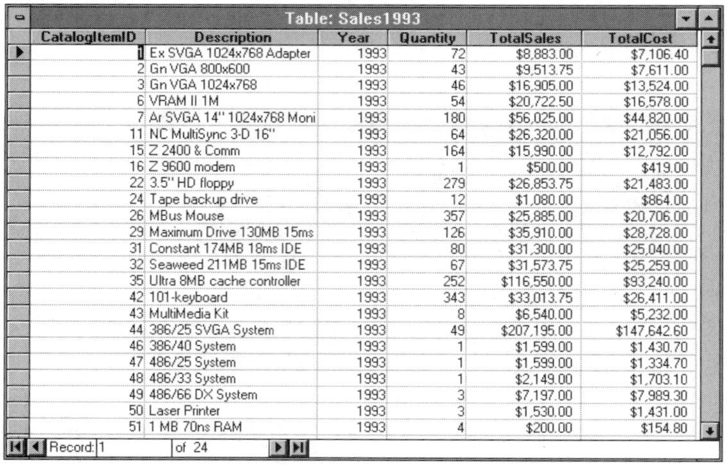

Table: Sales1993

CatalogItemID	Description	Year	Quantity	TotalSales	TotalCost
1	Ex SVGA 1024x768 Adapter	1993	72	$8,883.00	$7,106.40
2	Gn VGA 800x600	1993	43	$9,513.75	$7,611.00
3	Gn VGA 1024x768	1993	46	$16,905.00	$13,524.00
6	VRAM II 1M	1993	54	$20,722.50	$16,578.00
7	Ar SVGA 14" 1024x768 Moni	1993	180	$56,025.00	$44,820.00
11	NC MultiSync 3-D 16"	1993	64	$26,320.00	$21,056.00
15	Z 2400 & Comm	1993	164	$15,990.00	$12,792.00
16	Z 9600 modem	1993	1	$500.00	$419.00
22	3.5" HD floppy	1993	279	$26,853.75	$21,483.00
24	Tape backup drive	1993	12	$1,080.00	$864.00
26	MBus Mouse	1993	357	$25,885.00	$20,706.00
29	Maximum Drive 130MB 15ms	1993	126	$35,910.00	$28,728.00
31	Constant 174MB 18ms IDE	1993	80	$31,300.00	$25,040.00
32	Seaweed 211MB 15ms IDE	1993	67	$31,573.75	$25,259.00
35	Ultra 8MB cache controller	1993	252	$116,550.00	$93,240.00
42	101-keyboard	1993	343	$33,013.75	$26,411.00
43	MultiMedia Kit	1993	8	$6,540.00	$5,232.00
44	386/25 SVGA System	1993	49	$207,195.00	$147,642.60
46	386/40 System	1993	1	$1,599.00	$1,430.70
47	486/25 System	1993	1	$1,599.00	$1,334.70
48	486/33 System	1993	1	$2,149.00	$1,703.10
49	486/66 DX System	1993	3	$7,197.00	$7,989.30
50	Laser Printer	1993	3	$1,530.00	$1,431.00
51	1 MB 70ns RAM	1993	4	$200.00	$154.80

Record: 1 of 24

FIGURE 9-22. The results of the make table query shown in Figure 9-21.

Troubleshooting Action Queries

Microsoft Access analyzes your action query request and the data you are about to change before it commits changes to your database. When errors are identified, Access always gives you an opportunity to cancel the operation before proceeding with your action query.

Common Action Query Errors and Problems

Microsoft Access identifies *(traps)* four categories of errors during the execution of an action query:

1. *Duplicate primary keys.* This category of error occurs if you attempt to append a record to a table or update a record in a table when the result is a duplicate primary key or a duplicate of a unique index key value. Access will not update or append those rows that would create duplicate values in primary keys or unique indexes. For example, if the primary key of an employee table is employee ID, Access won't let you append a record that contains an employee ID already in the table. Before attempting to append the rows, you might have to change the primary key values in the source table to avoid the conflict.
2. *Data conversion errors.* This category of error occurs when you are inserting (appending) data to an existing table and the data type of the receiving field does not match that of the sending field (and the data in the sending field cannot be transformed into the appropriate data type). For example, if you're appending a text field to an integer field and the text field contains either alphabetic characters or a number string that is too large for the integer field, the error will occur. You can also encounter a conversion error in an update query if you use a formula that attempts a calculation on a field that contains characters. (For information on conversions and potential limitations, see Figure 6-17 in Chapter 6, "Modifying Your Database Design.")

3. *Locked records.* This category of error occurs when you're running a delete query or an update query on a table that you share with other users on a network. Access cannot update records that are in the process of being updated by others. You might want to wait and try again later to be sure your update or deletion occurs when no one else is using the affected records.
4. *Validation rule violations.* If any of the rows being inserted or any row being updated violates either a field validation rule or the table validation rule, Access notifies you of the error and does not insert or update any of the rows.

Another problem that occurs, although it isn't an error as such, is that Access might truncate data being appended to text or memo fields if the data does not fit. Access does not warn you when this happens. You must be sure (especially with append queries) that the receiving text and memo fields have been defined as large enough to store the incoming data.

An Error Example

Earlier in this chapter, in the section called "Inserting Data from Another Table," you saw how to append customer data from the NWIND database to the PROMPT database using an append query. At the time there were no problems with duplicate primary key values because the PROMPT Customers table was designed with a counter as the primary key. Also, the data types and lengths of the fields in the two tables matched.

But assume that the primary key (the CustomerID field) for the Customers table in PROMPT is a five-character text field just like the primary key in the Customers table in NWIND. And suppose you started with four records in the PROMPT Customers table, as shown in Figure 9-23.

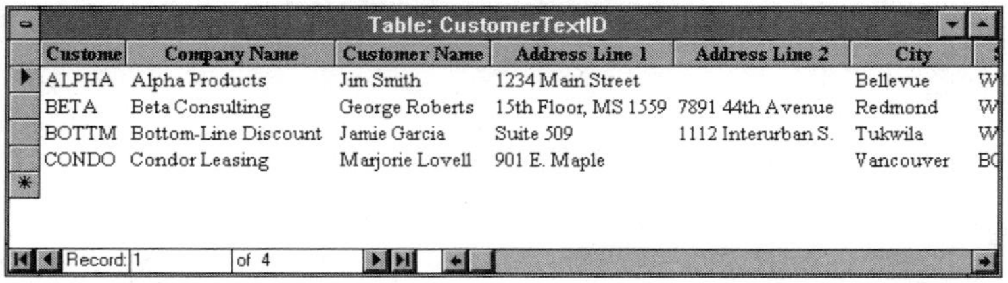
Table: CustomerTextID

Custome	Company Name	Customer Name	Address Line 1	Address Line 2	City	
ALPHA	Alpha Products	Jim Smith	1234 Main Street		Bellevue	W
BETA	Beta Consulting	George Roberts	15th Floor, MS 1559	7891 44th Avenue	Redmond	W
BOTTM	Bottom-Line Discount	Jamie Garcia	Suite 509	1112 Interurban S.	Tukwila	W
CONDO	Condor Leasing	Marjorie Lovell	901 E. Maple		Vancouver	BC

Record: 1 of 4

FIGURE 9-23. The PROMPT Customers table with a primary key (the CustomerID field) similar to the one in the NWIND Customers table.

In this append query, you'll need the Customer ID field from the Customers table in NWIND. Notice that there is a duplicate of one of the primary key values from the NWIND Customers table—BOTTM. In addition, imagine that the data type of the PhoneNumber field in the PROMPT Customers table had been changed from Text to Double. In NWIND you'll find that the phone numbers in the Customers table are really text fields with embedded parentheses and hyphens. Now if you try to append 12 records from the Customers table in NWIND to the Customers table in PROMPT, Access displays the dialog box shown in Figure 9-24.

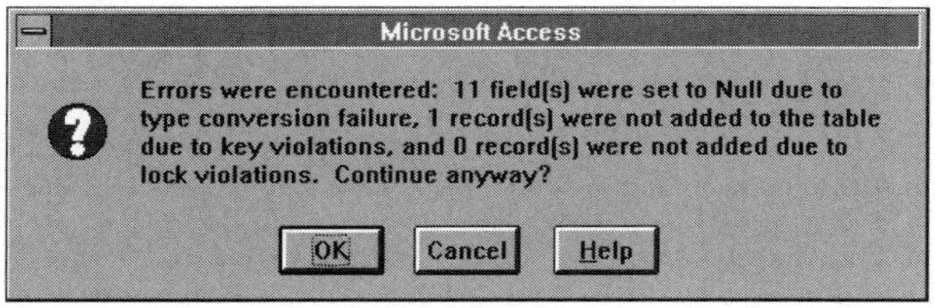

FIGURE 9-24.
The dialog box that declares there were action query errors.

The dialog box declares that one record won't be inserted; this error is the result of a duplicate primary key. Access also found 11 phone numbers in the rows selected from NWIND that can't be converted to a Double data type. Because this table isn't shared on a network, there aren't any locking errors. When you see this dialog box, you can click the OK button to proceed with the changes that Access can make without errors. You might find it difficult, however, to track down all the records that will not be updated successfully. Click the Cancel button to abort the append query.

If you clicked the OK button, you would see the result shown in Figure 9-25 on the next page. There's a BOTTM record, but it's the one that was in the PROMPT Customers table before running the append query, not the new record from NWIND. In Figure 9-25 the first four columns are frozen and the datasheet is scrolled to reveal that none of the records appended from NWIND have telephone numbers.

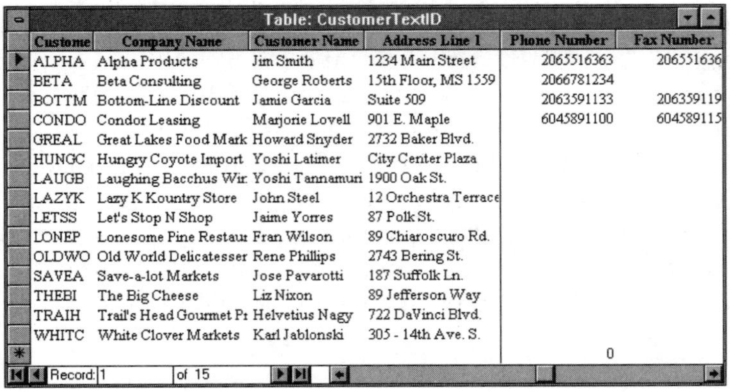

Table: CustomerTextID

Custome	Company Name	Customer Name	Address Line 1	Phone Number	Fax Number
ALPHA	Alpha Products	Jim Smith	1234 Main Street	2065516363	206551636
BETA	Beta Consulting	George Roberts	15th Floor, MS 1559	2066781234	
BOTTM	Bottom-Line Discount	Jamie Garcia	Suite 509	2063591133	206359119
CONDO	Condor Leasing	Marjorie Lovell	901 E. Maple	6045891100	604589115
GREAL	Great Lakes Food Mark	Howard Snyder	2732 Baker Blvd.		
HUNGC	Hungry Coyote Import	Yoshi Latimer	City Center Plaza		
LAUGB	Laughing Bacchus Wir	Yoshi Tannamuri	1900 Oak St.		
LAZYK	Lazy K Kountry Store	John Steel	12 Orchestra Terrace		
LETSS	Let's Stop N Shop	Jaime Yorres	87 Polk St.		
LONEP	Lonesome Pine Restau	Fran Wilson	89 Chiaroscuro Rd.		
OLDWO	Old World Delicatesser	Rene Phillips	2743 Bering St.		
SAVEA	Save-a-lot Markets	Jose Pavarotti	187 Suffolk Ln.		
THEBI	The Big Cheese	Liz Nixon	89 Jefferson Way		
TRAIH	Trail's Head Gourmet Pr	Helvetius Nagy	722 DaVinci Blvd.		
WHITC	White Clover Markets	Karl Jablonski	305 - 14th Ave. S.		
*				0	

Record: 1 of 15

FIGURE 9-25. The result of an append query after the errors declared in Figure 9-24 are accepted.

Example: Summarizing Detailed Sales by Month

Looking at individual action query examples is useful. Real business problems, however, are rarely as simple as a single query. To help you see some of the real potential of action queries, here's an example that shows how you might total some detailed sales figures and then append the result to a monthly history table.

Here's the problem statement: At the end of each month, Prompt Computer Solutions would like to total all the sales by item and save the result in a monthly sales total table. The first step is to build a query to calculate the totals. The second step is to convert the totals query to insert (append) the calculated totals into a history table. The next two sections describe how to accomplish these tasks.

Building a Query That Will Total Sales

To build a query that will total sales, start by opening a new Query window in Design view and including the Order, OrderItem, and Catalog tables. If you defined the relationships between the tables correctly, you should see relationship lines between the Order table and the OrderItem table in the OrderID field and between the OrderItem table and the Catalog table in the CatalogItemID field. At this point you need to click the Totals button on the toolbar (or choose the Totals command from the View menu) to add the Total row to the QBE grid.

You need the CatalogItemID field, so drag that field from either the OrderItem or the Catalog table to the QBE grid. Next, you need a Year field, so extract the year from the OrderDate field in the Order table by using the *Year* function. The entry on the QBE grid is *Year: Year([OrderDate])*. Similarly, you can use the *Month* function in the OrderDate field in the Order table to get the month of the order. The entry on the QBE grid is *Month: Month([OrderDate])*. Add parameters in the Criteria row to prompt for the year and month values when you run the query. Next, drag the Quantity field from the OrderItem table to the QBE grid. Set the Total row for the Quantity field to Sum, as shown in Figure 9-26.

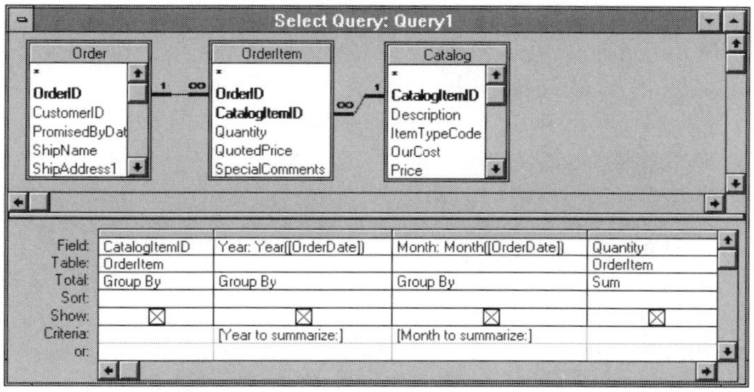

FIGURE 9-26.
The first four fields of the query that will generate monthly sales totals.

To get the total invoice amount, first create an expression that multiplies the Quantity field by the QuotedPrice field (both from the OrderItem table). The product is the invoice amount per item. You use the *Sum* function to calculate the total invoice amount from the per-item invoice amounts. To get the total cost, you need to create an expression that multiplies the Quantity field from the OrderItem table by the OurCost field from the Catalog table. When you're done you need to use the *Sum* function again to calculate the total cost from these costs per item. These fields on your QBE grid should look like the ones shown in Figure 9-27 on the next page.

Because the two query parameters are to be compared to values calculated from a function, you should define the data types for these parameters so that Microsoft Access can successfully compare the values you supply with the values returned from the functions. The *Year*

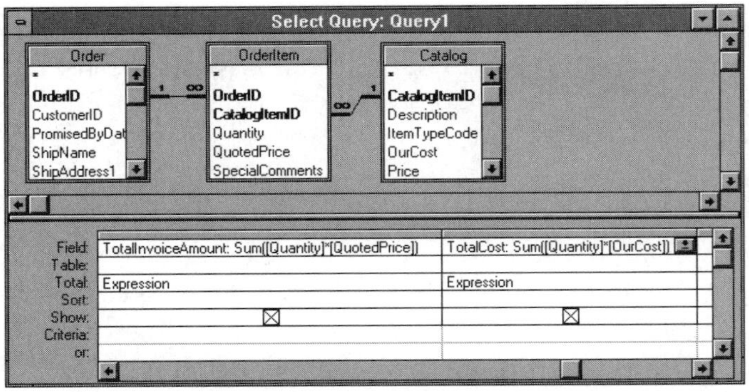

FIGURE 9-27. The last two fields of the query that will generate monthly sales totals.

and *Month* functions both return the Integer data type, so you should use the Integer data type for the two parameters in the Query Parameters dialog box, as shown in Figure 9-28.

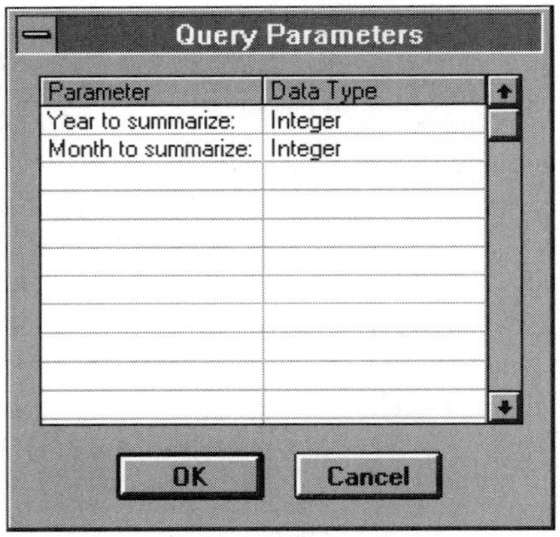

FIGURE 9-28. The data type settings for the parameters in the Figure 9-27 query.

Before converting this query to an append query, it's a good idea to run it as a select query to see whether you're getting the results you expect. Use the month of June 1994 for the prompts when you run the query. You can see the recordset shown in Figure 9-29.

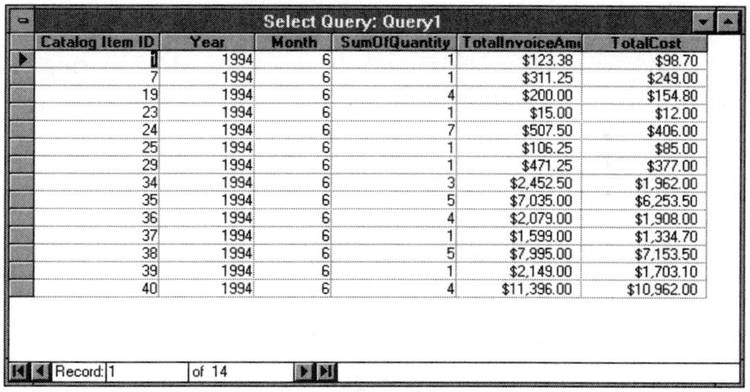

Catalog Item ID	Year	Month	SumOfQuantity	TotalInvoiceAm	TotalCost
1	1994	6	1	$123.38	$98.70
7	1994	6	1	$311.25	$249.00
19	1994	6	4	$200.00	$154.80
23	1994	6	1	$15.00	$12.00
24	1994	6	7	$507.50	$406.00
25	1994	6	1	$106.25	$85.00
29	1994	6	1	$471.25	$377.00
34	1994	6	3	$2,452.50	$1,962.00
35	1994	6	5	$7,035.00	$6,253.50
36	1994	6	4	$2,079.00	$1,908.00
37	1994	6	1	$1,599.00	$1,334.70
38	1994	6	5	$7,995.00	$7,153.50
39	1994	6	1	$2,149.00	$1,703.10
40	1994	6	4	$11,396.00	$10,962.00

FIGURE 9-29.
A test of the monthly sales summary generated by the select query in Figures 9-26 and 9-27.

Appending Totals to a Monthly Sales History Table

Creating a query to calculate monthly totals is only half the job. Now you need to convert the query to append rows to the monthly sales summary for the year. To do that, choose Append from the Query menu or click the Append Query button on the toolbar. Access responds with the Query Properties dialog box shown in Figure 9-30 to prompt you for the name of the table to which you want to append the total results. Enter *MonthlySalesHistory* in the dialog box.

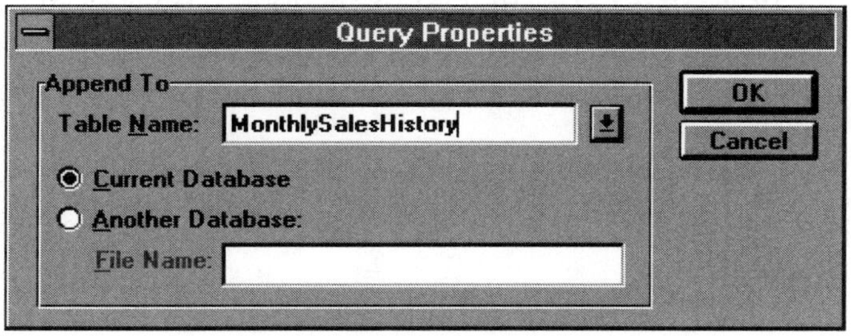

FIGURE 9-30.
The Query Properties dialog box for an append query.

When you run this query, you should see all the rows generated in the Totals query appended (added) to the MonthlySalesHistory table. If you use 1993 for the year and 6 for the month, you'll see the confirmation dialog box shown in Figure 9-31. Click OK to append the rows to the summary table.

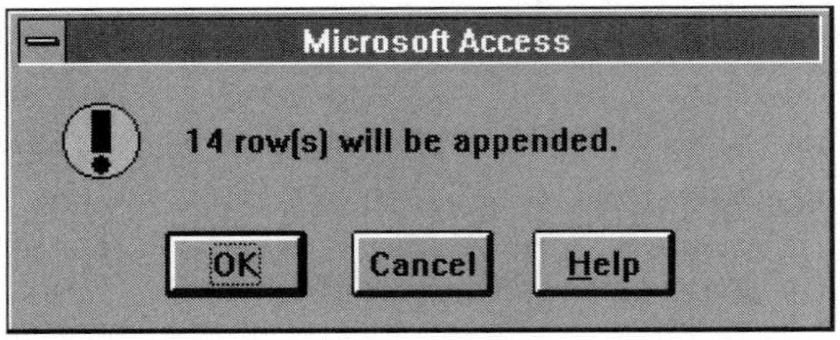

FIGURE 9-31.
A confirmation of summary rows to be appended.

See Also: For more examples of action queries, see Chapter 11, "Advanced Query Design—SQL."

At this point, you should have a reasonable understanding of how action queries can work for you. In the next chapter, you'll learn how to incorporate data from outside sources—text files, spreadsheets, other Microsoft Access databases, or data from other database management systems.

10

Importing, Attaching, and Exporting Data

Although you can use Microsoft Access as a self-contained database and application system, one of the primary strengths of the product (as its name implies) is that it allows you to work with many kinds of data in other databases, spreadsheets, or text files. In addition to using data in your local Microsoft Access database, you can *import* (copy in) or *attach* (connect to) data that's in other Access databases, dBASE files, Paradox files, FoxPro files, Btrieve files, and any other SQL database that supports the Open Database Connectivity (ODBC) software standard. You can also *export* (copy out) data from Access tables to the databases, spreadsheets, or text files of other applications.

A Word About Open Database Connectivity (ODBC)

If you look under the covers of Microsoft Access, you'll find that it uses a database language called *SQL (Structured Query Language)* to read, insert, update, and delete data. You can see the SQL statements that Microsoft Access uses by choosing the SQL command from the View menu or by clicking the SQL button whenever you're viewing a Query window in Design view. SQL grew out of a relational database research project conducted by IBM in the 1970s. It has been adopted as an official standard for relational databases by organizations such as the American National Standards Institute (ANSI) and the International Standards Organization (ISO).

See Also: Chapter 11, "Advanced Query Design—SQL," contains more details on how Microsoft Access uses SQL.

In an ideal world, any product that "speaks" SQL should be able to "talk" to any other product that understands SQL. You should be able to build an application that can work with the data in several relational database management systems using the same database language. Although standards exist for SQL, the reality is that most software companies have implemented variations on or extensions to the language to handle specific features of their products. Also, several products evolved before standards were well established, so the companies producing those products invented their own syntax, which differs from the adopted standard. An SQL statement intended to be executed by Microsoft SQL Server might require modification before it can be executed by other databases that support SQL, such as DB2 or Oracle or Rdb.

To solve this problem, several years ago a large group of influential hardware and software companies—more than 30 of them, including Microsoft Corporation—formed the SQL Access Group. Their goal was to define a common base SQL implementation that they could all use to "talk" to one another. They jointly developed the *Common Language Interface (CLI)* for all the major variants of SQL, and these companies committed themselves to building in support for their products that would allow any application using the CLI to work with their databases. About a dozen of these software companies jointly demonstrated this capability in early 1992.

In the meantime, Microsoft formalized the CLI for workstations and announced that all of its products—especially those designed for the Microsoft Windows operating system—would use this interface to access any SQL database. Microsoft has called this formalized interface the *Open Database Connectivity (ODBC)* standard. In the spring of 1992, Microsoft announced that more than a dozen database and application software vendors had committed to providing ODBC support in their products by the end of 1992. With Microsoft Access version 2, Microsoft is providing the basic ODBC driver manager and the driver to translate ODBC SQL to the Microsoft SQL Server and the Sybase SQL Server. Microsoft also has worked with several database vendors to develop drivers for other databases. The ODBC architecture is represented in Figure 10-1.

Microsoft Access is one of Microsoft's first ODBC-compliant products. You have an option to install ODBC when you install Access on your computer. Once you've added the drivers for the other SQL databases that you want to access, you can use Microsoft Access to build an application using data from any of these databases.

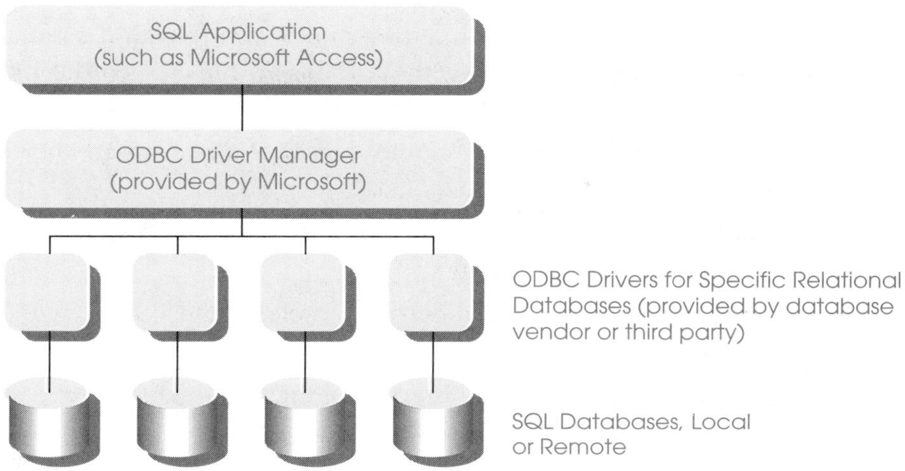

FIGURE 10-1.
The Microsoft Open Database Connectivity (ODBC) architecture.

See Also: Appendix A, "Installing Microsoft Access," contains details about installing and managing ODBC drivers on your computer.

Importing vs. Attaching Database Files

Because you have the choice of importing or attaching data from other databases, how can you know which type of access is best? Here are some guidelines.

Consider *importing* another database file when any of the following are true:

- The file you need is relatively small and is not changed frequently by users of the other database application.
- You don't need to share the data you create with users of the other database application.
- You're replacing the old database application, and you won't need to have the data in the old format any longer.

- You need the best performance while working with the data in the other database (because Access performs best with a local copy of the data in its native format).

On the other hand, you should consider *attaching* another database file when any of the following are true:

- The file is larger than the maximum capacity of a local Microsoft Access database (1 gigabyte).
- The file is changed frequently by users of the other database application.
- You must share the file with users of the other database application on a network.
- You'll be distributing your application to several individual users, and you might be offering updates to the application interface you develop. Separating the "application" (queries, forms, reports, macros, and modules) from the "data" (tables) can make it easier to update the application without having to disturb the user's accumulated data.

Importing Data and Databases

You can copy data from a number of different file formats to create a Microsoft Access table. In addition to copying data from a number of popular database file formats, Access can also create a table from data in a spreadsheet or a text file. When you copy data from another database, Microsoft Access uses information stored by the source database system to convert or name objects in the target Access table. You can import database data not only from other Access databases but also from dBASE, Paradox, FoxPro, Btrieve, and—using ODBC—any SQL database that supports the ODBC standard.

Importing dBASE Files

To import a dBASE file, do the following:

1. Open the Microsoft Access database that you want to receive the dBASE file. If you already have that database open, switch to the Database window.

2. Choose the Import command from the File menu. Access opens the Import dialog box, shown in Figure 10-2.

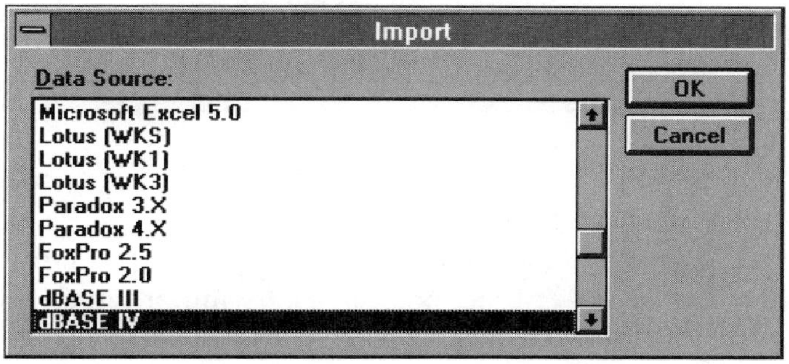

FIGURE 10-2.
The Import dialog box is used to select a data source.

3. Select dBASE III or dBASE IV as appropriate in the Data Source list and click OK. Access opens the Select File dialog box, shown in Figure 10-3, from which you can select the drive, directory, and name of the dBASE file that you want to import.

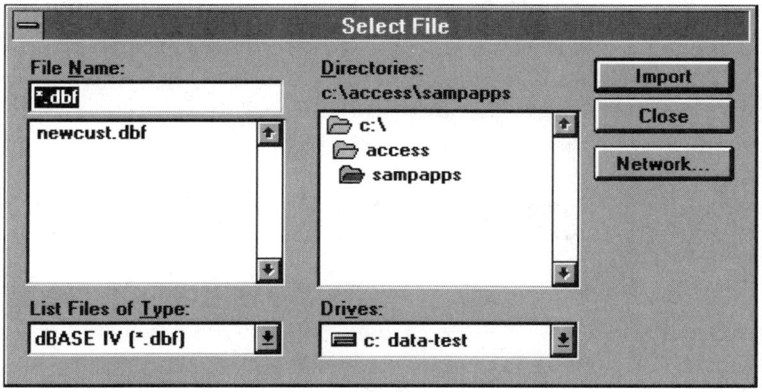

FIGURE 10-3.
The Select File dialog box is used to select a file to import.

4. Select a file, and click Import in the Select File dialog box to import the dBASE file you've chosen. Access opens a dialog box that informs you of the result of the import action, as shown in Figure 10-4 on the next page.

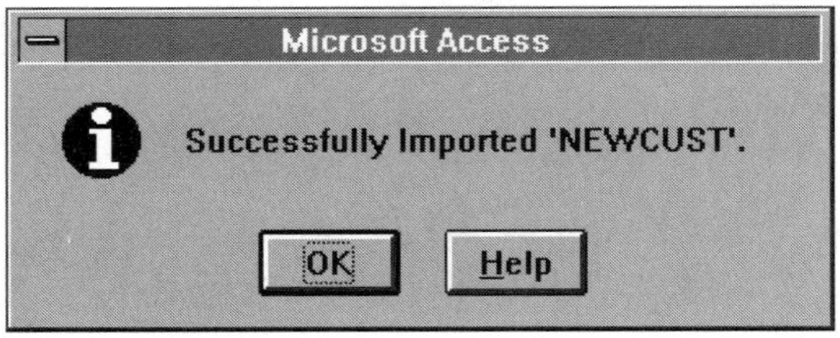

FIGURE 10-4.
This dialog box indicates the result of an import action.

If the import was successful, you'll find a new table in your database with the name of the DBF file. If Access finds a duplicate name, it generates a new name by adding a unique integer to the end of the name. For example, if you're importing a file named NEWCUST.DBF and you already have tables named NewCust and NewCust1, Access creates a table named NEWCUST2.

5. Click the OK button to dismiss the dialog box that confirms the import action. Access returns you to the Select File dialog box. You can select a new file and click the Import button, or you can click the Close button to dismiss the Select File dialog box.

You'll find a file named NEWCUST.DBF in the sample files you received with Microsoft Access. Follow the procedure described above to import this file into either PROMPT or NWIND. When you open the new table that Access creates from this dBASE format data, you'll see additional sample customer data, as shown in Figure 10-5.

FIGURE 10-5.
An imported dBASE file.

Table: NEWCUST

ADDRESS	CITY	CMPNY	CNTCT	COUNTRY	CUSTID
7384 Washington A	Portland	Live Oak Hotel Gift	Alan Thompson	USA	LIVEO
12405 Aurora Ave.	Seattle	Vine and Barrel, Inc	Willard Grant	USA	VINEA
2044 Seahorse Bay	Port Townsend	La Playa Mini Mart	Ursula Janacek	USA	LAPLA
89 Rain Way	Portland	Lillegard's Old Cour	Judy Pamona	USA	LILLO
213 E. Roy St.	Seattle	Bobcat Mesa West	Gladys Lindsay	USA	BOBCM
1029 - 12th Ave. S.	Seattle	White Clover Marke	Karl Jablonski	USA	WHITC
41 S. Marlon St., Su	Seattle	Bergstad's Scandin	Tammy Wong	USA	BERGS
210 Main St.	Port Townsend	Blue Lake Deli & Gi	Hanna Moore	USA	BLUEL
425 3rd Ave.	Seattle	Prince and Pauper	Mohan Chandrasek	USA	PRINA
44 McKnight Rd.	Portland	Lee's Oriental Food	Rita Morehouse	USA	LEESO
58 Bay View	Port Townsend	Rocky Mountain Gr	Liu Shyu	USA	ROCKM
89 Chiaroscuro Rd.	Portland	Lonesome Pine Re	Fran Wilson	USA	LONEP
89 Jefferson Way, S	Portland	The Big Cheese	Liz Nixon	USA	THEBI

Record: 1 of 13

When you look at the Table window in Design view for a table imported from dBASE, you'll find that Access has converted the data types, as shown in Figure 10-6.

dBASE Data Type	Converted to Access Data Type
Character	Text
Numeric	Number, FieldSize property set to Double
Float	Number, FieldSize property set to Double
Logical	Yes/No
Date	Date/Time
Memo	Memo

FIGURE 10-6.
The dBASE-to-Access data type conversions.

Importing Paradox Files

The procedure for importing Paradox files is similar to the procedure for importing dBASE files. To import a Paradox file, do the following:

1. Open the Microsoft Access database that you want to receive the Paradox file. If you already have that database open, switch to the Database window.
2. Choose the Import command from the File menu. Access opens the Import dialog box, shown in Figure 10-2 on page 295.
3. Select Paradox 3.x or Paradox 4.x, as appropriate, in the Data Source list and click OK. Access opens a Select File dialog box similar to the one shown in Figure 10-3 on page 295, from which you can select the drive, directory, and name of the Paradox file that you want to import.
4. Select a file, and click the Import button in the Select File dialog box to import the Paradox file you've chosen.
5. If the Paradox table is encrypted, Access prompts you for the password, as shown in Figure 10-7 on the next page. Type the correct password in the dialog box and click OK to proceed, or click Cancel to start over.

   When you proceed, Access responds with a dialog box, similar to the one shown in Figure 10-4, that indicates the result of the import action. (The dialog box you see might look different.) If the import was successful, you'll find a new table in your database with the name of the DB file. If Access finds a duplicate name, it generates a new name by adding a unique integer to the end of the name. For example, if you're importing a file named NEWCUST.DB and you already have tables named NewCust and NewCust1, Access creates a table named NEWCUST2.

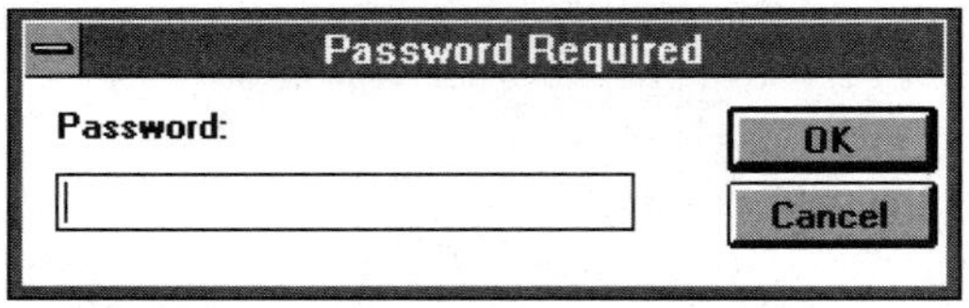

FIGURE 10-7.
The Password Required dialog box.

6. Click the OK button to dismiss the dialog box that confirms the import action. Access returns you to the Select File dialog box. You can select a new file and click the Import button, or you can click the Close button to dismiss the Select File dialog box.

When you look at a Table window in Design view for a table imported from Paradox, you'll find that Access has converted the data types, as shown in Figure 10-8.

Paradox Data Type	Converted to Access Data Type
Alphanumeric	Text
Number	Number, FieldSize property set to Double
Short Number	Number, FieldSize property set to Integer
Currency	Number, FieldSize property set to Double
Date	Date/Time

FIGURE 10-8.
The Paradox-to-Access data type conversions.

Importing FoxPro Files

The procedure for importing FoxPro files is similar to the procedure for importing dBASE files. To import a FoxPro file, do the following:

1. Open the Microsoft Access database that you want to receive the FoxPro file. If you already have that database open, switch to the Database window.
2. Choose the Import command from the File menu. Access opens the Import dialog box, shown in Figure 10-2 on page 295.
3. Select FoxPro 2.0 or FoxPro 2.5, as appropriate, in the Data Source list and click OK. Access opens a Select File dialog box similar to the one shown in Figure 10-3 on page 295, from which you can select the drive, directory, and name of the FoxPro file that you want to import.
4. Select a file, and click the Import button in the Select File dialog box to import the FoxPro file you've chosen.
5. If the FoxPro table is encrypted, Access prompts you for the password. The dialog box is similar to the one shown in Figure 10-7. Type the correct password in the dialog box and click OK to proceed, or click the Cancel button to start over.

   When you proceed, Access opens a dialog box, similar to the one shown in Figure 10-4 on page 296, that indicates the result of the import action. If the import was successful, you'll find a new table in your database with the name of the DBF file. If Access finds a duplicate name, it generates a new name by adding a unique integer to the end of the name. For example, if you're importing a file named NEWCUST.DBF and you already have tables named NewCust and NewCust1, Access creates a table named NEWCUST2.
6. Click OK to dismiss the dialog box that confirms the import action. Access returns you to the Select File dialog box. You can select a new file and click the Import button, or you can click the Close button to dismiss the Select File dialog box.

When you look at the Table window in Design view for a table imported from FoxPro, you'll find that Access has converted the data types, as shown in Figure 10-9 on the next page.

FoxPro Data Type	Converted to Access Data Type
Character	Text
Numeric	Number, FieldSize property set to Integer
Float	Number, FieldSize property set to Double
Date	Date/Time
Logical	Yes/No
Memo	Memo

FIGURE 10-9.
The FoxPro-to-Access data type conversions.

Importing Btrieve Tables

NOTE: To use Btrieve tables, you must have the Btrieve for Windows dynamic link library WBTRCALL.DLL, which is not provided with Microsoft Access. This DLL is provided with Novell Btrieve for Windows, Novell Netware SQL, and some other Windows-based products that use Btrieve.

To import a table from a Btrieve file, do the following:

1. Open the Microsoft Access database that you want to receive the Btrieve file. If you already have that database open, switch to the Database window.
2. Choose the Import command from the File menu. Access opens the Import dialog box, shown in Figure 10-2 on page 295.
3. Select Btrieve in the Data Source list, and then click OK. Access opens a Select File dialog box similar to the one shown in Figure 10-3 on page 295, from which you can select the drive, directory, and name of the Btrieve dictionary file containing the description of the tables you want to import. Click OK to open the dictionary. Access displays the list of tables in the dictionary file, as shown in Figure 10-10.

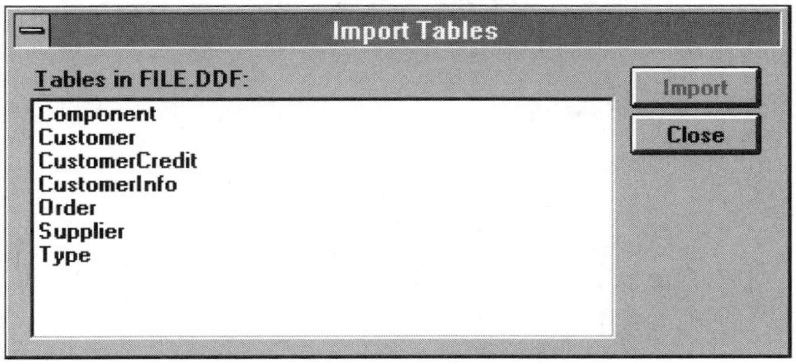

FIGURE 10-10. The Import Tables dialog box that's used for importing a table from a selected Btrieve dictionary file.

4. From the list of tables in the dictionary file, select the name of the table you want to import. Click the Import button in the Import Tables dialog box to import the Btrieve table you've selected.

5. If the Btrieve table is password protected, Access prompts you for the password with a dialog box similar to the one shown in Figure 10-7 on page 298. Type the correct password in the dialog box and click OK to proceed, or click the Cancel button to start over.

   When you proceed, Access responds with a dialog box, similar to the one shown in Figure 10-4 on page 296, that indicates the result of the import action. If the import was successful, you'll find a new table in your database with the name of the Btrieve table. If Access finds a duplicate name, it generates a new name by adding a unique integer to the end of the name. For example, if you're importing a table named NewCust and you already have tables named NewCust and NewCust1, Access creates a table named NewCust2.

6. Click OK to dismiss the dialog box that confirms the import action. Access returns you to the Import Tables dialog box. You can select a new table and click the Import button, or you can click the Close button to dismiss the dialog box.

When you look at the Table window in Design view for a table imported from Btrieve, you'll find that Microsoft Access has converted the data types, as shown in Figure 10-11 on the next page.

Btrieve Data Type	Converted to Access Data Type
String, lstring, zstring	Text
Integer, 1-byte	Number, FieldSize property set to Byte
Integer, 2-byte	Number, FieldSize property set to Integer
Integer, 4-byte	Number, FieldSize property set to Long Integer
Float or bfloat, 4-byte	Number, FieldSize property set to Single
Float or bfloat, 8-byte	Number, FieldSize property set to Double
Decimal or numeric	Number, FieldSize property set to Double
Money	Currency
Logical	Yes/No
Date or Time	Date/Time
Note	Memo
Lvar	OLE Object

FIGURE 10-11.
The Btrieve-to-Access data type conversions.

Importing SQL Tables

To import a table from another database system that supports ODBC SQL, you must first have the ODBC driver for that database installed on your computer. (For details, see the *User's Guide* that comes with Microsoft Access; also see Appendix A of this book.) Your computer must also be attached to the network that connects to the SQL server you want, and you must have an account on that server. Check with your system administrator for information about correctly connecting to the SQL server from which you want to import data.

To import data from an SQL table, do the following:

1. Open the Microsoft Access database that you want to receive the SQL data. If you already have that database open, switch to the Database window.
2. Choose the Import command from the File menu. Access opens the Import dialog box, shown in Figure 10-2 on page 295.

3. Select SQL Database in the Data Source list and click OK. Access opens the SQL Data Sources dialog box, shown in Figure 10-12, from which you can select the name of the SQL server that contains the table you want to import. Note that you can also use ODBC to access dBASE, FoxPro, Paradox, and other Microsoft Access databases. Using direct file access (see previous sections) might be faster for these other types of files if the files are on your local machine. Using ODBC might be faster if the files are on a remote server. Select a server and click OK. Access then displays the Login dialog box for the SQL data source that you selected, as shown in Figure 10-13.

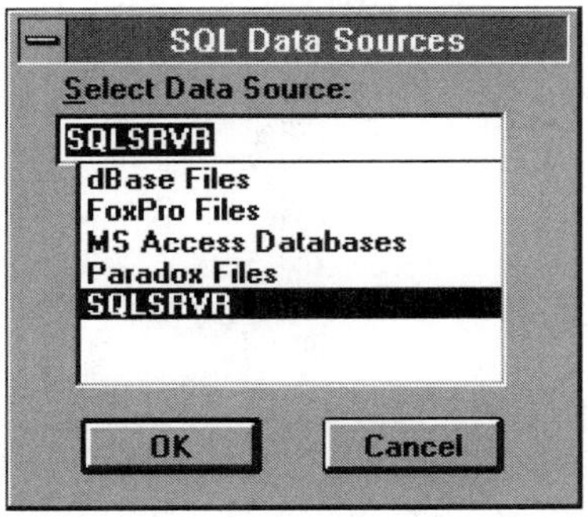

FIGURE 10-12. The SQL Data Sources dialog box.

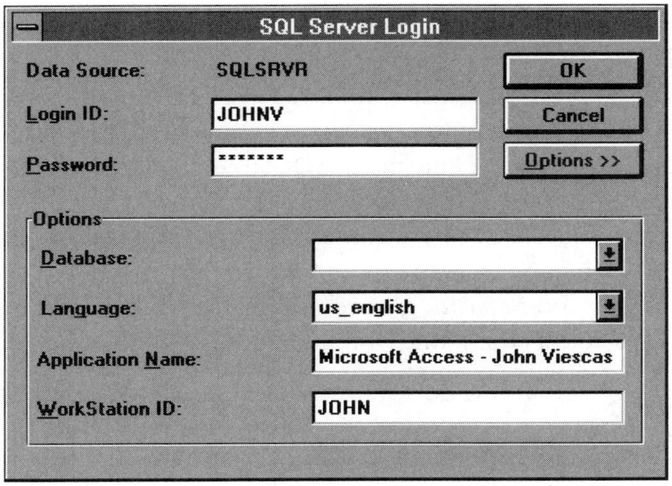

FIGURE 10-13. The SQL Server Login dialog box for an SQL data source.

4. Enter your user ID and your password, and click OK. If you want to connect to a specific database on the server, enter your user ID and password, and then click the Options button to open the lower part of the dialog box. When you click the Database box, Access logs you on to the server and returns a list of available database names. Choose the one you want and click OK. If you don't supply a database name and if multiple databases exist on the server, you'll be prompted to choose the database you want. When Access has connected you to the server, you'll see a list of available tables on that server, as shown in Figure 10-14.

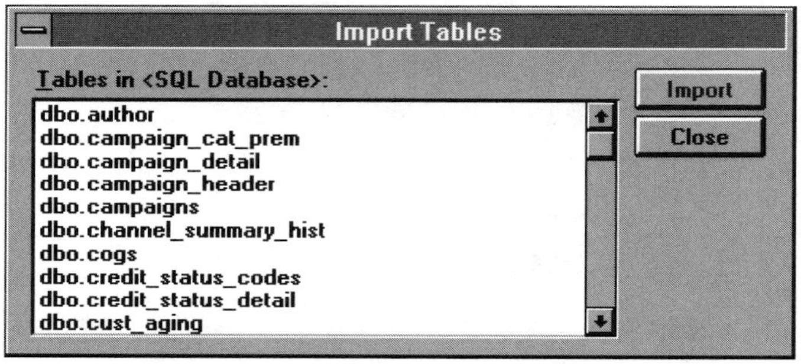

FIGURE 10-14. A table list for an SQL data source.

5. From the list of tables in the server, select the one you want to import. Click the Import button in the Import Tables dialog box to import the SQL table you've selected.

6. Microsoft Access opens a dialog box, similar to the one shown in Figure 10-4 on page 296, that indicates the result of the import action. If the import was successful, you'll find a new table in your database with the name of the SQL table. If Microsoft Access finds a duplicate name, it generates a new name by adding a unique integer to the end of the name. For example, if you're importing a table named *newcust* and you already have tables named *NewCust* and *NewCust1*, Access creates a table named *newcust2*. Access adopts the name of the table it is importing.

NOTE: You've no doubt noticed by now that the different databases have different style conventions—newcust, NewCust, NEWCUST—for names.

7. Click OK to dismiss the dialog box that confirms the import action. Access returns you to the Import Tables dialog box. You can select a new table and click the Import button, or you can click the Close button to dismiss the dialog box.

In general, Microsoft Access converts SQL data types to Access data types, as shown in Figure 10-15.

SQL Data Type	Converted to Access Data Type
CHAR[ACTER]	Text
VARCHAR	Text
TEXT	Memo
TINYINT	Numeric, FieldSize property set to Byte
SMALLINT	Numeric, FieldSize property set to Integer
INT	Numeric, FieldSize property set to Long Integer
REAL	Numeric, FieldSize property set to Double
FLOAT	Numeric, FieldSize property set to Double
DOUBLE	Numeric, FieldSize property set to Double
DATE	Date/Time
TIME	Date/Time
TIMESTAMP	Binary
IMAGE	OLE Object

FIGURE 10-15.
The SQL-to-Access data type conversions.

Importing Microsoft Access Objects

When the database from which you want to import data is another Microsoft Access database, you can import any of the six major types of Access objects: tables, queries, forms, reports, macros, and modules. To achieve the same result you can also open the source database, select the object you want, choose the Copy command from the Edit menu, open the target database, and then choose the Paste command from the Edit menu. Using the Import command, however, allows you to copy several objects without having to switch back and forth between the two databases.

To import an object from another Microsoft Access database, do the following:

1. Open the Microsoft Access database that you want to receive the object. If you already have that database open, switch to the Database window.
2. Choose the Import command from the File menu. Access opens the Import dialog box, shown in Figure 10-2 on page 295.
3. Select Microsoft Access in the Data Source list and click OK. Access opens a Select File dialog box, similar to the one shown in Figure 10-3 on page 295, from which you can select the drive, directory, and name of the MDB file containing the Access object that you want to import. Click OK.
4. Access then opens the Import Objects dialog box, shown in Figure 10-16. First select the object type, and then select the specific object you want to import. If the object is a table, you can choose to import the table structure (the table definition) only, or the structure <u>and</u> the stored data. Click Import to copy the object you selected to the current database.

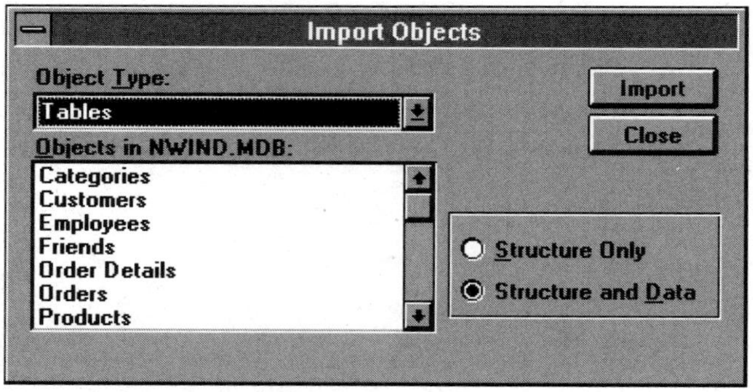

FIGURE 10-16. The Import Objects dialog box.

5. Access opens a dialog box, similar to the one shown in Figure 10-4, that indicates the result of the import action. If the import was successful, you'll find a new object in your database with the name of the object you selected. If Access finds a duplicate name, it generates a new name by adding a unique integer to the end of the name. For example, if you're importing a table named NewCust and you already have tables named NewCust and NewCust1, Access creates NewCust2. Because objects can refer to other objects by name within an Access database, you should carefully check preestablished name references to the new object if the object has to be renamed.
6. Click OK to dismiss the dialog box that confirms the import action. Access returns you to the Import Objects dialog box. You can select a new object and click the Import button, or you can click the Close button to dismiss the Import Objects dialog box.

Importing an Entire Microsoft Access Database

NEW!

With version 2, Microsoft Access has available several add-in utilities to make it easier to design and document applications. You can find these utilities by opening any database and choosing Add-ins from the File menu.

One of the add-in utilities lets you import all the objects from another database to the current database. This can be particularly useful if you've been developing a large application using a team of designers sharing a common database. Each of the objects in the development database will be owned by whomever created the object. When your team has completed the application, you can use the Import Database add-in to copy all the objects to a new database. This lets you assign ownership of all the objects to a single user to make it easier to assign security to the objects in your application before you distribute it. You can use the Change Owner command on the Security menu to reassign ownership, but you can reassign ownership only if you are the owner, and you must do the reassignment a single object at a time.

You'll need to create a copy of your existing database. For more information on creating accounts for new users, see Chapter 14 of the "Building Applications" manual that comes with Microsoft Access.

To create an entirely new database that is a copy of an existing database and in which all the objects are owned by a single new owner, do the following:

1. Create an account for the new user who is to own the database by logging on as the system administrator and creating a new-user account with the Users command on the Security menu.
2. Be sure that the new user account has Read Design authority over all the objects in the database you want to copy.
3. Log on using the new user account and create a new database.
4. Choose Add-ins from the File menu.
5. Choose Import Database. The import database utility shows you a file selection dialog box similar to the one shown in Figure 10-3 on page 295 (but titled Import Database) that allows you to choose the file containing the database you want to import.
6. Choose the file you want to import and click OK. The utility might run for several minutes if you're importing a large database. If the utility encounters an error (such as an object locked by another user), you're given the opportunity to abort the import, retry the failing object, or ignore the error and continue with other objects.

After the import database utility has imported the table, you'll find a copy of all the objects from the other database in your new database, with the new user account as the owner.

Importing Spreadsheet Data

Microsoft Access allows you to import data from spreadsheet files created by Lotus 1-2-3, Lotus 1-2-3 for Windows, and Microsoft Excel versions 2 and later. You can specify a portion of a spreadsheet or the entire spreadsheet file to import. (If you're working with a spreadsheet program that operates in the Microsoft Windows operating system and that supports Dynamic Data Exchange (DDE), you can also copy a single row or several rows of cells from a spreadsheet and paste them into any Access table that has matching fields.) If the first row of cells contains names suitable for field names in the resulting Access table, you can ask Access to use these names for your fields.

Preparing a Spreadsheet

You can append a range of spreadsheet cells or a whole spreadsheet directly to an existing table. To append data, either you must supply column names in the spreadsheet that match field names in the table or the columns must be in exactly the same sequence (and have the same data type) as fields in your target table. You create matching column names by entering them in the first row of your spreadsheet, as shown in Figure 10-17. If you don't provide column names, Access assigns a consecutive number to each field in the new table, starting with 1. You can open the Table window in Design view later to change these names.

If you're appending data to an existing table, the data types in the spreadsheet and in the table must match. Access can copy alphanumeric data into any Text or Memo field, numeric data into any Numeric or Currency field (as long as the FieldSize property is set large enough to contain the number value), and date or time data into any Date/Time field.

	A	B	C	D	E
1	CustID	Company	Contact	Title	Address
2	LIVEO	Live Oak Hotel Gift Shop	Alan Thompson	Accounting Manager	7384 Wa
3	VINEA	Vine and Barrel, Inc.	Willard Grant	Order Administrator	12405 Au
4	LAPLA	La Playa Mini Mart	Ursula Janacek	Sales Manager	2044 Se
5	LILLO	Lillegard's Old Country Deli	Judy Pamona	Owner	89 Rain
6	BOBCM	Bobcat Mesa Western Gifts	Gladys Lindsay	Marketing Manager	213 E. R
7	WHITC	White Clover Markets	Karl Jablonski	Owner	1029 - 12
8	BERGS	Bergstad's Scandinavian Groc	Tammy Wong	Order Administrator	41 S. Ma
9	BLUEL	Blue Lake Deli & Grocery	Hanna Moore	Owner	210 Mair
10	PRINA	Prince and Pauper Markets	Mohan Chandrasekharan	Sales Rep.	425 3rd
11	LEESO	Lee's Oriental Food Mart	Rita Morehouse	Sales Rep.	44 McKn
12	ROCKM	Rocky Mountain Grocery and D	Liu Shyu	Order Administrator	58 Bay V
13	LONEP	Lonesome Pine Restaurant an	Fran Wilson	Sales Manager	89 Chiar
14	THEBI	The Big Cheese	Liz Nixon	Marketing Manager	89 Jeffer
15					
16					
17					
18					

FIGURE 10-17. A Microsoft Excel spreadsheet with column names entered in the first row.

You can also import a spreadsheet to create a new table. Access can generate field names based on the names in the first row of the spreadsheet. You should also be aware that Access determines the data type for the fields in a new table from the values it finds in the first row of data being imported. When you import a spreadsheet into a new table, Access stores alphanumeric data as Text data type with an entry length of 255 characters, numeric data as Numeric with the FieldSize property set to Double, numeric data with currency formatting as Currency, and any date or time data as Date/Time.

> **TIP:** If you want to append a large spreadsheet but it doesn't exactly match your target table, import the entire spreadsheet as a new table and then use an append query to edit and to move the data to the table you want to update.

It might be worth your while to insert a single "dummy" row at the beginning of your spreadsheet with data values appropriate to the data type you want for the whole column. You can easily delete that row after you've imported the spreadsheet. For example, in the spreadsheet shown in Figure 10-18, suppose that the first entry in the Phone field is stored as a string of digits and that no value is specified in the first Credit Limit column. Access will interpret the entries in the Phone column as a Numeric data type and the entries in the Credit Limit column as a Text data type. The Credit Limit values in other records can be stored satisfactorily as text strings, but phone numbers in other records that have embedded parentheses, spaces, and hyphens cannot be stored as numbers.

	G	H	I	J	K	L
1	Region	Zip	Country	Phone	Fax	Credit Limit
2	OR	97229	USA	5035558946		
3	WA	98117	USA	(206) 555-3378	(206) 555-8202	$10,000
4	WA	98368	USA	(206) 555-8274		$7,000

FIGURE 10-18.

The initial entries in the Phone and Credit Limit columns in this Excel spreadsheet will generate the wrong data types for those fields when they are imported by Access. (The highlighted Phone column numbers must match the form of the other phone numbers, and the Credit Limit column must contain a dollar value to be saved as a Number data type.)

Importing a Spreadsheet

If a spreadsheet's column names and their data types match fields in an existing Access table, you can import the spreadsheet rows and append them to the table—and you can of course import a spreadsheet to create a new table.

To import a spreadsheet into a Microsoft Access database, do the following:

1. Open the Microsoft Access database that you want to receive the spreadsheet. If you already have that database open, switch to the Database window.
2. Choose the Import command from the File menu. Access opens the Import dialog box, shown in Figure 10-2.
3. Select the type of spreadsheet you want to import (Excel or Lotus 1-2-3) in the Data Source list and click OK. Access opens a Select File dialog box similar to the one shown in Figure 10-3.
4. Select the name of the spreadsheet file that you want and click the Import button. Access opens the Import Spreadsheet Options dialog box, shown in Figure 10-19.

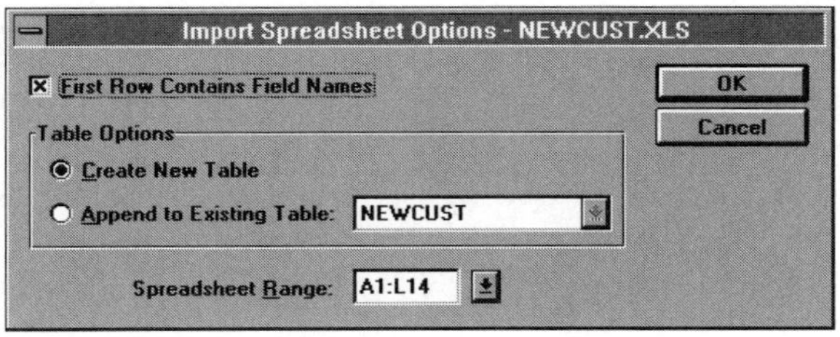

FIGURE 10-19. The Import Spreadsheet Options dialog box.

5. Click the First Row Contains Field Names check box if you've placed names at the tops of the columns in your spreadsheet. In the Table Options group box, you can choose to create a new table or to append data to an existing one. If you've included column names in your spreadsheet, the columns don't have to be in the same order as the fields in the table to which you want to append data. If you don't want to import the entire spreadsheet, specify the range of cells in the Spreadsheet Range box and be sure to include the column names row in the range if you've used

column names in the spreadsheet. For example, if the upper left corner of the range you want is C9 and the lower right corner is R50, enter *C9:R50* or *C9..R50* in the range box. Click OK to start the import process.

6. Access opens a dialog box, similar to the one shown in Figure 10-4 on page 296, that indicates the result of the import action. If the import was successful and you had elected to create a table, you'll find a new table in your database with the name of the spreadsheet you selected. If Access finds a duplicate name, it generates a new name by adding a unique integer to the end of the name. For example, if you're importing a spreadsheet named NEWCUST and you already have tables named NewCust and NewCust1, Access creates a new table named NEWCUST2.
7. Click OK to dismiss the dialog box that confirms the import action. Access returns you to the Select File dialog box. You can select a new spreadsheet and click the Import button, or you can click the Close button to dismiss the Select File dialog box.

Fixing Errors

In an earlier section in this chapter, titled "Preparing a Spreadsheet," you learned that Microsoft Access determines data types for the fields in a new table based on the values it finds in the first row of data being imported from a spreadsheet. Figure 10-18 on page 310 shows an example of spreadsheet data whose first row would generate wrong data types in a new Access table. The Numeric data type that Access would generate for the Phone field, based on the first entry, would not work for the remaining entries, which have parentheses, spaces, and hyphens in them.

If you were to import the data shown in Figure 10-18, Access would open a dialog box similar to the one shown in Figure 10-20.

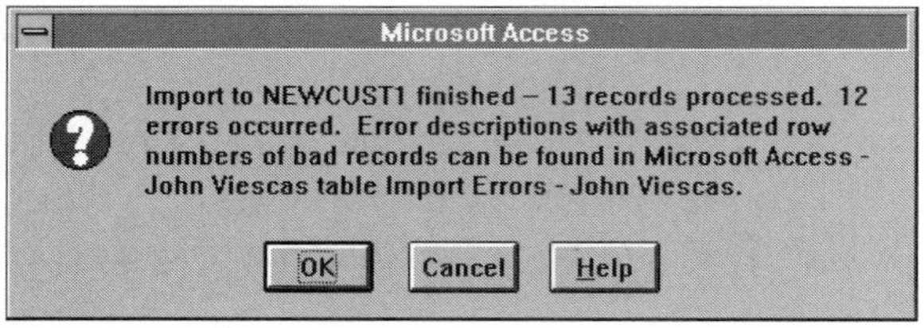

FIGURE 10-20. The dialog box that appears when an error occurs while you're importing data from a spreadsheet.

In any case, Access creates a table called Import Errors (with your name in the title) that contains a record for each error. Figure 10-21 shows the Import Errors table that Access creates when you import the spreadsheet from Figure 10-18. Access creates this table even when you click Cancel in the dialog box, enabling you to see what needs to be corrected in the spreadsheet before you try again. Notice that the Import Errors table lists not only the type of error but also the field and row in the spreadsheet where the error occurred. In this case, the second data row (the third row in the spreadsheet) and all subsequent entries in the Phone field are rejected for being text values. Be aware that when you append a spreadsheet to an existing table, you might also see rows rejected because of duplicate primary keys. Unless the primary key for your table is a Counter field, the rows you are appending from the spreadsheet must contain the primary key fields, and the values in these fields must be unique.

Table: Import Errors - John Viescas

Error	Field	Row
Type Conversion Failure	Phone	3
Type Conversion Failure	Phone	4
Type Conversion Failure	Phone	5
Type Conversion Failure	Phone	6
Type Conversion Failure	Phone	7
Type Conversion Failure	Phone	8
Type Conversion Failure	Phone	9
Type Conversion Failure	Phone	10
Type Conversion Failure	Phone	11
Type Conversion Failure	Phone	12
Type Conversion Failure	Phone	13
Type Conversion Failure	Phone	14

Record: 1 of 12

FIGURE 10-21. An Import Errors table resulting from the import of data shown in Figure 10-18.

If you look at the table that results from the import of the Figure 10-18 data, as shown in Figure 10-22 on the next page, you find that no phone numbers appear in the second and subsequent records. If you were to look at the data type for CreditLimit in Design view, you would find that this data has been saved as the Text data type, not as the Number data type.

Table: NEWCUST1

Region	Zip	Country	Phone	Fax	Credit Limit
OR	97229	USA	5035558946		
WA	98117	USA		(206) 555-8202	10000
WA	98368	USA			7000
OR	97219	USA		(503) 555-5994	12000
WA	98124	USA			8000
WA	98124	USA		(206) 555-4115	10000
WA	98104	USA		(206) 555-8832	10000
WA	98368	USA		(206) 555-4247	7000
WA	98101	USA		(206) 555-6044	12000
OR	97229	USA		(503) 555-6655	8000
WA	98368	USA			10000
OR	97219	USA		(503) 555-9646	9000
OR	97201	USA			15000

Record: 1 of 13

FIGURE 10-22.

The errors that were created by importing the data shown in Figure 10-18. (No phone numbers appear after the first one, which was incorrectly entered; and because the first CreditLimit field was left blank, the subsequent ones were saved as the Text data type.)

Some errors you can correct in the Table window in Design view. For example, you can change the data type of CreditLimit to Numeric, and because the text values in the second and subsequent rows are all valid numbers, Access can convert the data format correctly for all rows. (See Figure 6-16 in Chapter 6 for a table of data conversion limitations.) You have two choices for fixing the Phone field. You can add the missing phone numbers in the Table window in Datasheet view, or you can delete the imported records and then reimport this table after correcting the numeric value in the first row in the spreadsheet.

Importing Text Files

You can import data from a text file into Microsoft Access even though the data in a text file, unlike the data in a spreadsheet, isn't arranged in columns and rows in an orderly way. You can make it possible for Access to understand the data in a text file either by including special characters to delimit the fields in each record (sometimes called a *delimited text file*) or by placing each field in the same location in each record (called a *fixed-width file*) and defining those field locations for Access.

Preparing a Text File

You might be able to import some text files into Microsoft Access without changing them, especially if the text file was created by another program using standard field delimiters. In most cases, you'll have to modify the contents of the file or define the file for Access or do both before you can import it.

Setting Up Delimited Data

Microsoft Access needs some way of distinguishing where a field starts and ends in each incoming text string. Access supports three standard separator characters: comma, tab, and space. When you use a comma as the separator (a very common technique), the comma (or the carriage return at the end of the record) indicates the end of each field, and the next field begins with the first nonblank character. The commas aren't part of the data. To include a comma within a text string as data, you must enclose all text strings in single or double quotation marks. If any of your text strings contain double quotation marks, you must enclose the strings in single quotation marks, and vice versa. Access accepts only single or double quotation marks (but not both) as a text delimiter, so all embedded quotes in a file that you want to import to Access must all be of the same type. In other words, you can't include a single quotation mark in one field and a double quotation mark in another field within the same file. Figure 10-23 shows you a sample comma-separated and double-quote–delimited text file.

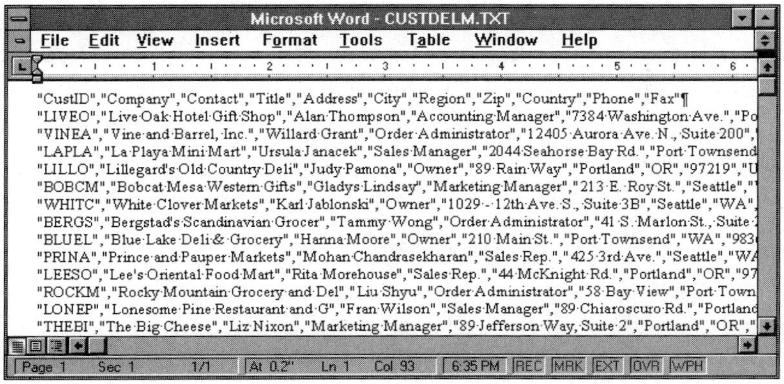

FIGURE 10-23.
A comma-separated and double-quote–delimited text file.

Another common way to separate data is to use the tab character between fields. In fact, when you save a spreadsheet file as text from most spreadsheet programs, the program stores the columns with tabs between them. Figure 10-24 shows the NEWCUST spreadsheet from Microsoft Excel saved as text. Notice that Excel has added double quotation marks around text strings that include commas, but not in any other case.

FIGURE 10-24.
A tab-separated text file.

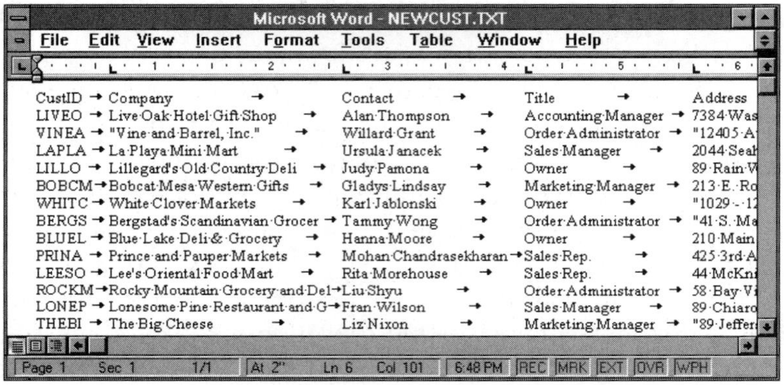

By default, Access assumes that fields in a delimited text file are separated by commas and that text strings are within double quotation marks. If you want to import a file that is delimited differently, you can define a new *import/export specification* and then refer to it when you import the data.

To define an import/export specification, open your database, click in the Database window, and then choose the Imp/Exp Setup command from the File menu. Access opens the Import/Export Setup dialog box, shown in Figure 10-25. In this dialog box, {tab} was selected from the Field Separator list and the change was saved with a new Specification Name entry: TabSeparator. (In the next section, you'll learn how to use the Field Information area to define fields in a fixed-width file.)

Setting Up Fixed-Width Data

Microsoft Access can also import text files when the fields appear in fixed locations in each record in the file, but you must first define the locations for Access. You might encounter this type of file if you download a print output file from a host computer.

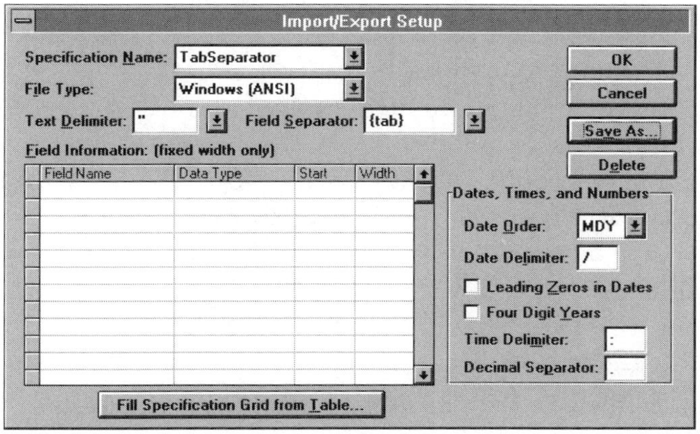

FIGURE 10-25.
An Import/Export Setup dialog box that defines a tab-separated specification.

Figure 10-26 shows a sample fixed-width text file. Notice that each field begins in exactly the same location in all the records. To prepare this type of file for import, you must first remove any heading or summary lines from the file. The file must contain only records, with the data you want to import in fixed locations. You must also create an import/export specification that Access can use to determine the data type and location of each field in the records.

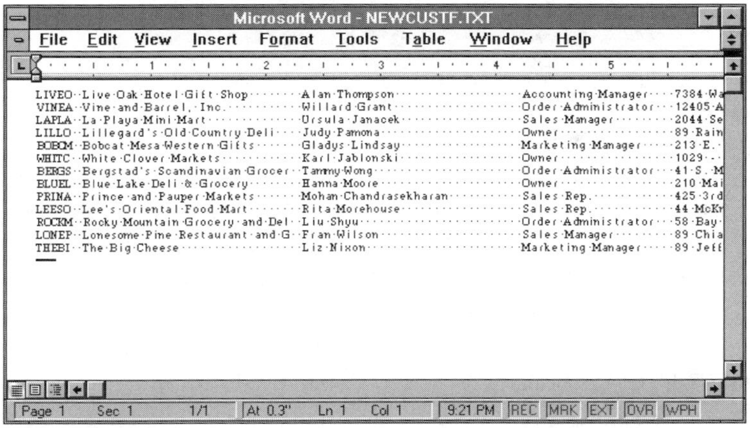

FIGURE 10-26.
A fixed-width text file.

To define an import/export specification, open your database, click in the Database window, and then choose the Imp/Exp Setup command from the File menu. Access opens the Import/Export Setup dialog box. In the Import/Export Setup dialog box, you can define each field in the file you want to import by filling in the Field Information area. Type the name you want to assign to the field in the resulting table, and then enter the data type, the starting location of the field data relative to the first character in each record, and the length of the field. (See Figure 10-27.) If your database contains a table that has field definitions similar to those of the data you're importing, you can fill in the field information grid by clicking the Fill Specification Grid From Table button and then choosing the table name in the subsequent dialog box. When you've finished defining a new specification, you can click Save As and type a name for the specification in the dialog box that opens. In Figure 10-27, the specification was saved as *NewCust In Fixed.*

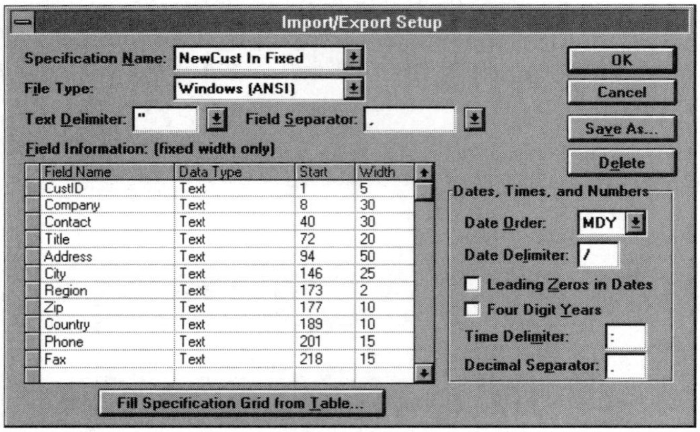

FIGURE 10-27.
An Import/Export Setup dialog box that defines a fixed-width specification.

In the Import/Export Setup dialog box, you can also indicate whether the text file was created using a program running under MS-DOS or under the Microsoft Windows operating system. For any file created with an application for Windows (such as Notepad), select the file type called *Windows (ANSI).* For files created with an MS-DOS program (such as EDIT.COM or EDLIN.EXE), select the file type called *DOS or OS/2 (PC-8).* For fixed-width files, you won't need to make a Text Delimiter selection or a Field Separator selection; you use these options to define a specification for delimited files only. In the lower right corner of the Import/Export dialog box, you can change the way Access recognizes date and time values and numeric fractions.

Importing a Text File

Before you can import a text file, you'll probably need to prepare the data or define the file for Microsoft Access, or both. (See the earlier section in this chapter, "Preparing a Text File.") After you've finished with that, you can import a text file into a Microsoft Access database by doing the following:

1. Open the Microsoft Access database that you want to receive the text data. If you already have that database open, switch to the Database window.
2. Choose the Import command from the File menu. Access opens the Import dialog box, shown in Figure 10-2 on page 295.
3. Select the type of text file you want to import, either Text (Delimited) or Text (Fixed Width), in the Data Source list, and click OK. Access opens a Select File dialog box, similar to the one shown in Figure 10-3 on page 295, from which you can select the drive, directory, and name of the file you want to import.
4. Select the name of the text file that you want and click the Import button.
5. For delimited files, Access opens the Import Text Options dialog box shown in Figure 10-28. You can choose to create a new table or to append a file to an existing table. Click the Options button to expand the dialog box, as shown in Figure 10-29 on the next page. You can then select a specification name or define different delimiters and separators. Click the First Row Contains Field Names check box if the first record in your delimited text file contains field names.

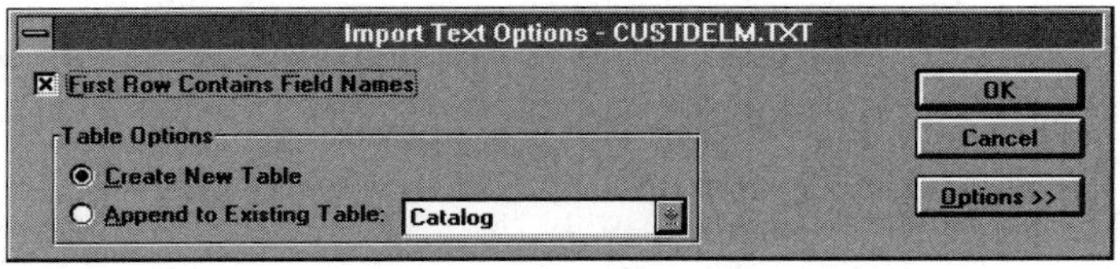

FIGURE 10-28.
The Import Text Options dialog box for delimited text files.

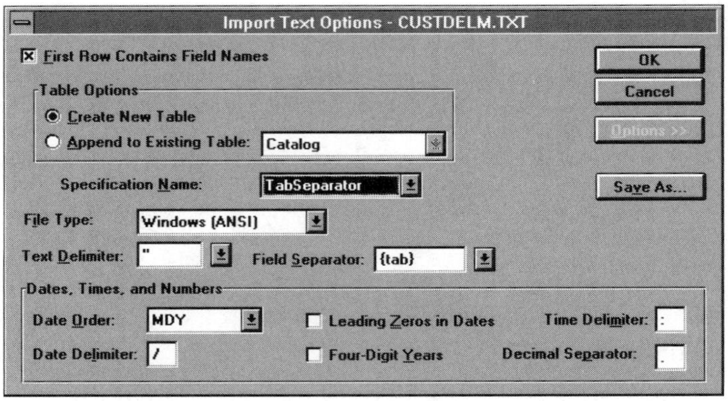

FIGURE 10-29. The Import Text Options dialog box for delimited text files, after the Options button is clicked.

For fixed-width files, Access shows you the Import Text Options dialog box shown in Figure 10-30. You can choose to create a new table or to append a file to an existing table. Choose the specification name you want Access to use from the drop-down list. If you haven't yet set up a specification, you can click the Edit Specs button to open the Import/Export Setup dialog box shown in Figure 10-27 on page 318.

Click OK to start the import process.

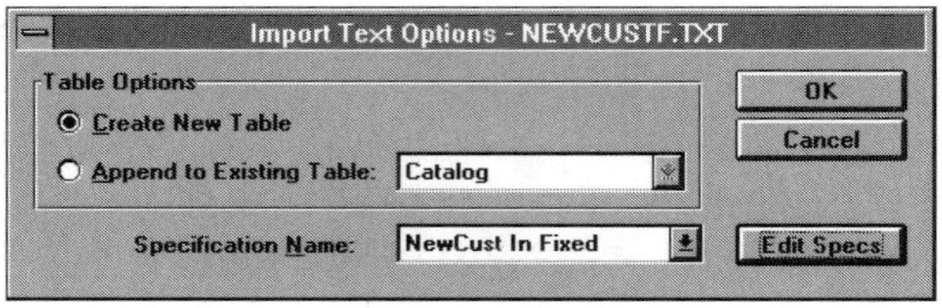

FIGURE 10-30. The Import Text Options dialog box for fixed-width text files.

6. Microsoft Access opens a dialog box indicating the result of the import action. If the import was successful and you had elected to create a table, you'll find a new table in your database with the name of the text file you selected. If Access finds a duplicate name, it generates a new name by adding a unique integer to the end of the name. For example, if you're importing a text file named NEWCUST and you already have tables named NewCust and NewCust1, Access creates a new table named NEWCUST2.

7. Click the OK button to dismiss the import action dialog box. Access returns you to the Select File dialog box. You can select a new text file and click the Import button, or you can click the Close button to dismiss the Select File dialog box.

Fixing Errors

You might encounter errors when importing text files that are similar to those explained earlier in the chapter, in the section titled "Importing Spreadsheet Data." When you append a text file to an existing table, you might see rows rejected because of duplicate primary keys. Unless the primary key for your table is a Counter, the rows you are appending from the text file must contain the primary key fields, and the values in those fields must be unique. For delimited text files, Microsoft Access determines the data type based on the fields in the first record being imported. If a number appears in a field in the first record that might later also contain text data, you need to enclose that number in quotes so that Access will use the Text data type for that field. If a number first appears without decimal places, Access uses the Number data type with the FieldSize property set to Integer. This setting will generate errors later if the numbers in other records contain decimal places.

Access opens an error dialog box, similar to the one shown in Figure 10-20, that summarizes any errors found. You can click OK to complete the import with the errors noted, or you can click Cancel to abort the operation. As when errors are produced while you're importing a spreadsheet, Access creates a table called Import Errors with your name appended to this title. The table contains a record for each error. Access creates this table even when you click Cancel in the dialog box that warns you of errors, enabling you to see what needs to be corrected before you try again. The Errors table lists not only the type of error but also the column and row in the text file in which the error occurred.

You can correct some errors in the Table window in Design view. For example, you can change the data type of fields provided that the content of the fields can be converted to the new data type. (See Figure 6-17 in Chapter 6 for data conversion limitations.) With other errors you must either add missing data in Datasheet view or delete the imported records and reimport the table after correcting the values in the text file that caused the errors originally.

Modifying Imported Tables

When you import data from an external source, Microsoft Access often has to use default data types or lengths that will accommodate the incoming data but that might not be correct for your needs. For example, Access assigns a maximum length of 255 characters to text data imported from a spreadsheet or text file. Even when the source of the data is another database, Access might choose numeric data types that can accept the data but that might not be correct. For example, numeric data in dBASE might be of the type Integer, but Access stores all numeric data from dBASE with a FieldSize setting of Double.

Unless you're importing data from an SQL or Paradox database that has a primary key defined, Access does not define a primary key in the new table. Also, if you did not include field names from a text or spreadsheet file, you'll probably want to enter meaningful names in the resulting table.

See Also: You can correctly specify most data types, change field names, and add a primary key in the Table window in Design view. For detailed information about modifying your table design, see Chapter 6, "Modifying Your Database Design."

Attaching Other Databases

You can attach tables from other Microsoft Access databases—whether the other databases are local or are on a network—and work with the data in them as if these tables were defined in your current Access database. If you want to work with data stored in another database format supported by Microsoft Access (FoxPro, dBASE, Paradox, Btrieve, or any SQL database that supports ODBC), you can attach the data directly as an alternative to importing it. In most cases, you can read data, insert new records, delete records, or change data just as though the attached file were an Access table. This ability to attach data is especially important when you need to access data on a host computer or share data from your application with many other users.

Security Considerations

If you attempt to attach a file or a table from another database system that is protected, Microsoft Access asks you for a password. If the security information you supply is correct and Access successfully attaches the secured data, Access stores the security information with the attached table entry so that you do not have to enter this information each time you or your application open the table. Although there is no way to directly access this information in your SYSTEM.MDB file from Microsoft Access, a knowledgeable person might be able to retrieve it by scanning the file with a dump utility. Therefore, if you have attached sensitive information to your Access database and have supplied security information, you should consider encrypting your database. Consult Chapter 3 in the *User's Guide* that comes with Access for information about securing and encrypting your Microsoft Access database.

Performance Considerations

Microsoft Access always performs best when working with its own files on your local machine. If you attach tables or files from other databases, you might notice slower performance. In particular, you can expect slower performance if you connect over a network to a table or a file in another database, even if the remote table is an Access table.

When sharing data over a network, you should consider how you and other people can use the data in a way that maximizes performance. For example, you should use queries with shared data whenever possible to limit the amount of data you need at any one time. When inserting new data in a shared table, you should use an Access form that is set only for data entry so that you don't have to access the entire table to add new data, as explained in Part 4 of this book, "Using Forms."

You should set options so that records are not locked if you are simply browsing through data. If you need to update data, your options should be set to lock only the records you are editing. When others are updating the data you are using, you'll occasionally notice that you cannot update a record. You can set options to limit the number of times

Access will retry an update to a locked record on your behalf and how long it will wait between retries. You can also control how often Access reviews updates made by other users to shared data. If this refresh interval is set very low, Access will be spending unnecessary time to perform this task repeatedly.

The original settings for Multiuser options are often appropriate when you share data over a network, so it's a good idea to consult your system administrator before making changes. If you need to alter the Multiuser options, you can choose the Options command from the View menu and select the Multiuser/ODBC category at the bottom of the list. The Options dialog box, with the Multiuser/ODBC category selected, is shown in Figure 10-31.

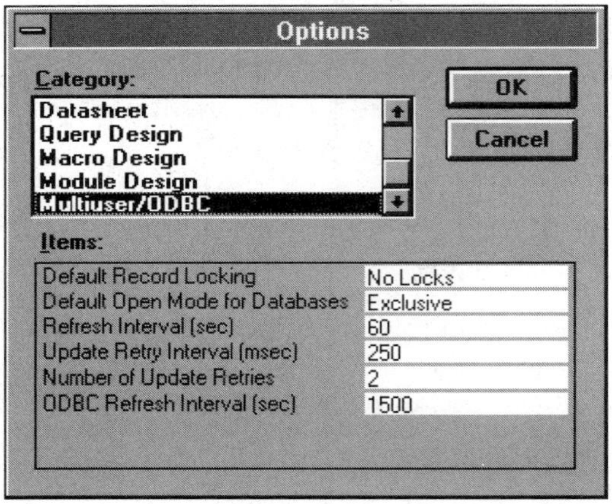

FIGURE 10-31. The Options dialog box with the Multiuser/ODBC category selected.

Attaching Microsoft Access Tables

To attach a table from another Microsoft Access database to your database, do the following:

1. Open the Microsoft Access database to which you want to attach the table. If you already have that database open, switch to the Database window.

2. Choose the Attach Table command from the File menu. Access opens the Attach dialog box, shown in Figure 10-32, which lists the types of databases you can attach.

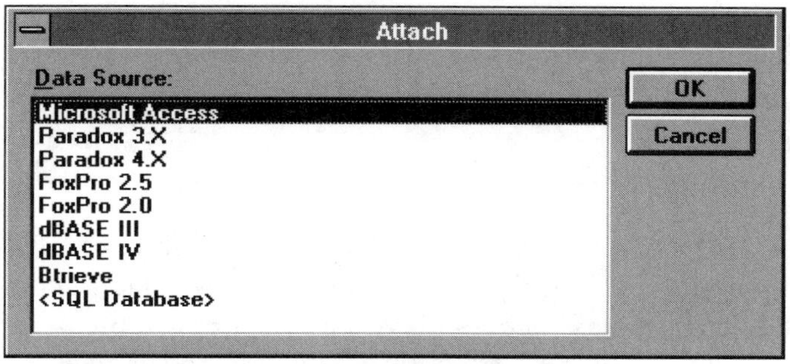

FIGURE 10-32.
The Attach dialog box, listing the types of databases that can be attached to Microsoft Access.

3. Select Microsoft Access in the Data Source list and click the OK button. Access opens a Select Microsoft Access Database dialog box, similar to the dialog box shown in Figure 10-3 on page 295, in which you can choose the drive, directory, and name of the MDB file that contains the table you want to attach. If you are connecting over a network, you can select the logical drive that is assigned to the network server containing the database you want. If you aren't always connected to the remote server that contains the Access table you want but you would like Access to connect each time you open the table, type the full network location in the File Name box instead of choosing a logical drive. For example, on a Microsoft LAN Manager network you might enter a network location such as this one:

   \\DBSVR\ACCESS\SHARED\NWIND.MDB

   You would then click OK.

4. Access opens the Attach Tables dialog box, as shown in Figure 10-33 on the next page, which lists the tables available in the database you've chosen. Select the table you want, and click the Attach button to connect the table you selected to the current database.

FIGURE 10-33. The Attach Tables dialog box.

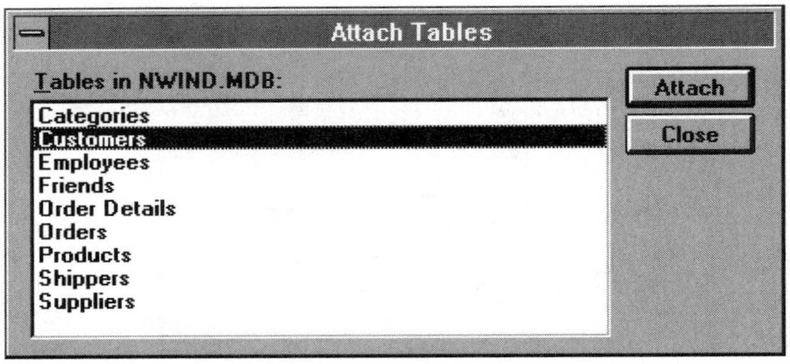

5. Access opens a dialog box, similar to the one shown in Figure 10-4 on page 296, that indicates the result of the attach action. If the attach action was successful, you'll find a new table in your database with the name of the table you selected. Access marks the icon for attached tables in the Database window with an arrow, as shown in Figure 10-34. If Access finds a duplicate name, it generates a new name by adding a unique integer to the end of the name. For example, if you're attaching a table named NEWCUST and you already have tables named NewCust and NewCust1, Access creates a table named NEWCUST2.

   Because objects such as forms, reports, macros, and modules might refer to this table by its original name, you should carefully check name references if Access has to rename an attached table.

FIGURE 10-34. The Database window showing dBASE, FoxPro, SQL (ODBC), Paradox, and Access attached tables. Icons marked with an arrow represent attached tables.

6. Click the OK button to dismiss the dialog box that confirms the attach action. Access returns you to the Attach Tables dialog box. You can select a new table and click the Attach button, or you can click the Close button to dismiss the Attach Tables dialog box.

Attaching dBASE, FoxPro, and Paradox Files and Btrieve Tables

Attaching tables from a foreign database is nearly as simple as attaching a Microsoft Access table. To attach a table from dBASE, FoxPro, Paradox, or Btrieve, do the following:

1. Open the Microsoft Access database to which you want to attach the table. If you already have that database open, switch to the Database window.
2. Choose the Attach Table command from the File menu. Access opens the Attach dialog box that lists the types of databases you can attach. (See Figure 10-32 on page 325.)
3. Select dBASE III, dBASE IV, FoxPro 2.0, FoxPro 2.5, Paradox 3.x, Paradox 4.x, or Btrieve, as appropriate, in the Data Source list and click OK. Access opens a Select File dialog box, similar to the dialog box shown in Figure 10-3 on page 295, in which you can choose the drive, directory, and name of the database file that you want to attach. If you're attaching a table from a Btrieve database, you'll select the dictionary file (a DDF file) at this time. If you're connecting over a network, select the logical drive that is assigned to the network server that contains the database you want. If you aren't always connected to the remote server that contains the file you want but you would like Access to automatically connect each time you open the attached file, type the full network location in the File Name box instead of choosing a "logical drive." For example, on a Microsoft LAN Manager network you might enter a network location such as this one:

   ```
   \\DBSVR\DBASE\SHARED\NEWCUST.DBF
   ```

   You would then click the Attach button to attach the selected dBASE, FoxPro, or Paradox file. Click OK to open the selected Btrieve dictionary file.

4. If you've chosen a dBASE or FoxPro file, Access next prompts you to identify any index files (NDX or MDX files) that are associated with the file you want to attach. Access opens the Select Index Files dialog box shown in Figure 10-35. You must inform Access of all related indexes if you want the indexes updated properly whenever you make a change to the dBASE file using Access. You must not move or delete these index files or the information (INF) file that Access builds when you attach the table; if you do, you will not be able to open the dBASE file from Access. You must also be sure that any dBASE application always maintains these indexes. Access can't open an attached dBASE table if its indexes are not current.

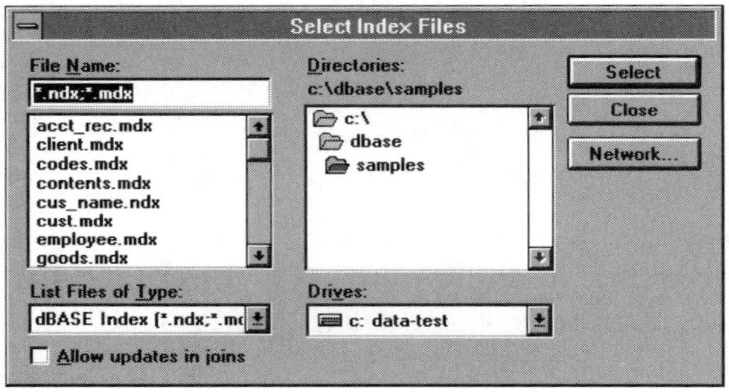

FIGURE 10-35. The Select Index Files dialog box, used to associate index files with dBASE files you attach to your Access database.

Select the index files you need to associate with the dBASE file you're attaching. Click the Select button once for each index file you want to add the information file. Click Close when you've selected all the indexes.

5. If you're attaching a Btrieve table, Access opens a Tables list box after you've selected a dictionary file in the Select File dialog box. The Tables list box shows the tables available in the dictionary you have chosen. Select the table you want, and click the Attach button to connect the table you selected to the current database. This tables list is in a dialog box similar to the one shown in Figure 10-10 on page 301.

6. If the file you selected requires a password to access it (because it's an encrypted Paradox file or a password-protected Btrieve table), Microsoft Access next prompts you for the correct password, as shown in Figure 10-7 on page 298. Access then opens a dialog box, similar to the one shown in Figure 10-4 on page 296, that indicates the result of the attach action. If the attach action was successful, you'll find a new table in your database with the name of the file you selected. If Access finds a duplicate name, it generates a new name by adding a unique integer to the end of the name. For example, if you're attaching a table named NEWCUST and you already have tables named NewCust and NewCust1, Access creates a new table named NEWCUST2.
7. Click the OK button to dismiss the dialog box that confirms the attach action. Access returns you to the Select File dialog box (or, in the case of Btrieve, to the Tables list box). You can select a new file and click the Attach button, or you can click the Close button to dismiss the dialog box.

Attaching SQL Tables

To attach a table from another database system that supports ODBC SQL, you must first have the ODBC driver for that database installed on your computer. (For details, see Chapter 9 of the *User's Guide* that comes with Access; also see Appendix A of this book.) Your computer must also be attached to the network that connects to the SQL server you want, and you must have an account on that server. Check with your system administrator for information about correctly connecting to the SQL server from which you want to attach a table.

To attach an SQL table, do the following:

1. Open the Microsoft Access database to which you want to attach an SQL table. If you already have that database open, switch to the Database window.
2. Choose the Attach Table command from the File menu. Access opens an Attach dialog box that lists the types of databases you can attach, as shown in Figure 10-32 on page 325.

3. Select SQL Database in the Data Source list and click the OK button. Access opens an SQL Data Sources dialog box, similar to the one shown in Figure 10-12 on page 303, in which you can select the name of the SQL server that contains the table you want to attach. Click OK, and Access displays a Login dialog box for the SQL data source that you selected. (See Figure 10-13 on page 303.) If you're using ODBC to attach via SQL to dBASE, FoxPro, Paradox, or another Microsoft Access database, you don't need to log on.

4. Enter your User ID and your password, and click OK. When Access has connected you to the server, you'll see a list of available tables on that server, as shown in Figure 10-14 on page 304.

5 From the list of tables on the server, select the one you want to attach. Click the Attach button in the Import Tables dialog box to attach the SQL table that you've selected.

6. Access then opens a dialog box, similar to the one shown in Figure 10-4 on page 296, that indicates the result of the attach action. If the attach action was successful, you'll find a new table in your database with the name of the SQL table. If Access finds a duplicate name, it generates a new name by adding a unique integer to the end of the name. For example, if you're attaching a table named newcust and you already have tables named NewCust and NewCust1, Access creates a new table named newcust2.

7. Click the OK button to dismiss the dialog box that confirms the attach action. Access returns you to the Import Tables dialog box. You can select a new table and click the Attach button, or you can click the Close button to dismiss the dialog box.

Modifying Attached Tables

You can make some changes to the definitions of attached tables to customize them for use in your Microsoft Access environment. When you attempt to open the Table window in Design view, Access opens a dialog box to warn you that you cannot modify certain properties in an attached table. You can still click OK to open the attached table in Design view.

For an attached table, you can open the Table window in Design view to change the Format, Decimal Places, Caption, Description, and Input Mask property settings for any field. You can set these properties to customize the way you look at and update data with Access forms and reports. You can also give any attached table a new name for use within your Access database (although the table's original name remains unchanged in the source database) to help you identify the table better or to enable you to use the table with the queries, forms, and reports that you've already designed.

Changing a table's design in Microsoft Access has no effect on the original table in its source database. Notice, however, that if the design of the table in the source database changes, you will have to reattach the table to Access. You must also detach and reattach any table when your User ID or your password to access the source database changes.

Unattaching Attached Tables

Unattaching tables attached to your Microsoft Access database is easy to do. Simply choose the table you want to detach in the Database window and press the Del key or choose Delete from the Edit menu. Access displays the confirmation dialog box shown in Figure 10-36. Click the OK button to unattach the table. Unattaching the table does not delete the table; it simply removes the attachment from your table list in the Database window.

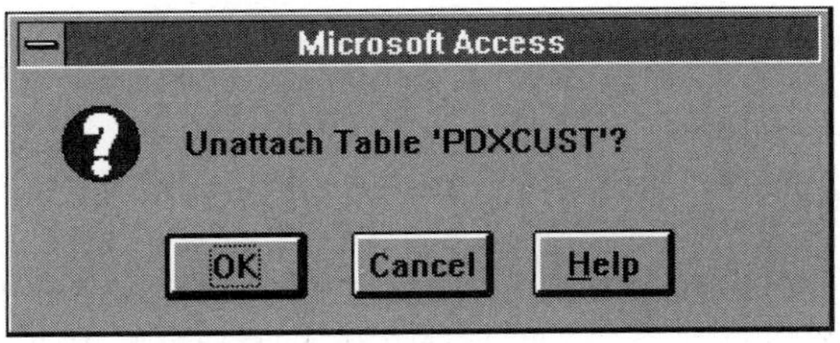

FIGURE 10-36. The unattach table confirmation dialog box.

Using the Attachment Manager

NEW!

Another handy utility provided in the Add-ins facility on the File menu is the Attachment Manager. If some or all of your attached tables move to a different location, you can update the location information easily by using this utility. To use the Attachment Manager, open the database that contains attached tables that need to be reattached, choose Add-ins from the File menu, and then choose Attachment Manager. The utility shows you a dialog box that displays all the attached tables in your database, as shown in Figure 10-37. Simply check the ones that you think need to be verified and updated, and then click OK. If any of the attached tables are now in a different location, the Attachment Manager prompts you with a dialog box similar to the one shown in Figure 10-3 on page 295 so that you can identify the new file location.

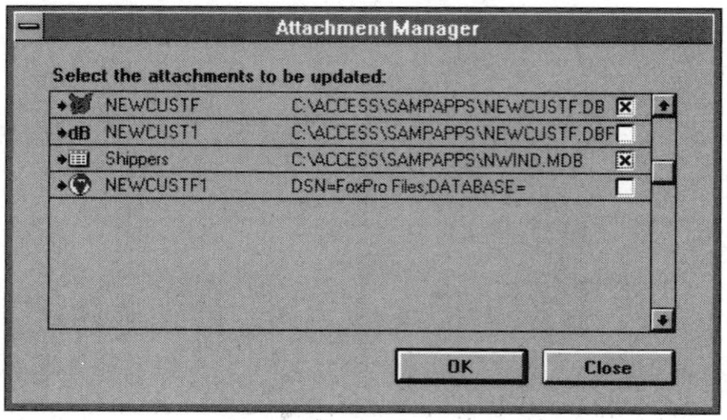

FIGURE 10-37. The Attachment Manager dialog box.

Exporting Data

You can export (copy) any object in a Microsoft Access database to any other Microsoft Access database. You can also export data from Access tables to spreadsheet files, other databases, or text files.

Exporting to Another Microsoft Access Database

Exporting objects from one Microsoft Access database to another works much like importing Access objects. To export any object from one Access database to another Access database, do the following:

1. Open the Microsoft Access database from which you want to export an object. If you already have that database open, switch to the Database window.

2. Choose the Export command from the File menu. Access opens the Export dialog box shown in Figure 10-38. Select Microsoft Access from the Data Destination list, and click OK.

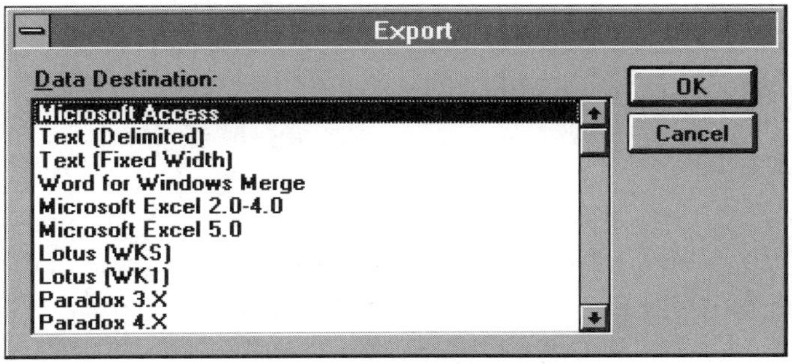

FIGURE 10-38.
The Export dialog box.

3. Access opens the Select Microsoft Access Object dialog box shown in Figure 10-39. In this dialog box, you can select the object type and then the specific object you want to export. If the object is a table, you can choose to export the table structure (table definition) only, or the structure <u>and</u> the stored data. After you've selected the object you want, click OK.

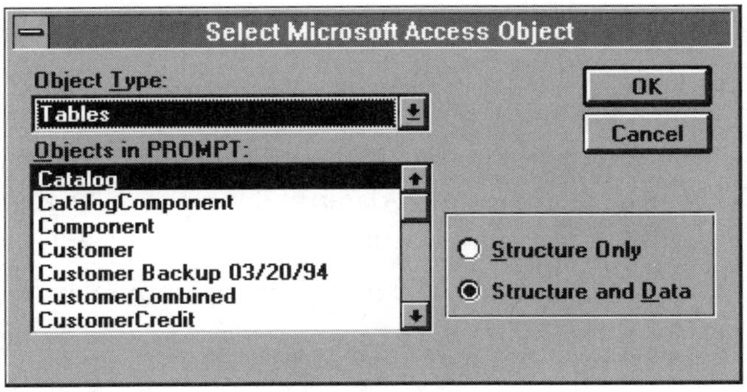

FIGURE 10-39.
The Select Microsoft Access Object dialog box that is used for exporting an object to another Access database.

4. Access opens the Export To File dialog box, shown in Figure 10-40 on the next page, from which you can select the drive, directory, and name of the MDB file to which you want to export objects. After you've selected these, click OK.

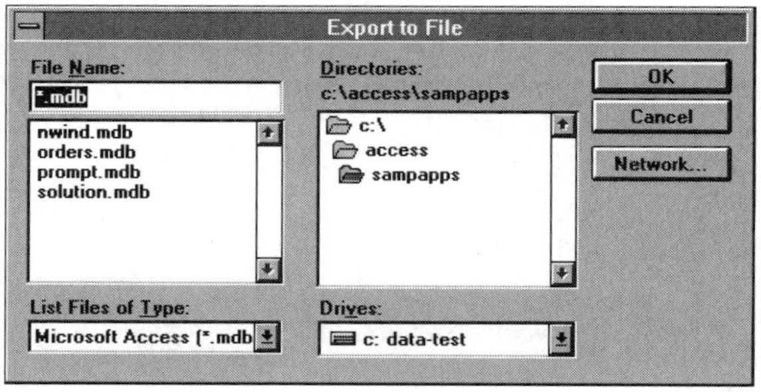

FIGURE 10-40. The Export To File dialog box.

5. Next, Access shows you the Export dialog box shown in Figure 10-41, which asks you to enter a name for the object in the receiving database. You can leave the name as is, or you can change it to meet your needs in the receiving database. Click OK to export the object.

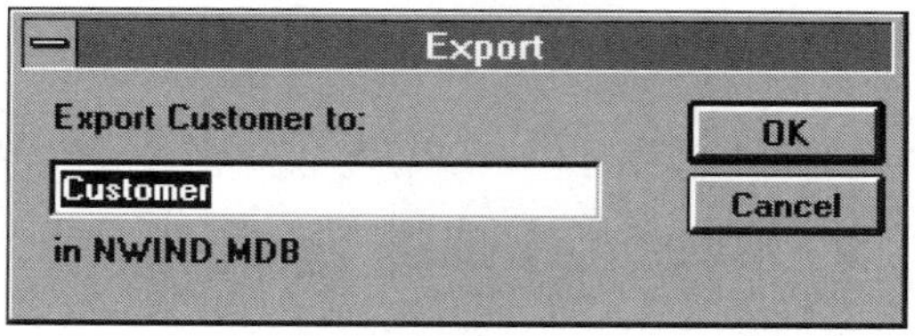

FIGURE 10-41. An Export dialog box that's used to name an exported Access object.

6. If the export name you've chosen already exists in the target database, Access warns you and asks whether you want to replace the existing object. Click OK to proceed, or click the Cancel button to stop the export action. If the export was successful, you'll find a new object in the target database. Because objects can refer to other objects by name within an Access database, you should carefully check name references in the receiving database.

Exporting to a Spreadsheet or to a dBASE, Paradox, or FoxPro File

NEW!

You can use the following procedure to export data from a table, a select query, or a crosstab query to a spreadsheet (Microsoft Excel or Lotus 1-2-3) or a database (dBASE, Paradox, or FoxPro file):

1. Open the Microsoft Access database from which you want to export the data in a table. If you already have that database open, switch to the Database window.
2. Choose the Export command from the File menu. Access opens the Export dialog box shown in Figure 10-38 on page 333. Select Excel, Lotus 1-2-3, dBASE III, dBASE IV, Paradox, or FoxPro from the Data Destination list, and click OK.
3. Access opens the Select Microsoft Access Object dialog box, shown in Figure 10-42, from which you can select the table or the query whose data you want to export. When you've selected the table or query you want, click OK.

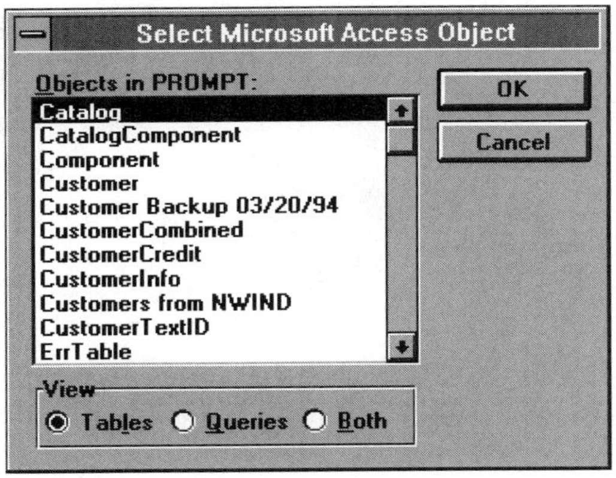

FIGURE 10-42.
The Select Microsoft Access Object dialog box for exporting data.

4. Access opens the Export To File dialog box, from which you can select the drive, directory, and filename to which you want to export your data. Click OK to export your data to that file in the application format you've chosen. (See Figure 10-40.)
5. If the export was successful, you'll find a new file that you can use with your spreadsheet or another database program. Figure 10-43 on the next page shows you an Access table that has been exported to a Microsoft Excel spreadsheet. (It's the sample dBASE file that was imported to Access in Figure 10-5 on page 296.)

NOTE: dBASE, Paradox, and FoxPro cannot support the 64-character field names available in Microsoft Access. Access truncates long field names when copying data to these files. If the truncated name results in a duplicate field name, Access reports an error and does not export your data.

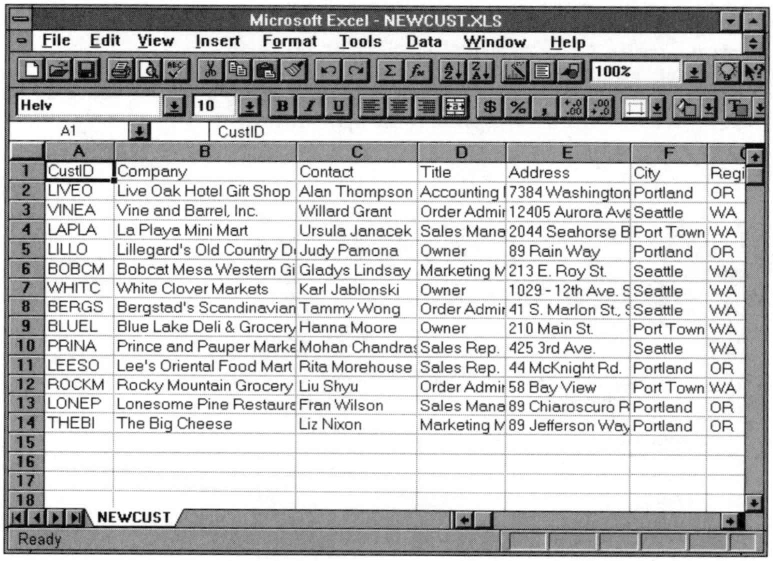

FIGURE 10-43. A Microsoft Access table exported to a Microsoft Excel spreadsheet.

TIP: Microsoft Access truncates long field names when copying data to dBASE, Paradox, or FoxPro files. If this results in a duplicate field name, Access will not export your data.

To correct this problem, make a temporary copy of your table, edit the field names in the temporary table to avoid duplicates, and retry the export using the temporary table. It's not a good idea to change the field names in your permanent table because you might cause errors in queries, forms, and reports that use the table.

Quick Export to Microsoft Excel

Microsoft Access also provides a quick facility to export the data in any table, select query, or crosstab query to a Microsoft Excel spreadsheet. Simply choose the table or query in the Database window whose data you want to export, choose Output To from the File menu and then choose Microsoft Excel in the dialog box that appears or click the Analyze It With MS Excel button on the toolbar. Access copies the table to a Microsoft Excel spreadsheet file and opens the file in Excel. If the filename already exists, Access asks you whether you want to replace the file. If you click No, Access asks you to provide a different filename. Figure 10-44 shows you the NEWCUST table (previously imported from dBASE) that has been output to Microsoft Excel.

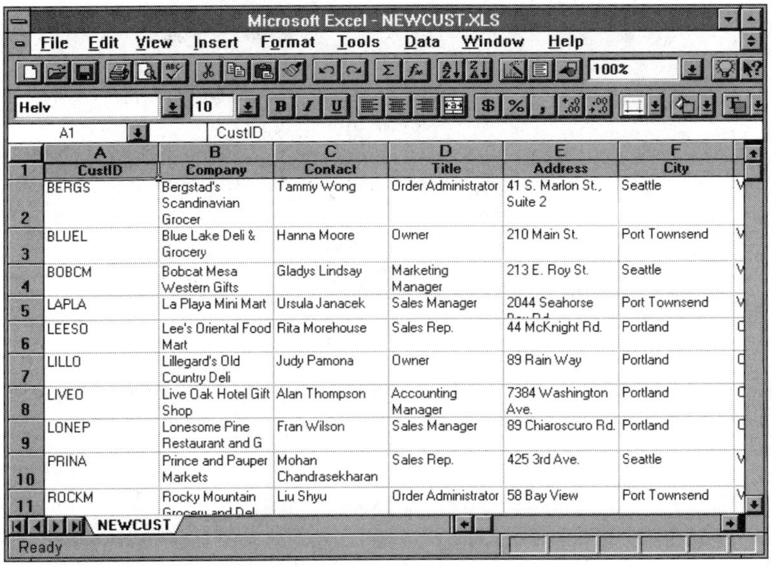

	A	B	C	D	E	F
1	CustID	Company	Contact	Title	Address	City
2	BERGS	Bergstad's Scandinavian Grocer	Tammy Wong	Order Administrator	41 S. Marlon St., Suite 2	Seattle
3	BLUEL	Blue Lake Deli & Grocery	Hanna Moore	Owner	210 Main St.	Port Townsend
4	BOBCM	Bobcat Mesa Western Gifts	Gladys Lindsay	Marketing Manager	213 E. Roy St.	Seattle
5	LAPLA	La Playa Mini Mart	Ursula Janacek	Sales Manager	2044 Seahorse	Port Townsend
6	LEESO	Lee's Oriental Food Mart	Rita Morehouse	Sales Rep.	44 McKnight Rd.	Portland
7	LILLO	Lillegard's Old Country Deli	Judy Pamona	Owner	89 Rain Way	Portland
8	LIVEO	Live Oak Hotel Gift Shop	Alan Thompson	Accounting Manager	7384 Washington Ave.	Portland
9	LONEP	Lonesome Pine Restaurant and G	Fran Wilson	Sales Manager	89 Chiaroscuro Rd.	Portland
10	PRINA	Prince and Pauper Markets	Mohan Chandrasekharan	Sales Rep.	425 3rd Ave.	Seattle
11	ROCKM	Rocky Mountain	Liu Shyu	Order Administrator	58 Bay View	Port Townsend

FIGURE 10-44.
A Microsoft Access table that's been output to Microsoft Excel.

Exporting to a Text File

You can export data from a Microsoft Access table or a select query or a crosstab query to a text file in one of two formats: delimited or fixed-width. You might find this procedure particularly useful for copying data from an Access table to a non-Windows word processor or text editor or for uploading the data to a host computer.

Before you export a table or a query as a delimited text file, you need to decide what field separators and text delimiters you want Access to use. By default, Access uses a comma to separate fields and encloses text data in double quotation marks.

To export a table in a fixed format, you must first define an import/export specification. To do this, first open the database from which you want to export data, click on the Database window, and then choose Imp/Exp Setup from the File menu. Access then opens the Import/Export Setup dialog box, shown in Figure 10-45.

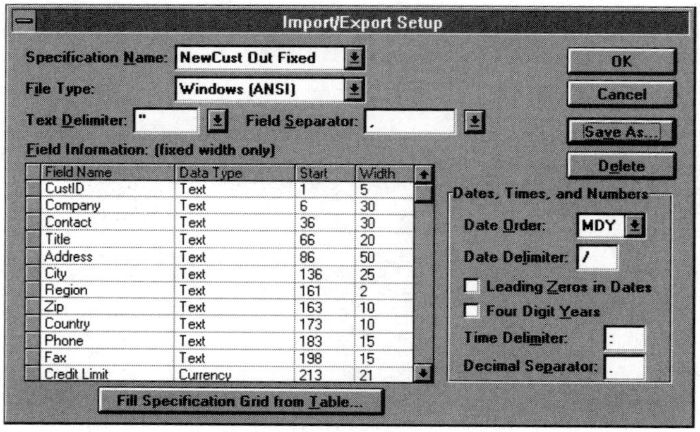

FIGURE 10-45. The Import/Export Setup dialog box with settings for a fixed-width export specification.

You can use the Fill Specification Grid From Table button to ask Access to fill in data type, start, and width specifications based on the table you're about to export. It's easy to customize the list to suit your needs. Or you can individually enter each field name from your table in the Field Name column, define the data type of the source field in the Data Type column, and specify the relative location in which you would like the output data to begin in the Start column (the first column in the resulting text file is 1) and the width of the field in the Width column. Click the Save As button to open a dialog box in which you can name the new specification. You can now use this specification to export data from a table or a query to a fixed-width text file.

To export the data from a Microsoft Access table to a text file, do the following:

1. Open the Microsoft Access database from which you want to export the data in a table. If you already have that database open, switch to the Database window.
2. Choose the Export command from the File menu. Access opens the Export dialog box shown in Figure 10-38 on page 333. Select Text (Delimited) or Text (Fixed Width) as appropriate from the Data Destination list, and then click OK.
3. Access opens the Select Microsoft Access Object dialog box, shown in Figure 10-39 on page 333, from which you can select the table whose data you want to export. After you've selected the table you want, click OK.
4. Access opens the Export To File dialog box, from which you can select the drive, directory, and filename to which you want to export your data. After you've entered the filename you want, click OK. (See Figure 10-40 on page 334.)
5. If you're exporting to a fixed-width text file, Access opens the Export Text Options dialog box shown in Figure 10-46. If you've previously created an import/export specification, choose it from the Specification Name drop-down list and click OK. If you haven't created an import/export specification, click the Edit Specs button. The Import/Export Setup dialog box appears, shown in Figure 10-45. Select the options you want, click the Save As button and name the specification, and then click OK to return to the Export Text Options dialog box. Click OK when you're done.

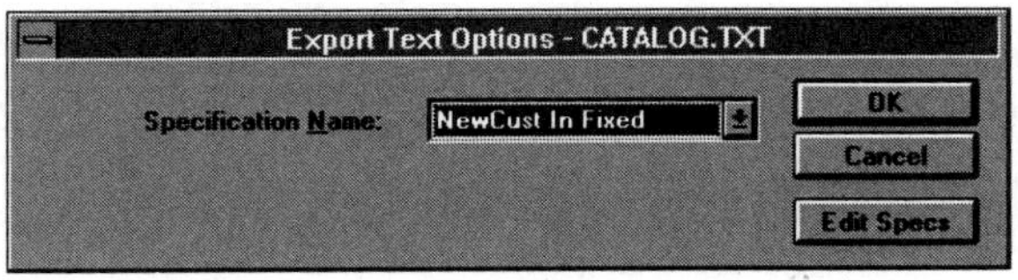

FIGURE 10-46.
The Export Text Options dialog box, used for exporting to a fixed-width text file.

6. If you're exporting to a delimited text file, Access opens the Export Text Options dialog box, shown in Figure 10-47 on the next page. You can use the default specification, or you can click Options to expand the dialog box, shown expanded in Figure 10-48 on the next page. Now you can create your own specification. Click OK when you're done.

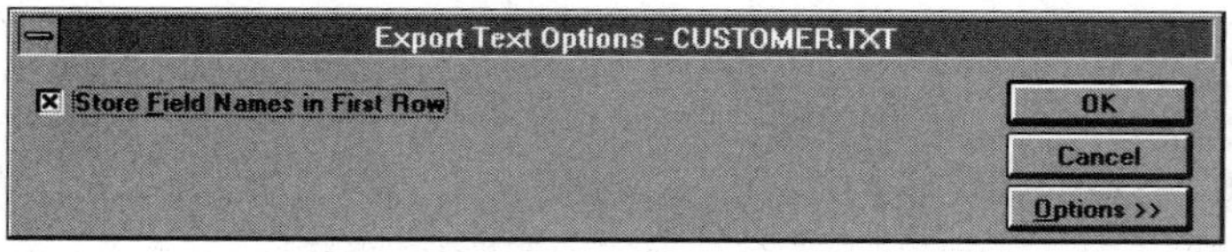

FIGURE 10-47. The Export Text Options dialog box, used for exporting to a delimited text file.

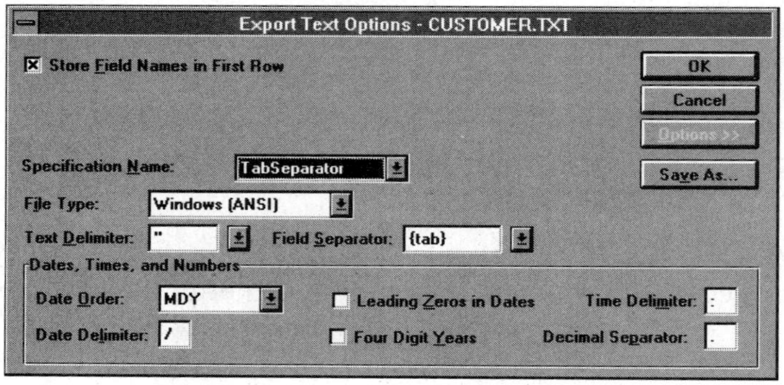

FIGURE 10-48. The Export Text Options dialog box expands when the Options button is clicked.

7. If the export was successful, you'll find a new file in the text format you selected.

NEW!

Exporting to Mail Merge in Microsoft Word for Windows

Perhaps one of the most useful features of Microsoft Access is its ability to integrate with Microsoft Word for Windows to allow you to embed data from an Access table or a query directly in a Word document. To embed data that is in your Microsoft Access database in a Microsoft Word for Windows document, do the following:

1. Open your database and choose the table or query whose data you want to embed in a Microsoft Word for Windows document.
2. Click the Merge It button on the toolbar to start the Mail Merge Wizard, shown in Figure 10-49.

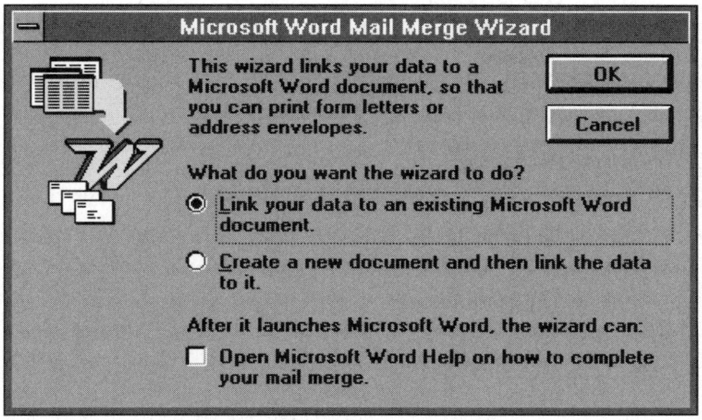

FIGURE 10-49.
The Microsoft Word Mail Merge Wizard in Microsoft Access.

3. Choose either an existing document or a new document. If you want to embed the data in an existing document, the Wizard asks you for the document location. Click the check box at the bottom of the dialog box if you want help on how to complete the mail merge. (Linking data to a document requires Word for Windows 6.0.) Click OK.

4. The Wizard starts Microsoft Word for Windows and activates a mail merge link to your table or query, shown in Figure 10-50. You can use the various features of the Mail Merge toolbar in Word to build your document with fields embedded from Microsoft Access.

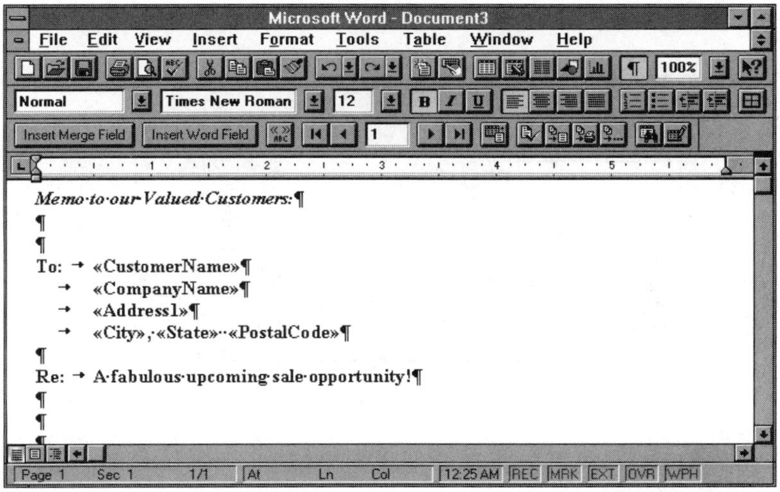

FIGURE 10-50.
Creating a mail merge document in Microsoft Word for Windows.

Exporting to a Btrieve Table

Before you can export data to a Btrieve table, a dictionary file must exist into which Microsoft Access can define the output table.

> NOTE: To use Btrieve tables, you must have the Btrieve for Windows dynamic link library WBTRCALL.DLL, which is not provided with Microsoft Access. This DLL is provided with Novell Btrieve for Windows, Novell Netware SQL, and some other Windows-based products that use Btrieve.

To export Access data to a Btrieve table, do the following:

1. Open the Microsoft Access database from which you want to export the data in a table. If you already have that database open, switch to the Database window.
2. Choose the Export command from the File menu. Access opens the Export dialog box. Select Btrieve from the Data Destination list, and click OK. (See Figure 10-38 on page 333.)
3. Access opens the Select Microsoft Access Object dialog box, shown in Figure 10-39 on page 333, from which you can select the table whose data you want to export. When you have selected the table you want, click OK.
4. Next, Access opens the Export To File dialog box, shown in Figure 10-51, from which you can select the drive and directory in which the dictionary file (a DDF file) is located. When you have selected the file you want, click OK.

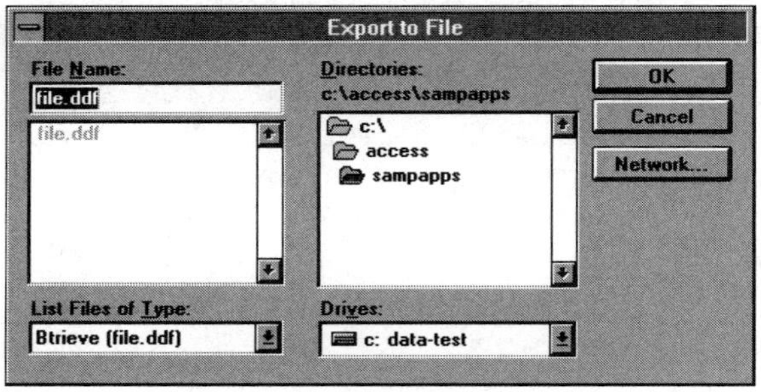

FIGURE 10-51. The Export To File dialog box with a Btrieve dictionary file listed.

5. Access next prompts you for a name for the Btrieve table. Type the name, as shown in Figure 10-52, and click OK to export the data in your table.

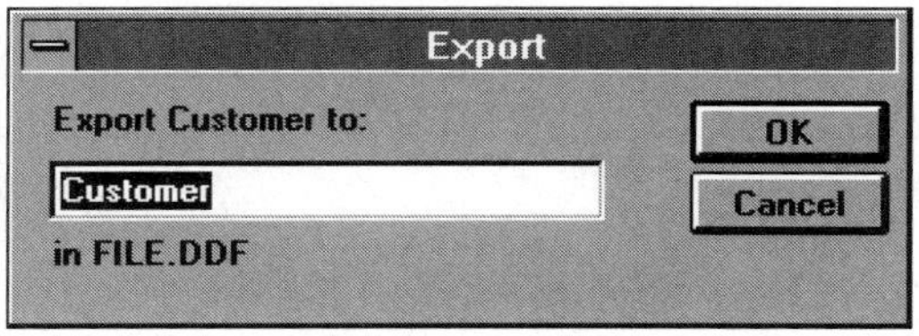

FIGURE 10-52.
The Export dialog box asks for the name of a table in the Btrieve dictionary into which data will be exported.

6. If the export was successful, you'll find a new Btrieve table defined in the dictionary you selected.

Exporting to an SQL Table

You can export data from a Microsoft Access table or query to define a new table in any SQL database that supports the ODBC standard. To export data in an Access table or query to another database system that supports ODBC SQL, you must first have the ODBC driver for that database installed on your computer. (For details, see Appendix D of the *User's Guide* that comes with Microsoft Access.) Your computer must also be attached to the network that connects to the SQL server you want, and you must have an account on that server. Check with your system administrator for information about correctly connecting to the SQL server to which you want to export data.

To export data to an SQL table, do the following:

1. Open the Microsoft Access database from which you want to export your data. If you already have that database open, switch to the Database window.
2. Choose the Export command from the File menu. Access opens the Export dialog box shown in Figure 10-38. Select SQL Database in the Data Destination list, and click OK.
3. Access opens the Select Microsoft Access Object dialog box, shown in Figure 10-42 on page 335, from which you can select the table or the query whose data you want to export. When you've selected the table you want, click OK.

4. Next, Access asks you what name you want to give the new table on the server. The dialog box is similar to the one shown in Figure 10-41 on page 334. Type the name you want, and click OK.
5. Access opens a dialog box in which you can select the name of the SQL server that will receive your data. This dialog box is similar to the one shown in Figure 10-12 on page 303. Select the server name, and click OK.
6. Access displays a Login dialog box for the SQL data source that you selected. This dialog box is similar to that in Figure 10-13 on page 303. Enter your User ID and your password, and click OK to create a new table on the server that contains your data.

Now you have all the information you need to import, attach, and export data using Microsoft Access. In Part 4 of this book, "Using Forms," you'll learn the really interesting stuff. Forms are what make your data "come alive" in a Microsoft Access application.

The next chapter, "Advanced Query Design—SQL," discusses in detail the Microsoft Access dialect of SQL. The discussion is intended for intermediate and advanced users. If you're not interested in advanced query design, skip to Chapter 12, "Form Basics."

11

Advanced Query Design—SQL

Underlying every query in Microsoft Access is the SQL database command language. Although you can design most queries using the simple query by example (QBE) graphical interface, Access stores every query you design as an SQL command. For some advanced types of queries that use the results of another query (called a *subquery*) as a comparison condition, you need to know SQL to be able to define the subquery. Also, you cannot use the QBE grid to construct all the types of queries available in the product. You must use SQL.

This chapter explores and explains the various syntax elements in the Microsoft Access variant of SQL that you can use to build the select, total, crosstab, make table, update, append, and delete queries. You'll find brief examples for each element that help explain how to use that element. At the end of this chapter are several complex examples you'll find implemented in the PROMPT database. The sample database uses some of the more complex features of SQL in Access to accomplish tasks described in Part 6 of this book. As you become more familiar with SQL, you can learn a lot about the language and how it's implemented in Access by using the QBE grid to design a query and then switching to SQL view to see how Access interprets the query in SQL statements.

NOTE: This chapter is appropriate for intermediate and advanced users who are interested in using the Microsoft Access dialect of SQL. If you prefer, you can skip to Chapter 12, "Form Basics."

A Brief History of SQL

A language called Structured English Query Language (SEQUEL) was invented by IBM in its research projects to build a relational database management system in the early 1970s. This language evolved into SEQUEL/2 and finally into Structured Query Language (SQL). Other companies became interested in the concept of relational databases and the emerging SQL interface. Relational Software, Inc. (now the Oracle Corporation) created a product called Oracle in 1979. IBM released its first product, called SQL Data System (SQL/DS), in 1981.

In 1982 the American National Standards Institute (ANSI), realizing the potential significance of the relational model, began work on a Relational Database Language (RDL) standard. By 1984 acceptance in the marketplace of such products as Oracle, SQL/DS, and IBM's DB2 caused the ANSI committee to focus on SQL as the basis for the new RDL standard. The first version of this standard, SQL-86, was adopted by both ANSI and the International Standards Organization (ISO) in October of 1986. An update to SQL-86 covering integrity enhancements was adopted in 1989. The current standard, often referred to as "SQL2" or "SQL-92," reflects extensive work by the international standards bodies to both enhance the language and correct many missing, confusing, or ambiguous features in the original 1986 standard.

The standard as it currently exists is both a common subset of the major implementations and a superset of almost all implementations. That is, the core of the standard contains features found in virtually every commercial implementation of the language, yet the entire standard includes enhanced features that many vendors have yet to implement.

As mentioned in the previous chapter, the SQL Access Group consortium of database vendors has published what could be regarded as the "commercial standard" for SQL—a variant of the language that can be "spoken" by (or mapped to) every major relational database product. Microsoft Corporation has promulgated the Open Database Connectivity (ODBC) application programming interface (API) to allow vendors to connect to each other via the SQL Access Group standard. Microsoft Access connects to many databases via the ODBC standard and also "speaks" a major subset of the SQL Access Group standard SQL.

SQL Syntax Conventions

The following table lists the SQL syntax conventions you'll encounter in this chapter:

SQL Convention	Meaning
UPPERCASE	Uppercase letters indicate keywords and reserved words that you must enter exactly as shown. Note that Microsoft Access understands keywords entered in either uppercase or lowercase.
Italics	Italicized words represent variables you supply.

(continued)

continued

<table>
<tr><th>SQL Convention</th><th>Meaning</th></tr>
<tr><td>Angle brackets <></td><td>Angle brackets enclose syntactic elements that you must supply. The words inside the angle brackets describe the element but do not show the actual syntax of the element.</td></tr>
<tr><td>Brackets [ ]</td><td>Brackets enclose optional items, separated by a pipe (|) character if more than one item is listed. Choose one or none of the elements. Do not enter the brackets or the pipe. Note that Microsoft Access in many cases requires you to enclose names in brackets. When brackets are required as part of the syntax of variables that you must supply in these examples, the brackets are italicized, as in [MyTable].[MyField].</td></tr>
<tr><td>Braces { }</td><td>Braces enclose one or more options, separated by a pipe (|) character if more than one is listed. Choose one option from the list. Do not enter the braces or the pipe.</td></tr>
<tr><td>Ellipses ,...</td><td>Ellipses indicate that you can repeat an item one or more times. When a comma is shown with an ellipsis, enter the comma between items.</td></tr>
</table>

You must enter all other characters, such as parentheses and colons, exactly as they appear in the syntax line.

TIP: When you work on a query in SQL Design view, you can insert a carriage return between elements to improve readability. In fact, Access inserts carriage returns between major clauses when you save and close your query. The only time you may not include carriage returns in an SQL statement is when you're defining an SQL statement on a string literal in Access Basic. Access Basic requires that a literal be defined as a single line in a procedure. (A literal is a value that is expressed as itself rather than as a variable's value or the result of an expression.)

NOTE: This chapter does not document all of the syntax variants accepted by Microsoft Access, but does cover all of the features of SELECT and of action queries. Wherever possible, ANSI standard syntax is shown to provide portability across other databases that also support some form of SQL. You might discover that Access modifies the ANSI standard syntax to a syntax that it prefers after you save a query definition.

SQL SELECT Syntax in Microsoft Access

The *SELECT* statement forms the core of the SQL database language. You'll use the SELECT statement to select or retrieve the rows and columns you want from your database tables. The SELECT statement syntax contains five major clauses, generally constructed as follows:

```
SELECT <field list>
  FROM <table list>
  [WHERE <row selection specification>]
  [GROUP BY <grouping specification>
  [HAVING <group selection specification>]]
  [ORDER BY <sorting specification>];
```

Microsoft Access implements four significant extensions to the language: *TRANSFORM*, to allow you to build crosstab queries; *IN*, to allow you to specify a remote database connection; *DISTINCTROW*, to define joined queries that can potentially allow updates; and *WITH OWNERACCESS OPTION*, to let you design queries that can be run by users who are authorized to use the query but who have no rights to the tables referenced in the query.

The following sections in this chapter are a reference guide to the Access implementation of SQL for select, total, and crosstab queries. The language elements are presented in alphabetic order.

Expression

Specifies a value in a predicate or in the select list of a SELECT statement or subquery.

Syntax:

```
[+|-] {function | (expression) | literal | column-name}
[{+|-|*|/|\|^|MOD|&} {function | (expression) |
literal | column-name}]...
```

Notes:

function—You can specify an SQL total function such as AVG, COUNT, MAX, MIN, STDEV, STDEVP, SUM, VAR, or VARP. You can also use any of the functions built into Microsoft Access or the functions you define using Access Basic.

(*expression*)—You can construct an expression from multiple expressions separated by operators. (See the examples later in this section.)

literal—You can specify a numeric or an alphanumeric constant. You must enclose an alphanumeric constant in single or double quotation marks. To include an apostrophe in an alphanumeric constant, enter the apostrophe character twice in the literal string. If the expression is numeric, you must use a numeric constant. Enclose a date/time literal within pound (#) signs.

column-name—You can specify the name of a column in a table or a query. You can only use a column name from a table or query that you've specified in the FROM clause of the statement. If the expression is an arithmetic expression, you must use a column that contains numeric data. If the same *column-name* appears in more than one of the tables or queries included in the query, you must fully qualify the name with the query name, table name, or correlation name, as in *[TableA].[Column1].*

+ | - | * | / | \ | MOD—You can combine multiple numeric expressions with arithmetic operators that specify a calculation. If you use arithmetic operators, all expressions within an expression must be able to be evaluated as numeric data types.

&—You can concatenate alphanumeric constants by using the special & operator.

Examples:

To specify the average of a column named COST, enter the following function:

```
AVG(COST)
```

To specify one-half the value of a column named PRICE, enter the following expression:

```
(PRICE * .5)
```

To specify a literal for 3:00 P.M. on March 1, 1993, enter the following:

```
#3/1/93 3:00PM#
```

To specify a character string that contains the name *Acme Mail Order Company*, enter the following literal (a literal is a value that is expressed as itself rather than as a variable's value or the result of an expression):

```
"Acme Mail Order Company"
```

To specify a character string that contains a possessive noun (requiring an embedded apostrophe), enter the following:

```
'Andy''s Hardware Store'
```

To specify a character string that is the concatenation of the fields containing a person's first and last name, enter the following:

```
[FirstName] & " " & [LastName]
```

See Also:

Predicates, SELECT statement, Subquery, and UPDATE statement.

FROM Clause

Defines the tables or queries that provide the source data for your query.

Syntax:

```
FROM {{table-name [[AS] correlation-name] |
 select-query-name [[AS] correlation-name]} |
 <joined table>},...
```

where *<joined table>* is

```
({table-name [[AS] correlation-name] |
 select-query-name [[AS] correlation-name] |
 <joined table>}
{INNER | LEFT | RIGHT} JOIN
 {table-name [[AS] correlation-name] |
 select-query-name [[AS] correlation-name] |
 <joined table>}
ON <join-specification>)
```

Notes:

You can optionally supply a correlation name for each table or query name. You can use this correlation name as an alias for the full table name when qualifying column names in the select list or in the WHERE clause and subclauses. If you're joining a table or a query to itself, you must use correlation names to clarify which copy of the table or query you're referring to in the select list, join criteria, or selection criteria. If a table name or query name is also an SQL reserved word (for example, "Order"), you must enclose the name in brackets.

If you include multiple tables in the FROM clause with no JOIN specification but do include a predicate that matches fields from the multiple tables in the WHERE clause, Microsoft Access in most cases optimizes how it solves the query by treating the query as a JOIN. For example,

```
SELECT *
  FROM TableA, TableB
  WHERE TableA.ID = TableB.ID
```

is treated by Microsoft Access as though you had specified

```
SELECT *
  FROM TableA
   INNER JOIN TableB
   ON TableA.ID = TableB.ID
```

When you list more than one table or query without join criteria, the source is the *Cartesian product* of all the tables. For example, *FROM TableA, TableB* asks Microsoft Access to search all the rows of TableA matched with all the rows of TableB. Unless you specify other restricting criteria, the number of logical rows that Access processes could equal the number of rows in TableA times the number of rows in TableB. Access then returns the rows in which the selection criteria specified in the WHERE and HAVING clauses are true.

Example:

To select information about customers and their purchases over $100, enter the following:

```
SELECT Cust.CustomerID, Cust.CompanyName, Ord.OrderDate,
       Cat.CatalogItemID, Cat.Description,
       OrderItem.Quantity, OrderItem.QuotedPrice
  FROM (Catalog AS Cat
    INNER JOIN ((Customer AS Cust
      INNER JOIN [Order] AS Ord
      ON Cust.CustomerID = Ord.CustomerID)
        INNER JOIN OrderItem
        ON Ord.OrderID = OrderItem.OrderID)
    ON Cat.CatalogItemID = OrderItem.CatalogItemID)
  WHERE (OrderItem.Quantity * OrderItem.Price) > 100;
```

See Also:

HAVING clause, IN clause, JOIN operation, SELECT statement, Subquery, and WHERE clause.

GROUP BY Clause

In a SELECT statement, specifies the columns used to form groups from the rows selected. Each group contains identical values in the specified column(s). In Microsoft Access, you use the GROUP BY clause to define a total query. You must also include a GROUP BY clause in a crosstab query. (See the TRANSFORM statement for details.)

Syntax:

```
GROUP BY column-name,...
```

Notes:

A column name in the GROUP BY clause can refer to any column from any table in the FROM clause, even if the column is not named in the select list. If the GROUP BY clause is preceded by a WHERE clause, Access creates the groups from the rows selected after the application of the WHERE clause. When you include a GROUP BY clause in a SELECT statement, the select list must be made up of either SQL total functions (AVG, COUNT, MAX, MIN, STDEV, STDEVP, SUM, VAR, or VARP) or column names specified in the GROUP BY clause.

Examples:

To find the largest order from any customer within each zip code, enter the following:

```
SELECT DISTINCTROW Customer.PostalCode,
       Max(Order.SubTotalCost) AS MaxOfSubTotalCost
  FROM Customer
    INNER JOIN [Order]
    ON Customer.CustomerID = Order.CustomerID
  GROUP BY Customer.PostalCode;
```

To find the average and maximum prices for items in the catalog by category, enter the following:

```
SELECT DISTINCTROW Type.TypeDescription,
       AVG(Catalog.Price) AS AvgOfPrice,
       MAX(Catalog.Price) AS MaxOfPrice
  FROM Type
    INNER JOIN Catalog
    ON Type.ItemTypeCode = Catalog.ItemTypeCode
  GROUP BY Type.TypeDescription;
```

See Also:

Total functions (beginning on page 384)—AVG, COUNT, MAX, MIN, STDEV, STDEVP, SUM, VAR, VARP; HAVING clause; Search-Condition; SELECT statement; and WHERE clause.

HAVING Clause

Specifies groups of rows that appear in the logical table (an Access recordset) defined by a SELECT statement. The search condition applies to columns specified in a GROUP BY clause, to columns created by total functions, or to expressions containing total functions. If a group doesn't pass the search condition, it is not included in the logical table.

Syntax:

```
HAVING search-condition
```

Notes:

If you do not include a GROUP BY clause, the select list must be formed using one or more of the total functions AVG, COUNT, MAX, MIN, STDEV, STDEVP, SUM, VAR, and VARP.

The difference between the HAVING clause and the WHERE clause is that the WHERE search condition applies to single rows before they are grouped, whereas the HAVING search condition applies to groups of rows.

If you include a GROUP BY clause preceding the HAVING clause, the search condition applies to each of the groups formed by equal values in the specified columns. If you do not include a GROUP BY clause, the search condition applies to the entire logical table defined by the SELECT statement.

Examples:

To find the largest purchase from each group (categorized by state) whose largest purchase is less than the average of purchases by all customers, enter the following:

```
SELECT DISTINCTROW Customer.State,
       Max(Order.SubTotalCost) AS MaxOfSubTotalCost
  FROM Customer
    INNER JOIN [Order]
    ON Customer.CustomerID = Order.CustomerID
  GROUP BY Customer.State
  HAVING (((MAX(Order.SubTotalCost)) <
    (SELECT AVG(SubTotalCost)
      FROM [Order])));
```

To find the average and maximum order amounts for customers in the state of Washington for every month in which the maximum order amount is under $4,000, enter the following:

```
SELECT DISTINCTROW Month([OrderDate]) AS Month,
       AVG(Order.SubTotalCost) AS AvgOfSubTotalCost,
       MAX(Order.SubTotalCost) AS MaxOfSubTotalCost
  FROM Customer
    INNER JOIN [Order]
    ON Customer.CustomerID = Order.CustomerID
  WHERE (((Customer.State) = "WA"))
  GROUP BY Month([OrderDate])
  HAVING (((Max(Order.SubTotalCost)) < 4000));
```

See Also:

Total functions (beginning on page 384)—AVG, COUNT, MAX, MIN, STDEV, STDEVP, SUM, VAR, VARP; GROUP BY clause; Search-Condition; SELECT statement; and WHERE clause.

IN Clause

Specifies the source for the tables in a query. The source can be another Microsoft Access database; a dBASE, FoxPro, or Paradox file; a Btrieve database; or any database for which you have an ODBC driver. This is an Access extension to standard SQL.

Syntax:

```
IN <"source database name"> <[source connect string]>
```

Enter *"source database name"* and *[source connect string]*. (Be sure to include the brackets.) If your database source is Microsoft Access, enter only *"source database name"*. Enter these parameters according to the type of database you are connecting, as follows:

Database Name	Source Database Name	Source Connect String
Microsoft Access	"*drive:\path\filename*"	(none)
dBASE III	"*drive:\path*"	[dBASE III;]
dBASE IV	"*drive:\path*"	[dBASE IV;]
Paradox 3.x	"*drive:\path*"	[Paradox 3.x;]
Paradox 4.x	"*drive:\path*"	[Paradox 4.x;]
Btrieve	"*drive:\path\filename*.DDF"	[Btrieve;]
FoxPro 2.0	"*drive:\path*"	[FoxPro 2.0;]
FoxPro 2.5	"*drive:\path*"	[FoxPro 2.5;]
ODBC	(none)	[ODBC; DATABASE= *defaultdatabase*; UID=*user*; PWD= *password*; DSN= *datasourcename*]

Notes:

The IN clause applies to all tables referenced in the FROM clause and any subqueries in your query. You can refer to only one external database within a query. If you need to refer to more than one external file or database, attach those files as tables in Access and use the logical attached table names instead.

For ODBC, if you omit DSN= or DATABASE=, Access prompts you with a dialog box showing available data sources so that you can choose the one you want. If you omit UID= or PWD= and the server requires a UserID and password, Access prompts you with a Login dialog box for each table accessed.

For dBASE, Paradox, FoxPro, and Btrieve databases, you can provide an empty string (" ") for *source database name* and provide the path or dictionary filename using the DATABASE= parameter in *source connect string* instead.

Examples:

To retrieve the Customer Name field in the NWIND sample database without having to attach the Customers table, enter the following:

```
SELECT DISTINCTROW Customers.[Company Name]
  FROM Customers
    IN 'C:\ACCESS\SAMPAPPS\NWIND.MDB';
```

To retrieve data from the CUST and ORDERS sample files distributed with dBASE IV, enter:

```
SELECT DISTINCTROW CUST.CUST_ID, CUST.CUSTOMER,
       ORDERS.DATE_TRANS, ORDERS.PART_ID,
       ORDERS.PART_QTY
  FROM CUST
    INNER JOIN ORDERS
    ON CUST.CUST_ID = ORDERS.CUST_ID
  IN "" [dBASE IV;DATABASE=C:\DBASE\SAMPLES;];
```

See Also:

SELECT statement.

JOIN Operation

Much of the power of SQL derives from its ability to combine (join) information from several tables or queries and present the result as a single logical recordset. In many cases, Microsoft Access lets you update the recordset of a joined query as if it were a single base table, provided you include the DISTINCTROW keyword.

Use a JOIN operation in a FROM clause to specify how you want two tables linked to form a logical recordset from which to select the information you need. You can ask Access to join only matching rows in both tables (called an INNER JOIN) or to return all rows from one of the two tables even when a matching row does not exist in the second table (called an OUTER JOIN). You can nest multiple join operations to join, for example, a third table with the result of joining two other tables.

Syntax:

```
({table-name [[AS] correlation-name] |
 select-query-name [[AS] correlation-name] |
 <joined table>}
{INNER | LEFT | RIGHT} JOIN
  {table-name [[AS] correlation-name] |
  select-query-name [[AS] correlation-name] |
  <joined table>}
ON <join-specification>)
```

where *<joined table>* is the result of another join operation, and where *<join-specification>* is a search condition made up of comparison predicates that compare fields in the first table with fields in the second table.

Notes:

You can optionally supply a correlation name for each table or query name. You can use this correlation name as an alias for the full table name when qualifying column names in the select list or in the WHERE clause and subclauses. If you're joining a table or a query to itself, you must use correlation names to clarify which copy of the table or query you're referring to in the select list, join criteria, or selection criteria. If a table name or query name is also an SQL reserved word (for example, "Order"), you must enclose the name in brackets.

Use INNER JOIN to return all the rows that match the join specification in both tables. Use LEFT JOIN to return all the rows from the first table joined on the join specification with any matching rows from the second table. When no row matches in the second table, Access returns Null values for the columns from that table. Conversely, RIGHT JOIN returns all the rows from the second table joined with any matching rows from the first table.

When you use only *equals* comparison predicates in the join specification, the result is called an *equi-join.* Access can graphically display equi-joins on the QBE grid but cannot display non-equi-joins. If you want to define a join on a non-equals comparison (<, >, <>, <=, or >=), then you must define the query using the SQL view. When you join a table to itself using an equals comparison predicate, the result is called a *self-join*.

Examples:

To select information about components and the supplier that provides each component, sorted by ComponentID, enter the following:

```
SELECT DISTINCTROW Component.*, Supplier.SupplierName,
       Supplier.SupplierAddress1,
       Supplier.SupplierAddress2,
       Supplier.SupplierCity,
       Supplier.SupplierState,
       Supplier.SupplierPostal,
       Supplier.SupplierPhone,
       Supplier.SupplierFax
  FROM Supplier
    INNER JOIN Component
    ON Supplier.SupplierID = Component.SupplierID
  ORDER BY Component.ComponentID;
```

To find out which suppliers do not provide component number 25, enter the following:

```
SELECT DISTINCTROW Component.ComponentID,
       Supplier.SupplierID,
       Supplier.SupplierName,
       Supplier.SupplierCity,
       Supplier.SupplierState
  FROM Supplier
    INNER JOIN Component
    ON Supplier.SupplierID <> Component.SupplierID
  WHERE Component.ComponentID = 25;
```

To find out which customers do not currently have an order outstanding, enter the following:

```
SELECT DISTINCTROW Customer.CompanyName, Customer.City,
       Customer.State
  FROM Customer
    LEFT JOIN [Order]
    ON Customer.CustomerID = Order.CustomerID
  WHERE (((Order.CustomerID) Is Null));
```

To see a list of products and the amounts currently on order, sorted by product type, enter the following:

```
SELECT DISTINCTROW Type.TypeDescription,
       Catalog.Description, OrderItem.OrderID,
       OrderItem.Quantity
  FROM Type
    INNER JOIN (Catalog
      INNER JOIN OrderItem
      ON Catalog.CatalogItemID = OrderItem.CatalogItemID)
    ON Type.ItemTypeCode = Catalog.ItemTypeCode
  ORDER BY Type.TypeDescription;
```

See Also:

FROM clause, HAVING clause, Predicate: Comparison, Search-Condition, SELECT statement, and WHERE clause.

ORDER BY Clause

Specifies the sequence of rows to be returned by a SELECT statement or an INSERT statement.

Syntax:

```
ORDER BY {column-name [ASC | DESC]},...
```

Notes:

You specify the column(s) on whose value(s) the rows returned are ordered by using column names. You can specify multiple columns in the ORDER BY clause. The list is ordered primarily by the first column name. If rows exist for which the values of that column are equal, they are then ordered by the next column name in the ORDER BY list. You can specify ascending (ASC) or descending (DESC) order for each column. If you do not choose ASC or DESC, ASC is assumed. Use of an ORDER BY clause in a SELECT statement is the only means of defining the sequence of the returned rows.

Examples:

To select customers who first did business in 1988 or earlier and list them in ascending order by zip code, enter the following:

```
SELECT DISTINCTROW Customer.CompanyName, Customer.City,
       PostalCode
  FROM Customer
  WHERE (((1988) >=
    (SELECT MIN(Year(OrderDate))
      FROM [Order]
      WHERE
        Order.CustomerID = Customer.CustomerID)))
  ORDER BY Customer.PostalCode;
```

To find all suppliers and all customers in the state of Washington and list them in descending order by zip code, enter the following:

```
SELECT DISTINCTROW Customer.CompanyName, Customer.City,
       PostalCode
  FROM Customer
  WHERE Customer.State = "WA"
UNION
  SELECT DISTINCTROW Supplier.SupplierName,
         Supplier.SupplierCity,
         Supplier.SupplierPostal
    FROM Supplier
    WHERE Supplier.SupplierState = "WA"
    ORDER BY PostalCode;
```

NOTE: In the example above, Microsoft Access derives output column names in a UNION query from the column names of the first table. The ORDER BY clause refers to the output column name.

See Also:

INSERT statement, SELECT statement, and UNION query operator.

PARAMETERS Declaration

Precedes an SQL statement to define the data types of any parameters you include in the query. You can use parameters to prompt the user for data values or to match data values in controls on an open form.

Syntax:

```
PARAMETERS {[parameter-name] data-type},... ;
```

Notes:

If your query prompts the user for values, each parameter name should describe the value that the user needs to enter. For example, [Print invoices from orders on date:] is much more descriptive than [Enter date:]. If you want to refer to a control on an open form, use the format

[Forms]![*Myform*]![*Mycontrol*]

To refer to a control on a subform, use the format

[Forms]![*Myform*]![*Mysubformcontrol*].[Form]![*ControlOnSubform*]

Valid data type entries are as follows:

SQL Parameter Data Type	Equivalent Access Data Type
Bit	Yes/No
Binary	Binary
Byte	Byte
Currency	Currency
DateTime	Date/Time
FLOAT	Double
IEEEDouble	Double
IEEESingle	Single
INT[EGER]	Long integer
Long	Long integer
LongBinary	OLE object
LongText	Memo
REAL	Single
Short	Integer
SMALLINT	Integer
Text	Text
Value	Value
VARCHAR	Memo

Example:

To create a parameter query that summarizes the sales and cost of goods for all items sold in a given month, enter the following:

```
PARAMETERS [Year to summarize:] Short,
           [Month to summarize:] Short;
SELECT DISTINCTROW OrderItem.CatalogItemID,
       SUM(OrderItem.Quantity) AS Quantity,
       SUM(OrderItem.[Quantity] *
          [QuotedPrice]) AS TotalSales,
       SUM(OrderItem.[Quantity] * [OurCost]) AS TotalCost
  FROM [Order]
    INNER JOIN (Catalog
      INNER JOIN OrderItem
      ON Catalog.CatalogItemID = OrderItem.CatalogItemID)
    ON Order.OrderID = OrderItem.OrderID
  WHERE (((Year([OrderDate])) = [Year to summarize:])
    AND ((Month([OrderDate])) = [Month to summarize:]))
  GROUP BY OrderItem.CatalogItemID;
```

See Also:

SELECT statement.

Predicate: BETWEEN

Compares a value with a range of values.

Syntax:

```
expression [NOT] BETWEEN expression AND expression
```

Notes:

The data types of all expressions must be compatible. Comparison of alphanumeric literals (strings) in Microsoft Access is case-insensitive.

Let *a*, *b*, and *c* be expressions. Then, in terms of other predicates, *a* BETWEEN *b* AND *c* is equivalent to the following:

```
a >= b AND a <= c
```

a NOT BETWEEN *b* AND *c* is equivalent to the following:

```
a < b OR a > c
```

The result is undefined if any of the expressions is NULL.

Example:

To determine whether the average of Quantity multiplied by QuotedPrice is greater than or equal to $500 and less than or equal to $10,000, enter the following:

```
AVG(Quantity * QuotedPrice) BETWEEN 500 AND 10000
```

See Also:

Expressions, SELECT statement, Subquery, and WHERE clause.

Predicate: Comparison

Compares the values of two expressions or the value of an expression and a single value returned by a subquery.

Syntax:

```
expression {= | <> | > | < | >= | <=}
{expression | subquery}
```

Notes:

Comparison of strings in Microsoft Access is case-insensitive. The data type of the first expression must be compatible with the data type of the second expression or with the value returned by the subquery. If the subquery returns no rows or more than one row, an error is returned except when the select list of the subquery is COUNT(*), in which case the return of multiple rows yields one value. If either the first expression, the second expression, or the subquery evaluates to Null, the result of the comparison is undefined.

Examples:

To determine whether the order date was in 1992, enter the following:

```
Year(OrderDate) = 1992
```

To determine whether the order ID is not equal to 50, enter

```
OrderID <> 50
```

To determine whether the amount owed is greater than 0, enter

```
AmountOwed > 0
```

To determine whether an order was placed in the first half of the year, enter

```
Month(OrderDate) < 7
```

To determine whether the maximum value for the total order amount in the group is less than the average total order amount found in the Order table, enter

```
MAX(SubTotalCost - (SubTotalCost * Discount)) <
  (SELECT AVG(SubTotalCost - (SubTotalCost * Discount))
    FROM [Order])
```

See Also:

Expressions, SELECT statement, Subquery, and WHERE clause.

Predicate: EXISTS

Tests the existence of at least one row that satisfies the selection criteria in a subquery.

Syntax:

```
EXISTS (subquery)
```

Notes:

The result cannot be undefined. If the subquery returns at least one row, the result is true; otherwise, the result is false. The subquery need not return values for this predicate; therefore, you can list any columns in the select list that exist in the underlying tables or queries (including *).

Example:

To find all suppliers that supply at least one component, enter

```
SELECT DISTINCTROW Supplier.SupplierName
  FROM Supplier
  WHERE Exists
    (SELECT *
      FROM Component
      WHERE Component.SupplierID = Supplier.SupplierID);
```

NOTE: In the preceding example, the inner subquery makes an outer reference to the Supplier table in the SELECT statement by specifically referring to a column in the outer table (Supplier.SupplierID in the WHERE clause of the subquery). This forces the subquery to be evaluated for every row in the SELECT statement, which might not be the most efficient way to achieve the desired result.

See Also:

Expression, SELECT statement, Subquery, and WHERE clause.

Predicate: IN

Determines whether a value is equal to any of the values or is unequal to all values in a set returned from a subquery or provided in a list of values.

Syntax:

```
expression [NOT] IN {(subquery) | ({literal},...) |
expression}
```

Notes:

Comparison of strings in Microsoft Access is case-insensitive. The data types of all expressions, literals, and the column returned by the subquery must be compatible. If the expression is Null or any value returned by the subquery is Null, the result is undefined. In terms of other predicates, *expression* IN *expression* is equivalent to the following:

```
expression = expression
```

expression IN (*subquery*) is equivalent to the following:

```
expression = ANY (subquery)
```

expression IN (*a*, *b*, *c*,...), where *a*, *b*, and *c* are literals, is equivalent to the following:

```
(expression = a) OR (expression = b) OR
(expression = c) ...
```

expression NOT IN ... is equivalent to the following:

```
NOT (expression IN ...)
```

Examples:

To determine whether State is on the West Coast, enter the following:

```
State IN ("CA", "OR", "WA")
```

To determine whether CustomerID is the same as any SupplierID in Washington, enter the following:

```
CustomerID IN
  (SELECT SupplierID
    FROM Supplier
    WHERE SupplierState = "WA")
```

See Also:

Expressions, Predicate: Quantified, SELECT statement, Subquery, and WHERE clause.

Predicate: LIKE

Searches for strings that match a pattern.

Syntax:

```
column-name [NOT] LIKE match-string
```

Notes:

String comparisons in Microsoft Access are case-insensitive. If the column specified by *column-name* contains a Null, the result is undefined. Comparison of two empty strings or an empty string with the special character * evaluates to true.

You provide a text string as a *match-string* value that defines what characters can exist in which positions for the comparison to be true. Access understands a number of *wildcard* characters that you can use to define positions that can contain any single character, zero or more characters, or any number, as follows:

Wildcard Character	Meaning
?	Any single character
*	Zero or more characters (used to define leading, trailing, or embedded strings that don't have to match any of the pattern characters)
#	Any single number

You can also specify that any particular position in the text or memo field can contain only characters from a list that you provide. To define a list of comparison characters for a particular position, enclose the list in brackets ([ ]). You can specify a range of characters within a list by entering the low value character, a hyphen, and the high value character, as in [A-Z] or [3-7]. If you want to test a position for any characters except those in a list, start the list with an exclamation point (!). If you want to test for any of the special characters *, ?, #, and [, you must enclose the character in brackets.

Examples:

To determine whether CustomerName is at least four characters long and begins with *Smi,* enter the following:

```
CustomerName LIKE "Smi?*"
```

To test whether PostalCode is a valid Canadian postal code, enter

```
PostalCode LIKE "[A-Z]#[A-Z] #[A-Z]#"
```

See Also:

Expressions, SELECT statement, Subquery, and WHERE clause.

Predicate: NULL

Determines whether the expression evaluates to Null. This predicate evaluates only to true or false and will not evaluate to undefined.

Syntax:

```
expression IS [NOT] NULL
```

Example:

To determine whether the customer phone number column has never been filled, enter the following:

```
PhoneNumber IS NULL
```

See Also:

Expressions, SELECT statement, Subquery, and WHERE clause.

Predicate: Quantified

Compares the value of an expression to some, any, or all values of a single column returned by a subquery.

Syntax:

```
expression {= | <> | > | < | >= | <=}
[SOME | ANY | ALL] (subquery)
```

Notes:

String comparisons in Microsoft Access are case-insensitive. The data type of the expression must be compatible with the data type of the value returned by the subquery.

When ALL is used, the predicate is true if the comparison is true for all the values returned by the subquery. If the expression or any of the values returned by the subquery is Null, the result is undefined. When SOME or ANY is used, the predicate is true if the comparison is true for any of the values returned by the subquery. If the expression is a Null value, the result is undefined. If the subquery returns no values, the predicate is false.

Examples:

To find the components whose cost is greater than all the components whose type code is 008, enter the following:

```
SELECT DISTINCTROW Component.Description,
       Component.OurCost
  FROM Component
  WHERE (Component.OurCost) > ALL
    (SELECT OurCost
      FROM Component
      WHERE ItemTypeCode = "008");
```

To find the components whose cost is greater than any component whose type code is 008, enter the following:

```
SELECT DISTINCTROW Component.Description,
       Component.OurCost
  FROM Component
  WHERE (Component.OurCost) > SOME
    (SELECT OurCost
      FROM Component
      WHERE ItemTypeCode = "008");
```

See Also:

Expressions, SELECT statement, Subquery, and WHERE clause.

Search-Condition

Describes a simple or compound predicate that is true, false, or undefined about a given row or group. Use a search condition in the WHERE clause of a SELECT statement, a subquery, a DELETE statement, or an UPDATE statement. It can also be used within the HAVING clause in a SELECT statement. The search condition defines the rows that should appear in the resulting logical table or the rows that should be acted upon by the change operation. If the search condition is true when applied to a row, that row is included in the result.

Syntax:

```
[NOT] {predicate | (search-condition)}
[{AND | OR | XOR | EQV | IMP}
[NOT] {predicate | (search-condition)}]...
```

Notes:

Microsoft Access effectively applies any subquery in the search condition to each row of the table that is the result of the previous clauses. Access then evaluates the result of the subquery with regard to each candidate row.

If you include a comparison predicate in the form *expression comparison-operator subquery*, an error is returned if the subquery returns no rows.

The order of evaluation of the Boolean operators is NOT, AND, OR, XOR (exclusive OR), EQV (equivalence), and IMP (implication). You can include additional parentheses to influence the order in which the Boolean expressions are processed.

> **TIP:** You can express AND and OR Boolean operations directly using the QBE grid. If you need to use XOR, EQV, or IMP, you must create an expression in the Field row, uncheck the Show box, and set Criteria to <> *False*.

In using the Boolean operator NOT, the following holds: NOT (True) is False, NOT (False) is True, and NOT (undefined) is undefined. The result is undefined whenever a predicate references a Null value. If a search condition evaluates to False or undefined when applied to a row, the row is not selected. Access returns True, False, or undefined values as a result of applying Boolean operators (AND, OR, XOR, EQV, IMP) against two predicates or search conditions according to the tables shown in Figure 11-1 on the next page.

Example:

To find all products whose cost is greater than $100 and whose number of days to build is equal to 2 or whose number in stock is less than 5, but not both, enter the following:

```
SELECT DISTINCTROW Catalog.CatalogItemID,
       Catalog.Description, Catalog.OurCost,
       Catalog.DaysToBuild, Catalog.NumberInStock
  FROM Catalog
  WHERE (Catalog.OurCost) > 100
    AND ((Catalog.DaysToBuild) = 2
    XOR (Catalog.NumberInStock) < 5);
```

See Also:

DELETE statement, Expressions, HAVING clause, Predicates, SELECT statement, Subquery, UPDATE statement, and WHERE clause.

AND	True	False	undefined (Null)
True	True	False	Null
False	False	False	False
undefined (Null)	Null	False	Null

OR	True	False	undefined (Null)
True	True	True	True
False	True	False	Null
undefined (Null)	True	Null	Null

XOR	True	False	undefined (Null)
True	False	True	Null
False	True	False	Null
undefined (Null)	Null	Null	Null

EQV	True	False	undefined (Null)
True	True	False	Null
False	False	True	Null
undefined (Null)	Null	Null	Null

IMP	True	False	undefined (Null)
True	True	False	Null
False	True	True	True
undefined (Null)	True	Null	Null

FIGURE 11-1.
Truth tables for SQL Boolean operators.

SELECT Statement

Performs the select, project, and join relational operations to create a logical table (recordset) from other tables or queries. The items in the select list identify the columns or values calculated on columns to be projected from the source tables to the table being formed. You identify the tables to be joined in the FROM clause, and you identify the rows to be selected in the WHERE clause. Use GROUP BY to specify how to form groups for a total query and HAVING to specify which resulting groups should be included in the result.

Syntax:

```
SELECT [ALL | DISTINCT | DISTINCTROW | TOP number
       [PERCENT]] select-list
  FROM {{table-name [[AS] correlation-name] |
   select-query-name [[AS] correlation-name]} |
   <joined table>},...
  [WHERE search-condition]
  [GROUP BY column-name,...]
  [HAVING search-condition]
  [UNION [ALL] select-statement]
  [ORDER BY {column-name [ASC | DESC]},...] |
  IN <"source database name"> <[source connect string]>
[WITH OWNERACCESS OPTION];
```

where *select-list* is

```
{* | {expression [AS output-column-name] | table-name.* |
query-name.* | correlation-name.*},...}
```

and where *<joined table>* is

```
({table-name [[AS] correlation-name] |
 select-query-name [[AS] correlation-name] |
 <joined table>}
{INNER | LEFT | RIGHT} JOIN
  {table-name [[AS] correlation-name] |
  select-query-name [[AS] correlation-name] |
  <joined table>}
ON <join-specification>)
```

Notes:

You can optionally supply a correlation name for each table or query name. You can use this correlation name as an alias for the full table name when qualifying column names in the select list or in the WHERE clause and subclauses. If you're joining a table or a query to itself, you must use correlation names to clarify which copy of the table or query you're referring to in the select list, join criteria, or selection criteria. If a table name or query name is also an SQL reserved word (for example, "Order"), you must enclose the name in brackets.

When you list more than one table or query without join criteria, the source is the Cartesian product of all the tables. For example, *FROM TableA, TableB* asks Microsoft Access to search all the rows of TableA matched with all the rows of TableB. Unless you specify other restricting criteria, the number of logical rows that Access processes could equal the number of rows in TableA times the number of rows in TableB. Access then returns the rows in which the selection criteria specified in the WHERE and HAVING clauses are true.

You can further define which rows Access includes in the output recordset by specifying ALL, DISTINCT, DISTINCTROW, TOP *n*, or TOP *n* PERCENT. ALL includes all rows that match the search criteria from the source tables, including potential duplicate rows. DISTINCT requests that Access return only rows that are different from any other row. You cannot update any columns in a query that uses ALL or DISTINCT.

DISTINCTROW (the default) requests that Access return only rows in which the concatenation of the primary keys from all tables supplying output columns is unique. Depending on the columns you choose, you might see rows in the result which contain duplicate values, but each row in the result is derived from a DISTINCT combination of ROWS in the underlying tables. You must specify DISTINCTROW to be able to update columns in a joined query. Specify TOP *n* or TOP *n* PERCENT to request that the recordset contain only the first *n* or first *n* percent of rows. The parameter *n* must be an integer and must be less than or equal to 100 if you include the PERCENT keyword. Note that if you do not include an ORDER BY clause (see more about this on the next page), the sequence of rows returned is undefined.

When you include a GROUP BY clause, the select list must be made up of one or more of the total functions (AVG, COUNT, MAX, MIN,

STDEV, STDEVP, SUM, VAR, and VARP) or one or more of the column names specified in the GROUP BY clause. A column name in a GROUP BY clause can refer to any column from any table in the FROM clause, even if the column is not named in the select list. If you want to refer to a calculated expression in the GROUP BY clause, you must assign an output column name to the expression in the select list and then refer to that name in the GROUP BY clause. If the GROUP BY clause is preceded by a WHERE clause, Access forms the groups from the rows selected after application of the WHERE clause.

If you use a HAVING clause but do not include a GROUP BY clause, the select list must be formed using total functions (AVG, COUNT, MAX, MIN, STDEV, STDEVP, SUM, VAR, or VARP). If you include a GROUP BY clause preceding the HAVING clause, then the HAVING search condition applies to each of the groups formed by equal values in the specified columns. If you do not include a GROUP BY clause, then the HAVING search condition applies to the entire logical table defined by the SELECT statement.

You specify the column(s) on whose value the rows returned are ordered by using column names. You can specify multiple columns in the ORDER BY clause. The list is ordered primarily by the first column name. If rows exist for which the values of that column are equal, they are then ordered by the next column name on the ORDER BY list. You can specify ascending (ASC) or descending (DESC) ordering for each column. If you do not choose ASC or DESC, ASC is assumed. Use of an ORDER BY clause in a SELECT statement is the only means of defining the sequence of the returned rows.

Normally, the person running the query not only must have rights to the query but also must have the appropriate rights to the tables used in the query. (These rights include reading data to select rows and updating, inserting, and deleting data using the query.) If there are multiple users of your application, you might want to secure the tables so that no user has direct access to any of the tables and all users still can run queries defined by you. Assuming you're the owner of both the queries and the tables, you can deny access to the tables but allow access to the queries. To ensure that the queries run properly, you must add the WITH OWNERACCESS OPTION clause to allow users to have the same access rights as the table owner when accessing the data via the query.

See Chapter 14 in the *Building Applications* manual that comes with Microsoft Access for more details on securing your applications.

Examples:

To select information about customers and their purchases over $100, enter the following:

```
SELECT Cust.CustomerID, Cust.CompanyName, Ord.OrderDate,
       Cat.CatalogItemID, Cat.Description,
       OrderItem.Quantity, OrderItem.QuotedPrice
  FROM (Catalog AS Cat
    INNER JOIN ((Customer AS Cust
      INNER JOIN [Order] AS Ord
      ON Cust.CustomerID = Ord.CustomerID)
        INNER JOIN OrderItem
        ON Ord.OrderID = OrderItem.OrderID)
    ON Cat.CatalogItemID = OrderItem.CatalogItemID)
  WHERE (OrderItem.Quantity * OrderItem.Price) > 100;
```

To find the largest order from any customer within each zip code, enter the following:

```
SELECT DISTINCTROW Customer.PostalCode,
       Max(Order.SubTotalCost) AS MaxOfSubTotalCost
  FROM Customer
    INNER JOIN [Order]
    ON Customer.CustomerID = Order.CustomerID
  GROUP BY Customer.PostalCode;
```

To find the average and maximum prices for items in the catalog by category, enter the following:

```
SELECT DISTINCTROW Type.TypeDescription,
       AVG(Catalog.Price) AS AvgOfPrice,
       MAX(Catalog.Price) AS MaxOfPrice
  FROM Type
    INNER JOIN Catalog
    ON Type.ItemTypeCode = Catalog.ItemTypeCode
  GROUP BY Type.TypeDescription;
```

To find the largest purchase from each group (categorized by state) whose largest purchase is less than the average of purchases by all customers, enter the following:

```
SELECT DISTINCTROW Customer.State,
       Max(Order.SubTotalCost) AS MaxOfSubTotalCost
  FROM Customer
    INNER JOIN [Order]
    ON Customer.CustomerID = Order.CustomerID
  GROUP BY Customer.State
  HAVING (((Max(Order.SubTotalCost)) <
    (SELECT AVG(SubTotalCost)
      FROM [Order])));
```

To find the average and maximum order amounts for customers in the state of Washington for every month in which the maximum order amount is under $4,000, enter the following:

```
SELECT DISTINCTROW Month([OrderDate]) AS Month,
       AVG(Order.SubTotalCost) AS AvgOfSubTotalCost,
       MAX(Order.SubTotalCost) AS MaxOfSubTotalCost
  FROM Customer
    INNER JOIN [Order]
    ON Customer.CustomerID = Order.CustomerID
  WHERE (((Customer.State) = "WA"))
  GROUP BY Month([OrderDate])
  HAVING (((Max(Order.SubTotalCost)) < 4000));
```

To find the number of different prices for items in the current inventory, you need two queries. For the query DistinctPrice, enter the following:

```
SELECT DISTINCT Price
  FROM Catalog
  WHERE NumberInStock > 0;
```

For the query CountDistinctPrice, enter the following:

```
SELECT COUNT(*)
  FROM DistinctPrice;
```

To select information about components and the supplier that provides each component, sorted by ComponentID, enter the following:

```
SELECT DISTINCTROW Component.*, Supplier.SupplierName,
       Supplier.SupplierAddress1,
       Supplier.SupplierAddress2,
       Supplier.SupplierCity,
       Supplier.SupplierState,
       Supplier.SupplierPostal,
```

(continued)

(continued)

```
            Supplier.SupplierPhone,
            Supplier.SupplierFax
       FROM Supplier
         INNER JOIN Component
         ON Supplier.SupplierID = Component.SupplierID
       ORDER BY Component.ComponentID;
```

To find out which suppliers do not provide component number 25, enter the following:

```
     SELECT DISTINCTROW Component.ComponentID,
            Supplier.SupplierID, Supplier.SupplierName,
            Supplier.SupplierCity, Supplier.SupplierState
       FROM Supplier
         INNER JOIN Component
         ON Supplier.SupplierID <> Component.SupplierID
       WHERE Component.ComponentID = 25;
```

To find out which customers do not currently have an order outstanding, enter the following:

```
     SELECT DISTINCTROW Customer.CompanyName, Customer.City,
            Customer.State
       FROM Customer
         LEFT JOIN [Order]
         ON Customer.CustomerID = Order.CustomerID
       WHERE (((Order.CustomerID) IS NULL));
```

To see a listing of products and the amount currently on order, sorted by product type, enter the following:

```
     SELECT DISTINCTROW Type.TypeDescription,
            Catalog.Description,
            OrderItem.OrderID, OrderItem.Quantity
       FROM Type
         INNER JOIN (Catalog
           INNER JOIN OrderItem
           ON Catalog.CatalogItemID = OrderItem.CatalogItemID)
         ON Type.ItemTypeCode = Catalog.ItemTypeCode
       ORDER BY Type.TypeDescription;
```

To select customers who first did business in 1988 or earlier and list them in ascending order by zip code, enter the following:

```
SELECT DISTINCTROW Customer.CompanyName, Customer.City,
       PostalCode
  FROM Customer
  WHERE (((1988) >=
    (SELECT MIN(Year(OrderDate))
      FROM [Order]
        WHERE Order.CustomerID = Customer.CustomerID)))
   ORDER BY Customer.PostalCode;
```

To find all suppliers and all customers in the state of Washington and list them in descending order by zip code, enter the following:

```
SELECT DISTINCTROW Customer.CompanyName, Customer.City,
       PostalCode
  FROM Customer
    WHERE Customer.State = "WA"
UNION
  SELECT DISTINCTROW Supplier.SupplierName,
         Supplier.SupplierCity, Supplier.SupplierPostal
    FROM Supplier
    WHERE Supplier.SupplierState = "WA"
    ORDER BY PostalCode;
```

To find all suppliers that supply at least one component, enter the following:

```
SELECT DISTINCTROW Supplier.SupplierName
  FROM Supplier
  WHERE Exists
    (SELECT *
      FROM Component
      WHERE Component.SupplierID = Supplier.SupplierID);
```

To find the components whose cost is greater than ALL the components whose type code is 008, enter the following:

```
SELECT DISTINCTROW Component.Description,
       Component.OurCost
  FROM Component
  WHERE (Component.OurCost) > ALL
    (SELECT OurCost
      FROM Component
      WHERE ItemTypeCode = "008");
```

To find all products whose cost is greater than $100 and whose number of days to build is equal to 2 or whose number in stock is less than 5, but not both, enter the following:

```
SELECT DISTINCTROW Catalog.CatalogItemID,
       Catalog.Description, Catalog.OurCost,
       Catalog.DaysToBuild, Catalog.NumberInStock
  FROM Catalog
  WHERE (Catalog.OurCost) > 100
    AND ((Catalog.DaysToBuild) = 2
    XOR (Catalog.NumberInStock) < 5);
```

To select from the Customer table and insert into a temporary table names of customers in the state of Oregon, enter the following:

```
INSERT INTO TempCust
  SELECT *
    FROM Customer
    WHERE State = "OR";
```

See Also:

INSERT statement, Search-Condition, and UNION query operator.

Subquery

Selects from a single column any number of values or no values at all for comparison in a predicate.

Syntax:

```
(SELECT [ALL | DISTINCT] select-list
  FROM {{table-name [[AS] correlation-name] |
   select-query-name [[AS] correlation-name]} |
   <joined table>},...
  [WHERE search-condition]
  [GROUP BY column-name,...]
  [HAVING search-condition])
```

where *select-list* is

```
{* | {expression | table-name.* |
query-name.* | correlation-name.*}}
```

and where *<joined table>* is

```
({table-name [[AS] correlation-name] |
 select-query-name [[AS] correlation-name] |
 <joined table>}
{INNER | LEFT | RIGHT} JOIN
  {table-name [[AS] correlation-name] |
  select-query-name [[AS] correlation-name] |
  <joined table>}
ON <join-specification>)
```

Notes:

You can use the special character asterisk (*) in the select list of a subquery only when the subquery is used in an EXISTS predicate or when the FROM clause within the subquery refers to a single table or query that contains only one column.

You can optionally supply a correlation name for each table or query name. You can use this correlation name as an alias for the full table name when qualifying column names in the select list or the WHERE clause and subclauses. If you're joining a table or a query to itself, you must use correlation names to clarify which copy of the table or query you're referring to in the select list, join criteria, or selection criteria. If a table name or query name is also an SQL reserved word (for example, "Order"), you must enclose the name in brackets.

When you list more than one table or query without join criteria, the source is the Cartesian product of all the tables. For example, *FROM TableA, TableB* asks Microsoft Access to search all the rows of TableA matched with all the rows of TableB. Unless you specify other restricting criteria, the number of logical rows that Access processes could equal the number of rows in TableA times the number of rows in TableB. Access then returns the rows in which the selection criteria specified in the WHERE and HAVING clauses are true.

In the search condition of the WHERE clause of a subquery, you can refer via an outer reference to the columns of any table or query that is defined in the outer queries. You must qualify the column name if the table or query reference is ambiguous.

A column name in the GROUP BY clause can refer to any column from any table in the FROM clause, even if the column is not named in the select list. If the GROUP BY clause is preceded by a WHERE clause, Access creates the groups from the rows selected after the application of the WHERE clause. When you include a GROUP BY clause in a SELECT statement, the select list must be made up of either SQL total functions (AVG, COUNT, MAX, MIN, STDEV, STDEVP, SUM, VAR, or VARP) or column names specified in the GROUP BY clause.

When you include a GROUP BY or HAVING clause, the select list must be made up of either total functions (AVG, COUNT, MAX, MIN, STDEV, STDEVP, SUM, VAR, or VARP) or column names specified in the GROUP BY clause. If a GROUP BY clause precedes a HAVING clause, the HAVING clause's search condition applies to each of the groups formed by equal values in the specified columns. If you do not include a GROUP BY clause, the HAVING clause's search condition applies to the entire logical table defined by the SELECT statement.

Examples:

To find all suppliers that supply at least one component, enter the following:

```
SELECT DISTINCTROW Supplier.SupplierName
  FROM Supplier
  WHERE Exists
    (SELECT *
      FROM Component
      WHERE Component.SupplierID = Supplier.SupplierID);
```

NOTE: In the example above, the inner subquery makes an outer reference to the Supplier table in the SELECT statement by specifically referring to a column in the outer table (Supplier.SupplierID in the WHERE clause of the subquery). This forces the subquery to be evaluated for every row in the SELECT statement, which might not be the most efficient way to achieve the desired result.

To find the largest purchase from each group (categorized by state) whose largest purchase is less than the average of purchases by all customers, enter the following:

```
SELECT DISTINCTROW Customer.State,
       Max(Order.SubTotalCost) AS MaxOfSubTotalCost
  FROM Customer
    INNER JOIN [Order]
    ON Customer.CustomerID = Order.CustomerID
  GROUP BY Customer.State
  HAVING (((MAX(Order.SubTotalCost)) <
    (SELECT AVG(SubTotalCost)
      FROM [Order])));
```

To select customers who first did business in 1988 or earlier and list them in ascending order by zip code, enter the following:

```
SELECT DISTINCTROW Customer.CompanyName, Customer.City,
       PostalCode
  FROM Customer
  WHERE (((1988) >=
    (SELECT MIN(Year(OrderDate))
      FROM [Order]
      WHERE Order.CustomerID = Customer.CustomerID)))
  ORDER BY Customer.PostalCode;
```

To find the inventory item name and supplier name for any item that has an inventory cost of less than $500, enter the following:

```
SELECT DISTINCTROW Component.Description,
       Supplier.SupplierName
  FROM Supplier
    INNER JOIN Component
    ON Supplier.SupplierID = Component.SupplierID
  WHERE EXISTS
   (SELECT *
     FROM Component C2
     WHERE Component.ComponentID = C2.ComponentID
       AND C2.NumberInStock > 0
       AND (C2.NumberInStock * C2.OurCost) < 500);
```

NOTE: In the example above, the inner subquery makes an outer reference to the Component table in the SELECT statement. Access is then forced to evaluate the subquery for every row in the SELECT statement, which might not be the most efficient way to achieve the desired result.

To find the components whose cost is greater than any component whose type code is 008, enter the following:

```
SELECT DISTINCTROW Component.Description,
       Component.OurCost
  FROM Component
  WHERE (Component.OurCost) > SOME
    (SELECT OurCost
      FROM Component
      WHERE ItemTypeCode = "008");
```

See Also:

Expressions, Predicates, and SELECT statement.

Total Function: AVG

In a logical table defined by a SELECT statement or subquery, creates a column value that is the numeric average of the values in the expression or column name specified. You can use the GROUP BY clause to create an average for each group of rows selected from the underlying tables or queries.

Syntax:

```
AVG(expression)
```

Notes:

You cannot use another total function reference within the expression. If you use a total function (AVG, COUNT, MAX, MIN, STDEV, STDEVP, SUM, VAR, or VARP) in the select list of a SELECT statement, any other columns in the select list must be derived using a total function, or the column name must appear in a GROUP BY clause. An expression must contain a reference to at least one column name, and the expression or column name must be a numeric data type.

Null values are not included in the calculation of the result. The data type of the result is generally the same as that of the expression or column name. If the expression or column name is an integer, the resulting average is truncated. For example, AVG(*n*)—where *n* is an integer and the values of *n* in the selected rows are equal to 0, 1, and 1—returns the value 0.

Examples:

To find the average and maximum prices for items in the catalog by category, enter the following:

```
SELECT DISTINCTROW Type.TypeDescription,
       AVG(Catalog.Price)  AS AvgOfPrice,
       MAX(Catalog.Price) AS MaxOfPrice
  FROM Type
    INNER JOIN Catalog
    ON Type.ItemTypeCode = Catalog.ItemTypeCode
  GROUP BY Type.TypeDescription;
```

To find the average inventory cost of items currently on hand (not counting items that are not in stock), enter the following:

```
SELECT DISTINCTROW Avg([OurCost] *
                   [NumberInStock]) AS AvgInventoryCost
  FROM Component
  WHERE Component.NumberInStock > 0;
```

See Also:

Expressions, GROUP BY clause, HAVING clause, SELECT statement, Subquery, and TRANSFORM statement.

Total Function: COUNT

In a logical table defined by a SELECT statement or subquery, creates a column value that is equal to the number of rows in the result table. You can use the GROUP BY clause to create a count for each group of rows selected from the underlying tables or queries.

Syntax:

```
COUNT({* | expression})
```

Notes:

You cannot use another total function reference within the expression. If you use a total function (AVG, COUNT, MAX, MIN, STDEV, STDEVP, SUM, VAR, or VARP) in the select list of a SELECT statement, any other columns in the select list must be derived using a total function, or the column name must appear in a GROUP BY clause. An expression must contain a reference to at least one column name.

Null values are not included in the calculation of the result. The data type of the result is a long integer.

Examples:

To find the number of customers who first did business in 1988 or earlier and group them by zip code, enter the following:

```
SELECT COUNT(*)
  FROM Customer
  WHERE (((1988) >=
    (SELECT MIN(Year(OrderDate))
      FROM [Order]
      WHERE Order.CustomerID = Customer.CustomerID)))
      GROUP BY Customer.PostalCode;
```

To find the number of different prices for items in the current inventory, you need two queries. For the query DistinctPrice, enter the following:

```
SELECT DISTINCT Price
  FROM Catalog
  WHERE NumberInStock > 0;
```

For the query CountDistinctPrice, enter the following:

```
SELECT COUNT(*) FROM DistinctPrice;
```

See Also:

Expressions, GROUP BY clause, HAVING clause, SELECT statement, Subquery, and TRANSFORM statement.

Total Function: MAX

In a logical table defined by a SELECT statement or subquery, creates a column value that is the maximum value in the expression or column name specified. You can use the GROUP BY clause to create a maximum value for each group of rows selected from the underlying tables or queries.

Syntax:

```
MAX(expression)
```

Notes:

You cannot use another total function reference within the expression. If you use a total function (AVG, COUNT, MAX, MIN, STDEV, STDEVP, SUM, VAR, or VARP) in the select list of a SELECT statement, any other columns in the select list must be derived using a total function, or the column name must appear in a GROUP BY clause. An expression must contain a reference to at least one column name.

Null values are not included in the determination of the result. The data type of the result is the same as that of the expression or column name.

Examples:

To find the largest order from any customer within each zip code, enter the following:

```
SELECT DISTINCTROW Customer.PostalCode,
       MAX(Order.SubTotalCost) AS MaxOfSubTotalCost
  FROM Customer
    INNER JOIN [Order]
    ON Customer.CustomerID = Order.CustomerID
  GROUP BY Customer.PostalCode;
```

To find the item currently on hand with the maximum inventory cost, enter the following:

```
SELECT ComponentID, Description, OurCost, NumberInStock
  FROM Component
  WHERE ([OurCost] * [NumberInStock]) =
   (SELECT MAX([OurCost] * [NumberInStock])
     FROM Component);
```

See Also:

Expressions, GROUP BY clause, HAVING clause, SELECT statement, Subquery, and TRANSFORM statement.

Total Function: MIN

In a logical table defined by a SELECT statement or subquery, creates a column value that is the minimum value in the expression or column name specified. You can use the GROUP BY clause to create a minimum value for each group of rows selected from the underlying tables or queries.

Syntax:

```
MIN(expression)
```

Notes:

You cannot use another total function reference within the expression. If you use a total function (AVG, COUNT, MAX, MIN, STDEV, STDEVP, SUM, VAR, or VARP) in the select list of a SELECT statement, any other columns in the select list must be derived using a total function, or the column name must appear in a GROUP BY clause. An expression must contain a reference to at least one column name.

Null values are not included in the determination of the result. The data type of the result is the same as that of the expression or column name.

Examples:

To find the smallest order from any customer within each zip code, enter the following:

```
SELECT DISTINCTROW Customer.PostalCode,
       MIN(Order.SubTotalCost) AS MinOfSubTotalCost
  FROM Customer
    INNER JOIN [Order]
    ON Customer.CustomerID = Order.CustomerID
  GROUP BY Customer.PostalCode;
```

To find the item currently on hand with the smallest inventory cost, enter the following:

```
SELECT ComponentID, Description, OurCost, NumberInStock
  FROM Component
  WHERE ([OurCost] * [NumberInStock]) =
    (SELECT MIN([OurCost] * [NumberInStock])
      FROM Component
      WHERE NumberInStock <> 0);
```

See Also:

Expressions, GROUP BY clause, HAVING clause, SELECT statement, Subquery, and TRANSFORM statement.

Total Functions: STDEV, STDEVP

In a logical table defined by a SELECT statement or subquery, creates a column value that is the standard deviation (square root of the variance) of the values in the expression or column name specified. You can use the GROUP BY clause to create a standard deviation for each group of rows selected from the underlying tables or queries. STDEVP produces an estimate of the standard deviation for the entire population based on the sample provided in each group.

Syntax:

```
{STDEV | STDEVP} (expression)
```

Notes:

You cannot use another total function reference within the expression. If you use a total function (AVG, COUNT, MAX, MIN, STDEV, STDEVP, SUM, VAR, or VARP) in the select list of a SELECT statement, any other columns in the select list must be derived using a total function, or the column name must appear in a GROUP BY clause. An expression must contain a reference to at least one column name, and the expression or column name must be a numeric data type.

Null values are not included in the calculation of the result. The data type of the result is a double number. If there are not at least two members in a group, STDEV returns a Null value. STDEVP returns an estimate if there is at least one non-Null value in the group.

Example:

To find the standard deviation and the population standard deviation of the cost of components, grouped by type of component, enter the following:

```
SELECT DISTINCTROW Type.TypeDescription,
       Count(Description) AS CountOfDescription,
       StDev(Component.OurCost) AS StDevOfOurCost,
       StDevP(Component.OurCost) AS StDevPOfOurCost
  FROM Type
    INNER JOIN Component
    ON Type.ItemTypeCode = Component.ItemTypeCode
  GROUP BY Type.TypeDescription;
```

See Also:

Expressions, GROUP BY clause, HAVING clause, SELECT statement, Subquery, and TRANSFORM statement.

Total Function: SUM

In a logical table defined by a SELECT statement or subquery, creates a column value that is the numeric sum of the values in the expression or column name specified. You can use the GROUP BY clause to create a sum for each group of rows selected from the underlying tables or queries.

Syntax:

```
SUM(expression)
```

Notes:

You cannot use another function reference within the expression. Also, a column name must not refer to a column in a query derived from a function. If you use a total function (AVG, COUNT, MAX, MIN, STDEV, STDEVP, SUM, VAR, or VARP) in the select list of a SELECT statement, any other columns in the select list must be derived using a total function, or the column name must appear in a GROUP BY clause. An expression must contain a reference to at least one column name, and the expression or column name must be a numeric data type.

Null values are not included in the calculation of the result. The data type of the result is generally the same as that of the expression or column name.

Examples:

To create a parameter query that summarizes the sales and cost of goods for all items sold in a given month, enter the following:

```
PARAMETERS [Year to summarize:] Short,
           [Month to summarize:] Short;
SELECT DISTINCTROW OrderItem.CatalogItemID,
      SUM(OrderItem.Quantity) AS Quantity,
      SUM(OrderItem.[Quantity] *
         [QuotedPrice]) AS TotalSales,
      SUM(OrderItem.[Quantity] *
         [OurCost]) AS TotalCost
```

```
FROM [Order]
  INNER JOIN (Catalog
    INNER JOIN OrderItem
    ON Catalog.CatalogItemID = OrderItem.CatalogItemID)
  ON Order.OrderID = OrderItem.OrderID
WHERE (((Year([OrderDate])) = [Year to summarize:])
  AND ((Month([OrderDate])) = [Month to summarize:]))
GROUP BY OrderItem.CatalogItemID;
```

To find the total inventory cost of items currently on hand, enter the following:

```
SELECT DISTINCTROW SUM([OurCost] *
       [NumberInStock]) AS SumInventoryCost
  FROM Component
  WHERE Component.NumberInStock > 0;
```

See Also:

Expressions, GROUP BY clause, HAVING clause, SELECT statement, Subquery, and TRANSFORM statement.

Total Functions: VAR, VARP

In a logical table defined by a SELECT statement or subquery, creates a column value that is the variance (average of the square of the difference from the mean) of the values in the expression or column name specified. You can use the GROUP BY clause to create a variance for each group of rows selected from the underlying tables or queries. VARP produces an estimate of the variance for the entire population based on the sample provided in each group.

Syntax:

```
{VAR | VARP} (expression)
```

Notes:

You cannot use another total function reference within the expression. If you use a total function (AVG, COUNT, MAX, MIN, STDEV, STDEVP, SUM, VAR, or VARP) in the select list of a SELECT statement, any other columns in the select list must be derived using a total function, or the column name must appear in a GROUP BY clause. An expression must contain a reference to at least one column name, and the expression or column name must be a numeric data type.

Null values are not included in the calculation of the result. The data type of the result is a double number. If there are not at least two members in a group, VAR returns a Null value. VARP returns an estimate if there is at least one non-Null value in the group.

Example:

To find the variance and population variance of the cost of components, grouped by type of component, enter the following:

```
SELECT DISTINCTROW Type.TypeDescription,
       Count(Description) AS CountOfDescription,
       Var(Component.OurCost) AS VarOfOurCost,
       VarP(Component.OurCost) AS VarPOfOurCost
  FROM Type
    INNER JOIN Component
    ON Type.ItemTypeCode = Component.ItemTypeCode
  GROUP BY Type.TypeDescription;
```

See Also:

Expressions, GROUP BY clause, HAVING clause, SELECT statement, Subquery, and TRANSFORM statement.

TRANSFORM Statement

Produces a crosstab query that lets you summarize a single value using the values found in a specified column or expression as the column headers and other columns or expressions to define the grouping criteria to form rows. The result looks similar to a spreadsheet and is most useful as input to a graph object.

Syntax:

```
TRANSFORM total-function-expression
  <select-statement>
PIVOT expression
```

where *total-function-expression* is an expression created using one of the total functions, and *<select-statement>* contains a GROUP BY clause.

Notes:

total-function-expression is the value that you want to appear in the "cells" of the crosstab datasheet. PIVOT *expression* defines the column or expression that provides the column heading values in the crosstab result. For example, you might use this value to provide a list of months with total rows defined by product categories in the *select-statement* GROUP BY clause. You can use more than one column or expression in the select statement to define the grouping criteria for rows.

Example:

To produce a total sales amount for each month in the year 1993, categorized by catalog item, enter:

```
TRANSFORM Sum(MonthlySales.TotalInvoiceAmount) AS
          SumOfTotalInvoiceAmount
SELECT Catalog.Description
  FROM Catalog
    INNER JOIN MonthlySales
    ON Catalog.CatalogItemID = MonthlySales.CatalogItemID
  GROUP BY Catalog.Description
  ORDER BY Catalog.Description,
    Format(DateSerial([Year],[Month],1),"mmm yy")
  PIVOT Format(DateSerial([Year],[Month],1),"mmm yy")
  IN ("Jan 93","Feb 93","Mar 93","Apr 93","May 93",
      "Jun 93","Jul 93","Aug 93","Sep 93","Oct 93",
      "Nov 93","Dec 93");
```

NOTE: The example above shows a special use of the IN predicate to define not only which months should be selected but also the sequence in which Microsoft Access displays the month in the resulting recordset.

See Also:

GROUP BY clause, HAVING clause, SELECT statement, and Total Functions.

UNION Query Operator

Produces a result table that contains the rows returned by both the first select statement and the second select statement. You must use SQL view to define a UNION query.

Syntax:

```
select-statement
UNION [ALL]
  select-statement
[ORDER BY {column-name [ASC | DESC]},...]
```

Notes:

If you specify ALL, Microsoft Access returns all rows in both logical tables. If you do not specify ALL, Access eliminates duplicate rows. The tables returned by each select statement must contain an equal number of columns, and each column must have identical attributes.

You must not use the ORDER BY clause in the select statements that are joined by query operators; however, you can include a single ORDER BY clause at the end of a statement that uses one or more query operators. This action will apply the specified order to the result of the entire statement. Access derives the column names of the output from the column names returned by the first select statement. Use the output column names to define ORDER BY criteria.

You can combine multiple select statements using UNION to obtain complex results. You can use parentheses to influence the sequence in which Access applies the operators, as shown here:

```
SELECT ... UNION (SELECT ... UNION SELECT ...)
```

Example:

To find the names of all suppliers, current customers, and potential customers from a new mailing list (NewCust) in the state of Washington, to eliminate duplicates, and to sort the names by zip code, enter the following:

```
SELECT DISTINCTROW Customer.CompanyName, Customer.City,
       PostalCode
  FROM Customer
    WHERE Customer.State = "WA"
UNION
  (SELECT DISTINCTROW Supplier.SupplierName,
         Supplier.SupplierCity, Supplier.SupplierPostal
  FROM Supplier
    WHERE Supplier.SupplierState = "WA"
UNION
```

```
SELECT DISTINCTROW NewCust.Company, NewCust.City,
       NewCust.Zip
  FROM NewCust
  WHERE NewCust.Region = "WA")
ORDER BY PostalCode;
```

See Also:

ORDER BY clause and SELECT statement.

WHERE Clause

Specifies a search condition in an SQL statement or clause. The DELETE, SELECT, and UPDATE statements and the subquery containing the WHERE clause operate only on those rows that satisfy the condition.

Syntax:

```
WHERE search-condition
```

Notes:

Microsoft Access applies the search condition to each row of the logical table assembled as a result of executing the previous clauses, and it rejects those rows for which the search condition does not evaluate to true. If you use a subquery within a predicate in the search condition (often called an *inner query*), Access must first execute the subquery before it evaluates the predicate.

In a subquery, if you refer to a table or query that you also use in an outer FROM clause (often called a *correlated subquery*), Access must execute the subquery for each row being evaluated in the outer table. If you do not use a reference to an outer table in a subquery, Access must execute the subquery only once. A correlated subquery can also be expressed as a join, which generally executes more efficiently. If you include a predicate in the search condition in the form

```
expression comparison-operator subquery
```

an error is returned if the subquery returns no rows.

The order of evaluation of the Boolean operators used in the search condition is NOT, AND, OR, XOR (exclusive OR), EQV (equivalence), and then IMP (implication). You can include additional parentheses to influence the order in which Access processes Boolean expressions.

Example:

To find all products whose cost is greater than $100 and whose number of days to build is equal to 2 or whose number in stock is less than 5, but not both, enter the following:

```
SELECT DISTINCTROW Catalog.CatalogItemID,
       Catalog.Description, Catalog.OurCost,
       Catalog.DaysToBuild, Catalog.NumberInStock
  FROM Catalog
  WHERE (Catalog.OurCost) > 100
    AND ((Catalog.DaysToBuild) = 2
    XOR (Catalog.NumberInStock) < 5);
```

See Also:

DELETE statement, Expressions, Predicates, Search-Condition, SELECT statement, Subquery, and UPDATE statement.

SQL Action Queries

Use SQL action queries to delete, insert, or update data or to create a new table from existing data. Action queries are particularly powerful because they allow you to operate on sets of data, not single rows. For example, an UPDATE statement or a DELETE statement affects all rows in the underlying tables that meet the selection criteria you specify.

DELETE Statement

Deletes one or more rows from a table or query. The WHERE clause is optional. If you do not specify a WHERE clause, all rows are deleted from the table or query that you specify in the FROM clause. If you specify a WHERE clause, the search condition is applied to each row in the table or query, and only those rows that evaluate to True are deleted.

Syntax:

```
DELETE [select-list]
  FROM {{table-name [[AS] correlation-name] |
   select-query-name [[AS] correlation-name]} |
   <joined table>},...
  [WHERE search-condition];
```

where *select-list* is

```
[* | table-name.* | column-list]
```

and where *<joined table>* is

```
({table-name [[AS] correlation-name] |
 select-query-name [[AS] correlation-name] |
 <joined table>}
{INNER | LEFT | RIGHT} JOIN
  {table-name [[AS] correlation-name] |
  select-query-name [[AS] correlation-name] |
  <joined table>}
ON <join-specification>)
```

Notes:

If you specify a query name in a DELETE statement, the query must not be constructed using the UNION query operator. The query also must not contain a total function (AVG, COUNT, MAX, MIN, STDEV, STDEVP, SUM, VAR, or VARP), the DISTINCT keyword, the GROUP BY or HAVING clause, or a subquery that references the same base table as the DELETE statement.

If you join two or more tables in the FROM clause, you may delete rows only from the "many" side of the relationship if the tables are related one-to-many, or on one of the "one" sides if the tables are related one-to-one. When you include more than one table in the FROM clause, you must also specify from which table the rows are to be deleted by using *table-name.** in the select list. When you specify only one table in the FROM clause, you do not need to provide a select list.

You can optionally supply a correlation name for each table or query name. You can use this correlation name as an alias for the full table name when qualifying column names in the WHERE clause and subclauses. You must use a correlation name when referring to a column name that occurs in more than one table in the FROM clause.

If you use a subquery in the search condition, you must not reference the target table or the query or any underlying table of the query in the subquery.

Examples:

To delete all rows in the MonthlySales table, enter the following:

```
DELETE FROM MonthlySales;
```

To delete all rows in the Component table that are "Hard drives," enter the following:

```
DELETE DISTINCTROW Component.*
  FROM Component
    INNER JOIN Type
    ON Component.ItemTypeCode = Type.ItemTypeCode
  WHERE Type.TypeDescription = "Hard drives";
```

See Also:

INSERT statement, Predicates, Search-Condition, and Subquery.

INSERT Statement (Append Query)

Inserts one or more new rows into the specified table or query. When you use the VALUES clause, only a single row is inserted. If you use a select statement, the number of rows inserted equals the number of rows returned by the select statement.

Syntax:

```
INSERT INTO table-name [({column-name},...)]
{VALUES({literal},...) |
select-statement}
```

Notes:

If you do not include a column name list, you must supply values for all columns defined in the table in the order in which they were declared in the table definition. If you include a column name list, you must supply values for all columns in the list, and the values must be compatible with the receiving column attributes. You must include in the list all columns in the underlying table whose Required attribute is Yes and that do not have a default value.

If you supply values by using a select statement, the statement's FROM clause cannot have the target table of the insert as its table name or as an underlying table. The target table also cannot be used in any subquery.

Because Microsoft Access allows you to define column value constraints, a table validation rule, and referential integrity checks, any values that you insert must pass these validations before Access allows you to run the query.

Examples:

To insert a new row in the Customer table, enter the following:

```
INSERT INTO Customer (CompanyName, CustomerName,
       Address1, Address2, City, State, PostalCode,
       Country, PhoneNumber, FaxNumber, CreditLimit,
       AmountOwed)
VALUES ("Books Unlimited", "12345 Camino Real", " "
        "San Jose", "CA", "95000", "USA",
        "(408) 881-2051", "(408) 881-2055", 9000, 0);
```

To calculate the sales totals for a given month and insert them into a summary working table, enter the following:

```
PARAMETERS [Year to summarize:] Short,
           [Month to summarize:] Short;
INSERT INTO zSumSalesWork (CatalogItemID, Quantity,
       TotalSales, TotalCost)
SELECT DISTINCTROW OrderItem.CatalogItemID,
       SUM(OrderItem.Quantity) AS SumOfQuantity,
       SUM([Quantity] * [QuotedPrice]) AS
         TotalInvoiceAmount,
       SUM([Quantity] * [OurCost]) AS TotalCost
  FROM [Order]
    INNER JOIN (Catalog
      INNER JOIN OrderItem
      ON Catalog.CatalogItemID =
         OrderItem.CatalogItemID)
    ON Order.OrderID = OrderItem.OrderID
  WHERE (((Year([OrderDate])) = [Year to summarize:])
    AND ((Month([OrderDate])) = [Month to summarize:]))
  GROUP BY OrderItem.CatalogItemID;
```

Although Microsoft Access accepts the ANSI-standard VALUES clause, you will discover that Access converts a statement such as

```
INSERT INTO MyTable (ColumnA, ColumnB)
VALUES (123, "Jane Doe");
```

to

```
INSERT INTO MyTable (ColumnA, ColumnB)
SELECT 123 As Expr1, "Jane Doe" as Expr2;
```

See Also:

DELETE statement, SELECT statement, and Subquery.

SELECT ... INTO Statement (Make Table Query)

Creates a new table from values selected from one or more other tables; make table queries are most useful to provide backup snapshots or to create tables with rolled-up totals at the end of an accounting period.

Syntax:

```
SELECT [ALL | DISTINCT | DISTINCTROW | TOP number
       [PERCENT]]
   select-list
INTO new-table-name
  FROM {{table-name [[AS] correlation-name] |
   select-query-name [[AS] correlation-name]} |
   <joined table>},...
  [WHERE search-condition]
  [GROUP BY column-name,...]
  [HAVING search-condition]
  [UNION [ALL] select-statement]
  [[ORDER BY {column-name [ASC | DESC]},...] |
  IN <"source database name"> <[source connect string]>
  [WITH OWNERACCESS OPTION];
```

where *select-list* is

```
{* | {expression [AS output-column-name] | table-name.* |
query-name.* | correlation-name.*},...}
```

and where <*joined table*> is

```
({table-name [[AS] correlation-name] |
 select-query-name [[AS] correlation-name] |
 <joined table>}
{INNER | LEFT | RIGHT} JOIN
  {table-name [[AS] correlation-name] |
  select-query-name [[AS] correlation-name] |
  <joined table>}
ON <join-specification>)
```

Notes:

A SELECT ... INTO query creates a new table with the name specified in *new-table-name.* If the table already exists, Microsoft Access prompts you to confirm deleting the table before creating a new one. The columns in the new table inherit the data type attributes of the columns produced by the select list.

You can optionally supply a correlation name for each table or query name. You can use this correlation name as an alias for the full table name when qualifying column names in the select list or in the WHERE clause and subclauses. If you're joining a table or a query to itself, you must use correlation names to clarify which copy of the table or query you're referring to in the select list, join criteria, or selection criteria. If a table name or query name is also an SQL reserved word (for example, "Order"), you must enclose the name in brackets.

When you list more than one table or query without join criteria, the source is the Cartesian product of all the tables. For example, *FROM TableA, TableB* asks Access to search all the rows of TableA matched with all the rows of TableB. Unless you specify other restricting criteria, the number of logical rows that Access processes could equal the number of rows in TableA <u>times</u> the number of rows in TableB. Access then returns the rows in which the selection criteria specified in the WHERE and HAVING clauses are true.

You can further define which rows Access includes in the output recordset by specifying ALL, DISTINCT, DISTINCTROW, TOP *n*, or TOP *n* PERCENT. ALL includes all rows that match the search criteria from the source tables, including potential duplicate rows. DISTINCT requests that Access return only rows that are different from any other row. You cannot update any columns in a query that uses ALL or DISTINCT.

DISTINCTROW (the default) requests that Access return only rows where the concatenation of the primary keys from all tables supplying output columns is unique. Depending on the columns you choose, you might see rows in the result that contain duplicate values, but each row in the result is derived from a DISTINCT combination of ROWS in the underlying tables. You must specify DISTINCTROW to be able to update columns in a joined query. Specify TOP *n* or TOP *n* PERCENT to request that the recordset contain only the first *n* or first *n* percent of rows. The parameter *n* must be an integer and must be less than or equal to 100 if you include the PERCENT keyword. Note that if you do not include an ORDER BY clause (see below), the sequence of rows returned is undefined.

When you include a GROUP BY clause, the select list must be made up of either total functions (AVG, COUNT, MAX, MIN, STDEV, STDEVP, SUM, VAR, or VARP) or column names specified in the GROUP BY clause. A column name in a GROUP BY clause can refer to any column from any table in the FROM clause, even if the column is not named in the select list. If you want to refer to a calculated expression in the GROUP BY clause, you must assign an *output-column-name* to the expression in *select-list* and then refer to that name in the GROUP BY clause. If the GROUP BY clause is preceded by a WHERE clause, Access forms the groups from the rows selected after application of the WHERE clause.

If you use a HAVING clause but do not include a GROUP BY clause, the select list must be formed using total functions (AVG, COUNT, MAX, MIN, STDEV, STDEVP, SUM, VAR, or VARP). If you include a GROUP BY clause preceding the HAVING clause, the HAVING search condition applies to each of the groups formed by equal values in the specified columns. If you do not include a GROUP BY clause, the HAVING search condition applies to the entire logical table defined by the SELECT statement.

You specify the column(s) on whose value the rows returned are ordered by using column names. You can specify multiple columns in the ORDER BY clause. The list is ordered primarily by the first column name. If rows exist for which the values of that column are equal, they are then ordered by the next column name on the ORDER BY list. You can specify ascending (ASC) or descending (DESC) ordering for each column. If you do not choose ASC or DESC, ASC is assumed. Use of an ORDER BY clause in a SELECT statement is the only means of defining the sequence of the returned rows.

Normally, the person running the query not only must have rights to the query but also must have the appropriate rights to the tables used in the query. (These rights include reading data to select rows, updating, inserting, and deleting data using the query.) If there are multiple users of your application, you might want to secure the tables so that no user has direct access to any of the tables and all users can still run queries defined by you. Assuming you are the owner of both the queries and the tables, you can deny access to the tables but allow access to the queries. So that the queries run properly, you must add the WITH OWNER-ACCESS OPTION clause to allow the users to have the same access rights as the table owner when accessing the data via the query. (See Chapter 14 in the *Building Applications* manual that comes with Microsoft Access for more details on securing your applications.)

Example:

To create a new table that summarizes all sales for the year 1993 by product from the MonthlySales totals table, enter the following:

```
SELECT DISTINCTROW MonthlySales.CatalogItemID,
       Catalog.Description, MonthlySales.Year,
       CLng(Sum([QuantitySold])) AS Quantity,
       Sum(MonthlySales.TotalInvoiceAmount) AS
           TotalSales,
       Sum(MonthlySales.TotalCost) AS TotalCost
INTO Sales1993
  FROM Catalog
    INNER JOIN MonthlySales
    ON Catalog.CatalogItemID = MonthlySales.CatalogItemID
  WHERE MonthlySales.Year = 1993
  GROUP BY MonthlySales.CatalogItemID,
           Catalog.Description, MonthlySales.Year;
```

See Also:

JOIN operation, Search-Condition, and SELECT statement.

UPDATE Statement

In the specified table or query, updates the selected columns (either to the value of the given expression or to Null) in all rows that satisfy the search condition. If you do not enter a WHERE clause, all rows in the specified table or query are affected.

Syntax:

```
UPDATE {{table-name [[AS] correlation-name] |
 select-query-name [[AS] correlation-name]} |
 <joined table>},...
SET {column-name = {expression | NULL}},...
[WHERE search-condition]
```

where *<joined table>* is

```
({table-name [[AS] correlation-name] |
 select-query-name [[AS] correlation-name] |
 <joined table>}
{INNER | LEFT | RIGHT} JOIN
  {table-name [[AS] correlation-name] |
  select-query-name [[AS] correlation-name] |
  <joined table>}
ON <join-specification>)
```

Notes:

If you provide more than one table name, you can update columns only in the table on the "many" side of a one-to-many relationship. If the tables are related one-to-one, you can update columns in either table. Microsoft Access must be able to determine the relationship between queries in order to update columns in a query. In general, if a table is joined by its primary key to a query, you can update columns in the query (because the primary key indicates that the table is on the "one" side of the join). You cannot update a table joined to a query. If you want to update a table with the results of a query, you must insert the query results into a temporary table that can be defined with a one-to-many or one-to-one relationship with the target table and then use the temporary table to update the target.

If you specify a search condition, you can reference only columns found in the target table or query. If you use a subquery in the search condition, you must not reference the target table or query or any underlying table of the query in the subquery.

In the SET clause, you cannot specify a column name more than once. Values assigned to columns must be compatible with the column attributes. If you assign the Null value, the column cannot have been defined Required=Yes.

Access lets you define column-value constraints, a table validation rule, or referential integrity checks, so any values that you update must pass these validations or Access will not let you run the query.

Examples:

To raise the price of all video boards by 10%, enter the following:

```
UPDATE DISTINCTROW Type
  INNER JOIN Catalog
  ON Type.ItemTypeCode = Catalog.ItemTypeCode
  SET Catalog.Price = [Price] * 1.1
  WHERE Type.TypeDescription = "Video Boards";
```

To discount the price of all items in the catalog by 5%, enter the following:

```
UPDATE Catalog
  SET Catalog.Price = [Price] * .95;
```

See Also:

Expressions, Predicates, Search-Condition, and WHERE clause.

Selected Complex Query Examples

Although the preceding sections provide many examples, it's useful to examine how two complex sets of queries are constructed for the PROMPT sample application. The first example shows you how to synchronize a total field in a parent table when a related value in a child table changes. The second example shows you how to update a table with results from a totals query (using an intermediate working table).

Example 1: Synchronizing Parent and Child Tables

As you learned in Chapter 4, "Designing Your Database Application," including calculated fields in your database design is not usually a good idea. In some cases, however, storing a calculated field in your database might be necessary to improve performance or simplify processing.

In the Prompt Computer Solutions database, items for sale are stored in the Catalog table. These items may be made up of one or more components, and each component has a separate component price. To calculate the cost of the assembled components, you could use totals queries to add up the prices, but the resulting totals query would not be updatable. To make working with Catalog data easier when entering customer orders into Microsoft Access, it is acceptable to store the calculated total cost in the Catalog record.

If you do this, you must be sure that any updates to the Catalog, CatalogComponent, or Component tables can be done only through forms. In Chapters 13 and 14, you'll learn how to build the forms to update Component and Catalog information. In Chapter 20, you'll find out how to connect the Catalog and Component forms to macros to ensure that the two tables remain synchronized. In addition, you'll need to build two queries that you can call from the update forms to ensure that the correct total price is stored in the Catalog table whenever any change occurs to a price in the Component table. Let's build those two queries now.

Calculating New Catalog Prices for a Component Price Change

Whenever the price of a component changes, you need a query that can calculate the changed price for all affected products in the catalog that contain the component. You'll know the ID of the changed component, so you can match that with the data in the linking CatalogComponent table to find all the items in the catalog that are affected by the price change. You can create a total query that will recalculate the price for all the identified catalog items.

The cost for each component is in the Component table. The quantity of each component of a particular catalog item is in the linking CatalogComponent table. Start by building a total query containing these two tables. You need the CatalogItemID from the CatalogComponent table. You also need a calculated sum of the Amount field (from the CatalogComponent table) times the OurCost field (from the

Component table). To find all the affected catalog items, you'll use a special test on CatalogItemID called a *subquery*. Include the CatalogItemID again on the QBE grid, and choose Where in the Total row. In the Criteria cell under this CatalogItemID, enter

```
IN (SELECT CatalogItemID
  FROM CatalogComponent
    WHERE ComponentID = [Component ID That Changed:])
```

You have used the IN comparison operator previously to check for a list of values. In this case, you're using a SELECT statement (the subquery) to generate the list. In plain English, the subquery asks for all the CatalogItemIDs from the CatalogComponent table in which the ComponentID field matches a parameter value. Your query should look like the one shown in Figure 11-2.

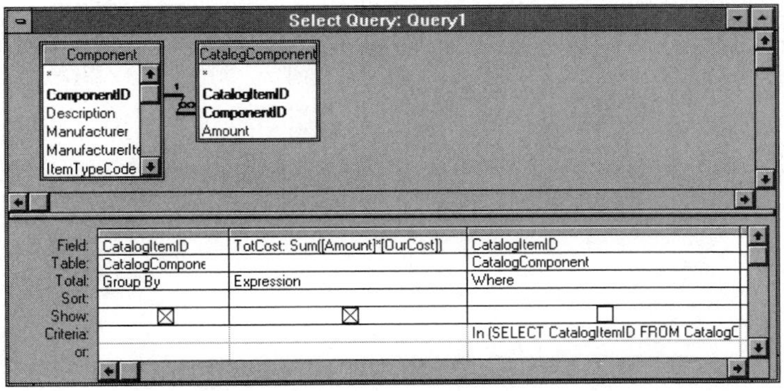

FIGURE 11-2.
A total query to calculate the total cost of components for selected catalog products.

If you run this query and enter *1* when you see Component ID That Changed, you'll see a total cost calculated for each item in the catalog that contains ComponentID number 1, as shown in Figure 11-3 on the next page.

It would be nice to save this query and join it to the Catalog table to perform a one-to-one join update by matching on CatalogItemID and updating the cost in the table from the cost in the query. Because Microsoft Access can't understand that the CatalogItemID in the total query is unique, it assumes that the query is on the "many" side of the join, not on the "one" side. This means that you can't update the table directly by joining with the query.

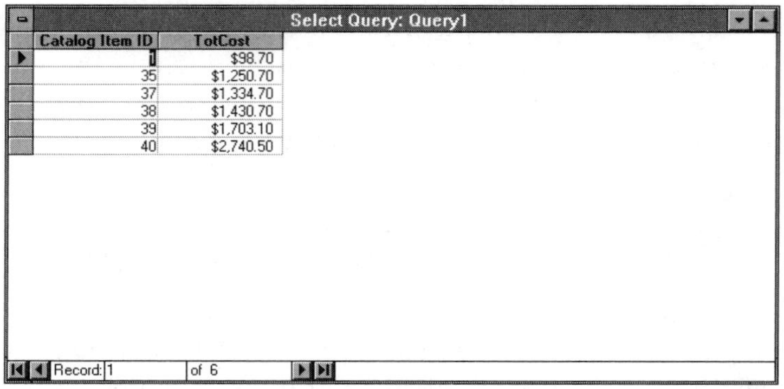

FIGURE 11-3. The total cost of all catalog items that contain Component 1.

One way to get around this is to design a "working" table that looks just like the query output but that has a primary key defined on CatalogItemID. Access will understand that any join between this table and the Catalog table is one-to-one because the join is on the unique CatalogItemID in each table. I like to define "working" tables with a "z" prefix to place them at the end of the list in the database window. The *zSumCatalogCost* working table looks like the one shown in Figure 11-4.

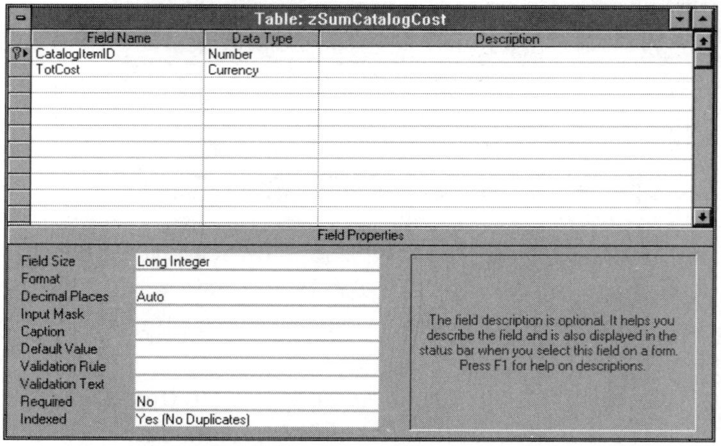

FIGURE 11-4. The working table for catalog item total calculations.

To populate this table, you need to save it and turn the query shown in Figure 11-2 into an append query. To do that, click the Append Query button on the toolbar or choose Append from the Query menu. Choose your new zSumCatalogCost table as the target for the append.

Because you named the output columns from the totals query the same as the columns in the working table, Access should map the column names, and the result should look like the one shown in Figure 11-5. Save this query and name it *Calc Catalog Cost.*

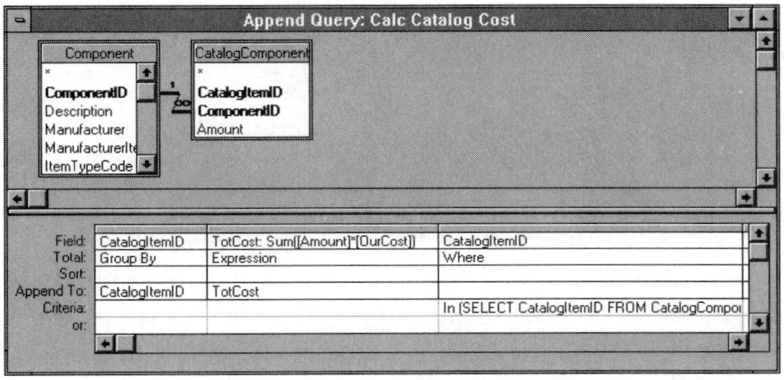

FIGURE 11-5. Appending calculated totals to a working table.

You might ask, "Why can't I use a make table query to create the working table each time I need to update the catalog item cost?" Unfortunately, there's no way to set the primary key of a table created by a make table query. Remember, you need to be able to tell Access that the relationship of this update data to the Catalog table is one-to-one. The only way to do that is with a unique index or primary key.

Because you want to be sure that the working table is empty each time you calculate the catalog item costs, you need a simple DELETE query to clear out the working table. Create a new query on the zSumCatalogCost table, convert it to a delete query, and save it as *Clear zSumCatalogCost*. In SQL view, the query should look like this:

```
DELETE DISTINCTROW zSumCatalogCost.*
  FROM zSumCatalogCost;
```

Finally, you need an update query to link the working table to the Catalog table and update the prices. Start a new query on the Catalog table and add the zSumCatalogCost table to the query. Convert the query to an update query, and then drag the OurCost field from the Catalog table to the QBE grid. Set the Update To row to *[TotCost]*, which is the total field from the working table. In SQL view, your query should look like this:

```
UPDATE DISTINCTROW zSumCatalogCost
  INNER JOIN Catalog
  ON zSumCatalogCost.CatalogItemID =
     Catalog.CatalogItemID
  SET Catalog.OurCost = [TotCost];
```

Save this query as *Update Catalog*. Now, after you change a price in the Component table, you can run the Clear zSumCatalogCost query, the Calc Catalog Cost query, and finally the Update Catalog query to ensure that the new price is reflected in all the related Catalog rows.

See Also: In Chapter 20, "Automating Your Application with Macros," you'll see how you can use a few simple macros to automatically run these queries whenever you change a price on the Components form.

Example 2: Updating a Table with Query Totals

In Chapter 9, you learned how to append monthly sales totals to a table that's accumulating monthly sales details for the year. Of course, you can use a total query to find out year-to-date totals at any time. But what if you're a large company with many thousands of products? It might also be efficient to have a year-to-date sales table that high-level executives can use directly rather than running a query against thousands of products.

To sum totals into a running total table, you'll need another "working" table just like the one in the previous example. In the PROMPT database, I call this table zSumSalesWork, and it looks like the one shown in Figure 11-6.

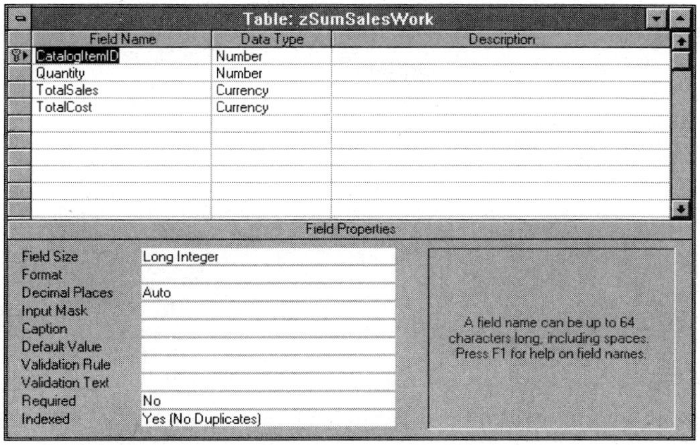

FIGURE 11-6.
A working table for monthly sales totals.

You can use a variation of the query you built in Figures 9-26 and 9-27 to create an append query that populates the working table. Simply change the target table to zSumSalesWork and save the query as Sum Monthly Sales Working Totals. In SQL view, the query looks like this:

```
PARAMETERS [Year to summarize:] Short,
           [Month to summarize:] Short;
INSERT INTO zSumSalesWork (CatalogItemID, Quantity,
       TotalSales, TotalCost)
SELECT DISTINCTROW OrderItem.CatalogItemID,
       Sum(OrderItem.Quantity) AS SumOfQuantity,
       Sum([Quantity] *
           [QuotedPrice]) AS TotalInvoiceAmount,
       Sum([Quantity] * [OurCost]) AS TotalCost
  FROM [Order]
    INNER JOIN (Catalog
      INNER JOIN OrderItem
      ON Catalog.CatalogItemID = OrderItem.CatalogItemID)
    ON Order.OrderID = OrderItem.OrderID
  WHERE (((Year([OrderDate])) = [Year to summarize:])
    AND ((Month([OrderDate])) = [Month to summarize:]))
  GROUP BY OrderItem.CatalogItemID;
```

You also need a delete query to clear out the working table before you insert the totals for a new month. Call this query *Clear zSumSalesWork*. The SQL statement for this query looks like this:

```
DELETE DISTINCTROW zSumSalesWork.*
  FROM zSumSalesWork;
```

Finally, you need a one-to-one join update query to update the YTDSales table with data that you total at the end of each month. Create this query by starting a query on the YTDSales table and adding the zSumSalesWork table to the query. Microsoft Access should automatically link the tables on CatalogItemID for you. Change the query to an update query and drag the Quantity, TotalSales, and TotalCost fields from the YTDSales table (not zSumSalesWork) to the QBE grid. In the Update To cell for each field, add the value from zSumSalesWork to the current value of the field. The expression for Quantity looks like this:

```
[YTDSales].[Quantity] + [zSumSalesWork].[Quantity]
```

When you've finished, the QBE grid should look like the one in Figure 11-7. Save this query as *Update YTD Sales*.

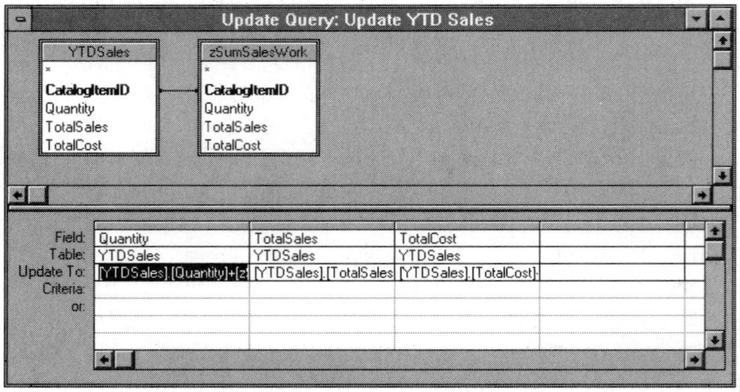

FIGURE 11-7.
A query to update YTD (year to date) sales totals.

The SQL statement for this query is as follows:

```
UPDATE DISTINCTROW YTDSales
  INNER JOIN zSumSalesWork
  ON YTDSales.CatalogItemID = zSumSalesWork.CatalogItemID
SET YTDSales.Quantity = [YTDSales].[Quantity] +
                        [zSumSalesWork].[Quantity],
    YTDSales.TotalSales = [YTDSales].[TotalSales] +
                          [zSumSalesWork].[TotalSales],
    YTDSales.TotalCost = [YTDSales].[TotalCost] +
                         [zSumSalesWork].[TotalCost];
```

At the end of each month, do the following to update year-to-date sales totals:

1. Execute the Clear zSumSalesWork query to be sure the working table is empty.
2. Run the Sum Monthly Sales Working totals query, and enter the current year and month to create the totals you need in the working table.
3. Run the Update YTD Sales query to add the totals to the YTDSales table.

At this point, you should have a good working understanding of how to build complex queries using the SQL syntax understood by Microsoft Access. In Parts 4 and 5 of this book, you'll learn how to build forms and reports that use queries. In Part 6, you'll learn how to use macros and Microsoft Access Basic to tie it all together.

PART 4

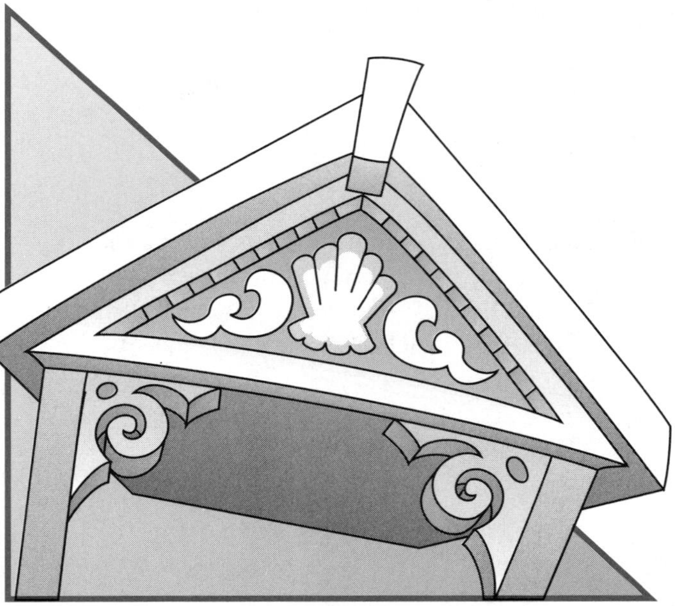

Using Forms

12

Form Basics

If you've worked through the book to this point, you should now understand all the mechanics of designing and building databases (and connecting to external ones), entering and viewing data in tables, and building queries. You need to understand tables and queries before you jump into forms because most forms you design will have an underlying table or recordset.

This chapter focuses on the external aspects of forms—why forms are useful, what they look like, and how to use them. The tour will look at samples from the Northwind Traders database (NWIND) that is included with Microsoft Access. Later you'll learn how to design and build your own forms by working to create the database application for Prompt Computer Solutions (PROMPT).

Uses of Forms

Forms are the primary interface between users and your Microsoft Access application. You can design forms for many different purposes:

- *Displaying and editing data.* This is the most common use of forms. Forms give you a way to customize the presentation of data in your database. You can also use forms to make it easier to change, add, or delete data in your database. You can set options in a form to make all or part of your data read-only, to fill in related information from other tables automatically, to calculate the values to be displayed, or to show or hide data based on either the values of other data in the record or the options chosen by the user of the form.
- *Controlling application flow.* You can design forms that work with macros or Microsoft Access Basic functions to automate the display of certain data or the sequence of certain actions. You can create special controls on your form, called *command buttons,* that run a macro or an Access Basic routine whenever the control is clicked. With macros and Access Basic routines, you can open other forms, run queries, restrict the data being displayed, execute a menu command, set values in records and on forms, display menus, print reports, and perform a host of other actions.

You can also design a form so that macros or Access Basic functions are run when different events occur—for example, when someone opens the form, tabs to a specific control, clicks an option on the form, or changes data on the form.

> **See Also:** See Part 6 of this book, "Creating an Application," for details on using macros and Microsoft Access Basic with forms to automate your application.

- *Accepting input.* You can design forms that are used only for entering new data in your database or for providing data values to help automate your application.
- *Displaying messages.* Forms can provide information about how to use your application or about upcoming actions. Microsoft Access also gives you a MsgBox macro action or an Access Basic function that you can use to display information, warnings, or errors. (See Chapter 19, "Adding Power with Macros," for details.)
- *Printing information.* Although you should design reports to print most information, you can also print the information that is on a form. Because you can specify one set of options when Access displays a form and another set of options when Access prints a form, a form can serve a dual role. For example, you might set up a form with two sets of display headers and footers, one set for entering an order and another set for printing the customer invoice from the order.

The Built-In Toolbar for the Form Window in Form View

It's useful to take a moment to look at the toolbar that Microsoft Access displays when you open a form. To open a form and then open the database you want, click the Form tab in the Database window, select the form you want from the list, and click the Open button.

From left to right, the buttons on the built-in Form view toolbar are:

Design View button. Click this button to see the Form window in Design view.

Form View button. This button appears pressed to indicate that you're looking at a Form window in Form view.

Datasheet View button. Click this button to see the Form window in Datasheet view, in which the data in the underlying table or query for the form is displayed.

Print button. Click this button to print the data displayed on the form.

Print Preview button. You can print most forms and the data displayed in them. Click this button to see a preview of the printed page.

New button. If you're allowed to add rows using this form, click this button to jump to the empty row at the end of the recordset to insert a new record.

Cut button. Click this button to copy the current selection to the Clipboard and delete the selection.

Copy button. Click this button to copy the current selection to the Clipboard. The data selected is not deleted.

Paste button. Click this button to paste data from the Clipboard to the currently selected row or control.

Find button. Click this button to initiate a search for values in any field.

NEW!

Sort Ascending button. Click anywhere in a control bound to a recordset field you want to sort, and then click this button to order the rows displayed based on ascending values in the selected column. You cannot sort data on a subform.

NEW!

Sort Descending button. Click anywhere in a control bound to a recordset field you want to sort, and then click this button to order the rows displayed based on descending values in the selected column. You cannot sort data on a subform.

Edit Filter/Sort button. You can restrict and sort the data you see on the form, much as you can specify selection criteria and sorting in a query or a table datasheet. Click this button to create or edit a filter or sorting criteria.

Apply Filter/Sort button. Click this button to apply any filter or sorting criteria you have created.

Show All Records button. Click this button to remove any filter and display all records in an underlying form recordset.

Show Database Window button. Click this button to place the focus on the Database window. This button also un-hides the window if you have hidden it and restores the window if you have minimized it.

Undo Current Field/Record button. Click this button to undo all changes to any field in the current record displayed on the form. The button is disabled when there are no changes that can be undone.

Undo button. Click this button to undo your last change. Undo has the same effect as Ctrl-Z or the Undo command on the Edit menu. The button is disabled when there are no changes that can be undone.

Cue Cards button. Click this button to open the main menu of the Cue Cards facility. Cue Cards lead you through step-by-step instructions for most common tasks.

Help button. Click this button to add a question mark to your mouse pointer. Click with this pointer on any displayed object to receive context-sensitive help about that object.

A Tour of Forms

The NWIND sample database included with the Microsoft Access software is full of interesting examples of forms. The rest of this chapter takes you on a tour of some of the major features of those forms. In the next chapter, you'll learn how to go about designing and building forms for the PROMPT database.

To start, open the NWIND database and click the Form tab in the Database window to see the list of available forms.

Headers, Details, and Footers

You will normally place the information that you want to display from the underlying table or query in the detail section in the center of the Form window. You can add a header at the top of the window or a footer at the bottom of the window to display information or controls that don't need to change with each different record.

An interesting form in NWIND that has both a header and a footer is Suppliers. Find the Suppliers form in the forms list in the Database window, select the form, and click the Open button to see a window similar to the one shown in Figure 12-1.

FIGURE 12-1. The Suppliers form in NWIND, with a header, a detail section, and a footer.

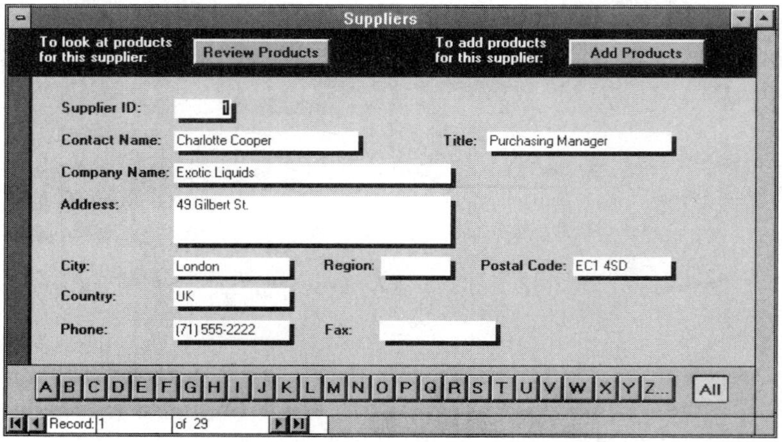

The black bar across the top of the window is the header for the form. Inside this header you can see some instructions and two command buttons that are used to activate other forms. At the bottom of the window is a gray panel with command buttons displaying the letters of the alphabet. This panel is the footer for the form. At the bottom left corner of the form is the record number box that you saw in tables and queries in Datasheet view. Click the arrow button immediately to the right of the record number, and you should see the next supplier record in the detail section of the form; notice that the header and footer don't change when you do this.

If you click the B command button in the footer, you should see details of the first company whose name begins with the letter *B*. The way the form is designed, each letter command button actually applies a filter to show you only suppliers with a company name starting with the letter you select. Click the All button to make all the supplier records available again on the form.

Multiple-Page Forms

When you have a lot of information from each record to display on a form, you can design a *multiple-page form*. Open the Employees form in NWIND to see an example. When you open the form, you'll see the first page of the employee data for the first employee. You can use the record number box and buttons in the lower left corner of the form to move through the records, viewing the first page of information for each employee. Figure 12-2 shows you the first page of the seventh employee record (that of Robert King). To see the second page of information for any employee, use the scroll bar at the right side of the form or press PgDn. Figure 12-3 on the next page shows the second page of the seventh record. (Notice that this form has a header, but no footer.) As you view different pages of a form, the black bar at the top of the form (with the employee's name) doesn't move. This name display on the header is actually a calculated field resulting from concatenating the First Name field and the Last Name field in the record.

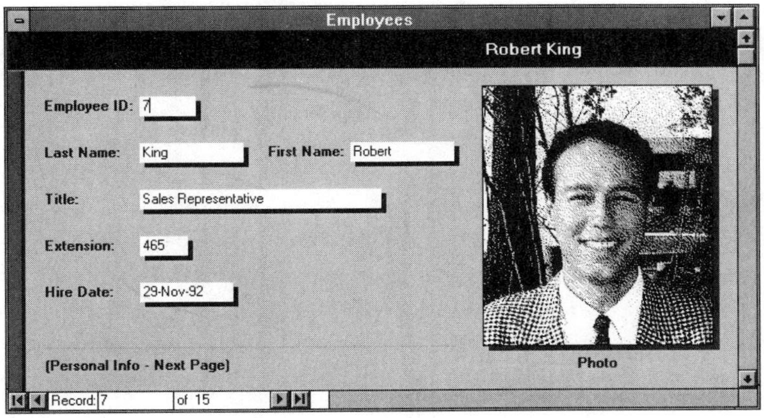

FIGURE 12-2. The first page of a record on the multiple-page Employees form.

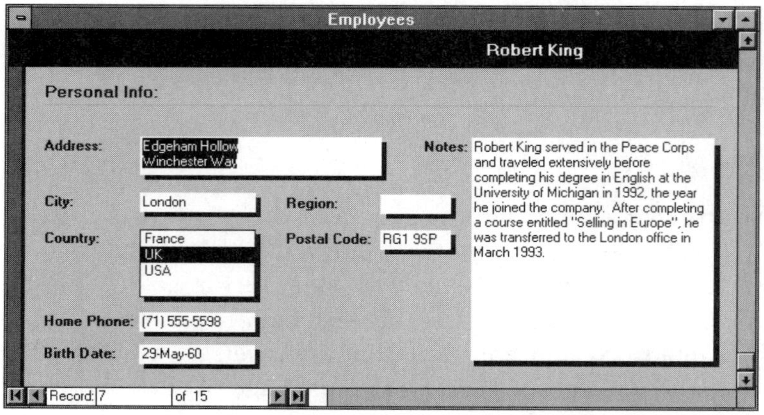
Employees
Robert King
Personal Info:
Address:
Edgeham Hollow
Winchester Way
Notes:
Robert King served in the Peace Corps and traveled extensively before completing his degree in English at the University of Michigan in 1992, the year he joined the company. After completing a course entitled "Selling in Europe", he was transferred to the London office in March 1993.
City:
London
Region:
Country:
France
UK
USA
Postal Code:
RG1 9SP
Home Phone:
(71) 555-5598
Birth Date:
29-May-60
Record: 7
of 15

FIGURE 12-3.
The second page of a record on the multiple-page Employees form.

Continuous Forms

You can create another type of form that is useful for browsing through a list of records when each record has just a few data fields. This form is a *continuous form*. Rather than showing you only a single record at a time, continuous forms display formatted records back to back, in the manner of a datasheet.

The Sales Totals form in NWIND, shown in Figure 12-4, is a continuous form. You can use the vertical scroll bar to move through the record display, or you can click the record number box and buttons in the lower left corner of the form to move from record to record. As you might guess, the records you see on this form are from a Totals query that joins information from the Employees table and the Orders table.

Subforms

A good example of a *subform* is the Orders form of NWIND, shown in Figure 12-5. Although the Orders form looks much like a single display panel, the center part of the window (which looks more like a datasheet than a form) is actually a subform embedded in the Orders form. The main part of the form displays information from a query that joins the Customers table, the Employees table, and the Orders table. The information on the subform comes from a query in the Order Details table and the Products table.

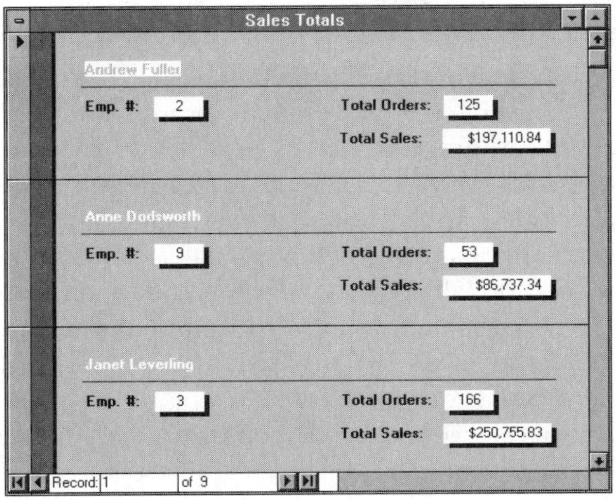

FIGURE 12-4. The Sales Totals form is a continuous form.

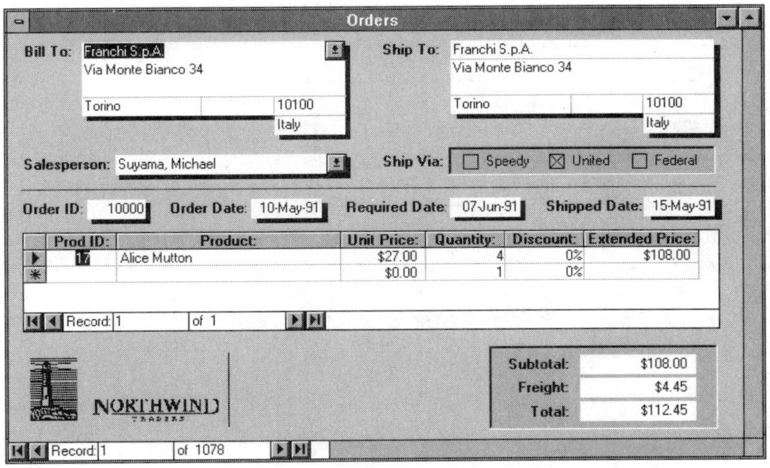

FIGURE 12-5. The Orders form with an embedded subform that can list products.

Although this form looks pretty complicated, it really isn't all that difficult to build. Because the NWIND database is well designed, it doesn't take much effort to build the two queries that extract information from five different tables. Most of the work of creating the form goes into selecting and placing the controls that display the data. To link a subform with a main form, you have to set only two properties that tell Access which linking fields to use. In Chapter 15, "Advanced Form Design," you'll build and link a form with a subform.

Modal Forms

As you add functionality to your application, you'll find situations in which you need to get some data or convey some important information before Microsoft Access can proceed. Access provides you with a special type of form—a *modal form*—that requires a response before you can continue working in the application. A sample modal form is the Print Reports Dialog dialog box in the NWIND database, shown in Figure 12-6. This dialog box normally opens when you choose the Print Reports button on the NWIND Main Switchboard form, but you can also open the form on which the dialog box is based directly from the Database window. You'll notice that as long as this dialog box is open, you can't select any other window or menu that you can see on the screen. So, in order to proceed, you must either select the type of report and click a button or close the Print Reports Dialog dialog box by double-clicking the Control-menu box in the upper left corner of the dialog box.

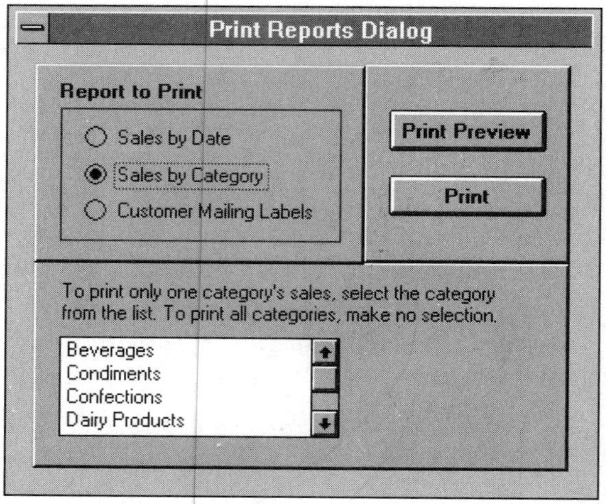

FIGURE 12-6. The Print Reports Dialog dialog box is a modal form.

This form might not look exactly like the one shown in Figure 12-6 when you first open it. Click the Sales By Category option button to see the category list at the bottom of the form. As you might suspect, when you click the Sales By Category option button, Access runs a simple macro that makes the category list visible. (Chapter 22, "Automating Your Application with Microsoft Access Basic," shows you how to build a similar form.)

Special Controls

The information on a form is contained in *controls*. The most common control you'll use on a form is a simple text box. A text box can display data from an underlying table or query, or it can display data calculated on the form itself. You've probably noticed that there are lots of controls on the forms that allow you to choose among several values or to see additional content. You can also use controls to trigger a macro. These controls are discussed under the next four headings.

Option Buttons, Check Boxes, Toggles, and Option Groups

Whenever the data you're displaying can have only two or three valid values, you can use controls such as option buttons, check boxes, and toggles to see or set the value you want in the field. For example, when there are two values, as in the case of a simple Yes/No field, you can use a check box to graphically display the value in the field: A check box that's checked means the value is "Yes," and a check box that's unchecked means the value is "No."

To provide a graphical choice among more than two values, you can place any of these controls in a group. Only one of the controls in a group can have a "Yes" value. For example, the Ship Via group shown in Figure 12-7 is from the Orders form in the NWIND database. This is an option group consisting of three check boxes. Because there are only three valid shipping methods in this application, the option group can show which shipping method is in effect for the current order. As you'll read in more detail later, Microsoft Access uses the relative numeric value of the control to determine the value in the underlying field.

FIGURE 12-7.
An option group containing three check boxes.

In the Print Reports dialog box shown in Figure 12-6, an option group is used in a slightly different way. When you click one of the option buttons in this group, you're setting a value. You'll notice that when you click the Sales By Category option button, a list of categories appears in the lower part of the form. This list appears because a macro tests the value set by the option button and triggers the display of the category list whenever the value corresponds to the second button in the option group. Later, when you click either the Print or the Print Preview command button on the form, a macro again tests this value to determine which report to run for you.

List Boxes and Combo Boxes

The list of categories discussed above is another control called a list box, an example of which is shown in Figure 12-8. A list box can show a list of values you entered when you designed the control, a list of values from an SQL statement, the value of a field in a table or query, or a list of field names from a table or query. In the example shown in Figure 12-8, the list includes the set of names from the Category Name field of the Categories table.

FIGURE 12-8.
A list box can show a list of values or a list of field names.

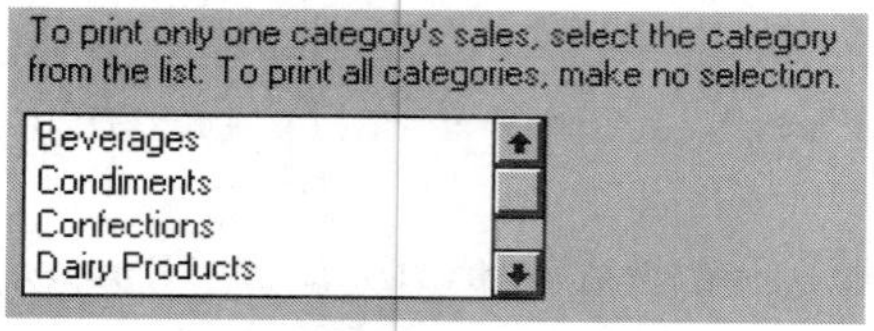
To print only one category's sales, select the category from the list. To print all categories, make no selection.
Beverages
Condiments
Confections
Dairy Products

When you select a category from the list, you set the value of the control. If the control represents a field in the underlying table or query, you update that field. In the example shown in Figure 12-8, the control is tested by the macro that runs the Sales By Category report to see whether the report should be restricted to a category chosen by you from the list. A list box like this one can use data from more than one field. You can, for example, display the more meaningful name of the Category field in the list but set a value of the related Category ID when the name is selected.

Combo boxes are similar to list boxes. The major difference is that a combo box has a text box and a drop-down list. One advantage of the combo box is that it requires space for only one of the values in the underlying list. The Salesperson field on the Orders form in NWIND is set using a combo box, as shown in Figure 12-9. The combo box uses two fields from the underlying table—Employee Name and Employee ID (which you can't see). When you select an employee name, the combo box sets the employee ID in the underlying field in the record—a very useful feature.

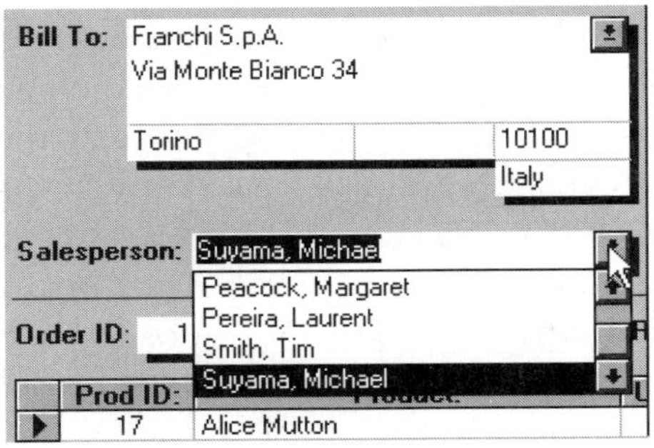

FIGURE 12-9. An open combo box.

OLE Objects

You've probably noticed pictures in several places on the NWIND forms. There's one on the Employees form. There's another on the Categories form. Both of these pictures are embedded in fields within database tables using the *Object Linking and Embedding (OLE)* technology. The logo in the lower left corner of the Orders form is a picture that Microsoft Access has stored as part of the form. The control you use to display pictures or any other OLE object is called an *object frame*. A bound object frame control is used to display OLE objects that are stored in fields in a table. An unbound object frame control is used to display an object that is not stored in a table.

See Also: The section in Chapter 15 titled "Working with Objects" contains more details about OLE objects.

When you include an object frame control on a form and bind the object frame control to an OLE object in the database, you can edit that object by selecting it and choosing the command at the bottom of the Edit menu that starts the object's application, as shown in Figure 12-10 on the next page. If the object is a picture, a graph, or a spreadsheet, you can see the object in the object frame control, and you can activate its application by double-clicking the object. If the object is a sound, you can hear it by double-clicking the object frame control.

Figure 12-10 shows you one of the pictures from the NWIND Categories table that is bound in an object frame control in the Categories form. When you select the picture and choose the Edit command or double-click the picture, Microsoft Access starts the Paintbrush application in which the picture was created. Paintbrush starts with the picture file open and ready to edit, as shown in Figure 12-11. You can update the picture using any of the Paintbrush tools. You can paste in a different picture by copying a picture to the Clipboard and choosing the Paste command from Paintbrush's Edit menu. Finally, after you've made your changes, choose the Update command from the File menu in Paintbrush, and then choose the Exit And Return To... command, also from Paintbrush's File menu.

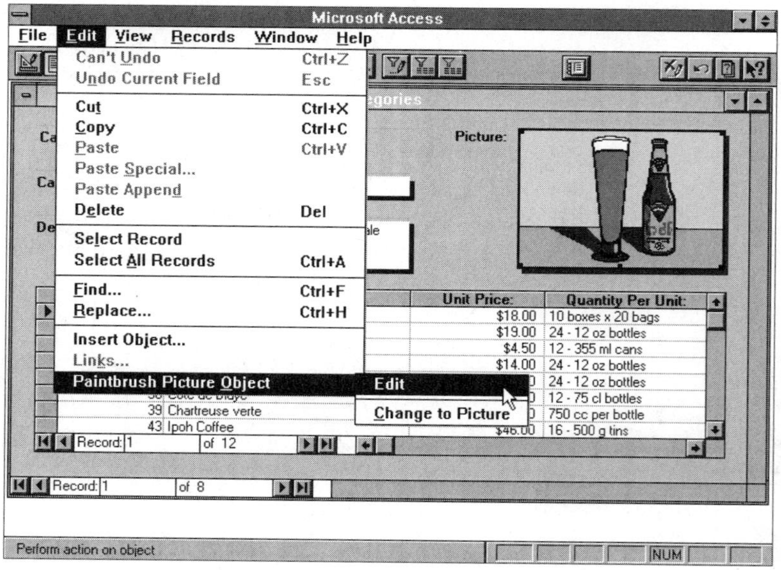

FIGURE 12-10. An OLE object (the picture in the upper right corner) has been selected on a form, and you can edit the object by choosing the Edit command on the Paintbrush Picture Object submenu at the bottom of the Edit menu.

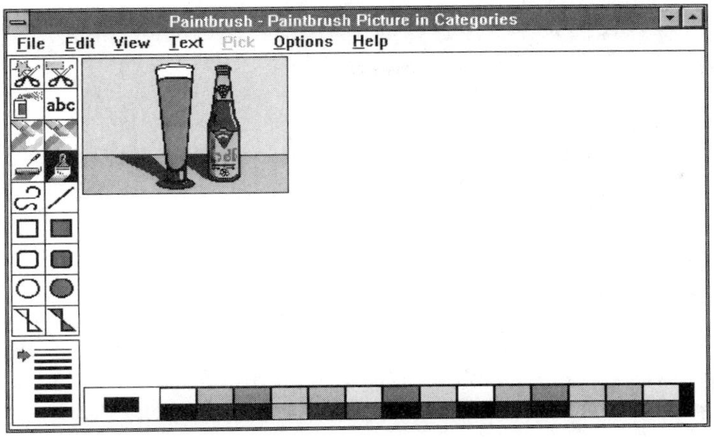

FIGURE 12-11.
The OLE object from Figure 12-10, in its original application and ready for editing.

Command Buttons

Although you can get a lot of work done by entering and reviewing data on individual forms, you can also link many forms together to create a complete database application using command buttons. In the Northwind Traders (NWIND) sample database, for example, most of the sample forms are tied to the Main Switchboard form, shown in Figure 12-12, from which command buttons launch various functions in the application. The advantage of command buttons is really quite simple—they offer an easy way to trigger a macro. The macro might do nothing more than open another form, print a report, or run an action query to update many records in your database. You can specify more than 40 different actions with a Microsoft Access macro. As you'll see by the time you get to the end of this book, you can easily build a fairly complex application using forms, reports, macros, and some simple Access Basic routines.

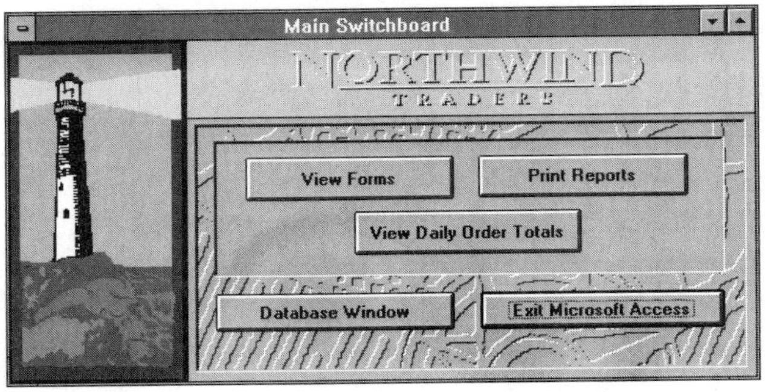

FIGURE 12-12.
The command buttons on the Main Switchboard form.

Moving Around in Forms and Working with Data

The rest of this chapter shows you how to move around and work with data on the various types of forms that were discussed earlier in this chapter.

Viewing Data

If you've read through Chapter 7, "Using Datasheets," and have followed along in this chapter with the form examples, you already have a pretty good idea of how to view data and move around on forms. While moving around on a form is similar to moving around on a datasheet, there are a few subtle differences between datasheets and forms (usually based on how a form was designed) that determine how a form works with data. You can use the Categories form in NWIND to explore how forms work.

To get to the Categories form, first open the NWIND sample database. Next, click the Form tab in the Database window. Select the Categories form from the list, and click the Open button to see the form shown in Figure 12-13.

FIGURE 12-13. The Categories form in the NWIND database.

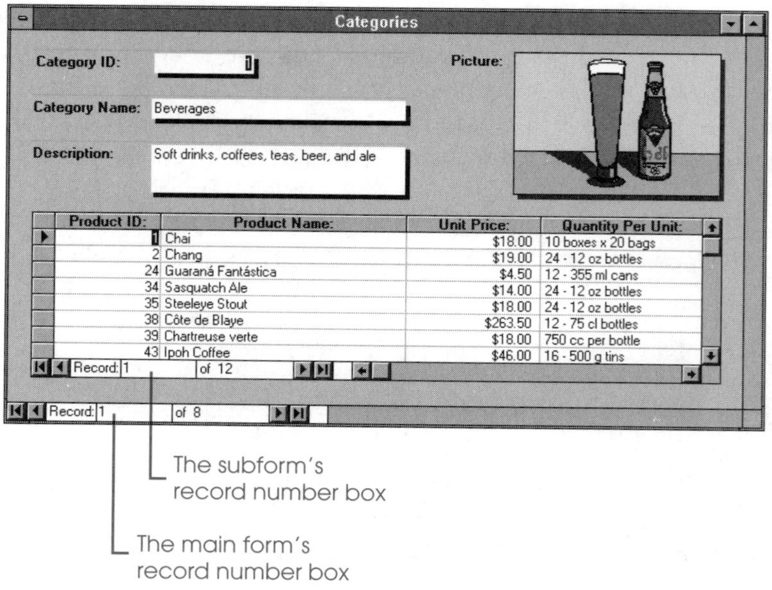

Moving Around

The way you move around on a form depends in part on the form design. For example, the Categories form contains a subform. To move back and forth between the form and the subform, you would use the Ctrl-Tab and Ctrl-Shift-Tab key combinations.

The Categories subform itself is a datasheet, and you move around on it as you would move around on any datasheet. The window for this subform is wide enough to display all the fields on the datasheet, but if some columns couldn't be displayed, you would see a horizontal scroll bar at the bottom of the subform that you could use to move the display left or right. On this subform you can use the vertical scroll bar at the right to move the display up or down. The subform can be toggled between two different views—Datasheet view (its current state) and Form view. If you want to see the Form view of the Categories subform, click in any of the fields on the subform datasheet (to ensure that the focus is on the subform), and then open the View menu. You'll notice that the Subform Datasheet command is checked. This command is a toggle. If you choose the Subform Datasheet command, the Categories subform will change to look like the one shown in Figure 12-14. Choose the Subform Datasheet command (which is no longer checked) from the View menu again to restore the datasheet display.

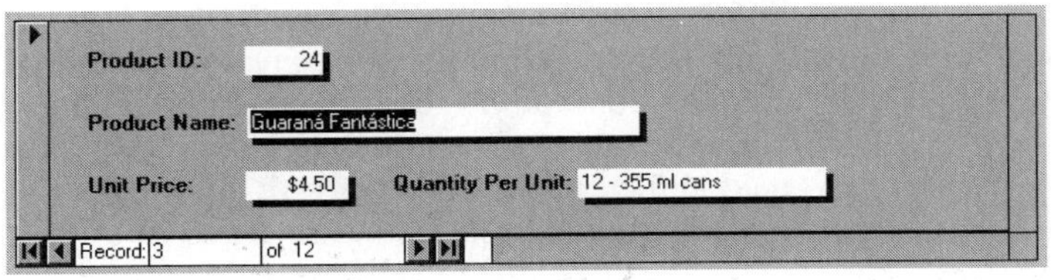

FIGURE 12-14. The Categories subform in Form view.

In the Categories form, you view different records by using one of two record number boxes. To change to the next category, use the main form's record number box; to see different products within a category, use the subform's record number box. (See Figure 12-13 on the next page.)

Using your keyboard, you can also choose the Go To command from the Records menu to move to the First, Last, Next, or Previous record on the main form or the subform. You can select any field you can see on the form by clicking anywhere in that field. To use the Go To command you must first move to the form or the subform, depending on which set of records you want to traverse.

Keyboard Shortcuts

If you're typing in new data, you might find it easier to use the keyboard rather than your mouse to move around on the form. Some of the keyboard shortcuts are listed in Figure 12-15 (for moving in fields and records) and in Figure 12-16 (for actions in a list box or a combo box).

Key(s)	Movement in Fields and Records
Tab	Moves to the next field.
Shift-Tab	Moves to the previous field.
Home	Moves to the first field of the current record.
End	Moves to the last field of the current record.
Up arrow	Moves to the current field of the previous record.
Down arrow	Moves to the current field of the next record.
Ctrl-Up arrow	Moves to the current field of the first record.
Ctrl-Down arrow	Moves to the current field of the last record.
Ctrl-Home	Moves to the first field of the first record.
Ctrl-End	Moves to the last field of the last record.
Ctrl-Tab	If on a subform, moves to the next field on the main form. If the subform is the last field in tab sequence on the main form, moves to the first field in the next main record. If not on a subform, moves to the next field.
Ctrl-Shift-Tab	If on a subform, moves to the previous field on the main form. If the subform is the first field in tab sequence on the main form, moves to the last field in the previous main record. If not on a subform, moves to the previous field.
Ctrl-Shift-Home	Moves to the first field on the main form.
F5	Moves to the record number box.

FIGURE 12-15.

The keyboard shortcuts for moving in fields and records.

Key(s)	Action in a List Box or a Combo Box
F4 or Alt-Down arrow	Opens a combo box or a drop-down list box.
Down arrow	Moves down one line.
Up arrow	Moves up one line.
PgDn	Moves down to next group of lines.
PgUp	Moves up to next group of lines.
Tab	Exits the box.

FIGURE 12-16.
The keyboard shortcuts for actions in a list box or a combo box.

Adding Records and Changing Data

You'll probably design most forms so that you can insert new records, change field values, or delete records in Form view or Datasheet view. The following sections explain procedures for adding new records and changing data.

Adding a New Record

The procedure for entering a new record varies depending on the design of the form. With a form that's been designed for data entry only, you open the form and type data in the (usually empty) data fields. Sometimes forms of this type open with default values in the fields or with data that's been entered by a macro. Another type of form displays data and allows you to add new records as well. Choose the Data Entry command from the Records menu or click the New button on the toolbar to shift the form into data-entry mode, as shown in Figure 12-17 on the next page.

When you've finished entering new records, you can choose the Show All Records command from the Records menu or click the Show All Records button on the toolbar to return to normal data display.

FIGURE 12-17.
The Categories form in data-entry mode.

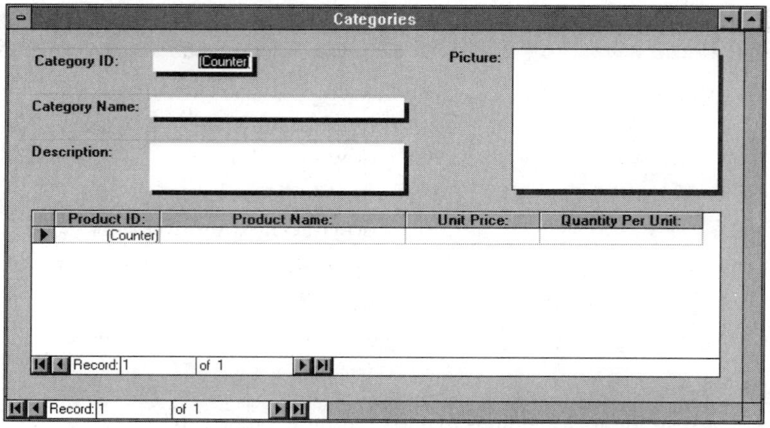

There's also a "blank" row at the end of the normal data display that you can use to enter new rows. You can jump to the blank row to begin adding a new record by choosing the Go To command from the Records menu and then choosing New on the submenu or by pressing Ctrl-+. Microsoft Access places the cursor in the first position of the first field when you start a new record. As soon as you begin typing, Access changes the indicator on the record selector (if your form shows the record selector) to the pencil icon to indicate that updates are in progress. Press Tab to move to the next field.

If you violate a field's validation rule, Access notifies you as soon as you attempt to leave the field. You must provide a correct value before you can move to another field. Press Shift-Enter at any point in the record or press Tab in the last field in the record to save your new record in the database. If the data you have entered violates a table validation rule, Access displays an error message and does not save the record. If you want to cancel the new record, press Esc twice or click the Undo Current Record button on the toolbar.

If you're adding a new record to a form such as Categories, you'll encounter a special case. You'll notice when you tab to the picture that you can't type anything in it. This is because the field in the underlying table is an OLE object. To enter data in this type of field in a new record, you must create the object in an application that supports OLE before you can store the data in Access. To do this, select the Picture field and choose the Insert Object command from the Edit menu. Access displays the Insert Object dialog box shown in Figure 12-18. Select the object type you want (in this case, Paintbrush Picture), and click OK. Access starts the Paintbrush application for you with a link established to the picture so that whatever you design in Paintbrush can be embedded in the field in the table.

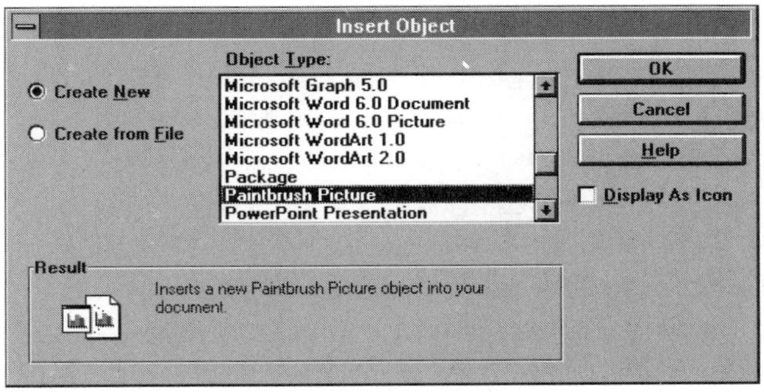

FIGURE 12-18.
The Insert Object dialog box.

If you already have an appropriate file available to copy into the OLE object in Access, choose the Create From File option button in the dialog box. Access changes the option list to let you enter the filename, as shown in Figure 12-19. You can click the Browse button to open the Browse dialog box, which lets you search for the file you want. When you've selected a file, click the Link check box to create an active link between the copy of the object in Access and the actual file. Whenever you change the file, the copy in Access also changes. Click the Display As Icon check box to display the Paintbrush application icon instead of the picture in Access.

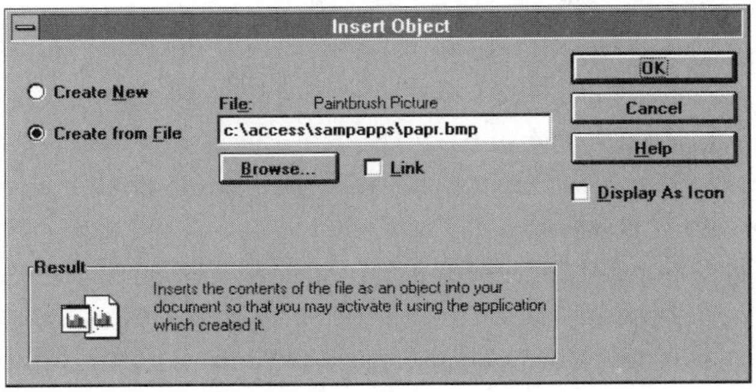

FIGURE 12-19.
Inserting an object from a file.

Try adding a new record to the Categories form. Open the form, choose the Go To command from the Records menu, and choose New from the submenu. You should see a screen similar to the one shown in Figure 12-17. You can start adding a new category for paper products. Type in a category name and follow the procedure discussed above to create a new picture. (The picture shown will not appear on your screen, and you need not draw it.)

> **NOTE:** As soon as you begin to enter new data for a table that has a counter field as its primary key, Microsoft Access assigns a new number to that field. You'll notice that Access assigns the value 9 to the Category ID field as soon as you start to type in a category name or create the new picture. If you decide to cancel adding the record, Access won't reuse this counter value. Access does this to ensure that multiple users sharing an Access database don't ever get the same counter value for a new table row.

To begin adding products in the Paper Products category, tab into the subform datasheet. Because the Product ID field is a Counter data type (and is the table's primary key), Microsoft Access will create a new value using the next available number in the Products table. Enter a product name, a unit price, and a quantity per unit, as shown in Figure 12-20. When you tab out of the last field or press Shift-Enter, Access adds the new product for you and assigns a product ID. Access also inserts the linking information required between the record in the main form and the new record in the subform. Here, Access adds a category ID of 9 to the new record in the Products table.

Changing and Deleting Data

If your form permits updates, you can easily change or delete existing data in the underlying table or query. If the form is designed to be used in Datasheet view, you can use the same techniques you learned in Chapter 7 to work with your data.

In Form view, your data might appear in one of several formats. If the form is designed to be a single form, you can see the data from only one record at a time in the form. If the form is designed as a continuous form, you might be able to see data from more than one record at a time.

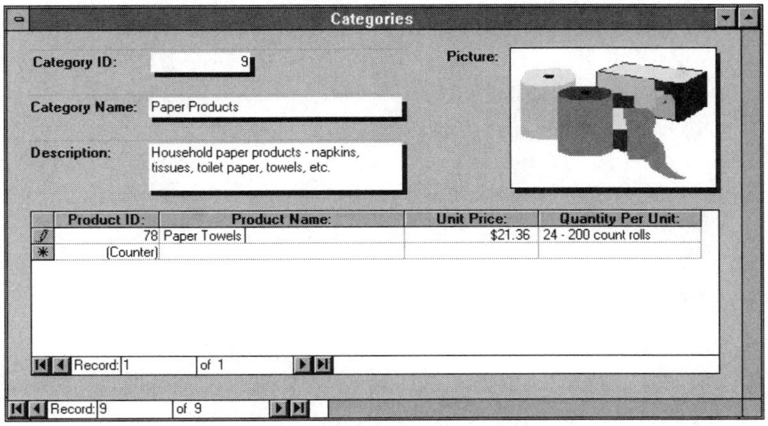

FIGURE 12-20.
The addition of a new record in the Categories form.

As with datasheets, you must select a field on the form in order to change the data in the field. To select a field on the form, either tab to the field or click in the field with the mouse. After you've selected a field, you can change the data in it using the same techniques for working with data in a datasheet. You can type over individual characters, replace a sequence of characters, or copy and paste data from one field to another.

You might find that you can't tab into or select some fields on a form. When you design a form, you can set the properties of the controls on the form so that a user can't select the control. These properties prevent users from changing fields you don't want updated, such as calculated values or fields from the "one" side of a query. You can also set the tab order to control the sequence of field selection when you use Tab or Shift-Tab to move around the form. (See Chapters 13 and 14 for details.)

Deleting a record on a single form or a continuous form is different from deleting a record on a datasheet. First you must select the record as you would select a record on a datasheet. If the form is designed with record selectors, simply click the record selector to select the record. If the form does not have a record selector, choose the Select Record command from the Edit menu. To delete a selected record, press the Del key or choose the Delete command from the Edit menu.

Searching for and Sorting Data

When you use forms to display and edit your data, you can search for data or sort it in a new sequence in much the same way as you search for and sort data in datasheets. (See Chapter 7.) The following sections show you how to use the Find command to search for data in a form or the Quick Sort commands to resequence your data.

Performing a Simple Search

You can use Microsoft Access's Find capability in a form just as you would in a datasheet. First select the field, and then choose the Find command from the Edit menu or click the Find button on the toolbar to open the Find dialog box that you saw in Figure 7-27. You can enter search criteria exactly as you would for a datasheet. Note that on a form you can also perform a search on any control that you can select, including controls that display calculated values.

NEW!

Performing a Quick Sort on a Form Field

As with a datasheet, you can choose just about any control that contains data from the underlying recordset and click the Sort Ascending or Sort Descending button on the toolbar to resequence the records you see, based on the contents of the selected field. You can't quick-sort fields in a subform. If you want to try to quick-sort, click in the Category Name field on the Categories form and then click the Sort Descending button on the toolbar. You should see the last category in alphabetic sequence displayed—Seafood.

Adding a Filter to a Form

One of Microsoft Access's most powerful features in a form is its ability to further restrict or sort the information displayed on the form without your having to create a new query. This restriction is accomplished with a filter that you define while you're using the form. When you apply the filter, you'll see only the data that matches the criteria you enter. You can apply a filter only to the records in a main form, not to the records in any subform.

To begin defining a new filter, click the Edit Filter/Sort button on the toolbar or choose the Edit Filter/Sort command from the Records menu. Open the Categories form and click the Edit Filter/Sort button. Access opens a Filter window, shown in Figure 12-21.

The Filter window looks similar to a Query window. In the top section of the window is the Categories field list for the table or query that provides data for the form. You can use the field list to select field names to place on the QBE grid. You can enter selection criteria exactly as you would for a query. You can also sort selected fields in ascending or descending alphabetic order. In the example in Figure 12-21, the category names are being restricted to those that begin with the letter *S*.

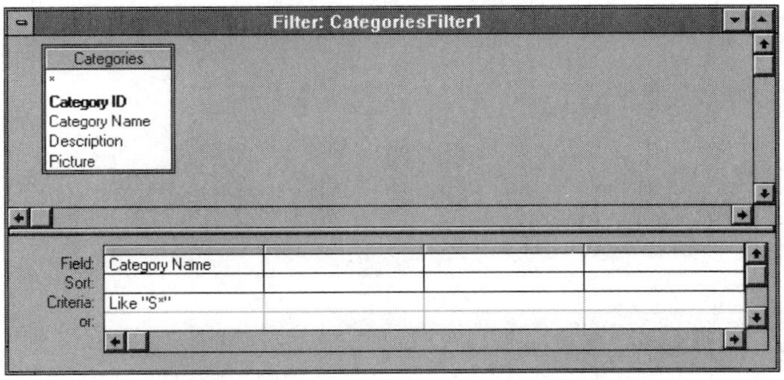

FIGURE 12-21. The Filter window for the Categories form.

When you've finished defining your filter, close the Filter window. To apply your filter, click the Apply Filter/Sort button on the toolbar or choose the Apply Filter/Sort command from the Records menu. To turn off the filter, click the Show All Records button on the toolbar or choose the Show All Records command from the Records menu.

> **NOTE:** If you used one of the Quick Sort buttons, you'll discover that Quick Sort uses the form's filter definition to create the sorting criteria. For example, if you did a quick sort to arrange category names in descending order, you'll find the Category Name field on the form filter with the Sort row set to Descending when you click the Edit Filter/Sort button.

If you find that you're often using the same filter with your form, you can save the filter as a query and give it a name. Open the Filter window and create the filter. Choose the Save As Query command from the File menu and type in a name for the query when prompted by Access. You can also load an existing query definition to use as a filter. Open the Filter window, and choose the Load From Query command from the File menu. Access presents you with a list of valid select queries (those that are based on the same table or tables as the form you're using). In this case, a Category List query sorts the category records in ascending order by category name rather than by category ID as in the form. If you select Category List from the list of valid select queries, the query will replace the existing filter in the Filter window with the information shown in Figure 12-22.

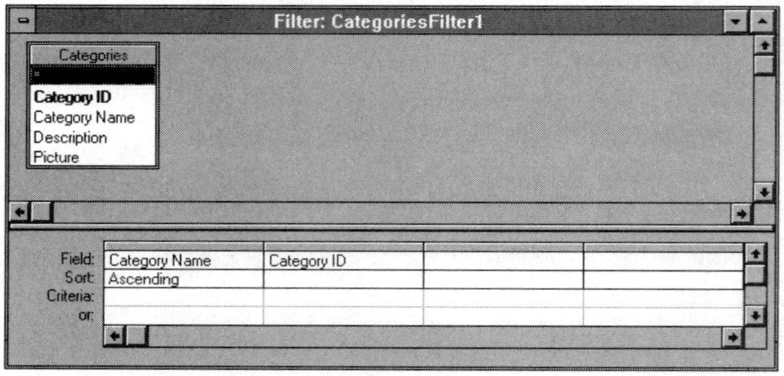

FIGURE 12-22. The Filter window for the Categories form, based on the Category List query.

Printing from a Form

You can use a form to print information from your table. When you design the form, you can specify different header and footer information for the printed version. You can also specify which controls are visible. For example, you might define some gridlines that are visible on the printed form but not on the screen.

An interesting form in NWIND to print is the Suppliers form. Open the form, and then click the Print Preview button on the toolbar or choose the Print Preview command from the File menu. You probably won't be able to read any of the data unless you have a large screen. Click the Zoom button and scroll to the top of the first page. You should see a screen that looks like the one shown in Figure 12-23. Notice that the form headers and footers that you saw in Figure 12-1 (on page 422) do not appear in the printed version.

You can use the scroll bars to move around on the page. Use the page number box in the lower left corner of the form in the same way that you can use the record number box on a form or datasheet. Click the Zoom button again to see the entire page on the screen.

Click the Print Setup button on the toolbar to customize the way the form prints. Access displays the Print Setup dialog box, shown in Figure 12-24. At the top of the dialog box you can select the printer you want to use. Click the Options button to open the Options dialog box for the printer you've chosen. See Chapter 7, "Using Datasheets," for details on choosing printer options.

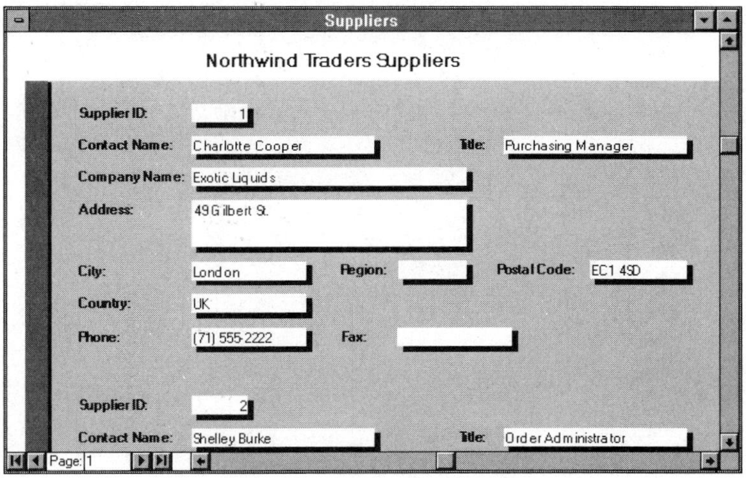

FIGURE 12-23.
The window for the Suppliers form, "zoomed" in Print Preview.

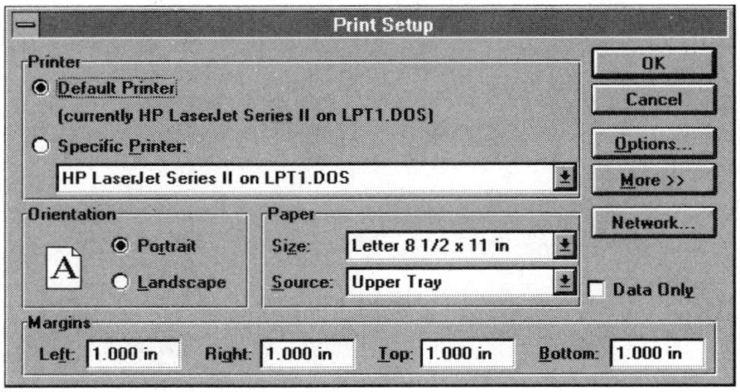

FIGURE 12-24.
The Print Setup dialog box for forms.

Just below the Printer group box, you can set options to print in portrait mode (vertically) or landscape mode (horizontally). In the Paper group box to the right, you can specify the size of paper you've loaded in your printer and the location of the paper tray (if your printer supports multiple trays). Finally, to the right of that area is a useful check box you can use to ask Microsoft Access to print only the data on the form and not any of the labels or other controls.

If you click the More button to see additional options, Access opens the margin and layout option sections at the bottom of the Print Setup dialog box, shown in Figure 12-25. If the data on your form appears in a fairly narrow width, you can ask Access to stack the data from the form either horizontally or vertically across the page. If you enter the settings shown in Figure 12-25 for the Suppliers form, you'll see the supplier data printed horizontally across the paper, three suppliers to a row and two rows on each page.

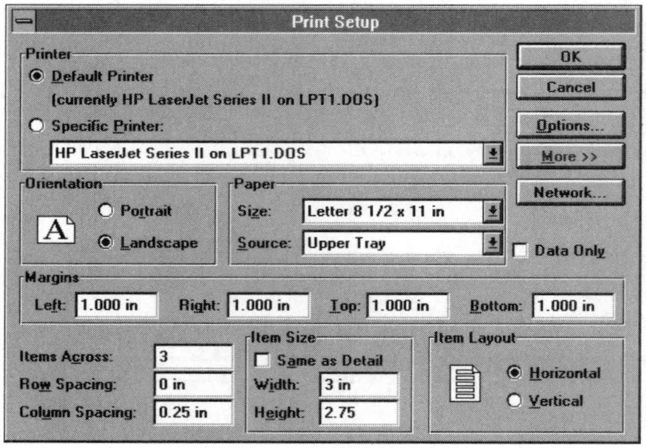

FIGURE 12-25. The Print Setup dialog box expands when you click the More button.

You should now have a good understanding of how forms work and of many of the design elements you can include when you build forms. Now on to the fun part—building your first form in Chapter 13.

13

Building a Form

From the perspective of daily use, forms are the most important objects you'll build in your Microsoft Access application. Forms are what users see and work with every time they run your application. This chapter shows you how to design and build forms in Access. You'll learn how to work with a Form window in Design view to build a basic form from a single table. You'll also learn how to use a Form Wizard to simplify the forms-creation process. The last section of this chapter shows you how to use some of the special forms controls to simplify data entry on your forms.

Forms and Object-Oriented Programming

Microsoft Access was not designed as a full object-oriented programming facility, yet it has many characteristics found in object-oriented application development systems. Before you dive into building forms, it's useful to examine how Access implements objects and actions, particularly if you come from the world of procedural application development.

In classic procedural application development, the data that you need for the application is clearly distinct from the programs you write to work on the data and from the results produced by your programs. Each program works independently on the data and generally has little structural connection with other programs in the system. An order-entry program might accept input from a clerk and write the order out to the application files. Later, a billing program is run to collect the orders and print invoices. Another characteristic of procedural systems is that events must occur in a specific order and cannot be executed out of sequence. A procedural system has difficulty looking up supplier or price information while in the middle of processing an order.

In an object-oriented system, however, all objects are defined in terms of a subject and an action on that subject. Objects can contain other objects as subjects. When an object defines a new action on another object, it inherits the attributes and properties of the other object and expands on the object's definition. In Access, queries define actions on tables, and the queries then become new logical tables known as *recordsets*. You can define a query based on another query with the same effect. Queries inherit the integrity and formatting rules defined for the tables. Forms further define actions on tables or queries, and the fields you include on forms initially inherit the underlying properties, such as formatting and validation rules, of the fields in the source tables or queries. You can define different formatting or more restrictive rules, but you cannot override the rules defined for the tables.

Within an Access database, you can interrelate application objects and data. For example, you can set an initial macro that prepares your application to run. That macro (called AUTOEXEC) will usually open a starting form in your application. Your starting form might act on some of the data in your database, or it might offer controls that open other forms, print reports, or close the application.

See Also: For more information about the AUTOEXEC macro, see Chapter 23, "The Finishing Touches."

Figure 13-1 on the next page shows the conceptual architecture of a Microsoft Access application. In addition to operating on tables or queries in your database, forms can contain other forms. These subforms can, in turn, define actions on other tables, queries, or forms, and can trigger additional macro actions or Microsoft Access Basic functions. As you'll learn when you read about advanced form design and create an application, macro actions or Access Basic functions can be triggered in many ways. The most obvious way to trigger an action is by clicking a command button on a form. But you can also define macros or functions that execute when an event occurs, such as clicking in a field, changing the data in a field, pressing a key, adding or deleting a row, or simply moving to a new row in the underlying table or query.

In Chapter 22, "Automating Your Application with Microsoft Access Basic," you'll build a sophisticated form to enter and review orders for

Prompt Computer Solutions. You'll also define many Access Basic procedures on the form that are triggered by events. Figure 13-2 shows just a few of those actions and events. For example, there's a command button to print the invoice for the order currently shown on the form.

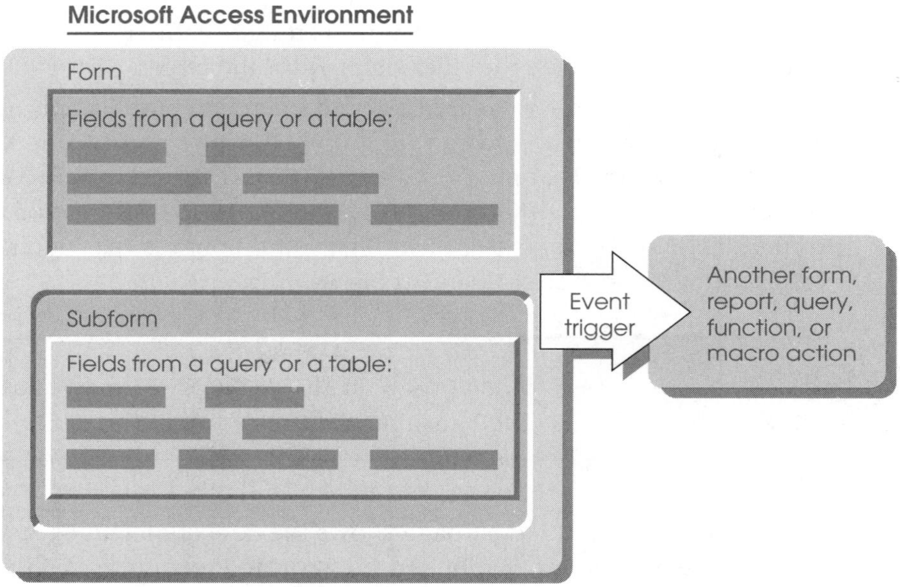

FIGURE 13-1. The relationship of objects in Microsoft Access.

When the invoice prints, another Access Basic procedure sets an indicator in the order to show that you've printed the invoice for this order. Whenever you add, change, or delete an order item, Access Basic procedures are triggered that recalculate the sales tax and total amount of the order. Even a small detail, such as changing the state the customer lives in, triggers an Access Basic procedure to determine a new sales tax percentage and calculate a new order total amount.

Object-oriented systems are not particularly sensitive to a required sequence of events. So an operator entering an order in Access can minimize the order-entry form and start a search in a products table for pricing information or start a search in a customers table for a customer's credit history without ending the order. You might provide a simpler way for the operator to do this in your application by means of a command button on the order-entry form.

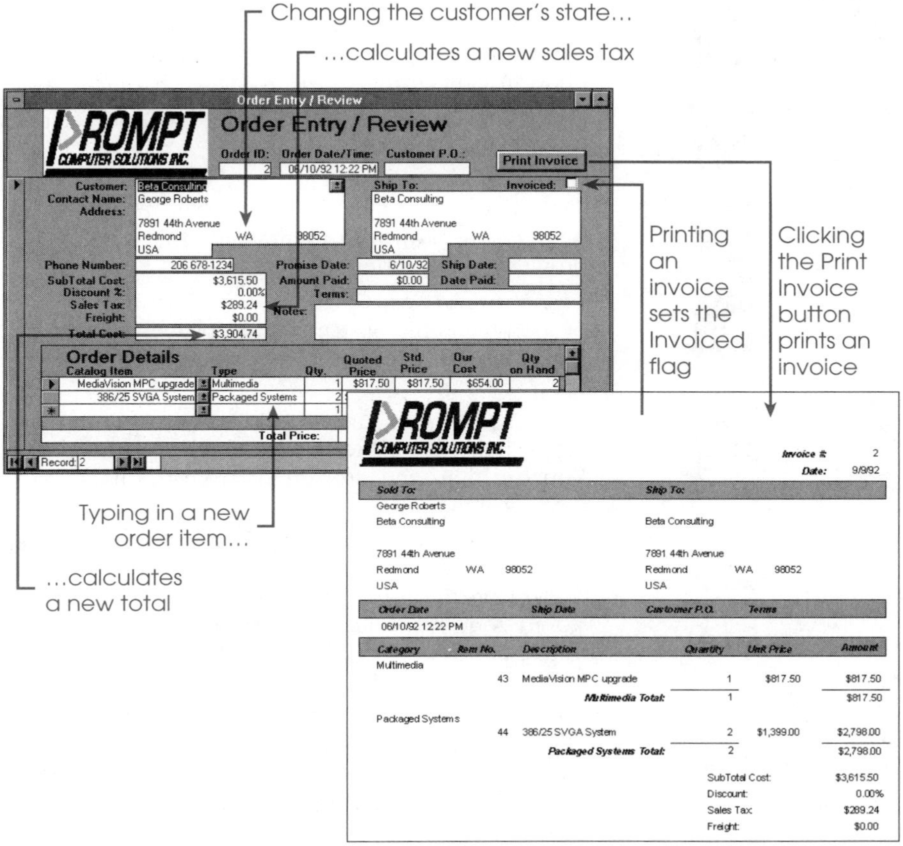

FIGURE 13-2.
The Microsoft Access environment in action.

The Built-In Toolbar for the Form Window in Design View

Microsoft Access provides you with a custom toolbar to use as you design forms. From left to right, the buttons are:

Design View button. This button appears pressed to indicate that you are in Design view.

Form View button. Click this button to see the Form window in Form view. While you're building a form, you can click here to see what your changes will look like after you save the form.

(continued)

(continued)

Datasheet View button. Click this button to see a datasheet containing the data in the underlying table or query for the form.

Save button. Click this button to save any changes.

Print Preview button. You can print most forms and the data displayed on them. Click this button to see a preview of the printed page.

Properties button. Click this button to show or hide the property sheet. You can define properties for the form as a whole, for each section of the form, and for any control on the form.

Field List button. Click this button to show or hide the list of fields available in the underlying table or query. You can drag and drop fields from the list onto your form design.

Code button. To view and edit any Microsoft Access Basic code stored with the form, select the form or any control on the form and then click this button. The stored code responds to events on the form or to the form's controls. (See Chapter 21, "Microsoft Access Basic Fundamentals," and Chapter 22, "Automating Your Application with Access Basic," for details.)

Toolbox button. Click this button to show or hide the toolbox. Use the toolbox to choose the type of control that you want to add to your form.

Palette button. Click this button to show or hide the Palette. Use the Palette to set the appearance and color of the form and controls.

Font Name box. When you select a control that contains text or data, you can use this box to select the font that will be used in the control.

Font Size box. When you select a control that contains text or data, you can use this box to select the font size that will be used in the control.

Bold button. Click this button to make the text in the selected control bold. Click the button again to make the text normal.

Italic button. Click this button to make the text in the selected control italic. Click the button again to make the text normal.

Left-Align Text button. Click this button to align the text in the selected control flush left.

Center-Align Text button. Click this button to center the text in the selected control.

Right-Align Text button. Click this button to align the text in the selected control flush right.

Database Window button. Click this button to place the focus on the Database window. This button also un-hides the window if you've hidden it and restores the window if you've minimized it.

Undo button. Click this button to undo the last change you made to the design.

Cue Cards button. Click this button to open the main menu of the Cue Cards facility. Cue Cards lead you through step-by-step instructions for most common tasks.

Help button. Click this button to add a question mark to your mouse pointer. Click with this pointer on any displayed object to receive context-sensitive help about that object.

Starting from Scratch—A Simple Input Form

To start, you'll learn how to create a simple form that accepts and displays data in the Supplier table in the PROMPT database. (See "Using the Companion Disk" on page xxiv.) Later, you'll learn how to create a form using a powerful Form Wizard.

Starting to Design a New Form

To begin building a new form, open your database and select in the Database window the table or query that you want to use for the form. Click the New Form button on the toolbar, and Microsoft Access opens the New Form dialog box, shown in Figure 13-3 on the next page.

Notice that Access displays the name of the table or query that you selected in the Database window in the combo box at the top of the New

Form dialog box. If you want to select a different table or query, you can open the combo box to see a list of all the tables and queries in your database. So that you understand all the components that go into designing a form, you'll build this first form without the aid of a Form Wizard.

FIGURE 13-3. The New Form dialog box.

Working with Design Tools

You start building a new form by clicking the Blank Form button. Microsoft Access opens the Form window in Design view and with it several design tools, as shown in Figure 13-4. (You might not see all the windows shown in Figure 13-4.) In this sample screen, the Form window is in the background, the toolbox is in the lower left corner, the field list is at the upper center, and the property sheet for the form is in the lower right corner. If you've experimented with forms in Design view before and moved some of the windows around, Access opens them where you last left them on the screen.

Access starts with a form that has only a white detail section grid. You can grab the edge of the detail section with your mouse pointer and drag the edge to make the detail section larger or smaller. You can remove the grid of dots from the detail section by choosing the Grid command from the View menu. If you want to add headers and footers, choose the Form Header/Footer command from the Format menu.

The detail section starts out at 5 inches (12.7 centimeters) wide by 1 inch (2.54 centimeters) high. The "inch" gradations that you can see on

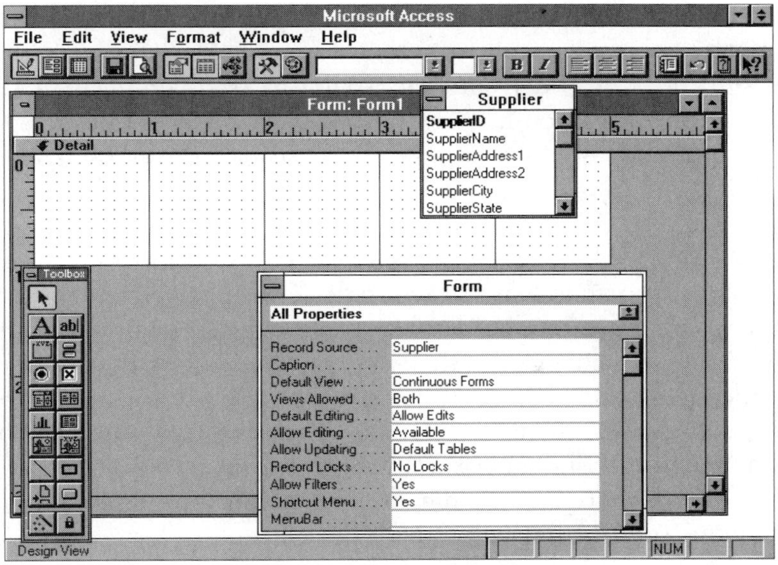

FIGURE 13-4.
The Form window in Design view with its design tools.

the rulers are relative to the size and resolution of your screen. On a standard 640-by-480-pixel VGA screen, the full screen is approximately 6.5 "inches" wide by 5 "inches" high. By default, Access sets the grid at 10 dots per inch horizontally and 12 dots per inch vertically. You can change the density of the grid dots by altering the Grid X and Grid Y settings on the form's property sheet.

The numbers you enter in Grid X and Grid Y tell Microsoft Access how many intervals per measure of unit you want in the design grid. You can provide a number from 1 (coarsest) through 64 (finest). You set the unit of measure you want using the Measurement field in the International section of the Windows Control Panel. Your unit of measure is inches if the Measurement setting is English or centimeters if the Measurement setting is Metric.

For example, if your unit of measurement is inches and you specify a Grid X value of 10, Access divides the grid horizontally into 0.1-inch increments. When your measurement is in inches and you set the Grid X and Grid Y values to 16 or less, Access displays the grid dots on the design grid. In centimeters, you can see the grid dots when you choose a

NEW!

setting of 6 or less. If you set a finer grid, Access won't display the grid dots but you can still use the grid to line up controls. Access always displays grid lines at 1-inch intervals (English) or 1-centimeter intervals (Metric), even when you have set fine Grid X or Grid Y values.

The sections that follow in this chapter describe some of the tools you can use to design a form.

The Toolbox

The toolbox, shown in Figure 13-5, is the "command center" of form design. You can move the toolbox around on your screen by dragging its title bar. You can change the shape of the toolbox by dragging its sides or corners. If you like, you can move the toolbox to the top of the workspace and "dock" it as a toolbar. You can close the toolbox by clicking the Control-menu box in the upper left corner of the toolbox or by choosing the Toolbox command again from the View menu or by clicking the Toolbox button on the toolbar.

TIP: If you don't see the toolbox in the form's Design view, choose the Toolbox command from the View menu or click the Toolbox button on the toolbar.

The toolbox contains buttons for all the controls you can use to design your form. When you want to place a particular control on your form, click the control's button in the toolbox. When you move the mouse pointer over the form, your mouse pointer turns into an icon that represents the tool you've chosen. Position the mouse pointer where you want the control, and click the left mouse button to put the selected control on your form. If you want to size the control as you place it, click and drag the mouse pointer to the size you want. (You can also size a control after it's placed by dragging its sides or corners.) If you want to bind a field in the underlying table or query to the control you've selected, find the field in the field list and drag the field onto the form.

FIGURE 13-5.
The toolbox. (If you place the cursor over a tool button, a pop-up label giving the name of the tool appears.)

Left to right, top to bottom, the tools in the toolbox are:

Pointer tool. This is the default tool. Use this tool to select, size, move, and edit controls.

Label tool. Use this tool to create label controls that contain fixed text on your form. By default, most controls have a label control attached. You can use this tool to create stand-alone labels for headings and instructions on your form.

Text Box tool. Use this tool to create text box controls for displaying text, numbers, dates, times, and memo fields on your form. You can bind a text box to one of the fields in the underlying table or query. If you allow a text box that is bound to a field to be updated, you can change the value (in the field in the underlying table or query) by entering a new value in the text box. You can also use a text box to calculate values using expressions.

Option Group tool. Use this tool to create option group controls that contain one or more toggle buttons, option buttons, or check boxes. (See the description of these controls on the next page.) You can assign a separate numeric value to each button or check box you include in the group. When you have more than one button or check

(continued)

(continued)

box in a group, you can select only one button or box at a time, and the value assigned to that selected button or box becomes the value for the option group. You can choose one of the buttons or boxes in the group as the default value for the group. If you bind the option group to a field in the underlying query or table, you can set a new value in the field by selecting a button or box in the group.

Toggle Button tool. Use this tool to create a toggle button control that holds an on/off, true/false, or yes/no value. When you click a toggle button, its value becomes –1 (to represent *on, true,* or *yes*) and the button appears pressed. Click the button again, and its value becomes 0 (to represent *off, false,* or *no*). You can include a toggle button in an option group and assign to the button a unique numeric value. If you create a group with multiple toggle buttons, any previously clicked toggle button, option button, or check box will turn *off* when you click a new toggle button *on*. If you bind the toggle button to a field in the underlying table or query, you can toggle the field's value by clicking the toggle button.

Option Button tool. Use this tool to create an option button control (also sometimes called a radio button control) that holds an on/off, true/false, or yes/no value. When you click an option button, its value becomes –1 (to represent *on, true,* or *yes*) and a filled circle appears in the center of the button. Click the button again, and its value becomes 0 (to represent *off, false,* or *no*). You can include an option button in an option group and assign to the button a unique numeric value. If you create a group with multiple option buttons, any previously clicked toggle button, option button, or check box turns *off* when you click a new option button *on*.

Check Box tool. Use this tool to create a check box control that holds an on/off, true/false, or yes/no value. When you click a check box, its value becomes –1 (to represent *on, true,* or *yes*) and an *X* appears in the box. Click the check box again, and its value becomes 0 (to represent *off, false,* or *no*) and the *X* disappears from the box. You can include a check box in an option group and assign to the check box a unique numeric value. If you create a group with multiple check boxes, any previously clicked toggle button, option button, or check box turns *off* when you click a new check box *on*. If you bind the check box to a field in the underlying table or query, you can toggle the field's value by clicking the check box.

Combo Box tool. Use this tool to create a combo box control that contains a list of potential values for the control and an editable text box. To create the list, you can enter the values in the Row Source property of the combo box. You can also specify a table or a query as the source of the values in the list. Microsoft Access displays the currently selected value in the text box. When you click the down arrow at the right side of the box, Access displays the values in the list. Choose a new value in the list to reset the value in the control. If the combo box is bound to a field in the underlying table or query, you can change the value in the field by choosing a new value in the list. You can bind multiple columns to the list, and you can hide one or more of the columns in the list by setting the column's list width to 0. You can bind the actual value in the control to a hidden column. Access displays the value in the first column whose width is greater than 0 when the combo box is closed. Access displays all nonzero-width columns when you open the combo list.

List Box tool. Use this tool to create a list box control that contains a list of potential values for the control. To create the list, you can enter the values in the Row Source property of the list box. You can specify a table or a query as the source of the values in the list. List boxes are always open, and Microsoft Access highlights the currently selected value in the list box. Select a new value in the list to reset the value in the control. If the list box is bound to a field in the underlying table or query, you can change the value in the field by choosing a new value in the list. You can bind multiple columns to the list, and you can hide one or more of the columns in the list by setting the column's list width to 0. You can bind the actual value in the control to a hidden column. Access displays all nonzero-width columns that fit within the defined width of the control.

Graph tool. Use this tool to add a Microsoft Graph object to your form. You can link the graph to a table or to a query, or you can import data into the graph from another source. Placing this tool on a form activates a Graph Wizard to assist you in designing the graph. (See Chapter 15, "Advanced Form Design," for details.)

Subform tool. Use this tool to embed another form in the current form. You can use the subform to show data from a table or query related to the data on the main form. Microsoft Access maintains the link between the two forms for you. (See Chapter 15 for details.)

(continued)

(continued)

Unbound Object Frame tool. Use this tool to add an object from another application that supports object linking and embedding (OLE) to your form. The object becomes part of your form, not part of the data from the underlying table or query. You can add pictures, sounds, graphs, or slides to enhance your form. (See Chapter 15 for details.)

Bound Object Frame tool. Use this tool to make available on your form an OLE object from your underlying data. Microsoft Access can display most pictures and graphs directly on your form. For other objects, Access displays the icon of the application in which the object was created. For example, if the object is a sound object created in Sound Recorder, you'll see a microphone icon on your form. (See Chapter 15 for details.)

Line tool. Use this tool to add lines to your form to enhance its appearance. (See Chapter 14, "Customizing Forms," for details.)

Rectangle tool. Use this tool to add filled or empty rectangles to your form to enhance its appearance. (See Chapter 14 for details.)

Page Break tool. Use this tool to add a page break between multiple pages on your form.

Command Button tool. Use this tool to create a command button control that can activate a macro or an Access Basic function. (See the section in Chapter 15 titled "Linking Forms with Command Buttons" for details.)

Control Wizards button. Click this toggle button to activate Control Wizards. When this button appears pressed, the Wizards help you enter control properties whenever you create a new option group, combo box, list box, or command button.

Tool Lock button. Click this button to keep the currently selected tool active after placing a control on the form. When the tool lock is off, the currently selected tool is deselected after you place a control on the form.

TIP: The Tool Lock button is useful if you plan to create several controls with the same tool—for example, a series of check boxes in an option group.

The Field List

Use the field list in conjunction with the toolbox to place bound controls (controls linked to fields in a table or query) on your form. You can open the field list by clicking the Field List button on the toolbar or by choosing the Field List command from the View menu. Microsoft Access displays the name of the underlying table or query in the window title bar, as shown in Figure 13-6. You can drag the edges of the window to resize the field list so that you can see any long field names. You can drag the title bar to move the field list out of the way. Use the scroll bar on the right side of the window to move through the list of available names.

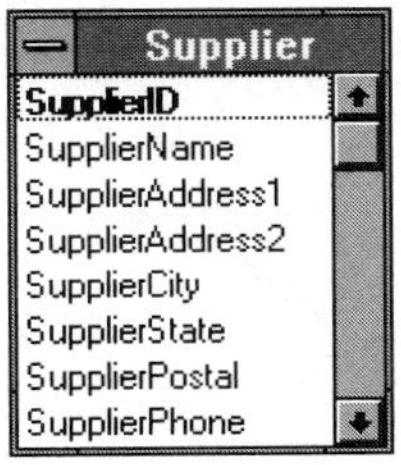

FIGURE 13-6.
A field list showing the names of the fields in the underlying table or query.

To use the field list to place a control for a field on your form, first click on the tool you want. (The default tool is for a text box control.) Then drag the field you want from the field list and drop it into position on the form. If you choose a control that's inappropriate for the data type, Access selects the default control for the data type. For example, if you choose anything but a bound object frame control for an OLE object, Access creates a bound object frame control for you anyway. If you try to drag and drop a field using the graph, subform, unbound object frame, line, rectangle, or page break control, Access creates a text box or bound object frame control instead.

The Property Sheet

The form, each section on the form (header, detail, footer), and every control on the form has a list of properties associated with it, and you set these properties using the property sheet. The kinds of properties you can specify vary depending on the object. To open the property sheet, click the Properties button on the toolbar or choose the Properties command from the View menu. Access opens a window that is similar to the window shown in Figure 13-7.

FIGURE 13-7. A property sheet for a form.

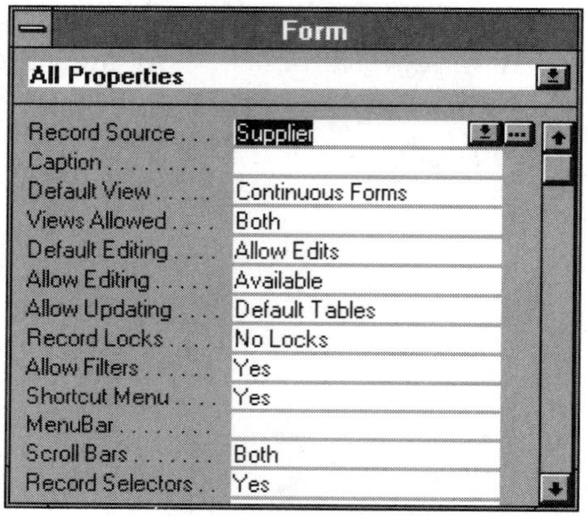

You can drag the title bar of the property sheet to move the window around on your screen. You can also drag the edges of the window to resize the property sheet so that you can see more of the longer property settings. Because a form has nearly 60 properties that you can set and because many controls have more than 30 properties, Access provides you with a combo box at the top of the property sheet so that you can choose either to display all properties (the default) or to display only data properties, layout properties, event properties, or other properties. The Form property sheet displaying only the data properties is shown in Figure 13-8.

NEW!

When you select a property that has a list of valid values, a down arrow button appears to the right of the field. Click this button, and a drop-down list of the values appears. For properties that can have a very long value setting, you can use Shift-F2 to open a *Zoom box*. The Zoom box provides an expanded text box for entering or viewing an entry.

NEW!

Even better than the Zoom box are the *builders* that help you create property settings for properties that can accept a complex expression, a query definition, or code (macro or module) to respond to an event. When a builder is available for a property setting, Access displays

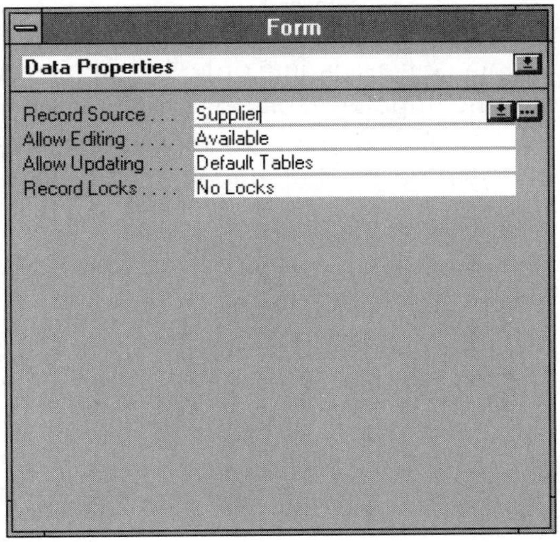

FIGURE 13-8.
The layout properties of a property sheet.

a small button with an ellipsis next to the property setting when you select the property; this is the Build button. If you click the Build button, Access responds with the appropriate builder dialog boxes. For example, display the data properties for the form on the property sheet, select the Record Source property, and then click the Build button next to Record Source on this form to start the Query Builder. Access asks whether you want to build a new query based on the table that currently is the source for this form. If you reply OK, Access shows you a new Query window in Design view with the Supplier table, as shown in Figure 13-9.

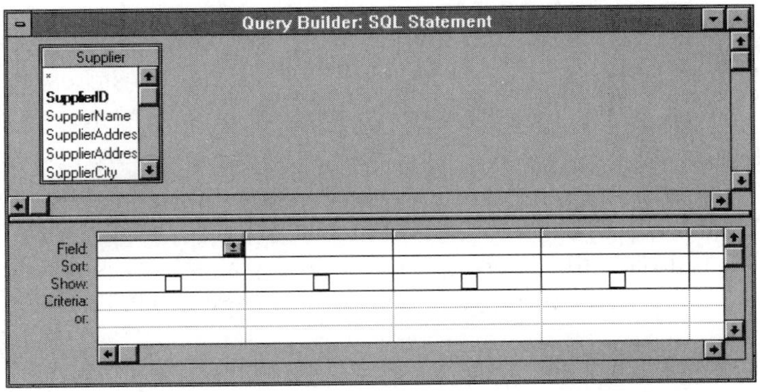

FIGURE 13-9.
Using the Query Builder for the form's Record Source property.

Rather than use the table directly, it might be nice to base this form on a query that sorts the suppliers in ascending order by supplier name. You'll need all the fields in the Supplier table for this form, so select them and drag them to the QBE grid. Under SupplierName, choose Ascending as the sorting order. Your result should look like that shown in Figure 13-10.

> **TIP:** To easily select all the fields from a table displayed on the query grid, double-click the title bar of the table's field list. Microsoft Access highlights all the fields for you. Simply click on any of them and drag them to the QBE grid.

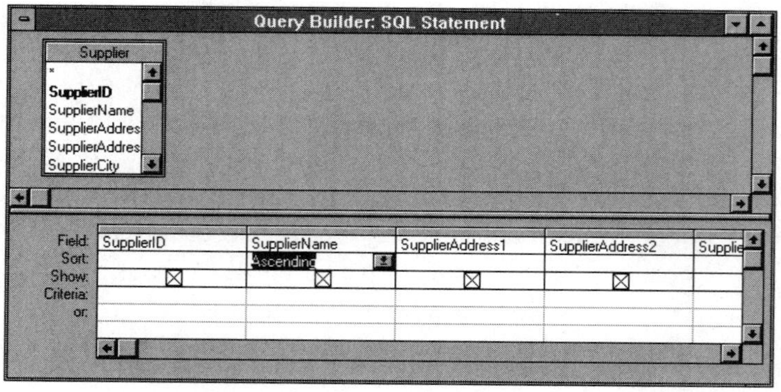

FIGURE 13-10. Building a query for the Record Source property of the Supplier form.

If you close the query window at this point, Access asks whether you want to update the property. If you reply Yes, Access stores the SQL text for the query in the Record Source property box. A better way is to save the query and give it a name such as *Supplier Sorted By Name,* so do that now. (This query is already defined in the PROMPT sample database.) When you close the query, Access asks whether you want to save the query and update the property. If you reply Yes, Access places the query name (rather than the SQL text) on the property sheet.

The Palette

The Palette provides a quick and easy way to alter the appearance and color of a control by allowing you to click options rather than to set properties. The Palette is also handy for setting background colors for sections of the form. To open the Palette shown in Figure 13-11, click the Palette button on the toolbar or choose the Palette command from the View menu.

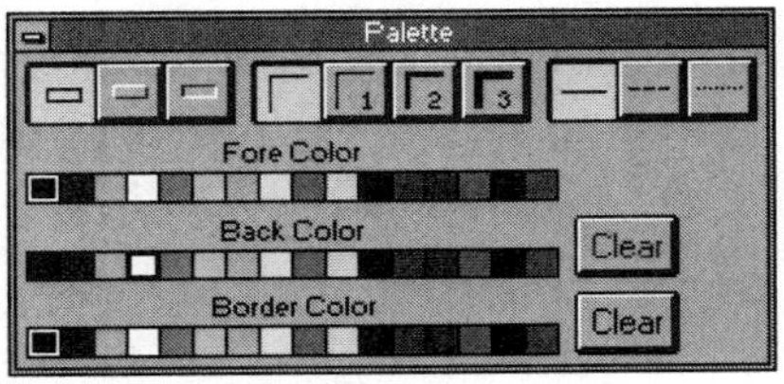

FIGURE 13-11.
The Palette.

Depending on the object you select, some of the Palette options might not be available. For example, you can't set text color on a bound object frame control. Nor can you set fill or border colors on a toggle button because these areas are always set to gray on a toggle button. If you have the property sheet open at the same time as the Palette and the property sheet is scrolled so that you can see the properties the Palette sets, you can watch the settings on the property sheet change as you click different options on the Palette.

Building a Simple Input Form for the Supplier Table

Here's where you actually create a simple input form for the Supplier table in PROMPT. If you've followed along to this point, you should have a blank form based on the Supplier Sorted By Name query that you created with the Query Builder. If you haven't done so already, go to the Database window, open the Tables list, select the Supplier table, and click the New Form button on the toolbar. Choose the Blank Form option in the New Form dialog box. You'll see the Form window in Design view and a set of design tools, as shown in Figure 13-4 on page 453. If necessary, open the toolbox, field list, and property sheet by clicking the appropriate buttons on the toolbar. Select the Record Source property, and then click the Build button and follow the procedures discussed on pages 460 through 462, whose results are shown in Figures 13-9 and 13-10; this will create the query you need and make it the source for the form.

In the blank form for Supplier, drag the bottom of the detail section down to give yourself some room to work. Because you'll be using default text boxes, you don't need to select a tool from the toolbox. If you'd like to practice, though, click on the Text Box tool and then the Tool Lock button in the toolbox before dragging fields from the field list. In this way, you can drag fields one at a time to the detail section of the form. Follow this procedure to drag the SupplierID field through the SupplierFax fields from the field list to the detail section. Your result should look something like that shown in Figure 13-12.

TIP: A quick way to place several successive fields on the form is to highlight the first field you want, scroll down until you can see the last field you want, and then hold down the Shift key while you click the last field. This procedure selects all the fields in between the first and last fields you selected. You can also double-click on the title bar of the field list to select all the fields. You can now click any of the highlighted fields and drag the fields as a group to the detail section of the form.

When you position the field icon that you're dragging from the field list, you should be aware that the point where you release your mouse button is the upper left corner of the new text box in the detail section of the form. For default text boxes, Microsoft Access attaches a label, using the field's Caption property (or field name, if you didn't specify a Caption property when you designed the field), 1 inch to the left of the text box. So you should drop each text box about 1.25 inches (3 centimeters) in from the left edge to leave room to the left of the icon for Access to place the control labels. If you don't leave room, the labels will overlap the text boxes.

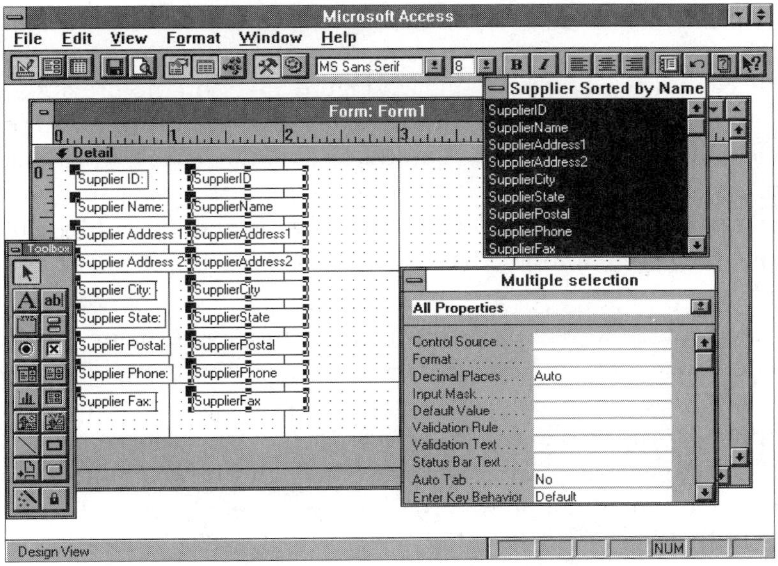

FIGURE 13-12.
The text box controls that are created on a form when you drag and drop fields from the Supplier list.

Notice in the example in Figure 13-12 that the property sheet indicates you have selected multiple controls. (In this case, all the selected fields were dragged to the form design grid at one time.) Whenever you select multiple controls on a form in Design view, Access displays the properties that are common to all the controls you selected. If you change a property on the property sheet while you have multiple controls selected, Access makes the change to all of the controls.

Moving and Sizing Controls

By default, Microsoft Access creates text boxes that are 1 inch wide and that have a label 1 inch to the left of the text box. For some of the fields, 1 inch is larger than necessary to display the field value—especially using the default font size of 8. For other fields, the text box isn't large enough. You probably also want to adjust the location of some of the controls.

To change a control's size or location, you usually need to select the control first. Be sure that the Tool Lock button is off and that you've selected the Pointer tool. Click the control you want to resize or move, and you'll see the moving and sizing *handles* appear around the control.

The handles are small boxes that appear at each corner of the control—except at the upper left corner, where the larger box indicates that this handle cannot be used for sizing. In Figure 13-12 on the previous page, you can see handles around all the text boxes, indicating that they are all selected. To select just one control, click anywhere in the blank area of the form; this changes the selection to the form detail section. Then click the control you want. If the control is wide enough or high enough, Access gives you additional handles at the midpoints of the sides of the control.

To change the size of a control, you can use the sizing handles on the sides, in either of the lower corners, or in the upper right corner. When you place your mouse pointer over one of these sizing handles, the pointer turns into a double arrow, as shown in Figure 13-13. Drag the edge of the control to a new size. You can practice on the Supplier form by shortening the SupplierID text box until it's 0.5 inch long. The name and address fields need to be stretched until they are about 1.75 inches long. You might also want to adjust the state, postal code, and phone number fields.

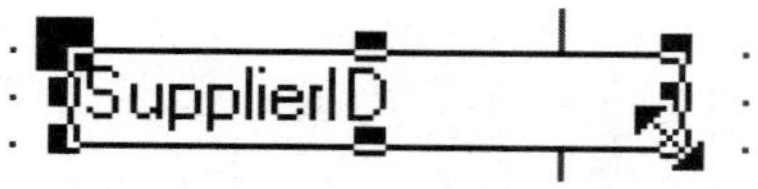

FIGURE 13-13.

The mouse pointer shaped like a double arrow can drag a corner handle of a selected control to size the control in width or height or both.

To move a control that is not currently selected, you can click anywhere on the control and drag it to a new location. After you've selected a control, you can grab and move it by placing your mouse pointer anywhere along the edge of the control between the handles. When you do that, the mouse pointer turns into a flat hand, as shown in Figure 13-14. When you see the flat hand, drag the control to a new location. Microsoft Access displays a shadow outline of the control as you move the control to help you locate it. When a control has an attached label, moving either the control or the label moves both.

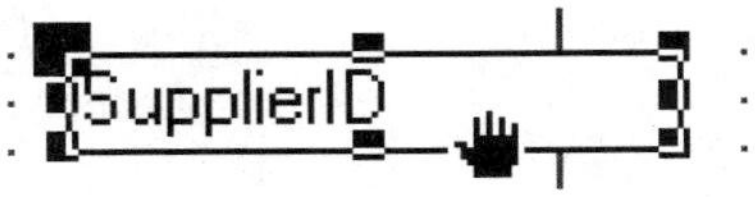

FIGURE 13-14.
The mouse pointer shaped like a flat hand can grab the edge of a selected control to move the control.

You can position a control and its attached label independently by grabbing the control by the larger square handle in the upper left corner. When you position your mouse pointer over this handle, the pointer turns into a hand with a pointing finger, as shown in Figure 13-15. Drag the control to a new location relative to its label. You can delete a label from its control by selecting the label and pressing the Del key. If you want to create a label that is independent of a control, you can use the Label tool. If you inadvertently delete a label from its control and you've made other changes so that you can no longer undo the delete, you can attach a new label by doing the following:

1. Create a new unattached label.
2. Select the label, and then choose Cut from the Edit menu to copy the label to the Clipboard and remove it.
3. Select the control to which you want to reattach a label, and then choose Paste from the Edit menu.

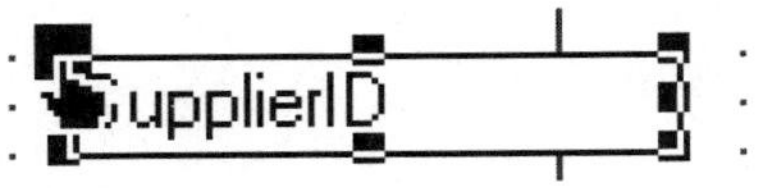

FIGURE 13-15.
The mouse pointer shaped like a hand with a pointing finger can drag the large handle of a selected control to move the control independent of its label.

Setting Text Box Properties

The next thing you might want to do is adjust some of the text box properties. Figure 13-16 on page 469 shows all the properties for the SupplierID control. Because the SupplierID field in PROMPT is a counter (which can't be changed by the user), you should change this control to prevent it from being selected on the form. To prevent the selection of a control, set the control's Enabled property to No. But Access shades a control that isn't enabled and that isn't locked. Set the Locked property to Yes to indicate that you won't be updating this control. The control will not be shaded, and you will not be able to tab to it or select it on the form in Form view.

If you specify a Format, Decimal Places, or Input Mask property setting when you define a field in a table, Access copies those settings into any text box that is bound to the field. Any data you enter using the form must conform to the validation rule defined in the table; however, you can define a more restrictive rule for this form. New rows inherit default values from the table unless you provide a different default value on the property sheet. The Status Bar Text property derives its value from the Description property setting you entered for the field in the table. In Figure 13-16, you can see properties labeled *Before Update*, properties labeled *After Update*, and a whole host of properties beginning with the word *On*. By entering macro names as values here, you can make certain events trigger certain actions (as explained in Chapter 19, "Adding Power with Macros"). You can also reference Access Basic functions that are stored separately in modules or locally with this form definition. (For details, see Chapter 21, "Microsoft Access Basic Fundamentals," and Chapter 22, "Automating Your Application with Microsoft Access Basic.") Other properties on this property sheet can be set to customize your form, as will be explained in the next chapter.

Setting Label Properties

You can also set separate properties for the labels attached to controls. Click on the label for SupplierID to see a property sheet, shown in Figure 13-17. Microsoft Access copies the Caption property from the field in the underlying table to the Caption property in the associated control label. Notice that in Figure 13-17 the caption has been changed from *Supplier ID* to *Supplier No*.

You also can correct the caption inside a label by selecting the label, moving the mouse pointer inside the label until the pointer changes into an I-beam pointer, and clicking again to set the insertion point inside the label text. You can delete unwanted characters, and you can

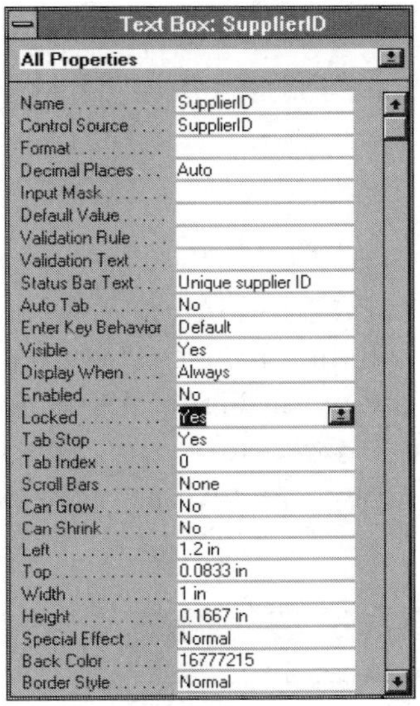

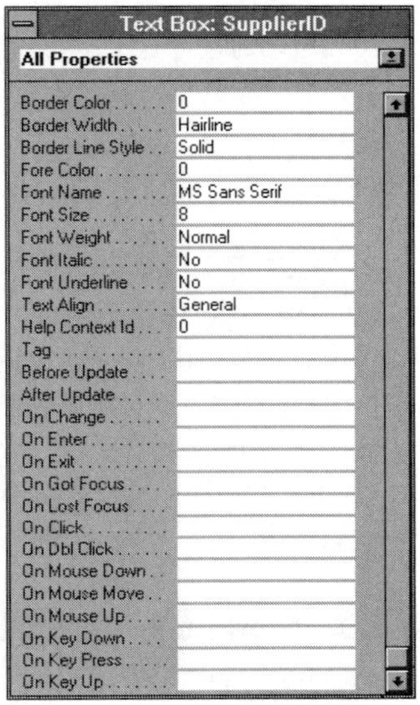

FIGURE 13-16.
The properties for the SupplierID text box control.

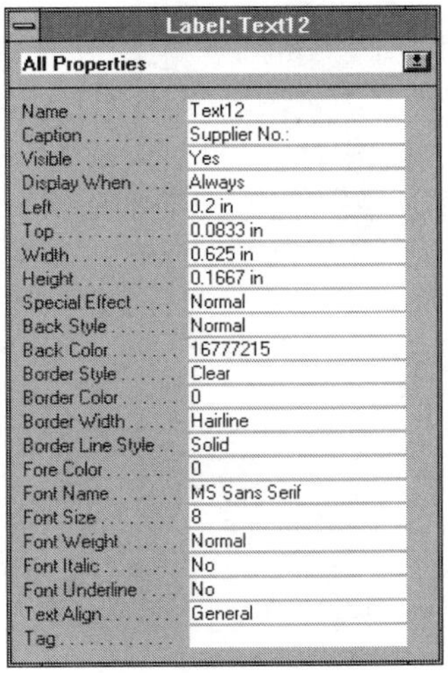

FIGURE 13-17.
The property sheet for the SupplierID label control.

type in new information. When you've finished correcting the label controls, you might find that the controls are either too large or too small to adequately display the new names. You can change settings using the property sheet to adjust the size of a label, or you can select the control and use the control's handles to fix the size and alignment.

> **TIP:** To quickly adjust the size of a label, click on the label and choose the Size To Fit command from the Format menu.

Setting Form Properties

Click anywhere outside the detail section of the form or choose the Select Form command from the Edit menu, and the property sheet will display the properties of the entire form, as shown in Figure 13-18. In that figure, the caption has been set to *Supplier Names/Addresses*. This value will be displayed on the Form window's title bar in Form view or in Datasheet view.

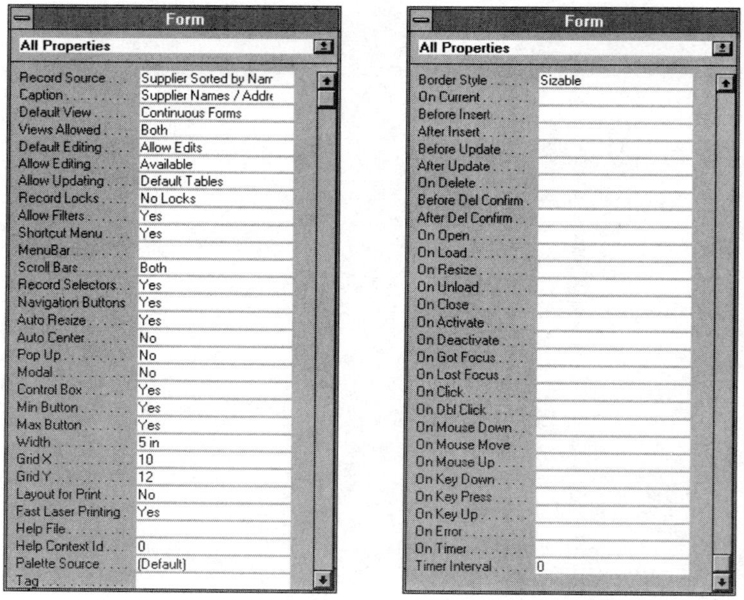

FIGURE 13-18. The property sheet for the Supplier form.

The properties from On Current through On Timer on the property sheet can be set to run macros or Microsoft Access Basic procedures. The events associated with the properties can trigger macro actions, as explained in the chapters in Part 6 of this book.

Toward the bottom of the first part of the list of properties, you can see the Grid X and Grid Y properties that control the density of dots on the grid. The defaults are 10 dots per inch across (X) and 12 dots per inch down (Y) if your Measurement setting in the International section of Windows Control Panel is English. For metric measurement, the defaults are 5 dots per centimeter in both directions. Access also draws a shaded line on the design grid every inch or centimeter to help you line up controls. If you decide to use the Snap To Grid command from the Layout menu to help you line up controls on your form, you might want to change the density of the grid dots to give you greater control over where you place objects on the form.

CAUTION: You won't be able to see the grid dots if you set either X or Y higher than 16 in English or 6 in Metric.

Checking Your Design Results

When you've finished working on this form in Design view, it might look something like the one shown in Figure 13-19 on the next page. To make the fields on the form stand out, you can click in the detail section and then open the Palette by clicking the Palette button or by choosing the Palette command from the View menu. In the Palette, set Back Color to a dark gray, as was done for the screen shown in Figure 13-19. If you also want to make the detail section fit snugly around the controls you have placed on the form, grab the edges of the detail area with your mouse pointer and drag the edges inward.

Click the Form View button on the toolbar to see your form. It will be similar to the form shown in Figure 13-20 on the next page. Notice that the captions of some of the labels have been changed. To go on to the next exercise, you'll need four records in the Supplier table. You can either copy four rows from the PROMPT Supplier table (AAA Computer Supply, Best Computer Wholesale, Computer Wholesale, Inc., and Lovell Electronics Supply) or add the rows yourself using this form. (You can invent addresses and phone numbers if you like.) Microsoft Access assigns consecutive numbers from 1 through 4 in the Supplier No. field. Save this form as *Suppliers*. (The master copy in the PROMPT database is called *Supplier*, without an "s" at the end, so you won't overwrite it if you use the plural name.)

First, click in the detail section…

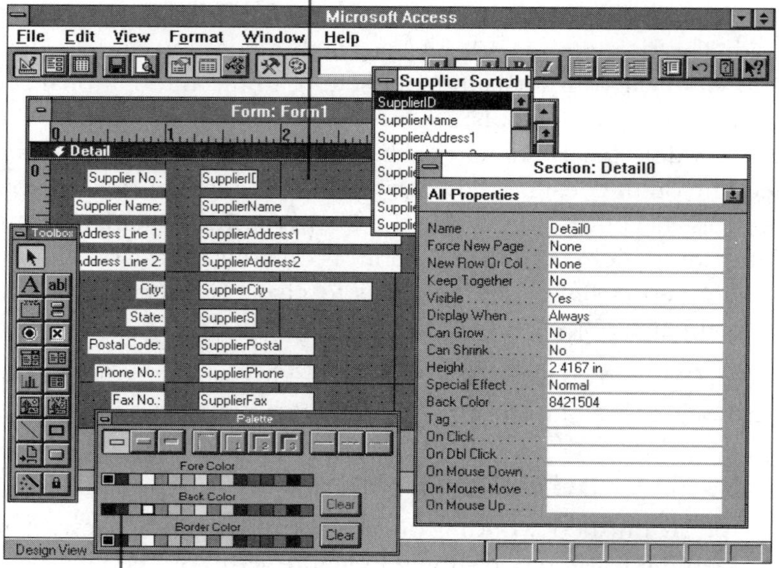

…and then click here to fill the detail section with dark gray color

FIGURE 13-19. The finished Suppliers form in Design view.

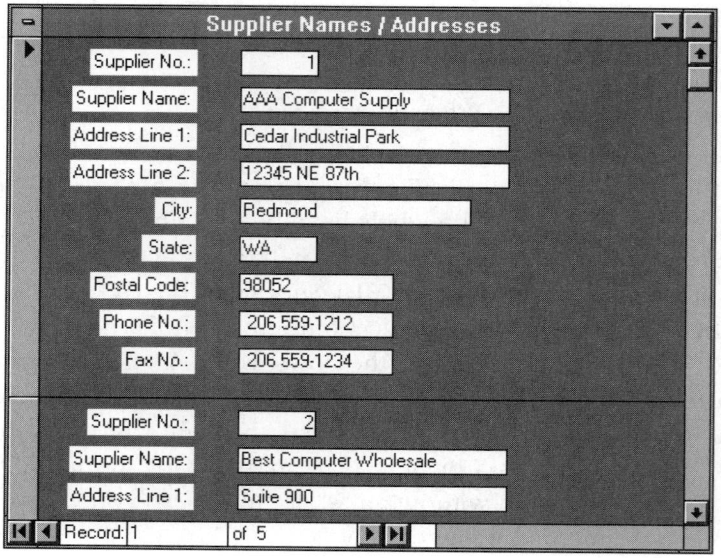

FIGURE 13-20. The finished Suppliers form in Form view.

Working with Form Wizards

The second form you'll build in this chapter is a bit more complex, so it might be a good idea to use a Form Wizard to get started. For this form, use the Component table in the PROMPT sample database.

Creating the Components Form with a Form Wizard

Begin by selecting the Component table in the PROMPT Database window and then clicking the New Form button on the toolbar. A dialog box opens, similar to the one shown in Figure 13-3 on page 452. Click the Form Wizards button; Microsoft Access opens the dialog box shown in Figure 13-21.

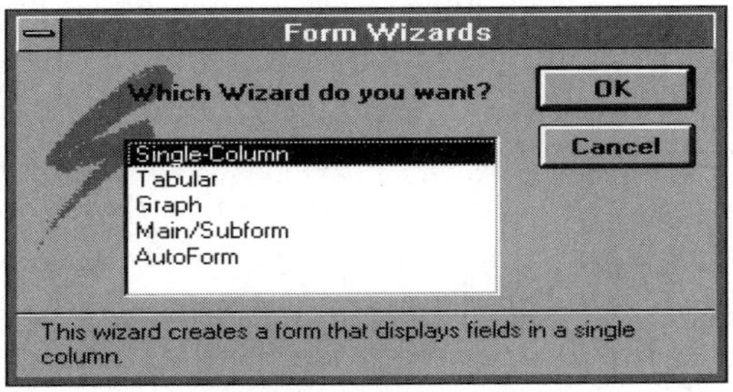

FIGURE 13-21.
The dialog box in which you select a Form Wizard.

As you can see, you have five choices in this dialog box: Single-Column, Tabular, Graph, Main/Subform, and AutoForm. (You'll read about most of these choices in Chapter 15, "Advanced Form Design.") For this example, select Single-Column and click OK. Access opens the dialog box shown in Figure 13-22 on the next page. You can select any field in the "Available fields" list box and click the single right arrow button to copy that field to the "Field order on form" list box. You can click the double right arrow button to copy all available fields to the "Field order on form" list box. If you copy a field in error, you can select the field in the "Field order on form" list box and click the single left arrow button to remove the field from the list. You can remove all fields and start over by clicking the double left arrow button. For this example, click the double right arrow button to use all the Component table's fields on the new form.

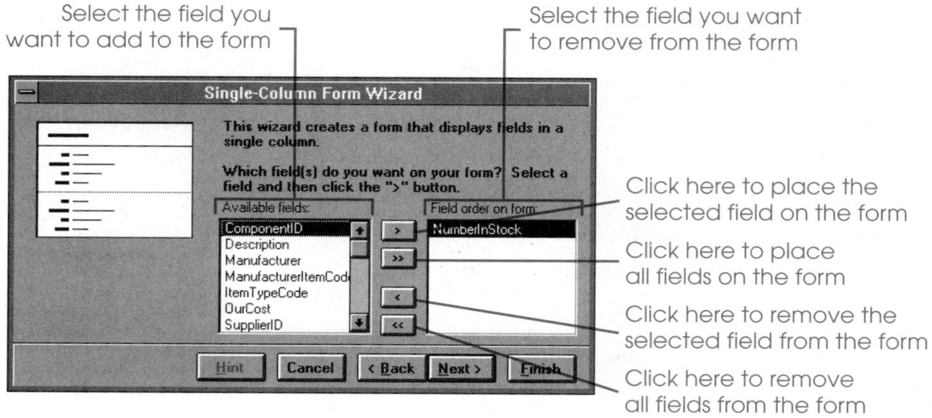

FIGURE 13-22. The Form Wizard dialog box for choosing fields.

At any time, you can click the Finish button to the right of Next to go directly to the last step. Click the Cancel button to stop creating your form.

After all the fields from the Component table are added to the form, click Next. Because you're working with the single-column format, Access opens a dialog box in which you can select the "look" for your form, as shown in Figure 13-23. The nice thing about this dialog box is that Access shows you a sample of what each selection looks like in the picture on the left. You can try them all to see the effect and decide which one you like best. In this example, choose Standard and click Next to go on to the last dialog box.

In the final dialog box, the Form Wizard asks you for a title for your form. Type in an appropriate title, such as *Components* (with an "s" at the end). Choose the "Open the form with data in it" option, and then click the Finish button to go directly to Form view. Choose "Modify the form's

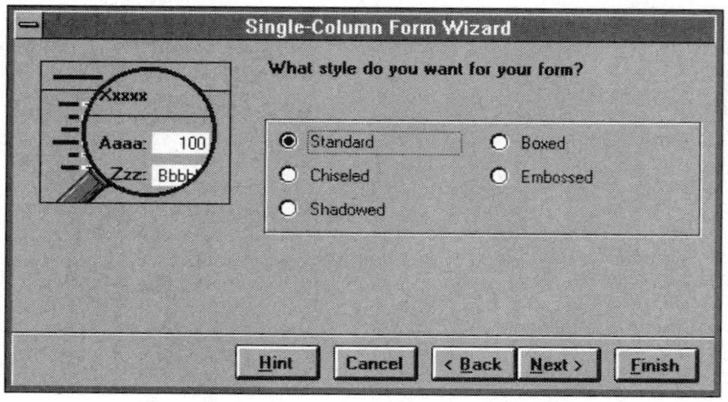

FIGURE 13-23. The Form Wizard dialog box for choosing the "look" of your form.

design" and click Finish to open the new form in Design view. The finished form is shown in Figure 13-24. Save the form as *Components.* (The master copy in the PROMPT sample database is called *Component,* so you won't overwrite it if you use the plural name.)

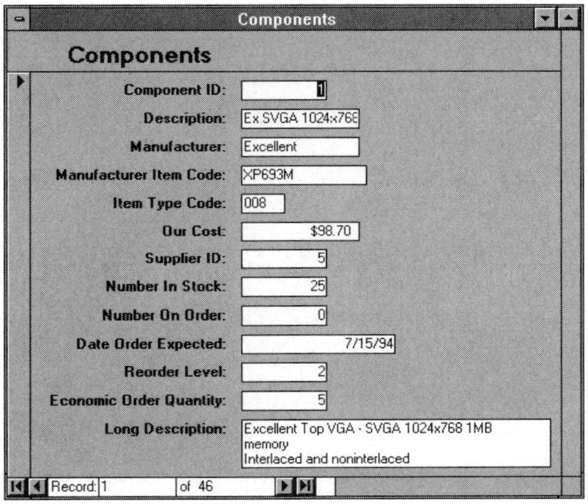

FIGURE 13-24.
The Components form in a single-column format.

If you're building the PROMPT database from scratch, you'll need a few valid entries in the Type table before you can add any components (because all components must be assigned a valid item type code). Here's the list of item type codes from the PROMPT sample database:

Item Type Code	Type Description	Item Type Code	Type Description
001	Cases, power supplies	010	Mice, pointing devices
002	Monitors	011	Multimedia
003	Keyboards	012	Software
004	Motherboards	013	Controllers
005	Floppies	014	Cables
006	Hard drives	015	Tape drives
007	RAM	016	Modems
008	Video boards	100	Packaged systems
009	Printers		

If you're curious about what the Tabular format looks like, you can start a new form on the Component table and click the Form Wizard button. Select Tabular in the first dialog box and click OK, copy all the fields in the second dialog box to the new form, and select Boxed for your form look. For a title, type *Components - Tabular*, and open the new form in Form view. It should look something like the one shown in Figure 13-25. Close this form when you've finished looking at it.

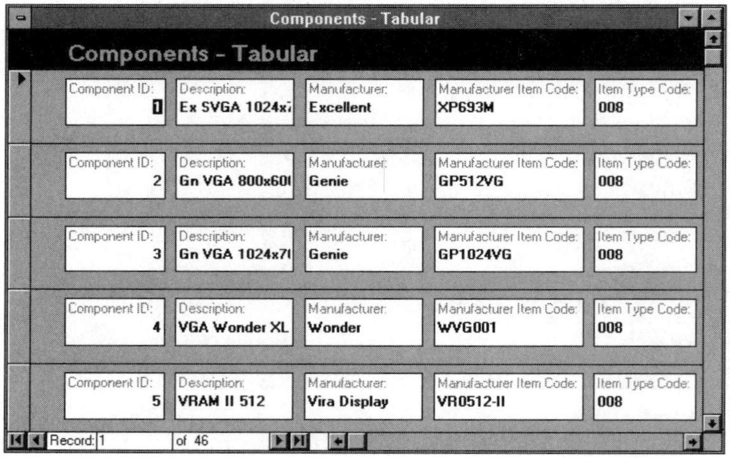

FIGURE 13-25.
The Components form in a tabular format.

Modifying the Components Form

The Form Wizard took care of some of the work, but there's a lot you can do to improve the appearance and usability of this form. The Form Wizard adjusted the control display widths, but they're still not perfect; the control displays for Description and Long Description need to be larger. Several other controls could be less wide. Also, you could make better use of the space on the form if you moved some of the fields into a second column.

Open the Components form in Design view. To help align controls, click outside the detail section so that the form is selected (or choose the Select Form command from the Edit menu), and set both Grid X and Grid Y on the form's property sheet to 16. (Leave the settings at X = 5 and Y = 5 if you're working in Metric.) Be sure the Grid command is checked on the View menu. Move controls around until the form looks similar to the one shown in Figure 13-26. (Some of the labels have been changed in this figure.) If you want to use this form in later exercises, place the ItemTypeCode control in the upper right corner of the form and reserve a fairly open space on the right half of the form for the SupplierID control.

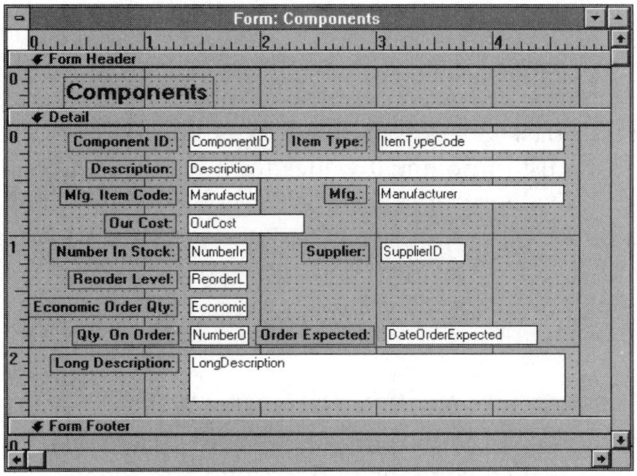

FIGURE 13-26.
The modified Components form in Design view.

Now switch to Form view. Your form should look something like the one shown in Figure 13-27. Save your work.

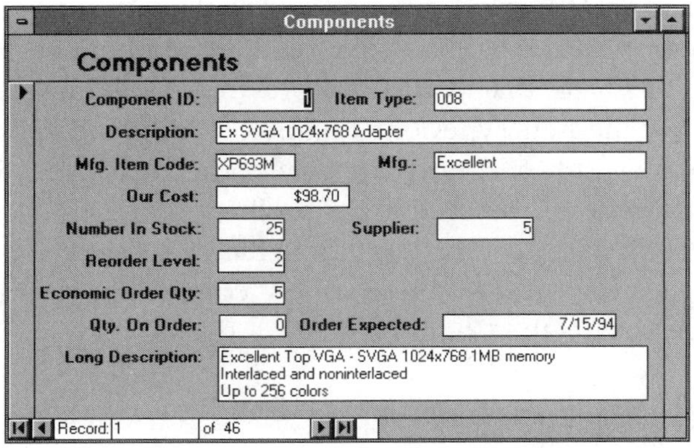

FIGURE 13-27.
The modified Components form in Form view.

Simplifying Data Input with a Form

One drawback to working with a relational database is that often you're dealing with information stored in multiple tables. That's not a problem when you're using a query to join data together, but multiple tables can be confusing if you're entering new data. Microsoft Access provides some great ways to show information from related tables, thus making data input much simpler.

Combo Boxes and List Boxes

In Chapter 12, "Form Basics," you saw that you can use a combo box or a list box to present a list of potential values for a control. To create the list, you can type the values in the Row Source property of the combo box or list box. You can also specify a table or a query as the source of the values in the list. Microsoft Access displays the currently selected value in the text box portion of the combo box or as a highlighted selection in the list.

Creating a Combo Box to Display Item Type

Codes don't mean much to the people who read a form, but for efficiency's sake you need a code, not a description, to identify component types in the Components table. You can build a combo box that shows the user the related code description fields but stores the code in the Components table when the user chooses a description.

To see how a combo box works, you can replace the ItemTypeCode text box control with a combo box on the Components form. Open the Components form that you saved previously. Change to Design view. First, select the ItemTypeCode text box control and press the Del key to remove the text box control from the form. Next, be sure the Control Wizards tool button is pressed in the toolbox, and then click the Combo Box tool button in the toolbox and drag the ItemTypeCode field from the field list to the form. You'll see a new control appear on the form, and then Access starts the Combo Box Wizard, as shown in Figure 13-28, to help you out.

NEW!

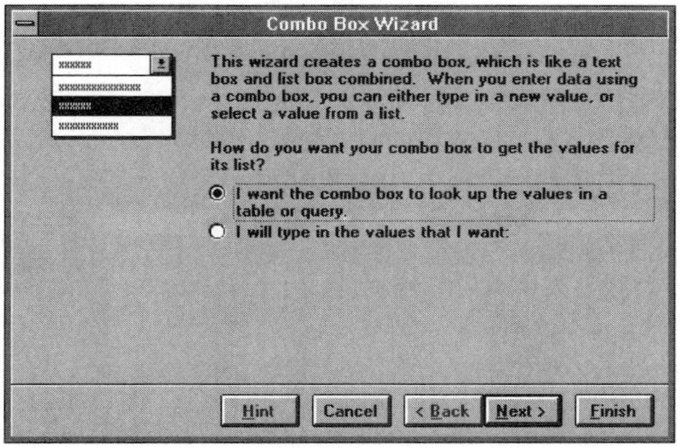

FIGURE 13-28. The first dialog box from the Combo Box Wizard.

Follow this procedure to build your combo box:

1. You want the combo box to display values from the Type table, so leave the first option checked and click the Next button to go on to the next dialog box.
2. In the second dialog box, Access displays a list of tables. Scroll down in the list until you can see the Type table, select it, and then click Next.
3. In the third dialog box, Access displays a list of available fields from the table and a list of columns in your combo box. Click the double right arrow button between the two lists to move both fields from the Type table to the columns in your combo box, and then click Next.
4. In the fourth dialog box, Access displays the two columns you selected and the data from the table. You use this dialog box to set the width of any columns you want displayed when you open the combo box on the form. Also, Access displays the data in the first column when the combo box is closed. You don't want to see the item type code, so grab the right edge of that column and move it to the left until the column disappears (which sets the width). Adjust the size of the remaining column so that you can see all the descriptions. Your result should look like that shown in Figure 13-29 on the next page. Now click Next.

FIGURE 13-29. The results of setting column widths in the fourth dialog box in the Combo Box Wizard.

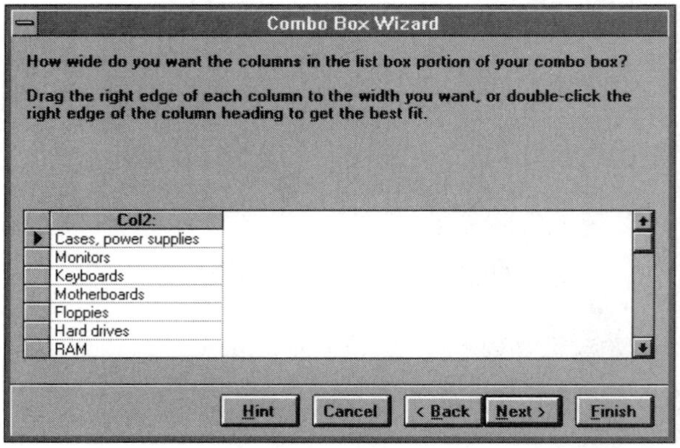

5. In the fifth dialog box, the Wizard asks you which column should be used to store the value in the control. You want to be able to choose from a list of type descriptions, but you want to store the related item type code. Be sure the ItemTypeCode field is selected, and then click Next.

6. In the sixth dialog box, the Wizard asks whether you want to bind the control to a value in the table or query that you're updating with this form or just save the value selected in an unbound control. You'll see in Part 6 of this book that unbound controls are useful for storing calculated values or working data. In this case, you want to update the item type code, so be sure to choose "Store that value in this field" and select ItemTypeCode from the field list shown on the screen. Click Next to go to the last step.

7. The Wizard shows you a final dialog box like the one shown in Figure 13-30. Notice that the Wizard has chosen the caption from the bound field as the label for the combo box. Because you'll be showing descriptions and not codes in the combo box, remove the word *Code* from the label. Click Finish, and you're all done.

If you have the property sheet open, you can study the properties set by the Combo Box Wizard, as shown in Figure 13-31. The Control Source property shows that the combo box is bound to the ItemTypeCode field. The Row Source Type property indicates that the data filling the combo box comes from a table or a query. You can also specify a list of values, or you can ask Access to create a list from the names of fields in the query or table specified in the Row Source property.

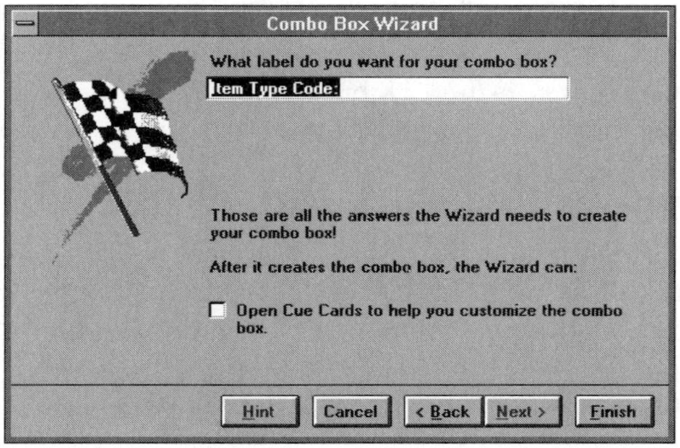

FIGURE 13-30.
The final dialog box in the Combo Box Wizard.

The Row Source property shows the SQL statement that the Wizard created to retrieve the ItemTypeCode and TypeDescription fields from the Type table. The Wizard doesn't specify any sorting criteria or save the query. You can click on the Row Source property and then click the Build button, as you learned earlier in this chapter. In the QBE grid, set the TypeDescription field to be sorted in ascending order and save the query as *Types Sorted By Description*. When you exit the Builder, ask it to update the Row Source property so that the property now refers to the query that sorts the descriptions.

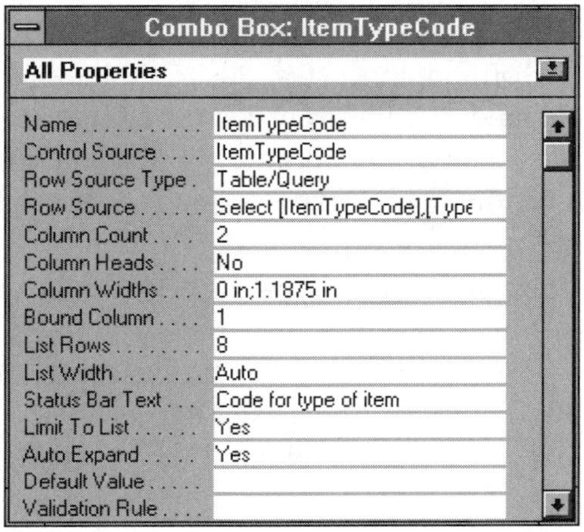

FIGURE 13-31.
The properties set by the Combo Box Wizard.

The Column Count property is set to 2 to indicate that two columns should be used from the query. You have the option of asking Access to display column headings when the combo box is open, but you don't need that for this example, so leave the Column Heads property set to No. Notice that the first entry in the Column Widths property is 0 inches. This is how you "hide" a column in a combo box. Remember, you don't want to show the item type code, but you do want to save it in the table when you choose a description from the combo box. The next property, Bound Column, indicates that the "hidden" first column (the ItemTypeCode field) is the one that sets the value of the combo box and, therefore, the bound field in the table.

One other property you should change is Limit To List. When this is set to No (as set by the Wizard), you can type entries in the combo box that aren't in the list. Because you don't want to be able to set an invalid type code in the Component table, you should change the property to Yes so that you can only select values in the list from the Type table. Save your changes.

> **TIP:** If you'd like Access to select the closest matching entry when you type a few leading characters in a combo box, set the Auto Expand property to Yes.

Now, when you open the form in Form view, it should look like the one shown in Figure 13-32. Notice that the Item Type combo box now shows meaningful descriptions instead of numbers, yet the item type you choose from the list will set the correct type code in the record.

You'll find that Microsoft Access sets the alignment of the data displayed in a combo box according to the data type of the Bound Column property. If the value of the Bound Column property is a number, the data will be right aligned, even though the actual data displayed is a text description. To correct the alignment, set the Text Align property to fit the data you want displayed—usually right-aligned for numbers and left-aligned for text.

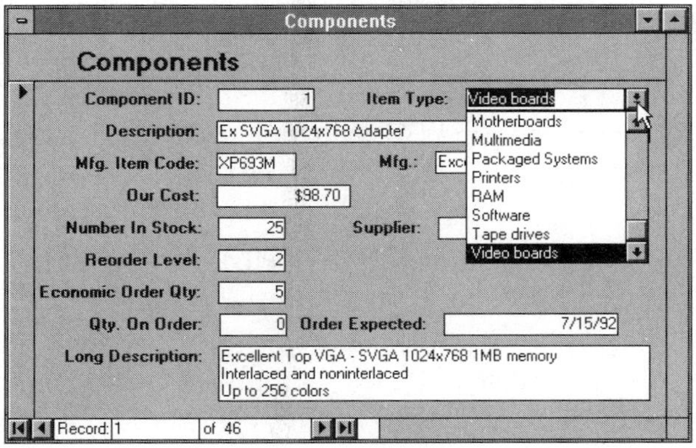

FIGURE 13-32. The finished Item Type combo box in operation.

Toggles, Check Boxes, and Option Buttons

If the list of values you want to display contains only a few values and those values are not likely to change, Microsoft Access has a few other controls that you might want to use to simplify data entry and display. Users can select from several choices with toggle buttons, check boxes, or option buttons. You can assign a separate numeric value to each button or check box you include in an option group. When you have more than one button or check box in a group, you can select only one button or check box at a time, and the value assigned to the selected button or check box becomes the value for the group. You can choose one of the buttons or check boxes in the group as the default value for the group. If you bind the option group to a field in the underlying table or query, selecting a button or check box sets a new value in the field.

Because you start with only four suppliers in PROMPT, it might be reasonable to represent the suppliers on a form as an option group. This works especially well because the SupplierID field is a counter that can be set directly by a numeric value, which is the result of selecting a button or check box in an option group. As you did earlier when you replaced an item type code with a list of item types, here you're replacing a relatively meaningless code with something recognizable.

Continue working with the Components form in Design view. To change the SupplierID control on the Components form, first delete the

SupplierID text box control. Because we're going to build this control "by hand," be sure the Control Wizards button is not pressed in the toolbox. Next, choose the Option Group tool and then drag the SupplierID field from the field list onto the form in the open space you left on the right side of the form. Stretch the group box so that it is large enough to contain four option buttons and associated labels.

Next, choose the Option Button tool and click the Tool Lock button so that you can use the Option Button tool more than once. Place four option buttons inside the option group control in a column down the left side of the group box. Select the option buttons (not their labels) one by one and look at the property sheet. Access should set the Option Value property for each button for you, using the consecutive numbers 1 through 4. Finally, click on the label for each option button, and type in the name of each of the four supplier companies so that their supplier ID numbers match the option values in the option buttons. You can find the supplier names and supplier ID numbers by opening the Supplier table in the PROMPT database. You might also want to correct the label for the option group itself to read *Supplier* instead of *Supplier ID.* Your form in Design view should now look like the one shown in Figure 13-33.

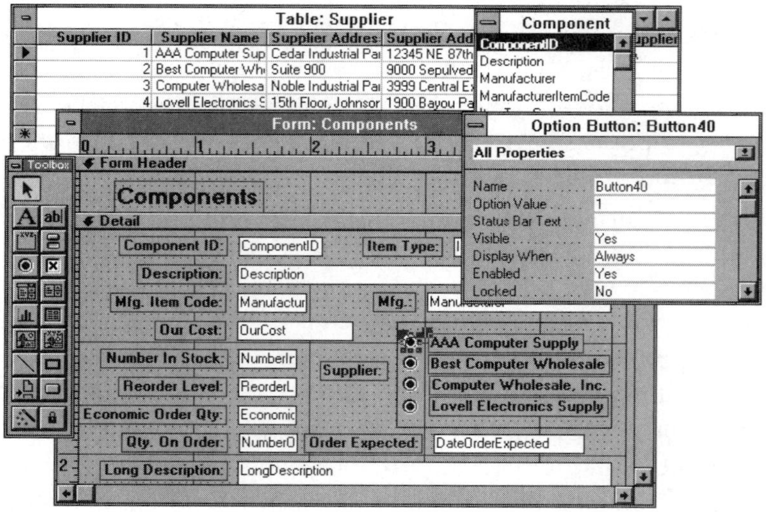

FIGURE 13-33. The Components form with an option group control for supplier names.

Click the Form View button to see the result. Your form should look like the one shown in Figure 13-34. You can test the Supplier option group by clicking one of the buttons and then switching to the Datasheet view for the form. You'll find that the SupplierID field in the record is set to the relative number of the option button you clicked.

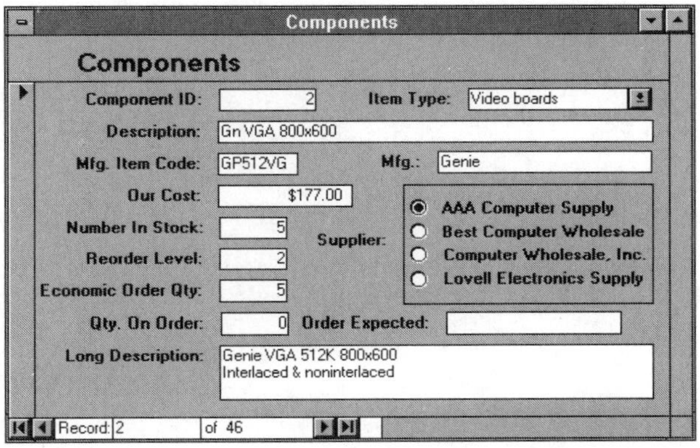

FIGURE 13-34.
The Components form with an option group for the SupplierID field.

Another common reason for using a large group of option or toggle buttons is to create a row of controls labeled with each letter of the alphabet. As you saw in Chapter 12, "Form Basics," the Suppliers form in NWIND uses this technique.

By now, you should be getting a feel for the process of designing and building forms. In the next chapter, you'll learn how to customize the appearance of your forms.

14

Customizing Forms

In the previous chapter, you learned how to create a basic form, both by building it from scratch and by using a Form Wizard. In this chapter, you'll look at ways you can refine your form's appearance and operation.

Creating a Custom Toolbar

NEW!

One of the nicest features offered by Microsoft Access is the ability to revise any of the built-in ("standard") toolbars or to define your own custom toolbars. You can build a custom toolbar for your application or to help you with design tasks. Because much of this chapter explains how to enhance the appearance of your forms, it might be nice to have a custom toolbar that gives you direct access to all the aligning and sizing commands—so let's create one.

See Also: In Chapter 23, you'll learn how to build and activate a control toolbar for the PROMPT application.

Defining a New Toolbar

First you need to create a new toolbar and then add the buttons you want to be able to use in form design. To do that, open your database and then open the Toolbars dialog box by choosing Toolbars from the View menu. You can also click with the right mouse button on any open toolbar to open the toolbar shortcut menu, and then choose Toolbars from that menu.

If the Toolbars command is grayed on the View menu, you might have inadvertently disabled all toolbars. Choose Options from the View menu and then be sure that the Built-In Toolbars Available option in the General category is set to Yes. The Toolbars dialog box is shown in Figure 14-1.

On the left side of the Toolbars dialog box, you can see the names of all the built-in toolbars that Microsoft Access provides. At the bottom of the list are three special built-in toolbars that Access displays only if you choose them in this dialog box and click the Show button:

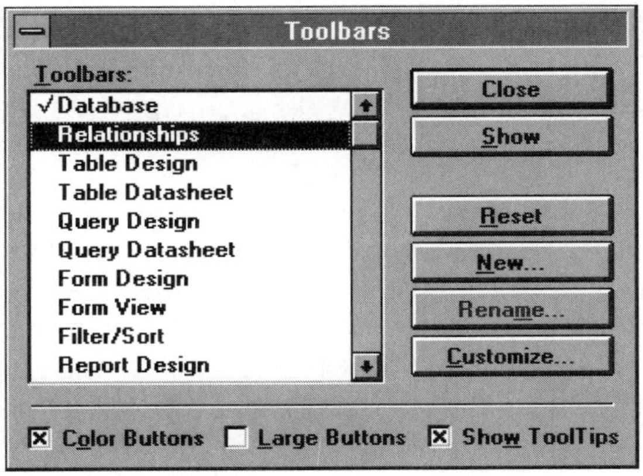

FIGURE 14-1. The Toolbars dialog box.

Microsoft, Utility 1, and Utility 2. (Note: The Show button changes to a Hide button if you select a toolbar currently displayed in the window that is open.) The Microsoft toolbar contains buttons to launch seven different Microsoft applications: Microsoft Excel, Word, Mail, PowerPoint, FoxPro, Project, and Schedule+. The two utility toolbars are empty, so you can customize these by adding buttons of your choice.

Across the bottom of the dialog box you can see check boxes to select buttons with color icons, to select large buttons, and to display ToolTips. If you're working on a large monitor at a high resolution (1024 by 768 or 1280 by 1024), you might want to choose the larger toolbar buttons to make them easier to distinguish. The large buttons are approximately 50 percent wider and taller than the standard ones.

If you have made changes to one of the built-in toolbars, you can select it in the dialog box and click the Reset button to return the toolbar to its installation default. Access prompts you to confirm the reset so that you don't inadvertently erase any custom changes you've made.

NOTE: Any new toolbar you define is available only in the database that you had open at the time you created the toolbar. If you want to define a custom toolbar that is available to all databases, you must use one of the built-in toolbars. Access provides two "blank" toolbars—Utility 1 and Utility 2—that you can use to create a custom set of toolbar buttons that is available in any database. The only drawback to these two toolbars is that you cannot give them custom names.

You can click the New button to begin defining a new toolbar. Access will prompt you for a name for your new toolbar. You'll see the new name appear at the bottom of the list, and a new small gray window will open in the Access workspace.

Because you'll probably want to use form alignment tools in every database that you design, it's a good idea to "borrow" one of the blank utility toolbars to define your custom buttons. Scroll down in the Toolbars list until you see the Utility 1 toolbar name. Select it and click the Show button to open the toolbar. The Utility 1 toolbar appears as a small gray box in the Access workspace. Then, click the Customize button to open the Customize Toolbars dialog box.

The Customize Toolbars dialog box is shown in Figure 14-2. This dialog box allows you to change the buttons on any open toolbar. On the left side of the dialog box is a list of all the button categories that Microsoft Access provides. Because you want buttons to help with sizing and alignment in form design, select the Form Design category to see the Buttons group shown in Figure 14-2. As you move your mouse pointer over the various buttons in the group, Access displays a description of the control in the box at the bottom of the dialog box. If you have ToolTips turned on, you'll also see a short description appear just below the mouse pointer.

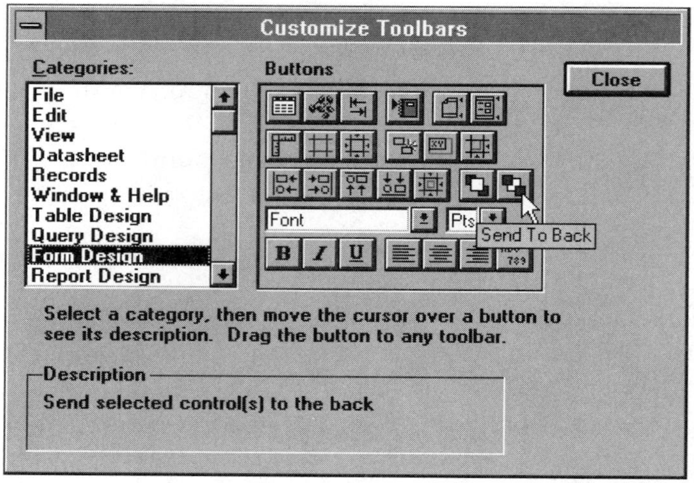

FIGURE 14-2. The Customize Toolbars dialog box and the Form Design category buttons.

Some useful buttons to have for form design include the Tab Order button (the third button in the top row), all the buttons in the second row (Show/Hide Ruler, Show/Hide Grid, Snap To Grid, Duplicate Control, Size To Fit, Size To Grid), and all the buttons in the third row (Align Controls Left, Align Controls Right, Align Controls Top, Align Controls Bottom, Align To Grid, Bring To Front, Send To Back). Drag and drop these buttons one at a time onto your new toolbar. You might find it easiest to line up the buttons in the proper order if you add them to the toolbar from right to left. You'll notice that Access displays the name of your toolbar as soon as you've added enough buttons to make the toolbar wide enough to show the entire name. Your toolbar with all the added buttons should look something like that shown in Figure 14-3.

FIGURE 14-3.
The Utility 1 custom toolbar under construction, with added form design buttons.

Unless you're building the toolbar while a form is open in Design view, all buttons will appear gray (disabled). As soon as you open a form in Design view, the appropriate buttons become available for use.

Customizing the Look of Your New Toolbar

After you've built a toolbar, you can rearrange the buttons and add spacing between them. To make any changes, first open the toolbar. Then open the Toolbars dialog box and click the Customize button.

> **TIP:** You can click with the right mouse button on the toolbar to open the toolbar shortcut menu and choose Customize from that menu.

When you open the Customize Toolbars dialog box, all toolbar buttons become editable:

- You can remove any button from any open toolbar (including all built-in ones) by clicking the button and dragging it to the Buttons group in the dialog box.
- You can rearrange buttons by clicking one and dragging it to a new location.
- You can add more buttons by finding the one you want in the Buttons group and dragging it to any toolbar.

To make buttons easier to use, it's often useful to "cluster" buttons that have a similar function and create a space between clusters of buttons. To create a space in front of any button, hold down the Shift key and then click the button and move it to the right. (You might need to resize the toolbar window to make the space visible.) On the Utility 1 toolbar, the Tab Order and Duplicate Control buttons should probably stand on their own. The Show/Hide Ruler and Show/Hide Grid buttons could be clustered next. The Snap To Grid, Size To Fit, and Size To Grid buttons would make a good group. The five alignment buttons seem logical together, followed finally by the Bring To Front and Send To Back buttons. After you've made these modifications, your toolbar should look like the one shown in Figure 14-4. Close the Customize Toolbars dialog box when you've finished.

FIGURE 14-4.
The Utility 1 custom toolbar with buttons arranged in clusters.

> **TIP:** You can drag the edges of the toolbar to change its shape. You can also "dock" the toolbar at the top, sides, or bottom of the workspace.

Adding a Custom Button to a Built-In Toolbar

It might be nice to have a button on the built-in Form Design toolbar to open and close your new Utility 1 toolbar. To do this, you need a small Microsoft Access Basic procedure, a macro, and a custom button added to the built-in Form Design toolbar.

A Simple Function to Open and Close Your Custom Toolbar

The custom buttons that you add to any toolbar have a couple of limitations. First, they can do only simple things like open a table or form, run a query, open a report in Print Preview, or run a macro. Second, you can't create a custom toolbar button that acts like a toggle. For example, the built-in Toolbox button on the Form Design toolbar is a toggle: Click it once, and it opens the toolbox and stays pressed; click it again, and it closes the toolbox and pops up.

So you can create a custom button that runs a macro that opens the Utility 1 toolbar, but you have to use the toolbar shortcut menu (or the Control-menu box on the toolbar when it's floating) to close the toolbar. You can, however, emulate a toggle button by writing a simple Access Basic procedure known as a *function procedure* (also called a *function*) and a macro to run the function. Unfortunately, you can't run an Access Basic function directly from a custom toolbar button; if you could, you wouldn't need the macro.

You will explore Access Basic in some depth in Chapter 21, "Microsoft Access Basic Fundamentals," and Chapter 22, "Automating Your Application with Access Basic." For now, follow these simple steps to create a toolbar toggle (open/close) function:

1. Go to the Database window and click the Module tab. Click the New button to open a new Access Basic module. You'll see a window like the one shown in Figure 14-5.

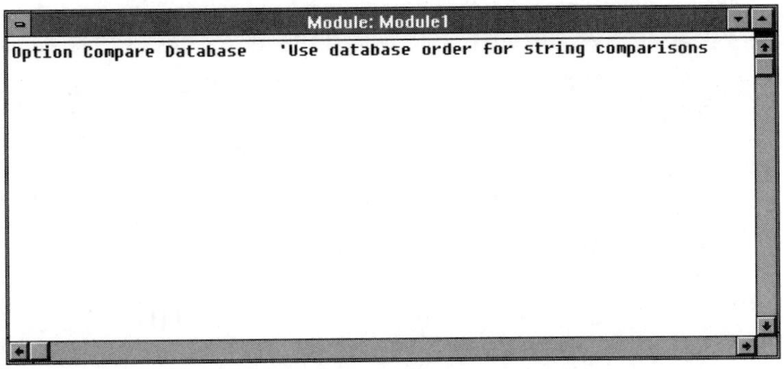
Module: Module1
Option Compare Database 'Use database order for string comparisons

FIGURE 14-5. The Module window for a new Access Basic module.

2. On the second line of the window, type the following:

```
Global intFormTool As Integer        'On/Off switch for
                                     'custom toolbar
```

3. From the Edit menu, choose the New Procedure command. Access displays the dialog box shown in Figure 14-6. Enter the name for the new function as shown in the figure.

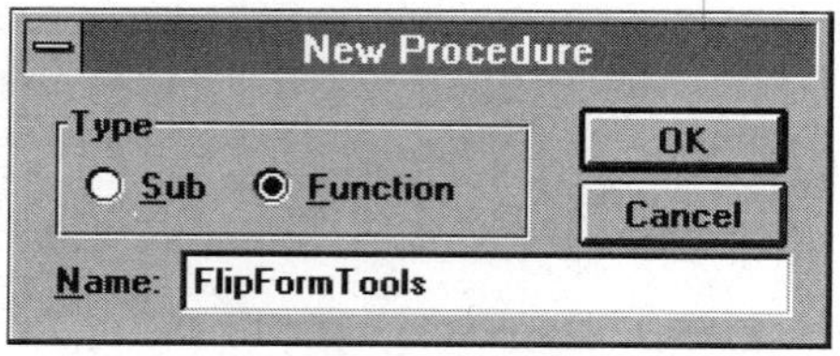
New Procedure
Type
Sub
Function
OK
Cancel
Name:
FlipFormTools

FIGURE 14-6. Starting a new function in an Access Basic module.

4. Click OK. Access displays the new, empty function. Beginning on the third line, type the following code:

```
If intFormTool Then
  intFormTool = False
  DoCmd ShowToolbar "Utility 1", A_TOOLBAR_NO
Else
  intFormTool = True
  DoCmd ShowToolbar "Utility 1", A_TOOLBAR_YES
End If
```

In a nutshell, this function tests the variable you created in step 2. If the variable is True, the function calls a macro action called "ShowToolbar" to close the Utility 1 toolbar and set the variable to False. If the variable is False (it will be False the first time this code is executed), the function opens the toolbar and sets the variable to True. Your result should look like the window shown in Figure 14-7.

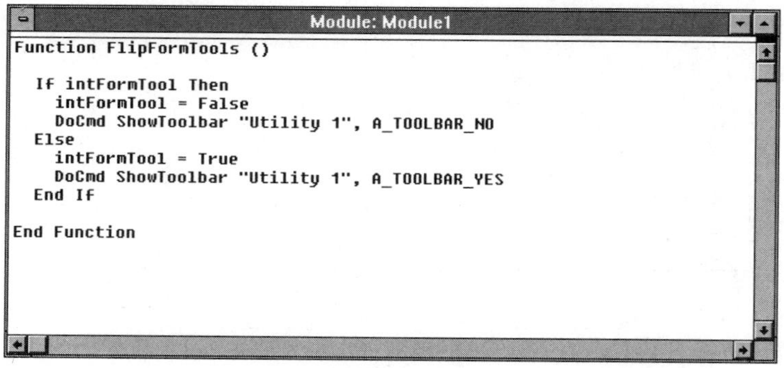
Module: Module1
Function FlipFormTools ()
If intFormTool Then
intFormTool = False
DoCmd ShowToolbar "Utility 1", A_TOOLBAR_NO
Else
intFormTool = True
DoCmd ShowToolbar "Utility 1", A_TOOLBAR_YES
End If
End Function

FIGURE 14-7. A function to toggle (open/close) the Utility 1 toolbar.

5. Choose Save from the File menu, name the module *ToolbarFunction,* and then close the Module window.

A Macro to Run Your Toggle Function

You also need a macro that you can call from your custom toolbar button to run the function you just created. Go to the Database window and click the Macro tab. Click New to open a new macro design window, shown in Figure 14-8. In the first Action row, type *RunCode,* or choose RunCode from the drop-down list in the Action row. Press F6 to jump down to the Function Name parameter box, and type your new function name followed by open and close parentheses: *FlipFormTools().* Choose Save from the File menu and name your macro *Form Tools.*

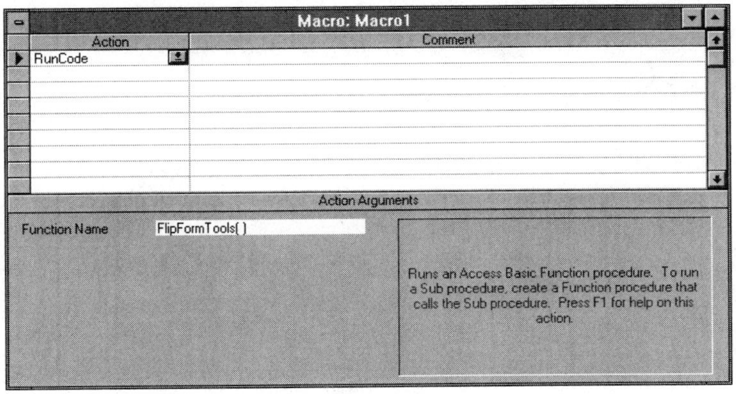

FIGURE 14-8.
A macro to run the FlipFormTools Access Basic function.

Now you're ready to add a custom button to the Form Design toolbar.

Defining a Button to Run Your Macro

You'll now be spending some time working with the Components form that you built in the last chapter. Open the Components form in Design view. This should also show you the Form Design toolbar. If you can't see the toolbar, choose Options from the View menu and be sure that the Built-In Toolbars Available option is set to Yes.

Move your mouse pointer to the toolbar and click with the right mouse button on the toolbar to open the shortcut menu, shown in Figure 14-9 on the next page. Choose Customize from this menu to open the Customize Toolbars dialog box again.

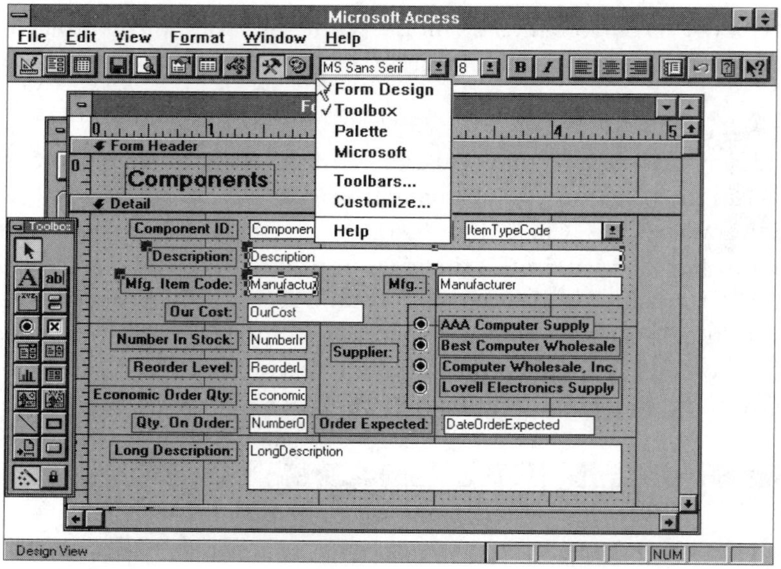

FIGURE 14-9.
Using the shortcut menu to open the Customize Toolbars dialog box.

If you're working on a screen with a 640-by-480 resolution or if you've turned on the large toolbar buttons, you might want to remove one of the standard buttons from the Form Design toolbar to make room for a new button. (I don't know about you, but I rarely have a need to see a form in Print Preview.) You can click the Print Preview button and drag it to the Buttons group in the dialog box to remove it.

Next, you need to find the macro you just created. Scroll down in the Categories list and select All Macros. Microsoft Access displays all the macros in your database in the Objects list of the Customize Toolbars dialog box, as shown in Figure 14-10. In this case, I'm using the completed version of the PROMPT database, so the example shows many macro names that you'll create later in this book.

Click on your new *Form Tools* macro, drag it to the Form Design toolbar, and drop it between the existing Toolbox and Palette buttons. Your result should look like the toolbar shown in Figure 14-11.

The default picture that Access displays when you create a button to run a macro is the macro icon. As you can see, the ToolTip says *Run macro 'Form Tools.'* Fortunately, Access lets you improve both the icon and the ToolTip. While you still have the Customize Toolbars dialog box open, click with the right mouse button on your new button to open a shortcut menu containing the Choose Button Face option. Select this option to open the Choose Button Face dialog box, shown in Figure 14-12.

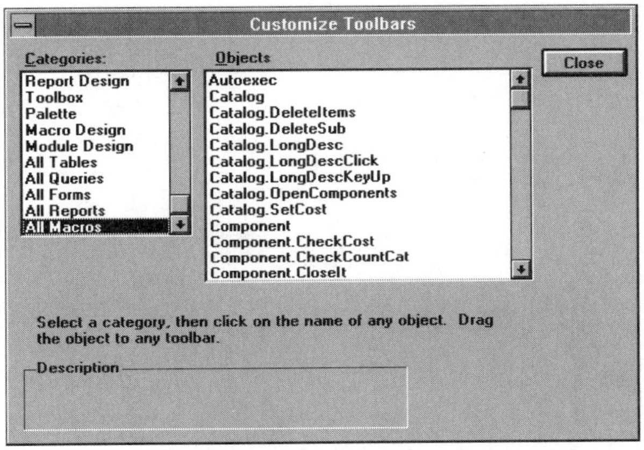

FIGURE 14-10. Choosing a macro to use for a custom toolbar button.

FIGURE 14-11. Placing a custom toolbar button on the Form Design toolbar.

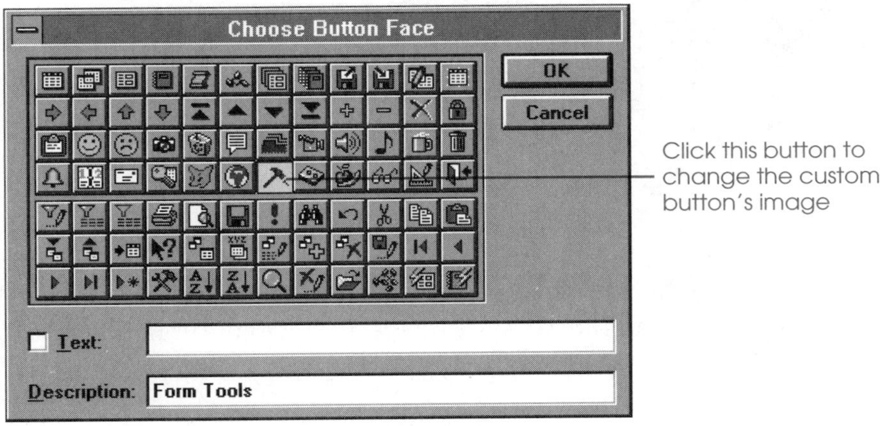

FIGURE 14-12. Choosing a custom button icon and description in the Choose Button Face dialog box.

There's a handy hammer-and-nail icon near the center of the set of available icons that will do quite nicely for this new button. You can also shorten the description to say simply "Form Tools"—this description will show up as a ToolTip when you move the mouse pointer over the button. Click OK to change the icon on your new button. Close the Customize Toolbars dialog box. You can now click your new toolbar button to open and close the Utility 1 toolbar that contains your custom set of form design buttons, as shown in Figure 14-13.

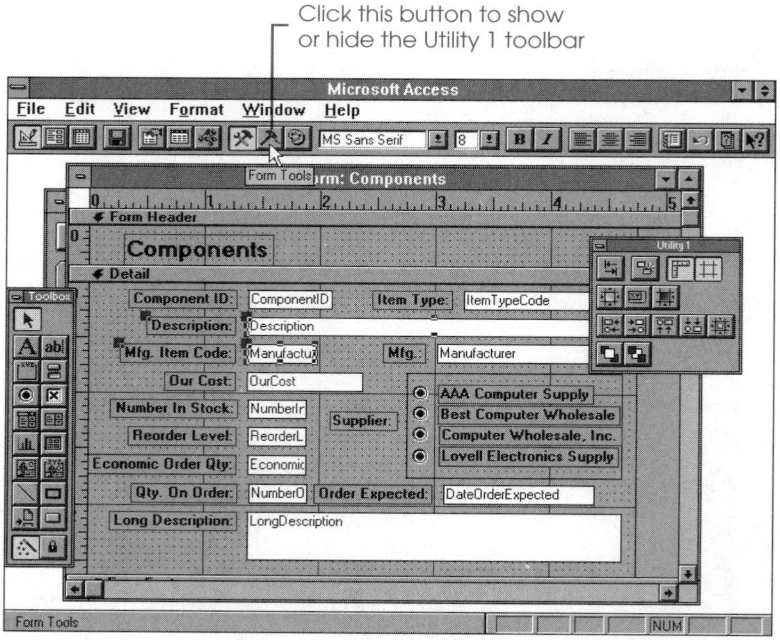

FIGURE 14-13.
A new custom toolbar button to open/close the Utility 1 toolbar.

When the Utility 1 toolbar is open, you can "dock" it at the top, bottom, or sides of your workspace or leave it floating. You'll find it useful to help line up your Components form in the next section. If you want to continue to use this custom toolbar in other databases, be sure to copy the *Form Tools* macro and the Toolbar Function module to those databases.

Aligning and Sizing

In Chapter 13, you built a form from the Components table, shown in Figure 14-13. This form looks pretty good, but the labels and fields are different sizes and are out of alignment. If you've just thrown the form together to help you enter some data (as you did to create a simple Supplier input form in Chapter 13), it probably doesn't matter if the form's appearance isn't perfect. But if you've designed this form to be used continuously in an application you're building, it's worth making the extra effort to fine-tune the form's design. Otherwise, your database will look less than "professional," and users might suffer eyestrain and fatigue.

To check out the alignment and relative size of controls on your form, you can open the property sheet in Design view, choose Layout Properties from the drop-down list at the top of the property sheet, and click various controls. For example, Figure 14-14 shows the property sheet for the NumberInStock and ReorderLevel controls. You can see by looking at the values for the Left property (the distance from the left edge of the form) that the ReorderLevel control is a little bit closer to the left margin than the NumberInStock control.

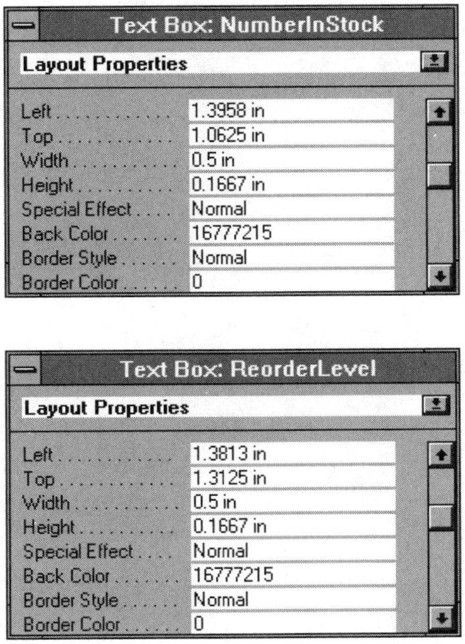

FIGURE 14-14.
The properties that define the placement and size of the NumberInStock and ReorderLevel controls.

Now, you could go around the form and adjust controls so that they fit your data. You could painstakingly enter values for each control's Left property to get all controls in a column to line up exactly and then set the Top property (defining the distance from the top of the form section) for controls that you want to appear in a row. You could also adjust the values for the Width and Height properties so that controls and labels are the same width and height where appropriate. Fortunately, there are easier ways to fix all of these problems.

Sizing Controls to Fit Content

One of the first things you can do with this form is be sure all the boxes you have drawn are the right size for displaying your data. Microsoft Access has a command that sizes label controls to fit around the text you have typed in them. This command also ensures that text, combo, and list boxes are tall enough to display your data using the font size you've chosen.

Because you built all controls and labels on this form using the same font, it makes sense to resize them all at once. First, choose Select All from the Edit menu to highlight all the controls on your form. To select a specific group of labels or controls, click on the first one and then hold down the Shift key as you click on each control or label you want selected. You can also drag the mouse pointer across your form (as long as you don't start the drag over a control!), and the mouse pointer will delineate a selection box. (See the following tip.) Any controls that are inside the selection box when you release the mouse button will be selected. When you have the controls that you want selected, choose the Size To Fit command from the Format menu. (If the custom Form Design toolbar that you created earlier in this chapter is open, you can click the Size To Fit button on that toolbar. The result on the design grid should look something like the one shown in Figure 14-15.

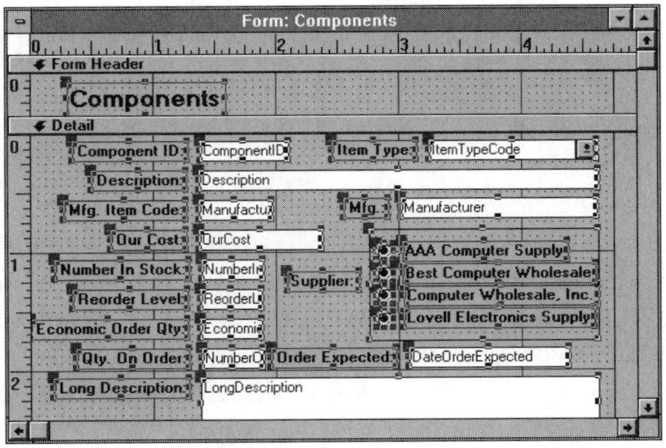

FIGURE 14-15.

The Components form after you select the controls and choose the Size To Fit command.

TIP: If you think you'll be selecting multiple controls often, you might want to experiment with an option setting that governs how dragging your mouse pointer over multiple controls works. From the View menu, choose Options and select the Form & Report Design category. When you choose a Selection Behavior of Partially Enclosed, the selection box you draw with your mouse pointer need only touch any part of a control to select it. If you choose Fully Enclosed, the selection box must contain all of the control for the control to be selected. Fully Enclosed is most useful for complex forms with many controls close to each other—that way you don't have to worry about inadvertently selecting controls that you partially touch with the selection box.

You can also select all controls in a vertical or horizontal band by making the rulers visible and then dragging your mouse pointer along the top or side ruler.

> **TIP:** You can "size to fit" any individual control or label by double-clicking its lower left corner.

"Snapping" Controls to the Grid

It's a good idea to verify that all your controls are spaced evenly down the form. One way to do this is to take advantage of the grid. You can adjust the density of the grid using the Grid X and Grid Y properties of the form. Be sure that the property sheet is open, and then choose Select Form from the Edit menu. Also, be sure that the Grid command in the View menu has a check mark in front of it.

In this example, set the values for the Grid X and Grid Y properties to 16 (0.0625 inch between grid points). This works well for the default MS Sans Serif font in 8-point size because the "sized to fit" text boxes will be 0.17 inches high. You can place these text boxes every 0.25 inch (four grid points) down the form and leave adequate space between the controls.

Choose the Snap To Grid command from the Format menu. You can see a check mark in front of this command when Snap To Grid is active. Now grab each control and position it vertically every 0.25 inch (every fourth grid point) down the grid. When you release the mouse button, you'll see the upper left corner of the control "snap" to the nearest grid point. As you saw in Chapter 13, "Building a Form," Microsoft Access moves a control and its label as a unit. So, if you've previously moved the label up or down independently of the attached control, you might need to use the positioning handle in the upper left corner of the control or its label to align them horizontally.

If you're having difficulty moving the controls to the nearest quarter inch, you can try setting Grid X to 8 or 4. Don't worry about vertical alignment yet. You'll take care of that shortly. When you've finished, your form might look something like the one shown in Figure 14-16.

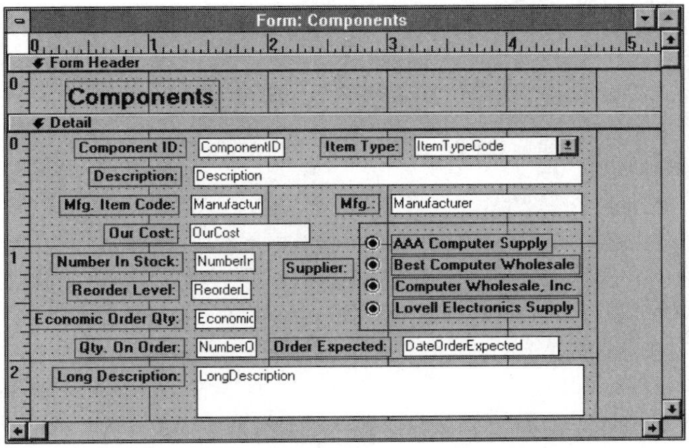

FIGURE 14-16.
The Components form after you "snap" the controls to the grid.

Lining Up Controls

You now have your controls spaced evenly down the form, but they probably look a little jagged from left to right. That's easy to fix. Select all the labels in the far left column. Do this by clicking on the first label (not its associated control) and then pressing the Shift key. Hold down the Shift key as you click on all the remaining labels in the column. When you have them all selected, your design grid should look something like the one shown in Figure 14-17 on the next page. Notice that Microsoft Access also shows handles for all the related controls but no sizing handles on the controls. With this method, you see the related control but you know that you've selected only the labels.

The labels will look best if their right edges align. You have two choices at this point. If you turn off the Snap To Grid command, you can have Access line up all the labels with the label whose right edge is farthest to the right, even if that edge is between dots on the grid. If you leave on Snap To Grid, you can have Access line up the labels with the label farthest to the right and then snap the entire group to the nearest grid point.

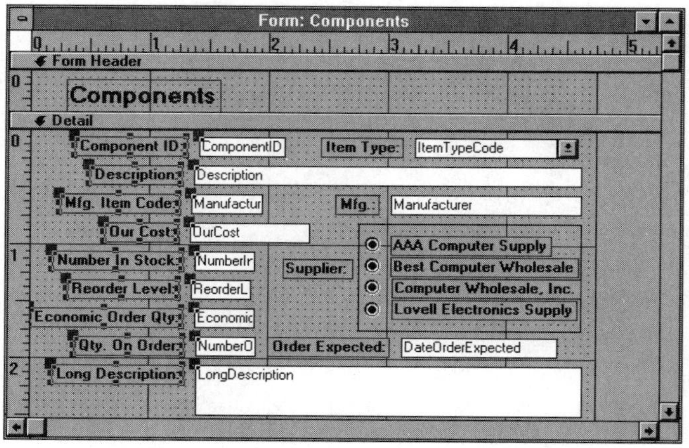

FIGURE 14-17. The Components form with a column of labels selected.

When you're ready to line up the selected controls on your form, choose the Align command from the Format menu. This command opens a submenu, as shown in Figure 14-18. Choose the Right command from the submenu, and click inside the grid. Your form should look similar to the one shown in Figure 14-19. (Again, if you're using the Utility 1 toolbar, you can simply click the Align Right button instead of using the menus.)

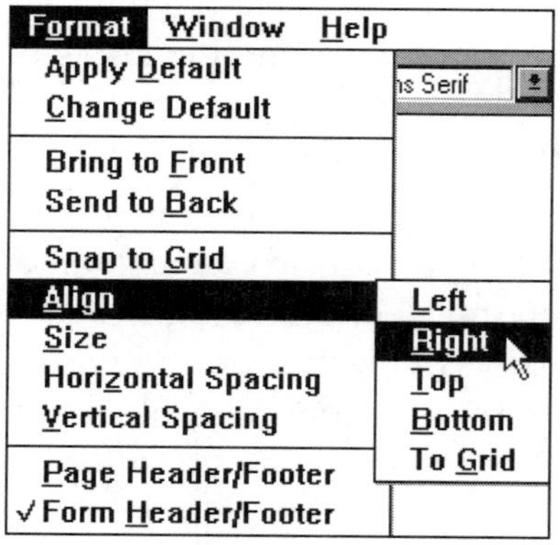

FIGURE 14-18. The Align command and its submenu.

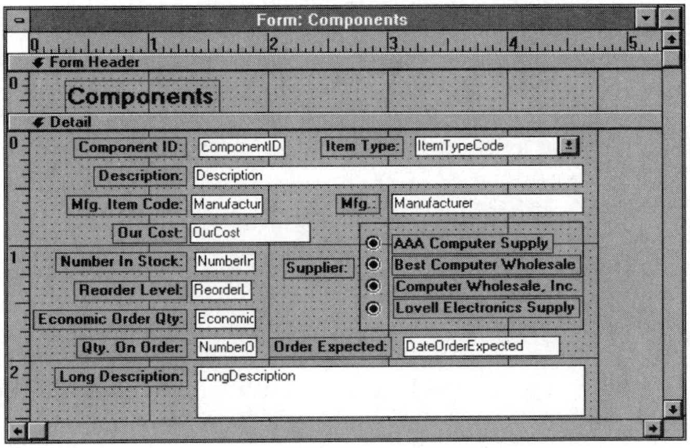

FIGURE 14-19. The labels from Figure 14-17 are right-aligned.

To complete alignment of the Components form, use the Align submenu commands (shown in Figure 14-18) to do the following:

1. Select the Item Type, Mfg., and Order Expected labels (not the controls), and align them using the Align Right command.
2. Select the ComponentID, Description, ManufacturerItemCode, OurCost, NumberInStock, ReorderLevel, EconomicOrderQty, NumberOnOrder, and LongDescription controls (not the labels), and align them using the Align Left command.
3. Select the ItemTypeCode control, the Manufacturer control, the SupplierID option group, and the DateOrderExpected control. Do not include the Description and LongDescription controls in this group. Align the group using the Align Right command.
4. Select the Component ID and Item Type labels and corresponding controls, and align them using the Align Top command.
5. Select the Description label and control, and align them using the Align Top command.
6. Select the Mfg. Item Code and Manufacturer labels and corresponding controls, and align them using the Align Top command.
7. Select the Our Cost label and its control and the SupplierID option group (but not its label), and align them using the Align Top command.

8. Select the Number In Stock label and its control, and the label for the SupplierID option group, and align them using the Align Top command.
9. Select the Qty. On Order and Order Expected labels and corresponding controls (the NumberOnOrder control's caption is Qty. On Order), and align them using the Align Top command.
10. Select the Supplier label (not the SupplierID option group) and the Order Expected label, and align them using the Align Left command.
11. Use the Align Top command to individually align the remaining controls and their labels.

When you've completed these steps, your form should look something like the one shown in Figure 14-20.

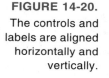

FIGURE 14-20. The controls and labels are aligned horizontally and vertically.

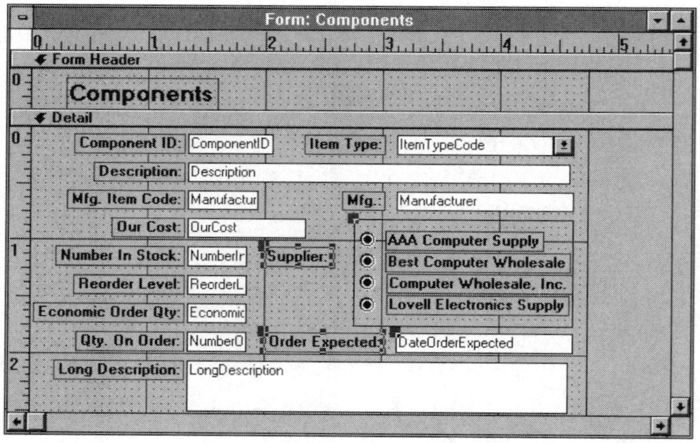

Making Control Length Adjustments

Two long controls—Description and LongDescription—stretch most of the way across the form. You lined up their left edges, but it would be nice if their right edges also lined up with the items in the second column on the form. You can do that by adjusting the Width property for the two long controls.

To figure out what adjustment you need (if any), first take a look at the Left and Width properties of the ItemTypeCode control's property sheet, as shown in Figure 14-21. In this example, the ItemTypeCode combo box starts 3.125 inches from the left edge of the form and is 1.5 inches long. This means that the right edge is 4.625 inches from the left edge of the form. Next, take a look at the Left and Width properties of the LongDescription text box. You don't want to move this text box from its location 1.3396 inches from the left edge because it's lined up with the other controls in that column. The sum of the Left and Width properties should equal 4.625 inches in order to line up the right edge of the Description control with the right edge of the ItemTypeCode control. So you need to change the Description control's Width property to 3.2854 inches (4.625 minus 1.3396) to achieve the desired result. (Access adjusts this length to 3.2847 inches to line up with the nearest display pixel.) You should make a similar adjustment to the Width property for the LongDescription control.

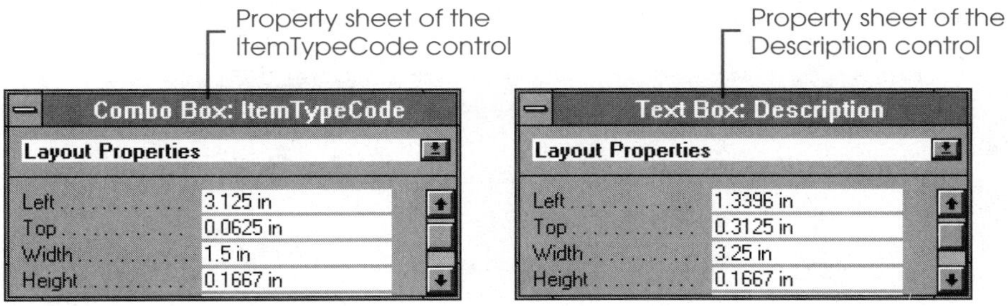

FIGURE 14-21.
The values for the Left and Width properties can be compared and adjusted to align the right edges of two controls.

As a final touch, you should adjust controls in a column to the same length where it makes sense to do so. For example, you could make the ComponentID and ManufacturerItemCode controls the same length (about 0.6 inch works well). You can select the ComponentID control and the ManufacturerItemCode control and then set the width for both at the same time in the property sheet. Similarly, the NumberInStock, ReorderLevel, EconomicOrderQty, and NumberOnOrder controls can be the same length. If you decide to make the ItemTypeCode, Manufacturer, and DateOrderExpected controls the same length, you might have to realign them on the right.

When you're all done, switch to Form view and move the Form window to the upper left corner of your screen. Choose Size To Fit Form from the Window menu to resize the Form window to show only the controls. (Notice that you must move the form to the top left of your screen before choosing the Size To Fit Form command because this command expands a form only to the right and down.) Your form should look something like the one shown in Figure 14-22. Choose Save Form from the File menu to save your design changes.

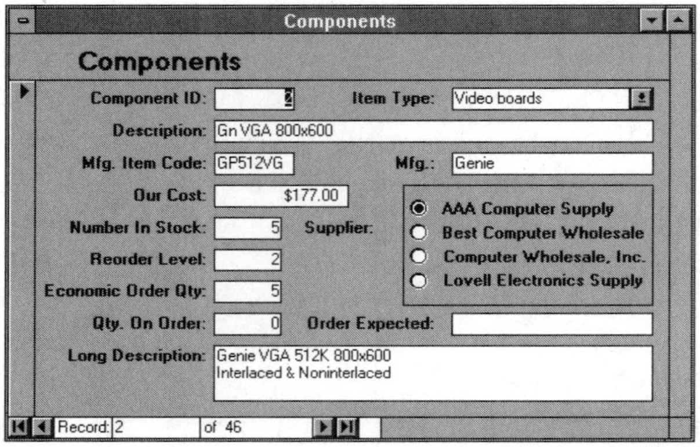

FIGURE 14-22. The Components form with controls aligned and sized.

TIP: Forms have an Auto Resize property. If you set this property to Yes, Microsoft Access sizes the form's window to fit the detail section whenever you open the form. Note that Access won't automatically resize a form if you've switched from Design view to Form view.

There's also an Auto Center property that you can set to Yes to ask Access to center the form's window in the current Access workspace.

Special Effects

When you first built the Components form using a Form Wizard and asked for Standard format, the Wizard automatically added one special effect—a gray background color. In this section, you'll learn about a few more enhancements you can make to your form's design.

Lines and Rectangles

Microsoft Access comes with two drawing tools that you can use to enhance the appearance of your forms. Lines can be added to visually separate parts of your form. Rectangles are useful for surrounding and setting off a group of controls.

On the Components form, it might be helpful to separate the primary information about the component ID and its description at the top of the form from the rest of the information on the form. To make room to add a line under this information, you need to move the ManufacturerItemCode and Manufacturer controls and all the controls below them down two grid points. The easiest way to do this is to switch to Design view, use the pointer tool to highlight all the affected controls and labels, and then move them as a group. Start by clicking on the left ruler (if you can't see the rulers, be sure Ruler is checked on the View menu) just above the ManufacturerItemCode control and then dragging down the ruler until the selection box surrounds the LongDescription control. Release the mouse button, and Access will have selected all the controls that were inside the selection box. Grab a handle on any of the controls and slide the whole selection box down two grid points. You might have to first drag the bottom margin of the detail section downward to provide room to do this.

> **TIP:** If you want to move one or more controls only horizontally or vertically, hold down the Shift key when you select the control (or the last control in a group) that you want to move and then drag your mouse either up/down or left/right. When Access detects movement either horizontally or vertically, it "locks" the movement and won't let the objects stray in the other plane. If you inadvertently start to drag horizontally when you meant to move vertically (or vice versa), click the Undo button and try again.

Next, select the Line tool from the toolbox. To draw your line, click the left side of the form, about one grid row below the Description label, and drag across to the right edge. If the line isn't exactly straight, you can drag the right end up or down to adjust it. You can also set its height to 0 in the property sheet. Click the third width button on the Palette to make the line a little thicker. Your form should now look similar to the one shown in Figure 14-23.

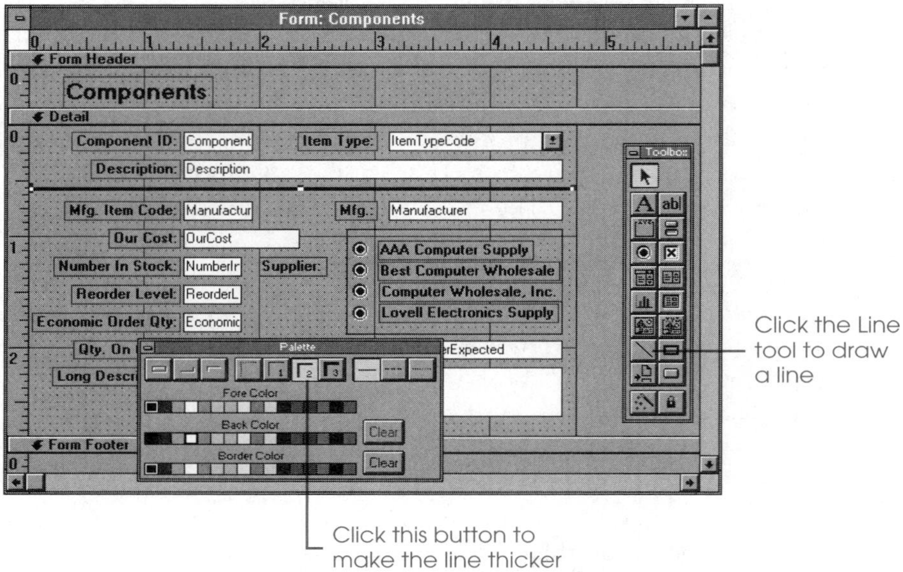

FIGURE 14-23. The Line tool is used to draw a line on a form, and the Palette is used to adjust the line width.

You can add emphasis to the SupplierID option group by drawing a rectangle around it. To do this, you might first need to move the SupplierID option group down and to the left a bit. The idea is to make the top and right edges of the new rectangle line up where the top and right edges of the option group used to be. Select the option group (if necessary) and move it down and to the left one point on the grid. Select the SupplierID label and drag it until it's again lined up with the ReorderLevel control. Now select the Rectangle tool, click where you want to place one corner of the rectangle, and drag to the intended location of the opposite corner. When you draw a rectangle around the SupplierID option group, the option group will look similar to the one shown in Figure 14-24.

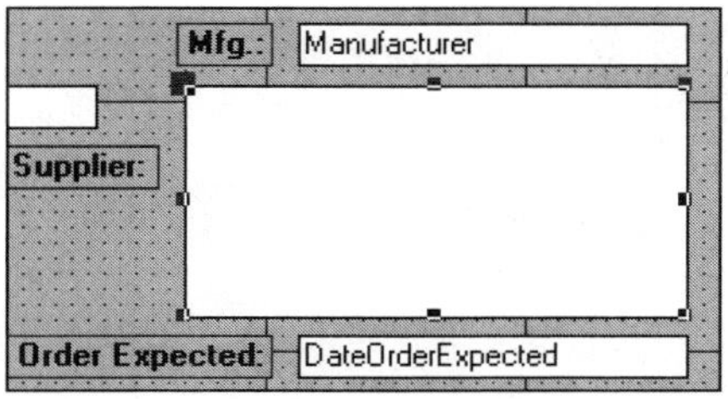

FIGURE 14-24.
A rectangle with a white background color is created, and it covers the option group.

The SupplierID option group is covered up because the default background color for the interior of the rectangle is white, not clear. Whenever you overlap one control with another, Access places the last-defined control on top. You have two choices with the rectangle selected. You can click the Clear box in the Back Color row on the Palette to make the rectangle clear and allow the SupplierID option group to show through, or you can choose the Send To Back command from the Format menu and effect the change shown in Figure 14-25. Because the default background color for labels is gray, you should select the labels and set their background color to clear if you choose the Send To Back command.

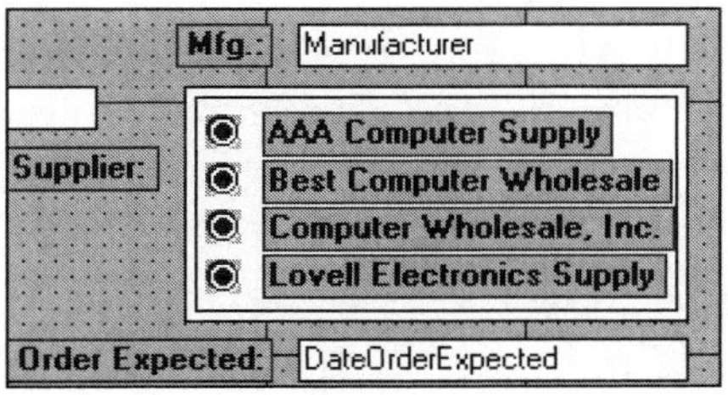

FIGURE 14-25.
The rectangle has been sent to the back of the option group control, exposing the option group that was covered in Figure 14-24.

Now you can switch to Form view and choose Size To Fit Form from the Window menu. (Remember: The form must be in the upper left part of the screen before it can be properly sized.) Your Components form should now look similar to the one shown in Figure 14-26 on the next page. Now is a good time to save your result.

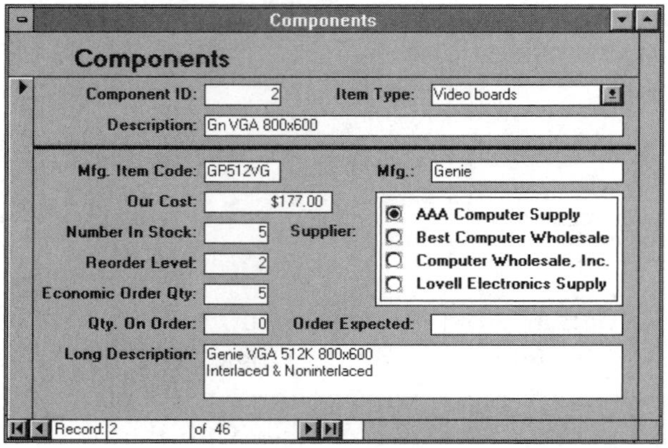

FIGURE 14-26. The Components form with a line and a rectangle added.

Color and Raised Effect

The Form Wizard added a light gray color to the background of the form for you. You can do additional things with color and special effects to highlight objects on your form. For example, you can make the SupplierID option group appear to "float" on the form. To do so, switch to Design view and select the rectangle behind the SupplierID option group. (It might take a bit of practice to select the rectangle instead of the group.) Open the Palette and click the dark gray color in the second box of the Back Color line. Your form will now look similar to the one shown in Figure 14-27.

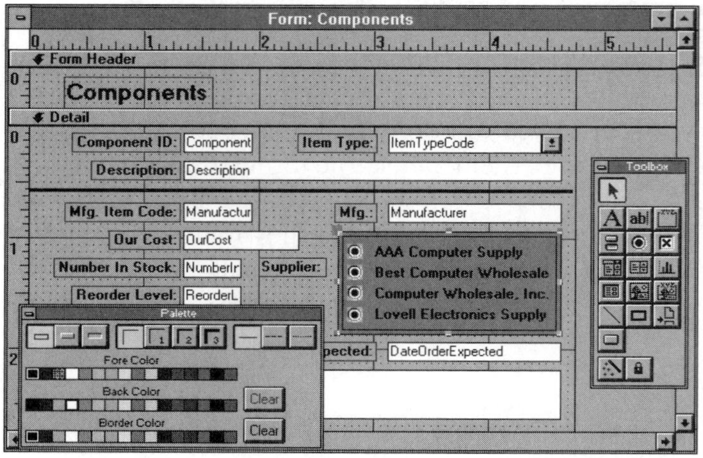

FIGURE 14-27. The rectangle behind the SupplierID option group is filled with a dark gray color.

Because the default background color of the option group is clear, the dark gray color of the rectangle behind the group shows through. Because you're using black letters for the option names, you need to make the option group lighter to improve readability. You could make the background color of the SupplierID option group light gray or white if you prefer. Access also provides a number of interesting special effects. Here's one: Select the SupplierID option group. (Again, selecting the option group and not the rectangle might be difficult, but you can keep the property sheet open nearby to verify that you've selected the group.) Click the light gray background color, and then click the Clear button (so that the button appears no longer pressed). Now click the Raised Appearance button on the Palette, as shown in Figure 14-28.

Switch to Form view to see the result of your work. The SupplierID option group now appears to "float" in the dark gray rectangle on the form, as shown in Figure 14-29 on the next page.

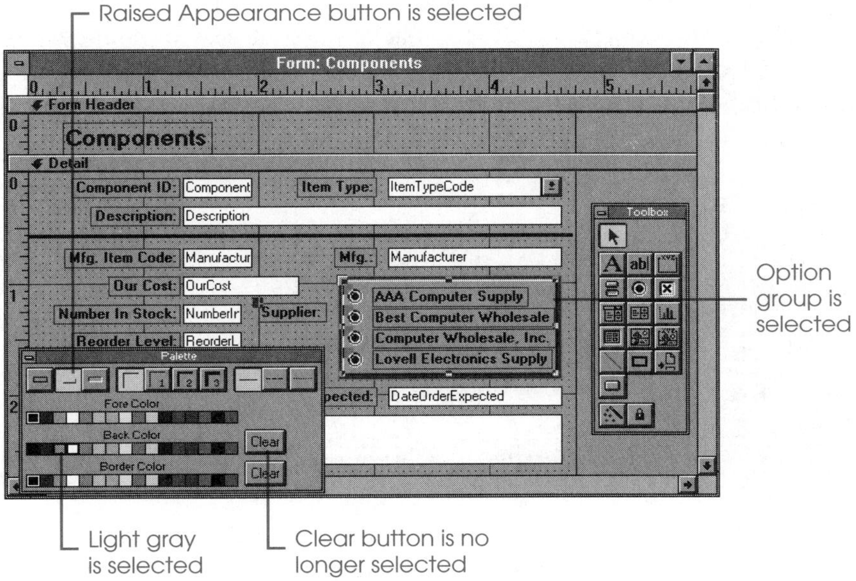

FIGURE 14-28. The SupplierID option group is a lighter color than the rectangle and appears raised.

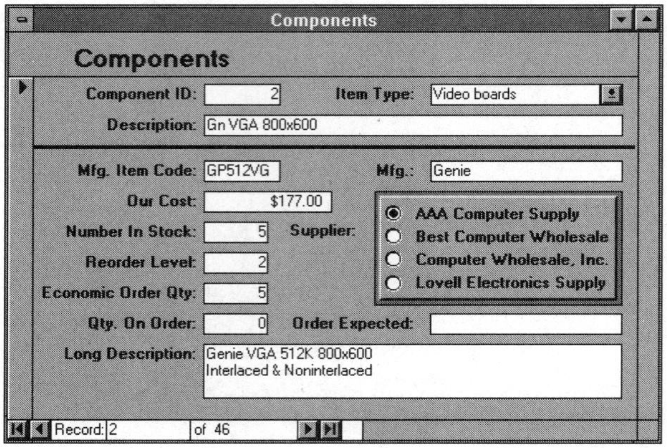

FIGURE 14-29. A "floating" SupplierID option group.

Fonts

Another way you can enhance the appearance of your forms is by varying the fonts and font sizes you use. When you select any control or label that can display text or data, Microsoft Access adds font, font size, and font attribute controls to the toolbar to make it easy to change how that control or label looks. Simply click the down arrow next to the Font combo box to open a list of all the available fonts, shown in Figure 14-30. Choose the font you want for the selected control or label.

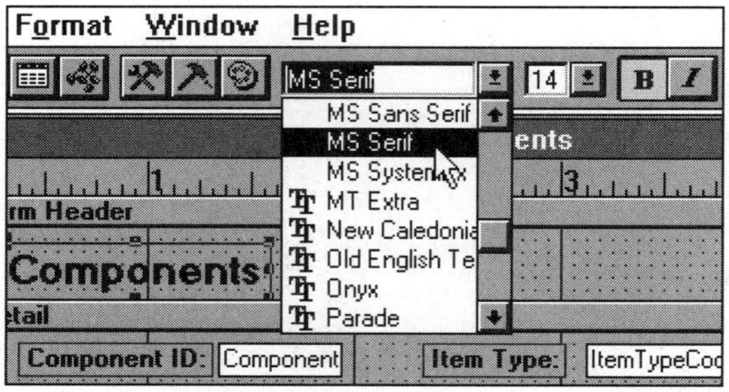

FIGURE 14-30. An open list in the Font combo box.

In this case, it might be interesting to add some character to the Components label in the form header. Select the label in the form header, and change the font from MS Sans Serif to MS Serif. Open the Font Size combo box to the right of the Font combo box and select a size of 18 points. Click the Italic button to add an italic tilt. You might find that you must resize the label in order to fit the larger text. Use a handle to resize the label, or choose Size To Fit from the Format menu. When you've finished, the label will look similar to the one shown in Figure 14-31.

You should note that a form with too many fonts or font sizes will look busy and jumbled. In general, you should choose only two or three fonts per form. Use one font and font size for most data in controls and labels. Make the label text bold or colored for emphasis. Choose a second font for controls in the headers and perhaps a third for information you include in the form footer.

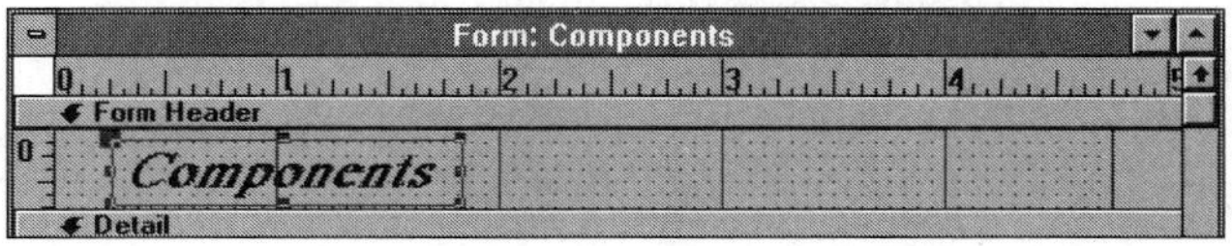

FIGURE 14-31.
The header Components label with new font, font size, and italic settings.

Setting Control Properties

Microsoft Access gives you several additional properties for each control to allow you to customize the way your form works. These properties affect formatting, the presence or absence of scroll bars, and the enabling or locking of records.

Format

In the property sheet of each text box, combo box, and list box, you can find three properties that you can set to determine how Access displays your data on the form. These properties are Format, Decimal Places, and Input Mask, shown in Figure 14-32 on the next page.

See Also: You can find a detailed discussion of the Input Mask property in Chapter 5, "Building Your Database in Microsoft Access."

Access copies these properties from the definition of the fields in the underlying table. If you haven't specified a Format property in the field definition, Access chooses a default Format property for the control, depending on the data type of the field bound to the control. You can customize the appearance of your data by choosing a format setting from the list that you can open on the Format entry of the control's property sheet or by entering a custom set of formatting characters. The following sections present the format settings and formatting characters available for each data type.

FIGURE 14-32. The list of format settings for the NumberInStock control, a Number data type.

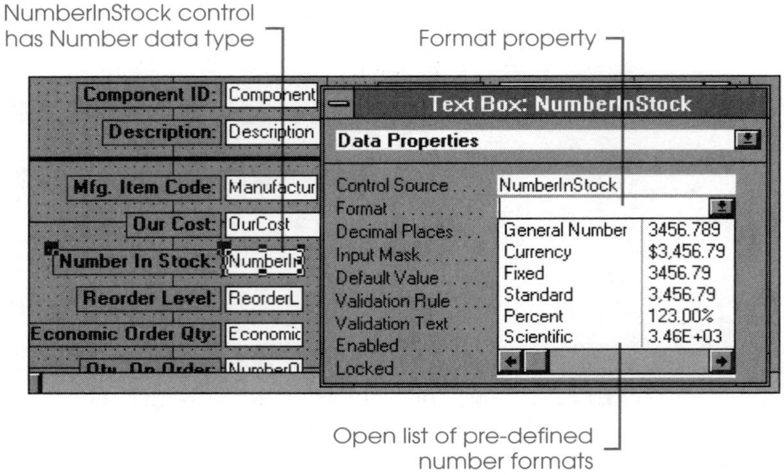

Numbers and Currency

If you don't specify a Format property setting for a control that displays a number or currency value, Microsoft Access displays numbers in a General Number format and currency in a Currency format. You can choose from six format settings, as shown in Figure 14-33.

You can also create your own custom format. You can specify a different display format for Access to use (depending on whether the numeric value is positive, negative, 0, or Null) by providing up to four format specifications in the Format property. The specifications must be separated by semicolons. When you enter two specifications, Access uses the first for all non-negative numbers and the second for negative numbers. When you provide three specifications, Access uses the third specification to display numbers with a value of 0. Provide the fourth specification to indicate how you want Null values handled.

To create a custom number format, use the formatting characters shown in Figure 14-34. Notice that you can include text strings in the format and specify a color to use to display the number on the screen.

Number/Currency Format	Description
General Number	Displays numbers as entered with up to 11 significant digits. When the number contains more than 11 significant digits, Microsoft Access first rounds the number to 11 decimal places and then uses exponential format for very large or very small numbers (more than 10 digits to right or left of the decimal point).
Currency	Displays numeric data according to the Currency setting in the International section within the Control Panel of the Microsoft Windows operating system. For the U.S. layout, Access uses a leading dollar sign, maintains two decimal places (rounded), and encloses negative numbers in parentheses.
Fixed	Displays numbers without thousands separator and with two decimal places.
Standard	Displays numbers with thousands separator and with two decimal places.
Percent	Multiplies value by 100, displays two decimal places, and adds a trailing percent sign.
Scientific	Displays numbers in scientific (exponential) notation.

FIGURE 14-33.
The format settings for the Number and Currency data types.

Formatting Character(s)	Usage
Decimal separator	Use to indicate where you want Microsoft Access to place the decimal point. Use the decimal separator defined in the International section of the Control Panel in the Microsoft Windows operating system. In the U.S. layout, the separator is a period (.).

FIGURE 14-34. *(continued)*
The formatting characters for the Number and Currency data types.

FIGURE 14-34. *continued*

Formatting Character(s)	Usage
Thousands separator	Use to indicate placement of the thousands separator character that is defined in the International section of the Windows Control Panel. In the U.S. layout, the separator is a comma (,).
0	Use to indicate digit display. If no digit exists in the number in this position, Access displays 0.
#	Use to indicate digit display. If no digit exists in the number in this position, Access displays a blank.
- + $ ( ) space	Use these characters anywhere you want in your format string.
"text"	Use double quotation marks to embed any text you want displayed.
\	Use to always display the immediately following character (the same as including a single character in double quotes).
!	Use to force left alignment.
*	Use to generate the immediately following character as a fill character. Access normally displays formatted data right-aligned and filled with blanks to the left.
%	Use to multiply the value by 100 and include a trailing percent sign.
E– or e–	Use to generate scientific (exponential) notation and display a minus sign preceding negative exponents. It must be used with other characters, as in *0.00E–00*.
E+ or e+	Use to generate scientific (exponential) notation and display a minus sign preceding negative exponents and a plus sign preceding positive exponents. It must be used with other characters, as in *0.00E+00*.
[*color*]	Use brackets to display the text in the color specified. Valid color names are Black, Blue, Green, Cyan, Red, Magenta, Yellow, and White. A color name must be used with other characters, as in *0.00[Red]*.

For example, if you want to display a number with two decimal places and comma separators when positive, surrounded by parentheses and shown in red when negative, "Zero" when 0, and "Not Entered" when Null, specify

#,##0.00;(#,##0.00)[Red];"Zero";"Not Entered"

To format a U.S. phone number and area code from a numeric field, specify

(000) 000-0000

Text

If you don't specify a Format property setting for a control that displays a text value, Access displays the data in the control left-aligned. You can also specify a custom format with one to three entries separated by semicolons. If you include a second format specification, Access uses that specification to show Null and empty values. If you include a third format specification, Access uses the second specification to show empty values and the third specification to show Null values. Notice that when you specify formatting for text, Access displays the data in the control right-aligned.

If a text field contains more characters than the number of formatting characters you provide, Access uses up the formatting characters and then appends the extra characters at the end with the fill character (if any) in between. Figure 14-35 lists the formatting characters applicable to character strings.

Formatting Character(s)	Usage
@	Use to display any available character or a space in this position.
&	Use to display any available character in this position. If no characters are available to display, Microsoft Access displays nothing.
<	Use to display all characters in lowercase.
>	Use to display all characters in uppercase.

FIGURE 14-35. *(continued)*

The formatting characters for the Text data type.

FIGURE 14-35. *continued*

Formatting Character(s)	Usage
- + $ ( ) space	Use these characters anywhere you want in your format string.
"text"	Use double quotation marks to embed any text you want displayed.
\	Use to always display the immediately following character (the same as including a single character in double quotes).
!	Use to force left alignment. It also forces placeholders to fill left to right instead of right to left.
*	Use to generate the immediately following character as a fill character. Access normally displays formatted data right-aligned and filled with blanks to the left. The asterisk must be used with other characters, as in >*@-@@@.
[*color*]	Use brackets to display the text in the color specified. Valid color names are Black, Blue, Green, Cyan, Red, Magenta, Yellow, and White. A color name must be used with other characters, as in >*[Red]*.

For example, if you want to display a six-character text part number with a hyphen between the second character and the third character, left-aligned, specify

```
!@@-@@@@
```

To format a check amount string in the form of "Fourteen Dollars and 59 Cents" so that Access displays an asterisk (*) to fill any available space between the word "and" and the cents amount, specify

```
**@@@@@@@@
```

Using the above format in a text box wide enough to display 62 characters, Access displays

"Fourteen Dollars and 59 Cents"

as

"Fourteen Dollars and *********************************59 Cents"

and

"One Thousand Two Hundred Dollars and 00 Cents"

as

"One Thousand Two Hundred Dollars and ****************00 Cents"

Date/Time

If you don't specify a Format property setting for a control that displays a Date/Time value, Microsoft Access displays the Date/Time in the General Date format. You can also choose one of the seven format settings shown in Figure 14-36.

Date/Time Format	Description
General Date	Displays the date as numbers separated by the date separator character. Displays the time as hours and minutes separated by the time separator character and followed by an AM/PM indicator. If the value has no time part, Microsoft Access displays the date only. If the value has no date part, Access displays the time only. Example: 3/15/94 06:17 PM.
Long Date	Displays the date according to the Long Date format in the International section of the Control Panel in the Windows operating system. Example: Monday, March 15, 1994.
Medium Date	Displays the date as dd-mmm-yy. Example: 5-Mar-94.
Short Date	Displays the date according to the Short Date format in the International section of the Windows Control Panel. Example: 3/15/94.
Long Time	Displays the time according to the Time format in the International section of the Windows Control Panel. Example: 6:17:12 PM.

FIGURE 14-36. *(continued)*

The format settings for the Date/Time data type.

FIGURE 14-36. *continued*

Date/Time Format	Description
Medium Time	Displays the time as hours and minutes separated by the time separator character and followed by an AM/PM indicator. Example: 06:17 PM.
Short Time	Displays the time as hours and minutes separated by the time separator character using a 24-hour clock. Example: 18:17.

You can also specify a custom format with one or two entries separated by semicolons. If you include a second format specification, Access uses that specification to show Null values. Figure 14-37 lists the formatting characters applicable to Date/Time data.

Formatting Character(s)	Usage
Time separator	Use to show Microsoft Access where to separate hours, minutes, and seconds. Use the time separator defined in the International section of the Windows Control Panel. In the U.S. layout, the separator is a colon (:).
Date separator	Use to show Access where to separate days, months, and years. Use the date separator defined in the International section of the Windows Control Panel. In the U.S., the separator is a forward slash (/).
c	Use to display the General Date format.
d	Use to display the day of the month as one or two digits, as needed.
dd	Use to display the day of the month as two digits.
ddd	Use to display the day of the week as a three-letter abbreviation. Example: Saturday = Sat.

FIGURE 14-37. *(continued)*
The formatting characters for the Date/Time data type.

FIGURE 14-37. *continued*

Formatting Character(s)	Usage
dddd	Use to display the day of the week fully spelled out.
ddddd	Use to display the Short Date format.
dddddd	Use to display the Long Date format.
w	Use to display a number for the day of the week. Example: Sunday = 1.
ww	Use to display the week of the year (1–54).
m	Use to display the month as a one-digit or two-digit number, as needed.
mm	Use to display the month as a two-digit number.
mmm	Use to display the name of the month as a three-letter abbreviation. Example: March = Mar.
mmmm	Use to display the name of the month fully spelled out.
q	Use to display the calendar quarter number (1–4).
y	Use to display the day of the year (1–366).
yy	Use to display the last two digits of the year.
yyyy	Use to display the full year value (within the range 0100–9999).
h	Use to display the hour as one or two digits, as needed.
hh	Use to display the hour as two digits.
n	Use to display the minutes as one or two digits, as needed.
nn	Use to display the minutes as two digits.
s	Use to display the seconds as one or two digits, as needed.
ss	Use to display the seconds as two digits.
ttttt	Use to display the Long Time format.
AM/PM or am/pm	Use to display 12-hour clock values with trailing AM or PM, as appropriate.

(continued)

FIGURE 14-37. *continued*

Formatting Character(s)	Usage
A/P or a/p	Use to display 12-hour clock values with trailing A or P, as appropriate.
AMPM	Use to display 12-hour clock values using forenoon/afternoon indicators as specified in the International section of the Windows Control Panel.
- + $ ( ) space	Use these characters anywhere you want in your format string.
"text"	Use quotation marks to embed any text you want displayed.
\	Use to always display the immediately following character (the same as including a single character in double quotes).
!	Use to force left alignment.
*	Use to generate the immediately following character as a fill character. Access normally displays formatted data right-aligned and filled with blanks to the left. The asterisk must be used with other characters, as in *A/P*#*.
[*color*]	Use brackets to display the text in the color specified. Valid color names are Black, Blue, Green, Cyan, Red, Magenta, Yellow, and White. A color name must be used with other characters, as in *ddddd[Red]*.

For example, to display a date as full month name, day, and year (say, *December 20, 1992*) with a color of cyan, you would specify

```
mmmm dd, yyyy[Cyan]
```

Yes/No

You can choose from one of three standard formats—Yes/No, True/False, On/Off—to display Yes/No data type values, as shown in the table in Figure 14-38. Of the three, the Yes/No format is the default. As you've seen earlier, it's often more useful to display Yes/No values in a check box or an option button rather than in a text box.

Yes/No Format	Description
Yes/No (the default)	Displays 0 as No and any nonzero value as Yes.
True/False	Displays 0 as False and any nonzero value as True.
On/Off	Displays 0 as Off and any nonzero value as On.

FIGURE 14-38.
The format settings for the Yes/No data types.

NEW!

You can also specify your own custom word or phrase for Yes and No values. To do that, specify a format string containing three parts separated by semicolons. Leave the first part empty, specify a string enclosed in double quotation marks (and with an optional color modifier) in the second part for Yes values and another string (also with an optional color modifier) in the third part for No values.

For example, to display "True" for Yes and "False" for No in a Yes/No field, you would specify

```
True/False
```

To display "Invoice Sent" in red for Yes and "Not Invoiced" in blue for No, you would specify

```
;"Invoice Sent"[Red];"Not Invoiced"[Blue]
```

NOTE: If you specify both an Input Mask setting (see Chapter 5, "Building Your Database in Microsoft Access") and a Format setting, Access uses the Input Mask setting to display data when you move the focus to the control and uses the Format setting at all other times. If you don't include a Format setting but do include an Input Mask setting, Access formats the data using the Input Mask setting. Be careful not to define a Format setting that conflicts with the Input Mask. For example, if you define an Input Mask setting for a phone number that looks like this:

```
!\(###") "000\-0000;0;_
```
(this stores the parentheses and hyphen with the data)

and a Format setting that looks like this:

(&&&) @@@-@@@@

your data will display as

(2060 5) 55--1212

Format Specifications for Components

To format the data in the Components form's controls, you might want to set the Format and Decimal Places properties as indicated in Figure 14-39. The Components form in Form view will then look similar to the one shown in Figure 14-40. (Notice that I updated one of the NumberIn-Stock values to a number greater than 1000 to show the comma generated by the Standard format.)

Control	Data Type	Format	Decimal Places
OurCost	Currency	Currency	Auto
NumberInStock	Number	Standard	0
ReorderLevel	Number	Standard	0
EconomicOrderQty	Number	Standard	0
NumberOnOrder	Number	Standard	0
DateOrderExpected	Date/Time	Long Date	Auto

FIGURE 14-39.
The settings for the Format and Decimal Places properties of some Components form controls.

Scroll Bars

When you have a control that can contain a long data string (for example, the LongDescription control on the Components form), it's a good idea to provide a scroll bar in the control to make it easy to scan through all the data. This scroll bar appears whenever you select the control. If you don't add a scroll bar, you must use the arrow keys to move down and up through the data.

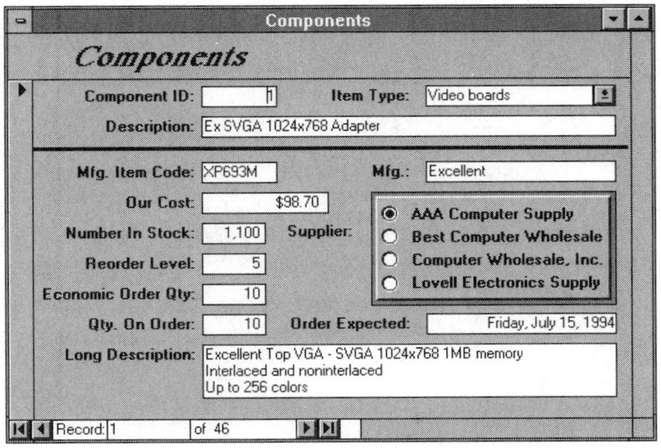

FIGURE 14-40. The Components form with control formats specified.

To add a scroll bar, first open the Components form in Design view. Select the LongDescription control and open the property sheet. Then set the Scroll Bars property to Vertical. If you open the Components form in Form view and tab to (or click inside) the LongDescription text box, the vertical scroll bar appears, as shown in Figure 14-41.

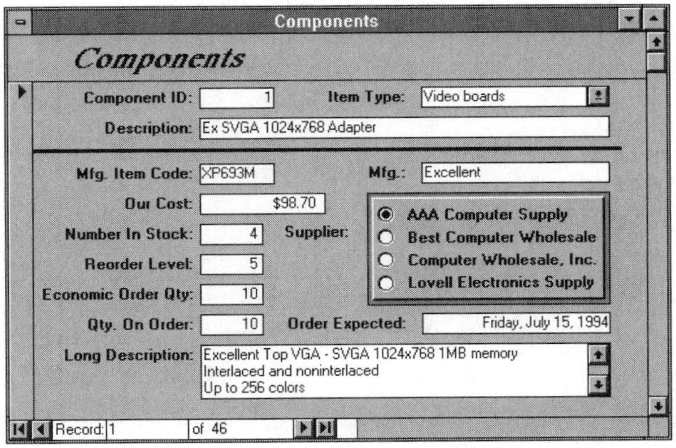

FIGURE 14-41. The Long-Description control with a scroll bar added.

Enabling and Locking

You might not want users of your form to select or update certain controls. You can set these conditions with the control's Enabled and Locked properties. For example, because the ComponentID control on the Components form is a counter and Access always provides the counter's value, it's a good idea to set the control's Enabled property to No (so that the user can't select it) and the control's Locked property to Yes (so that the user can't update it). Figure 14-42 shows the effects of the Enabled and Locked property settings.

Enabled	Locked	Description
Yes	Yes	Control can have the focus. Data is displayed normally and can be copied but not changed.
No	No	Control can't have the focus. Control and data appear dimmed.
Yes	No	Control can have the focus. Data is displayed normally and can be copied and changed.
No	Yes	Control can't have the focus. Data is displayed normally but can't be copied or changed.

FIGURE 14-42.
The combinations of settings for the Enabled and Locked properties.

NEW!

In some cases, you might want to allow a control to be selected with the mouse but be skipped over as you tab through the controls on the form. You can set the control's Tab Stop property to No while leaving its Enabled property set to Yes. This might be useful for controls for which you also set the Locked property to Yes to prevent updating. Setting the Tab Stop property to No keeps you from tabbing into the control as you enter data, but you can select the control with the mouse to use the Find command or to copy the data in the control to the Clipboard.

Setting Form Properties

There are a number of properties for the form itself that you can use to control its appearance and how it works.

Default View and Views Allowed

When the Form Wizard built the original form for you, it set the Default View property for the form to Single Form. This is the view you'll see first whenever you open the form. Note that with the Single Form setting, you can see only one record at a time. You have to use the record number box, the arrows to the left and right of the record number box, or the Go To command on the Records menu to move to another record. If you set the Default View property for the form to Continuous Forms, you can see multiple records on a short form, and you can use the scroll bar on the right side of the form to move down through the records. Because one record's data in the Components table fills the form, the Single Form setting is probably the best choice.

With another property, Views Allowed, you can control whether a user can change to a Datasheet view of the form. The default setting is Both, meaning that a user can use the toolbar or the View menu to switch between views. If you're designing a form to be used in an application, you will usually want to eliminate either Form or Datasheet view. For the Components form, set the Views Allowed property to Form; you should see the Datasheet button on the toolbar become gray (disabled).

Setting the Tab Order

After the Form Wizard built the form, you moved several controls around and changed the ItemTypeCode control to a combo box and the SupplierID control to an option group. As you design a form, Access sets up the tab order for the controls in the order in which the controls are defined. You can set the tab order you want, however. Choose the Tab Order command from the Edit menu to see the Tab Order dialog box, as shown in Figure 14-43.

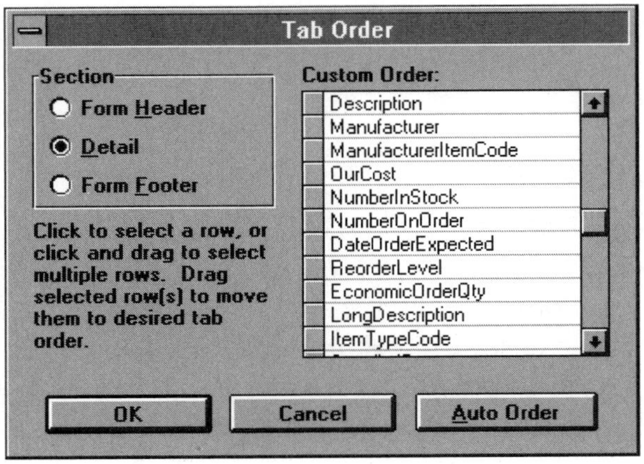

FIGURE 14-43.
The Tab Order dialog box.

As you can see, the ItemTypeCode control is near the bottom of the list in Figure 14-43, even though you positioned it at the top of the form. Click the Auto Order button to reorder the controls so that the tab order corresponds to the arrangement of the controls on the form, from left to right and from top to bottom. You can make additional adjustments to the list (such as moving the SupplierID option group to last in the list) by clicking the selector button for a control to highlight it, and then clicking the selector button again and dragging the control to the location in the list you want. Click OK to save your changes to the tab order list.

NEW! You can also set the tab order for an individual control by changing the control's Tab Index property. The Tab Index property of the first control on the form is 0, the second 1, and so on. If you assign a new Tab Index setting to a control and some other control already has that Tab Index setting, Access resequences the Tab Index settings as though you had dragged the control to that relative position in the Tab Order dialog box.

Setting Record Selectors, Scroll Bars, and Navigation Buttons

Because the form you've been designing displays one record at a time, it might not be all that useful to show the record selector on the left side of the form. You've also designed the form to show all the data in a single window, so a scroll bar down the right side of the window really isn't necessary. You probably should keep the record number box at the bottom of the form, but you don't need the horizontal scroll bar. To make these changes, set the form's Record Selectors property on the property sheet to No, the Scroll Bars property to Neither, and the Navigation Buttons property to Yes. Your form should look something like the one shown in Figure 14-44.

Creating a Pop-Up or Modal Form

You might occasionally want to design a form that stays in view on top of all other forms even when it doesn't have the focus. You might have noticed that the toolbox, property sheet, field list, and Palette in Design view all have this characteristic. These are called *pop-up forms.* You make the Components form a pop-up form by setting the form's Pop Up

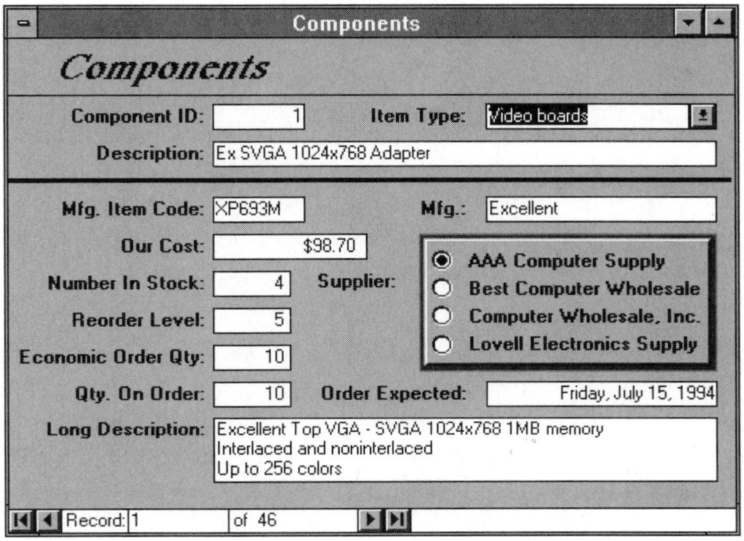

FIGURE 14-44.
The Components form without a record selector or scroll bars.

property to Yes. Figure 14-45 shows the Components form as a pop-up form in front of the Database window that has the focus. (Note: Be sure to set the form's Pop Up property back to No.)

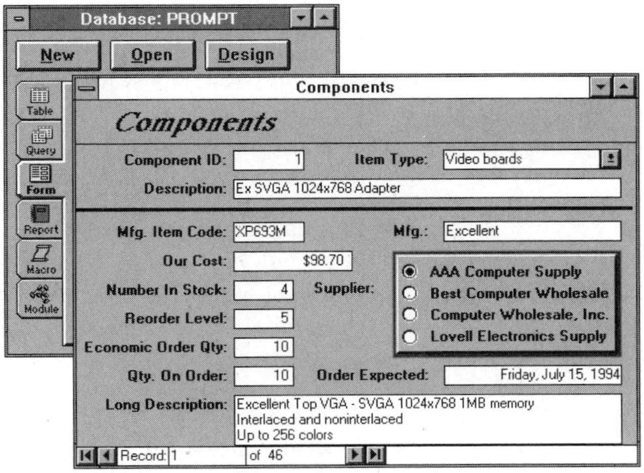

FIGURE 14-45.
The Components form as a pop-up form in front of the Database window that has the focus.

As you'll learn in Part 6 of this book, it's sometimes useful to create forms that ask the user for some information that's needed to perform the next task. Forms have a Modal property that you can set to Yes to "lock" the user into the form when it's open. (The form must be saved before Access will recognize this change.) The user has to make a choice on the form or close the form to be able to go on to other tasks. While a modal form is open, you can switch to another application, but you can't select any other form, menu, or toolbar button in Access until you dismiss the modal form. You've probably noticed that most dialog boxes are modal forms. Modal isn't a good choice for the Components form, but you'll use it later to help control application flow. (Note: Be sure to set the Components form's Modal property back to No.)

Controlling Editing

You can set several properties on forms to control whether data on the form can be updated or whether data in the underlying tables can change. These properties and their settings are shown in this table:

Default Editing	Determines whether a user can update data in controls on the form, including controls that are not bound to fields. The possible settings are:	
	Allow Edits	Lets you update data in any controls.
	Read Only	Disallows any updating, including unbound controls.
	Data Entry	Sets the form for appending records only. You cannot display existing records. You can return to edit mode by choosing the Show All Records command from the Records menu.
	Can't Add Records	Allows updating but disallows adding rows. The user can't access the "new" row beyond the end of the current set of records or choose the Data Entry or Go To New command from the Records menu.
Allow Editing	Determines whether the Editing Allowed command on the Records menu is enabled. The Editing Allowed command allows users to update data even if the Default Editing property is set to Read Only. The possible settings are:	
	Available	Enables the Editing Allowed command on the Records menu.
	Not Available	Disables the Editing Allowed command on the Records menu.

<table>
<tr><td>Allow Filters</td><td colspan="2">Determines whether a user can see selected records by applying filter and sorting criteria and whether the user can see all records by choosing the Show All Records command on the Records menu. If you set the Default Editing property to Data Entry and set the Allow Filters property to No, the user can only enter new data with this form and cannot change the form to view other existing records. The valid settings for the Allow Filters property are Yes and No.</td></tr>
<tr><td>Allow Updating</td><td colspan="2">Determines which, if any, fields in tables you can update through this form. The possible settings are:</td></tr>
<tr><td></td><td>Default Tables</td><td>Allows you to change information only in underlying tables or queries of the form. If the underlying object is a single table, you can change all fields except calculated fields. If the underlying object is a query, you can change only fields in the table that are updatable. (See Chapter 8, "Adding Power with Select Queries," for details on update rules for joined tables.)</td></tr>
<tr><td></td><td>Any Tables</td><td>Allows you to update any field in any underlying table or query. Access does not enforce rules for updating joined tables when you choose this option. Use this option with care.</td></tr>
<tr><td></td><td>No</td><td>Does not allow you to update any fields in tables, although you can update unbound controls.</td></tr>
</table>

Setting the Control Box, Min Button, and Max Button Properties

In some cases, you might not want to allow the user to open the Control menu on the form (the Control menu contains the Restore, Move, Size, Minimize, Maximize, Close, and Next commands) or to minimize or maximize the form. If you have special processing that you want to do before a form closes, you might want to provide a command button to do the processing and then close the form. You can set the form's Control Box property to No to remove the Control-menu box from the upper left corner of the form window. You can set the form's Min Button property to No to remove the form's Minimize button (this also grays the

Minimize command on the form's Control menu). You can also set the form's Max Button property to No to remove the form's Maximize/Restore button (this also grays the Minimize and Restore commands on the form's Control menu).

CAUTION: If you remove the form's Control-menu box, the only way to close the form is to use the Ctrl-F4 key combination. If you create an *Autokeys* macro (see Chapter 23, "The Finishing Touches") that intercepts the Ctrl-F4 key combination, you must provide an alternative way to close the form—most likely with a command button. See Part 6 for information on building a command button to close a form.

Setting Border Style

In most cases, you'll want to create forms that have a normal border that allows you to size the window and move it around. Forms have a Border Style property that lets you define both the look of the border and whether the window can be sized or moved. The Border Style property has the following settings:

None	The form has no borders, Control-menu box, title bar, or Minimize and Maximize buttons. You cannot resize or move the form when it is open. You can select the form and press Ctrl-F4 to close it unless you have also set the form's Pop Up property to Yes. You should take care to provide an alternative way to close this type of form.
Thin	The form has a thin border, signifying that the form cannot be resized.
Sizable	This is the default setting. The form can be resized.
Dialog	If the Pop Up property is set to Yes, the form's border is a thick double line (like that of a true Windows dialog box), signifying that the form cannot be resized. If the Pop Up property is set to No, the Dialog setting is the same as the Thin setting.

Setting Control Defaults

You can use the Apply Default and Change Default commands on the Format menu to apply and change the defaults for the various controls you can use on your form. If you've placed a control on your form and modified the control but you don't like the way it turned out, you can restore the control's default property settings by selecting the control and choosing Apply Default from the Format menu. If you want to change the default property settings for all new controls of a particular type, select a control of that type, set the control's properties to the desired default values, and then choose the Change Default command from the Format menu. The settings of the currently selected control will become the default settings for any subsequent definitions of that type of control on your form.

For example, you might want all labels to have blue text on a white background. To accomplish this, place a label on your form and set the label's Fore Color property to blue and the Back Color property to white using the Palette. Choose the Change Default command from the Format menu while this label is selected. Any new labels you place on the form will have the new settings.

You can also create a special form to define new default properties for all your controls. To do this, open a new blank form, place controls on the form for which you want to define default properties, modify the properties of the controls to your liking, and save the form with the name *Normal*. The Normal form becomes your *form template*. Any new control that you place on a form (except forms for which you've already changed the default for one or more controls) will use the new default property settings you defined for that control type on the Normal form.

Setting Form Design Options

You can also customize the way you work with forms in Design view by setting the Form & Report Design options. Choose the Options command from the View menu and select the Form & Report Design category, as shown in Figure 14-46 on the next page.

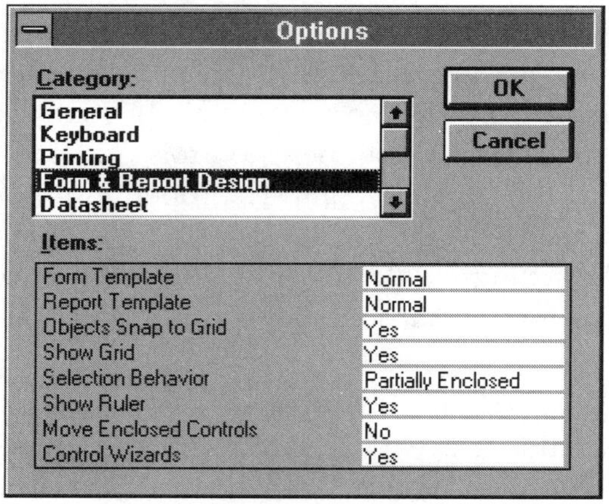

FIGURE 14-46. The Options dialog box with the Form & Report Design category selected.

With these options you can change the name of your form template from Normal to something else. You can also set whether the Snap To Grid command is on and whether you can see the grid and the ruler. You can set Selection Behavior to Fully Enclosed so that any selection box you draw on the grid must fully enclose a control in order to select it. With the Partially Enclosed setting, only part of a control must be inside a selection box for the control to be selected. If you set Move Enclosed Controls to Yes, you can select a control that covers or surrounds other controls. You can then move that control, and Microsoft Access will move all enclosed controls with it. Finally, you can set an option that determines whether Control Wizards are active when you create an option group, a combo box, a list box, or a command button.

Now you should be comfortable with designing forms and adding special touches to make your forms more attractive and usable. In the next chapter, you'll learn about "power forms": using queries with data from multiple tables in forms, building forms within forms, adding pictures and graphs, and doing simple form linking with command buttons.

15

Advanced Form Design

In the last two chapters, you learned how to design a form that works with data in a table. Although you saw how to display some data from another table by using a combo box or a list box, you haven't learned how to consolidate in a form the information from multiple tables. In this chapter, you'll find out how to

- Create a form using a query that joins multiple tables
- Embed a *subform* in a *main form* so that you can work with related data from two tables or queries at the same time
- Enhance forms with pictures or graphs
- Link two related forms with a simple command button

Basing a Form on a Query

In Chapter 8, you learned how to bring together data from multiple tables using queries. The result you get when you run a select query is called a *recordset.* A recordset contains all the information you need, but it's in the unadorned Datasheet view format. Forms enable you to present this data in a more attractive and meaningful way. And in the same way that you can update data in queries, you can also update data using a form that is based on a query.

A Many-to-One Form

As you discovered in the past few chapters, it's easy to design a form that allows you to view and update the data from a single table. You also learned how to include selected single fields from related tables using a list box or a combo box. But what if you would like to see more information from the related tables? The best way to do this is to design a query based on the two (or more) related tables and use that query as the basis of your form.

Most of the time when you create a query with two or more tables, you're working with one-to-many relationships between the tables. As you learned earlier, Microsoft Access lets you update any data in the table that is on the "many" side of the relationship and any nonkey fields on the "one" side of the relationship. So, when you base a form on a query, you can update all of the fields in the form that come from the "many" table and most of the fields from the "one" side. Because the primary purpose of the form is to search and update records on the "many" side of the relationship while reviewing information on the "one" side, this is called a *many-to-one* form.

In the last two chapters, for example, you created and customized a form to view and update data from the Component and Supplier tables in the PROMPT database. You created an option group to deal with setting the supplier ID on the assumption that there are four suppliers and there won't ever be any others. This was probably a bad assumption, but it provided an interesting exercise for learning how to build option groups.

Suppose instead that there will ultimately be dozens of suppliers. How to best handle this? You could simply add a combo box to display the supplier name to help set the supplier ID correctly for each component. Be aware, however, that you want to use this form for more than just data entry. If you're using the Components form to search for items low in stock, it would be nice to have the supplier address and phone number handy when you find a component you need to reorder. You could base your form on a query that selects information from the Component and Supplier tables. Every supplier might produce many components, but each component has just one supplier. You'll be building a many-to-one form.

Designing a Many-to-One Query

First, you must design a query that contains the fields you need. Open a new Query window in Design view and add the Component and Supplier field lists using the Add Table command from the Query menu. You should see a relationship line from the SupplierID field in the Supplier field list to the SupplierID field in the Component field list. If you don't, you need to close the Query window and go back to the Database window, choose the Relationships command from the Edit menu, add the appropriate one-to-many relationship between the Supplier and Component tables, and then open a new Query window and add the Component and Supplier field lists.

Because you want to be able to update all fields in the Component table, drag the special "all fields" indicator (*) from the Component field list to the QBE grid. From the Supplier table, you need the SupplierName, SupplierAddress1, SupplierAddress2, SupplierCity, SupplierState,

SupplierPostal, and SupplierPhone fields. Do not include the SupplierID field from Supplier; you want to be able to update the SupplierID field, but only in the Component table. If you include the SupplierID field from the Supplier table, it might confuse you later as you design the form.

You should end up with a query that looks like the one shown in Figure 15-1. Save this query as *Components And Suppliers*. (If you're working in the sample PROMPT database, you'll find this query already defined.)

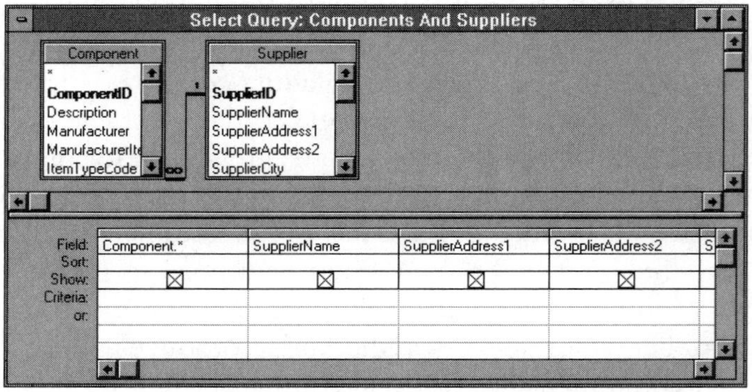

FIGURE 15-1. The Components And Suppliers query in Design view.

Designing a Many-to-One Form

Open the Components form you created earlier in Design view. In the property sheet for the form, change the Record Source setting from Component (the table) to *Components And Suppliers* (the query), as shown in Figure 15-2.

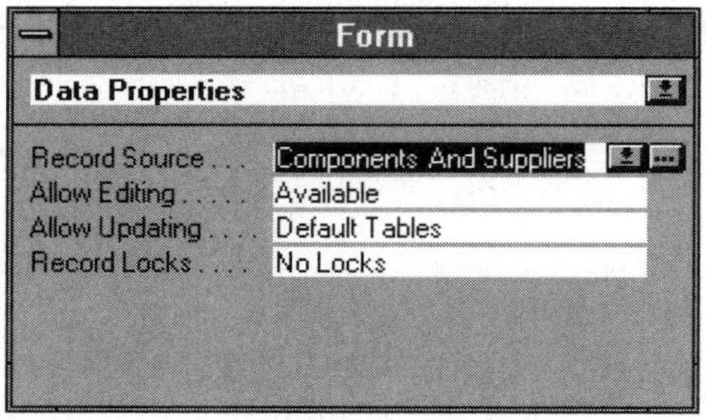

FIGURE 15-2. The form's Record Source setting has been changed to the new Components And Suppliers query.

Now you need to delete the old Supplier option group and replace that group with a combo box for the SupplierID field and text boxes for the SupplierAddress1, SupplierAddress2, SupplierCity, SupplierState, SupplierPostal, and SupplierPhone fields. As shown in Figure 15-3, you can leave the shaded rectangle to provide emphasis for the supplier data. Use the technique you learned earlier for building the ItemType-Code combo box (described in the Chapter 13 section titled "Creating a Combo Box to Display Item Type") to display the supplier name in the SupplierID control. With this technique you tie the supplier ID display to the SupplierID and SupplierName columns from the Supplier table—and then you hide the first column (SupplierID). The appropriate settings for the combo box property sheet are shown in Figure 15-3.

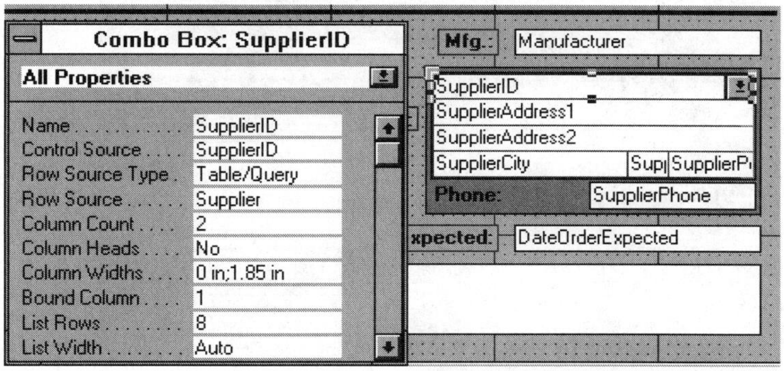

FIGURE 15-3. The new supplier controls and the property sheet for the SupplierID control.

Remember: Access lets you update any nonkey fields on the "one" (Supplier) side of a query. In this case, you can change the supplier's address, city, state, zip, and phone number fields. Once you change any of these fields, however, the change becomes effective for all components provided by this supplier. Perhaps it would be a good idea to issue a warning if a user tries to update these fields in this form. (You'll learn how to do that in Chapter 22.) For now, set the Enabled property to No and the Locked property to Yes for the SupplierAddress1, Supplier-Address2, SupplierCity, SupplierState, SupplierPostal, and SupplierPhone controls. With these settings, you won't be able to tab to or select any of these controls. For the SupplierID control, be sure to leave the Enabled property set to Yes and the Locked property set to No so that you can update the data in that control.

The results of these changes in Form view are shown in Figure 15-4 on the next page. When you find the component you want, you can immediately see the relevant supplier name, address, and phone information. You can also update the supplier ID in the Components form by opening the combo box and selecting a new supplier name. Notice that because the underlying SupplierID field is a number, you have to set the Text Align property of the SupplierID control to Left if you want to see the text value for the supplier name correctly aligned with the supplier address information.

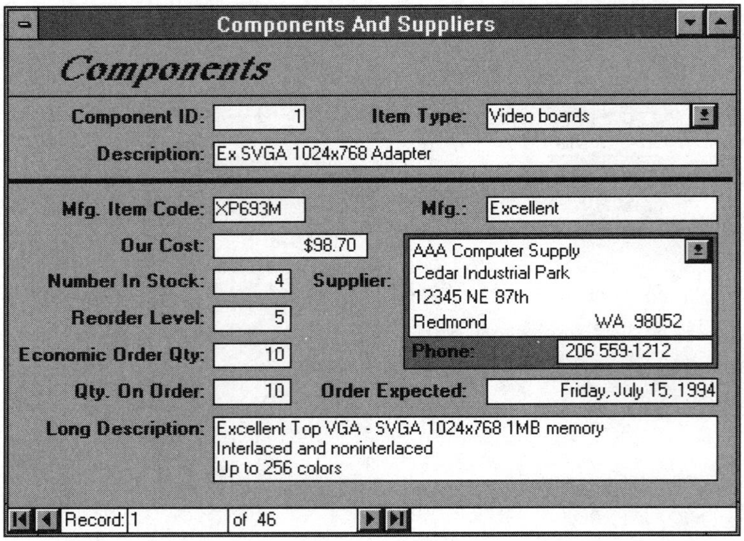

FIGURE 15-4. The Components form is now a Components And Suppliers many-to-one form.

TIP: If you want to end up with a white box and no lines for the supplier information (as shown in Figure 15-4), you can use combo boxes and text boxes with no border. To do this, click the Clear button in the Border Color row on the Palette. To create the outline around the supplier information, you can add a clear rectangle behind the controls. Finally, you can carefully enter settings for the Left, Top, Width, and Height properties so that the text boxes all touch each other and appear as a single display area.

A Form on a Joined Crosstab Query

In Chapter 8, in the section titled "Crosstab Queries," you built a crosstab query to display sales totals by catalog item and month. The resulting query in Datasheet view was interesting, but not very usable. You could convert the query to a make table query and export the result to a spreadsheet program to format or graph the data. But why do that when you can format and graph the crosstab query data directly using a form?

Designing the Crosstab Query

Imagine that at the end of each year you copy the monthly sales data to a sales summary for the year. In this example, you'll create a crosstab query named *1993 Sales Crosstab,* which displays and formats the data in a form. Start with the crosstab query for Monthly Item Sales Query from Chapter 8, and save it as *1993 Sales Crosstab.* Use the Add Table command on the Query menu to add the Type field list to the Query window. Drag the TypeDescription field to the QBE grid. Set its Crosstab row to Row Heading and its Sort row to Ascending. In the expression for the date, you can remove the "yy" formatting characters because you're going to select only 1993 data. As shown in Figure 15-5, the expression reads *Expr1: Format(DateSerial([Year],[Month],1),"mmm").*

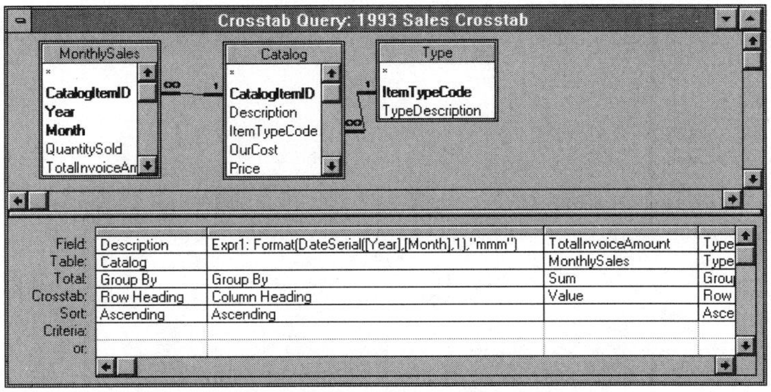

FIGURE 15-5. The first three fields of the 1993 Sales Crosstab query in Design view.

For variety, also drag the OurCost and Price fields from the Catalog field list to the QBE grid. Set their Total rows to Group By (the default) and their Crosstab rows to Row Heading. Drag the Year field from the MonthlySales field list to the QBE grid, set the Total row to Where, and add *1993* to the Criteria row, as shown in Figure 15-6. Finally, remove the fixed column headings for the crosstab query by choosing the Properties command from the View menu, clicking in the top section of the QBE grid to see the query properties, and removing the settings in the Column Headings property in the property sheet. You'll use the form to set the months in the order you want.

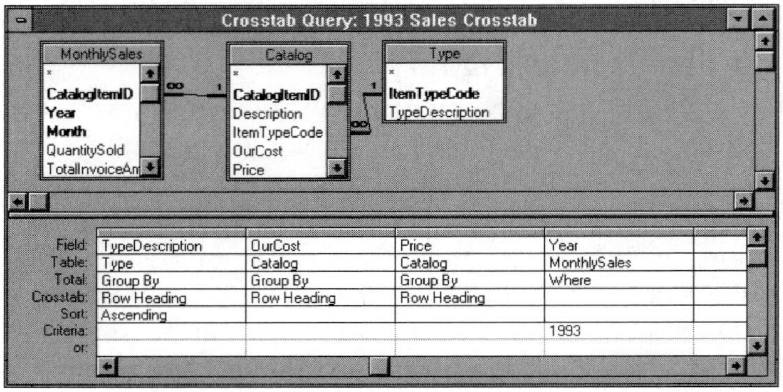

FIGURE 15-6.
The last four fields of the 1993 Sales Crosstab query in Design view.

When you run the query shown in Figure 15-6, you should get a recordset similar to the one shown in Figure 15-7. Save the 1993 Sales Crosstab query with your changes. (If you're working in the PROMPT sample database, you'll find this query already defined.) Now you're ready to build the form to handle this data.

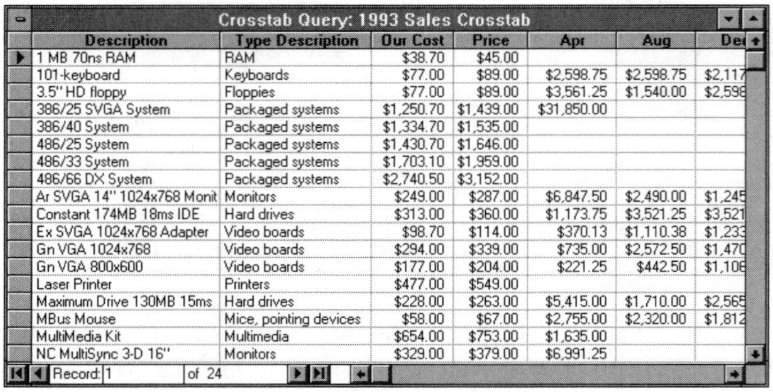
Crosstab Query: 1993 Sales Crosstab

Description	Type Description	Our Cost	Price	Apr	Aug	De
1 MB 70ns RAM	RAM	$38.70	$45.00			
101-keyboard	Keyboards	$77.00	$89.00	$2,598.75	$2,598.75	$2,117
3.5" HD floppy	Floppies	$77.00	$89.00	$3,561.25	$1,540.00	$2,598
386/25 SVGA System	Packaged systems	$1,250.70	$1,439.00	$31,850.00		
386/40 System	Packaged systems	$1,334.70	$1,535.00			
486/25 System	Packaged systems	$1,430.70	$1,646.00			
486/33 System	Packaged systems	$1,703.10	$1,959.00			
486/66 DX System	Packaged systems	$2,740.50	$3,152.00			
Ar SVGA 14" 1024x768 Monit	Monitors	$249.00	$287.00	$6,847.50	$2,490.00	$1,245
Constant 174MB 18ms IDE	Hard drives	$313.00	$360.00	$1,173.75	$3,521.25	$3,521
Ex SVGA 1024x768 Adapter	Video boards	$98.70	$114.00	$370.13	$1,110.38	$1,233
Gn VGA 1024x768	Video boards	$294.00	$339.00	$735.00	$2,572.50	$1,470
Gn VGA 800x600	Video boards	$177.00	$204.00	$221.25	$442.50	$1,106
Laser Printer	Printers	$477.00	$549.00			
Maximum Drive 130MB 15ms	Hard drives	$228.00	$263.00	$5,415.00	$1,710.00	$2,565
MBus Mouse	Mice, pointing devices	$58.00	$67.00	$2,755.00	$2,320.00	$1,812
MultiMedia Kit	Multimedia	$654.00	$753.00	$1,635.00		
NC MultiSync 3-D 16"	Monitors	$329.00	$379.00	$6,991.25		

Record: 1 of 24

FIGURE 15-7.
The 1993 Sales Crosstab query in Datasheet view.

Designing the Crosstab Form

Create a new form based on the crosstab query you've just designed. The easiest way to get started is to use the Form Wizard. Select the single-column design and the standard format. When the Form Wizard displays the list of fields you can place on the form, you should see the fields you added to the 1993 Sales Crosstab query and a list of months in alphabetic sequence. If you choose the fields in calendar sequence, the Form Wizard will place them on the form in that order. Choose the standard format, and title this new form *1993 Sales By Month And Quarter.*

After you have the basic form built by the Form Wizard, you can create four columns of numbers on the form, one for each calendar quarter, as shown in Figure 15-8. Add column labels to enhance the appearance of your form. Because you only want to view data in this form, it's a good idea to set the properties for every control on the form to the following settings: Default Editing property to Read Only, Allow Editing property to Unavailable, and Allow Updating property to No Tables. You can set the form's Default View property to Single Form (sales totals for one item at a time) or to Continuous.

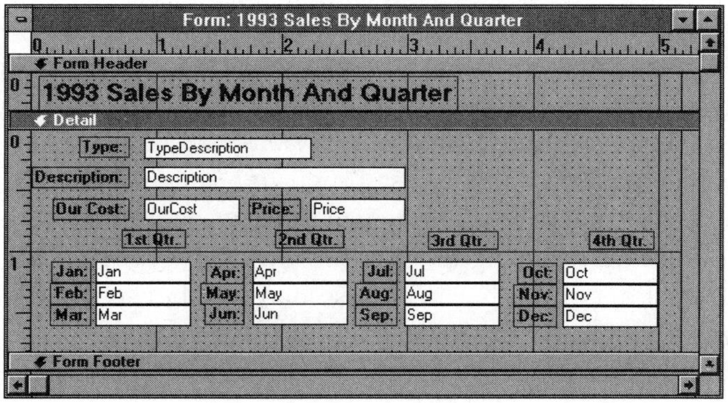

FIGURE 15-8.
A form based on the 1993 Sales Crosstab query.

When you switch to Form view, you can see the result, as shown in Figure 15-9 on the next page. (You might need to view another record to see numbers in all the text boxes.)

FIGURE 15-9.
The Form view of the form shown in Figure 15-8.

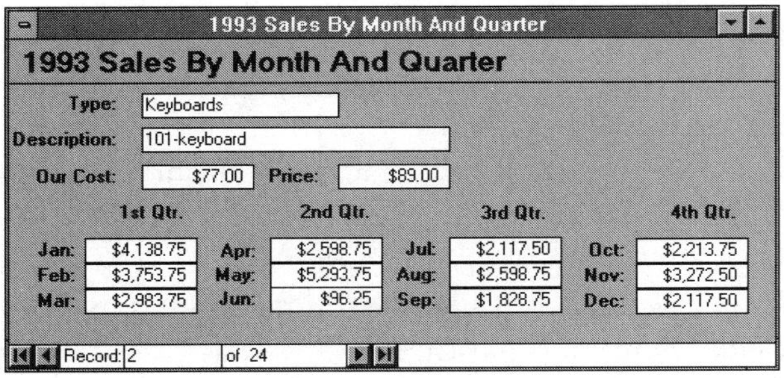

The form in this example is a single-form view with no vertical scroll bars. You can move to different records by clicking the arrows to the left and right of the record number box.

Adding Calculated Values

The form shown in Figure 15-9 is a much more interesting view of the crosstab recordset than the query's Datasheet view, but even here you've only begun to tap the capabilities of Microsoft Access. For example, you can add some totals for each quarter and a grand total for the year. To generate totals, you add some text boxes that aren't bound to any fields in the underlying query. Simply select the Text Box tool from the toolbox, and then click in the form at the location where you want to place the upper left corner of the text box control. Add four quarterly total controls under each column of months. Delete all labels attached to these controls except the first one, as shown in Figure 15-10. Set each total control's Format property to Currency. Change each control's Name property to something meaningful, such as Qtr1Tot, Qtr2Tot, Qtr3Tot, and Qtr4Tot. You'll need to reference these names when you create the calculation for the grand total, and these names make more sense than the "Field*nn*" names that Access creates by default

You can display the result of any calculated expression in an unbound text box control. Simply enter the expression preceded by an equal sign (=) in the control's Control Source property in the property sheet. You can also select the control, click in the text box area, and then type the expression directly. An even easier way is to use the Expression Builder. Select the Qtr1Tot text box control, click in the Control Source property box in the property sheet, and then click the Build button (not the drop-down button) that appears on the far right of the property box. The Expression Builder window opens, as shown in Figure 15-11.

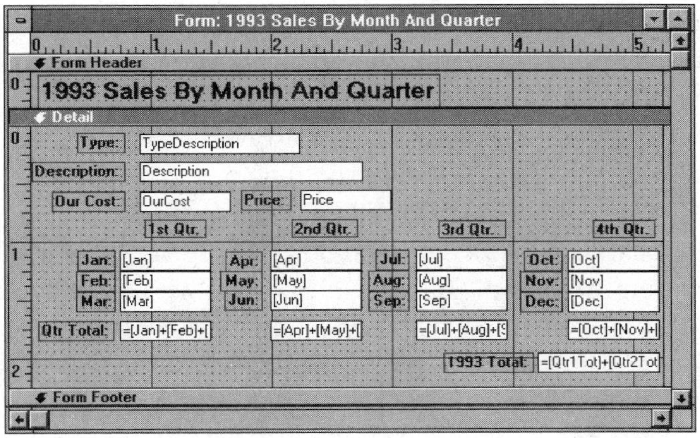

FIGURE 15-10.
The four quarterly total controls and the grand total control have been added to the form.

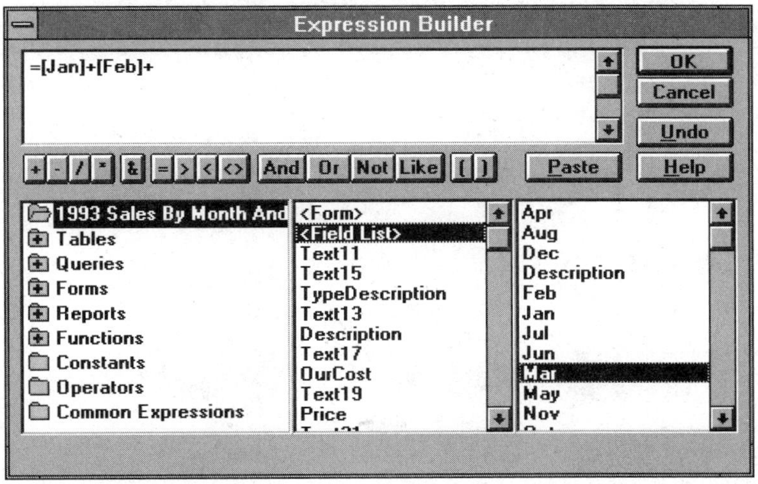

FIGURE 15-11.
A summation expression being created with the Expression Builder.

The expression you're building appears in the top text box. In the lower left list box are all the types of objects in your database as well as handy folders containing constants, special operators, and common expressions. At the top of the list is the current object, the form you are designing. In the center list box, the Expression Builder displays controls or fields for the object you've selected in the left list box. The right list box shows properties of the object you've selected in the center list box.

When you first open the window, the Expression Builder selects the current form in the left list box, selects the <Form> object in the center list box, and shows you the form properties in the right list box.

When you create an expression using data in bound controls, you can refer either to the control name (shown farther down the list in the center list box) or to the field name from the underlying query. To see field names, choose the second item in the center list box, <Field List>, and the Expression Builder shows you the list of field names in the right list box.

As you can see in Figure 15-11, I've begun to build a simple expression to add the data from the first three months of the year. I first clicked the Equal Sign button, then picked Jan in the right list box and clicked Paste, then clicked the Plus Sign button, then added Feb, and so on. You'll notice that Access adds brackets around field and control names in expressions. Because you can use spaces in names in Access, you need to add open and close brackets to delimit names that contain spaces in expressions. Although you can leave out the brackets for simple names such as these that don't have embedded spaces, it's a good idea to get in the habit of always adding the brackets. When you finish building your expression, click OK to paste it into the Control Source property box.

Create a similar grand total unbound text box and label in the lower right corner of the form. Use the Expression Builder window to create an expression that adds together the four quarterly total controls you created. Your result should look something like that shown in Figure 15-12.

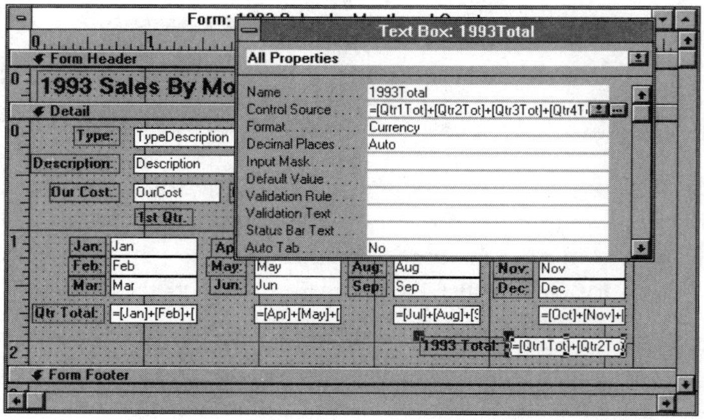

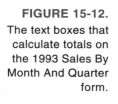

FIGURE 15-12. The text boxes that calculate totals on the 1993 Sales By Month And Quarter form.

Figure 15-13 shows the form in Form view. I happened to pick a product that didn't have any sales in the month of April. You'll notice that the April box is blank—as are the second quarter total and the grand total! This is because crosstab queries return a Null value if there's no matching data for a particular column. Although totals functions in queries can ignore Nulls, when you reference a field or control that contains a Null value in a calculated numeric expression, the result is always Null. So the second quarter total is Null because April is Null, and the grand total is Null because the second quarter total is Null.

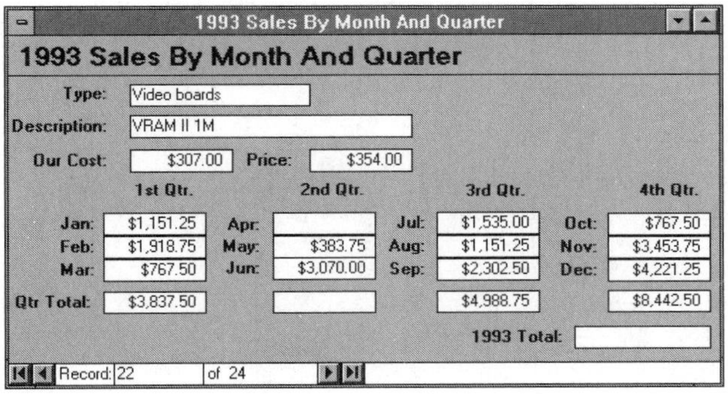

FIGURE 15-13. The Form view of the form shown in Figure 15-12.

To fix this, you can add a special function expression to either the month controls or the quarterly total controls to substitute 0 for Null values. It's a bit more work to fix all twelve month controls, but because it would be nice to display a *0* in the month, it'll be worth the effort. Rather than making the control source for each month the field from the query, substitute a special function called *IsNull* to test for a Null value and use the *IIF* function to return the field value if it isn't Null or a 0 if it is. The expression for the Jan control looks like this:

```
=IIF(IsNull([Jan]),0,[Jan])
```

Basically, the *IsNull* function tests the value you include in parentheses; it returns True if the value is Null or False if the value is not Null. The *IIF* function tests the first value (the *IsNull*) for True or False. If the value is True, *IIF* returns the second value; otherwise, *IIF* returns the third value. So, if the value of the [Jan] field is Null, the expression returns a 0, but if the value of the [Jan] field is not Null, the expression returns the value of the [Jan] field.

Because you're now specifically referencing the field from the underlying query (Jan) in a control that the Form Wizard also named "Jan," you need to change the name of the control so that you don't have the control's expression referring to itself. A name like "JanTot" will work fine. You also need to change the expression in the quarter total controls to refer to [JanTot], [FebTot], and so on so that you're adding the values in the controls instead of the fields from the underlying query. Finally, because you're now using an expression to display the month total values, Access doesn't know that you want the values displayed as currency. Set the Format property of the monthly controls to Currency to display dollar values instead of unformatted numbers. After you make all these changes, your result should look like that shown in Figure 15-14. Save this form—you'll use it later to learn how to work with graphs.

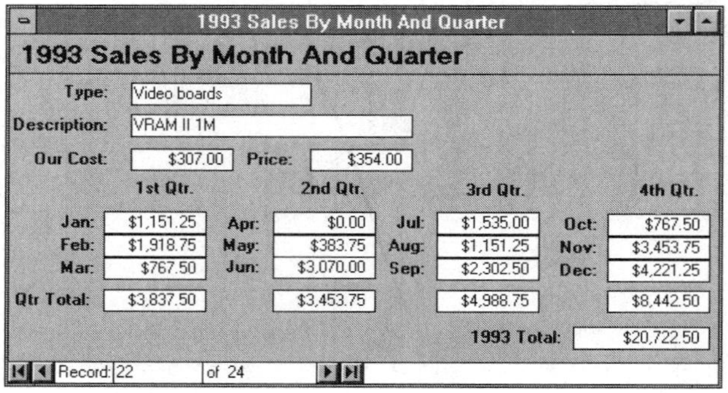

FIGURE 15-14.
The 1993 Sales By Month And Quarter form with the Null problem fixed.

Creating Subforms

If you want to show data from several tables and be able to update the data in more than one of the tables, you probably need something more complex than a standard form. In the PROMPT database, the company's products are listed in the Catalog table. Because Prompt Computer Solutions sells assembled systems, there's also a separate Component table of component parts.

There's another table, called CatalogComponent, that links the Catalog and Component tables. The CatalogComponent table lists the components in each assembled system. The Catalog table is related one-to-many to the CatalogComponent table (because an assembled system can be made of many components). The Component table is also related one-to-many to the CatalogComponent table (because a component—for example, a disk drive—might be included in several system configurations).

You could create a single form to display rows from the Catalog table and the related components, but you would be able to see only one component of a product at a time. You would possibly have to scroll through several displays to see all the components that make up a given product. Trying to add a component to a product would be very cumbersome because you wouldn't be able to tell at a glance whether that component was already part of that product.

The combined query linking rows from the Catalog, CatalogComponent, and Component tables would allow you to create a new product in the catalog, add a new component, or link existing components to existing products. To link a new component to a new product, you would have to be very careful to first enter the catalog and component data and then type in the matching linking data in the CatalogComponent table. Also, such a query would not allow you to delete, for example, an obsolete catalog product that no longer had any related components.

To be able to see a catalog product and all related components in a single-form view, you need to create a form with another form embedded: a *main form* to handle rows from the Catalog table and a *subform* to handle rows from the CatalogComponent table. When you build such a form/subform, Microsoft Access allows you to create a link to keep the two forms synchronized; you see on the CatalogComponent subform only those components that belong to the catalog product displayed on the main form.

Designing the Subform Source

You can embed forms within forms up to three layers deep. You should always start by designing the innermost form and work outward. Begin by deciding on the source of data for the subform.

In the problem stated above, you want to create or update rows in the CatalogComponent table to create, modify, or destroy links between systems in the Catalog table and components in the Component table. Also, you'll want to modify the display; the CatalogComponent table contains only two linking fields and a quantity—not very useful information to display on a form. You need to include the Component table in the subform so that you can display component descriptions, and you need to include the Types table so that you can show the kind of component you're adding.

Start by opening a new query. Use the Add Table command on the Query menu to add the field lists for the CatalogComponent, Component, and Type tables to the Query window. You want to be able to update all the fields in the CatalogComponent table, so copy them to the QBE grid. You will set the ComponentID control on the subform to display the Description field from the Component table, so you don't need to add the Description field to the QBE grid. Instead, add the OurCost field from the Component table so that you can calculate the total cost of the component in an unbound text box on the subform. Add the TypeDescription field from the Type table so that you can also display the related component type without resorting to a combo box or a list box. Your query should look similar to the one shown in Figure 15-15.

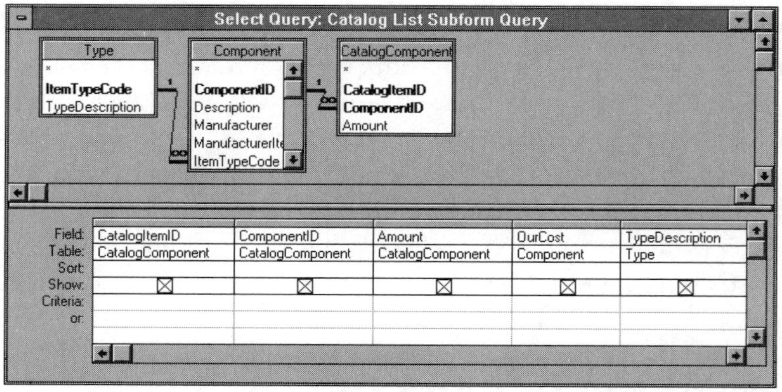

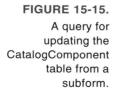

FIGURE 15-15. A query for updating the CatalogComponent table from a subform.

Notice that the Type table is related to the Component table one-to-many, and the Component table is related to the CatalogComponent table one-to-many. This means that you can update any field in the CatalogComponent table (including both key fields as long as you don't create a duplicate row) because the CatalogComponent table is at the "bottom" of the hierarchy. You can update any of the nonkey fields in either the Type table or Component table, but not the ItemTypeCode field in the Type table or the ComponentID field in the Component table. Your focus is on the CatalogComponent table, so you won't be taking advantage of the ability to update fields in the Type table or Component table. Save the query and name it *Catalog List Subform Query* so that you can use it as you design the subform. (If you're working in the PROMPT sample database, you'll find this query already defined.)

Designing the Subform

It would be nice to display the component name, type, amount, and cost in Datasheet view with multiple rows that you could scroll through to see all the parts that belong to a particular assembled computer system. But you can't display a form header or footer in Datasheet view. However, you can build a form that <u>looks</u> and acts like a datasheet but also has a customized header and a footer for displaying a calculated total. Start by opening a new form based on the Catalog List Subform query you just created. Try creating the form without using the Form Wizard.

Figure 15-16 on the next page shows the design for the subform. If you line up controls of equal height in a row in the detail section, and then size the section so that it shows only those controls, and finally set the Default View property of the form to Continuous Forms, the form will look like a datasheet when you switch to Form view. At the same time, in Design view you can add a header and a footer by choosing the Form Header/Footer command from the Layout menu. Notice that this form includes in the footer a total of cost multiplied by amount for all the rows on the form—another use of a calculation in an unbound control.

This form design also uses a combo box to update the ComponentID in the CatalogComponent table. The ID by itself isn't very meaningful, so the combo box displays the ComponentDescription field from a query that sorts component information by ItemTypeCode and then by Description. You can use the Query Builder on the Row Source property to build a query that contains the ComponentID and ComponentDescription fields sorted on ComponentDescription. In the sample PROMPT database, you'll find a Component Sorted By Type query that does this. (Refer to the section titled "Combo Boxes and List Boxes" in Chapter 13 for details on using the Query Builder to set a combo box's Row Source property.) The settings for the combo box are shown in Figure 15-16.

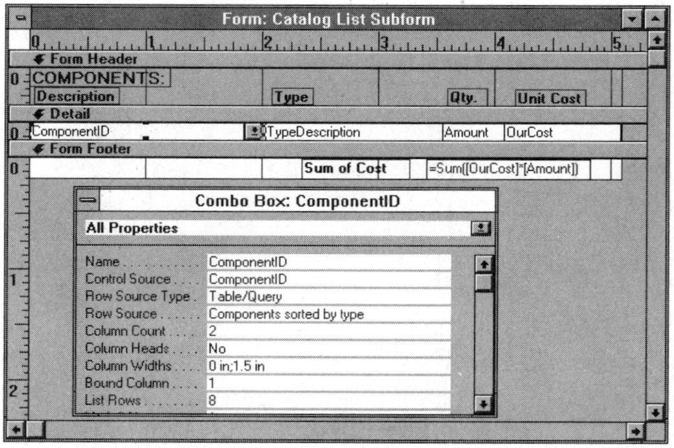

FIGURE 15-16. The Catalog List Subform form that will eventually be embedded as a subform.

If you're curious, you can open this Catalog List Subform form in Form view. Because you haven't yet limited catalog item ID numbers to unique values by embedding this form as a subform, you'll get a row for every component in every catalog product—including duplicates—and a grand total cost at the bottom, as shown in Figure 15-17. Notice that this form looks like a Datasheet view even though it's really a continuous Form view, with a header, a footer, and an embedded combo box.

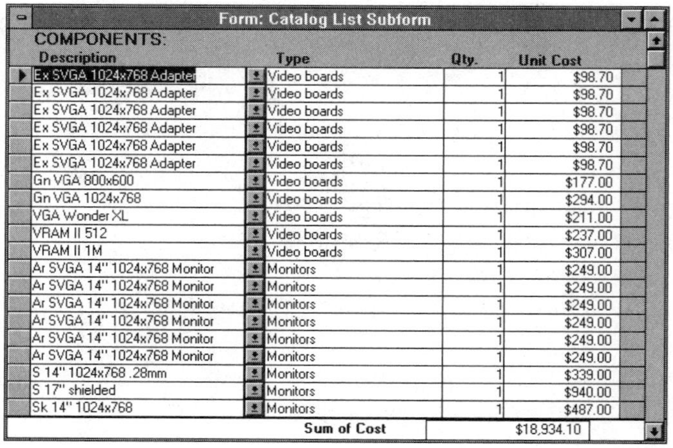
Form: Catalog List Subform

COMPONENTS:

Description	Type	Qty.	Unit Cost
Ex SVGA 1024x768 Adapter	Video boards	1	$98.70
Ex SVGA 1024x768 Adapter	Video boards	1	$98.70
Ex SVGA 1024x768 Adapter	Video boards	1	$98.70
Ex SVGA 1024x768 Adapter	Video boards	1	$98.70
Ex SVGA 1024x768 Adapter	Video boards	1	$98.70
Ex SVGA 1024x768 Adapter	Video boards	1	$98.70
Gn VGA 800x600	Video boards	1	$177.00
Gn VGA 1024x768	Video boards	1	$294.00
VGA Wonder XL	Video boards	1	$211.00
VRAM II 512	Video boards	1	$237.00
VRAM II 1M	Video boards	1	$307.00
Ar SVGA 14" 1024x768 Monitor	Monitors	1	$249.00
Ar SVGA 14" 1024x768 Monitor	Monitors	1	$249.00
Ar SVGA 14" 1024x768 Monitor	Monitors	1	$249.00
Ar SVGA 14" 1024x768 Monitor	Monitors	1	$249.00
Ar SVGA 14" 1024x768 Monitor	Monitors	1	$249.00
Ar SVGA 14" 1024x768 Monitor	Monitors	1	$249.00
S 14" 1024x768 .28mm	Monitors	1	$339.00
S 17" shielded	Monitors	1	$940.00
Sk 14" 1024x768	Monitors	1	$487.00
	Sum of Cost		$18,934.10

FIGURE 15-17. The Catalog List Subform form in Form view.

Choosing the Main Form Source

Now it's time to move on to the main form. You'll need a table or query as the source of the form. You want to be able to view, update, add, and delete catalog products, so you could use the Catalog table as the source. However, your principal concern is assembled systems, not all catalog products. By creating a Catalog Main Form query instead of using the Catalog table as the source of your form, you can sort the catalog items based on item type code and ensure that assembled systems appear first in the form. Figure 15-18 shows the query you need. An easy way to create your query is to drag all Catalog fields at once to the QBE grid (using *) and then to add the ItemTypeCode field with the Show check box unchecked. Save the query and name it *Catalog Main Form Query* to use in your main form. (If you're working in the PROMPT sample database, you'll find this query already defined.)

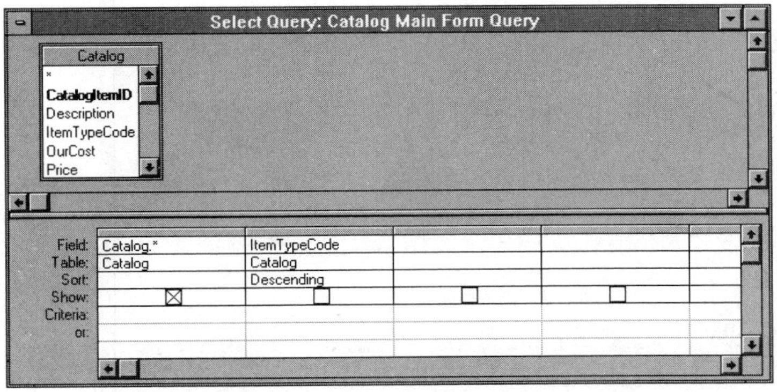

FIGURE 15-18.
A query for updating the Catalog table from a main form.

Creating the Main Form

Building the form for catalog products is fairly straightforward. In fact, you can select the Catalog Main Form Query and use a Form Wizard to build the basic form in both single-column and shadowed formats. If you decide to use these formats, you must be careful when you move controls around because the shadow boxes behind the controls are actually separate rectangle controls. The best way to drag and move the shadow and the control together is to drag the mouse pointer to create a selection box around both the control and its shadow and move them as a group. If you want to change the width or height of a control box and its shadow rectangle, choose both controls and then type in the new width or height value in the property sheet.

Look at the form shown in Figure 15-19. The CatalogItemID field has been placed in the form header because it's a counter that Microsoft Access maintains. You can also use the Combo Box Wizard to create a combo box for the ItemTypeCode field based on the TypeDescription field to make it easy to choose the code for a catalog item.

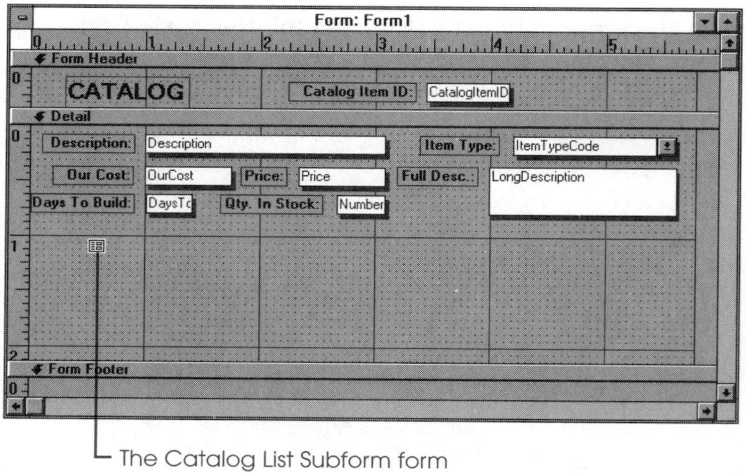

FIGURE 15-19. The Catalog List Subform form is being dragged to the Catalog main form, where it will appear as a subform.

Although you can use the Subform tool to add a subform control, the easiest way to add the subform to the main form is to drag and drop the subform onto the main form. To do this, move the Form window in Design view to the side so that you can see the Database window; click the Forms tab in the Database window, click the Catalog List Subform form, and drag and drop it onto the open main form that you're building. (See Figure 15-18.) When you do this, Microsoft Access sizes the width of the subform control based on the width of the subform. With the subform in place, you should make the subform control high enough to display four or five rows of content—perhaps 1¼ inches high. You can further adjust the size of the subform after you've seen how it looks in Form view. Your result should look like that shown in Figure 15-20.

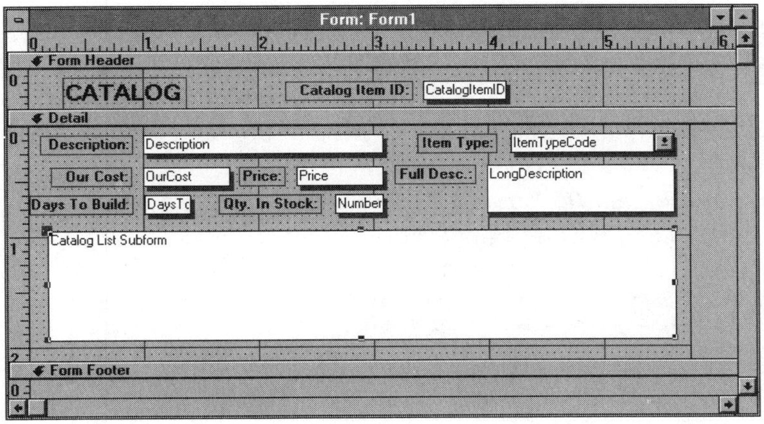

FIGURE 15-20. The Catalog main form with the subform added in Design view.

> **TIP:** You can use the Size To Fit command on the Format menu to help you size a subform control or any control that displays multiple lines. Size To Fit sets the width of the control based on the size of the subform. In addition, this command "shrinks" the height of the form to the next full line. If you want to stretch a multiple-line control to handle one more line, drag the bottom of the control down a little more than one line width and then use Size To Fit to "snap" the control back to the nearest whole line.

Linking the Main Form and the Subform

To link the main form and the subform, you need to set three properties for the subform control. The property sheet is shown in Figure 15-21 on the next page. If you used the Subform tool to create an unbound subform control, you need to enter the name of the form you want to use as a subform for the Source Object property. The name in this case is Catalog List Subform. If you dragged and dropped the subform onto the main form, Microsoft Access set the Source Object property for you. In the Link Master Fields property box, you must enter the name of the control on the main form whose value determines what Access displays on the subform; in this case, it's the *CatalogItemID* field from the Catalog table. Likewise, type the name of the linking field on the subform in the Link Child Fields property box. The linking field also happens to be named *CatalogItemID,* but the linking field is on the subform and originates in the CatalogComponent table.

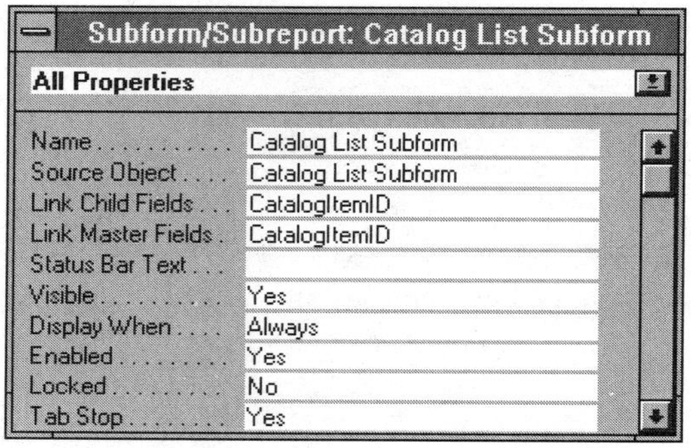

FIGURE 15-21. The property sheet for the subform control in the Catalog main form.

NOTE: If the source of the main form and the subform is a table (not a query), and if you've defined a relationship between the two tables, Microsoft Access generates the link properties (Link Master Fields and Link Child Fields) for you using the related fields when you drag and drop the subform onto the main form. Access also links a subform to a main form when the main form is based on a table and there's a field on the subform with the same name as the primary key of the main form's source table.

When you've finished, click the Form View button on the toolbar to see the completed form, as shown in Figure 15-22. If you see a partial row displayed on the subform, return to Design view and adjust the height of the subform control. Save your form and name it *Catalog List.* Next, you'll make your form more interesting using pictures.

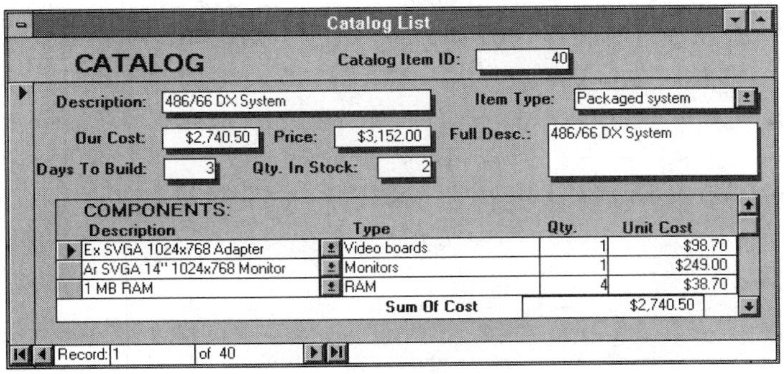

FIGURE 15-22.
The Catalog List form with subform.

By the way, you can also use a Form Wizard to create a form/subform for you. When you do that, the Form Wizard creates a single-column form for the main form and a Datasheet view of the subform. In this case, because you did some special designing of the subform, making the Datasheet view inappropriate, you used only the Form Wizard to create the main form.

Working with Objects

Microsoft Access makes it easy to work with objects created by any application that supports Object Linking and Embedding (OLE). One way you can enhance a form is to add pictures to the form design. Many of the forms in the NWIND database are designed with pictures. In this section, you'll add an unbound logo and a bound picture from the Catalog table to the Catalog List form. You'll also briefly revisit the 1993 Sales By Month And Quarter form, which you created earlier in this chapter, to learn how to add a graph to a form.

Adding an Unbound Picture

Start by opening the heading of the form and making room on the left side for an area about 1 inch high by 2 inches wide. Select the Object Frame tool in the toolbox, and place the object frame control in the upper left corner of the form. Microsoft Access responds with an Insert Object dialog box, shown in Figure 15-23 on the next page, asking you what type of object you would like to insert on the form.

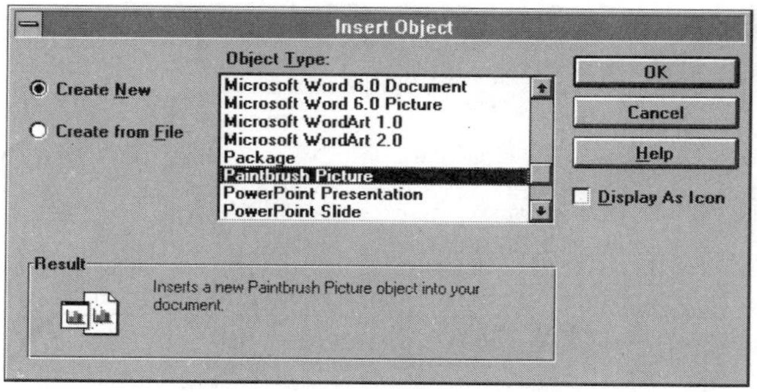

FIGURE 15-23. The Insert Object dialog box invoking an application for creating a new OLE object.

If you haven't already saved the object as a file, you can choose from any drawing application that supports OLE—including Microsoft Draw, Microsoft WordArt, Microsoft Paintbrush, and Microsoft PowerPoint. Select an application such as Paintbrush, and click OK to start the application to create a new picture. After Access opens the application, you use it to create your drawing. Choose Update from that application's File menu to store your work back on your form, and then exit the application.

If you've already saved the object as a file, select Create From File in the Insert Object dialog box to change the dialog box, as shown in Figure 15-24, to allow you to enter a filename. Click the Browse button to open a file search dialog box to specify the file you want. In this case, I have a bitmap file (prlogo.bmp) containing the Prompt Computer Solutions logo that I want to insert on the form.

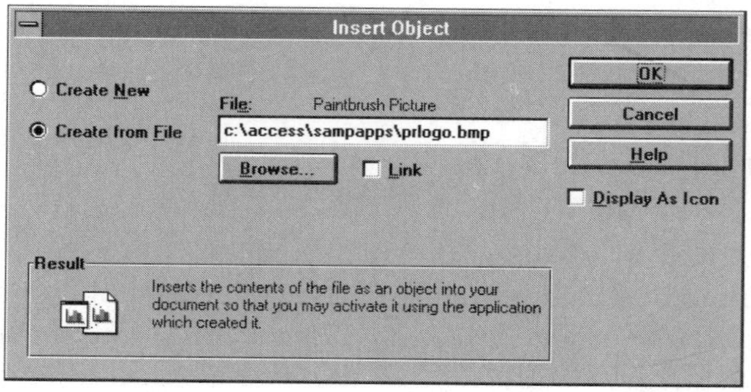

FIGURE 15-24. The Insert Object dialog box is used to create an object from a file.

If you specify a file, Access copies it directly into the object frame control. You have the option of copying the entire file into your Access form or linking to the original file by selecting the Link check box. When you choose Link, Access establishes a link to the original file and updates the image in your form whenever that file changes.

This example will use a sample logo for Prompt Computer Solutions that was scanned in from a letterhead and then sized as small, medium, and large bitmap (BMP) files compatible with Paintbrush. The result is shown in Figure 15-25.

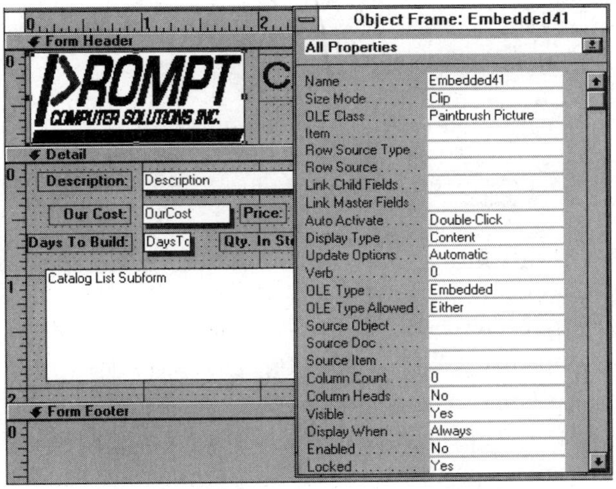

FIGURE 15-25.
A picture object is embedded in an object frame control, and its properties are set.

For the Size Mode property, you have three choices. *Clip* (the default) leaves the picture the original size, places the picture in the upper left corner of the control, and clips the picture on the bottom and right if it's too large to fit. *Stretch* shrinks or enlarges the picture horizontally and vertically to fit the control, and it distorts the proportion of your picture if the control doesn't match the original picture proportions. *Zoom* shrinks or enlarges your picture but maintains the aspect ratio. In this case, the Clip setting was chosen because the original bitmap is the correct size.

When you create an object frame control and embed a nonlinked picture (Access stores a copy of the file in your form), Access sets the control's Enabled property to No and its Locked property to Yes. Access assumes you're adding the picture to enhance the appearance of the form, and therefore you don't need to select or update it. Now when you open the form in Form view, you can see a logo in the upper left corner, as shown in Figure 15-26.

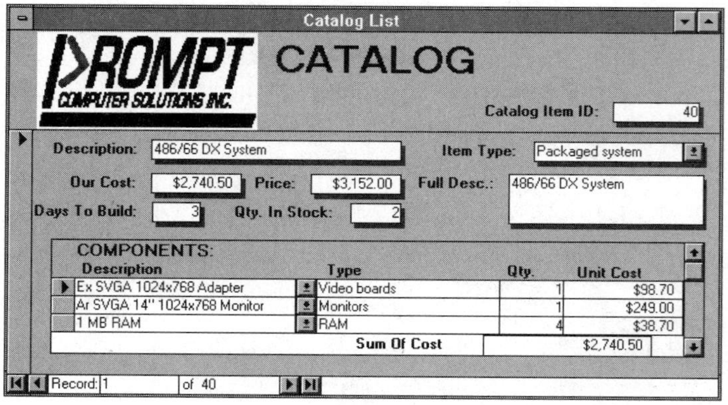

FIGURE 15-26. The Catalog List form with an embedded picture (a logo).

If you create an object frame that's linked to a file from another application, Access displays a copy of the image on your form and maintains a link to the original file. If you change the original source file, you can set the Update Options property to Automatic to ensure that the copy on the form is updated. The Source Object property will point to the original source file, and the Source Item property might contain information used by the owning application to locate data in the file (such as spreadsheet cell ranges). If you enable the control, you can set the Auto Activate property to Double-Click, GetFocus, or Manual to activate the source application on a mouse double-click event, on a GetFocus event (when you select the object), or on a manual event (when you use the Edit menu to activate the source application). For source applications that support the Object Linking and Embedding standard version 2 (OLE 2), verb settings are available that let you "activate" the source application within the bound control.

Adding a Bound Picture

If you look at the Catalog table in Design view, you'll notice that there's a field named Diagram that is an OLE object in each record. This field stores a picture of each major item in the catalog. The picture can be displayed on the screen or printed in fliers to be mailed to customers. If you want to be able to update all the Diagram objects in the Catalog table from your Catalog List form, you need to add a Bound Object Frame control to the form.

Open the Catalog List form in Design view. Drag the bottom border down to enlarge the form. Clear some space on the right side of the form by moving the ItemTypeCode and LongDescription controls to the left. Click the Object Frame tool, and then click the Diagram field in the field list and drag the field to the form. Size the Bound Object Frame control so that it's about 1½ inches square, as shown in Figure 15-27.

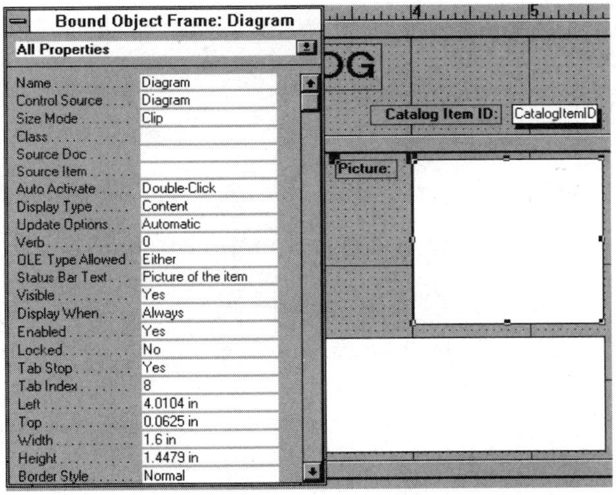

FIGURE 15-27.
A Bound Object Frame control and its property sheet.

You can easily replace a picture in the Bound Object Frame control. If you have Microsoft PowerPoint or a similar graphics program, you can probably find a clip art graphic of a personal computer to try out as a replacement. Or you can scan in and size any crisp black-and-white picture and save it as a bitmap file and then switch to Form view, select the picture control, and choose the Insert Object command from the Edit menu. You'll see an Insert Object dialog box, as shown in Figure 15-23 on page 560. Choose an object type, and click OK to open the related application; or click the Create From File option button in the dialog box to copy the image directly from a picture file.

In this example, a PC graphic was chosen from a PowerPoint clip art file, pasted into Paintbrush, and saved as a bitmap file. It was then inserted into the picture control of the Catalog List form in Form view. The result is shown in Figure 15-28.

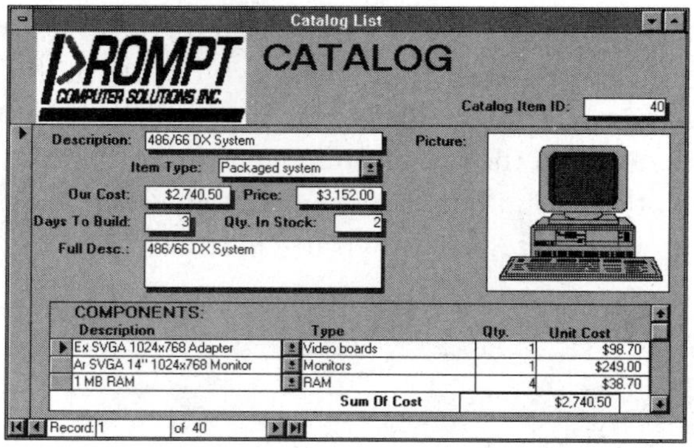

FIGURE 15-28. The Catalog List form with a new picture object, in Form view.

Using Graphs

Graphs are another kind of object you can embed in a form. For example, it would be interesting to add a graph showing sales by month for each product to the 1993 Sales By Month And Quarter form you created earlier in this chapter. To do this, you need a slightly different version of the crosstab query you created for the form to supply data for the graph. Open the 1993 Sales Crosstab, and remove the TypeDescription, Price, and OurCost fields. By default, the Graph Wizard attempts to graph all numeric fields. If you leave these fields in the input query, you'll have to do some extra work later to customize your graph. You also need to set the Column Headings property for the query so that the alphabetic months appear in the correct order. Your new query should look like the one shown in Figure 15-29. Save this query as *1993 Sales Crosstab For Graph*.

You could also use a totals query to provide the same data for the graph, but if you do that you'll have to go through extra steps in the Graph Wizard to define which output columns form the X and Y axis for the graph. Also, if any product has no sales in a month, the resulting graph won't show those months. When you use a crosstab query, the Graph Wizard can automatically figure out which columns form the axes. The graph from a crosstab query shows all months, even when a product did not have any sales in one or more months.

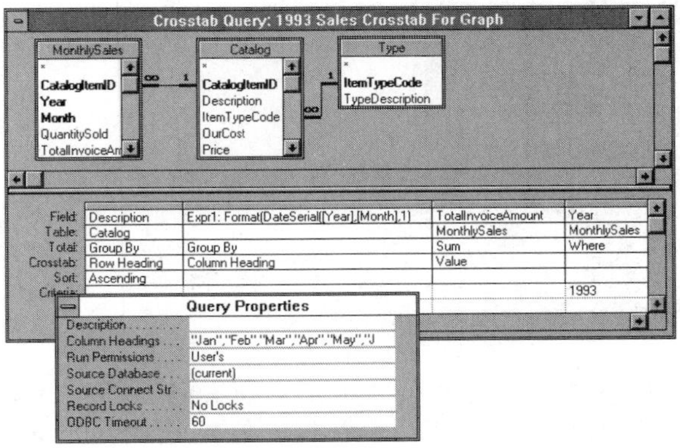

FIGURE 15-29.
The crosstab query to provide sales data to graph on the 1993 Sales By Month And Quarter form.

Next, open in Design view the 1993 Sales By Month And Quarter form you created earlier. Open a space in the upper right corner of the form by moving the monthly totals down and stacking the other fields on the left. The result is shown in Figure 15-30.

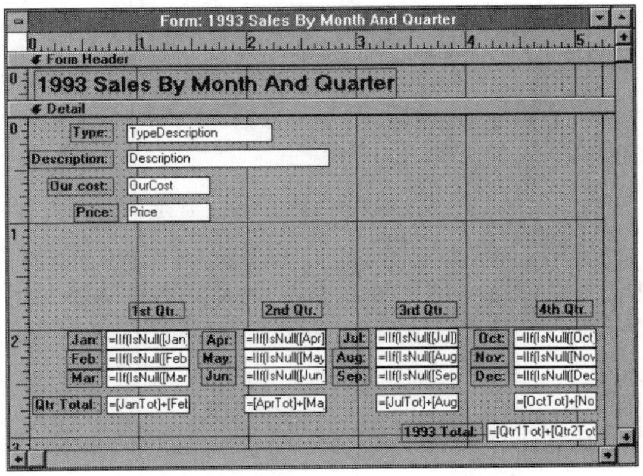

FIGURE 15-30.
The controls on this form are re-arranged to make room for a graph in the upper right corner.

Now click the graph tool in the toolbox, and place a graph control in the new blank space on your form. Microsoft Access responds with a Graph Wizard dialog box, as shown in Figure 15-31 on the next page.

The Graph Wizard screens are similar to those you'll see if you choose the Graph option on the Form Wizard. In fact, one good way to create a graph is to use the Graph option on the Form Wizard to create a new form that has only the graph you want. You can then cut and paste the result to any form or report.

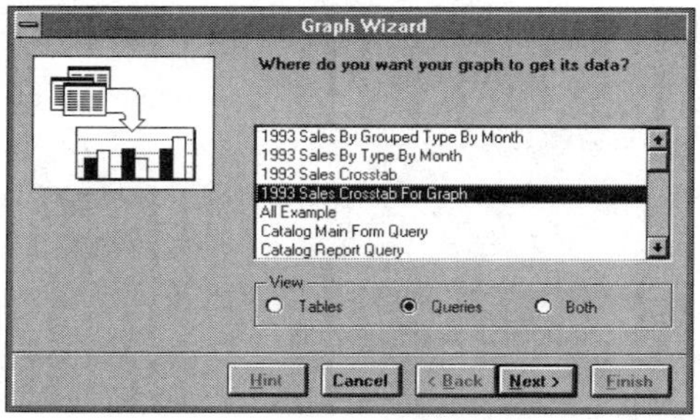

FIGURE 15-31. The first Graph Wizard screen.

To use the Graph Wizard shown in Figure 15-31, you must first choose the source for the graph. In this example, you want to graph the monthly sales data from the new crosstab query you just created. Select the Queries option button (so that the wizard displays all the queries in your database), choose the 1993 Sales Crosstab For Graph query, and click Next.

On the next screen, shown in Figure 15-32, the Graph Wizard lets you choose the "look" for your graph and whether you want to use the data from the rows or the columns of the crosstab to create the graph. The area chart in the upper left corner is a good choice. Also, you want to plot sales for each product description (the data in rows) by month, so choose Data Series in Rows.

Click the Next button to see the final Graph Wizard screen, shown in Figure 15-33. You don't need a title on this graph, so leave that blank. Because you'll finally link the graph to the data displayed in the form, you don't need a legend either. Choose No under the options to display a legend, and then click Finish to complete your graph. Your result should look something like that shown in Figure 15-34.

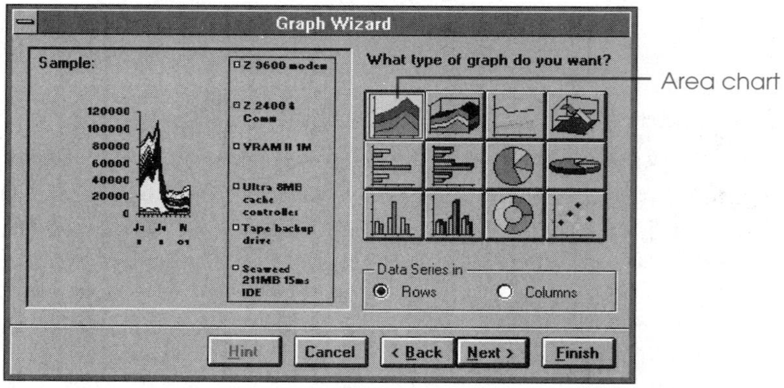

FIGURE 15-32. The second Graph Wizard screen for a crosstab query, where you choose the "look" of your graph and whether you want to graph by rows or columns.

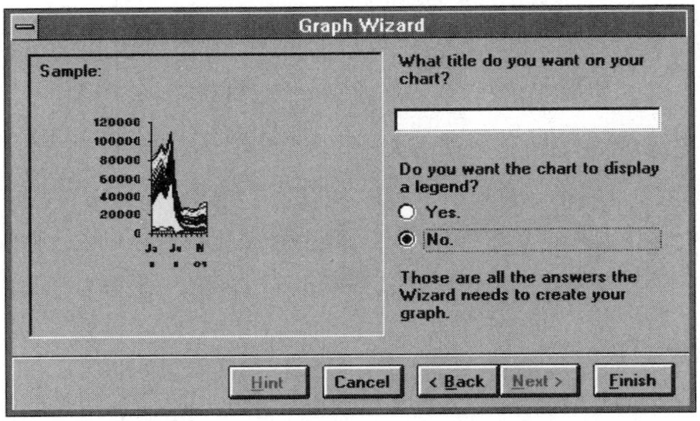

FIGURE 15-33.
The final options screen in the Graph Wizard.

You need to tell the Microsoft Graph program that you want to link its display to the value of a field in the current record on the form. In this case, you want to plot the sales data for the current product. Because both the form and the graph query contain the Description field, you can use it to link the graph to the form. To do that, select the graph object, open its property sheet, and type *Description* in the Link Child Fields and Link Master Fields properties as shown in Figure 15-34.

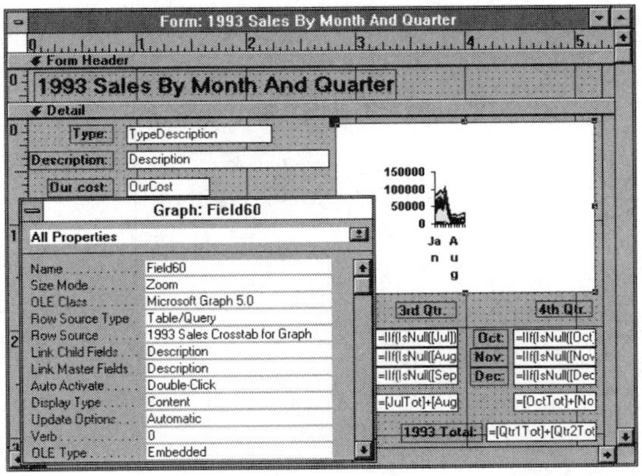

FIGURE 15-34.
The first draft of your graph created by the Graph Wizard is shown on your form in Design view.

Next, you need to adjust the graph design so that the graph program formats the values on the Y (vertical) axis as dollar amounts. You also need to "stretch" the graph picture to display all the label values properly. To accomplish this, double-click on the graph object to open it inside the Microsoft Graph application, as shown in Figure 15-35 on the next page.

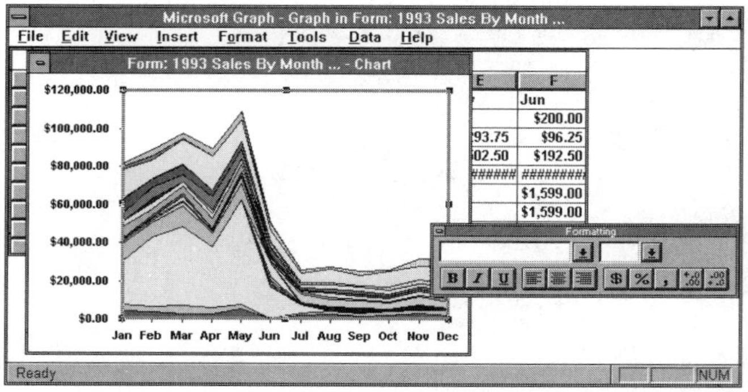

FIGURE 15-35. Adjusting the graph design using Microsoft Graph.

When you first open the graph inside the Microsoft Graph application, the graph picture might be "hiding" behind the datasheet that shows the values being displayed on the graph. You can move the graph picture to the front by ensuring that the Datasheet option on the View menu is unchecked. Click and drag the edges of the graph display window to make it large enough to display all values on both the horizontal and vertical axes. Click in the white area just above the area chart to select the chart boundary, as shown in Figure 15-35. You can drag the edges of this gray rectangle to adjust the size of the chart display. With a little practice, you can make the chart fill the graph window at a size large enough to display all the month abbreviations across the bottom.

When the chart looks the way you want it to, choose Update from the File menu. Finally, choose Exit And Return To Form... from the File menu to see your "customized" graph, shown in Figure 15-36.

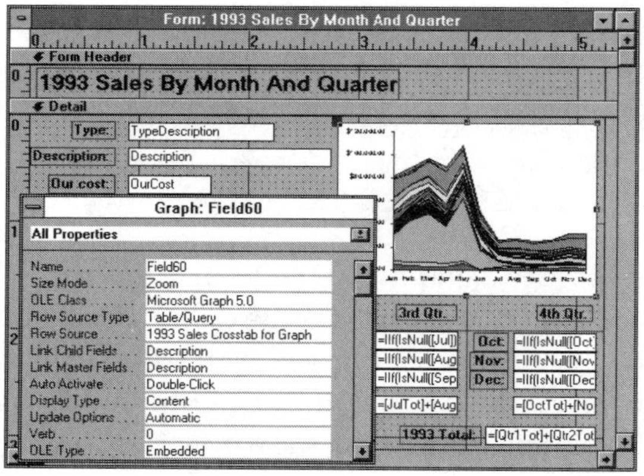

FIGURE 15-36. The customized graph now stored in your form.

Change to Form view to see the records and their related sales charts, shown in Figure 15-37. Each time you move to a new record, Microsoft Access links to the Microsoft Graph program to produce a new chart on the form. You can see that the capability of Access approaches the capability of many spreadsheet programs, linking data directly from your database into useful charts that you can view and print.

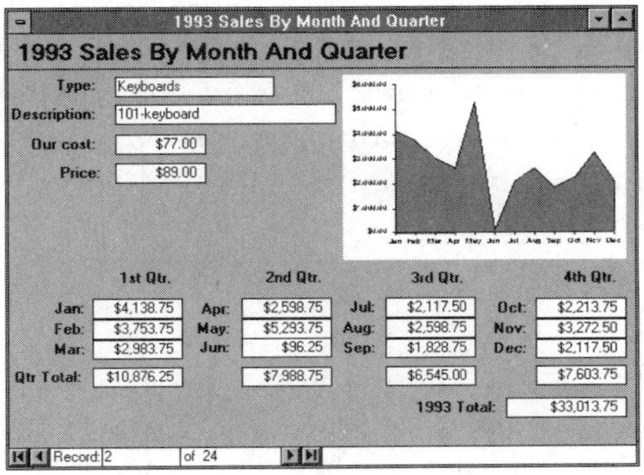

FIGURE 15-37.
The form in Form view with the linked graph.

As of version 2, Microsoft Access links to Microsoft Graph 5, which fully supports the OLE 2 standard. If you change the Enabled property of the graph object on your form to Yes and the Locked property to No, you can double-click on the graph object when the form is in Form View to start up Microsoft Graph right inside your form. You'll notice that Graph adds items to the menu bar and pops open a custom toolbar, as shown in Figure 15-38. You can use Graph tools to change the look of your graph without leaving Microsoft Access.

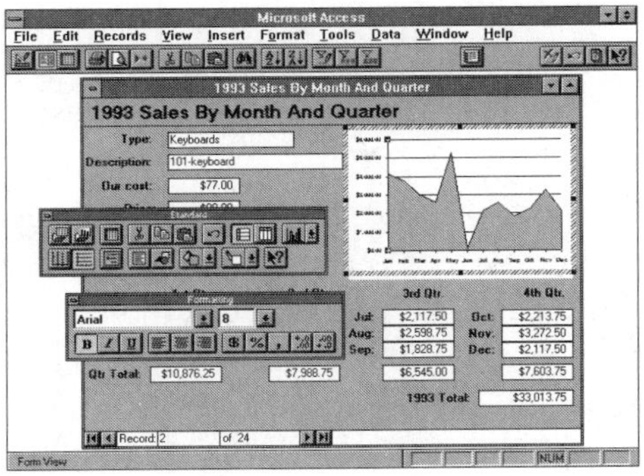

FIGURE 15-38.
Microsoft Graph is opened inside the Microsoft Access form to change the graph format.

Linking Forms with Command Buttons

One of the most exciting features of Microsoft Access is its ability to trigger macros by events on forms. Suppose you're working in the Catalog List form, listing new systems. Every time you realize that you're missing a new component, you don't have to go to the Database window, find the Components form that you designed earlier, create your new component, and then switch back to the Catalog List form. Access provides an easy way to open the Components form directly from the Catalog List form. You can create a command button in your form in Design view that uses a macro to open another form.

Creating a Macro

If you've looked at any of the form or control property sheets in any detail, you've probably noticed several properties with names like *On Load, Before Update, On Close,* and the like. These properties refer to events for which you can define actions that you want Microsoft Access to execute when the event happens. For example, selecting a control, clicking a button, and typing characters in a text box are events to which Access can respond.

You can define most of the actions you'll ever need with a macro. Access also gives you the option of handling events with Access Basic—either as functions attached to your forms and reports or as separate modules. (You'll learn more about both macros and Access Basic in the last part of this book.)

Macros give you more than 40 different actions you can use as responses to events. To define a simple macro, go to the Database window, click the Macro tab, and then click the New button. Access opens the Macro window, as shown in Figure 15-39.

The Macro window looks a lot like the Table window in Design view and works in much the same way. You enter action names and comments in the top section of the window, and you use the F6 function key to jump down to the bottom section of the window to set arguments for each action. When you choose an action at the top of the window, Access asks for the appropriate arguments at the bottom of the window. You don't even have to remember the names of all the actions. If you

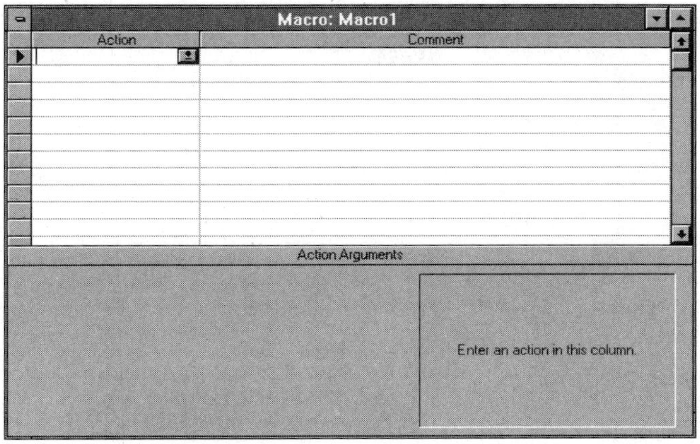

FIGURE 15-39.
The Macro window.

click in the Action column, Access shows you a drop-down list button, which you can click to reveal a list of all macro actions.

It's time to try creating your own macro. Your macro will open the Components form you created previously.

Open a new Macro window. Move the Macro window to the side a bit so that you can see the Database window. Find your Components form in the Database window, and drag and drop it onto the top section of the Macro window, as shown in Figure 15-40. When you drop a form onto a Macro window, Access creates an OpenForm action for you with all the correct arguments filled in, as shown in Figure 15-41 on the next page.

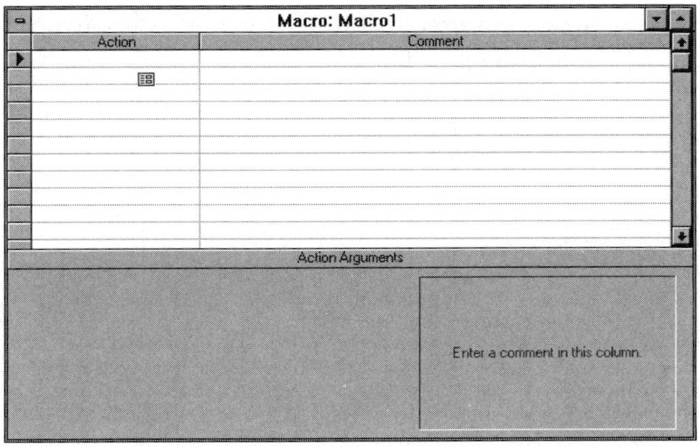

FIGURE 15-40.
Dragging and dropping a form onto a Macro window.

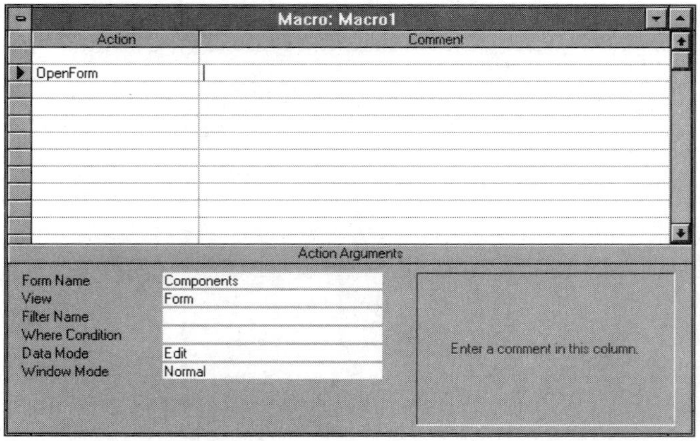

FIGURE 15-41. A new macro, created by Access when a form is dropped onto a Macro window, with an OpenForm action to open the Components form.

You might want to type an appropriate comment in the Comment field next to the OpenForm action. Now all you have to do is save your macro. Choose the Save As command from the File menu, and name your macro *Open Components.*

Adding a Command Button

It's easy to create a command button for your newly created macro. Open the Catalog List form in Design view. Move the Form window to the side a bit so that you can see the Database window again. Locate your new Open Components macro in the Database window, and drag and drop it onto the form header area of your Catalog List form. Microsoft Access creates a command button for you to run the macro you picked. The result is shown in Figure 15-42.

You'll notice that Access didn't size the button quite large enough to show you the entire "Open Components" caption—only "Open" shows. Choose Size To Fit from the Format menu, save the Catalog List form, and open it in Form view. Click the Open Components button, and you will see the Components form open conveniently on top of the Catalog List form, as shown in Figure 15-43.

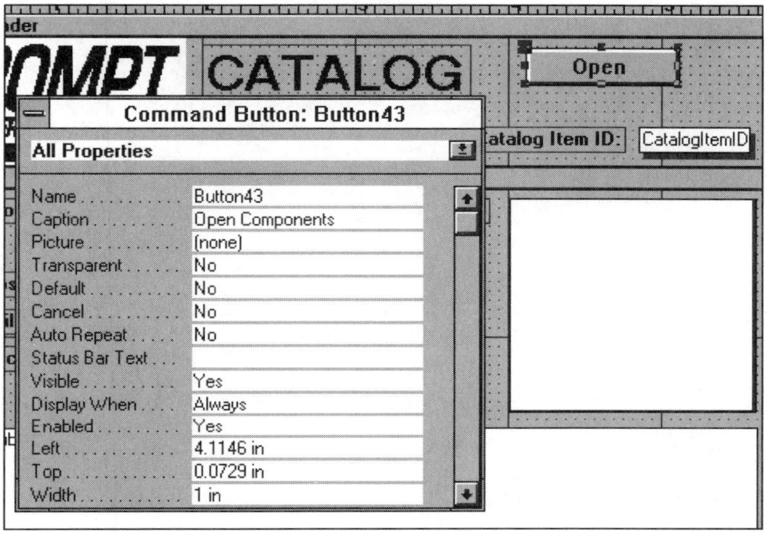

FIGURE 15-42.
An Open Components command button added to the Catalog List form.

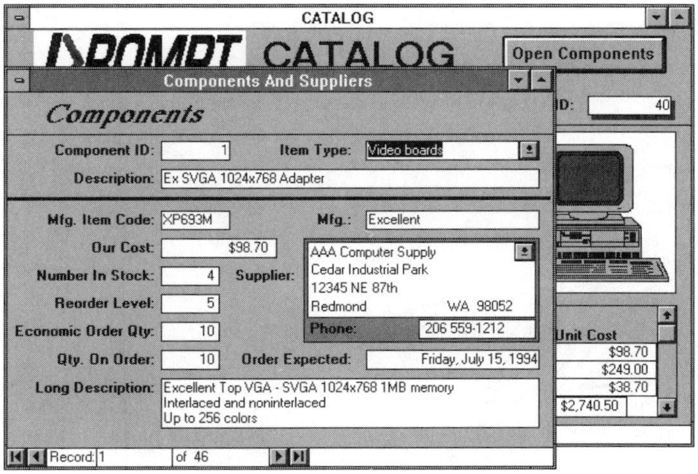

FIGURE 15-43.
The Components form opens when the new Open Components button is clicked.

This is the last chapter on forms. You'll learn a few more design tricks when you start to build an application using macros and Microsoft Access Basic in Part 6 of this book. Now it's time to learn about reports in the three chapters of Part 5, "Building Reports."

PART 5

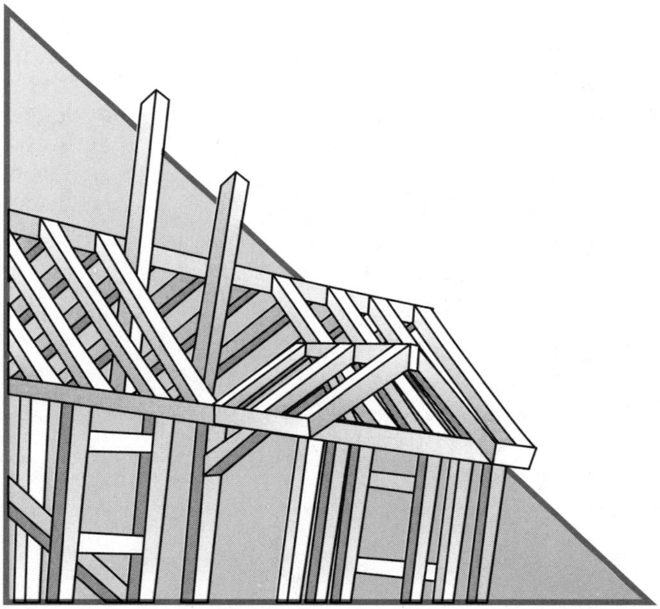

Building Reports

16

Report Basics

Previously you learned that you can format and print tables and queries in Datasheet view. You can use this technique to produce a printed copy of simple lists of information. Later you found that you could use forms not only to view and modify data, but also to print data—including data from several tables. However, because the major focus of forms is to allow you to view single records or small groups of related records displayed on screen in an attractive way, forms aren't the best way to print and summarize large sets of data in your database.

This chapter explores the external aspects of reports—why you should use a report instead of other methods of printing data and what features reports offer. Because you aren't building any reports for Prompt Computer Solutions yet, this chapter uses examples you can readily find in the NWIND sample database that you received with Microsoft Access. After you understand what you can do with reports, you'll look at the process of building reports for Prompt in the following two chapters.

Uses for Reports

Reports are the best way to create a printed copy of information extracted or calculated from data in your database. Reports have two principal advantages over other methods of printing data:

- Reports can compare, summarize, and subtotal large sets of data.
- Reports can be created to produce attractive invoices, purchase orders, mailing labels, presentation materials, and other output you might need to efficiently conduct business.

Reports are designed to group data, to present each grouping separately, and to perform calculations. They work as follows:

- You can define up to 10 grouping criteria to separate the levels of detail.
- You can define separate headers and footers for each group.
- You can perform complex calculations not only within a group or set of rows but also across groups.
- In addition to page headers and footers, you can define a header and a footer for the entire report.

As with forms, you can embed pictures or graphs in any section of a report. You can also embed subreports or subforms within report sections.

A Tour of Reports

You can take a tour of reports by exploring many of the features designed into the samples in NWIND. A good place to start is the Percentages Of Sales report. Open the NWIND database and click the Report tab in the Database window. Scroll down the list of reports in the Database window until you see the Percentages Of Sales report, as shown in Figure 16-1. Double-click that report (or select it and click the Preview button) to see the report in Print Preview—a view of how the report will look when printed.

FIGURE 16-1.
The Reports list in the Database window.

The Percentages Of Sales report is based on the Employee Sales By Country query, which brings together information from the Employees, Orders, and Order Details tables. You'll be prompted for two parameters: a beginning date and an ending date. For this exercise, enter *January 1, 1993* and *December 31, 1993* (or enter *1/1/93* and *12/31/93*) when prompted by the Enter Parameter Value dialog boxes. When the Percentages Of Sales report opens in Print Preview, you'll see a view of the report in the Report: Percentages Of Sales window, as shown in Figure 16-2 on the next page.

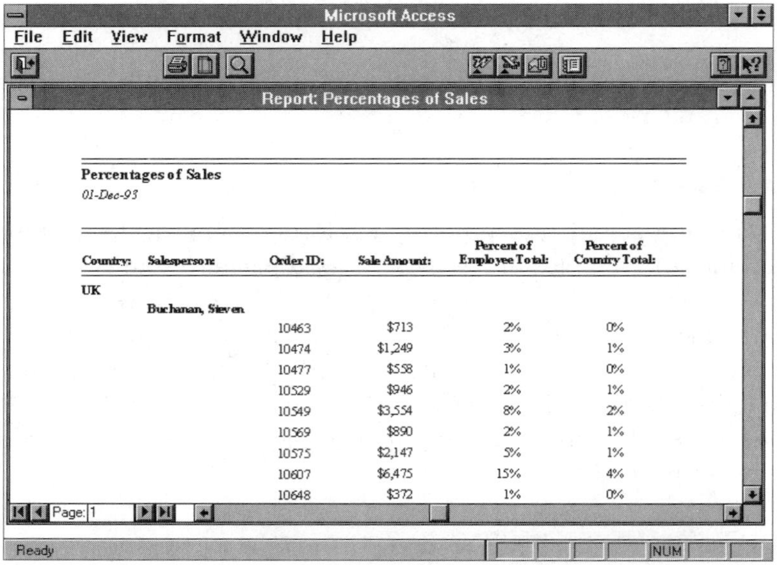

FIGURE 16-2. The NWIND Percentages Of Sales report in Print Preview.

The Built-In Toolbar for Print Preview

When you open a report in Print Preview, Microsoft Access displays a toolbar with 10 buttons, as shown in Figure 16-2. From left to right, the buttons are:

Close Window button. Click this button to close the Print Preview window and return to the previous window. If you entered Print Preview from the Database window, Microsoft Access returns you to the Database window. If you entered Print Preview from report design, Access returns you to design mode.

Print button. Click this button to send the report to your printer.

Print Setup button. Click this button to define the destination printer and the overall layout for the report (margins, orientation, columns).

Zoom button. Click this button to zoom out to see the entire page layout or to zoom in to see details. You can also place your mouse pointer over any area of the report and click to zoom out or in.

Publish It With MS Word button. Saves the report output as an RTF (Rich Text Format) file and opens the file in Microsoft Word for Windows.

Analyze It With MS Excel button. Saves the report output as an XLS format file and opens the file in Microsoft Excel.

Mail It button. Saves the report output as an XLS, RTF, or text format file and starts a new message with the file embedded in Microsoft Mail.

Database Window button. Click this button to place the focus on the Database window. This button also un-hides the window if you've hidden it and restores the window if you've minimized it.

Cue Cards button. Click this button to open the main menu of the Cue Cards facility. Cue Cards lead you through step-by-step instructions for most common tasks.

Help button. Click this button to add a question mark to your mouse pointer. Click with this pointer on any displayed object to receive context-sensitive help about that object.

More About Print Preview

You can expand the window in Print Preview so that it's easy to see a large portion of the Percentages Of Sales report at one time. You should be able to use the vertical and horizontal scroll bars to position the report so that you can see most of the top half of the first page, as shown in Figure 16-2. You can also use the arrow keys to move the page up, down, left, and right.

To view other pages of the report, use the page number box at the bottom left of the window, as shown in Figure 16-3 on the next page. To move forward one page at a time, click the arrow button immediately to the right of the page number box. You can also click on the page number (or press F5 to select the page number), change the number, and press Enter to skip to the page you want. As you might guess, the left arrow button immediately to the left of the page number box moves you backward one page, and the two outer arrows (pointing into a vertical bar) on either end of the page number box move you to the first or last page of the report. You can also move to the top of the page by pressing Ctrl-up arrow, move to the bottom of a page by pressing Ctrl-down arrow, move to the left margin of the page by pressing Home or Ctrl-left arrow, and move to the right margin of the page by pressing End or Ctrl-right arrow. Pressing Ctrl-Home moves you to the upper left corner of the page, and pressing Ctrl-End moves you to the lower right corner of the page.

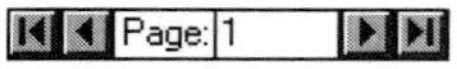

FIGURE 16-3.
The page number box in a Report window in Print Preview.

Headers, Details, Footers, and Groups

Although the Percentages Of Sales report shown in Figure 16-2 appears simple at first glance, it actually contains a lot of information. On the first page you can see a report header that provides a title for the overall report and also displays the date on which you open the report. Below that is a page header that you'll see at the top of every page. As you'll see later when you design reports, you can choose whether or not to print this header on the page that also displays the report header.

Next is a simple group header that Microsoft Access prints each time the country changes. This first page begins with data for salespeople in the United Kingdom. Below that is the group header you'll see for each salesperson. The Salesperson field is calculated in the query on which the report is based by concatenating the Last Name field, a comma, and the First Name field from the Employees table. You could also perform this calculation in the report rather than in the query.

Below the Salesperson header, Access prints the detail information, one line for each row in the recordset formed by the query. Also in the detail section, Access calculates for each order the percentage it represents of total sales by salesperson as well as the percentage it represents of total sales in the country.

CAUTION: If you're working in a report with many pages, it might take a long time to move to the top or bottom of a page or back one page. Press Esc to cancel your movement request. Microsoft Access leaves you on the most recent page it attempted to format.

On the fourth page of the Percentages Of Sales report (although the page number might vary slightly depending on the printer you're using), you can see the group footer for one of the salespeople, the group footer for the country, and the next country and salesperson group headers, as shown in Figure 16-4. Notice that the salesperson footer contains the salesperson's total sales figure and the percentage this represents of sales within the country. In the country footer, Access has calculated the total country sales and the percentage this represents of the grand total sales (which you'll see on the last page). The report continues with data for the first salesperson in the USA. At the bottom of the page is a page number, which is the content of the page footer.

Country:	Salesperson:	Order ID:	Sale Amount:	Percent of Employee Total:	Percent of Country Total:
		10791	$1,830	4%	1%
		10794	$315	1%	0%
		10804	$2,278	5%	1%
		10822	$238	1%	0%
		10826	$730	2%	0%
		10833	$907	2%	1%
	Total for Suyama, Michael:		$45,001		26%
Total for UK:			$173,981		
Percent UK is of Grand Total:			27%		
USA					
	Callahan, Laura				
		10435	$632	1%	0%
		10437	$393	1%	0%

FIGURE 16-4. The NWIND Percentages Of Sales report has subtotals and percentage calculations in group footers.

If you skip to the last page of the report (about page 12), you can see the total and percentage calculations for USA sales and the grand total sales for the report, as shown in Figure 16-5. The grand total is the content of the report footer.

Country:	Salesperson:	Order ID:	Sale Amount:	Percent of Employee Total:	Percent of Country Total:
		10807	$18	0%	0%
		10816	$8,446	7%	2%
		10830	$1,974	2%	0%
		10843	$159	0%	0%
	Total for Peacock, Margaret:		$118,196		25%
Total for USA:			$472,591		
Percent USA is of Grand Total:			73%		
Grand Total:			$646,572		

FIGURE 16-5. The NWIND Percentages Of Sales report has the grand total calculation in the report footer.

Reports Within Reports

Just as you can embed subforms within forms, you can also embed subreports (or subforms) within reports. Sometimes you might find it useful to calculate summary information in one report and also include the information in a report that shows detailed information. You don't have to define the summary report twice. Simply include it as a subreport within the detail report and—presto—Microsoft Access links the summary information with the related details.

You can see an example of this use of a subreport in the Sales By Year report and the Sales By Year Subreport in NWIND. Open the Sales By Year Subreport in Design view by selecting the subreport in the Database window and clicking the Design button, as shown in Figure 16-6. The Report window in Design view is shown in Figure 16-7.

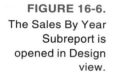

FIGURE 16-6. The Sales By Year Subreport is opened in Design view.

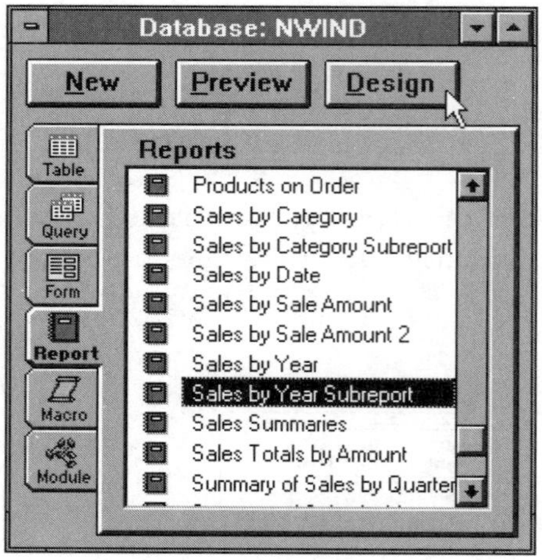

Notice that there isn't a detail section on this subreport. You can see one header for the column titles and two footers—one footer for the quarter totals (the footer repeats once for each quarter) and another footer for the year total. Because this report is intended to be embedded in another report, no report or page headers or footers are included. Open the subreport in Print Preview, and enter *1/1/93* and *12/31/93* in reply to the two parameter prompts from the query. You'll see a summary for 1993 sales, as shown in Figure 16-8.

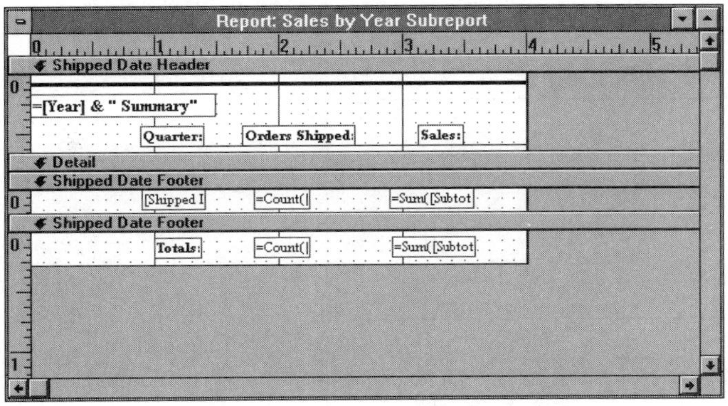

FIGURE 16-7. The Report window for the Sales By Year Subreport, in Design view.

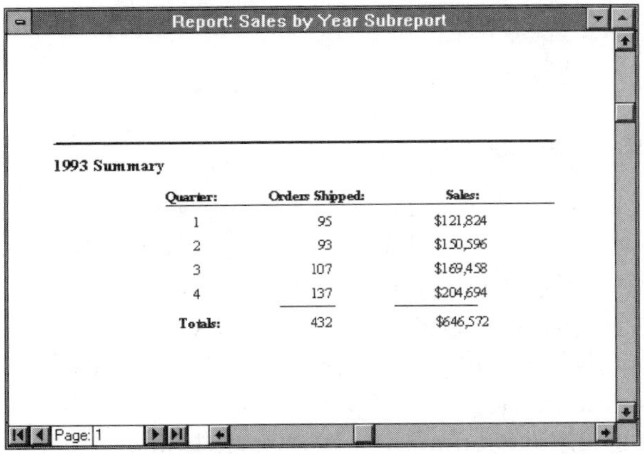

FIGURE 16-8. The data for 1993 on the Sales By Year Subreport.

Close the subreport and run the Sales By Year report. Access prompts you for a beginning date and an ending date. If you enter, say, *1/1/93* and *12/31/93*, you'll see the first page of the report, as shown in Figure 16-9 on the next page. There's a report header to provide a title and run date. Within the group header for the year, you can see the embedded subreport, followed by the column headings for the subsequent detail.

You can see another interesting feature in reports in the detail lines. Notice that there are four order entries for the January 1, 1993, date and three order entries for the January 8, 1993, date. But these dates are not repeated in the Shipped Date column, and neither is *1993* repeated in the Year column. Microsoft Access lets you set an option for detail lines to avoid printing duplicate values. In contrast, if you had

FIGURE 16-9.
The Sales By Year report with the embedded subreport.

Sales by Year

01-Jun-94

1993 Summary

Quarter:	Orders Shipped:	Sales:
1	95	$121,824
2	93	$150,596
3	107	$169,458
4	137	$204,694
Totals:	432	$646,572

Details

Year:	Shipped Date:	Orders Shipped:	Sales:
1993	01-Jan-93	10429	$1,441
		10431	$1,892
		10432	$485
		10435	$632
	04-Jan-93	10439	$1,078
	05-Jan-93	10436	$1,995
	06-Jan-93	10437	$393
	07-Jan-93	10434	$321
	08-Jan-93	10425	$360
		10438	$454
		10443	$517
	12-Jan-93	10442	$1,792

been looking at this data in a regular datasheet or a form, you would have seen the value *1993* repeated 12 times, the value *01-Jan-93* repeated four times, and *08-Jan-93* repeated three times.

Another good use for embedding one report within another is to display several groups of data that are related many-to-many. In NWIND, the Sales Summaries report contains no detail—only two subreports. These subreports summarize 1993 sales both by salesperson and by item category. Without subreports, it would be difficult to bring this information together because of the many-to-many relationship between the data in the two tables—a salesperson can sell items in many categories, and a category can contain items sold by many different salespeople.

Objects in Reports

As with forms, you can embed OLE (Object Linking and Embedding) objects in reports. The objects embedded in or linked to reports are usually pictures or charts. You can embed a picture or a chart as an unbound object in the report itself, or you can link a picture or a chart as a bound object from data in your database.

The Catalog report in the NWIND database has both unbound and bound objects. When you open the Catalog report in Print Preview, you can see the Northwind Traders logo (a lighthouse) embedded in the report title as an unbound Microsoft Draw object, as shown in Figure 16-10. This drawing is actually a part of the report design.

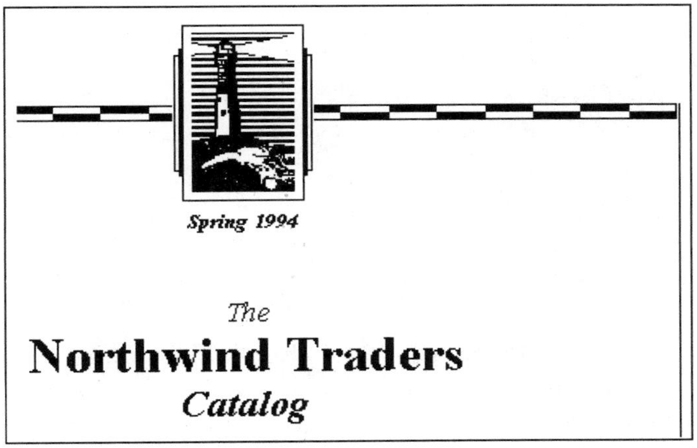

FIGURE 16-10.
An unbound Microsoft Draw object (the Northwind Traders logo) embedded in the Catalog report.

If you skip forward to page 3 of the report, you can see a picture displayed on the form, as shown in Figure 16-11. This picture is a bound Paintbrush object from the Categories table.

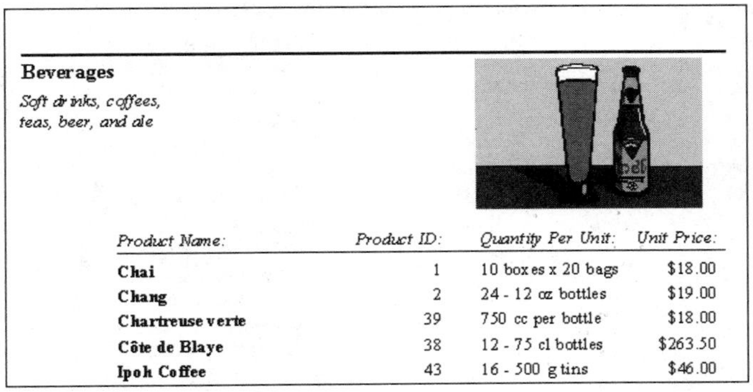

Beverages
Soft drinks, coffees, teas, beer, and ale

Product Name:	*Product ID:*	*Quantity Per Unit:*	*Unit Price:*
Chai	1	10 boxes x 20 bags	$18.00
Chang	2	24 - 12 oz bottles	$19.00
Chartreuse verte	39	750 cc per bottle	$18.00
Côte de Blaye	38	12 - 75 cl bottles	$263.50
Ipoh Coffee	43	16 - 500 g tins	$46.00

FIGURE 16-11.
A bound Paintbrush object (beer glass and bottle) linked to the Catalog report.

Printing Reports

Previously you learned the basics of viewing a report in Print Preview. Here are a few more tips and details about setting up reports for printing.

Print Setup

When you decide you want to print a report, you might first want to check its appearance and then change the printer setup. Open the Sales By Year report you looked at earlier, select the report in the Database window, and click the Preview button to run the report. Enter *1/1/93* and *12/31/93* as the beginning and ending dates when you're prompted. After Microsoft Access shows you the report, click the Zoom button and then enlarge the window to see the full-page view, as shown in Figure 16-12. You can see that the report does not occupy a lot of space on the page. You might be able to increase the amount of data per page by asking Access to print data in a two-column format. To do that, you need to modify some parameters in the Print Setup dialog box.

You can open the Print Setup dialog box by clicking the Print Setup button on the Print Preview toolbar. You can also define the printer

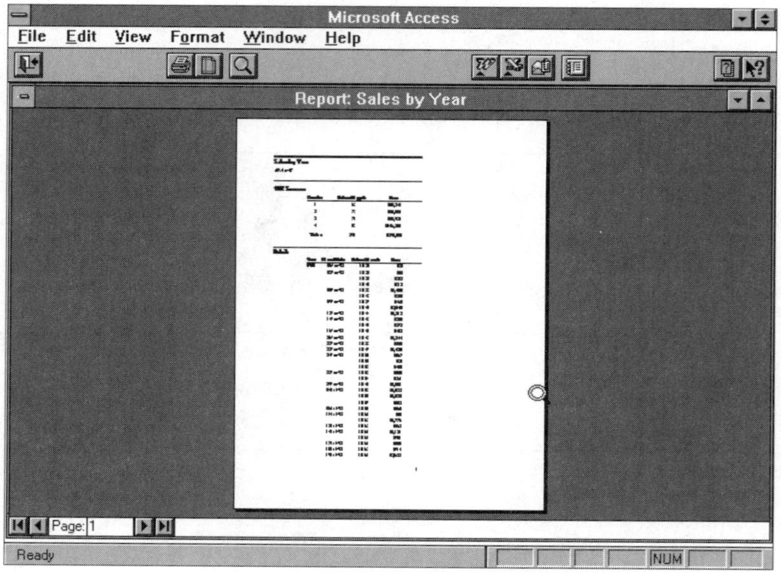

FIGURE 16-12. The full-page view of the Sales By Year report, in Print Preview.

setup for a report by selecting the report in the Database window and choosing the Print Setup command from the File menu. Microsoft Access displays a dialog box similar to the one in Figure 16-13. You can expand the dialog box by clicking the More button. The expanded Print Setup dialog box is shown in Figure 16-14.

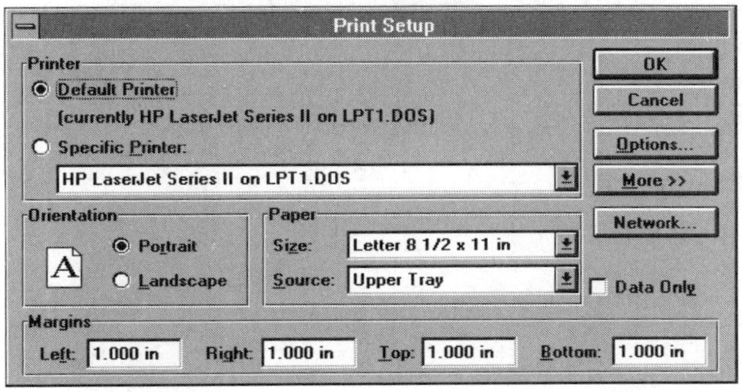

FIGURE 16-13.
The Print Setup dialog box.

To print the Sales By Year report in two columns, change the printer's orientation setting from Portrait (vertical orientation) to Landscape (horizontal orientation). Set Items Across to *2* and set Column Spacing to *0.5 in*. Indicate to Access that you want the detail information arranged vertically on the page to retain the original sequence of the printing in two columns. Figure 16-14 shows the correct settings.

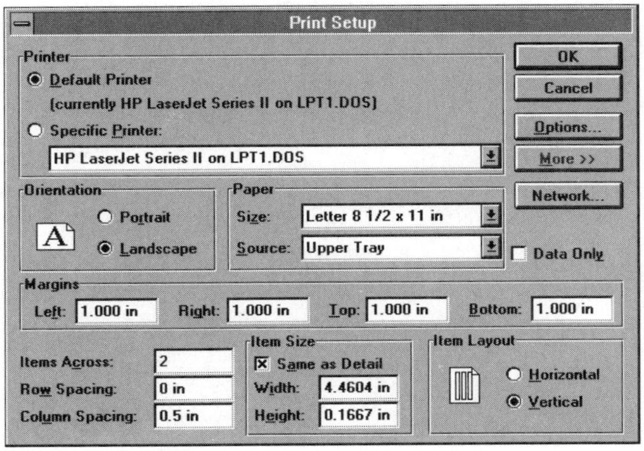

FIGURE 16-14.
The expanded Print Setup dialog box, with settings to print the Sales By Year report in two columns.

When you've entered the settings shown in Figure 16-14, your report in Print Preview will look like the one shown in Figure 16-15.

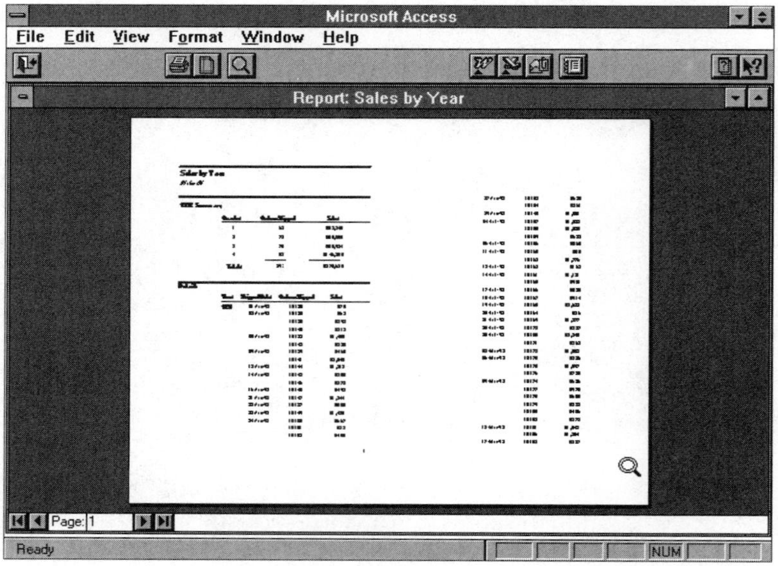

FIGURE 16-15. The Sales By Year report in Print Preview, displayed in landscape orientation and in two columns.

That covers the fundamentals of reports and how to view them and set them up for printing. The next two chapters show you how to design and build reports for your application.

17

Constructing a Report

Constructing a report is very similar to building a form. In this chapter, you'll apply many of the techniques you used in working with forms, and you'll learn how to apply some of the unique features reports offer. After a quick tour of the report design facilities, you'll build a simple report for Prompt Computer Solutions, and then you'll use a Report Wizard to create the same report.

See Also: Chapter 18, "Advanced Report Design," shows you how to apply advanced techniques to report design.

Starting from Scratch—A Simple Report

In this section, you'll build a relatively simple report as you tour the report design facilities. Because you're most likely to use reports to look at the "big picture," you'll usually design a query that brings together data from several related tables as the basis for your reports.

The report you'll build uses the Catalog and Type tables in the PROMPT database, available on the companion disk included with this book. (See "Using the Companion Disk" on page xxiv.)

Designing the Report Query

To construct this report for the PROMPT database application, you need the CatalogItemID, Description, ItemTypeCode, OurCost, Price, and LongDescription fields from the Catalog table. It would be interesting to add the TypeDescription field and also to calculate the total stock on hand and the average cost by item type. You could include a list box on the report to extract the TypeDescription field from the Type table, but it's more efficient to include that information in a query that provides the data for the report rather than to include the information in the report directly.

Figure 17-1 shows the query you'll need for this first report. To create the query, go to the Database window, select the Catalog table, click the New Query button on the toolbar, and choose New Query (not Query Wizards) in the New Query dialog box. Use the Add Table command from the Query menu to add the Type table to the query. Drag all the fields from the Catalog table, and the TypeDescription field from the Type table, to the QBE grid. Save the query and name it *Catalog Report Query*. (You can find the query named *Inventory Report Query* in the PROMPT database on the companion disk.)

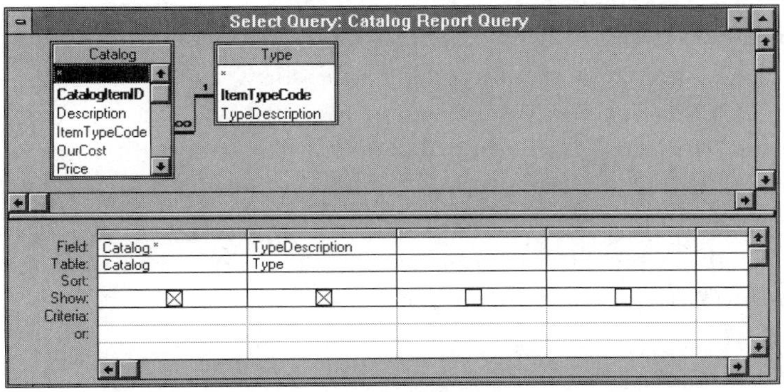

FIGURE 17-1.
A query that selects catalog item data for a report.

Starting to Design a New Report

Now you're ready to start constructing a report. Select in the Database window the query that you just built, and then click the New Report button on the toolbar. Microsoft Access displays the dialog box shown in Figure 17-2.

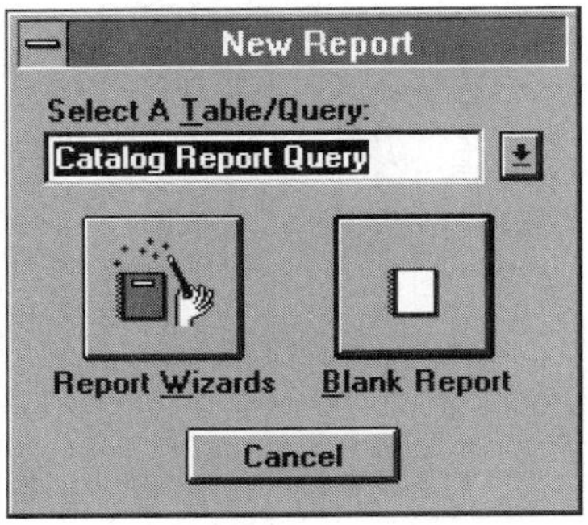

FIGURE 17-2.
The New Report dialog box.

Access shows you the name of the query you just selected in the combo box at the top of the dialog box. (If you want to select a different table or query, you can open the drop-down list to see a list of all the tables and queries in your database, and select another.) You'll use a Report Wizard later in this chapter to create a report. For now, click the Blank Report button to open a new Report window in Design view.

Working with Design Elements

When you open a blank report, Microsoft Access shows you a Report window in Design view similar to the one shown in Figure 17-3. The toolbar for the Report window is at the top of the Microsoft Access window. As with form design, the Report window itself is in the background (but on top of the Database window), with the field list, property sheet, and toolbox open to assist you as you build your report. (If necessary, you can use the Field List, Properties, and Toolbox commands on the View menu to open these windows.)

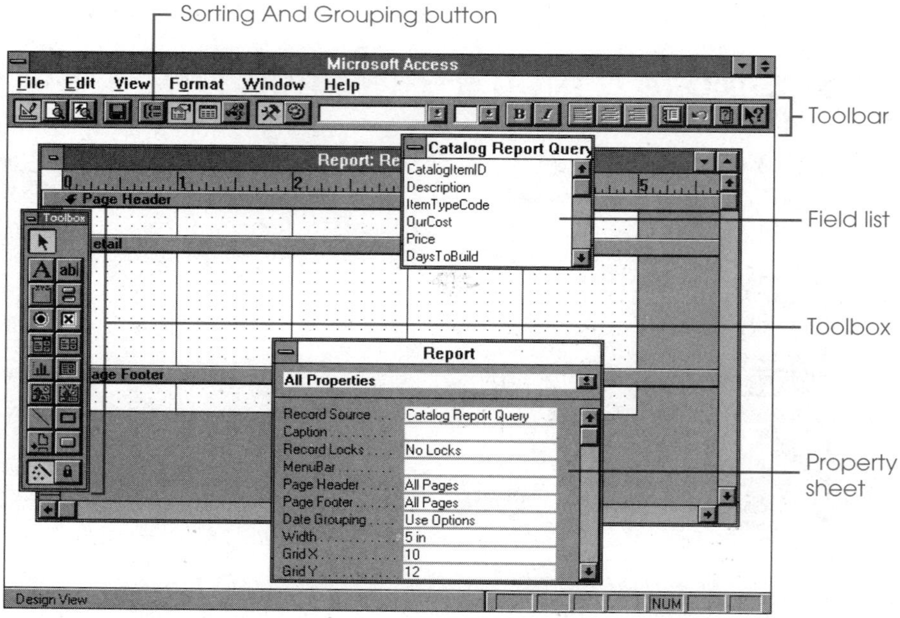

FIGURE 17-3. The Report window in Design view.

On the blank report, Access starts you out with page header and page footer sections and a 5-inch-wide-by-1-inch-high detail section in the center. The rulers at the top and left of the Report window help you plan space on the printed page. If you plan to have 0.5-inch side margins, you can design the body of the report up to 7.5 inches wide for a normal 8.5-by-11-inch page. The space you can use vertically depends on how you design your headers and footers and how you define the top and bottom margins. As with forms, you can drag the edge of any section to make the section larger or smaller. Note that the width of all sections must be the same, so if you change the width of one section, Access changes the width of all other sections to match.

Within each section you can see an initial design grid that has 10 dots per inch horizontally and 12 dots per inch vertically, with a solid gray line displayed at 1-inch intervals. If you're working in centimeters, Access divides the grid into 5 dots per centimeter both vertically and horizontally. You can change these settings using the Grid X and Grid Y properties on the property sheet for the report. (If the dots are not visible in your Report window, choose the Grid command from the View menu. If the Grid command is checked and you still can't see the dots, try resetting the Grid X and Grid Y properties on the property sheet.)

The page header and page footer will print in your report at the top and bottom of each page. You can also add a report header that prints once at the beginning of the report and a report footer that prints once at the end of the report. To add these sections to a report, choose the Report Header/Footer command from the Format menu. You can use the Page Header/Footer command on this same menu to add or remove the page header and page footer sections. You'll learn how to add group headers and group footers later in this chapter.

See Also: The field list, the property sheet, the toolbox, and the Palette are similar to the elements you used in building forms. See Chapter 13, "Building a Form," for a detailed description of their use.

The Toolbar for the Report Window in Design View

Microsoft Access provides you with a custom toolbar to use as you design reports. From left to right, the buttons are as follows:

Design View button. This button appears pressed to indicate that you are in Design view.

Print Preview button. Click this button to see a preview of the printed page using the actual data from the report's query.

Sample Preview button. Click this button to see a preview of the printed page using sample data generated by Microsoft Access. Using Sample Preview to get an idea of the report layout can be much faster than using the actual data, especially if the report is complex.

Save button. Click this button to save any changes.

Sorting And Grouping button. Click this button to show or hide the Sorting And Grouping window. Reports ignore any sorting specification in the source query. You must use the Sorting And Grouping window to define the sequence of data in your report and the groups to be formed for totals.

Properties button. Click this button to show or hide the property sheet. You can define properties for the report as a whole, for each section in the report, and for any control on the report.

Field List button. Click this button to show or hide the list of fields available in the underlying table or query. You can drag and drop fields from the list onto your report.

Code button. Select the report or any control on the report and then click this button to view and edit any Microsoft Access Basic code that responds to events on the report or to the report's controls. (See Chapter 21, "Microsoft Access Basic Fundamentals," and Chapter 22, "Automating Your Application with Access Basic," for details.)

Toolbox button. Click this button to show or hide the toolbox. Use the toolbox to choose the type of control you want to add to your report.

Palette button. Click this button to show or hide the Palette. Use the Palette to set the appearance and color of the report and the controls.

Font Name box. When you select a control that contains text or data, you can use this box to select a font that will be used in the control.

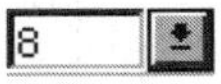

Font Size box. When you select a control that contains text or data, you can use this box to select a font size that will be used in the control.

Bold button. Click this button to make the text in the selected control bold. Click the button again to make the text normal.

Italic button. Click this button to make the text in the selected control italic. Click the button again to make the text normal.

Left-Align Text button. Click this button to align the text in the selected control flush-left.

Center-Align Text button. Click this button to center the text in the selected control.

Right-Align Text button. Click this button to align the text in the selected control flush-right.

Database Window button. Click this button to place the focus on the Database window. This button also un-hides the window if you've hidden it and restores the window if you've minimized it.

Undo button. Click this button to undo the last change you made to the design.

Cue Cards button. Click this button to open the main menu of the Cue Cards facility. Cue Cards lead you through step-by-step instructions for most common tasks.

Help button. Click this button to add a question mark to your mouse pointer. Click with this pointer on any displayed object to receive context-sensitive help about that object.

Sorting and Grouping

One way in which reports are different from forms is that you can group information for display on reports using the Sorting And Grouping window. Click the Sorting And Grouping button on the toolbar (shown in Figure 17-3 on page 594) to open the Sorting And Grouping window, as shown in Figure 17-4 on the next page. In this window you can define up to 10 fields or expressions that you will use to form groups on the report. The first item on the list determines the main group, and subsequent items define groups within groups. (You saw this nesting of groups in the previous chapter within the Percentages Of Sales report in NWIND; there was a main group for each country and a subgroup within that main group for each salesperson in that country.)

FIGURE 17-4.
The Sorting And Grouping window.

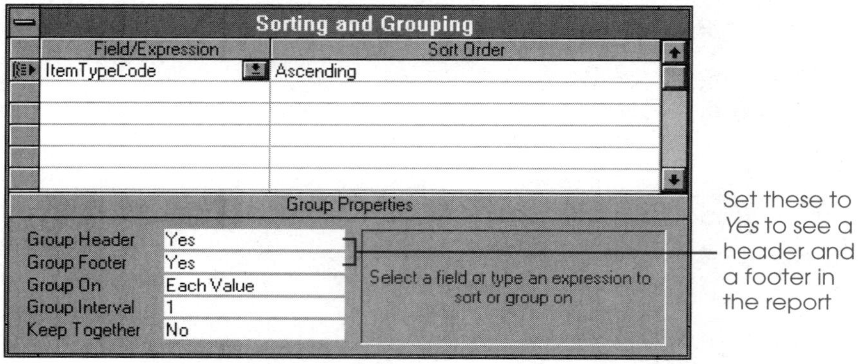

In the simple report you're creating for Catalog Items, you need to group data by item type code so that you can calculate the total number of items on hand and an average cost by item type. If you click in the first row of the Field/Expression column, a down arrow appears in the right corner. Click this arrow (or press Alt-down arrow) to open the list of fields from the underlying table or query. Select the ItemTypeCode field to place it in the Field/Expression column. You can also use the Field/Expression column to enter an expression based on any field in the underlying query or table. By default, Microsoft Access sorts each grouping value in ascending order. You can change the sorting order by choosing Descending from the drop-down list that appears when you click in the Sort Order column.

You need a place to put a header for each group (at least for the TypeDescription field) and a footer for the calculated fields (the total and the average values). To add those sections, change the settings for the Group Header and the Group Footer properties to *Yes* in the Sorting And Grouping window, as shown in Figure 17-4. When you do that, Access will add those sections to the Report window for you. You'll see how to use the Group On, Group Interval, and Keep Together properties in the next chapter. For now, leave them set to their default values. Click the Sorting And Grouping button on the toolbar to close the Sorting And Grouping window.

Constructing a Simple Report for Catalog Items

Now you're ready to finish building an inventory report based on the Catalog Item table. First, save your report as *Inventory Report,* and then perform the following steps to construct a report similar to the one shown in Figure 17-5 on the next page.

1. Place a label control on the page header and type *Catalog Item Inventory* as the label's caption. Select the label control and then, from the toolbar, select the Arial font in 18-point bold. Choose Size To Fit from the Format menu to set the control size to accommodate the new font size.

2. Click and drag the TypeDescription field from the field list to the ItemTypeCode header. Use Arial 10-point bold for the label and the control. Change the caption in the label from *Type Description* to *Category:*.

3. You'll need some column labels in the ItemTypeCode header. The easiest way to create them is to open the detail section to give yourself some room, and then drag and drop the fields CatalogItemID, Description, OurCost, and NumberInStock from the field list to the detail section. Select the label for CatalogItemID, and then choose the Cut command from the Edit menu (or press Ctrl-X) to separate the label from the control and place the label on the Clipboard. Click on the ItemTypeCode header bar, and then choose the Paste command from the Edit menu (or press Ctrl-V) to paste the label into the upper left corner of the header section. You can now place the label independently in the ItemTypeCode header section. (If you try to move the label before you separate it from the control to which it's attached, the control moves with it.) Now separate the labels from the Description, OurCost, and NumberInStock controls, and move the labels to the ItemTypeCode header section of the report.

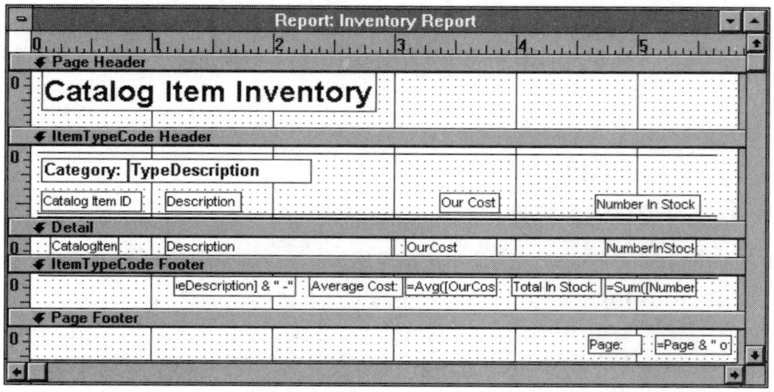

FIGURE 17-5. The Report window in Design view for the Inventory Report report.

4. Line up the column labels in the ItemTypeCode header, placing CatalogItemID near the left margin, placing Description about 1.2 inches from the left margin, placing OurCost about 3.5 inches from the left margin, and placing NumberInStock about 4.75 inches from the left margin. You can set these distances in the Left property of each label's property sheet. Now is a good time to line up the tops of the labels. Select all four labels using the Pointer tool to drag a selection box around them, and then choose the Align Top command from the Format menu.

5. You can enhance the appearance of the report by placing a line control across the top of the ItemTypeCode header and a double line control across the bottom of the ItemTypeCode header. Click on the Line tool in the toolbox, and drag your lines across the report.

6. Line up the controls for CatalogItemID, Description, OurCost, and NumberInStock under their respective headers. The controls for CatalogItemID, OurCost, and NumberInStock can be made smaller. You'll need to make the Description control about 2 inches wide.

7. The depth of the detail section on a report determines the spacing between lines on the report. You don't need any space between report lines, so make the detail section smaller until it's only as high as the row of controls for displaying your data.

8. Now add a line across the top of the ItemTypeCode footer, and add three unbound text boxes below the line.
9. Delete the label from the first text box, and then select the text box control. Go to the property sheet for the control, and then type *=[TypeDescription] & "-"* as the setting for the Control Source property. With this setting, the item category will be displayed in the footer, concatenated with a hyphen. Line up this control under the Description control.
10. Change the caption in the label of the second text box to read *Average Cost*. In the Control Source property of the second text box, enter the formula *=Avg([OurCost])*. This formula calculates the average of all the cost values within the group. Set the Format property to Currency so that the average will be preceded by a dollar sign. Line up this control under the OurCost control.
11. Change the caption in the label of the third text box to read *Total In Stock*. In the Control Source property of the third text box, enter the formula *=Sum([NumberInStock])*. This formula calculates the total of all the in-stock values within the group. Line up this control under the NumberInStock column.
12. Finally, create an unbound text box in the lower right corner of the page footer section. Type *Page:* as the caption of the label and enter the formula *=Page & " of " & Pages* in the Control Source property of the text box. *Page* is a system variable that contains the current page number. *Pages* is a different system variable that contains the total number of pages in the report.

When you've finished, click the Print Preview button on the toolbar to see your results, as shown in Figure 17-6 on the next page. Notice that in this figure, the detail lines are not sorted in any particular order. You can add the Description field to the Sorting And Grouping box and set the sort order to Ascending to see the components sorted by name.

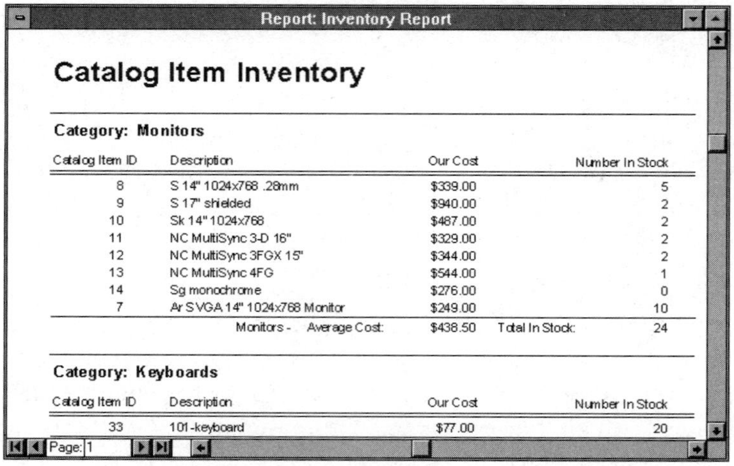

Report: Inventory Report

Catalog Item Inventory

Category: Monitors

Catalog Item ID	Description	Our Cost	Number In Stock
8	S 14" 1024x768 .28mm	$339.00	5
9	S 17" shielded	$940.00	2
10	Sk 14" 1024x768	$487.00	2
11	NC MultiSync 3-D 16"	$329.00	2
12	NC MultiSync 3FGX 15"	$344.00	2
13	NC MultiSync 4FG	$544.00	1
14	Sg monochrome	$276.00	0
7	Ar SVGA 14" 1024x768 Monitor	$249.00	10
	Monitors - Average Cost:	$438.50	Total In Stock: 24

Category: Keyboards

Catalog Item ID	Description	Our Cost	Number In Stock
33	101-keyboard	$77.00	20

Page: 1

FIGURE 17-6. The Inventory Report report in Print Preview.

Working with Report Wizards

Similar to the Form Wizards you used to create forms are the Report Wizards that Microsoft Access provides to assist you in constructing reports. To practice using a Report Wizard, you can build the Inventory Report report again. Open the Database window, click the Query tab, and select the Catalog Report Query you built earlier. Click the New Report button on the toolbar, and click the Report Wizards button in the New Report dialog box.

Choosing a Report Type

The Microsoft Access Report Wizards offer you seven report format options, several of which are shown in Figure 17-7. Here are the format options:

Single-Column	This report is very similar in format to the single-column form you saw in Chapter 13, "Building a Form." The Single-Column Report Wizard builds a simple report header and footer and displays in a column the data from fields you select. Labels are placed to the left of the column.

Group/Totals	This report displays in a single row across the report the data from the fields you select. The Group/Totals Report Wizard provides subtotals for all numeric fields within each group of fields you select. (You'll use this Report Wizard in the next section to duplicate the Inventory Report report.)
Mailing Label	This Report Wizard lets you select name and address fields and format them to print mailing labels. You can choose from a number of popular label types. The Report Wizard will size your labels correctly.
Summary	This report is like a Group/Totals report, but with no detail lines printed. This Report Wizard generates totals and, optionally, percentages of totals for the groups you select.
Tabular	This Report Wizard displays in a single row across the report the data from fields you select, but it does not generate any totals.
AutoReport	Using this Report Wizard is the same as clicking the AutoReport button on the toolbar. This is a tabular report in Presentation style.
MS Word Mail Merge	Using this Report Wizard is the same as clicking the Merge It button on the toolbar when viewing tables or queries in the Database window.

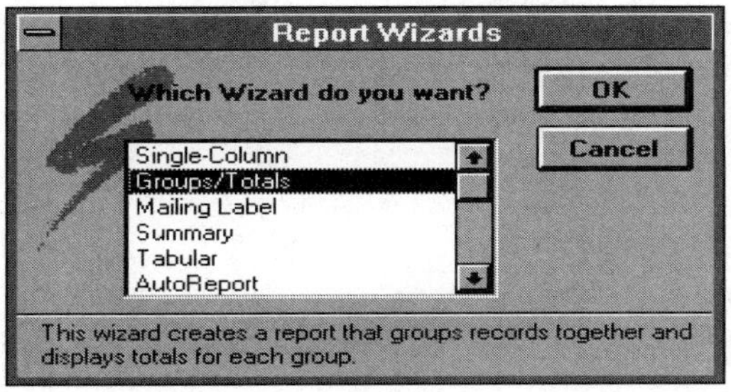

FIGURE 17-7.
The Microsoft Access Report Wizards dialog box.

Because the report you built earlier included a group and subtotals, select the Group/Totals option in the Microsoft Access Report Wizards dialog box, as shown in Figure 17-7, and click OK.

Specifying Parameters for a Group/Totals Report

The next dialog box that the Microsoft Access Report Wizard displays, shown in Figure 17-8, will allow you to select the fields you want in your report. You can select all available fields in the sequence in which they appear in the underlying query or report by clicking the double right arrow (>>) button. If you want to select only some of the fields or if you want to choose the order in which the fields appear on the report, select one field at a time in the list box on the left, and click the single right arrow (>) button to move the field into the list box on the right. If you make a mistake, you can select from the list box on the right the field you placed in the report in error and then click the single left arrow (<) button to remove the field from the list box. Click the double left arrow (<<) button to remove all selected fields from the right list box and start over.

FIGURE 17-8. The Group/Totals Report Wizard dialog box for selecting fields.

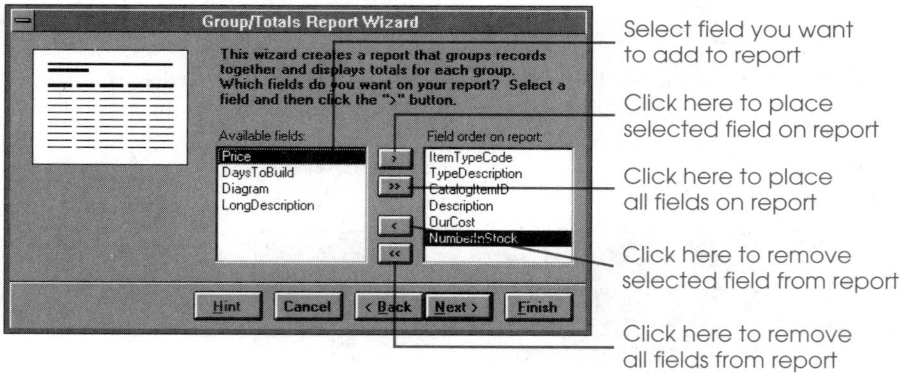

To create an Inventory Report report, you should first select the ItemTypeCode field. You also want to display the TypeDescription, CatalogItemID, Description, OurCost, and NumberInStock fields, in that order. When you've finished selecting fields, click the Next button to go on to the next step.

In the next Report Wizard dialog box, shown in Figure 17-9, the Report Wizard asks which fields you want to use for grouping records. You can select up to four fields. The Report Wizard doesn't allow you to enter an expression as a grouping value—something you can do when you build a report from scratch. If you want to use an expression as a grouping value in a Report Wizard, you have to include that expression in the underlying query. For this report, you should select ItemTypeCode as the field by which you want to group records, as shown in Figure 17-9. Click the Next button to go on to the next step.

In the next Report Wizard dialog box, shown in Figure 17-10, the Report Wizard asks you to specify how you want to group data in each grouping field you've selected.

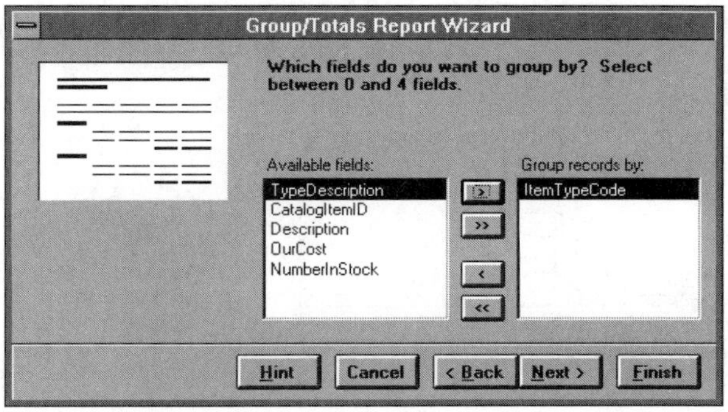

FIGURE 17-9.
The Group/Totals Report Wizard dialog box for selecting the fields by which you want to group.

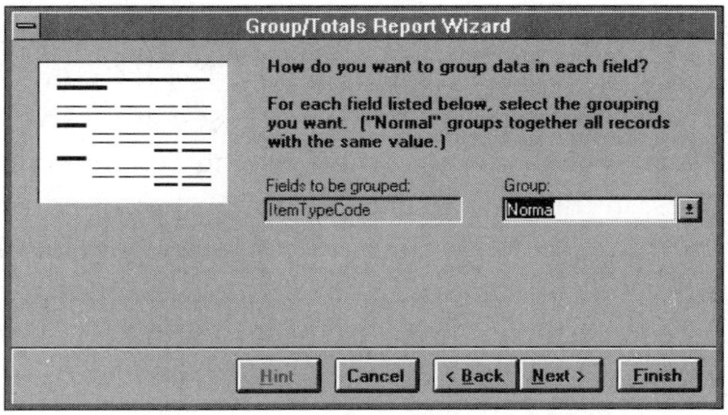

FIGURE 17-10.
The Group/Totals Report Wizard dialog box for selecting how you want to group data.

For text fields, you can group by the entire field or by one to five of the leading characters in the fields. For date/time fields, you can group by individual values or by year, quarter, month, week, day, hour, or minute. For numeric fields, you can group by individual values or in increments of 10, 50, 100, 500, 1000, and so on, up to 500,000. The ItemTypeCode field, although it contains numbers, is actually a text field. Select the Normal grouping to create a new group for each unique item type code. Click the Next button to see a dialog box that asks you to select any additional fields to determine sorting within the detail section of the report, as shown in Figure 17-11. You can select CatalogItemID and then click Next.

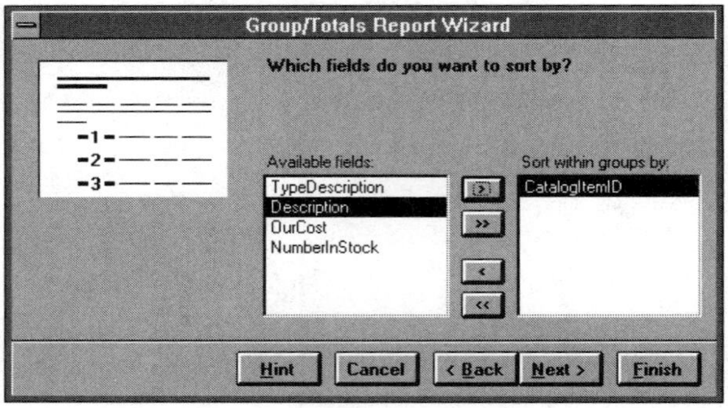

FIGURE 17-11. The Group/Totals Report Wizard dialog box for selecting the fields by which you want to sort.

The next-to-last Report Wizard dialog box is shown in Figure 17-12. It lets you choose between three formatting styles. When you click any option button, the Report Wizard shows you a sample of that report style in the display box on the left of the dialog box. The Executive style is a crisp format with lines dividing sections. The Presentation style uses a larger font and thick lines to separate sections. The Ledger style surrounds all data in boxes, in the style of a spreadsheet. You can also decide to format the report in either Portrait mode (vertical orientation) or Landscape mode (horizontal orientation). You can choose the spacing you want between lines. Because you're trying to emulate the report you built "by hand" earlier, choose 0 inches spacing. Click the Executive option button and then click the Next button.

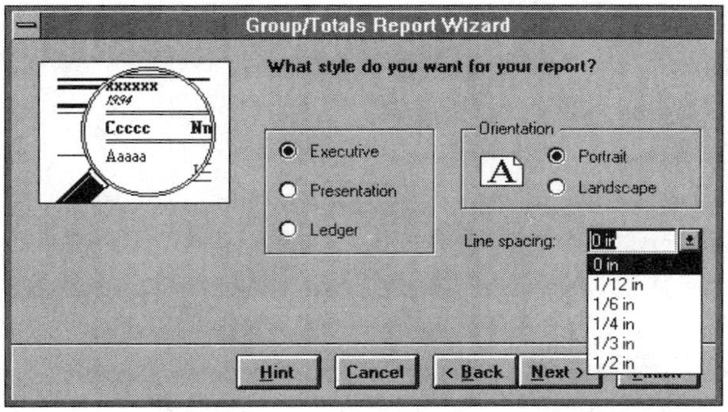

FIGURE 17-12. The Group/Totals Report Wizard dialog box for selecting a formatting style.

In the final Report Wizard dialog box, which is shown in Figure 17-13, you can type a report title. You can also ask the Report Wizard to attempt to fit all fields on one page. If you click the Calculate Percentages Of The Total check box, the Report Wizard generates additional controls below each total that show you what percentage each group is of the overall total.

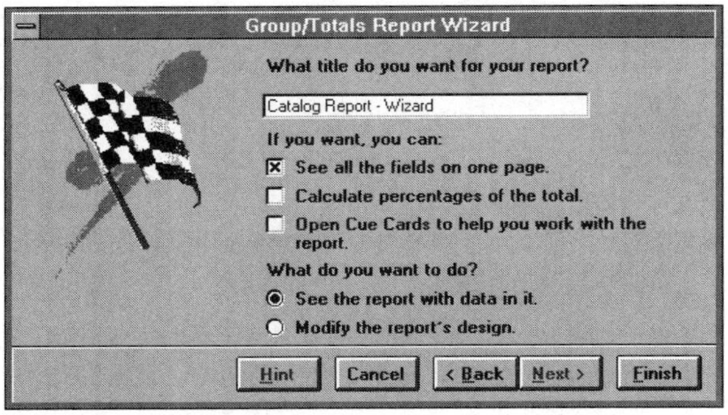

FIGURE 17-13. The Group/Totals Report Wizard dialog box for selecting a title.

If you are using the Report Wizard to start the design for a complex report with many fields, clicking the See All The Fields On One Page check box causes the Report Wizard to lay the fields one on top of another in a single row. You might find it difficult to sort out the overlapped fields when you customize the report in Design view. If you do not click the See All The Fields On One Page check box, the Report Wizard places only the fields that fit across your report, starting with the first field in your list. You can add fields when you customize the design by using the toolbox and the field list. For this report, you have only a few fields, so you should ask the Report Wizard to attempt to fit all fields on a single page.

Viewing the Report Wizard Result

Click the See The Report With Data In It option, and then click the Finish button in the final Report Wizard dialog box (shown in Figure 17-13 on the previous page) to create the report and display the result in Print Preview, as shown in Figure 17-14.

You can press Esc to return to Design view. It's easy to use Design view to modify a few minor items (such as changing the cost total to an average and deleting the total that the Report Wizard created for the CatalogItemID field) to obtain a result nearly identical to the report you constructed earlier. You can save this report as *Inventory Wizard.* As you might imagine, Report Wizards are a good way to get a head start on more complex report designs.

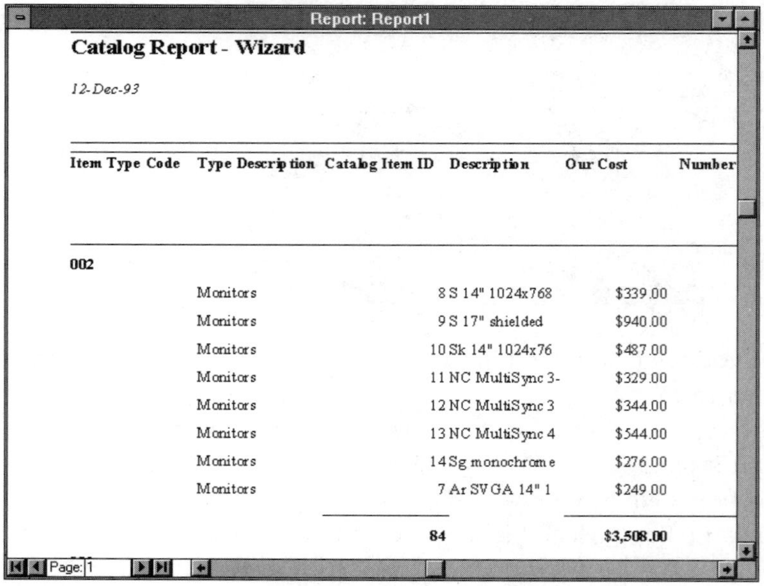

FIGURE 17-14. The Inventory Wizard report as created by the Group/Totals Report Wizard.

You should now feel comfortable with constructing reports. In the next chapter, you'll learn how to build a complex report with a subreport and embedded pictures—the Prompt Computer Solutions customer invoice.

18

Advanced Report Design

In the last chapter, you learned how to create a relatively simple report with a single subtotal level. You also saw how a Report Wizard can assist you in constructing a new report. This chapter shows you how to

- Design a report with multiple subtotal groups
- Add complex calculations to your report
- Display or hide information based on a condition
- Embed a report within another report
- Add pictures to enhance your report
- Create a complex "spreadsheet" report

To learn how to work with these features, you'll build an invoice report for the PROMPT database. (The companion disk that comes with this book contains all the tables, queries, forms, reports, macros, and modules of the PROMPT database. See "Using the Companion Disk," on page xxiv.) You'll also build a complex sales summary report.

Creating the Invoice Query

As noted in the previous chapter, because reports tend to bring together information from many tables, you are most likely to begin constructing a report by designing a query to retrieve the data you need for the report. For this example, you need information from the Catalog, Customer, Order, OrderItem, and Type tables in the PROMPT database. Open a new Query window in Design view and add these tables to the query. The top section of the Query window should look similar to the one shown in Figure 18-1 on the next page. If you created all the table relationships properly, Microsoft Access links the tables for you. Even if you didn't create relationships for all the tables, Access creates links by matching field names and data types. Add the fields listed in Figure 18-2 on the next page to the QBE grid of this query. Drag and drop the * from the Order field list onto the QBE grid to create the Order.* field.

FIGURE 18-1.
The Invoice Main Query query for the Invoice report.

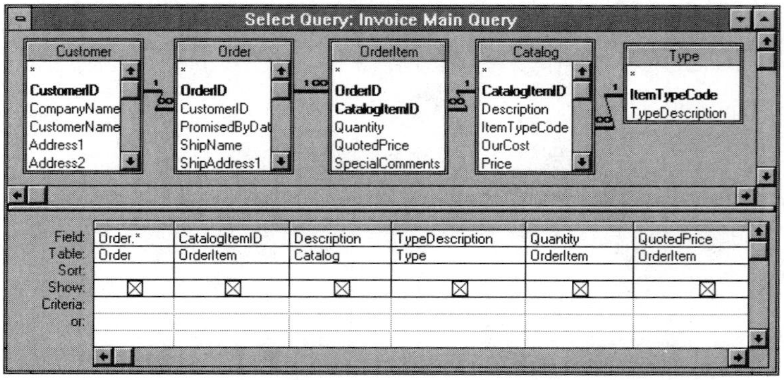

FIGURE 18-2.
The fields in the Invoice Main Query query.

Field	Source Table
Description	Catalog
CompanyName	Customer
CustomerName	Customer
Address1	Customer
Address2	Customer
City	Customer
State	Customer
PostalCode	Customer
Country	Customer
CatalogItemID	OrderItem
Quantity	OrderItem
QuotedPrice	OrderItem
Order.*	Order
TypeDescription	Type
ItemTypeCode	Type

Save the query and name it *Invoice Main Query*. (This query is already constructed on the companion disk containing the PROMPT database.) Select this query in the Database window and click the New Report button on the toolbar. Click the Blank Report button in the New Report dialog box to open the Report window in Design view. (Because there are so many fields in this report, it is easier to build the report without a Report Wizard.)

Defining the Groups Query

The first thing you need to do is define the sorting and grouping criteria for the report. Click the Sorting And Grouping button on the toolbar to open the Sorting And Grouping window. Because you might decide to print several invoices in one print run, you should start with a grouping based on the OrderID field. Select Yes for the Group Header and Group Footer properties.

Notice that when you set Group Header or Group Footer to Yes for any field or expression in the Sorting And Grouping window, Microsoft Access shows you a grouping symbol on the row selector for that row. Let's assume that your largest customers have also asked for a subtotal by item type in the report, so add a grouping based on the TypeDescription field and also set its Group Header and Group Footer properties to *Yes*. (You could use the ItemTypeCode field for this grouping, but it would be nice to have these category descriptions sorted alphabetically using the TypeDescription field.) Set the Keep Together property for the TypeDescription grouping to *Whole Group* so that Access will attempt to fit entire product categories on one page. Finally, you should sort the Description field within each detail group alphabetically. Even if you've specified this sorting on the Invoice Main Query query, you must also define the sorting you want in the report definition. Reports ignore any sorting specification from the source query. Your result should look something like Figure 18-3.

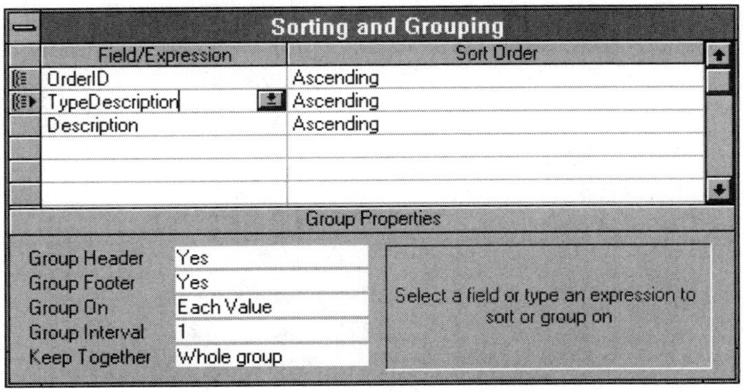

FIGURE 18-3.
The sorting and grouping settings for the Invoice report.

Setting Group Ranges by Data Type

For each field or expression at the top of the Sorting And Grouping window, you can define Group On and Group Interval properties. Normally, you want to start a new grouping of data whenever the value of your field or expression changes. You can, however, specify that a new grouping starts based on a range of values. The kind of range you can specify varies depending on the data type of the field or expression.

For text grouping fields, you can ask Microsoft Access to start a new group based on a change in value of one or more leading characters in the string. For example, you could create a new group based on a change in the first letter of the field, rather than on a change anywhere in the field, to create one group per letter of the alphabet—a group of items beginning with *A*, a group of items beginning with *B*, and so on. To group on a prefix, set the Group On property to Prefix Characters, and set the Group Interval property to the number of leading characters you want to determine each group.

For numbers, you can set the Group On property to Interval. When you select this setting, you can enter a setting for the Group Interval property that will cluster multiple values within a range. Microsoft Access calculates ranges from 0. For example, if you choose 10 as the interval value, you'll see groups for the values –20 through –11, –10 through –1, 0 through 9, 10 through 19, 20 through 29, and so on.

For date/time fields, you can set the Group On property to calendar or time subdivisions and multiples of those subdivisions, such as Year, Qtr, Month, Week, Day, Hour, and Minute. Include a setting for the Group Interval property if you want to group on a multiple of the subdivision—for example, set Group On to Year and Group Interval to 2 if you want groupings for every two years.

NOTE: When you create groupings in which the Group Interval property is set to something other than Each Value, Microsoft Access sorts only the grouping value, not the individual values within each group. If you want the detail items within the group sorted, you must include a separate sort specification for that field. For example, if you group on the first two letters of a Name field and also want the names within each group sorted, you must enter *Name* as the field in the Sorting And Grouping window with Group Header (and possibly Group Footer) set to *Yes*, Sort Order set to Ascending, Group On set to Prefix Characters, and Group Interval set to *2*, and then you must enter *Name* as the field again with Sort Order set to Ascending and Group On set to Each Value.

Creating the Basic Invoice Report

Now that you've defined the groups, you're ready to start building the report. Before you go further, choose the Save As command from the File menu, and save the report as *Invoices*. (You can find the completed report in the PROMPT sample database saved as *Invoice*.) You can create the basic report by performing the following steps. Refer to Figure 18-4 to see the results of the steps described.

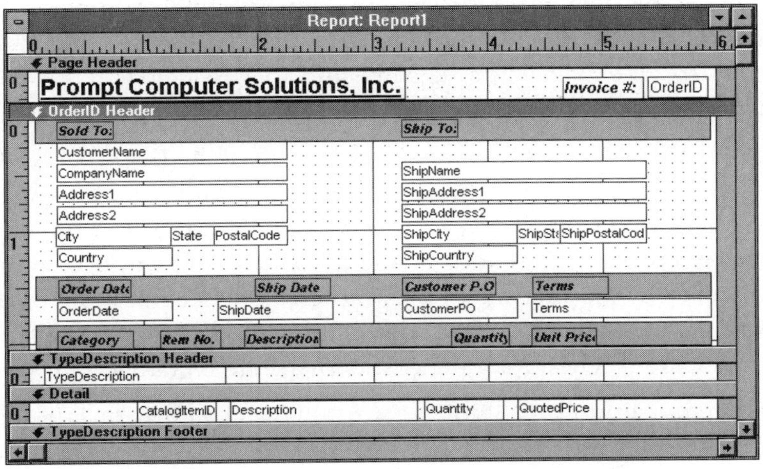

FIGURE 18-4.
The top section of the Invoices report in Design view.

1. Place a label in the page header and type *Prompt Computer Solutions, Inc*. Select the label, set the font to Arial, and choose a font size of 14 points from the toolbar. Click the Bold button to make the title stand out. Open the property sheet and set the Font Underline property to Yes to add emphasis. Choose the Size To Fit

command from the Format menu to expand the label to fit your text. Drag the right border of the detail section to widen the report to about 6 inches. Drag the OrderID field to the page header near the right margin, and then select the control's label and change it to read *Invoice #*. Make the label bold and italic.

2. Move from the page header section to the OrderID header section. Expand the OrderID header section to give yourself at least 2 inches of vertical working space. At the top of the OrderID header section, add a rectangle about 0.2 inch high and extend it to almost the width of the report. Open the Palette. Be sure the rectangle's border color is black, and set its background color to light gray. Create two labels, one reading *Sold To:* and the other *Ship To:*, and place them on the rectangle, as shown in Figure 18-4 on the previous page. Make their text bold italic, and click the Clear button on the Back Color line of the Palette for both of these labels.

3. Under the *Sold To:* label, add text box controls (but delete their labels) for the CustomerName, CompanyName, Address1, Address2, City, State, PostalCode, and Country fields. Under the *Ship To:* label, add shipping name and address field text box controls (but delete their labels).

4. Select the rectangle you created at the top of the OrderID header section, choose the Duplicate command from the Edit menu to create a duplicate copy of the rectangle, and position the copy below the name and address fields. Choose the Duplicate command from the Edit menu again to create a second copy of the rectangle. Drag the second copy of the rectangle a little lower in the header section than the first copy of the rectangle.

5. Drag the OrderDate, ShipDate, CustomerPO, and Terms fields to the OrderID header section. Position them below the second gray rectangle. Grab the move handle in the upper left corner of each label and place the label in the second gray rectangle, above its corresponding text box. Change the text in the labels to bold italic for emphasis. In the Palette, click the Clear button on the Back Color line for these labels.

6. Drag the TypeDescription field to the TypeDescription header section. Select its label and choose the Cut command on the Edit menu to disconnect the label from the control. Choose the Paste command on the Edit menu to paste the label into the detail section (although the label won't be connected to the control anymore), and then move this label to the third gray rectangle in the OrderID header section and change its caption to read *Category* in bold italic. In the Palette, click the Clear button on the Back Color line. Position the TypeDescription text box immediately below the Category label and at the very top of the TypeDescription header section. Widen the TypeDescription text box. Shrink the TypeDescription header section so that there's no space above or below the control.

7. Drag the CatalogItemID, Description, Quantity, and QuotedPrice fields to the detail section of the report. Separate each label from its control (using the Cut and Paste commands), and place the labels above their respective controls in the third gray rectangle you created in the OrderID header section. Change the CatalogItemID caption to *Item No*. Change the QuotedPrice caption to *Unit Price*. Leave some room at the right side of the report to add one more control later in this exercise. Change the text in the labels to bold italic for emphasis. In the Palette, click the Clear button on the Back Color line for these labels.

8. Next, scroll down in the Report window until you can see the TypeDescription footer and OrderID footer sections. Close up the TypeDescription footer section to 0 height for now; you'll add some controls to show totals here later. Drag the SubtotalCost, Discount, SalesTax, and FreightCharge fields to the OrderID footer, in one of the columns to the right. Change the FreightCharge label to *Freight:*. Your result should look something like the one shown in Figure 18-5 on the next page. Because you want to force each invoice to start on a new page, click the OrderID header bar and set its Force New Page property to *Before Section*.

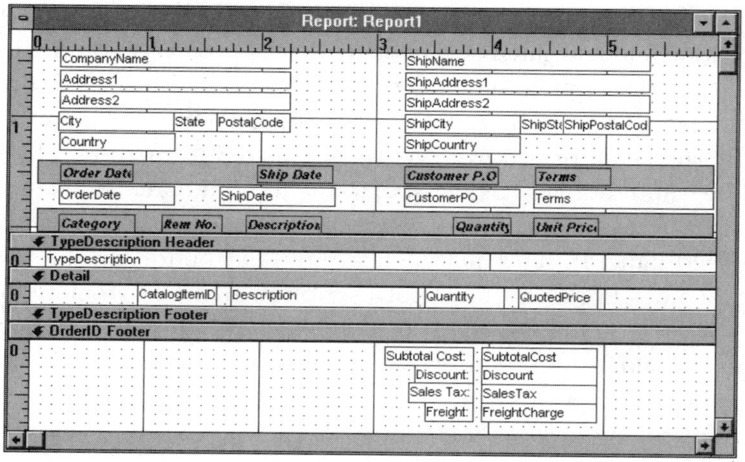

FIGURE 18-5. The bottom section of the Invoices report in Design view.

When you click the Print Preview button on the toolbar and maximize the Report window, your result should look something like the one shown in Figure 18-6.

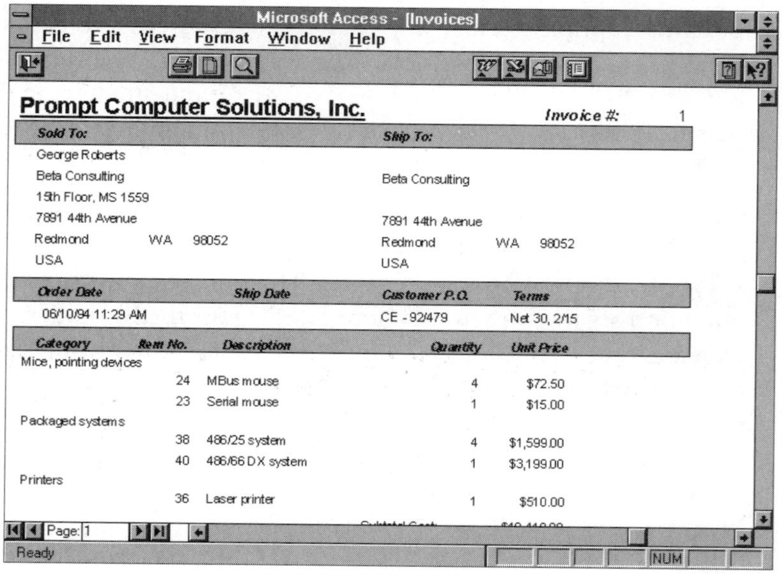

FIGURE 18-6. The Invoices report in Print Preview.

NOTE: Many laser printers that support the HP PCL printer language might not display dark type on a colored background or white type on a black background properly. To ensure that type overlaid on a colored background always prints properly, use a TrueType font. Also, choose Print Setup from the File menu, click the Options button, and be sure the Print TrueType As Graphics check box is clicked.

Understanding Section and Report Properties

You've probably noticed that Microsoft Access has a property sheet for each section in the Report window in Design view. You've already set one of the section properties in the exercise above so that each invoice starts on a new page. There's also a property sheet for the report as a whole. You don't need to change any more of these properties at this time, but the following sections explain the available property settings.

Section Properties

Click in the blank area of any group section or detail section of a report, and Microsoft Access displays a property sheet, such as the one shown in Figure 18-7.

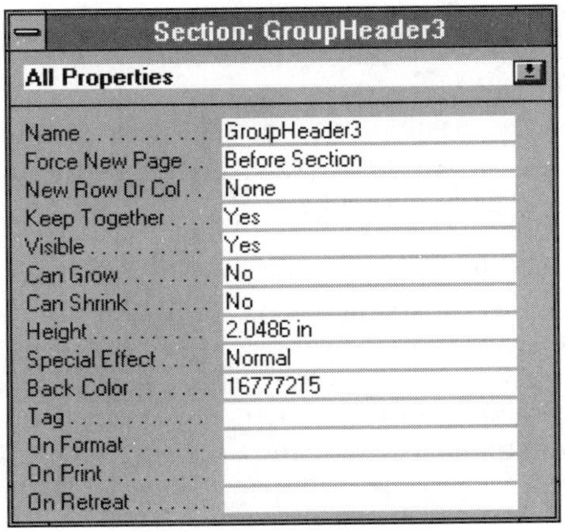

FIGURE 18-7.
A property sheet for a report section.

The available properties and their uses are described below:

Name	Microsoft Access automatically generates a section name for you and numbers each one for uniqueness. Especially if you write macros or Microsoft Access Basic code that reference report sections, you might want to create your own more meaningful names.
Force New Page	Set this property to Before Section to force this section to print at the top of a new page. Set this property to After Section to force the next section to print at the top of a new page.
New Row Or Col	When you use Print Setup to format your report with more than one column (vertical) or more than one row (horizontal) of sections, you can set this property to Before Section, After Section, or Before & After to force Access to produce the section again at the top or the bottom (or both) of a new column or row. This property is useful for forcing headers to print again at the top of each column on a multiple-column report.
Keep Together	Set this property to No to allow Access to flow a section across page boundaries. The default Yes setting tells Access to attempt to keep all lines within a section together on a page. You can ask Access to attempt to keep lines with group headers and footers together by setting the Keep Together property to Yes for the grouping specification in the Sorting And Grouping window.
Visible	Set this property to Yes to make the section visible or to No to make the section invisible. This is a handy property to set from a macro or from an Access Basic routine while Access formats and prints your report. You can make sections disappear, depending on data values in the report. (See Chapter 19, "Adding Power with Macros," for details.)
Can Grow	Access sets this value to Yes when you include any control in the section that also has its Can Grow property set to Yes. This allows the section to expand to accommodate controls that might expand because they display memo fields or long text strings. You can design a control to

	display one line of text, but you should allow the control to expand to display more lines of text as needed.
Can Shrink	This property is similar to Can Grow. You can set it to Yes to allow the section to become smaller if controls in the section become smaller to accommodate less text. You'll use Can Shrink later in this chapter to make a control disappear when the control contains no data.
Tag	NEW! Use this property to store additional identifying information about the section. You can use this property in macros and Microsoft Access Basic to temporarily store information that you want to pass to another routine.
On Format	Enter the name of a macro or module function you want Access to execute when it begins formatting this section. (See Chapters 19 and 21 for details.)
On Print	Enter the name of a macro or module function you want Access to execute when it begins printing this section or when it displays the section in Print Preview. (See Chapter 19 for details.)
On Retreat	NEW! Enter the name of a macro or module function you want Access to execute when it has to "back up" over a section after it finds that the section won't fit on the current page and you've set Keep Together to Yes. This event happens after On Format but before On Print, so you can use it to undo settings you might have changed in your On Format routine. Access calls On Format again when it formats the section on a new page.

The remaining properties on the property sheet (Height, Special Effect, and Back Color) control how the section looks. Whenever you adjust the height of the section by dragging its lower border, Microsoft Access resets the section's Height property. You can set the Special Effect and Back Color properties using the Palette.

For page and report headers and footers, only the Name, Visible, Height, Special Effect, Back Color, Tag, On Format, and On Print properties are available.

Report Properties

If you choose the Select Report command from the Edit menu or click beyond the right edge of the detail section, Microsoft Access displays the report's properties on the property sheet, as shown in Figure 18-8.

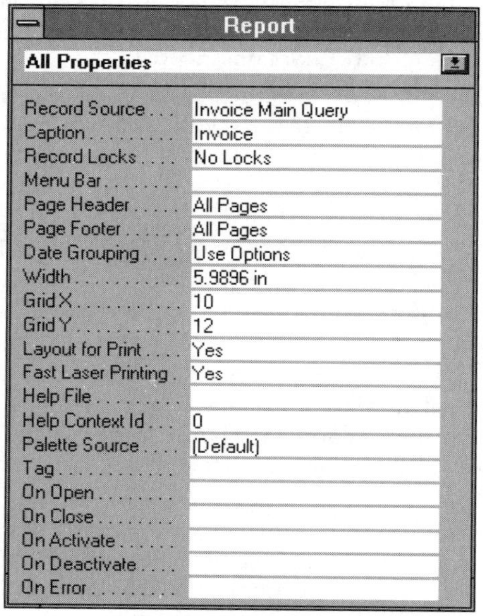

FIGURE 18-8. The property sheet for a report.

The available properties and their uses are described below:

NEW!

Record Source	This setting displays the name of the table or query that provides the data for your report.
Caption	Use this property to enter the text that appears in the title bar when you open the report in Print Preview.
Record Locks	Set this property to Yes if the data for your report is on a server shared by others and you want to be sure no one can update the records in the report until Access creates every page in the report. You should not set this property to Yes for a report you plan to view in Print Preview because you'll be locking out other users for the entire time that you're viewing the report on your screen.

Menu Bar	Enter the name of the macro that defines a custom menu bar that Access displays when you open the report in Print Preview. (See Chapter 23 for details.) If you want to hide the menu bar when your report opens, set this property to True.
Page Header	This property controls whether the page header appears on all pages. You can choose not to print the page header on the first and last pages if these pages contain a report header or a report footer.
Page Footer	This property controls whether the page footer appears on all pages. You can choose not to print the page footer on the first and last pages if these pages contain a report header or a report footer.
Date Grouping	Use this property to determine how Access groups date and time values you've specified in the Sorting And Grouping window. You can set this property to *US Defaults* or *Use Options*. For *US Defaults,* the first day of the week is Sunday, and the first week of the year starts on January 1. You can choose *Use Options* and then select Options from the View menu to set the First Weekday and First Week properties. You can set a week to start on any day. You can set the first week to start on January 1, the first 4-day week, or the first full week.
Width	This property is set by Access when you stretch the width of the report on the design grid.
Grid X, Grid Y	Specify the number of horizontal (X) or vertical (Y) divisions per inch or per centimeter for the dots in the report design area. When you are using inches (because Measurement is set to English in the International section of the Control Panel in Microsoft Windows), you can see the dots whenever you choose a value of 16 or less for both X and Y. In centimeters (Measurement is set to Metric), you can see the dots when you choose values of 6 or less.
Layout For Print	When this property is set to Yes, you can choose from several TrueType and printer fonts in your design. When set to No, screen fonts are available.

Fast Laser Printing	Some laser printers support drawing lines (such as the edges of rectangles, the line control, or the edges of text boxes) with rules. If you set Fast Laser Printing to Yes, Access sends rule commands instead of graphics to your printer to print rules. Rules print faster than graphics.
Help File, Help Context ID	You can create custom help text using the Microsoft Windows Help Compiler provided in the Microsoft Windows Software Development Kit or in the Microsoft Access Developer's Toolkit. (See the development kit documentation for details.)
Palette Source	If you have a color printer, you can specify a device-independent bitmap file (DIB), Microsoft Windows Palette file (PAL), Windows icon file (ICO), or Windows bitmap file (BMP) to provide a palette of colors different from those in the Access default.
Tag	Use this property to store additional identifying information about the report. You can use this property in macros and in Microsoft Access Basic to temporarily store information that you want to pass to another routine.
On Open	Enter the name of a macro or module function you want Access to execute when it begins printing this report or when it displays the report in Print Preview. (See Chapter 19, "Adding Power with Macros," for details.)
On Close	Enter the name of a macro or module function you want Access to execute when you close Print Preview or when Access has finished sending the report to your printer or to Print Manager in Microsoft Windows. (See Chapter 19 for details.)
On Activate	Enter the name of a macro or module function you want Access to execute when the Report window gains the focus in Print Preview. This property provides a convenient method of opening a custom toolbar.
On Deactivate	Enter the name of a macro or module function you want Access to execute when the Report window loses the focus in Print Preview. This property provides a convenient method of closing a custom toolbar.

On Error	Enter the name of a macro or module function you want Access to execute when any errors occur in the report.

Using Calculated Values

Some of the true power of Microsoft Access reports comes from the ability to perform both simple and complex calculations on the data from your underlying table or query. Access also provides dozens of built-in functions that you can use to work with your data or to add information to your report. The following sections show you samples of the types of calculations you can perform.

Adding Print Date and Page Numbers

One of the pieces of information you might add most frequently to a report is the date on which you prepared the report. You'll probably also want to add page numbers. For dates, Microsoft Access provides two built-in functions that you can use to add the current date and time to your report. The *Date( )* function returns the current system date as a Date/Time variable with no time component. The *Now( )* function returns the current system date and time as a Date/Time variable.

To add the current date to your report, create an unbound text box control and set its Control Source property to *=Date( )*. Then, in the Format property box, choose a date/time setting. Go back to the report and type a meaningful caption for the label. You can see an example in Figure 18-9. The result in Print Preview is shown in Figure 18-10 on the next page.

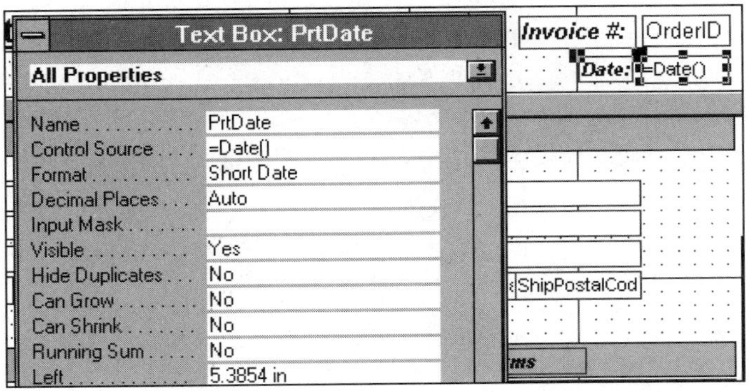

FIGURE 18-9.
The *Date()* function is used to add the date to a report.

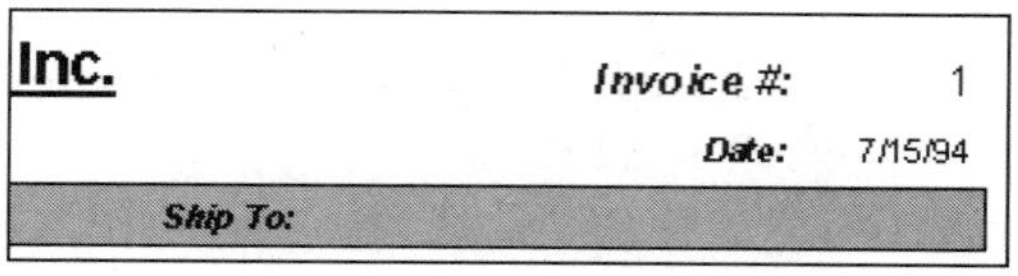

FIGURE 18-10. The current date is displayed on the Invoices report in Print Preview.

To add a page number, use the Page property for the report. You can't see this property on any of the property sheets because it is maintained by Microsoft Access. To add the current page number to your report (in this example, in the page footer section), create an unbound text box control and set its Control Source property to *=Page,* as shown in Figure 18-11.

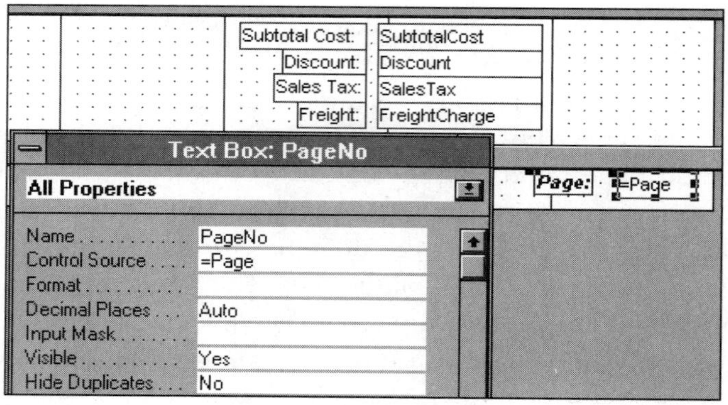

FIGURE 18-11. The Page property is used to add page numbers to a report.

You can reset the value of the Page property in a macro or module function that you activate from an appropriate report property. For example, if you schedule several invoices to print at one time, you probably want each invoice for a different customer to start with a page number of 1. You can accomplish that by entering a single line of code in the On Format property box of the OrderID header section to set the page number back to 1 each time Access starts to print an invoice for a different order.

To reset the page number on each order, do the following:

1. Select the OrderID header section. Scroll down in the property sheet and select the On Format property, as shown in Figure 18-12.

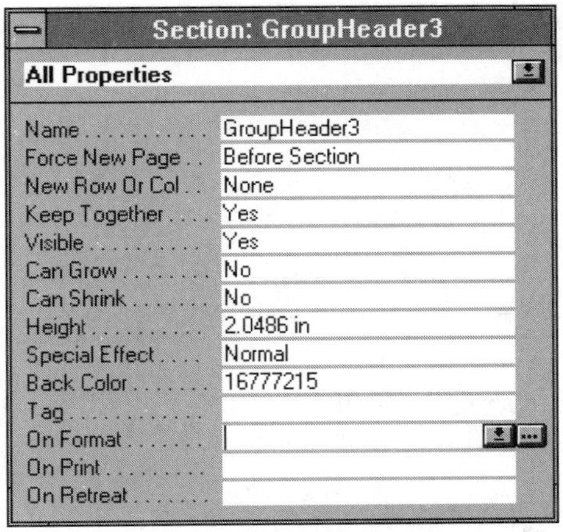

FIGURE 18-12.
Selecting the On Format property for the OrderID header section (which makes the Build button appear).

2. Click the Build button (the one with three dots) at the far right of the On Format property box. Microsoft Access displays the dialog box shown in Figure 18-13.

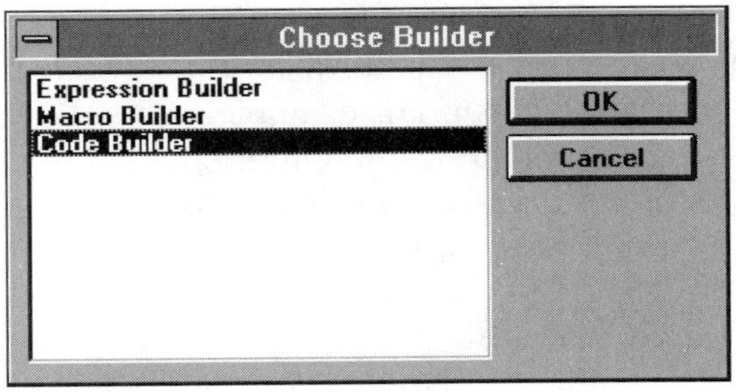

FIGURE 18-13.
The Code Builder is selected.

3. Choose the Code Builder option and click OK. Access shows you the code module for the report with the template of the function you need filled in.
4. Type in a statement to set the system Page property back to 1 each time Access formats a new OrderID header section, as shown in Figure 18-14 on the next page.

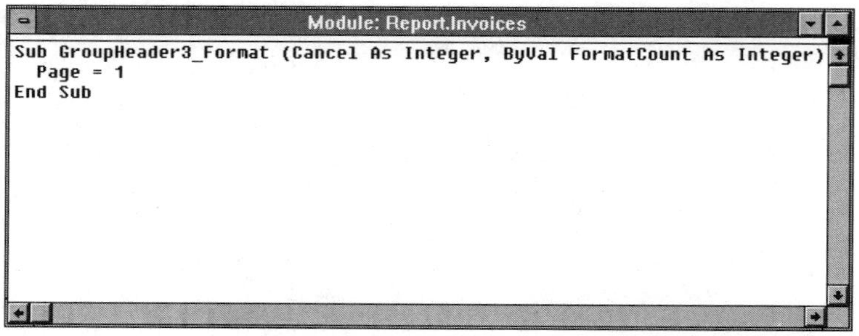

FIGURE 18-14. This procedure sets the system Page property back to 1 each time Access starts to print a new order.

When you open the report in Print Preview, you'll find that Access now starts over with page number 1 for each order.

Arithmetic Calculations

Another task you might perform frequently is calculating extended values from detail values in your tables. You might remember from the exercise in which you designed your database tables in Chapter 4 that it's usually redundant and wasteful of storage space to define in your tables the fields that you calculate from other fields. (The one time that this is acceptable is when saving the calculated value greatly improves performance in parts of your application. For example, in the PROMPT database, there's an extended subtotal in the Order table so that you don't have to fetch all the order items in an order when you want to know only the total amount due for the order.)

Calculation on a Detail Line

The OrderItem table contains a Quantity field and a QuotedPrice field but not a calculation of the extended amount (quantity times price). Your customers will probably want to see the extended amount on the invoice, so you need to calculate that value in your report. Remember that there's some room at the right side of the detail section in the Invoice report. Create an unbound text box control and place it there, next to the QuotedPrice control. Cut and paste the control's label, and move the label onto the last gray rectangle in the OrderID header section. Change the label's caption to *Amount*, select the label, format it in bold italic, and click the Clear button on the Back Color line of the Palette. Choose the Size To Fit command from the Format menu to size the label. Change the text box's Name property to *Amount*. The calculation of the extended amount will be the content of the new unbound text box control. To refer to the name of any control in a calculation expression, simply type the name of the control enclosed in brackets.

You can add arithmetic operators and parentheses to create complex calculations. You can also use any of the many built-in functions or any of the functions you define yourself in a module. If you like, you can use the Expression Builder that you learned about in Chapter 8 and Chapter 17 to build the expression for this control. Because you want to multiply the value in the Quantity control by the value in the QuotedPrice control, enter *=[Quantity]*[QuotedPrice]* in the Control Source property of the new control, as shown in Figure 18-15. Set the Format property to Currency to display the number correctly.

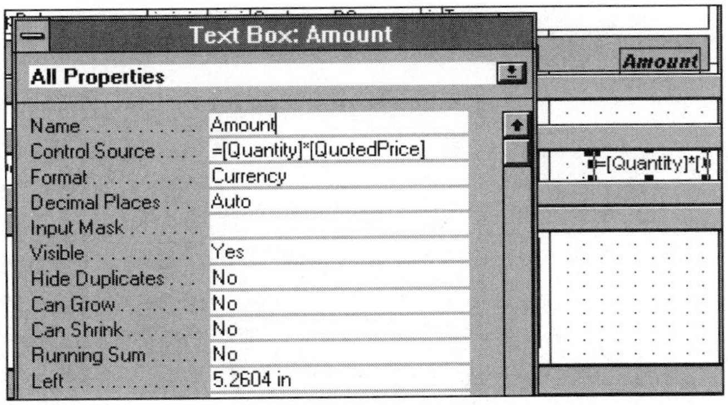

FIGURE 18-15. A calculated expression is set as the source of a control.

Figure 18-16 on the next page shows you the result in Print Preview. (This figure shows some additional total values that you'll add in the next section.) You can see that Microsoft Access has performed the required calculation on each line and displayed the result.

Total Across a Group

Another task commonly used in reports is adding values across a group. You already learned how to do that for uncalculated values (in Chapter 17) using the built-in *Sum* function. You can also use the *Sum* function to add calculated values such as the extended amount. You might think that you can use the name of the unbound control (in this case, *[Amount]*) with the *Sum* function to get a total of the extended amounts listed in the Amount control. However, Microsoft Access doesn't actually store the calculated values in the control, so *Sum([Amount])* would be trying to add nothing. To get the sum of calculated values, you need to repeat the calculation formula as the parameter for the *Sum* function.

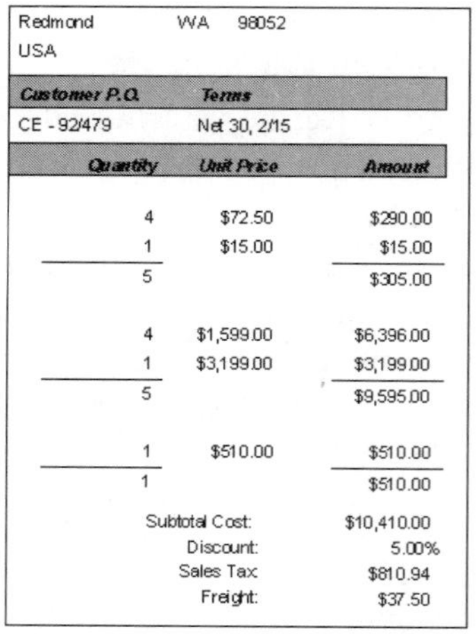
Redmond WA 98052
USA
Customer P.O.
Terms
CE - 92/479
Net 30, 2/15
Quantity
Unit Price
Amount
4 $72.50 $290.00
1 $15.00 $15.00
5 $305.00
4 $1,599.00 $6,396.00
1 $3,199.00 $3,199.00
5 $9,595.00
1 $510.00 $510.00
1 $510.00
Subtotal Cost: $10,410.00
Discount: 5.00%
Sales Tax: $810.94
Freight: $37.50

FIGURE 18-16. The calculation (of quantity times quoted price) is displayed in the Amount column of the report in Print Preview.

For example, to calculate the subtotal of the number of items ordered and the subtotal of the amount for each, you can add unbound text boxes to the TypeDescription footer section under the Quantity and Amount columns. (You'll first need to drag down the TypeDescription footer section.) Enter *=Sum([Quantity])* in the Control Source property box for the first text box, and then enter *=Sum([Quantity]*[QuotedPrice])* in the Control Source property box for the second text box, as shown in Figure 18-17. Delete the labels bound to these text box controls and set the Format property of the second text box control to Currency. You might also want to add a line control immediately above each text box to indicate that you are displaying a total.

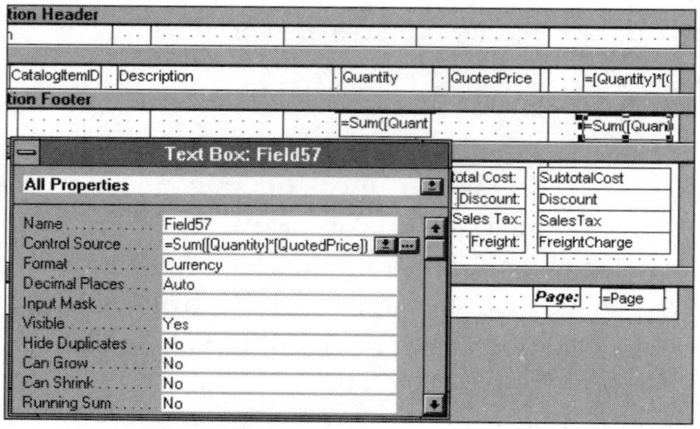

FIGURE 18-17. A sum of calculated values is set as the source of a control.

Notice the interesting new property for controls on reports—Running Sum. You can set this property to ask Access not to reset totals at the end of a group. If you set the Running Sum property to Over Group, Access accumulates the total over all groups at this level until a new group value is encountered at the next-highest level. In this case, you could total the quantity or the amount over all product categories and display that incremental total in the TypeDescription footer section. The total would reset to 0 with every new OrderID. You can also set the Running Sum property to Over All, which allows you to accumulate a total and not have it reset for new groups. You could, for example, show the total amount accumulated up to the current point for all previous product categories within all orders.

Creating a Grand Total

In the OrderID footer section, you placed the calculated subtotal from the Order table along with other fields for discount percent, sales tax, and freight charge. You should now create a grand total for these items at the bottom of the report. To do this, drag the Page footer section down to make some space below the FreightCharge text box control so that you can add an unbound text box control labeled Total Due, whose Format property is set to Currency. The formula for the calculation used by this control is a bit complicated because it uses the Discount field, which contains a percentage by which the subtotal must be reduced. You could type

```
[Subtotal] - ([Subtotal] * [Discount])
```

to multiply the percentage by the subtotal and then subtract that amount from the subtotal. Or you could type

```
[Subtotal] * (1 - [Discount])
```

to subtract the percentage from 1 and then multiply the result by the subtotal. Either formula will yield the correct result.

A problem that is introduced when you multiply or divide a currency value by another value is that the result might have more than two decimal places. To ensure that you get the correct result when you add a series of calculated currency values, you should always multiply the result by 100 and truncate it using the *CLng* (convert to long integer) function, and then divide by 100 and use the *CCur* (convert to currency) function to round off the result to the nearest penny and store it as a currency value. You need to use this function in the discount calculation before you add the SalesTax and FreightCharge values. The complete formula you need, shown in Figure 18-18 in the Control Source property box, is

```
=(CCur(CLng([SubtotalCost] * (1 – [Discount]) * 100) / ↵
100)) + [SalesTax] + [FreightCharge]
```

After you've finished setting up the calculations, Print Preview should yield a result similar to the one shown in Figure 18-19.

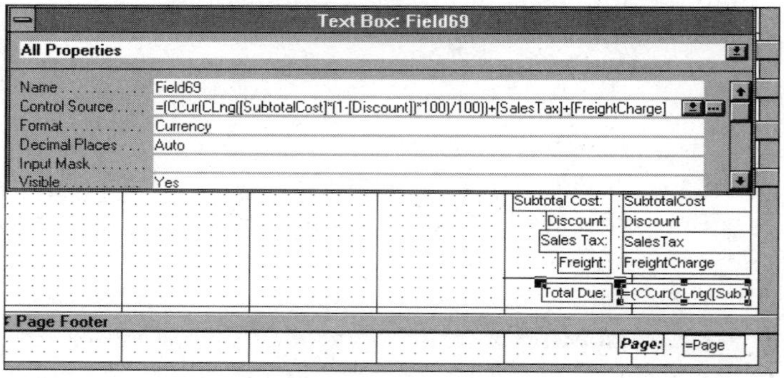

FIGURE 18-18. A grand total calculation (using the *CLng* and *CCur* functions) is set as the source of a control.

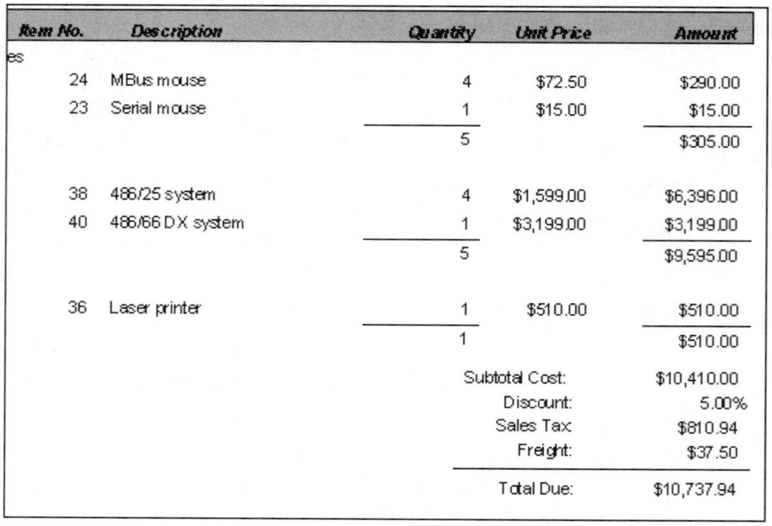

FIGURE 18-19. The grand total (Total Due) is displayed in the report in Print Preview.

Concatenating Text Strings

You can add labels to your report to provide descriptive information. Sometimes it's useful to combine descriptive text with a value from a text field in the underlying query or table or to combine multiple text fields in one control. In Figure 18-20, you can see descriptive labels (created by a single text box control) on the subtotal lines. These labels concatenate the information from the TypeDescription field followed by the word *Total,* as shown in Figure 18-21. Certainly, you could define a text box followed by a label to create the same display. The advantage of using a single control is that you don't have to worry about lining up two controls or about setting the font characteristics twice.

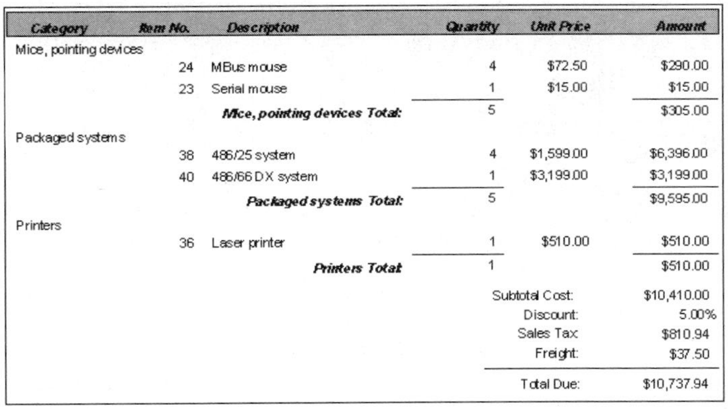

Category	Item No.	Description	Quantity	Unit Price	Amount
Mice, pointing devices					
	24	MBus mouse	4	$72.50	$290.00
	23	Serial mouse	1	$15.00	$15.00
		Mice, pointing devices Total:	5		$305.00
Packaged systems					
	38	486/25 system	4	$1,599.00	$6,396.00
	40	486/66 DX system	1	$3,199.00	$3,199.00
		Packaged systems Total:	5		$9,595.00
Printers					
	36	Laser printer	1	$510.00	$510.00
		Printers Total:	1		$510.00
				Subtotal Cost:	$10,410.00
				Discount:	5.00%
				Sales Tax:	$810.94
				Freight:	$37.50
				Total Due:	$10,737.94

FIGURE 18-20.
The descriptive labels on the subtotal lines are concatenations of a text field and a text string.

Figure 18-21 shows the concatenation as a setting of the Control Source property. The special character *&* (ampersand) indicates a concatenation operation of two text strings. To get the proper spacing between the descriptions, set the text box control's Text Align property to Right.

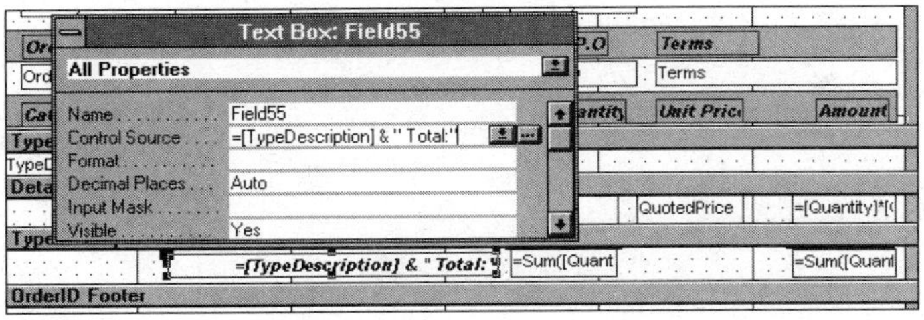

FIGURE 18-21.
A text field and a text string are concatenated as the source of a control.

Microsoft Access provides an alternative syntax for concatenating text string variables. You can include any control name inside the double quotation marks that delimit a string, as long as you type the pipe character (|) before and after the name of the control whose value you want inserted in the string. Enclosing an expression bound by pipe characters inside a string asks Microsoft Access to evaluate the expression enclosed in pipes and substitute the resulting value in the string. On the Invoices report, it would be nice to display the city, state, and postal code as a single string, with a comma separating city and state. To do this, delete the City, State, and PostalCode text boxes, insert an unbound text box control, and delete the attached label control. Figure 18-22 shows the alternative syntax for combining these three fields.

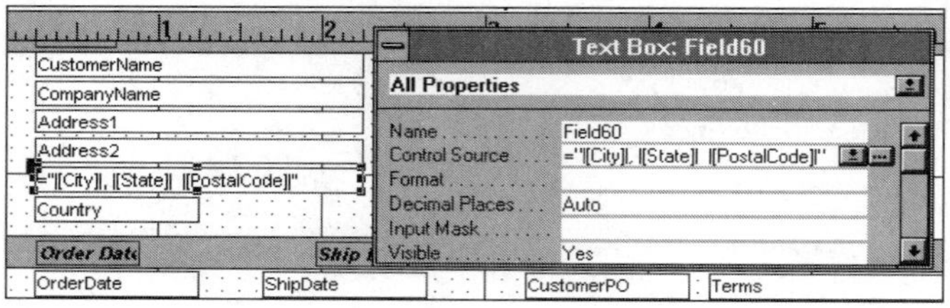

FIGURE 18-22. A concatenation of three text fields is set as the source of a control.

When you look at the report in Print Preview, you can see the city, state, and zip code placed together as a single string, as shown in Figure 18-23. One advantage of concatenating address fields in this way is that Access adjusts the position of the state name relative to the length of the city name. Using the separate field method, you'd always have to show the state in a fixed location.

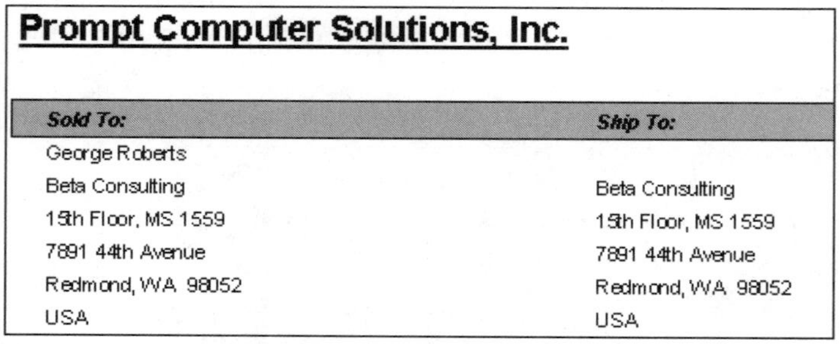
Prompt Computer Solutions, Inc.
Sold To:
Ship To:
George Roberts
Beta Consulting
15th Floor, MS 1559
7891 44th Avenue
Redmond, WA 98052
USA
Beta Consulting
15th Floor, MS 1559
7891 44th Avenue
Redmond, WA 98052
USA

FIGURE 18-23. The City, State, and PostalCode fields displayed as a single string in Print Preview.

Conditional Data Display

Sometimes you don't want to show certain fields on your report, depending on their value or the value of other controls. For example, on the Invoices report you might not want to display the Discount field to all your customers if only some customers receive discounts. Microsoft Access provides a conditional testing function named *Immediate If(IIF)* that returns one of two values depending on whether the test is true or false. You provide to the function in the first parameter the condition you want tested, in the second parameter the value you want returned if the test is true, and in the third parameter the value you want returned if the test is false.

You can now display the Discount control conditionally using the *IIF* function. You'll also use some of the calculated values previously discussed to change the Discount control so that it displays the dollar amount of the discount as well as the percentage. The first step is to delete the Discount control from your report and add in its place an unbound text box control with no label. You need to size this text box so that it's about 2 inches wide because it will include a label, the discount percent value, and the calculated amount when the discount value is greater than 0. Examine the Top and Height properties to be sure that the top edge of the control doesn't overlap the Subtotal Cost control and the bottom edge doesn't overlap the Sales Tax control. If the edges overlap, you won't be able to make this control "disappear" when you want it to. Figure 18-24 shows how to position this control.

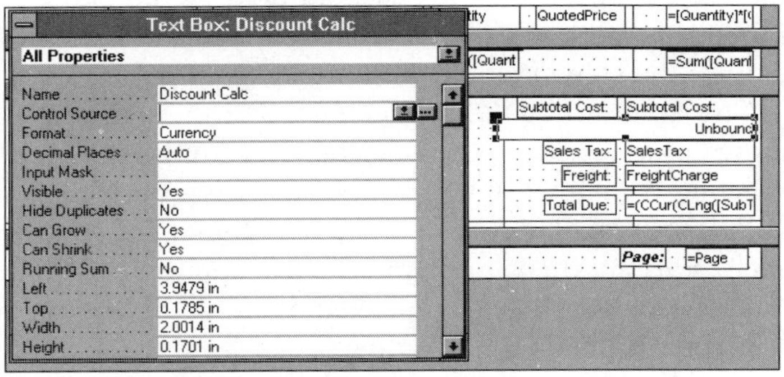

FIGURE 18-24.
The position of the Discount control, which will display conditionally.

The formula you need to enter is quite long and complex, so it would be a good idea to open the Expression Builder window from the property sheet. To do so, click in the Control Source property box for the unbound text box control you just added, and then click the Build button (the one with three dots) at the far right of the property box. Access opens the Expression Builder window, shown in Figure 18-25.

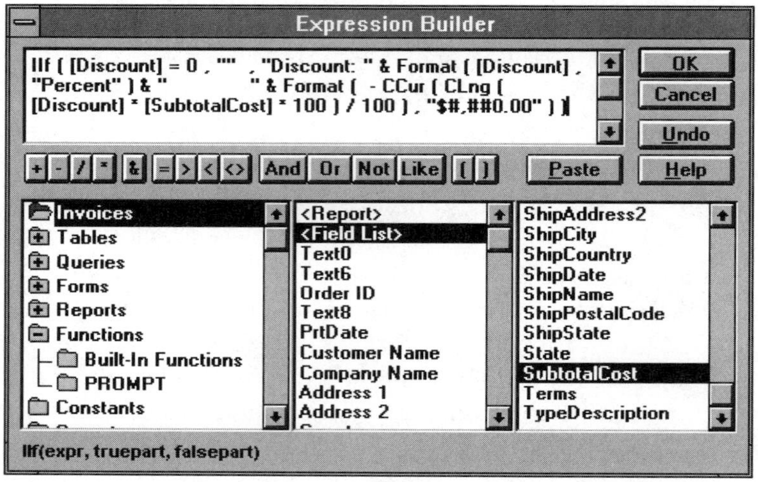

FIGURE 18-25. A conditional display statement is set as the source of a control.

Find the *IIF* function in the list of built-in program flow functions and paste a copy into the text box. In this case, you want to test whether the value in the Discount field is 0, so select the *<<expr>>* part of the *IIF* function, and then double-click the Discount field on the Field List list. Next, click the = operator, click *<<Expr>>,* and type *0* to complete the first parameter. If the value in the Discount field is 0, you don't want to display anything at all. Click the *<<truepart>>* of the expression, and pick the Empty String constant (" ") from the Constants list to set no display in the second parameter. If the value in the Discount field is not 0, you want to display a label, the value in the Discount field as a percent, some spaces to separate the values, and the discount expressed in dollars and cents. These displays are connected by using the concatenation symbol (&) in your formula.

Click the *<<falsepart>>* argument, and type a double quotation mark. Your label is created by entering the word *Discount,* a colon, some spaces, and another double quotation mark. There's another built-in function, named *Format,* that returns a value formatted according to a format name or string. Click the & button, click *<<Expr>>*, and then select the *Format* function from the built-in function Text list. Click the *<<expr>>* part of the *Format* function and double-click the Discount field in the Field List list for this report. Click the *<<fmt>>* part of the *Format* function and type *"Percent"*. Move just beyond the closing parenthesis of the *Format* function, and click the & button. Type about a dozen spaces enclosed in double quotation marks. (Eleven or twelve spaces is about right to line up the columns on the report properly.) Click the & button to separate the percentage and the total. You need to calculate the second value as a negative number that's the result of multiplying the value in the Discount field by the subtotal. (Remember: Because you're multiplying a currency value by a noncurrency value, you should use the *CLng* and *CCur* functions to round off and truncate the result before you display it.) You also need the *Format* function to create a currency value. So, starting with the *Format* function again, enter the following expression:

```
Format( - CCur( CLng( [Discount] * [SubtotalCost] * 100)→
 / 100),"$#,##0.00 "))
```

Click OK to close the Expression Builder window and store the result.

Be sure that this control has the Text Align property set to Right. You must also set the Can Shrink property to Yes so that the control will "disappear" when its value is an empty string (when Discount is 0). If you check the result in Print Preview, you should see a result similar to the one shown in Figure 18-26 when the order has a discount.

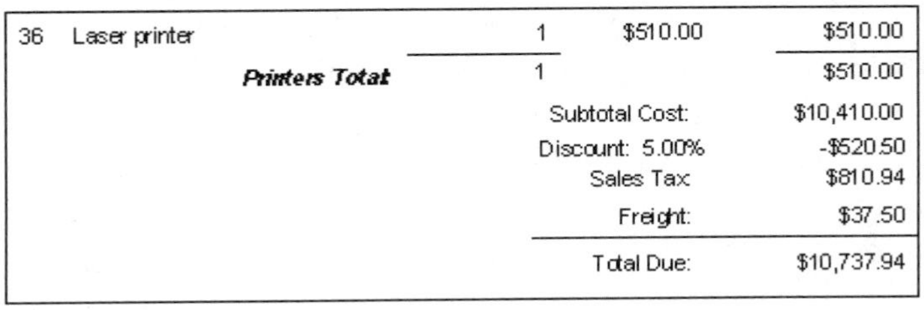

36 Laser printer		1	$510.00	$510.00
	Printers Total	1		$510.00
			Subtotal Cost:	$10,410.00
			Discount: 5.00%	-$520.50
			Sales Tax	$810.94
			Freight:	$37.50
			Total Due:	$10,737.94

FIGURE 18-26.
A Discount line is displayed in Print Preview when the customer receives a discount.

Figure 18-27 shows the result when the Discount is 0. Notice that the Discount line has disappeared and the sales tax and freight charge values have moved up.

FIGURE 18-27.
A Discount line is not displayed in Print Preview when the customer receives no discount.

35	386/25 SVGA system	2	$1,399.00	$2,798.00
	Packaged systems Total:	2		$2,798.00
			Subtotal Cost:	$3,615.50
			Sales Tax	$296.47
			Freight:	$0.00
			Total Due:	$3,911.97

Embedding a Subreport

In the Prompt Computer Solutions database, products in the Catalog table are set up so that you can sell an individual component (such as a video card) or a whole system. When customers purchase a packaged system, it would be nice to itemize for them all the pieces they're getting in the system. You can add that information to the Invoices report by designing a subreport based on the related information in the CatalogComponent table and the Component table.

Designing the Subreport

Because you need information from more than one table, you should first design a query for the subreport. You need the CatalogItemID from the Catalog table and the Amount field from the CatalogComponent table (to determine the quantity of each component included in the system), and you need the Description field from the Component table. Because you don't need this detailed information for anything but packaged systems, you will want to include the ItemTypeCode field from the Catalog table so that you can perform a test—to determine when to shrink the subreport (if, say, only a component is present rather than a system).

Your resulting query should look something like the one shown in Figure 18-28. Save the query and name it *Invoice Subreport Query*. (If you're working in the PROMPT sample database, you'll find the Invoice

Subreport Query query already defined.) Select the query in the Database window, and click the New Report button on the toolbar. Click the Blank Report button in the New Report dialog box to open the Report window in Design view.

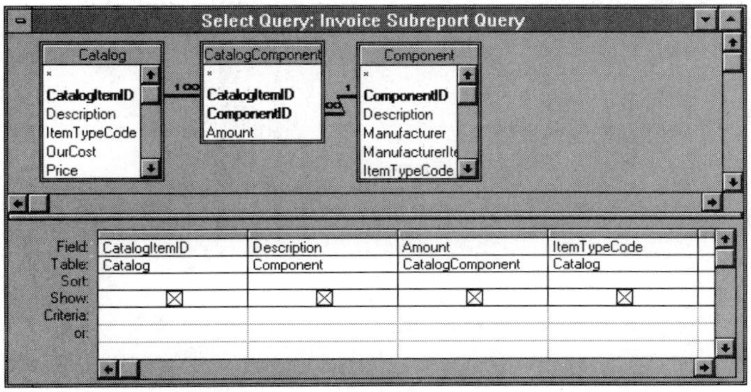

FIGURE 18-28. The design of the Invoice Subreport Query query.

Open the Format menu and be sure the Page Header/Footer option is not checked. Access won't display page headers and footers in a subreport. You need only one control on the report, a text box control (without an attached label) to display the Amount and Description fields when the value in the ItemTypeCode field equals 100 (the code for packaged systems). Choose the Sorting And Grouping command from the View menu. Select Description as the Field/Expression and Ascending as the sort order. Close the Sorting And Grouping window.

Figure 18-29 on the next page shows you the formula to enter in the Control Source property box for the text box control. You want a display when the test is true, so you must define the display string in the second parameter of the *IIF* function. Include an empty string (" ") as the last parameter. Be sure to set the Can Shrink property to Yes for this control so that the control disappears if the ItemTypeCode isn't 100. Set the detail section's Can Shrink property to Yes as well. Save the report and name it *Invoices Subreport*. Now you're ready to embed this subreport in the main report.

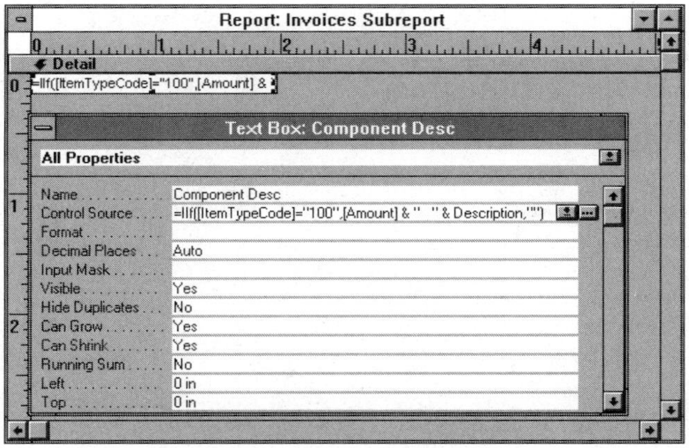

FIGURE 18-29.
A conditional display statement is set as the source of a subreport control.

Embedding the Subreport

Go back to the Invoices report and open a small area below the Description field in the detail section. Click the Subform/Subreport tool in the toolbox, create a Subform/Subreport control in the empty space in the detail section, and size the control to about 0.17 inch high—high enough to display one line.

To insert your subreport, enter *Report.Invoices Subreport* in the Source Object property box of the subreport control, as shown in Figure 18-30. Because you could also include a form in the report, the *Report.* prefix tells Microsoft Access to include a report, not a form. As you did with a subform, you need to define linking fields. In this case, the CatalogItemID field on the main report (set in the Link Master Fields property box) matches the CatalogItemID field on the subreport (set in the Link Child Fields property box). You need to set the Can Shrink and Can Grow properties to Yes to allow the subreport to expand or shrink as necessary.

You might notice that this sample includes a text box as a "disappearing" title in a text box control above the subreport control. The title displays the word *Contains* when an item is a system. You can build the conditional display statement for this control exactly as you built one earlier for the Discount control in the subreport. Figure 18-31 shows the property settings you need for this text box.

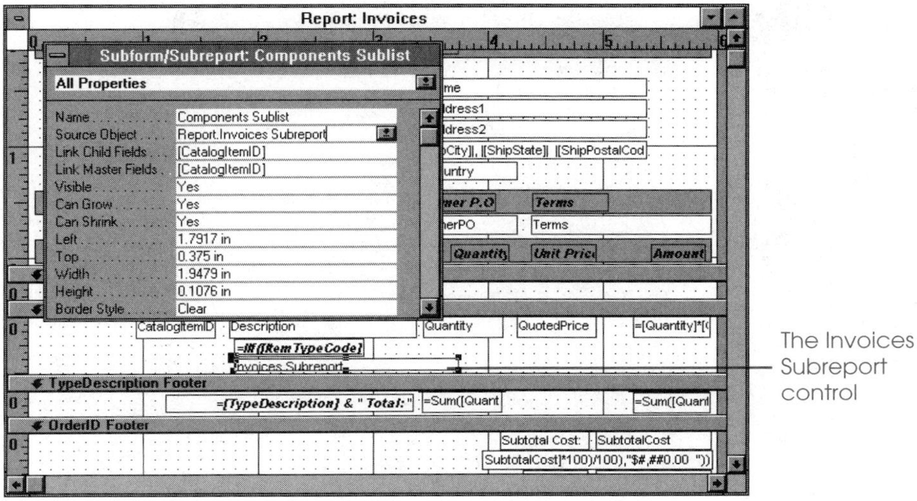

FIGURE 18-30. The subreport is linked to the main report.

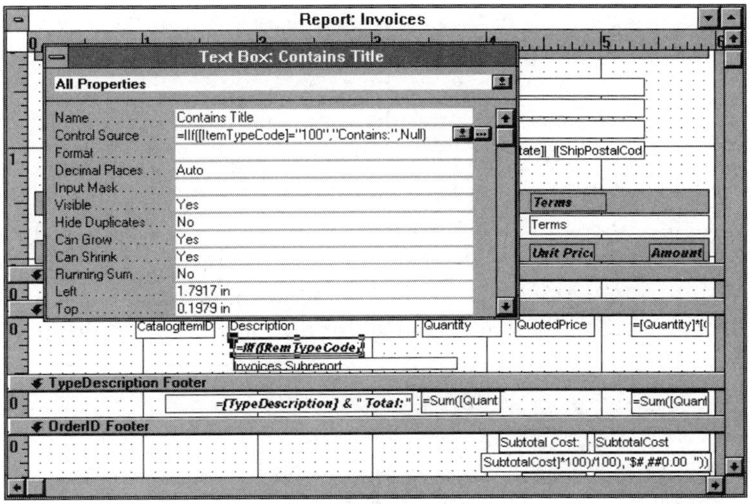

FIGURE 18-31. A conditional display statement for the control that titles the subreport shown in Figure 18-29.

Viewing the Embedded Result

After you've finished the preceding exercise, the result should look similar to the one shown in Figure 18-32 on the next page. Notice that no subreport shows for the individual mouse entries. The subreport and its title do appear for the 486/25 and the 486/66 packaged systems.

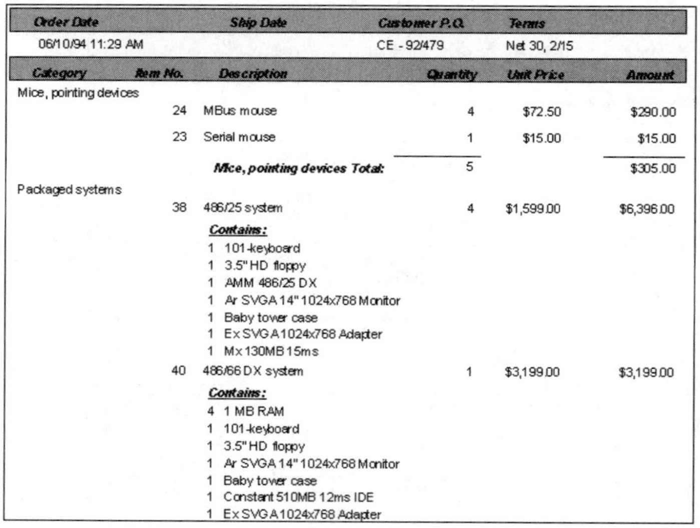

Order Date		Ship Date	Customer P.O.	Terms	
06/10/94 11:29 AM			CE - 92/479	Net 30, 2/15	

Category	Item No.	Description	Quantity	Unit Price	Amount
Mice, pointing devices					
	24	MBus mouse	4	$72.50	$290.00
	23	Serial mouse	1	$15.00	$15.00
		Mice, pointing devices Total:	5		$305.00
Packaged systems					
	38	486/25 system	4	$1,599.00	$6,396.00
		Contains:			
		1 101-keyboard			
		1 3.5" HD floppy			
		1 AMM 486/25 DX			
		1 Ar SVGA 14" 1024x768 Monitor			
		1 Baby tower case			
		1 Ex SVGA 1024x768 Adapter			
		1 Mx 130MB 15ms			
	40	486/66 DX system	1	$3,199.00	$3,199.00
		Contains:			
		4 1 MB RAM			
		1 101-keyboard			
		1 3.5" HD floppy			
		1 Ar SVGA 14" 1024x768 Monitor			
		1 Baby tower case			
		1 Constant 510MB 12ms IDE			
		1 Ex SVGA 1024x768 Adapter			

FIGURE 18-32. A title and a list of components are displayed in Print Preview when an invoice contains a system for which an embedded report has been prepared.

If you find that you need to make some adjustments to the subreport (or, for that matter, to any subreport or subform), you can edit it directly from the Design view of the main report or form. Be sure that the subreport isn't selected, and then double-click on the subreport control to open the subreport in Design view. Save and close the subreport in its Report window after you've finished making changes. To update the subreport control to reflect these changes in the main report's Report window, select the subreport control, click on it, and highlight the source object name in the upper left corner of the control. Press Enter to update the subreport definition in the main report.

Embedding Objects

As a finishing touch, you can add an embedded picture to display the company logo. As you might suspect, you can also add a bound object frame to display pictures or graphs stored in your data. With a graph control, you can graphically represent numeric data. You embed objects in reports in the same way that you embed objects in forms. (For an explanation of the process, see the section titled "Working with Objects" in Chapter 15.)

In the Invoice example, you can remove the company title from the page header and substitute a "picture" logo as an unbound object frame, as shown in Figure 18-33.

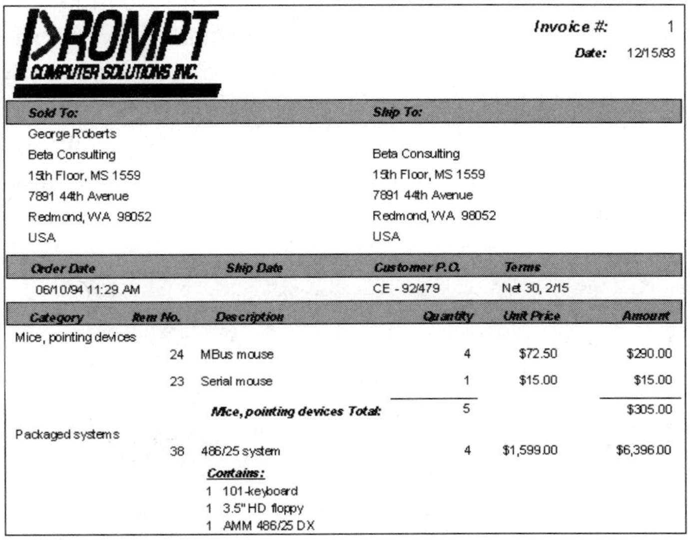

PROMPT COMPUTER SOLUTIONS INC.

Invoice #: 1
Date: 12/15/93

Sold To:	*Ship To:*
George Roberts	
Beta Consulting	Beta Consulting
15th Floor, MS 1559	15th Floor, MS 1559
7891 44th Avenue	7891 44th Avenue
Redmond, WA 98052	Redmond, WA 98052
USA	USA

Order Date	*Ship Date*	*Customer P.O.*	*Terms*
06/10/94 11:29 AM		CE - 92/479	Net 30, 2/15

Category	*Item No.*	*Description*	*Quantity*	*Unit Price*	*Amount*
Mice, pointing devices					
	24	MBus mouse	4	$72.50	$290.00
	23	Serial mouse	1	$15.00	$15.00
		Mice, pointing devices Total:	5		$305.00
Packaged systems					
	38	486/25 system	4	$1,599.00	$6,396.00
		Contains:			
		1 101-keyboard			
		1 3.5" HD floppy			
		1 AMM 486/25 DX			

FIGURE 18-33. The Invoice report with an unbound object frame embedded, the Prompt Computer Solutions logo.

Creating a "Spreadsheet" Report

Any decent report generator can create sophisticated reports with grouped totals down the page, like the Invoices report you built in the previous sections. But what happens when the sales manager wants a monthly summary of units and dollars by item category? Crosstab queries work great for summarizing data by categories and dates, but they can display only a single summarized value.

You could export the data to a Microsoft Excel spreadsheet, but that's an unnecessary step, and you would still have to work with the data extensively in Excel to create a two-column summary. You can use the reporting facilities in Access to create what you want.

Designing a Sales Summary Query

First, you need a query to summarize sales for the year by type of product and by month. This query will be very similar to the crosstab query you designed in Chapter 8, but it creates totals for the QuantitySold and TotalInvoiceAmount fields from the MonthlySales table. In this example, you need only the sales from 1993, so add a test to summarize only that data. Your result should look like the one shown in Figure 18-34.

Save the query as *1993 Sales By Type By Month*. You'll find this query already defined in the PROMPT database. Your result should look like the one shown in Figure 18-34.

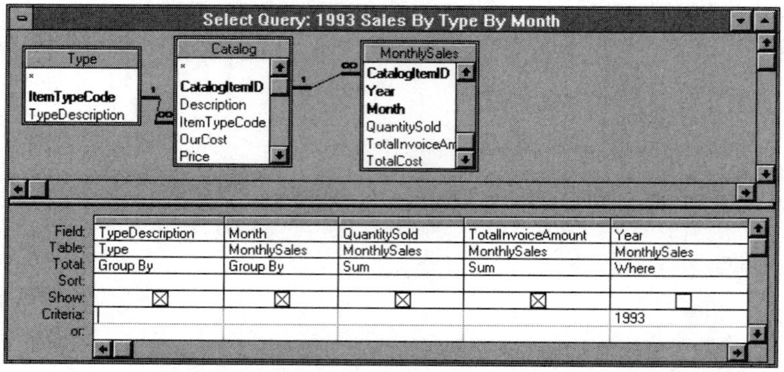

FIGURE 18-34. A query to summarize 1993 sales by product type and by month.

Designing a "Summaries Only" Report

The report you need to display both quantity and sales dollars by month in a spreadsheet-like format won't actually have any detail lines. Start by selecting the 1993 Sales By Type By Month query you created above, and then click the New Report button on the toolbar. Open a blank report. Start by defining a group on the TypeDescription field, and set the Group Footer property to Yes. Access will display a TypeDescription footer for you. Your Sorting And Grouping window should look like the one shown in Figure 18-35.

Open the Report Header and Report Footer sections by choosing Report Header/Footer from the Format menu. Be sure you also have a page header and a page footer. In the report header, place a label control as a title for the report. (The sample in the PROMPT database uses the Times New Roman TrueType font in 18-point bold text.)

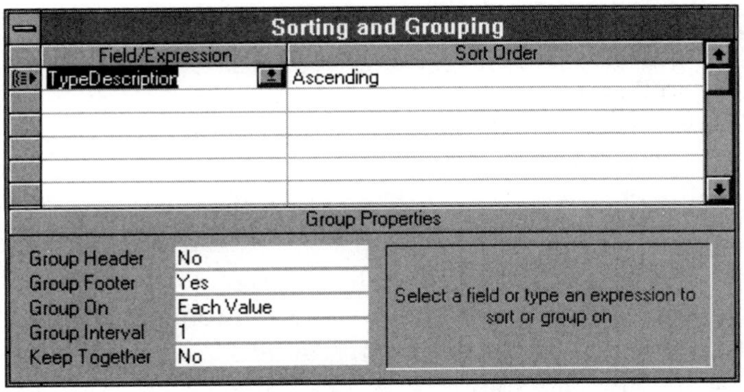

FIGURE 18-35. Sorting and grouping criteria for the "spreadsheet" report.

In the page header, you need to insert an Item Type label at the left edge. Move about 1½ inches (3.8 centimeters) to the right and start inserting labels for each of the month groups. Place a label holding the month name centered above the two labels Qty. Sold and Sales Amt. Draw a rectangle around each month group to highlight the "columns" you'll be creating below. Each group of labels should be 1½ inches wide or less. Create six groups for the months January through June, extending the report to 10 inches wide. Drag and drop the TypeDescription field from the field list into the TypeDescription footer, remove its label, and set it to display Arial 10-point bold text. Your result should look something like that shown in Figure 18-36.

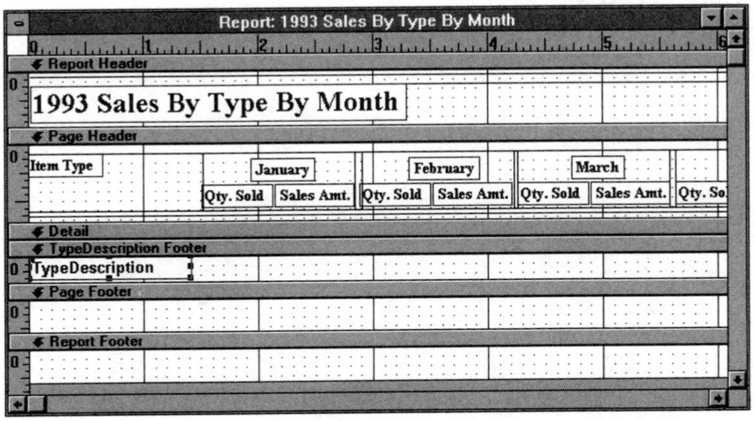

FIGURE 18-36. A spreadsheet report under construction.

To create the monthly totals you want, you need two unbound text boxes per month in the TypeDescription footer—one to display the sum of the quantity sold and the other to display the sum of the total invoice amount. You want to use the *Sum* function to total the SumOfQuantity-Sold and SumOfTotalInvoiceAmount fields from the query. However, for each month, you want the *Sum* function to add up only the values for the month in that column. Here's where the *IIF* function comes in handy again. In the unbound text box control for the total quantity in January, simply test to see whether the month in the "current" row being processed by the *Sum* function has a month value of 1. If the month is 1, give the *Sum* function the SumOfQuantitySold value to work with (as shown in Figure 18-13 on page 629). If the month is not 1, pass a 0 to the *Sum* function. The formula in the Control Source property box is

=Sum(IIf([Month]=1,[SumOfQuantitySold],0))

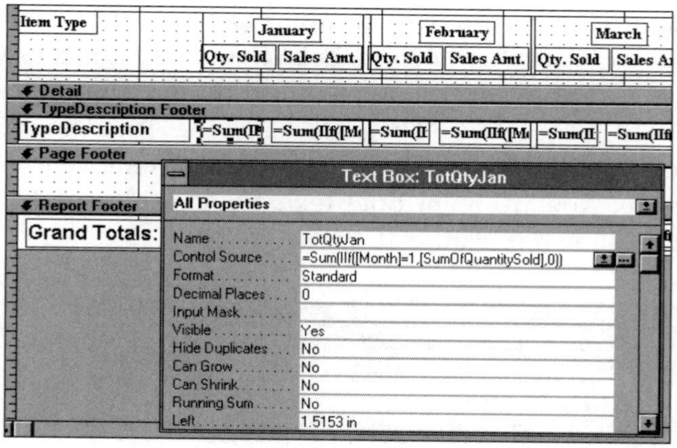

FIGURE 18-37. Creating a total of selected month values.

You'll enter a similar formula for the controls that total sales. The formula for January looks like this:

=Sum(IIF([Month]=1,[SumOfTotalInvoiceAmount],0))

For the controls in the other months, simply change the month number to pick out the total values you want to display in that column. (February is 2, March is 3, and so on.) In the sample report in PROMPT, a rectangle was drawn around each group of monthly total controls so that they would line up with the rectangles in the page header.

You'll notice that only the first six months fit within a 10-inch-wide report, and that won't print across a standard 8½-inch-wide page. To fix that, choose Print Setup from the File menu, select Landscape mode, and set the left and right margins to 0.5 inch. This gives you a 10-inch-wide print area on standard 8½-by-11-inch paper.

To set up the second logical page for the last six months, stretch your report to 20 inches wide. Select all the controls in the first "half" of the report, section by section, and choose Duplicate from the Edit menu. You can move these duplicated controls to the area between 10 and 20 inches. Change the month labels and change each of the formulas to test for the month in that column. You'll see when you print this report that Access shows you the first six months on the first page and that the second six months overflows onto a second page.

To create grand totals on the report, simply copy all the calculation controls from the TypeDescription footer to the Clipboard, select the Report Footer section, and paste the controls there. You don't have to make any changes to any of the formulas, although you'll need to delete the TypeDescription controls and add labels for the grand totals. The totals in the TypeDescription footer will be for the rows matching that type. The totals in the Report Footer will be for all rows returned by the query. Your Design view should now look something like that shown in Figure 18-38.

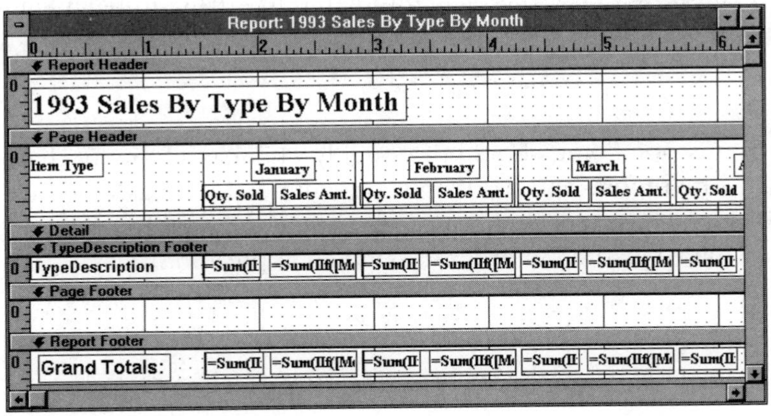

FIGURE 18-38.
The completed spreadsheet report in Design view.

Switch to Print Preview, and your result should look similar to that shown in Figure 18-39.

FIGURE 18-39. The spreadsheet report in Print Preview.

1993 Sales By Type By Month

Item Type	January		February		March		Ap
	Qty. Sold	Sales Amt.	Qty. Sold	Sales Amt.	Qty. Sold	Sales Amt.	Qty. Sold
Controllers	34	$15,725	22	$10,175	28	$12,950	39
Floppies	34	$3,273	28	$2,695	44	$4,235	37
Hard drives	40	$14,513	23	$8,444	31	$11,415	29
Keyboards	43	$4,139	39	$3,754	31	$2,984	27
Mice, pointing device	34	$2,465	45	$3,263	27	$1,958	38
Modems	22	$2,145	35	$3,413	25	$2,438	38
Monitors	41	$13,861	39	$13,539	45	$14,906	39
Multimedia	0	$0	3	$2,453	0	$0	2
Packaged systems	5	$22,750	8	$36,400	9	$40,950	7
Printers	0	$0	0	$0	0	$0	0
RAM	0	$0	0	$0	0	$0	0
Tape drives	5	$450	0	$0	7	$630	0
Video boards	11	$2,578	19	$4,526	19	$5,015	6
Grand Totals:	269	$81,898	261	$88,660	266	$97,480	262

In the PROMPT sample database, you can find this report saved as 1993 Sales By Type By Month. There's another version of this report that uses an Access Basic function rather than the *IIF* function. A third version of this report, called 1993 Sales By Type By Month - Grouped, shows you how to use the *Switch* function to create artificial summary groups by testing the value in the ItemTypeCode field.

At this point, you should thoroughly understand the mechanics of constructing reports and working with complex formulas. The final part of this book (Chapters 19 through 23) shows you how to bring together all that you've learned in order to build an application.

PART 6

Creating an Application

19

Adding Power with Macros

In Microsoft Access, you can define a macro to execute just about any task you would otherwise initiate with the keyboard or the mouse. The unique power of macros in Access is their ability to automate responses to many types of events. The event might be a change in the data, the opening or closing of a form or report, or even a change of focus from one control to another. Within a macro, you can include multiple actions and define condition checking so that different actions are performed depending on the values in your forms or reports.

In this chapter, first you'll learn about the various types of actions you can define in macros. Next you'll tour the macro design facility and learn how to build both a simple macro and a macro with multiple defined actions. You'll also learn how to manage the many macros you need for a form or report by creating a macro group. Finally, you'll see how to add conditional statements to a macro to control the actions Microsoft Access performs. At the end of the chapter, you'll find summaries of the macro actions and of the events that can trigger a macro. You might find these sections useful as a quick reference when you're designing macros for your applications.

Uses of Macros

Microsoft Access provides various types of macro actions that you can use to automate your application:

- You can use macros to open any table, query, form, or report in any available view. You can also use a macro to close any open table, query, form, or report.
- You can use macros to open a report in Print Preview or to send a report directly to the printer. You can also send the output data from a report to a rich text format (RTF) file or to a Microsoft Excel (XLS) file and then open the file in Microsoft Word for Windows or in Microsoft Excel. Or you can send the output data from a report as an RTF, an XLS, or a text file embedded in an electronic mail message (provided you have Microsoft Mail or other electronic mail software that adheres to the Microsoft Windows Mail Application Programming Interface, or MAPI, standard).

NEW!

- You can use macros to execute a select query (which opens its Datasheet view) or an action query. You can base the parameters of a query on controls in any open form.
- You can use macros to base the execution of an action on any condition that tests values in your database, in a form, or in a report. You can use macros to execute other macros or Microsoft Access Basic modules. You can halt the current macro or all macros, cancel the event that triggered the macro, or quit the application.
- You can use macros to set the value of any form or report control. You can also emulate keyboard actions and supply input to system dialog boxes. With macros you can also refresh the values in any control based on a query.
- You can use macros to apply a filter to, go to any record in, or search for data in the underlying table or query of a form.

NEW!

- You can use macros with any form to define a custom menu bar to replace the standard menu bar offered by Microsoft Access. You can also open and close any of the standard Access toolbars or your own custom toolbars.
- You can use macros to execute any of the commands on any of the Access menus.
- You can use macros to move and size, minimize, maximize, or restore any window within the Access workspace. You can change the focus to a window or to any control within a window. You can select the page of a report to display in Print Preview.
- You can use macros to display informative messages and sound a computer tone to draw attention to your messages. You can also disable certain warning messages when executing action queries.

NEW!

- You can use macros to rename any object in your database. You can make another copy of a selected object in your database or copy an object to another Access database. You can delete objects in your database. With macros you can also import, export, or attach other database tables, or import or export spreadsheet or text files.

- You can use macros to start another application, in either the Microsoft Windows or the MS-DOS operating system, and exchange data with the application using Dynamic Data Exchange (DDE) or the Clipboard. You can send data from a table, query, form, or report to an output file and then open that file in the appropriate application. You can also send keystrokes to the target application.

NEW!

Consider some of the other possibilities for macros. For example, you can make it easy to move from one task to another using command buttons that open and position forms and set values. You can create very complex editing routines that validate data entered on forms, including checking data in other tables. You can even check something like the customer name entered on an order form and open another form so that the user can enter detailed data if no record exists for that customer.

NOTE: Macros are particularly useful for building small, personal applications or for prototyping larger ones. As you'll learn in Chapter 21, you probably should use Access Basic for complex applications or for applications that will be shared by several users over a network. Even if you think you're ready to jump right into Access Basic, you should study all the macro actions first. You'll find that you'll use nearly all of the available macro actions in Access Basic, so learning macros is an excellent introduction to programming in Microsoft Access in general.

The Toolbar for the Macro Window

Microsoft Access provides a custom toolbar for working with macros. Open the PROMPT database, click the Macro tab in the Database window, and click the New button to open a new Macro window. From left to right, the buttons on the Macro window toolbar are:

Save button. Click this button to save any changes.

Macro Names button. Click this button to show or hide the Macro Name column in the Macro window. Within this column you can assign names to macros in a macro group.

(continued)

(continued)

Conditions button. Click this button to show or hide the Condition column in the Macro window. With this column you can define conditions that must be true in order to execute the associated action.

Run button. Click this button to run your macro. You must save the macro and give it a name before you can run it.

Single Step button. Click this button to step through a macro one action at a time. This option is useful for debugging complex macros. After you set this option, it remains active until you turn it off. (See the section titled "Testing Your Macro" later in this chapter for details.)

Database Window button. Click this button to place the focus on the Database window. This button also un-hides the window if you've hidden it and restores the window if you've minimized it.

NEW!

Build button. Microsoft Access provides a sophisticated Expression Builder dialog box to assist you in defining entries for macro action parameters. Click in a macro parameter box where you want to use a complex expression, and click this button to start the Expression Builder.

Undo button. Click this button to undo the last change you made to the macro design.

Cue Cards button. Click this button to open the main menu of the Cue Cards facility. Cue Cards lead you through step-by-step instructions for most common tasks.

Help button. Click this button to add a question mark to your mouse pointer. Click with this pointer on any displayed object to receive context-sensitive information about that object.

Creating a Simple Macro

Near the end of Chapter 15, "Advanced Form Design," you learned how to create a macro that opens a form when a button is clicked on another form. This section explains the macro design facility in Microsoft Access in more detail.

Macro Window

When you opened a new Macro window to take a look at the toolbar, you saw an empty window similar to the one shown in Figure 19-1. There are two columns, Action and Comment, at the top of the window.

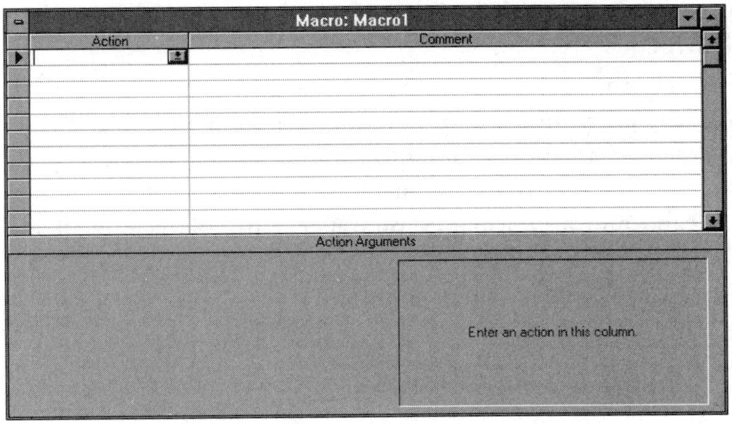

FIGURE 19-1.

A new Macro window.

Notice that the area at the bottom right of the Macro window displays a short Help message. The message changes, depending on where your cursor is located in the Macro window. (Remember: You can always press F1 to open a context-sensitive Help topic.)

In the Action column, you can specify any one of more than 40 macro actions provided by Access. If you click anywhere in a box in the Action column, you'll see a down arrow button at the right side of the box. This button opens a drop-down list of the macro actions, as shown in Figure 19-2.

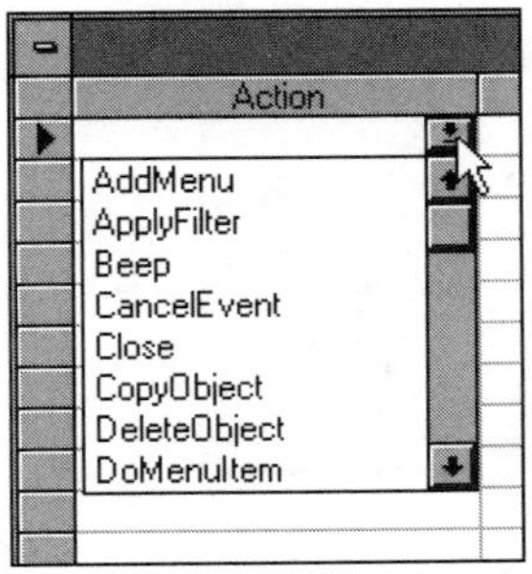

FIGURE 19-2.

An open drop-down list of macro actions.

To see how the Macro window works, try selecting the MsgBox action now. You can use the MsgBox action to open a pop-up modal dialog box with a message in it. It's a great way to display a warning or an informative message or information in your database without defining a separate form.

Now, assume this message will be a greeting, and type *Greeting message* in the corresponding box in the Comment column of the Macro window. You'll find the Comment column especially useful for documenting large macros that contain many actions. In the Comment column, you can enter additional comments on any blank line (that is, any line without an action next to it).

After you select an action such as MsgBox, Access displays argument boxes near the bottom of the Macro window (shown in Figure 19-3) in which you enter settings, called *arguments,* for the action.

> **TIP:** As with the Table and Query windows in Design view, you can use the F6 key to move between the top and bottom portions of the Macro window.

FIGURE 19-3.

A macro that displays a greeting message.

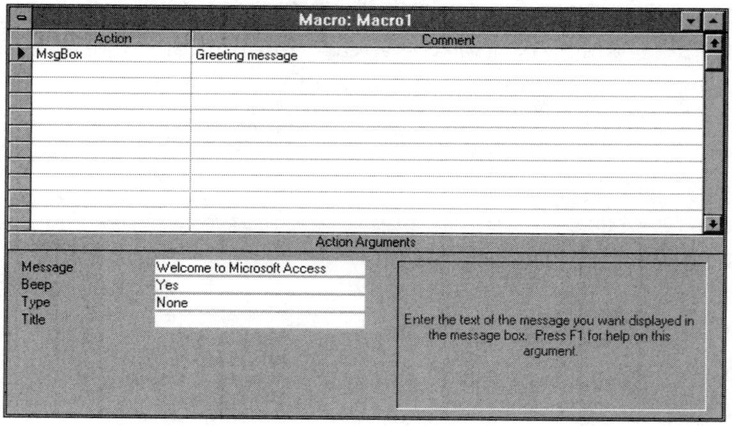

The setting in the Message argument box is the message that you want Access to display in the dialog box you're creating. The setting in the Beep argument box will tell Access whether to sound a beep when the message is displayed. In the Type argument box, you can set a graphic indicator, such as a red stop sign, that will appear along with your message. In the Title argument box, you can type the contents of your dialog box's title bar. Use the settings shown in Figure 19-3 in your macro.

Saving Your Macro

You must save any macro before you can run it. Choose the Save (or Save As) command from the File menu. Access opens the dialog box shown in Figure 19-4. Enter the name *Test Greeting* and click OK to save your macro.

FIGURE 19-4.
The Save As dialog box for saving a macro.

Testing Your Macro

Some macros (such as the simple one you just created) can be run directly from the Database window or from the Macro window because they don't depend on controls on an open form or a report. If your macro does depend on a form or a report, you must link the macro to the appropriate event and run it that way. (You'll learn how to do this later in this chapter.) However you run your macro, Microsoft Access provides you with a good way to test it, by allowing you to single-step through the macro actions.

To activate single-stepping, first go to the Database window, click the Macro tab, select the macro you want to test, and click the Design button. These steps will open the macro in a Macro window in Design view. You can then either click the Single Step button on the toolbar or choose the Single Step command from the Macro menu.

When you run your macro after clicking the Single Step button, Access will open the Macro Single Step dialog box before executing each step. In this dialog box, you'll see the macro name, the action, and the action arguments.

Try this procedure with the *Test Greeting* macro you just created. Open the Macro window in Design view, click the Single Step button, and then click the Run button. The Macro Single Step dialog box opens, as shown in Figure 19-5. If you click the Step button in the dialog box, the action you see in the dialog box will run, and you'll see the modal dialog box with the message you created, as shown in Figure 19-6. Click the OK button in the modal dialog box to dismiss it. If your macro had had more than one action defined, you would have returned to the Macro Single Step dialog box, which would have shown you the next action. In this case, your macro has only one action, so Access returns you to the Macro window in Design view.

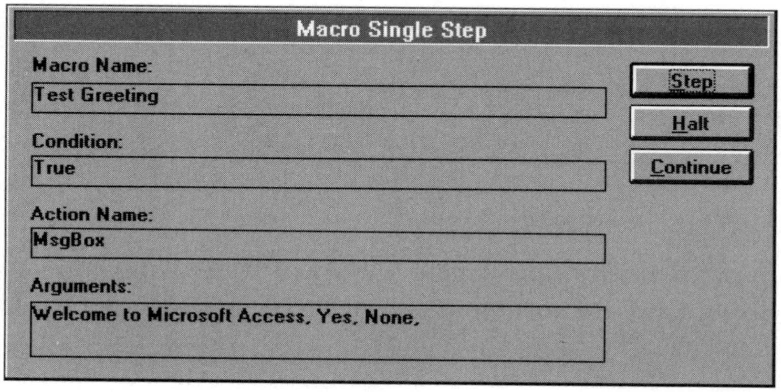

FIGURE 19-5.
The Macro Single Step dialog box.

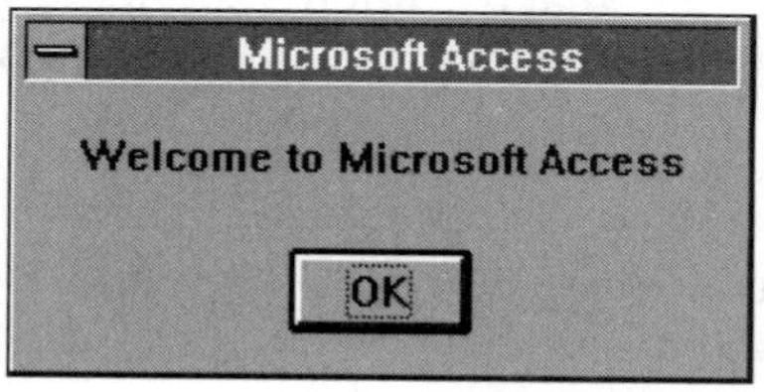

FIGURE 19-6.
The dialog box you created with the macro in Figure 19-3.

If you encounter an error in any macro during normal execution of your application, Access first displays a dialog box explaining the error it found. You'll then see an Action Failed dialog box, similar to the Macro Single Step dialog box, with information about the action that caused the problem. At this point, you can click only the Halt button. You can then edit your macro to fix the problem.

Before you read on in this chapter, you might want to return to the Macro window and click the Single Step button again so that it's no longer selected. Otherwise you'll continue to single-step through every macro you run in a database until you close and restart Access.

Defining Multiple Actions

In Microsoft Access, you can define more than one action within a macro, and you can define the sequence in which you want the actions performed. The NWIND sample database contains several good examples of macros containing more than one action. Open the NWIND database, click the Macro tab in the Database window, and scroll down to the macro named *Sample AutoExec*. Select the macro and click the Design button to open the macro in a Macro window in Design view. The macro is shown in Figure 19-7.

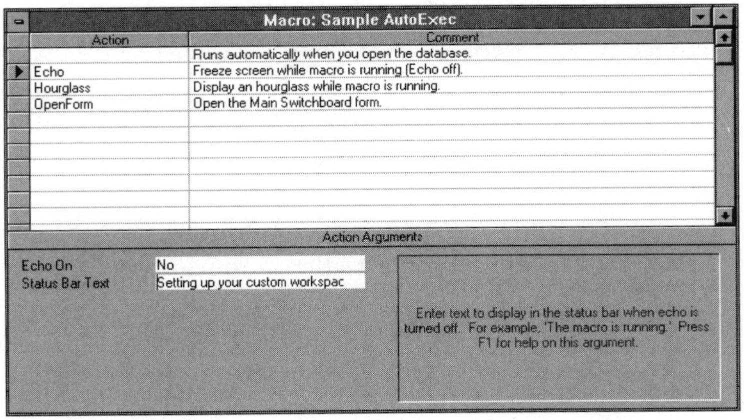

FIGURE 19-7. The *Sample AutoExec* macro, which defines multiple actions in the NWIND database.

This macro can be used to start the Main Switchboard form in the Northwind Traders application each time you open the NWIND database.

> **TIP:** If you create a macro and name it *AutoExec*, Access runs the macro each time you open the database in which it is stored. (For details, see Chapter 23.)

In this macro, you can see three actions defined. The Echo action sets Echo On to No so that you don't see any extraneous actions flashing on the screen while the macro runs. The Echo action also defines an informative message that displays on the status bar while the macro is running, to tell you what's happening. The Hourglass action sets Hourglass

On to Yes so that an hourglass mouse pointer is displayed while the macro is running. The OpenForm action opens the Main Switchboard form that contains the NWIND logo and buttons to activate the various features in the application.

Macro Groups

You'll find that most of the forms you design for an application require multiple macro actions—some to edit fields, some to open reports, and still others to respond to command buttons. You could design a macro for each of these actions, but you'd soon have hundreds of separate macros in your application. A simpler design is created by defining a macro group for each form or report. In a macro group, you can define a number of macros. You give each macro in the group a name in the Macro Name column of the Macro window. When you save your macro group and give it a name, the name appears in the list of macros in the Database window.

Figure 19-8 shows the Main Switchboard form in the NWIND database in Form view. This form contains five command buttons, each of which triggers a different macro. The macros are all contained within a macro group called Main Switchboard Buttons. To look at the macro group, go to the Database window, click the Macro tab, and then select Main Switchboard Buttons in the list of macros in the Database window. Click the Design button to open this macro group in a Macro window. The macro group is shown in Figure 19-9.

FIGURE 19-8.
The NWIND Main Switchboard form.

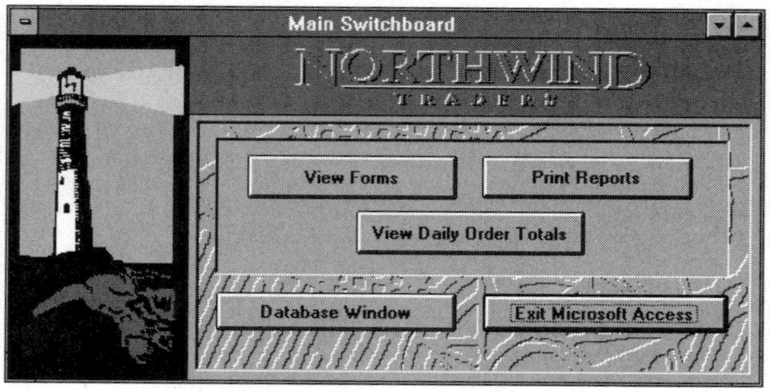

The Main Switchboard Buttons macro group has a Macro Name column. (If you don't see the Macro Name column, click the Macro Names button on the toolbar.) Each of the five names in this column represents a macro within the group. The first three macros open other forms. The fourth macro moves the focus to the Database window. The last macro closes all open objects and exits Access.

If you open the Main Switchboard form in Design view and look at the properties for each of the command buttons, you'll see that the On Click property contains two names separated by a period. The name before the period is the name of the macro group. The name after the period is the name of the macro within the group. So, for the first command button control, the On Click property has been set to *Main Switchboard Buttons.View Forms*. When the user clicks this button, Access runs the *View Forms* macro in the Main Switchboard Buttons group.

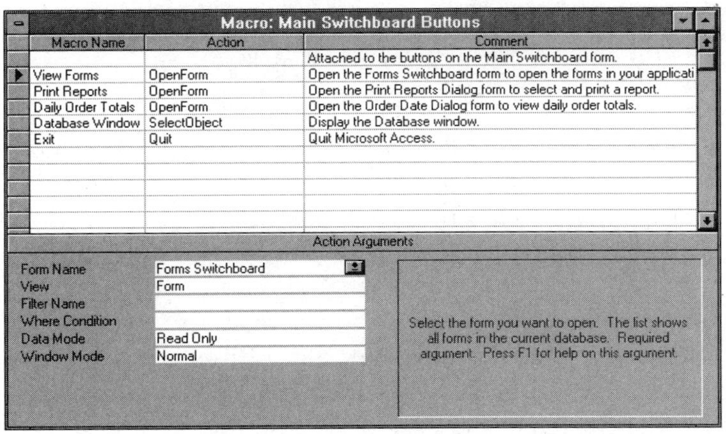

FIGURE 19-9.
The Main Switchboard Buttons macro group.

Conditional Expressions

In some macros, you might want to execute some actions only under certain conditions. For example, you might want to update a record, but only if new values in the controls in a form pass validation tests. Or you might want to display or hide certain controls based on the value of other controls.

The *Great Job* macro in the NWIND database is a good example of a macro that uses conditions to test whether an action should proceed. Select *Great Job* in the NWIND macro list, and click the Design button to see the Macro window shown in Figure 19-10. If you can't see the Condition column, click the Conditions button on the toolbar.

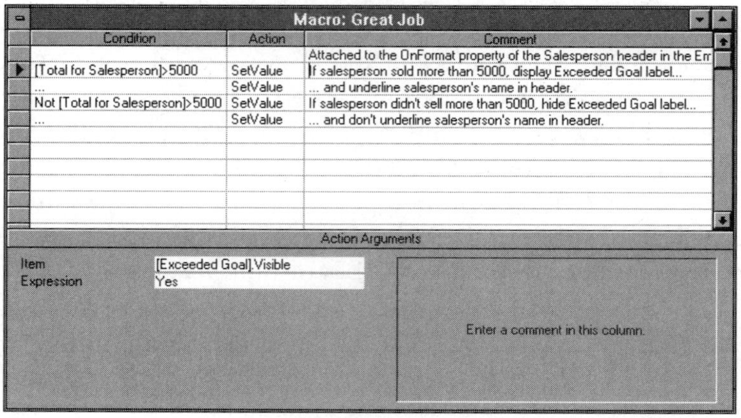

FIGURE 19-10. The NWIND *Great Job* macro.

This macro is triggered by the On Format property of the Salesperson header in the Employees Sales By Country 2 report. The idea is to test each salesperson's total sales and print an indication on the report when these sales exceed $5,000. The first condition checks to see whether the Total For Salesperson field has a value greater than 5000. Note that the report must be open for this macro to work; the macro must be able to find the Total For Salesperson field. If the test is true (sales exceed the goal), Microsoft Access executes the action listed in the Action column of the Macro window. In this case, the SetValue action sets the Visible property of the Exceeded Goal control to Yes. In other words, it lets Access print the contents of that control, which is a label containing the message "Exceeded Goal" in bold italics next to the salesperson's name.

Notice that the line following the first test has three periods specified in the Condition column. This indicates that if the previous condition is true, you also want the actions on this line performed. This is a handy way to group several actions that you want to run based on the results from one test. In this case, when the sales exceed $5,000, the second SetValue action also sets the Visible property of the Salesperson Line control to Yes. This "turns on" a line control that is placed just below the salesperson's name. The second test checks for sales below the goal and ensures that both the "Great Job" label and the underline are not visible if the salesperson did not exceed the goal.

The rest of this chapter summarizes all the actions you can include in macros and the events that trigger macros. You'll find it useful to browse through these sections on first reading to become familiar with the available actions and events before going on to the next chapter, in which you'll learn how to automate a major part of the Prompt Computer Solutions application. As you build this application, you'll find these last two sections useful as a quick reference to actions and events.

Summary of Macro Actions

This section summarizes the actions available for you to use in macros. The summaries are organized in the following functional categories:

- Opening and closing tables, queries, forms, and reports
- Printing data
- Executing a query
- Testing conditions and controlling action flow
- Setting values
- Searching for data
- Building a custom menu and executing menu commands
- Controlling display and focus
- Informing the user of actions
- Renaming, copying, deleting, importing, and exporting objects
- Running another application for MS-DOS or Microsoft Windows

Opening and Closing Tables, Queries, Forms, and Reports

Macro Action	Purpose
Close	Closes either the specified window or the active window for a table, query, form, or report. If the Database window has the focus when you run a Close action with no window specified, Access closes the database.
OpenForm	Opens a form in Form, Datasheet, or Design view or in Print Preview. You can also apply a filter or a Where condition in Datasheet view or Form view or in Print Preview.
OpenModule	Opens a module in Design view and displays the named procedure.
OpenQuery	Opens a query in Datasheet or Design view or in Print Preview. If you specify an action query, Microsoft Access performs the updates specified by the query. (See RunSQL in the upcoming section titled "Executing a Query" to specify parameters for an action query.)
OpenReport	Opens a report in Print Preview (the default), prints the report, or opens the report in Design view. For Print and Print Preview, you can also specify a filter or a Where condition.
OpenTable	Opens a table in Datasheet or Design view or in Print Preview.

NEW!

Printing Data

Macro Action	Purpose
OpenForm	Can optionally open a form in Print Preview. You can specify a filter or a Where condition.
OpenQuery	Can optionally open a query in Print Preview.

(continued)

continued

Macro Action	Purpose
OpenReport	Prints a report or opens a report in Print Preview. You can specify a filter or a Where condition.
OpenTable	Can optionally open a table in Print Preview.
OutputTo	Outputs the named table, query, form, report, or module to a Microsoft Excel (XLS), Microsoft Word for Windows (RTF), or Windows Notepad text (TXT) file and optionally starts the application to edit the file. For forms, the data output is from the form's Datasheet view. For reports, Microsoft Access outputs all controls containing data (including calculated controls) except memo, OLE, and subform or subreport controls.
Print	Prints the active datasheet, form, or report. You can specify a range of pages, the print quality, the number of copies, and collation. Use an Open action first if you want to apply a filter or a Where condition.

NEW!

Executing a Query

Macro Action	Purpose
OpenQuery	Runs a select query and displays the recordset in Datasheet view or in Print Preview. Executes an action query. To specify parameters for an action query, use the RunSQL action.
RunSQL	Executes the specified SQL INSERT, DELETE, SELECT...INTO, or UPDATE statement. You can refer to form controls in the statement to limit the affected records.

Testing Conditions and Controlling Action Flow

Macro Action	Purpose
CancelEvent	Cancels the event that caused this macro to be executed. You can't use a CancelEvent action in a macro that defines menu commands or in the OnClose event for a report. CancelEvent can cancel the following events: BeforeDelConfirm, BeforeInsert, BeforeUpdate, DblClick, Delete, Exit, Format, KeyPress, MouseDown, Open, Print, and Unload.
DoMenuItem	Executes a command on a standard Microsoft Access menu. You can use a DoMenuItem action in a macro that defines a custom menu to make selected Access menu commands available on the custom menu.
Quit	Closes all Microsoft Access windows and exits Access.
RunCode	Executes an Access Basic function procedure. Other actions following this action execute after the function is completed. (Note: To execute an Access Basic sub procedure, call that procedure from a function procedure.)
RunMacro	Executes another macro. Actions following this action execute after the other macro is completed.
StopAllMacros	Stops all macros, including any macros that called this macro.
StopMacro	Stops the current macro.

Setting Values

Macro Action	Purpose
Requery	Refreshes the data in a control that is bound to a query (such as a list box, a combo box, a subform, or a control based on an aggregate function such as *DSum*). When other actions (such as inserting or deleting a row in the underlying query) might affect the contents of a control that is bound to a query, use the Requery action to update the control values. Use Requery without an argument to refresh the data in the active object (form or datasheet).
SendKeys	Stores keystrokes in the keyboard buffer. If you intend to send keystrokes to a modal form or a dialog box, you must execute the Send-Keys action before opening the modal form or the dialog box.
SetValue	Changes the value of any control or property you can update. For example, you can use the SetValue action to calculate a new total in an unbound control or to affect the Visible property of a control (which determines whether you can see that control).

Searching for Data

Macro Action	Purpose
ApplyFilter	Restricts the information displayed in a form or report by applying a named filter or query or an SQL WHERE clause to the underlying table or query of the form.
FindNext	Finds the next record that meets the criteria previously set by a FindRecord macro action or in the Find dialog box.

(continued)

continued

Macro Action	Purpose
FindRecord	Finds a record that meets the search criteria. You can specify in the macro action all the parameters available in the Find dialog box.
GoToRecord	Moves to a different record and makes it current in the specified table, query, or form. You can move to the first, last, next, or previous record. When you specify "next" or "previous," you can move by more than one record. You can also go to a specific record number or to the new-record placeholder at the end of the set.

Building a Custom Menu and Executing Menu Commands

NEW!

Macro Action	Purpose
AddMenu	Adds a drop-down menu to a custom menu bar for a form or report. This is the only action allowed in a macro referenced by a Menu Bar property. The arguments to AddMenu specify the name of this menu bar and the name of another macro that contains all the named commands for the menu and the actions that correspond to those commands. An AddMenu action can also refer to another macro that uses an AddMenu action to build submenus.
DoMenuItem	Executes a command on one of the standard Microsoft Access menus. Use this macro action within a custom menu bar to make selected Access menu commands available in the custom menu.

Controlling Display and Focus

Macro Action	Purpose
Echo	Controls the display of intermediate actions while a macro runs.
GoToControl	Sets the focus to the specified control.
GoToPage	Moves to the specified page in a report or form.
Hourglass	Sets the mouse pointer to an hourglass icon while a macro runs.
Maximize	Maximizes the active window.
Minimize	Minimizes the active window.
MoveSize	Moves and sizes the active window.
RepaintObject	Forces the repainting of the window for the specified object. Forces recalculation of any formulas in controls on that object.
Requery	Refreshes the data in a control that is bound to a query (such as a list box, a combo box, a subform, or a control based on an aggregate function such as *DSum*). When actions (such as inserting or deleting a row in the underlying query) might affect the contents of a control that is bound to a query, use the Requery macro action to update the control values. Use Requery without an argument to refresh the data in the active object (form or datasheet).
Restore	Restores a maximized or minimized window to its previous size.
SelectObject	Selects the window for the specified object. Restores the window if it was minimized.
SetWarnings	When enabled, causes an automatic Enter key response to all system warning or informational messages while a macro runs. For warning messages displayed in a dialog box, pressing the Enter key selects the default button (usually OK or Yes). Does not halt the display of error messages. Use this macro action with the Echo action set to Off to avoid displaying the messages.
ShowAllRecords	Removes any filters previously applied to the active form.
ShowToolbar	Shows or hides any of the standard toolbars or any custom toolbar.

NEW!

Informing the User of Actions

Macro Action	Purpose
Beep	Produces a sound.
MsgBox	Displays a warning or an informational message and optionally produces a sound. You must click OK to dismiss the dialog box and proceed.
SetWarnings	When enabled, causes an automatic Enter key response to all system warning or informational messages while a macro runs. For warning messages displayed in a dialog box, pressing the Enter key selects the default button (usually OK or Yes). Does not halt the display of error messages. Use this macro action with the Echo action set to Off to avoid displaying the messages.

Renaming, Copying, Deleting, Importing, and Exporting Objects

Macro Action	Purpose
CopyObject	Copies any object in the current database with a new name or with any specified name to another Microsoft Access database.
DeleteObject	NEW! Deletes any table, query, form, report, macro, or module.
OutputTo	NEW! Outputs the named table, query, form, report, or module to a Microsoft Excel (XLS), Microsoft Word for Windows (RTF), or Windows Notepad text (TXT) file and optionally starts the application to edit the file. For forms, the data output is from the form's Datasheet view. For reports, Microsoft Access outputs all controls containing data (including calculated controls) except memo, OLE, and subform or subreport controls.

(continued)

continued

Macro Action	Purpose
Rename	Renames the specified object in the current database.
SendObject	Outputs a table datasheet, a query datasheet, a form datasheet, data in text boxes on a report, or a module listing to a Microsoft Excel (XLS), Microsoft Word for Windows (RTF), or Windows Notepad text (TXT) file and embeds the data in an electronic mail message. You can specify to whom the message is to be sent, the message subject, additional message text, and whether the message can be edited before it is sent. You must have electronic mail software installed that conforms to the Mail Application Programming Interface (MAPI) standard.
TransferDatabase	Exports data to or imports data from another Microsoft Access, dBASE, Paradox, FoxPro, Btrieve, or SQL database. You can also use this action to attach tables or files from other Access, dBASE, Paradox, FoxPro, Btrieve, or SQL databases.
TransferSpreadsheet	Exports data to or imports data from Microsoft Excel or Lotus 1-2-3 spreadsheet files.
TransferText	Exports data to or imports data from text files.

NEW!

Running Another Application for MS-DOS or Microsoft Windows

Macro Action	Purpose
RunApp	Starts another application for MS-DOS or Microsoft Windows.

Summary of Events That Trigger Macros

Microsoft Access provides more than 40 event properties on forms and reports that can trigger macros (or Access Basic procedures). This section summarizes those events and organizes them in the following functional categories:

- Opening and closing forms and reports
- Changing data
- Detecting focus changes
- Trapping keyboard and mouse events
- Printing
- Activating a custom form, report, or application menu
- Trapping errors
- Detecting timer expiration

Opening and Closing Forms and Reports

Event Property	Event Name	Description
On Close	Close	Runs the specified macro or user-defined event procedure when you close a form or report but before Microsoft Access clears the screen. You can't use a CancelEvent macro action in the On Close routine. The Close event occurs after the Unload event.
On Load	Load	Runs the specified macro or user-defined event procedure when Access loads a form and displays the records in the form. You can use the event procedure to set values in controls or to set form or control properties. You cannot cancel a Load event because the Load event occurs after the Open event and before the Resize event.
On Open	Open	Runs the specified macro or user-defined event procedure when you open a form or report but before Access displays the first record. To access a control on the form or report, the routine must specify a GoToControl action to set the focus on the control. The Open event occurs before Access retrieves the form or report recordset, so you can use the event procedure to prompt the user for parameters and to apply filters.

(continued)

continued

Event Property	Event Name	Description
NEW! On Resize	Resize	Runs the specified macro or user-defined event procedure when a form changes size. This event also occurs when a form opens, after the Load event but before the Activate event. You can use this event to force immediate repainting of the resized form or to recalculate variables that are dependent on the size of the form.
NEW! On Unload	Unload	Runs the specified macro or user-defined event procedure when you close a form but before Microsoft Access removes the form from the screen. You can cancel an Unload event if you determine that a form should not be closed. (Caution: You must carefully test any routine that can cancel the unload of a modal form.)

Changing Data

Event Property	Event Name	Description
After Del Confirm	AfterDelConfirm	Runs the specified macro or user-defined event procedure after a row has been deleted via a form and the user has confirmed the delete. The AfterDelConfirm event also occurs if the event procedure for the BeforeDelConfirm event cancels the delete. In an Access Basic procedure, you can test a status variable to determine whether the delete was completed, was canceled by the event procedure for the BeforeDelConfirm event, or was canceled by the user. If the delete was successful, you can use the Requery action within the event procedure for the AfterDelConfirm event to refresh the contents of the form or combo boxes. You can also provide automatic deletion of dependent rows in another table (for example, of all the orders for the customer just deleted) by executing a delete query. You cannot cancel this event.
After Insert	AfterInsert	Runs the specified macro or user-defined event procedure after a new row has been inserted. You can use this event to requery a recordset after Microsoft Access has inserted a new row. You cannot cancel this event.

NEW!

NEW!

(continued)

continued

Event Property	Event Name	Description
After Update	AfterUpdate	Runs the specified macro or user-defined event procedure after the data in the specified form or control has been updated. You cannot cancel this event. You can, however, use a DoMenuItem action to choose the Undo command from the Edit menu. This event applies to all forms and to combo boxes, list boxes, option groups, and text boxes as well as to check boxes, option buttons, and toggle buttons that are not part of an option group.
NEW! Before Del Confirm	BeforeDelConfirm	Runs the specified macro or user-defined event procedure after rows have been deleted via a form but before Access displays the standard Confirm Delete dialog box. If you cancel this event, Access replaces the deleted rows and does not display the Confirm Delete dialog box. In an Access Basic routine, you can display a custom confirmation dialog box and then set a return parameter to suppress the standard confirmation dialog box.
Before Insert	BeforeInsert	Runs the specified macro or user-defined event procedure when you type the first character in a new row. This event is useful for providing additional information to a user who is about to add records. If you cancel this event, Access erases any new data on the form. This event occurs before the BeforeUpdate event. (Note: This event replaces the OnInsert event in Access versions 1.0 and 1.1.)

(continued)

continued

Event Property	Event Name	Description
Before Update	BeforeUpdate	Runs the specified macro or user-defined event procedure before the changed data in the specified form or control has been saved to the database. You can cancel this event to stop the update and place the focus on the updated control or record. This event is most useful for performing complex validations of data on forms or in controls. This event applies to the same controls as the AfterUpdate event.
On Change	Change	Runs the specified macro or user-defined event procedure whenever you change any portion of the contents of a combo box or text box control. You cannot cancel this event. (Caution: You can cause an endless loop if you change the contents of this control within the event procedure for the Change event.)
On Delete	Delete	Runs the specified macro or user-defined function just before one or more rows are deleted. You can use this event to provide a customized warning message. You can also provide automatic deletion of dependent rows in another table (for example, of all the orders for the customer about to be deleted) by executing a delete query. You can cancel this event if you need to stop the rows from being deleted.

NEW!

(continued)

continued

Event Property	Event Name	Description
NEW! On Not in List	NotInList	Runs the specified macro or user-defined event procedure when you type an entry in a combo box that does not exist in the Row Source property for the combo box. You cannot cancel this event. You can use this event to allow a user to create a new entry for the combo box Row Source (perhaps by adding a row to the table on which the Row Source property is based). In Access Basic, you can examine a parameter passed to the event procedure that contains the unmatched text. You can also set a return value to cause Access to display the standard error message, display no error message (after you have issued a custom message), or requery the list after you've added data to the Row Source property.
NEW! On Updated	Updated	Runs the specified macro or user-defined event procedure after the data in a form's object frame control changes. You cannot cancel this event. In an Access Basic procedure, you can examine a status parameter to determine how the change occurred.

Detecting Focus Changes

NEW!

Event Property	Event Name	Description
On Activate	Activate	Runs the specified macro or user-defined event procedure in a form or a report when the Form or Report window receives the focus and becomes the active window. You cannot cancel this event. This event is most useful for displaying custom toolbars when a form or a report receives the focus. This event does not occur for pop-up or modal forms. This event also does not occur when a normal Form or Report window regains the focus from a pop-up or modal form, unless the focus moves to another form or report.
On Current	Current	Runs the specified macro or user-defined event procedure in a form when a new record receives the focus but before Microsoft Access displays that record. The macro or procedure specified is also triggered when you open a form after the Activate event. This event is most useful for keeping two open and related forms synchronized. You cannot cancel this event. You can, however, use a GoToRecord or other action to move to another record if you decide you do not want to move to the new record.

(continued)

continued

Event Property	Event Name	Description
On Deactivate	Deactivate	Runs the specified macro or user-defined event procedure when a form or a report loses the focus to another window inside the Access application that is not a pop-up or modal window. This event is useful for closing custom form or report toolbars. You cannot cancel this event.
On Enter	Enter	Runs the specified macro or user-defined event procedure when the focus moves to a bound object frame, a combo box, a command button, a list box, an option group, or a text box, as well as when the focus moves to a check box, an option button, or a toggle button that is not part of an option group. You cannot cancel this event. This event occurs only when the focus moves from another control on the same form. If you change the focus to this control with the mouse, this event occurs before the MouseDown and MouseUp events in this control. If you change the focus to this control using the keyboard, this event occurs after the KeyDown event in the control you leave but before the KeyUp and the KeyPress events in this control.

(continued)

continued

Event Property	Event Name	Description
On Exit	Exit	Runs the specified macro or user-defined event procedure when the focus moves from a bound object frame, a combo box, a command button, a list box, an option group, or a text box, as well as when the focus moves from a check box, option button, or toggle button that is not part of an option group, to another control on the same form. You cannot cancel this event. This event does not occur when the focus moves to another window. If you leave a control using the mouse, this event occurs before the MouseDown and MouseUp events in the new control. If you leave a control using the keyboard, the KeyDown event in this control occurs, and then the Exit KeyUp and KeyPress events occur in the new control.
On Got Focus	GotFocus	NEW! Runs the specified macro or user-defined event procedure when an enabled form control receives the focus. If a form receives the focus but has no enabled controls, then the GotFocus event occurs for the form. You cannot cancel this event. The GotFocus event occurs after the Enter event. Unlike the Enter event, which occurs only when the focus moves from another control on the same form, the GotFocus event occurs every time a control receives the focus, including from other windows.

(continued)

continued

NEW!

Event Property	Event Name	Description
On Lost Focus	LostFocus	Runs the specified macro or user-defined event procedure when an enabled form control loses the focus. The LostFocus event for the form occurs whenever a form that has no enabled controls loses the focus. You cannot cancel this event. The LostFocus event occurs after the Exit event. Unlike the Exit event, which occurs only when the focus moves to another control on the same form, the LostFocus event occurs every time a control loses the focus, including to other windows.

Trapping Keyboard and Mouse Events

Event Property	Event Name	Description
On Click	Click	Runs the specified macro or user-defined event procedure when you click a command button or click on an enabled form or control. You cannot cancel this event. (Note: This event replaces the OnPush event in Access versions 1.0 and 1.1.)

(continued)

continued

Event Property	Event Name	Description
On Dbl Click	DblClick	Runs the specified macro or user-defined event procedure when you double-click a bound object frame, a combo box, a command button, a list box, an option group, or a text box, as well as when you double-click a check box, an option button, or a toggle button that is not part of an option group. Microsoft Access runs the macro before showing the normal result of the double-click. You can cancel the event to prevent the normal response to a double-click on a control, such as activating the application for an OLE object in a bound control or highlighting a word in a text box.
On Key Down	KeyDown	Runs the specified macro or user-defined event procedure when you press a key or a combination of keys. You cannot cancel this event. In an Access Basic procedure, you can examine parameters to determine the key code and whether the Shift, Ctrl, or Alt key was also pressed. You can also set the key code to 0 in Access Basic to prevent the control from receiving keystrokes. If the form has a command button whose Default property is set to Yes, KeyDown events do not occur when the Enter key is pressed. If the form has a command button whose Cancel property is set to Yes, KeyDown events do not occur when the Esc key is pressed.

(continued)

continued

Event Property	Event Name	Description
On Key Press	KeyPress	Runs the specified macro or user-defined event procedure when you press a key or a combination of keys. You cannot cancel this event. In an Access Basic procedure, you can examine the ANSI key value.
On Key Up	KeyUp	Runs the specified macro or user-defined event procedure when you release a key or a combination of keys. You cannot cancel this event. In an Access Basic procedure, you can examine parameters to determine the key code and whether the Shift, Ctrl, or Alt key was also pressed. If the form has a command button whose Default property is set to Yes, KeyDown events do not occur when the Enter key is pressed. If the form has a command button whose Cancel property is set to Yes, KeyDown events do not occur when the Esc key is pressed.
On Mouse Down	MouseDown	Runs the specified macro or user-defined event procedure when you press any mouse button. You cannot cancel this event. In an Access Basic procedure, you can determine which mouse button was pressed (left, right, or middle); whether the Shift, Ctrl, or Alt key was also pressed; and the X and Y coordinates of the mouse pointer (in twips) when the button is pressed. (Note: A *twip* is $\frac{1}{20}$ point, or $\frac{1}{1440}$ inch.)

(continued)

continued

Event Property	Event Name	Description
On Mouse Move	MouseMove	NEW! Runs the specified macro or user-defined event procedure when you move the mouse over a form or a control. You cannot cancel this event. In an Access Basic procedure, you can determine whether a mouse button was pressed (left, right, or middle) and whether the Shift, Ctrl, or Alt key was also pressed. You can also determine the X and Y coordinates of the mouse pointer (in twips) when the button was released.
On Mouse Up	MouseUp	NEW! Runs the specified macro or user-defined event procedure when you release any mouse button. You cannot cancel this event. In an Access Basic procedure, you can determine which mouse button was released (left, right, or middle); whether the Shift, Ctrl, or Alt key was also pressed; and the X and Y coordinates of the mouse pointer (in twips) when the button was released.

Printing

Event Property	Event Name	Description
On Format	Format	Runs the specified macro or user-defined event procedure just before Microsoft Access formats a report section to print. This event is useful for hiding or displaying controls in the report section based on data values. If Access is formatting a group header, you have access to the data in the first row of the detail section. Similarly, if Access is formatting a group footer, you have access to the data in the last row of the detail section. You can test the value of the FormatCount property to find out whether the Format event has occurred more than once for a section (due to page overflow). You can use the CancelEvent action to keep a section from appearing on the report.
On Print	Print	Runs the specified macro or user-defined event procedure just before Access prints a formatted section of a report. If you use the CancelEvent action in a macro triggered by a Print event, Access leaves a blank space on the report where the section would have printed.
NEW! On Retreat	Retreat	Runs the specified macro or user-defined event procedure when Access has to retreat past already formatted sections when it discovers that it cannot fit a "keep together" section on a page. You cannot cancel this event.

Activating a Custom Form, Report, or Application Menu

Event Property	Event Name	Description
Menu Bar	(N/A)	Defines the macro that creates the custom menu for a form or report. The macro triggered by the Menu Bar property must contain only named AddMenu actions. Each AddMenu action refers to another macro that defines the individual commands for that menu. (Note: This property replaces the On Menu property in Microsoft Access versions 1.0 and 1.1.) You can include additional AddMenu actions in macros referenced by an AddMenu action to define submenus. From a Microsoft Access Basic macro or procedure, you can set the Application.MenuBar property to define a custom menu bar for the database. Set the Menu Bar property to =True to hide the menu bar when this form or report has the focus.

NEW!

NEW!

Trapping Errors

Event Property	Event Name	Description
On Error	Error	Runs the specified macro or user-defined event procedure whenever a run-time error occurs while the form or report is active. This event does not trap errors in Microsoft Access Basic code; use On Error in the Access Basic procedure instead. You cannot cancel this event. If you use an Access Basic procedure to trap this event, you can examine the error code to determine an appropriate action.

Detecting Timer Expiration

NEW!

Event Property	Event Name	Description
On Timer	Timer	Runs the specified macro or user-defined event procedure when the timer interval defined for the form elapses. The form's Timer property defines how frequently this event occurs in milliseconds. If the Timer property is 0, no Timer events occur. You cannot cancel this event. However, you can set the Timer property for the form to 0 to stop further timer events from occurring.

You should now have a basic understanding of macros and how you might use them. In the next chapter, you'll see macros in action.

20

Automating Your Application with Macros

Now it's time to begin to put into action all you've learned about building tables, queries, forms, and reports. In this chapter, you'll see how to automate one of the forms you built in a previous chapter and link it to another form using macros.

Connecting Tasks to Forms and Reports

In Chapter 4, "Designing Your Database Application," you saw how to lay out several key tasks for the PROMPT database application, which are shown in Figure 20-1. You need to define suppliers before you can add components, and you need components in order to build items for the catalog. When you bring together customers with products from the catalog, you can record an order and ultimately print an invoice.

In previous chapters, you created some of the objects you'll need to accomplish these tasks:

- The Suppliers form in Chapter 13
- The Components form in Chapter 13
- The Catalog List form in Chapter 15
- The Invoices report in Chapter 18

In the following sections, you'll learn how to link and automate the Suppliers, Components, and Catalog List forms within the PROMPT database. The next chapter gives you an introduction to Microsoft Access Basic, and in the final two chapters you'll build the Customers, Orders, Invoices Selector, and Main Menu forms and finish linking these tasks using Access Basic and the menu macros.

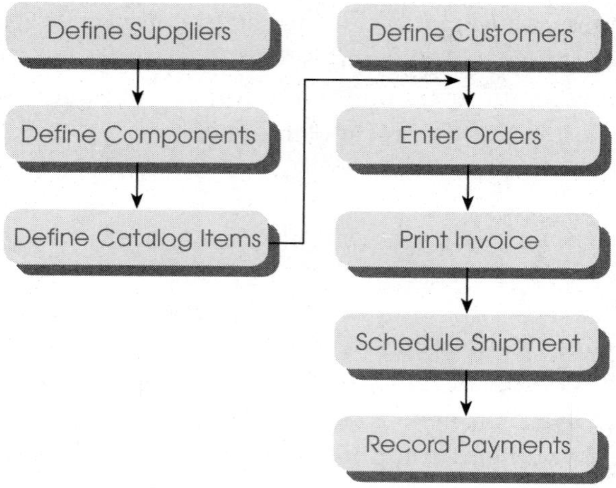

FIGURE 20-1. The task flow in the PROMPT database application.

Referencing Form and Report Objects

In linking and automating these forms and reports, you'll often need to refer to a form, a report, or a control on a form or a report to set properties or values. The syntax for referencing reports, forms, controls, and properties is described in the following sections.

Rules for Referencing Forms and Reports

You can refer to a form or a report by name, but you must first tell Microsoft Access which *collection* contains the named object. Forms are in the *Forms collection,* and reports are in the *Reports collection.* You follow the collection name with an exclamation point to separate it from the name of the object. If the object name contains no blanks or special characters, you can simply enter the name. You must enclose an object name that contains blanks or special characters in brackets ([ ]). It's a good idea to always enclose an object name in brackets so that your name reference syntax is consistent.

So, to reference a form named Catalog List, you should enter

```
Forms![Catalog List]
```

To reference a report named Inventory Report, you should enter

```
Reports![Inventory Report]
```

Rules for Referencing Form and Report Properties

To reference a property on a form or a report, follow the form or report name with a period and the property name. You can see a list of most property names for a form or a report by viewing a form or a report in Design view and opening the property sheet while you have the form or the report selected. (Note: The names of properties do not contain embedded blanks, even though the property sheet shows blanks between name parts. For example, the name of the property listed as Back Color in the property sheet is BackColor.) As of version 2, you can change most form or report properties while the form is in Form view or while the report is in Print Preview.

NEW!

To reference the ScrollBars property of a form named Suppliers, enter the following:

```
Forms![Suppliers].ScrollBars
```

To reference the MenuBar property of a report named Invoices, enter the following:

```
Reports![Invoices].MenuBar
```

Rules for Referencing Form and Report Controls and Their Properties

To reference a control on a form or a report, follow the form or report name with an exclamation point and then the control name enclosed in brackets. To reference a property of a control, follow the control name with a period and the name of the property. You can see a list of most property names for controls by opening a form or a report in Design view, selecting a control (note that different control types have different properties), and opening the property sheet. (Note: The names of properties do not contain embedded blanks, even though the property sheet shows blanks between name parts. For example, the name of the property listed as Back Color in the property sheet is BackColor.) As of version 2, you can change most control properties while the form is in Form view.

NEW!

To reference a control named CustomerID on the Customers form, enter the following:

```
Forms![Customers]![CustomerID]
```

To reference the Visible property of a control named Great Job on the report named Sales Summary, enter

```
Reports![Sales Summary]![Great Job].Visible
```

Rules for Referencing Subforms and Subreports

When you embed a form inside another form or report, the form is contained in a subform control. A report embedded within another report is contained in a subreport control. You can reference a subform or a subreport control exactly as you would any other control on a form or a report. For example, to reference the subform control named Catalog Subform on the Catalog List form, enter

```
Forms![Catalog List]![Catalog Subform]
```

Likewise, you can reference properties of a subform or a subreport by following the control name with a period and the name of the property. To reference the Visible property of the above subform control, enter

```
Forms![Catalog List]![Catalog Subform].Visible
```

Subform controls have a special Form property that lets you reference the form that's embedded within the subform control. Likewise, subreport controls have a special Report property that lets you reference the report embedded in the subreport. You can follow this special property name with the name of a control on the subform or the subreport to access the control's contents or properties. For example, to reference the ComponentID control on the form embedded in the Catalog Subform control on the Catalog List form, enter

```
Forms![Catalog List]![Catalog Subform].Form![ComponentID]
```

To reference the FontWeight property of the above control, enter

```
Forms![Catalog List]![Catalog→
 Subform].Form![ComponentID].FontWeight
```

Automating the Catalog Form

At the end of Chapter 15, you learned how to build a complex catalog form with an embedded subform and how to open another form with a command button. This is a very simple way to automate the use of forms and other objects within your database. In the sections below, you'll see that Microsoft Access also allows you to automate more complex functions. For example, you'll learn how to do the following:

- Copy the data from one field into another field
- Automatically calculate new values on a single form
- Automatically recalculate dependent values in a table when the source value in another table changes
- Trap delete events that would cause a "cascade" to issue custom warning messages
- Open a form by double-clicking a control
- Test whether a form is open
- Resynchronize data between two open forms

Creating a Macro Group

It's a good idea to keep all the macros that respond to events on a form or report in a single macro group. It's also a good idea to give the macro group the same name as the form or the report so that you can easily see which macros are related to which forms or reports. In Chapter 15, you created a macro named *Open Components* to respond to clicking the Open Components button on the Catalog List form. In this chapter, you'll create several additional macros for the Catalog List form, so it would be a good idea to start collecting all macros for this form in a single macro group.

In the Database window, click the Macro tab, select the *Open Components* macro, and choose Rename from the File menu. Change the name to *Catalog List.* Next, open the Catalog List Macro window in Design view, and click both the Macro Names button and the Conditions button on the toolbar to open up these columns in the Macro window. Type *OpenComponents* in the Macro Name column on the line that contains your OpenForm action. Add a comment that describes what causes this macro to run (the user clicking the command button) and what it does. Your result should look like the one shown in Figure 20-2. Save this macro. Later in this chapter, you'll see that you can build additional routines into this macro.

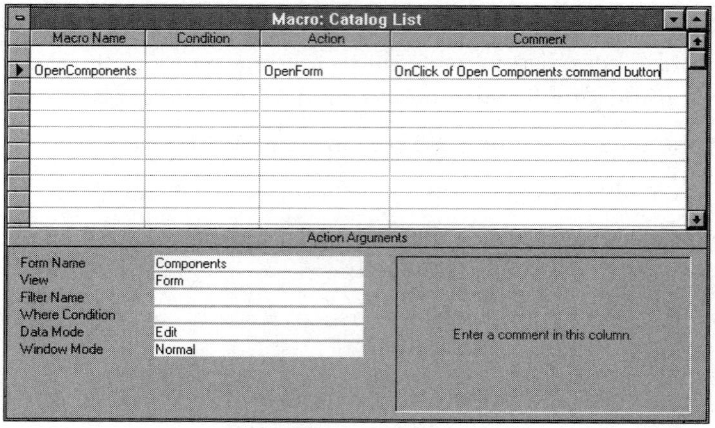

FIGURE 20-2. Starting a macro group for the Catalog List form.

> **TIP:** Giving a macro group that contains macros for a single form or report the same name as the form or the report makes it easy to find the macros related to a specific form or report later.

Open the Catalog List form in Design view and select the Open Components command button that you created in Chapter 15. As you may remember, Access set the On Click property of the command button to point to the *Open Components* macro when you dragged and dropped the macro onto the form. When a property refers only to a macro group, Access runs the first unnamed macro in the macro group. Because there was only one macro without a name in the *Open Components* macro group, that macro ran when you clicked the command button.

Now you want to create several macros within one macro group in order to make it easy to find all the macros for this form. To do this, you must now set event properties to refer to the macro group, followed by a period and the name of the macro that you want to run. So, change the On Click property of the Open Components command button in the Catalog List form to *Catalog List.OpenComponents,* as shown in Figure 20-3. Save and close the form.

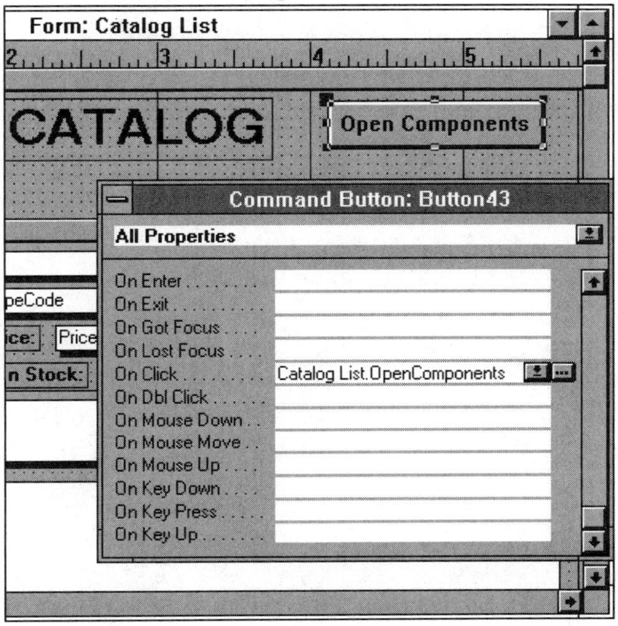

FIGURE 20-3. Resetting the On Click property of the Open Components command button to refer to a macro within a macro group.

Calculating Values

Macros are extremely useful for providing automatic calculations whenever certain events occur. For example, you can automatically add default entries to a blank field if the field is empty when you tab into it. You can also recalculate values automatically when records are added, changed, or deleted in the database.

Assisting Data Entry

In the Catalog List form, there is a Description control and a LongDescription control. The long description is usually a repeat of the description but with some information added. To make data entry easier, you can use a macro to automatically copy the entry from the Description control into the LongDescription control when the LongDescription control is empty. You can call this macro *LongDesc* and create it as part of the Catalog List macro group. Open the Catalog List Macro window in Design view, place the cursor on the first line, and choose Insert Row from the Edit menu several times to open up some space ahead of the *OpenComponents* macro.

> **TIP:** It's a good idea to enter macros in alphabetic order in a macro group to make them easy to find later.

Figure 20-4 shows the *LongDesc* macro. Here's a good use of the Condition column: testing whether you want the macro to run. If the LongDescription field already contains data, you don't want to erase it by setting the value of the field. If, however, the LongDescription field is Null or empty, you want to help out by copying the existing data from the Description field to the LongDescription field. So the macro condition tests to see whether the LongDescription is Null (has never been updated) or contains a zero length string (might have been updated and then cleared). The full condition string is

IsNull([LongDescription]) Or [LongDescription]=""

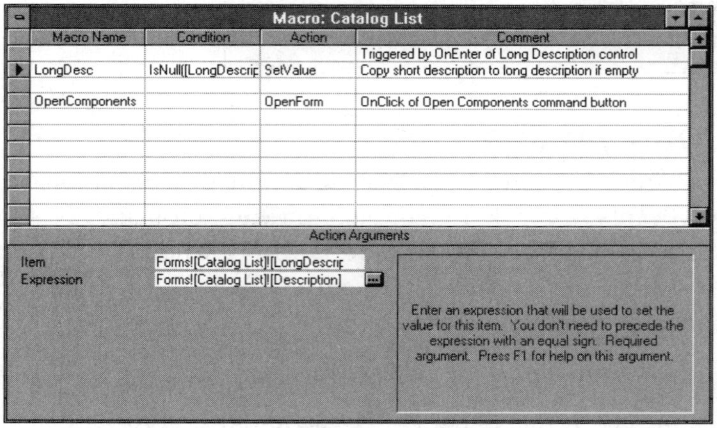

FIGURE 20-4.
The *LongDesc* macro automatically copies data from the Description field to the LongDescription field if LongDescription is Null or empty.

The settings for the *LongDesc* macro are shown in Figure 20-5.

Action	Argument Box	Setting
SetValue	Item	Forms![Catalog List]![LongDescription]
	Expression	Forms![Catalog List]![Description]

FIGURE 20-5.
The settings for the *LongDesc* macro.

> **TIP:** When a macro runs from an event on a form or a report, you don't have to fully qualify control names with a prefix such as *Forms!* and the name of the form. Nevertheless, it's a good practice to always fully qualify names in macro parameters with the form name and the control names (unless the online Help for the macro parameter specifically states that you should not fully qualify these names).

If either condition in the macro's Condition column is True when this macro runs, the SetValue macro action copies the data from the Description field to the LongDescription field. You can trigger this macro action from the On Enter property of the LongDescription control (so that data is copied when focus enters the LongDescription control). Figure 20-6 shows how to trigger the macro from the On Enter property of the LongDescription control.

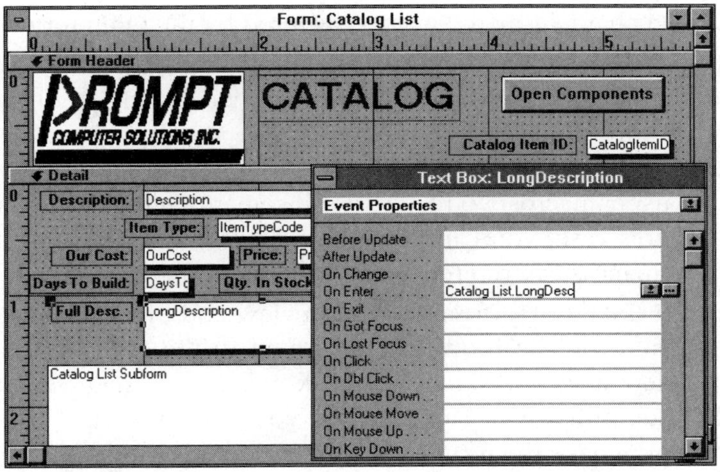

FIGURE 20-6. The LongDescription control's On Enter property is set to trigger the *LongDesc* macro.

Save both the macro and the form, and then open the form in Form view. Go to a new record and type something in the Description field. Tab to or click in the LongDescription field, and you should see your macro copy the data from the Description field to the LongDescription field.

Now, it would be nice if after the macro copied the data it would place the cursor at the end so that typing in additional information was easy. Every text box and combo box control has a property named SelStart that sets or returns either the position of the cursor or the starting point of the currently selected data. You can reset SelStart in your macro to reposition the cursor. If you set SelStart to a value larger than the number of characters currently in the text box or the combo box, Access adjusts the value and places the cursor immediately after the last character in the control.

It would seem simple to follow the SetValue action that copies the data with another SetValue to set the SelStart property of the LongDescription control to some high value, such as 255. This will work whenever you tab into the field, but it won't work if you click in the field. This is because the Click event happens after the Enter event, and Access doesn't finally position the cursor until the Click event. So you can also reset the cursor position in a macro called by the OnClick event to do the job, but you don't want to move the cursor every time you click in the LongDescription field. You want to reset the cursor only after the value has been changed by the macro triggered by the OnEnter event.

To detect this sequence of events, you need to pass a value from the macro triggered by the OnEnter event to macros triggered by the OnClick and OnKeyUp events. If you were using Microsoft Access Basic, you could set something called a global variable to accomplish this, but when you're using macros, you have to use something that both macros can "see." In this case, you can use a control on the Catalog List form because both macros can reference any control on the form.

Open the Catalog List form in Design view and place a check box control anywhere on the form—perhaps next to the LongDescription field—and delete its label. Name the check box *LongDescReset*, and set its Default Value property to False. So that you won't see this "variable" control when you have the form in Form view, set its Visible property to No. You can see the settings for this control in Figure 20-7.

The trick is to set the LongDescReset check box to True whenever you have changed the value of the LongDescription field. You need to add a line to the *LongDesc* macro to set the LongDescReset check box whenever you copy the data from the Description field to the LongDescription field. Remember that the three dots in the Condition column

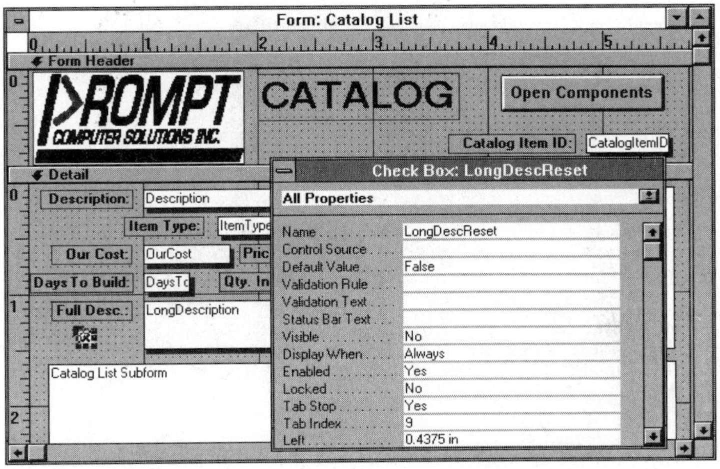

FIGURE 20-7. The settings for a control that is used to pass a value from one macro to another.

on the second line of the macro means: "If the condition on the previous line is true, then run this macro action." In this case, if you change the value of the LongDescription field, then the macro also sets the check box to True.

If you enter the LongDescription control by tabbing into it, the OnKeyUp event occurs after the Enter event. If you enter the Long-Description control by clicking it, the Click event occurs after the Enter event and after Access has positioned the cursor where you clicked in the text box. You can test your check box control using macros triggered by the OnKeyUp and OnClick events to see whether you should send the cursor to the end of the field. You should also reset the check box to False to be sure you send the cursor to the end of the field only once.

So you need two additional macros, one called *LongDescClick* and the other called *LongDescKeyUp*. You can see these two additional macros in Figure 20-8 on the next page. The condition on the first line for both macros reads as follows:

```
Forms![Catalog List]![LongDescReset]
```

Notice that because you used a check box for your macro variable, it can contain either a True or a False value. So, when you place the control name in the Condition column, the action runs if the control contains a True value and does not run if the control contains a False value.

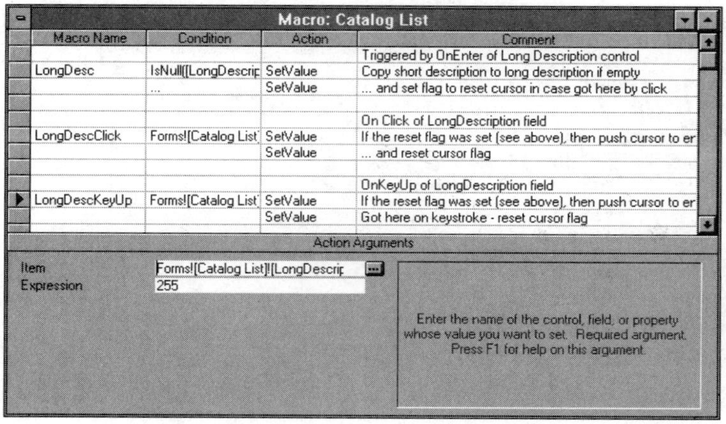

FIGURE 20-8.
The macros that are used to copy the value from the Description field to the LongDescription field and set the cursor to the end of the field.

The final settings for the *LongDesc* macro are shown in Figure 20-9.

Action	Argument Box	Setting
SetValue	Item	Forms![Catalog List]![LongDescription]
	Expression	Forms![Catalog List]![Description]
SetValue	Item	Forms![Catalog List]![LongDescReset]
	Expression	True

FIGURE 20-9.
The final settings for the *LongDesc* macro.

The actions in the *LongDescClick* and *LongDescKeyUp* macros are the same, as shown in Figure 20-10.

Action	Argument Box	Setting
SetValue	Item	Forms![Catalog ➘ List]![LongDescription].SelStart
	Expression	255
SetValue	Item	Forms![Catalog List]![LongDescReset]
	Expression	False

FIGURE 20-10.
The settings for the *LongDescClick* and *LongDescKeyUp* macros.

The last step you need to perform is to set the properties of the LongDescription text box, as shown in Figure 20-11. Switch to Form view and try out your new macros. If you have a value in the Description field and you clear out the LongDescription field, your macros should copy the Description field to the LongDescription field and set the cursor at the end of the field whenever you click or tab into the LongDescription field.

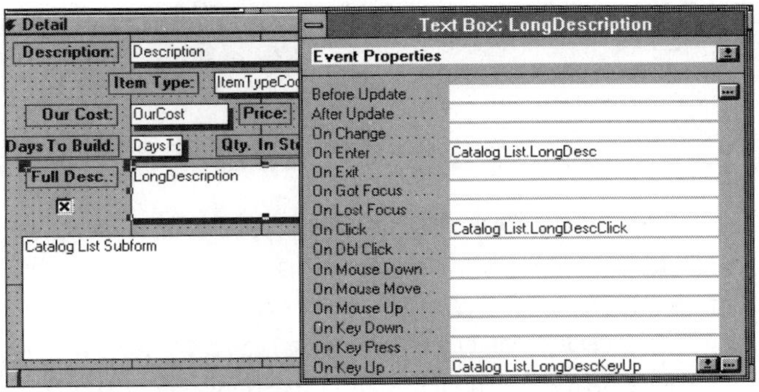

FIGURE 20-11. The event properties for the LongDescription text box.

Performing Automatic Calculations

The Catalog Subform form has an OurCost and an Amount field for each component of a product in the catalog. There is also a SumOfCost field, which multiplies the value in the OurCost field by the value in the Amount field for each component and then calculates the sum of the results, to provide a total cost of the catalog item. It would be nice if every time this total cost changed, the new cost was reflected in the Catalog List main form's OurCost field. A new suggested price could also be calculated. You can perform both of these calculations by creating a macro called *SetCost,* which is triggered by the After Update and After Del Confirm properties of the subform, as shown in Figure 20-12 on the next page.

Figure 20-13 on page 711 shows the *SetCost* macro that recalculates the cost in the main form, sets a new price, and saves the result. The settings are shown in Figure 20-14 on page 711. (The condition statement is explained on page 712.)

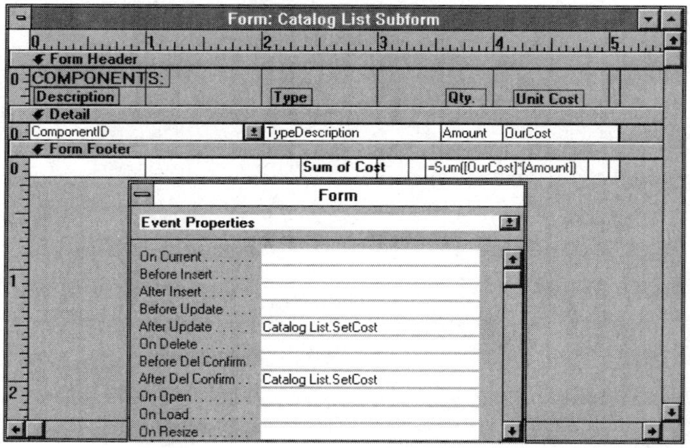

FIGURE 20-12. The subform's After Update property is set to trigger the *SetCost* macro.

NOTE: The calculated OurCost field in the Catalog table compromises the relational design of this database. As you'll see in Chapter 22, this field makes it very easy to create orders. If this field didn't exist, you would have to sum the prices of all the component parts and then apply a standard markup to derive a suggested retail price when creating an order. By placing the OurCost field in the Catalog table, you make it easy to set individual prices and to avoid having to look up all the components when you create an order. However, you can see from the steps in this section that you must take great care to ensure that this calculated field always reflects the sum of the costs times the quantity ordered from the related Component table.

The first SetValue action in the *SetCost* macro calls an aggregate function named *DSum* to recalculate the total cost for all the items on the subform. You might think that you could just copy the value in the SumOfCost control on the subform to the main form, but this won't work. The reason you can't copy the value is that many actions in Microsoft Access happen asynchronously. The AfterUpdate event triggers the macro after any changed row is saved but before all controls on the subform might have finished recalculating. Because the *DSum* function takes perhaps half a second to perform, the new SumOfCost value isn't available when the *SetCost* macro runs. So you have to do the SumOfCost calculation as part of the SetValue action in the macro to be sure you get the correct amount.

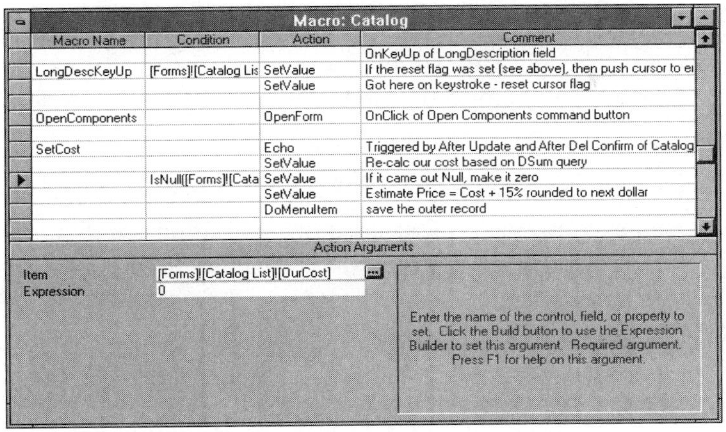

FIGURE 20-13.

The *SetCost* macro calculates a new cost and suggested price after a component's cost information is changed.

Action	Argument Box	Setting
Echo	Echo On	Yes
	Status Bar Text	Copying Sum Cost to Our Cost
SetValue	Item	Forms![Catalog List]![OurCost]
	Expression	DSum("[OurCost]*[Amount]", "[Catalog Subform Query]", "[CatalogItemID]=Forms![Catalog List]![CatalogItemID]")
Set Value	Item	Forms![Catalog List]![OurCost]
	Expression	0
SetValue	Item	Forms![Catalog List]![Price]
	Expression	CCur(CLng((Forms![Catalog List]![OurCost]*1.15)+0.5))
DoMenuItem	Menu Bar	Form
	Menu Name	File
	Command	Save Record
	Subcommand	(none)

FIGURE 20-14.

The settings for the *SetCost* macro.

The condition for the second SetValue macro action checks to see whether *Dsum* returned a Null value. If *Dsum* returned a Null value, the action sets the OurCost field to 0. The full condition statement is

```
Forms![Catalog List]![OurCost] Is Not Null
```

The third SetValue macro action adds 15 percent to the total cost to determine a suggested price. The calculation by the third SetValue macro action involves a currency, so you have to convert to an integer to be sure fractional penny amounts are rounded correctly. The *[OurCost]*1.15+0.5* part of the expression calculates the 15 percent margin in pennies. The *CLng* function converts the result to a long integer, rounding to the nearest penny. Converting back to a currency value (via the *CCur* function) yields the desired result accurate to the penny.

The DoMenuItem macro action ensures that the new subtotal value is saved to the database each time something changes on the subform.

Triggering a Query to Update Totals

The *SetCost* macro you built above takes care of propagating changes in the CatalogComponent table to the OurCost and Price fields in the Catalog table. If you delete or add a row or change the quantity of components in a particular product via the Catalog form, your macro corrects the price fields for you. But what if you change the cost of an individual component using the Components form? You need to figure out which products in the catalog are affected by the price change and then calculate new OurCost and Price fields. You can do that by executing some of the advanced queries you saw in the examples at the end of Chapter 11. As you might have guessed, some macros attached to the Components form will do the trick.

At the end of Chapter 11, in the example that dealt with synchronizing "parent" and "child" tables, you built a totals query to recalculate the prices of products that contain a certain component. You also created a temporary table named zSumCatalogCost and a delete query (named Clear zSumCatalogCost) to clear the table. You converted the totals query to append its results to the temporary table (and named the append query Calc Catalog Cost), and then you created an update query (named Update Catalog) that uses a one-to-one join with the Catalog table to update the OurCost field in the Catalog table.

You need to make a slight change to the Calc Catalog Cost query to change its parameter to point to your Components form. When you detect a change in the price of a component, you want this query to use the current component displayed on the form to calculate its totals. Open the Calc Catalog Cost query in Design view and change the subquery on CatalogItemID to read as follows:

```
IN (SELECT CatalogItemID FROM CatalogComponent
  WHERE   CatalogComponent.ComponentID=
  [Forms]![Components]![ComponentID])
```

You also need to change the query parameters to identify Forms!-[Components]![ComponentID] as a long integer. Notice that the parameter contains a fully qualified name of a control on your Components form. If the form is open when you run this query, Access won't prompt you for the ComponentID value. Instead, Access will use the current value in the ComponentID control on your Components form.

There's a table validation rule on the Catalog table to ensure that the selling price of a component is never less than its purchase cost. You need to make a small adjustment to the Update Catalog query not only to set the new value in the OurCost field but also to update the Price field to ensure that it's greater than the component's cost. You can use the expression you used in the *SetCost* macro to create a price that's 15 percent higher than your cost. Open the Update Catalog query in Design view, add the Price field from the Catalog table to the QBE grid, and set the Update To line to read as follows:

```
CCur(CLng(([TotCost]*1.15)+0.5))
```

Your result should look like the one shown in Figure 20-15 on the next page. Save this query as *Update Catalog Prices*.

The really simple solution would be to attach a macro to the After Update property on the Components form to correct the prices each time the data in the Components table changes. But running the three queries (delete, append, and update) could take a few seconds, and you really don't want to run these queries unless the price has changed and there are products in the Catalog table that would be affected.

In the BeforeUpdate event of a form, you can examine a special control property called OldValue to see if the value of a control has changed. In a macro attached to the Before Update property of the form,

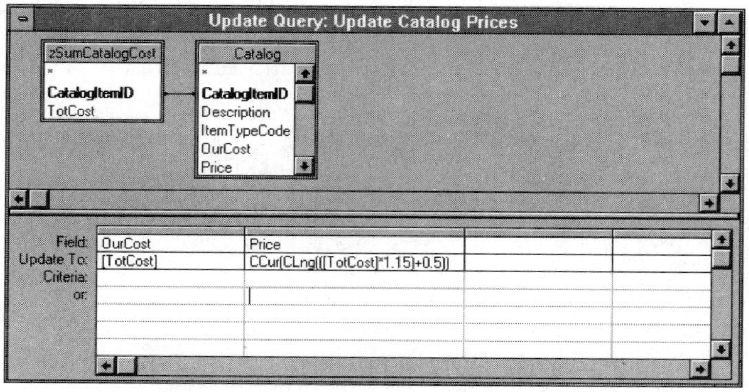

FIGURE 20-15. An update query to change both the OurCost and Price fields in the Catalog table when the price of a component changes.

you can first test to see whether the value of the OurCost field has changed. If the value has changed, you can call another macro (using the RunMacro macro action) to see whether any products in the Catalog are affected by this change, using the *DCount* aggregate function. You could code both tests in one condition, but Access evaluates all expressions in a condition before evaluating whether the condition is true or false. The test to compare [OurCost].OldValue to [OurCost] is very fast, and it should be the first test because you would expect this test to fail much of the time. Only when the cost has changed do you need to do a lookup in the Catalog table to determine whether any products are affected. Coding both tests in one condition would mean that Access will compare the values <u>and</u> do the table lookup any time any change occurs on the form.

If you find that the OurCost control has changed, and some products will be affected, you should display a warning message to give the user the opportunity to cancel the change. Use the *MsgBox* function (not the MsgBox macro action) in the Condition column of a macro for this. You can display a warning and ask the *MsgBox* function to display an OK and a Cancel button. The function returns the value 1 if the user clicks OK, so you can check the return value to decide whether to proceed or not. If the return value from the *MsgBox* function confirms the change, you should set a flag on the form indicating that the three queries should be run during the AfterUpdate event. The reason you want to do this is that there might be some other update test on the form or a system error that causes the update to fail. The AfterUpdate event occurs after the update is completed, so you know it's safe to go ahead and update the prices in the Catalog table.

Open the Components form in Design view and add a check box similar to the one you created on the Catalog List form. Name the check box *CostUpdt*. Set its properties as shown in Figure 20-16.

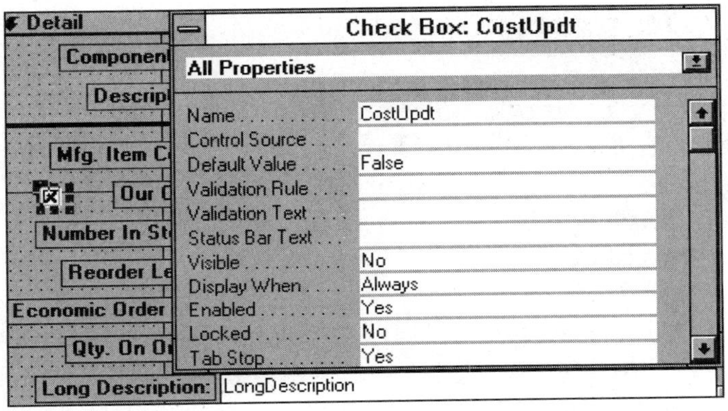

FIGURE 20-16.
The hidden CostUpdt check box that you set when an OurCost field in the Components table changes.

Now you're ready to create a macro for the Components form. In the Database window, click the Macro tab and then click New to start a new macro group. You need four macros to do the job. The first macro, named *CheckCost,* will be called from the BeforeUpdate event of the Components form. It contains a single command to run the *CheckCountCat* macro if the condition test is true. The condition statement looks like this:

```
Forms![Components]![OurCost] <>➘
 Forms![Components]![OurCost].OldValue
```

In the *CheckCountCat* macro, test to see whether any products in the Catalog table contain the component whose price is about to change; you do this by using the *DCount* function on the CatalogComponent table. If this test succeeds, run the *MsgCostUpdt* macro, which uses the *MsgBox* function to verify the update. On the second line in the *CheckCountCat* macro, enter a SetValue action to set the CostUpdt check box on the form to True. The test that uses the *DCount* function looks like this:

```
DCount("[CatalogItemID]", "[CatalogComponent]",➘
  "[ComponentID]=Forms![Components]![ComponentID]")<>0
```

In the *MsgCostUpdt* macro, use the *MsgBox* function in the Condition column to verify the change. The function looks like this:

```
MsgBox("Changing the cost for component
|[Description]|
affects one or more Catalog Items!",49,↵
 "Component Cost Warning")<>1
```

NOTE: You can embed carriage-return and line-feed characters in the middle of the message string to control the length of the lines in the message by pressing Ctrl-Enter as you type the string. (This character has been embedded in the four lines of code above.)

Notice that the Description field from the form is embedded in the message to make the message more informative. The second parameter for the *MsgBox* function, the number 49, asks the function to display the exclamation-point Warning icon and the OK and Cancel buttons. If the value returned by the function is not equal to 1 (the OK button was not clicked), use the CancelEvent macro action to cancel the update and to return the user to the form with the change not saved. Follow this with a StopAllMacros macro action to exit without returning to the *CheckCountCat* macro that called this macro.

The settings for the *CheckCost, CheckCountCat,* and *MsgCostUpdt* macros are shown in Figure 20-17.

The last macro you need—the *PriceFix* macro—will be attached to the After Update property of the Components form. Test the CostUpdt control to see whether it was set by the macros that run in Before Update. If the flag is set, turn off action query warnings, run the three queries, and reset the flag. The Condition column is simply the fully qualified name of the CostUpdt control which checks to see whether it is True or False. Figure 20-18 shows you the parameters for the actions in this macro. Figure 20-19 on page 718 shows you all four macros in the macro design window.

Macro Name	Action	Argument Box	Setting
CheckCost	RunMacro	Macro Name	Components.➘ CheckCountCat
CheckCountCat	RunMacro	Macro Name	Components.➘ MsgCostUpdt
	SetValue	Item	Forms![Components]!➘ [CostUpdt]
		Expression	True
MsgCostUpdt	CancelEvent		
	StopAllMacros		

FIGURE 20-17.
The three macros triggered by the Before Update property of the Components form.

Action	Argument Box	Setting
SetWarnings	Warnings On	No
OpenQuery	Query Name	Clear zSumCatalogCost
	View	Datasheet
	Data Mode	Edit
OpenQuery	Query Name	Calc Catalog Cost
	View	Datasheet
	Data Mode	Edit
OpenQuery	Query Name	Update Catalog Prices
	View	Datasheet
	Data Mode	Edit
SetWarnings	Warnings On	Yes
SetValue	Item	Forms![Components]![CostUpdt]
	Expression	False

FIGURE 20-18.
The settings for the *PriceFix* macro.

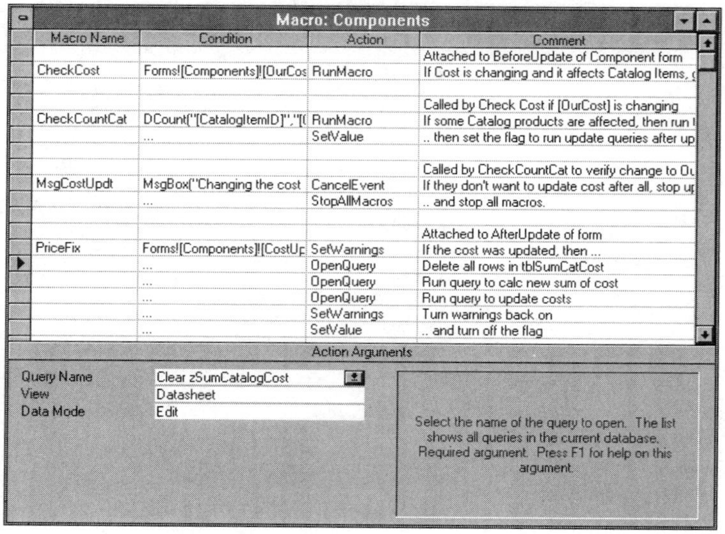

FIGURE 20-19. The four macros that are used to propagate a Component price change in the Catalog table.

If you look at the Component macro group in the sample PROMPT database, you'll find one additional action at the end of the *PriceFix* macro. This action opens an informative dialog box that lists all the products in the Catalog table that were affected by the price change.

The last step is to open the Components form in Design view and set the Before Update and After Update properties of the form to point to the *CheckCost* and *PriceFix* macros. Your property sheet for the Components form should look like the one shown in Figure 20-20.

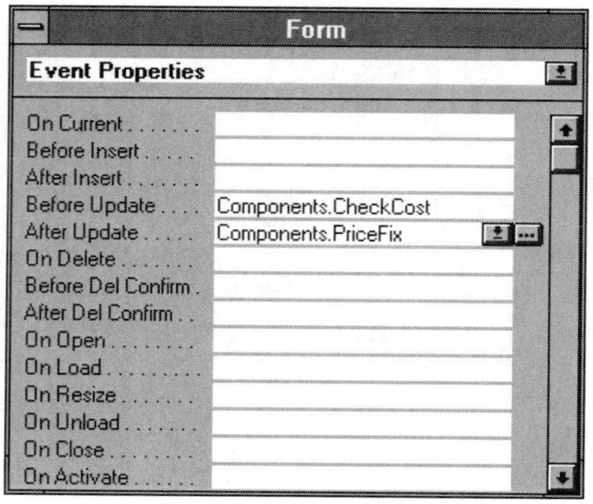

FIGURE 20-20. The property settings for the Components form that update the price of a product in response to a change in the price of a component.

You can now test your macros. Open the Components form in Form view and change the price of one of the components that is a part of several products in the catalog. If you're working in the PROMPT database, the first item in the Catalog table is used in six products.

Cascading a Delete

If you've correctly defined all the relationships in the PROMPT database and turned on referential integrity, Microsoft Access ensures that you haven't entered any orders for nonexistent customers. Access also ensures that you haven't defined any components for nonexistent catalog items. Access protects the integrity of your database by removing rows from the CatalogComponents table if you delete a row in the Catalog table. It does this because the referential integrity constraint between the Catalog and CatalogComponent tables has been set to "cascade" deleted rows.

However, it's probably a good idea to intercept a request to delete a Catalog entry. First, you can check to see whether any rows in the OrderItem table reference this product. If so, you can display a more informative message than the standard message from Access, which is: "Can't delete or change record. Since related records exist in table 'OrderItem', referential integrity rules would be violated." Second, if no rows in the Order table refer to this product, you can request a verification before you let Access delete the product and all its related CatalogComponent rows. To do this, you can create a macro that's triggered by the On Delete property of the Catalog List form.

The macro triggered by the On Delete property must first verify that no orders are outstanding for the current product displayed on the Catalog List form. You can use the *DCount* function to "count" matching rows in the OrderItem table. If there are zero rows, you can go on to the next step. If matching rows exist (that is, there are outstanding orders for the current product), you display a custom message with the MsgBox macro action and then use the CancelEvent action to stop the delete before Access issues its own message. Also include a StopMacro action to halt the macro when you detect this condition. The expression in the Condition column of your macro should look like this:

```
DCount("[CatalogItemID]","[OrderItem]",→
 "[CatalogItemID]=Forms![Catalog List]![CatalogItemID]")<>0
```

If no matching rows exist, you can use the *MsgBox* function in the Condition column of a following action to display a warning message and to let the delete proceed only if you click the OK button to confirm. The Condition column should look something like this:

```
MsgBox("Are you sure you want to delete
Catalog product |[Description]|
and all its components?",33,"Delete Catalog Product")<>1
```

NOTE: If the expression in the Condition column of a macro is true, Microsoft Access runs the macro action in that row and all of the immediately following actions with an ellipsis (...) in the Condition column. It then continues to run any additional actions in the macro with a blank Condition column until it reaches another expression, a macro name, or the end of the macro. If the expression in the Condition column of a macro is false, Access ignores the macro action and any immediately following actions with an ellipsis in the Condition column and moves to the next action row that contains an expression or a blank Condition column.

Notice that the first parameter uses the technique of embedding a control name surrounded by solid-pipe characters in order to insert variable information into the message. (You can enter this text using the Zoom edit box by placing the cursor in the Condition column and pressing Shift-F2.) You can use the Ctrl-Enter key combination at the end of each line to create a multiple-line message. You must begin this parameter with an equal sign and enclose the string in quotes so that Access knows this is an expression that must be evaluated. The parameter mode value 33 is the sum of the 1 mode value (indicating a dialog box with an OK and a Cancel button) and the 32 mode value (indicating a question-mark Warning icon). (See the Help topic on the *MsgBox* function for details on other mode values.) If you click OK in the dialog box created by the *MsgBox* function, the function returns a 1. If you don't click OK, the macro action on this line, a CancelEvent action, stops the action that triggered this macro—the deletion of the Catalog record.

Figure 20-21 shows the other settings for the *DeleteItems* macro. Figure 20-22 shows the completed macro in the Macro window.

Action	Argument Box	Setting
MsgBox	Message	="Orders still exist for Catalog Item |Description|. Delete all orders for this item before proceeding."
	Beep	Yes
	Type	Warning!
	Title	Delete Catalog Product - Action Required
CancelEvent	(none)	(none)
StopMacro	(none)	(none)
CancelEvent	(none)	(none)

FIGURE 20-21.
The settings for the *DeleteItems* macro.

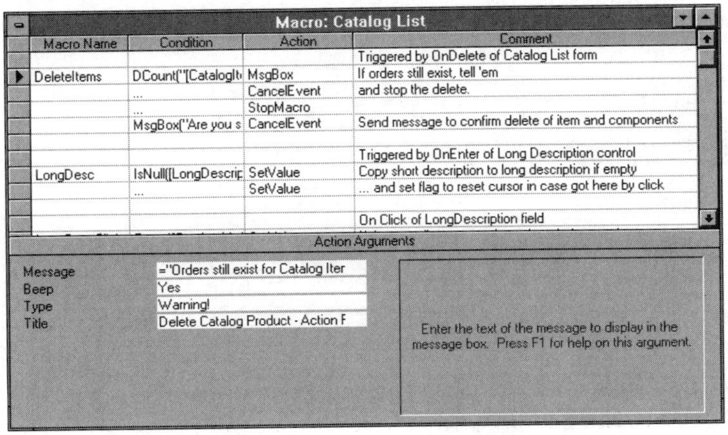

FIGURE 20-22.
The completed *DeleteItems* macro for the Catalog List form.

Open the Catalog List form in Design view and enter *Catalog List.-DeleteItems* in the On Delete property box of the form. Switch to Form view and try deleting a product in the catalog that you know is in one or more orders to test your macro.

You can perform a similar check for related rows in the Catalog-Component table before you allow a delete to proceed from the Components form. Look at the Component form and the *Component* macro in the PROMPT sample to see how to do this.

Linking Forms with a Mouse Event

You learned how to open the Components form from the Catalog List form using a command button. Now you can link the Suppliers form to the Components form in a different way.

Instead of using a command button, it's possible to open the Suppliers form by double-clicking the SupplierID control on the Components form. Figure 20-23 shows you how to set the properties for the SupplierID control to do this. The On Dbl Click property is set to trigger a macro called *NewSupplier* in the Components macro group. It's also a good idea to change the control's status bar text (using the control's Status Bar Text property) to inform you that double-clicking the control will open the Suppliers form to add a new supplier to the list.

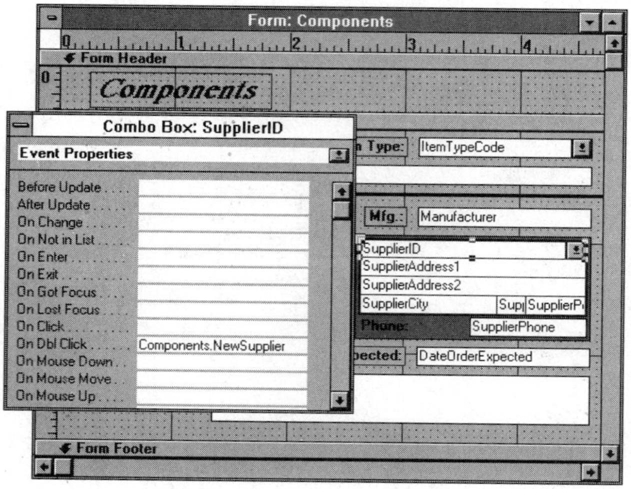

FIGURE 20-23. The SupplierID control's On Dbl Click property is set to trigger the *NewSupplier* macro.

Open the Components macro group in Design view. The *NewSupplier* macro is simply an OpenForm macro action to open the Suppliers form. You want to define a new supplier when you double-click the SupplierID control on the Components form, so you need to set the Data Mode argument box for the OpenForm action to Add, as shown in Figure 20-24. The Add setting causes the Suppliers form to open ready for data entry, as shown in Figure 20-25. You can type in your new supplier information and then close the form to save the record and return to the Components form.

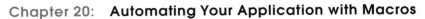

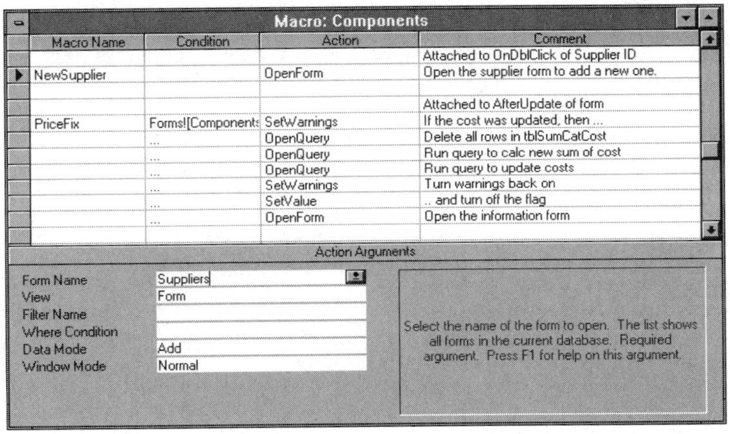

FIGURE 20-24.
The *NewSupplier* macro will open the Suppliers form.

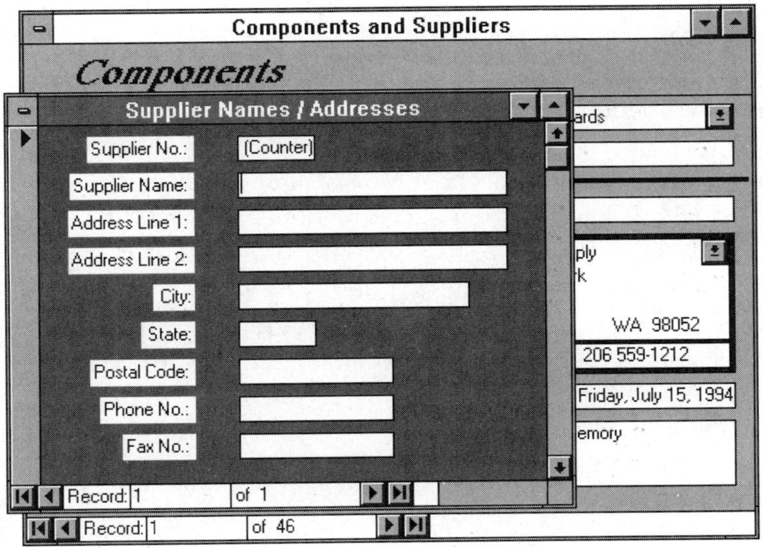

FIGURE 20-25.
The Suppliers form has been opened by double-clicking the SupplierID control and is ready for the addition of a new supplier.

Testing for an Open Form and Resynchronizing Data

After you type in new supplier information and close the Suppliers form, it would be nice to see that new information appear immediately on your Components form. You can create a macro triggered by the On Close property of the Suppliers form to update the information on the Components form when Microsoft Access returns to it. However, you might want to open the Suppliers form by itself, so the macro needs to be able to detect whether the Components form is open. The macro will end in an error if it tries to update controls on the Components form when the form isn't open.

Testing for an Open Form—An Introduction to Modules

In this section, you'll learn a little about Microsoft Access Basic modules. (The next chapter covers Access Basic in more detail.) To be able to verify whether a form is open, you need a function that is not a standard function in Microsoft Access. But you can find the function you need in the NWIND module named *Utility Functions*. To locate it, open the NWIND database, and click the Module tab in the Database window. Select the Utility Functions module, and click the Design button to open the module. You'll see a Module window similar to the one shown in Figure 20-26.

In Figure 20-26 you see the declarations section of the module, in which the programmer can set global options and variables. On the toolbar, the second combo box lists the available procedures in this module. Open the list in this box and scroll until you can see a function called *IsLoaded*. Select the *IsLoaded* function, and the Access Basic code will appear in the Module window, as shown in Figure 20-27.

To copy this code to your working copy of the PROMPT database, select the contents of the function in the Module window (but not the first and last lines). Choose the Copy command from the Edit menu and close the NWIND database. Open your PROMPT database, click the Module tab in the Database window, and click the New button. Choose the New Procedure command from the Edit menu, and type the name *IsLoaded2* in the New Procedure dialog box. (You'll find this function saved in the PROMPT database as *IsLoaded*.) Click inside the new blank

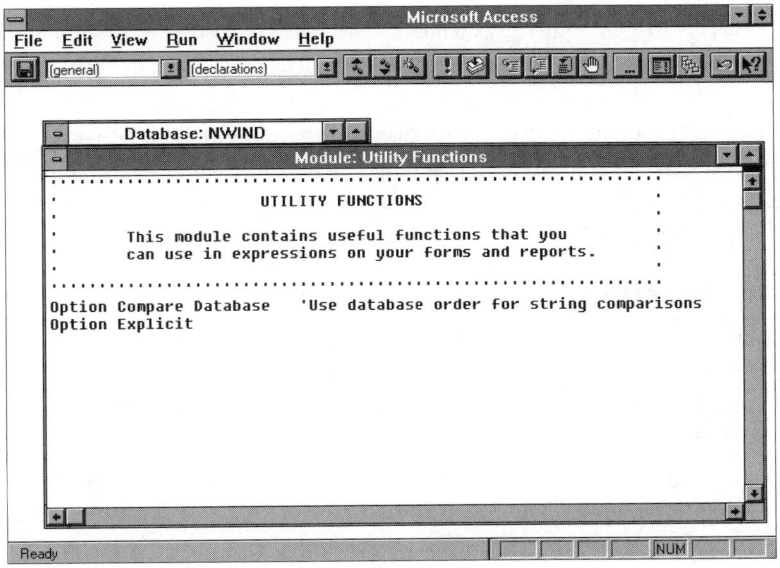

FIGURE 20-26. The initial view of the Utility Functions module in the NWIND database.

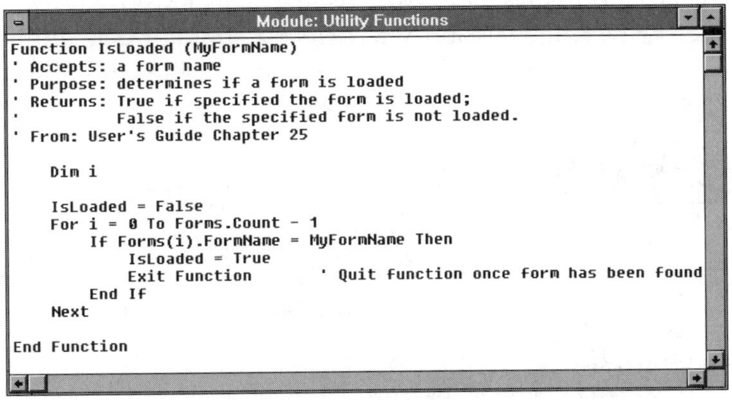
Module: Utility Functions
This module contains useful functions that you
Function IsLoaded (MyFormName)
' Accepts: a form name
' Purpose: determines if a form is loaded
' Returns: True if specified the form is loaded;
' False if the specified form is not loaded.
' From: User's Guide Chapter 25
Dim i
IsLoaded = False
For i = 0 To Forms.Count - 1
If Forms(i).FormName = MyFormName Then
IsLoaded = True
Exit Function ' Quit function once form has been found
End If
Next
End Function

FIGURE 20-27. The Access Basic code for the *IsLoaded* function.

procedure somewhere near the left border and then choose Paste from the Edit menu to copy the code to your module. Choose the Save command from the File menu and give your new module the name *MyFunctions*. Now the custom function *IsLoaded2* can be used anywhere in your database in the same way you'd use any built-in function. The *IsLoaded2* function can be used to test for open forms, as explained in the next section.

NOTE: If you already have a function with the name you type in the New Procedure dialog box in your database (for example, because you are working with the PROMPT database from the companion disk included with this book), Microsoft Access will not let you give this new function the same name. You'll need to rename the other function or save this function with a different name.

Resynchronizing Two Forms

You can open the Suppliers form from the Components form. If you add a new supplier to the Suppliers form, you can use a macro so that the new supplier information, including SupplierID data, appears immediately in the Components form.

Create a Suppliers macro group, and in the Macro window you can create the *RefreshComponent* macro shown in Figure 20-28. (Notice that you can also see a *CheckComponents* macro that is attached to the On Delete property of the Suppliers form. You can find this macro in the Supplier macro group in the PROMPT database. Its purpose is to display a friendly error message if you try to delete a supplier that still has related rows in the Component table.) The macro is shown in Figure 20-28, and its settings are shown in Figure 20-29.

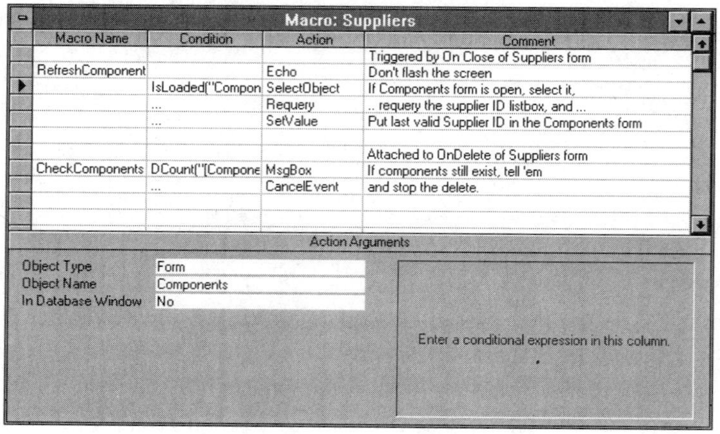

FIGURE 20-28. The *Refresh-Component* macro automatically adds new supplier information to the Components form.

Action	Argument Box	Setting
Echo	Echo On	No
	Status Bar Text	(none)
SelectObject	Object Type	Form
	Object Name	Components
	In Database Window	No
Requery	Control Name	SupplierID
SetValue	Item	Forms![Components]!➘ SupplierID]
	Expression	Forms![Suppliers]!➘ [SupplierID]

FIGURE 20-29.
The settings for the *RefreshComponent* macro.

Because several things are happening in this macro that might be distracting to the user, the first macro action sets Echo to No. The second line in the macro checks to see whether the current value in the SupplierID field on the Suppliers form is valid. The condition statement is

```
IsLoaded("Components") And Forms![Suppliers]![SupplierID]➘
 Is Not Null
```

The condition checks whether a valid SupplierID was entered and whether the Components form is open. If you opened the Suppliers form but didn't add a new record, you don't want to copy information from an invalid Null supplier record to the Components form.

If the SupplierID is valid and the Components form is open, the SelectObject macro action will move the focus to the Components form. Notice the ellipses in the Condition column of Figure 20-28; an ellipsis signifies that the condition still applies to the macro action on this line. The Requery macro action refreshes the SupplierID control on the Components form. Finally, the SetValue macro action copies the SupplierID information from the Suppliers form to the Components form.

You have a similar resynchronization problem between the Components form and the Catalog List form. If, when you change a price in the Components form, the Catalog List form is open, you should refresh the Catalog List form to be sure that it reflects the latest prices. At the end of your *PriceFix* macro for the Components form, it would be a good idea to add two additional lines, as shown in Figure 20-30.

Condition	Action	Argument Box	Setting
IsLoaded→ ("Catalog List")	RepaintObject	Object Type	Form
		Object Name	Catalog List
...	SelectObject	Object Type	Form
		Object Name	Components
		In Database Window	No

FIGURE 20-30.
The settings for the *PriceFix* macro.

You can see that there's a lot of power in the macro facility in Microsoft Access. If you want to explore other techniques, be sure to look at the macros for the Catalog, Component, and Supplier forms in the sample PROMPT database. These macros automate other functions on the Catalog, Component, and Supplier forms in the sample database.

In Chapter 21, you'll learn more about the power of Microsoft Access Basic, and in Chapter 22, you'll learn how to perform some of these same tricks using functions.

21

Microsoft Access Basic Fundamentals

You've already had a brief taste of Microsoft Access Basic. In Chapter 14, you used it to handle opening a custom toolbar, and in Chapter 20, you used it to determine whether a form is open. In this chapter and in the following one, you'll learn more about Access Basic and how to use it to automate your application.

Choosing Modules Instead of Macros

As you saw in Chapters 19 and 20, you can make lots of magic happen with macros. In fact, as you explore the NWIND and ORDERS sample databases that come with Microsoft Access or the PROMPT sample database on the companion disk that comes with this book, you'll discover many additional ways you can use macros to automate tasks in your database.

Macros, however, have certain limitations. For example, you learned from examining the list of available events in Chapter 19 that many events require or return parameters that can't be passed or read from a macro. Also, although you can write a macro to handle general errors on forms and reports, you can't really analyze errors effectively within a macro or do much to recover from an error.

When to Use Macros

Use macros in your application in any of these circumstances:

- You don't need to trap errors.
- You don't need to evaluate or set parameters passed by certain events, such as AfterDelConfirm, BeforeDelConfirm, Error, KeyDown, KeyPress, KeyUp, MouseDown, MouseMove, MouseUp, NotInList, and Updated.
- Your application involves only a few forms and reports.
- Your application might be used by nonprogrammers who will want to understand your code and possibly modify or enhance it.
- You're developing an application prototype, and you want to rapidly automate a few features to demonstrate your design.

There are actually a few things that can only be done with macros:

- Create custom menus and submenus for forms.
- Create the routine that Microsoft Access runs when your database opens.
- Define alternative actions for certain keystrokes.

You'll learn about these specialized tasks for macros in the final chapter of this book, "The Finishing Touches."

When to Use Modules

Although macros are extremely powerful, there are a number of tasks either that you cannot do with macros or that are better implemented using a Microsoft Access Basic module. Use a module instead of a macro in any of these circumstances:

- You need discrete error handling in your application.
- You want to define a new function.
- You need to handle events that pass parameters or accept return values (other than Cancel).
- You need to create new objects (tables, queries, forms, or reports) in your database from application code.
- Your application needs to interact with another Microsoft Windows application via dynamic data exchange (DDE).
- You want to be able to directly call Windows API functions.
- You want to place part of your application code in a library. (You can't execute macros in a library, only functions.)
- You want to be able to manipulate data in a recordset on a record-by-record basis.
- You need to use some of the native facilities of the database management system that handles your attached tables (such as SQL Server procedures or data definition facilities).
- You want the utmost performance in your application. Because modules are compiled, they execute slightly faster than macros. You'll probably notice a difference only on 386/25 or slower processors.

The Microsoft Access Basic Development Environment

As with all the other objects in a Microsoft Access database, you'll find a custom set of tools for defining the Microsoft Access Basic code you need to automate your application. There's also a comprehensive set of analysis tools to help you test and confirm the proper execution of the code you write.

The Built-In Module Design Toolbar

Microsoft Access provides a custom toolbar for working with modules. Open the PROMPT database, click the Form tab in the Database window, choose your Catalog List form and click the Design button, and then click the Code button on the toolbar (or choose Code from the View menu) to open the Module window for the form. From left to right, here are the elements on the Module window toolbar:

Save button. Click this button to save any changes.

NEW!

Object list box. When editing a form or report module, open this list to select the form or report, a section on the form or report, or any control on the form or report that can generate an event. The Procedure list box then shows the available event procedures for the selected object. Choose *(general)* to select the Declarations section of the module. When you're editing a module object, this list displays only the (general) option.

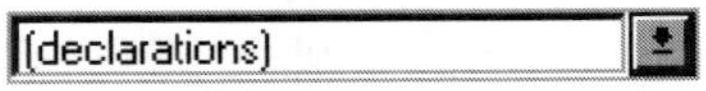

Procedure list box. Open this list to choose a procedure in the module and display that procedure in the Module window. When you're editing a form or report module, this list shows the available event procedures for the selected object and displays a check mark next to event procedures that you have coded and attached to

(continued)

(continued)

the form or report. When you're editing a module object, the list displays all the procedures you've coded in the module in alphabetic sequence.

Previous Procedure button. Click this button to move to the previous procedure in alphabetic sequence.

Next Procedure button. Click this button to move to the next procedure in alphabetic sequence.

New Procedure button. Click this button to start a new procedure in the current module.

Run button. Click this button to continue execution of your procedure after halting on a breakpoint.

Compile Loaded Modules button. Click this button to compile all procedures in all modules in the current database. If you save a changed procedure without compiling it, Microsoft Access compiles the module the first time you run the procedure.

Step Into button. After halting on a breakpoint, click this button to step through a procedure one statement at a time. When a statement calls another procedure, Step Into halts on the first line in the called procedure to allow you to step through each statement in the called procedure.

Step Over button. After halting on a breakpoint, click this button to step through code one statement at a time, treating a call to a procedure as a single statement. When a statement calls another procedure, Step Over runs all statements in the called procedure before halting on the next statement in the halted procedure.

Reset button. After procedure execution has halted (either due to an error or halting on a breakpoint), click this button to terminate execution of any Microsoft Access Basic procedure and clear all its variables.

Breakpoint button. Click any statement in a procedure, and then click this button to set a breakpoint on that statement. Access displays the statements on which you have set a breakpoint in boldface type. When you run a procedure containing a breakpoint, Access halts just before it executes the statement on which you have set the breakpoint. Click the Run button on the toolbar to continue execution. Click the Step Into button to execute statements one at a time, or click the Step Over button to execute procedures one at a time. Click the statement on which you have set a breakpoint, and click this button again to clear the breakpoint.

Build button. Access provides a sophisticated Expression Builder utility to assist you in defining Access Basic statements. Click anywhere in the Module window in which you want to insert a new statement, and click this button to start the Expression Builder utility.

Immediate Window button. Click this button to open the Immediate Window, in which you can enter Access Basic statements that you want to execute immediately. When procedure execution is halted, you can use this window to display and change variables used in the procedure. You can also use this window to start a procedure.

Calls button. After procedure execution has halted, click this button to open a dialog box showing the sequence of procedures that your code has called. You can select any called procedure and click the Show button in the dialog box to display the code for that procedure.

Undo button. Click this button to undo the last change you made to the procedure design.

Help button. Click this button to add a question mark to your mouse pointer, and then click with this pointer on any displayed object to receive context-sensitive help about that object.

Close the Catalog List Module window and the Catalog List form to return to the Database window.

Modules

You save all Microsoft Access Basic code in your database in modules. Microsoft Access provides two ways to create modules: as a module object or as part of a form or report object.

Module Objects

You can view the module objects in your database by clicking the Module tab in the Database window. Figure 21-1 on the next page shows the modules in the PROMPT sample database. You should use module objects to define procedures that can be used from queries or from several forms or reports in your application. A procedure defined in a module object can be called from anywhere in your application.

To create a new module, click the New button while viewing the Modules list. It's a good idea to name modules based on their purpose. For example, a module that contains procedures to perform custom calculations for queries might be named Query Functions, and a module containing procedures to work directly with Microsoft Windows functions might be named Windows API Functions.

FIGURE 21-1. The module objects in the PROMPT sample database.

NEW!

Form and Report Modules

To make it easy to create Microsoft Access Basic procedures that respond to events on forms or reports, Microsoft Access provides a module associated with each form or report that can contain procedures to respond directly to events. You can also create special procedures within a form or report module that are to be used only by that form or report. You can edit the module for a form or report by opening the form or report in Design view and then clicking the Code button on the toolbar or choosing Code from the View menu.

Form and report modules have two main advantages over module objects:

- All the code you need to automate a form or report resides with that form or report. You don't have to remember the name of the module you used to store the commands you created to respond to form or report events.

- Access loads module objects in a database when you open the database, but it loads the code for a form or a report only when the form or the report is open. Therefore, form and report modules consume application memory on your machine only when you're using the form or the report to which they are attached.

The Module Window

When you open a module in Design view, Microsoft Access shows you the Module window for the module and places you in the Declarations section, in which you define any variables that are shared by all procedures in the module. Click the Module tab in the Database window, choose the Toolbar Function module you created in Chapter 14, and click the Design button to see the Module window for the Toolbar Function module, as shown in Figure 21-2.

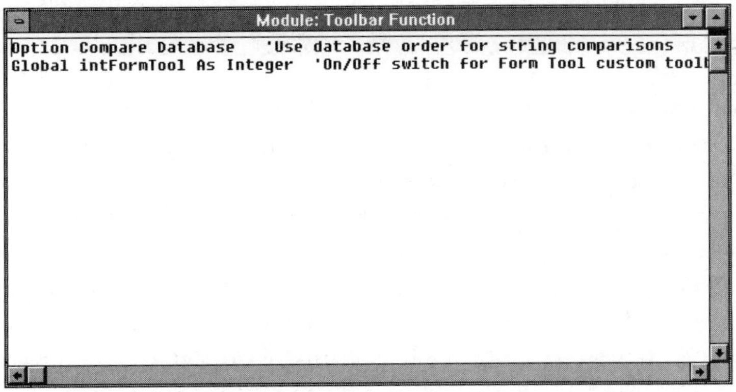

FIGURE 21-2. The Toolbar Function module from Chapter 14, open in a Module window.

In Figure 21-2, you can see the Declarations section of the module, in which you declared a global variable named *intFormTool* that you want to be shared by all procedures in the database (and not be reset each time a procedure runs). Within a Module window, you can use the arrow keys to move left and right and up and down. You'll find there's one blank line after the last line in this section on which you can enter additional variable declarations. When you enter a new line of code and press Enter, Access verifies the syntax of the new line and warns you of any problems it finds.

From the Declarations section, you can press the PgDn key to move to the first procedure in this module. You can also select any procedure by using the Procedure list box on the toolbar. When you press PgDn while in the Toolbar Function module, you see the *FlipFormTools* function procedure you created in Chapter 14, as shown in Figure 21-3.

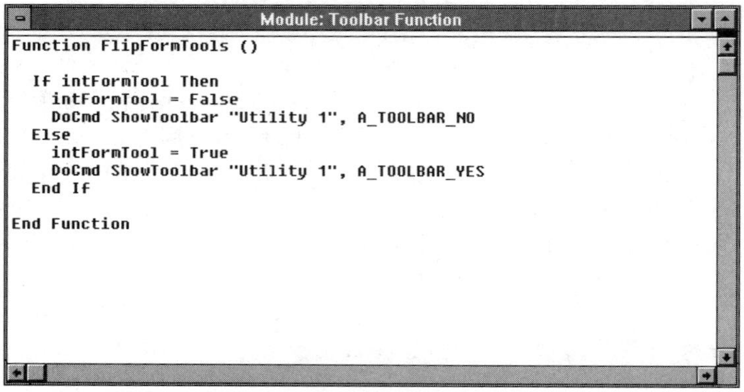

Module: Toolbar Function
Function FlipFormTools ()
If intFormTool Then
intFormTool = False
DoCmd ShowToolbar "Utility 1", A_TOOLBAR_NO
Else
intFormTool = True
DoCmd ShowToolbar "Utility 1", A_TOOLBAR_YES
End If
End Function

FIGURE 21-3. The *FlipFormTools* function procedure from Chapter 14, as it appears in the Toolbar Function module.

If you want to create a new procedure in a module, you can type in either a *Function* statement or a *Sub* statement on any line and then press Enter or click the New Procedure button on the toolbar or choose New Procedure from the Edit menu. When you type in a new *Function* or *Sub* statement on any line in a module and press Enter, Access starts a new procedure for you (it does not embed the new procedure in the one you were editing) and inserts an *End Function* or *End Sub* statement for you. If you're working in a form or report module, you can choose an object in the Object list box on the toolbar and then open the Procedure list box to see all the available events for that object. A check mark next to the event name means you have created a procedure to handle that event. Choose an event without a check mark to create a procedure to handle that event.

The Immediate Window

Perhaps one of the most useful tools for working with modules is the Immediate window. While you have a Module window open, click the Immediate Window button on the toolbar (or choose Immediate Window from the View menu) to see the Immediate window, shown in Figure 21-4.

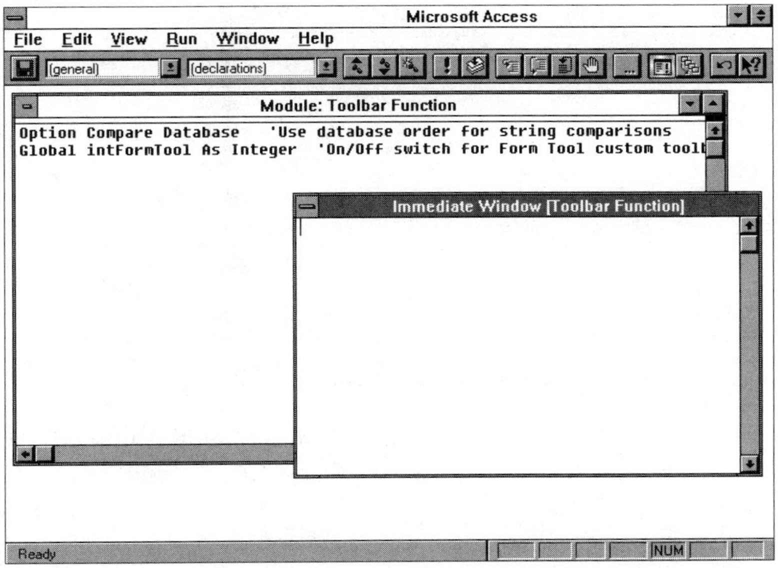

FIGURE 21-4.
The Immediate window for the Toolbar Function module.

In the Immediate window, you can type and immediately execute any legal Microsoft Access Basic statement. For example, you can set the value of the *intFormTool* variable to *1* by typing

```
intFormTool = 1
```

and pressing the Enter key.

The object used to debug Access Basic code is called *Debug*. The Debug object has a special method called *Print* that you can use to display the value of data in the Immediate window. So, to display the current value of the *intFormTool* variable in the Immediate window, type

```
Debug.Print intFormTool
```

in the Immediate window and press Enter. You can try out these commands using the Immediate window for the Toolbar Function module. Set the value of *intFormTool* to some integer, and then use the *Debug.Print* method to display the value you just set, as shown in Figure 21-5 on the next page.

Debug.Print also has a shorthand syntax—a single question mark (?). Therefore,

```
?intFormTool
```

is the same as:

```
Debug.Print intFormTool
```

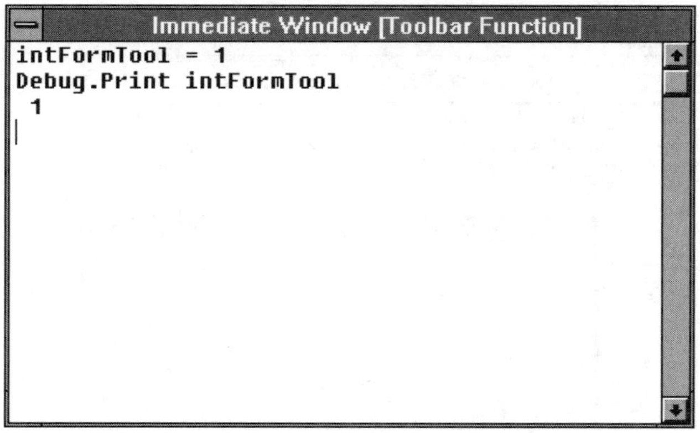
Immediate Window [Toolbar Function]
intFormTool = 1
Debug.Print intFormTool
1

FIGURE 21-5. Setting and displaying a variable in the Immediate window.

If you want to run a function procedure from the Immediate window, you can either assign the return value of the function procedure to a variable or use *Debug.Print* to run the function and display the value (if any) that it returns. If you want to try this out with your Toolbar Function module, first set the value of *intFormTool* to *0* (False), and then enter

```
?FlipFormTools()
```

You should see a result similar to the one shown in Figure 21-6—your Utility 1 toolbar opens. Run the function again to close the toolbar.

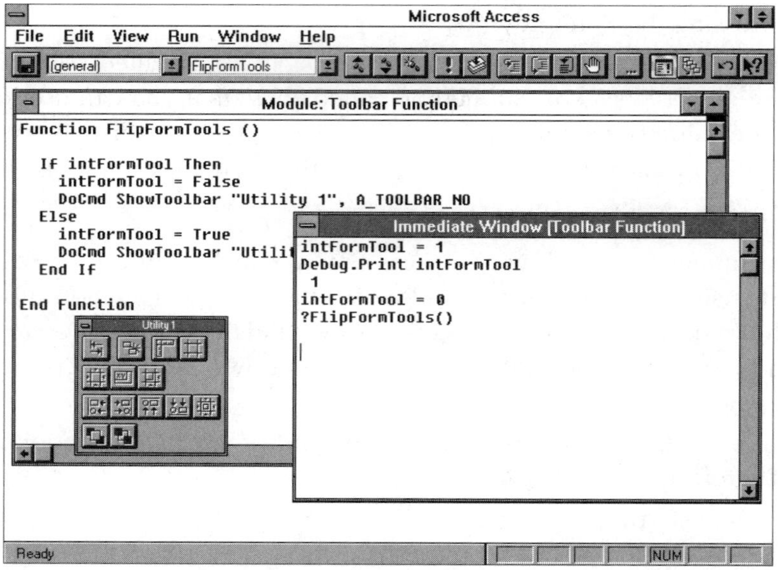
Microsoft Access
File
Edit
View
Run
Window
Help
(general)
FlipFormTools
Module: Toolbar Function
Function FlipFormTools ()
If intFormTool Then
intFormTool = False
DoCmd ShowToolbar "Utility 1", A_TOOLBAR_NO
Else
intFormTool = True
DoCmd ShowToolbar "Utili
End If
End Function
Utility 1
Immediate Window [Toolbar Function]
intFormTool = 1
Debug.Print intFormTool
1
intFormTool = 0
?FlipFormTools()
Ready
NUM

FIGURE 21-6. Using the Immediate window to run the *FlipFormTools* function procedure.

Variables and Constants

In addition to being able to work with the controls on any open forms or reports (as you can in macros), you can declare and use named variables in your Microsoft Access Basic code for storing values temporarily, calculating a result, or manipulating any of the objects in your database. So instead of defining "hidden" controls on forms to hold data you want to pass from one routine to another, you can define a global variable (as you did in the Toolbar Function module).

A constant is a data object that has a fixed value that you cannot change. You've already encountered some of the "built-in" constants in Microsoft Access—Null, True, and False. Access Basic also has a large number of "intrinsic" constants that you can use to test for such things as data types or can use as fixed arguments in functions and expressions. You can view the list of intrinsic constants by searching for the Constants topic in Help. You can also declare your own constant values to use in code you write.

In the following sections, you'll learn about variables to store and calculate data and variables you can declare to work with database objects.

Data Types

Microsoft Access Basic supports data types that are similar to the data types you use to define fields in tables in your database. The data types are described in the following table:

Data Type	Size	Data Typing Character	Can Contain
Integer	2 bytes	%	Integers from –32,768 through 32,767 or the values True (–1) or False (0)
Long	4 bytes	&	Integers from –2,147,483,648 through 2,147,483,647

(continued)

continued

Data Type	Size	Data Typing Character	Can Contain
Single	4 bytes	!	Floating-point numbers from approximately -3.4×10^{38} through 3.4×10^{38}
Double	8 bytes	#	Floating-point numbers from approximately -1.79×10^{308} through 1.79×10^{308}
Currency	8 bytes	@	A scaled integer with four decimal places from −922,337,203,685,477.5808 through 922,337,203,685,477.5807
String	1 byte per character	$	Any text or binary string up to 65,535 bytes in length, including text, memo data, and "chunks" from an OLE object
Variant	1 byte through approximately 65,535 bytes	(none)	Any data, including Empty, Null, and Date/Time data (Use the *VarType* function to determine the current data type of the data in the variable.)
User-defined	Depends on elements defined	(none)	Any number of variables of any of the above data types

You can implicitly define the data type of a variable by appending a data-typing character, as noted in the above table, the first time you use the variable. For example, a variable named *MyInt%* is an integer variable. If you do not explicitly declare a data variable that you reference in your code and do not supply a data type character, Microsoft Access assigns the Variant data type to the variable. Note that while the Variant data type is the most flexible (and, in fact, is the data type for all controls on forms and reports), it is also the least efficient because Access must do extra work to determine the current data type of the data in the variable before working with it in your code. The Variant data type is also the only data type that can contain the Null value.

> **TIP:** It's a good idea to include an *Option Explicit* statement in the Declarations section of every module in your database. When you do this, Access won't let you use any variable in your code that you haven't properly declared in a *Dim, Global, ReDim, Static,* or *Type* statement or as part of the parameter list in a *Function* statement or a *Sub* statement (see below). Using an *Option Explicit* statement helps you find variables that you may have misspelled when you designed your code.

Microsoft Access also lets you define variables that can contain object definitions. (See the section later in this chapter titled "Collections, Objects, Properties, and Methods" for details about objects that you can work with in Access Basic.) The object data types are Container, Control, Form, Database, Document, Field, Group, Index, Parameter, Property, QueryDef, Recordset, Relation, Report, TableDef, User, and Workspace.

Variable and Constant Scope

The scope of a variable or constant determines whether the variable or constant is known to just one procedure, all procedures in a module, or all procedures in your database. You can create variables or constants that can be used by any procedure in your database (global scope). You can also create variables or constants that apply only to the procedures in a module or only to a single procedure (local scope). You can pass variables from one procedure to another using a parameter list (see the sections on the *Function*, *Sub*, and *Call* statements, later in this chapter), but the variables might be known by different names in the two procedures.

To declare a global variable, use the *Global* statement in the Declarations section of a module object. To declare a global constant, use the Global keyword with a *Const* statement in the Declarations section of a module object. (You cannot use the Global keyword in a form or report module.) The name of a global data object (variable or constant) must be unique across all procedures in your database.

To declare a variable or constant that can be used by all procedures in a module, define that variable or constant in the Declarations section of the module object or the form or report module. No data object in a module can have the same name as any global data object. To declare a variable or constant used only in a particular procedure, define that variable or constant as part of the procedure. A data object in a procedure cannot have the same name as any global data object or any data object you define in the Declarations section of the module in which the procedure resides.

Syntax Conventions

The following conventions describe the Microsoft Access Basic syntax for statements you'll encounter in this chapter.

<table>
<tr><th>Convention</th><th>Meaning</th></tr>
<tr><td>Bold</td><td>Bold letters indicate keywords and reserved words that you must enter exactly as shown. Note that Microsoft Access understands keywords entered in uppercase, lowercase, and mixed case.</td></tr>
<tr><td>Italic</td><td>Italicized words represent variables that you supply.</td></tr>
<tr><td>Angle brackets < ></td><td>Angle brackets enclose syntactic elements that you must supply. The words inside the angle brackets describe the element but do not show the actual syntax of the element. Do not enter the angle brackets; they're not part of the element.</td></tr>
<tr><td>Brackets [ ]</td><td>Brackets enclose optional items. If more than one item is listed, the items are separated by a pipe character (|). Choose one or none of the elements. Do not enter the brackets or the pipe; they're not part of the element. Note that Microsoft Access in many cases requires you to enclose names in brackets. When brackets are required as part of the syntax of variables that you must supply in these examples, the brackets are italicized, as in: [MyTable].[MyField].</td></tr>
</table>

(continued)

continued

<table>
<tr><th>Convention</th><th>Meaning</th></tr>
<tr><td>Braces { }</td><td>Braces enclose one or more options. If more than one option is listed, the items are separated by a pipe character (|). Choose one item from the list. Do not enter the braces or the pipe.</td></tr>
<tr><td>Ellipsis ,...</td><td>Ellipses indicate that you can repeat an item one or more times. When a comma is shown with an ellipsis, enter a comma between items.</td></tr>
</table>

You must enter all other symbols, such as parentheses and colons, exactly as they appear in the syntax line.

The following sections show the syntax of the statements you can use to define variables in your modules and procedures.

Const Statement

Use a *Const* statement to define a constant.

Syntax:

```
[Global] Const {constantname = <const expression>},...
```

Notes:

Include the Global keyword in the Declarations section of a module object (not a form or report module) to define a constant that is available to all procedures in all modules in your database.

The *<const expression>* cannot include any user-defined functions, any Microsoft Access functions, any variables, the exponentiation operator (^), or the string concatenation operator (&). You can include simple literals and other previously defined constants.

You can append a data typing character to *constantname* (see the table in the "Data Types" section earlier in this chapter) to explicitly define the data type of your constant. If you do not include a data typing character, Microsoft Access uses the simplest data type that can contain the value of *<const expression>*. Access provides a number of built-in constants that have special prefixes to help avoid name conflicts. You should avoid creating constants that begin with any of the following prefixes: A_, DATA_, DB_, LB_, OBJSTATE_, OLE_, and SYSCMD_.

Example:

To define the constant PI to be available to all procedures in all modules, enter the following in the Declarations section of any module object:

```
Global Const PI = 3.14159
```

TIP: It's a good idea to use all uppercase characters to define constant names. This makes constants easy to identify in your code.

Dim Statement

Use a *Dim* statement in the Declarations section of a module to declare a variable or a variable array that can be used in all procedures in the module. Use a *Dim* statement within a procedure to declare a variable used only in that procedure.

Syntax:

```
Dim {variablename [([<array dimension>],... )]→
 [As data type]},...
```

where *<array dimension>* is

```
[lowerbound To ] upperbound
```

Notes:

You cannot declare an array using an object data type. You can declare arrays using a *Dim* statement only in the Declarations section of a module. To declare an array in a procedure, use a *ReDim* or *Static* statement. If you do not include an *<array dimension>* specification, you must include a *ReDim* statement in each procedure that uses the array to dynamically allocate the array at runtime. You can define an array with up to 60 dimensions. If you do not include a *lowerbound* in an *<array dimension>* specification, the default lower bound is 0. You can reset the default lower bound to 1 by including an *Option Base 1* statement in the module Declarations section. You must specify a *lowerbound* of at least –32,768 and an *upperbound* not exceeding 32,767.

Valid data type entries are Container, Control, Currency, Database, Document, Double, Field, Form, Group, Index, Integer, Long, Parameter, Property, QueryDef, Recordset, Relation, Report, Single, String (variable-length string), String * *length* (fixed-length string), TableDef, and Variant (the default). You can also declare a user-defined variable structure using the *Type* statement and then use the user type name as a data type.

Microsoft Access initializes declared variables at compile time. Numeric variables are initialized to zero (0); variant variables are initialized to empty; variable-length string variables are initialized as zero-length strings; and fixed-length string variables are filled with ANSI zeros (Chr(0)). If you use a *Dim* statement within a procedure to declare variables, Access reinitializes the variables each time you run the procedure.

Examples:

To declare a variable named *intMyInteger* as an integer, enter

```
Dim intMyInteger As Integer
```

To declare a variable named *dbMyDatabase* as a database object, enter

```
Dim dbMyDatabase As Database
```

To declare an array named *strMyString* that contains fixed-length strings that are 20 characters long and contains 50 entries from 51 through 100, enter

```
Dim strMyString (51 To 100) As String * 20
```

TIP: Especially if you create complex procedures, it's a good idea to prefix all variable names you create with a notation that indicates the data type of the variable. This will help you to be sure that you aren't attempting to assign or calculate incompatible data types. (For example, the names will make it obvious that you're creating a potential error if you try to assign the contents of a long integer variable to an integer variable.) It also helps you to be sure you pass variables of the correct data type to procedures. Finally, including a prefix helps you to be sure that you do not create a variable name that is the same as a Microsoft Access reserved word. The following table suggests data type prefixes you can use for many of the most common data types:

Data Type	Prefix	Data Type	Prefix
Integer	int	Control	ctl
Long	lng	Form	frm
Single	sgl	Report	rpt
Double	dbl	Database	db
Currency	cur	Field	fld
String	str	Index	idx
Variant	var	QueryDef	qry
User-defined (using the *Type* statement)	usr	Recordset	rcd
		TableDef	tbl

Global Statement

Use a *Global* statement in the Declarations section of a module object (not a form or report module) to declare variables that you can use in any procedure anywhere in your database.

Syntax:

```
Global {variablename [([<array dimension>],... )]¬
 [As data type]},...
```

where *<array dimension>* is

```
[lowerbound To ] upperbound
```

Notes:

You cannot declare an array using an object data type. If you do not include an *<array dimension>* specification, you must include a *ReDim* statement in each procedure that uses the array in order to dynamically allocate the array at runtime. You can define an array with up to 60 dimensions. If you do not include a *lowerbound* in an *<array dimension>* specification, the default lower bound is 0. You can reset the default lower bound to 1 by including an *Option Base 1* statement in the module Declarations section. You must specify a *lowerbound* of at least –32,768 and an *upperbound* not exceeding 32,767.

Valid data type entries are Container, Control, Currency, Database, Document, Double, Field, Form, Group, Index, Integer, Long, Parameter, Property, QueryDef, Recordset, Relation, Report, Single, String (variable-length string), String * *length* (fixed-length string), TableDef, and Variant (the default). You can also declare a user-defined variable structure using the *Type* statement; you can then use the user type name as a data type.

Microsoft Access initializes declared variables at compile time. Numeric variables are initialized to zero (0); variant variables are initialized to empty; variable-length string variables are initialized as zero-length strings; and fixed-length string variables are filled with ANSI zeros (Chr(0)).

Example:

To declare a long variable named *lngMyNumber* that can be used in any procedure in the database, enter

```
Global lngMyNumber As Long
```

ReDim Statement

Use a *ReDim* statement to dynamically declare an array within a procedure or to re-dimension a declared array within a procedure at runtime.

Syntax:

```
ReDim [Preserve] {variablename (<array dimension>,...)→
 [As type]},...
```

where *<array dimension>* is

```
[lowerbound To ] upperbound
```

Notes:

If you're dynamically allocating an array that you previously defined with no *<array dimension>* in a *Dim* or a *Global* statement, your array can have no more than 8 dimensions. If you declare the array only within a procedure, your array can have up to 60 dimensions. If you do not include a *lowerbound* in an *<array dimension>* specification, the default lower bound is 0. You can reset the default lower bound to 1 by including an *Option Base 1* statement in the module Declarations section. You must specify a *lowerbound* of at least –32,768 and an *upperbound* not exceeding 32,767. If you previously specified dimensions in a *Global* or a *Dim* statement or in another *ReDim* statement within the same procedure, you cannot change the number of dimensions.

Include the Preserve keyword to ask Microsoft Access to not reinitialize existing values in the array. When you use Preserve, you can change the bounds of only the last dimension in the array.

Valid data type entries are Currency, Double, Integer, Long, Single, String (variable-length string), String * *length* (fixed-length string), and Variant (the default). You can also declare a user-defined variable structure using the *Type* statement and then use the user type name as a data type. You cannot change the data type of an array that you previously declared with a *Dim* or a *Global* statement. After you have established the number of dimensions for an array that has module or global scope, you cannot change the number of its dimensions using a *ReDim* statement.

Access initializes declared variables at compile time. Numeric variables are initialized to zero (0); variant variables are initialized to empty; variable-length string variables are initialized as zero-length strings; and fixed-length string variables are filled with ANSI zeros (Chr(0)). If you use a *ReDim* statement within a procedure to both declare and allocate an array (and you have not previously defined the array with a *Dim* or *Global* statement), Access reinitializes the array each time you run the procedure.

Example:

To dynamically allocate an array named *strProductNames* that contains 20 strings, each with a fixed length of 25, enter

```
ReDim strProductNames (20) As String * 25
```

Static Statement

Use a *Static* statement within a procedure to declare a variable used only in that procedure that Microsoft Access does not reinitialize while the module containing the procedure is open. Access opens all module objects when you open the database containing those objects. Access keeps form or report modules open only while the form or the report is open.

Syntax:

```
Static {variablename [({<array dimension>},...)]→
 [As data type]},...
```

where *<array dimension>* is

```
[lowerbound To ] upperbound
```

Notes:

You cannot declare an array using an object data type. You can define an array with up to 60 dimensions. If you do not include a *lowerbound* in an *<array dimension>* specification, the default lower bound is 0. You can reset the default lower bound to 1 by including an *Option Base 1* statement in the module Declarations section. You must specify a *lowerbound* of at least –32,768 and an *upperbound* that does not exceed 32,767.

Valid *data type* entries are Container, Control, Currency, Database, Document, Double, Field, Form, Group, Index, Integer, Long, Parameter, Property, QueryDef, RecordSet, Relation, Report, Single, String (variable-length string), String * *length* (fixed-length string), TableDef, and Variant (the default). You can also declare a user-defined variable structure using the *Type* statement and then use the user type name as a *data type*.

Microsoft Access initializes declared variables at compile time. Numeric variables are initialized to zero (0); variant variables are initialized to empty; variable-length string variables are initialized as zero-length strings; and fixed-length string variables are filled with ANSI zeros (Chr(0)).

Examples:

To declare a static variable named *intMyInteger* as an integer, enter

```
Static intMyInteger As Integer
```

To declare a static array named *strMyString* that contains fixed-length strings that are 20 characters long and contains 50 entries from 51 through 100, enter

```
Static strMyString (51 To 100) As String * 20
```

Type Statement

Use a *Type* statement in a Declarations section to create a user-defined data structure containing one or more variables.

Syntax:

```
Type typename
  {variablename As data type}
  ...
End Type
```

Notes:

A *Type* statement is most useful for declaring sets of variables that can be passed to procedures (including Windows API functions) as a single variable. You can also use the *Type* statement to declare a record structure. After you declare a user-defined data structure, you can use the *typename* in any subsequent *Dim*, *Global*, or *Static* statement to create a variable of that type. You can reference variables in a user-defined data structure variable by entering the variable name, a period, and the name of the variable within the structure. (See the second part of the example that follows.)

You must enter each *variablename* entry on a new line. You must indicate the end of your user-defined data structure using an *End Type* statement. Valid data type entries are Currency, Double, Integer, Long, Single, String (variable-length string), String * *length* (fixed-length string), and Variant (the default).

Example:

To define a user type structure named *MyRecord* containing a long integer and three string fields and then to declare a variable named *usrContacts* using that user type and set the first string to Jones, enter

```
Type MyRecord
    lngID As Long
    strLast As String
    strFirst As String
    strMid As String
End Type
```

Within a procedure, enter

```
Dim usrContacts As MyRecord
usrContacts.strLast = "Jones"
```

Collections, Objects, Properties, and Methods

You've already dealt with two of the main collections supported by Microsoft Access—Forms and Reports. The Forms collection contains all the forms that are open in your application, and the Reports collection contains all the open reports.

You don't need a thorough understanding of *collections, objects, properties,* and *methods* to perform most application tasks in Microsoft Access. It's useful, however, for you to know how Access organizes these items so that you can better understand how Access works. If you want to study advanced code examples available in the Microsoft Access Solutions Pack or the many sample databases you can download from public forums, you'll need to understand collections, objects, properties, and methods and how to correctly reference them.

The Microsoft Access Application Architecture

Microsoft Access has two major components—the application engine, which controls the programming and end-user interface to the product, and the JET DBEngine, which controls the storage of data and the definition of all the objects in your database. (Figure 21-7 shows the architecture of Microsoft Access.) When you open a database, the application engine uses the DBEngine to determine the names of all the tables, queries, forms, reports, macros, and modules to display in the Database window. The application engine establishes the Forms collection (all the open forms) and the Reports collection (all the open reports). The application engine also creates two special objects, the Application object and the Screen object.

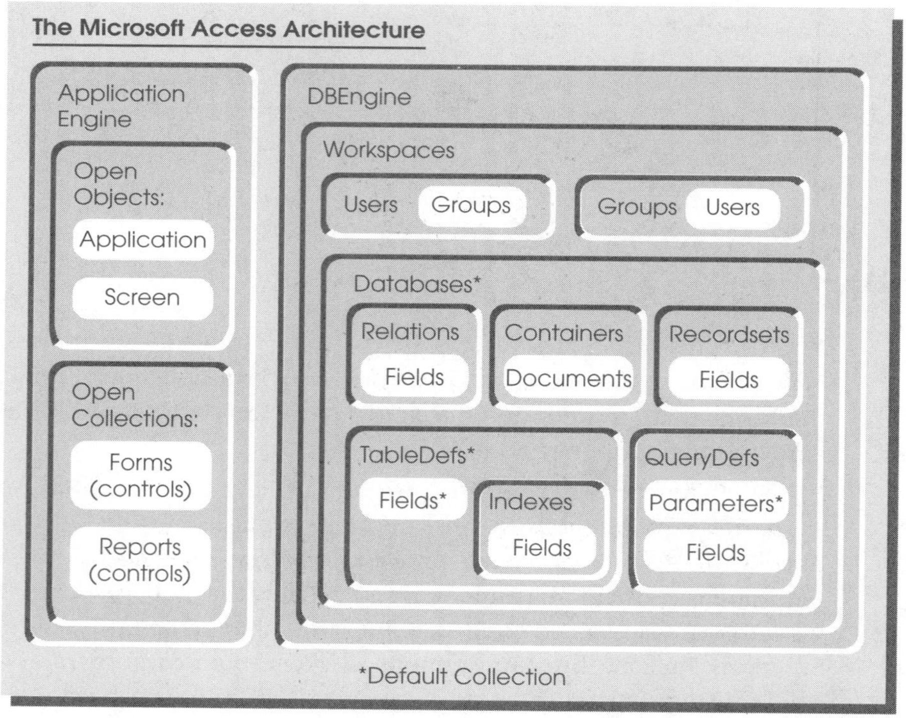

FIGURE 21-7. The Microsoft Access architecture.

NOTE: All collections except the DBEngine also have objects with singular names.

The Application object contains three properties: CurrentObject-Name, CurrentObjectType, and MenuBar. You can examine the value of the CurrentObjectName property to determine the name of the currently active object. You can compare the value of the CurrentObjectType property to the intrinsic constants A_TABLE, A_QUERY, A_FORM, A_REPORT, A_MACRO, and A_MODULE to determine the type of the current object. You can set the MenuBar property to the name of a menu bar macro to establish a custom menu bar for the Database window.

See Also: Chapter 23 contains details about menu bar macros.

The Screen object has four very useful properties: ActiveControl, ActiveForm, ActiveReport, and PreviousControl. Without having to know the actual names, you can reference the control (if any) that currently has the focus, the form (if any) that has the focus, the report (if any) that has the focus, or the name of the control that previously had the focus. (Additional details about referencing properties of objects appear later in this chapter.)

The DBEngine controls all the objects in your database through a hierarchy of collections, objects, and properties. When you open a Microsoft Access database, the DBEngine first establishes a *Workspaces* collection and a default Workspace object. If your database is secured, you'll notice that Access prompts you for a password and a user ID so that the DBEngine can create a User object and a Group object within the default workspace. If your database is not secured, the DBEngine creates a default user called Admin in a default group also called Admin.

Finally, the DBEngine creates a Database object within the default Workspace object. The DBEngine uses the current User and/or Group object information to determine whether you're authorized to access any of the objects within the database.

After a database is open, the application engine checks to see whether a macro group named Autoexec exists in the database. If it finds Autoexec, the application engine runs this macro group to start your application. If no such macro group exists, the application engine displays the Database window and waits for you to choose the next action from the user interface.

See Also: See also Chapter 23, "The Finishing Touches," for details on creating an Autoexec macro group.

You can create Microsoft Access Basic procedures that are called by the Autoexec macro group or by an event triggered from a form or a report that can create additional Database objects in the Databases collection by opening additional MDB files. Each open Database object has a Containers collection that the DBEngine uses to store the definition (using the Documents collection) of all your tables, queries, forms, reports, macros, and modules.

You can use the TableDefs collection to examine and modify existing tables. You can also create new TableDef objects within this collection. Likewise, the Relations collection contains Relation objects that define how tables are related and what integrity rules apply between tables. The QueryDefs collection contains QueryDef objects defining all the queries in your database. You can modify existing queries or create new ones. Finally, the Recordsets collection contains a Recordset object for each open recordset in your database.

NOTE: In the example at the end of this chapter, you'll see how to create a new TableDef object and then open a Recordset object in which the new table can insert rows.

Referencing Collections, Objects, and Properties

In the previous chapter, you learned the most common way to reference objects in the Forms and Reports collections and controls on those objects and their properties. Two alternative ways can be used to reference an object within a collection. The three ways to reference an object within a collection are:

- *CollectionName![Object Name].* This is the method you used in Chapter 20. For example: *Forms![My Form].*
- *CollectionName("Object Name").* This method is similar to the first method but uses a string constant to supply the object name, as in *Forms("My Form").*
- *CollectionName(RelativeObjectNumber).* Access numbers objects within a collection from zero (0) to *CollectionName.Count* minus 1. For example, you can determine the number of open forms by referring to the Count property of the Forms collection: *Forms.Count.* You can refer to the second open form in the Forms collection as *Forms(1).*

Forms and Reports are relatively simple because they are *top-level* collections within the application engine. As you can see from the diagram in Figure 21-7 on page 754, when you reference a collection or object maintained by the DBEngine, the hierarchy of collections and objects is quite complex. If you want to find out how many Workspace objects exist in the Workspaces collection, you need to reference the Count property of the Workspaces collection. For example, you reference the Count property like this:

```
DBEngine.Workspaces.Count
```

(You can create additional workspaces from Microsoft Access Basic code.)

Using the third method shown above to reference an object, you can reference the default Workspace object by entering

```
DBEngine.Workspaces(0)
```

Likewise, refer to the currently open database by entering

```
DBEngine.Workspaces(0).Databases(0)
```

When you want to refer to an object that exists in the default (or only collection) of a collection (see Figure 21-7), you do not need to include the collection name. So, because the Databases collection is the default collection for the Workspaces collection, you can also refer to the currently open database by entering

```
DBEngine.Workspaces(0)(0)
```

You can see that, even with this shorthand method, names can become quite cumbersome if you want to refer, for example, to a particular field within an index definition for a table within the current database in the default Workspace object. (Whew!) If for no other reason, object variables are quite handy to help minimize name complexity. For example, you can create a Database object, set it to *DBEngine.Workspaces(0)(0),* and then use the Database object name as a starting point to reference the TableDefs, QueryDefs, and Recordsets that it contains. (See page 759 for the syntax of the *Set* statement.)

When to Use "!" and "."

You've probably noticed that a complex, fully qualified name of an object or a property in Microsoft Access contains exclamation points (!) and periods (.) separating the parts of the name. Use an exclamation point preceding a name when the name refers to an object that is <u>in</u> the preceding object or collection of objects. Names following an exclamation point can contain embedded spaces and should always be enclosed in brackets ([ ]).

Use a period preceding a name that refers to a collection name, a property name, or the name of a method you can perform against the preceding object. Names following a period should never contain spaces. In other words, use a period when the following name is <u>of</u> the preceding name (as in the TableDefs collection <u>of</u> the Databases(0) object, or the Count property <u>of</u> the TableDefs collection, or the *MoveLast* method <u>of</u> the Recordset object). This distinction is particularly important when referencing something that has the same name as the name of a property. For example, the reference

```
DBEngine.Workspaces(0).Databases(0).TableDefs(0).Name
```

refers to the name of the first TableDef object in the current database. In the PROMPT sample database, if you use *Debug.Print* to display this reference, Access returns the value *Catalog*. However, the reference

```
DBEngine.Workspaces(0).Databases(0).TableDefs(0)![Name]
```

refers to the contents of a field called Name (if one exists) in the first TableDef object in the current database. In the PROMPT sample database, this reference returns an error because there is no Name field in the Catalog table.

Assigning an Object Variable— The *Set* Statement

As noted earlier, you can use object variables to simplify name references. Also, using an object variable is much faster than using a fully qualified name. At runtime, Microsoft Access must always parse a qualified name to first determine the type of object and then determine which object or property you want. If you use an object variable, you have already defined the type of object, so Access can quickly go to that object. This is especially important if you plan to reference, for example, many controls on a form. If you create a form variable first and assign the variable to point to the form, referencing controls on the form via the form variable is much simpler and faster than using a fully qualified name for each control.

Syntax:

```
Set variablename = objectreference
```

Notes:

You must first declare *variablename* using a *Dim*, *Global*, or *Static* statement as a Container, Control, Database, Document, Field, Form, Group, Index, Parameter, Property, QueryDef, Recordset, Relation, Report, or TableDef object. The object type must be compatible with the object type of *objectreference*. You can use another object variable in an *objectreference* to qualify an object at a lower level. (See the examples below.) You can also use an object *method* to create a new object in a collection and assign that object to an object variable. For example, it's common to use the *OpenRecordset* method against a QueryDef or TableDef object to create a new Recordset object. (See the example in the next section, "Object Methods.")

An object variable is a reference to an object, not a copy of the object. So you can assign more than one object variable to point to the same object and change a property of the object, and all variables referencing the object will reflect the change as well. The one exception is that several Recordset variables can refer to the same recordset, but each can have its own Bookmark property pointing to different rows in the recordset.

Examples:

To create a variable reference to the current database, enter

```
Dim dbMyDB As Database
Set dbMyDB = DBEngine.Workspaces(0).Databases(0)
```

To create a variable reference to the Catalog table in the current database, using the *dbMyDB* variable defined above, enter

```
Dim tblMyTable As TableDef
Set tblMyTable = dbMyDB![Catalog]
```

Notice that in the above example you do not need to explicitly reference the TableDefs collection of the database (as in *dbMyDB.TableDefs![Catalog]* or *dbMyDB.TableDefs("Catalog")*) because TableDefs is the default collection of the database. Access assumes that *[Catalog]* refers to the name of an object in the default collection of the database.

To create a variable reference to the Description field in the Catalog table using the *tblMyTable* variable defined above, enter

```
Dim fldMyField As Field
Set fldMyField = tblMyTable![Description]
```

Object Methods

When you want to apply an action against an object in your database (such as open a query as a recordset or go to the next row in a recordset), you apply a *method* against either the object or an object variable that you have assigned to point to the object. In some cases, you'll use a method to create a new object. Many methods accept parameters that you can use to further refine how the method acts on the object. For example, you can tell the *OpenRecordSet* method whether you're creating a recordset against a local table, a dynaset (an updatable recordset), or a read-only snapshot.

Microsoft Access supports many different object methods—far more than there's room to properly document in this book. Perhaps one of the most useful groups of methods is the group you can use to create a recordset and then read, update, insert, and delete rows in the recordset.

To create a recordset, you must first declare a Recordset object variable. Then open the recordset using the *OpenRecordSet* method against the current database (specifying a table name, a query name, or an SQL string to create the recordset) or against a QueryDef, TableDef, or other Recordset object. You can specify options to indicate whether you're opening the recordset as a local table (which means you can use the *Seek* method to quickly locate rows based on a match with an available index), as a dynaset, or as a read-only snapshot. For updatable recordsets, you can also specify that you want to deny other updates, deny other reads, open a read-only recordset, open the recordset for append only, or open a read-only forward scroll recordset (which allows you to move only forward through the records).

For example, to declare a recordset for the Catalog table in the PROMPT database and open the recordset as a table so that you can use its indexes, enter

```
Dim dbPrompt As Database
Dim rcdCatalog As RecordSet
Set dbPrompt = DBEngine.Workspaces(0).Databases(0)
Set rcdCatalog = dbPrompt.OpenRecordSet("Catalog",→
 DB_OPEN_TABLE)
```

To open the Catalog Main Form Query as a dynaset, enter

```
Dim dbPrompt As Database
Dim rcdCatQry As RecordSet
Set dbPrompt = DBEngine.Workspaces(0).Databases(0)
Set rcdCatQry = dbPrompt.OpenRecordSet("Catalog Main→
 Form Query")
```

(Note that opening a recordset as a dynaset is the default when the source is a query.)

After you open a recordset, you can use one of the *Move* methods to move to a specific record. Use *recordset.MoveFirst* to move to the first row in the recordset. Other *Move* methods include *MoveLast, MoveNext,* and *MovePrevious*. If you want to move to a specific row in the recordset, use one of the *Find* methods. You must supply a string variable containing the criteria for finding the records you want. The criteria looks exactly like an SQL WHERE clause (see Chapter 11) but without the WHERE keyword. For example, to find the first item in the Catalog Main Form Query whose price is less than $1,000, using the recordset created in the example above, enter

```
rcdCatQry.FindFirst "Price > 1000"
```

To delete a row in an updatable recordset, simply move to the row in the recordset you want to delete and then use the *Delete* method. For example, to delete the first row in the Catalog Main Form Query recordset whose price is greater than $1,000, enter

```
Dim dbPrompt As Database
Dim rcdCatQry As RecordSet
Set dbPrompt = DBEngine.Workspaces(0).Databases(0)
Set rcdCatQry = dbPrompt.OpenRecordSet("Catalog Main→
 Form Query")
rcdCatQry.FindFirst "Price > 1000"
' Test the recordset NoMatch property for "not found"
If Not rcdCatQry.NoMatch Then
  rcdCatQry.Delete
End If
```

If you want to update rows in a recordset, you move to the row you want to update and then use the *Edit* method to lock the row and make it updatable. You can then refer to any of the fields in the row by name to change their values. Use the *Update* method on the recordset to save your changes before moving to another row. For example, to lower the price of the first row in the Catalog Main Form Query whose price is greater than $1,000, enter

```
Dim dbPrompt As Database
Dim rcdCatQry As RecordSet
Set dbPrompt = DBEngine.Workspaces(0).Databases(0)
Set rcdCatQry = dbPrompt.OpenRecordSet("Catalog Main→
 Form Query")
rcdCatQry.FindFirst "Price > 1000"
' Test the recordset NoMatch property for "not found"
If Not rcdCatQry.NoMatch Then
  rcdCatQry.Edit
  rcdCatQry![Price] = 999.95
  rcdCatQry.Update
End If
```

Finally, to insert a new row into a recordset, use the *AddNew* method to start a new row. Set the values of all required fields in the row, and then use the *Update* method to save the new row. For example, to insert a new customer into the PROMPT Customer table, enter

```
Dim dbPrompt As Database
Dim rcdCust As RecordSet
Set dbPrompt = DBEngine.Workspaces(0).Databases(0)
Set rcdCust = dbPrompt.OpenRecordSet("Customer")
rcdCust.AddNew
rcdCust![CompanyName] = "Microsoft Corporation"
rcdCust![CustomerName] = "Bill Gates"
rcdCust![Address1] = "One Microsoft Way"
rcdCust![City] = "Redmond"
rcdCust![State] = "WA"
rcdCust![PostalCode] = "98052"
rcdCust![Country] = "USA"
rcdCust![PhoneNumber] = "(206) 882-8080"
rcdCust.Update
```

For further information about object methods, search for "Methods" in Microsoft Access Help.

Functions and Subroutines

You can create two types of procedures in Microsoft Access Basic—functions and subroutines (also known as Function procedures and Sub procedures). Both types of procedures can accept parameters—data variables that you pass to the procedure that can determine how the procedure operates. Functions can return a single data value, but subroutines cannot. In addition, you can execute a function from anywhere in Microsoft Access, including from expressions in queries and from macros. You can execute a subroutine only from a function, from another subroutine, or as an event procedure in a form or report.

Function Statement

Use a *Function* statement to declare a new function, the parameters it accepts, the variable type it returns, and the code that performs the function procedure.

Syntax:

```
[Static] [Private] Function functionname
  ([<arguments>]) [As data type]
  [<function statements>]
  [functionname = <expression>]
  [Exit Function]
  [<function statements>]
  [functionname = <expression>]
End Function
```

where *<arguments>* is

```
{[ByVal] argumentname [As data type]},...
```

Notes:

Include the Static keyword to preserve the value of all variables declared within the procedure, whether explicitly or implicitly, as long as the module containing the procedure is open. This is the same as using the *Static* statement (see earlier in this chapter) to explicitly declare all variables created in this function.

Use the Private keyword to make this function available only to other procedures in the same module. By definition, all functions and subroutines in a form or report module are private. When you declare a function as private in a module object, you cannot call that function from a query or macro or from a function in another module. A private function, however, can have the same name as some procedure in another module.

You can use a type declaration character at the end of *functionname* or the *As* clause to declare the data type of the variable returned by this function. If you do not declare a data type, Microsoft Access assumes that the function returns a variant result. You set the return value in code by assigning an expression of a compatible data type to the function name.

You should declare the data type of any arguments that the function can accept in its parameter list. If you declare an argument list, you must always supply a matching number of arguments with matching data types whenever you call this function. Note that the names of the variables passed by the calling procedure can be different from the names of the variables as known by this procedure. If you use the ByVal keyword to declare an argument, Access passes a copy of the argument to your function. Any change you make to a ByVal argument does not change the original variable in the calling procedure. If the argument passed by the calling procedure is an expression, Access treats it as though you had declared it a ByVal.

Use the *Exit Function* statement anywhere in your function to clear any error conditions and exit your function normally, returning to the calling procedure. If Access runs your code until it encounters the *End Function* statement, control is passed to the calling procedure, but any errors are not cleared. If this function causes an error and terminates with the *End Function* statement, Access passes the error to the calling procedure. (See the section titled "Trapping Errors," later in this chapter, for details.)

Example:

To create a function named *MyFunction* that accepts an integer argument and a string argument and returns a double value, enter

```
Function MyFunction (intArg1 As Integer, strArg2 As→
 String) As Double
  <function statements>
End Function
```

Sub Statement

Use a *Sub* statement to declare a new subroutine, the parameters it accepts, and the code in the subroutine.

Syntax:

```
[Static] [Private] Sub subroutinename ([<arguments>])→
  [As data type]
  [ <subroutine statements> ]
  [Exit Sub]
  [ <subroutine statements> ]
End Sub
```

where *<arguments>* is

```
{[ByVal] argumentname [As data type]},...
```

Notes:

Include the Static keyword to preserve the value of all variables declared within the procedure, whether explicitly or implicitly, as long as the module containing the procedure is open. This is the same as using the *Static* statement (see earlier in this chapter) to explicitly declare all variables created in this subroutine.

Use the Private keyword to make this subroutine available only to other procedures in the same module. By definition, all functions and subroutines in a form or report module are private. When you declare a subroutine as private in a module object, you cannot call that subroutine from a procedure in another module. A private subroutine, however, can have the same name as a procedure in another module.

You should declare the data type of all arguments that the subroutine accepts in its argument list. If you declare an argument list, you must always supply a matching number of arguments with matching data types whenever you call this subroutine. Note that the names of the variables that are passed by the calling procedure can be different from the names of the variables as known by this procedure. If you use the ByVal keyword to declare an argument, Microsoft Access passes a copy of the argument to your subroutine. Any change you make to a ByVal argument does not change the original variable in the calling procedure. If the argument passed by the calling procedure is an expression, Access treats it as though you had declared it a ByVal.

Use the *Exit Sub* statement anywhere in your subroutine to clear any error conditions and exit your subroutine normally, returning to the calling procedure. If Access runs your code until it encounters the *End Sub* statement, control is passed to the calling procedure, but any errors are not cleared. If this subroutine causes an error and terminates with the *End Sub* statement, Access passes the error to the calling procedure. (See the section titled "Trapping Errors," later in this chapter, for details.)

Example:

To create a subroutine named *MySub* that accepts two string arguments but can modify only the second argument, enter

```
Function MySub (ByVal strArg1 As String, strArg2 As→
 String)
  <subroutine statements>
End Sub
```

Controlling Flow

Microsoft Access Basic provides you with many ways to control the flow of statements in your procedures. You can call other procedures, loop through a set of statements either a calculated number of times or based on a condition, or test values and conditionally execute sets of statements based on the result of the condition test. You can also go directly to a set of statements or exit a procedure at any time. The following sections demonstrate some (but not all) of the ways you can control flow in your procedures.

Call Statement

Use a *Call* statement to transfer control to a subroutine.

Syntax:

```
Call subroutinename [(<arguments>)]
```

or

```
subroutinename [<arguments>]
```

where *<arguments>* is

```
{[ByVal] <expression> },...
```

Notes:

If the subroutine accepts arguments, you must always supply a matching number of arguments with matching data types. The names of the variables passed by the calling procedure, however, can be different from the names of the variables as known by the subroutine. If you use the ByVal keyword to declare an argument, Microsoft Access passes a copy of the argument to the subroutine. The subroutine cannot change the original variable in the calling procedure. If the argument passed by the calling procedure is an expression, Access treats it as though you had declared it a ByVal.

Examples:

To call a subroutine named *MySub* and pass it an integer variable and an expression, enter

```
Call MySub (intMyInteger, curPrice * intQty)
```

An alternative syntax is

```
MySub intMyInteger, curPrice * intQty
```

Do ... Loop Statement

Use a *Do ... Loop* statement to define a block of statements that you want executed multiple times. You can also define a condition that terminates the loop when the condition is false.

Syntax:

```
Do [{While | Until} <condition>]
  [<procedure statements>]
  [Exit Do]
  [<procedure statements>]
Loop
```

or

```
Do
  [<procedure statements>]
  [Exit Do]
  [<procedure statements>]
Loop [{While | Until} <condition>]
```

Notes:

The *<condition>* is a comparison predicate or expression that Microsoft Access can evaluate to true (nonzero) or false (zero or Null). The *While* clause is the opposite of the *Until* clause. If you specify a *While* clause, execution continues as long as the *<condition>* is true. If you specify an *Until* clause, execution of the loop stops when *<condition>* is true. If you place a *While* or an *Until* clause in the *Do* clause, the condition must be met for the statements in the loop to execute at all. If you place a *While* or an *Until* clause in the *Loop* clause, Access executes the statements within the loop before testing the condition.

You can place one or more *Exit Do* statements anywhere within the loop to exit the loop before reaching the *Loop* statement. Generally you'll use the *Exit Do* statement as part of some other evaluation statement structure, such as an *If ... Then ... Else* statement.

Example:

To read all the rows in the Customer table until you reach end of the recordset, enter

```
Dim dbPrompt As Database
Dim rcdCust As RecordSet
Set dbPrompt = DBEngine.Workspaces(0).Databases(0)
Set rcdCust = dbPrompt.OpenRecordSet("Customer")
Do Until rcdCust.EOF
  <procedure statements>
  rcdCust.MoveNext
Loop
```

For ... Next Statement

Use a *For ... Next* statement to execute a series of statements a calculated number of times. A *For ... Next* statement is most useful for iterating through elements of an array or members of a collection.

Syntax:

```
For counter = first To last [Step stepamount]
  [<procedure statements>]
  [Exit For]
  [<procedure statements>]
Next [counter],...
```

Notes:

The *counter* must be a numeric variable that is not an array or a record element. Microsoft Access initially sets the value of *counter* to *first.* If you do not specify a *stepamount,* the default *stepamount* is +1. If the *stepamount* is positive or 0, Access executes the loop as long as *counter* is less than or equal to *last.* If the *stepamount* is negative, Access executes the loop as long as *counter* is greater than or equal to *last.* Access adds *stepamount* to *counter* when it encounters the corresponding *Next* statement. You can change the value of *counter* within the *For* loop, but this might make your procedure more difficult to test and debug. Changing the value of *last* within the loop does not affect execution of the loop.

You can nest one *For* loop inside another. When you do that, you must choose a different name for each *counter.* You can end multiple nested *For* loops with a single *Next* statement by listing the *counter* names with the *Next* statement—first list the *counter* name for the innermost *For* loop, then list the *counter* name for the next innermost *For* loop, and so on.

Example:

To list the names of all the tables in the PROMPT database in the Immediate window, enter

```
Dim dbPrompt As Database
Dim intNumTables As Integer, i as Integer
Set dbPrompt = DBEngine.Workspaces(0).Databases(0)
intNumTables = dbPrompt.TableDefs.Count
For i = 0 To intNumTables - 1
  Debug.Print dbPrompt.TableDefs(i).Name
Next i
```

GoTo Statement

Use a *GoTo* statement to jump unconditionally to another statement in your procedure.

Syntax:

```
GoTo {label | linenumber}
```

Notes:

You can label a statement line by starting the line with a string no more than 40 characters long that starts with an alphabetic character and ends with a colon (:). A line label cannot be a Microsoft Access reserved word. You can also optionally number the statement lines in your procedure. Each line number must contain only numbers, must be different from all other line numbers in the procedure, must be the first nonblank characters in a line, and must contain 40 characters or less. To jump to a line number or a labeled line, use the *GoTo* statement and the appropriate *label* or *linenumber*.

Example:

To jump to the statement line labeled *SkipOver:*, enter

```
GoTo SkipOver
```

If ... Then ... Else Statement

Use an *If ... Then ... Else* statement to conditionally execute statements based on the evaluation of a condition.

Syntax:

```
If <condition1> Then
  [<procedure statements 1>]
[ElseIf <condition2> Then
  [<procedure statements 2>]]...
[Else
  [<procedure statements n>]]
End If
```

or

```
If <condition> Then <thenstmt> [Else <elsestmt>]
```

Notes:

The *<condition>* is a numeric or string expression that Access can evaluate to true (nonzero) or false (0 or Null). The *<condition>* can also be the special *TypeOf ... Is* test to evaluate a control variable. The syntax for this test is

```
TypeOf <ControlObject> Is <ControlType>
```

where *<ControlObject>* is the name of a control variable and *<ControlType>* is one of the following: BoundObjectFrame, CheckBox, ComboBox, CommandButton, Label, Line, ListBox, ObjectFrame, OptionButton, OptionGroup, PageBreak, Rectangle, Subform, Subreport, TextBox, or ToggleButton.

If the *<condition>* is true, then Microsoft Access executes the statement or statements immediately following the Then keyword. If the *<condition>* is false, Access evaluates the next *ElseIf* *<condition>* or executes the statements following the Else keyword, whichever occurs next.

The alternate syntax does not need an *End If* statement, but you must enter the entire *If ... Then* statement on a single line. Both *<thenstmt>* and *<elsestmt>* can be either a single Microsoft Access Basic statement or multiple statements separated by colons (:).

Example:

To set an integer value depending on whether a string begins with a letter from A through F, from G through N, or from O through Z, enter

```
Dim strMyString As String, strFirst As String,→
  intVal As Integer
strFirst = UCase$(Mid$(strMyString, 1, 1))
If strFirst >= "A" And strFirst <= "F" Then
  intVal = 1
ElseIf strFirst >= "G" And strFirst <= "N" Then
  intVal = 2
ElseIf strFirst >= "O" And strFirst <= "Z" Then
  intVal = 3
Else
  intVal = 0
End If
```

Select Case Statement

Use a *Select Case* statement to execute statements conditionally based on the evaluation of an expression compared to a list or range of values.

Syntax:

```
Select Case <test expression>
  [Case <comparison list 1>
    [<procedure statements 1>]]
  ...
  [Case Else
    [<procedure statements n>]]
End Select
```

where *<test expression>* is any numeric or string expression; where *<comparison list>* is

```
{<comparison element>,...}
```

where *<comparison element>* is

```
{expression |→
 expression To expression |→
 Is <comparison operator> expression}
```

and where *<comparison operator>* is

```
{= | <> | < | > | <= | >=}
```

Notes:

If the *<test expression>* matches one of the *<comparison elements>* in a *Case* clause, Microsoft Access executes the statements following that clause. If the *<comparison element>* is a single expression, the *<test expression>* must equal the *<comparison element>* for the statements following that clause to be executed. If the *<comparison element>* contains a To keyword, the first expression must be less than the second expression (either in numeric value if the expressions are numbers or in collating sequence if the expressions are strings) and the *<test expression>* must be between the first expression and the second expression. If the *<comparison element>* contains the Is keyword, the evaluation of *<comparison operator> expression* must be true.

If more than one *Case* clause matches the *<test expression>*, Access executes only the set of statements following the first *Case* clause that matches. You can include a block of statements following a *Case Else* clause that Access executes if none of the previous *Case* clauses match the *<test expression>*. You can nest another *Select Case* statement within the statements following a *Case* clause.

Example:

To assign an integer value to a variable depending on whether a string begins with a letter from A through F, from G through N, or from O through Z, enter

```
Dim strMyString As String, intVal As Integer
Select Case UCase$(Mid$(strMyString, 1, 1))
  Case "A" To "F"
    intVal = 1
  Case "G" To "N"
    intVal = 2
  Case "O" To "Z"
    intVal = 3
  Case Else
    intVal = 0
End Select
```

Stop Statement

Use a *Stop* statement to suspend execution of your procedure.

Syntax:

```
Stop
```

Notes:

A *Stop* statement has the same effect as setting a breakpoint on a statement. You can use the Microsoft Access debugging tools, such as the Step Into and the Step Over buttons and the Immediate window, to evaluate the status of your procedure after Access halts on a *Stop* statement.

While ... Wend Statement

Use a *While ... Wend* statement to continuously execute a block of statements as long as a condition is true.

Syntax:

```
While <condition>
  [<procedure statements>]
Wend
```

Notes:

A *While ... Wend* statement is similar to a *Do ... Loop* statement with a *While* clause, except that you can use an *Exit Do* statement to exit from a *Do* loop. Microsoft Access provides no similar *Exit* clause for a *While* loop. The *<condition>* is an expression that Access can evaluate to true (nonzero) or false (0 or Null). Execution continues as long as the *<condition>* is true.

Example:

To read all the rows in the Customer table until you reach end of the recordset, enter

```
Dim dbPrompt As Database
Dim rcdCust As RecordSet
Set dbPrompt = DBEngine.Workspaces(0).Databases(0)
Set rcdCust = dbPrompt.OpenRecordSet("Customer")
While Not rcdCust.EOF
  <procedure statements>
  rcdCust.MoveNext
Wend
```

Running Macro Actions

Within Microsoft Access Basic, you can also execute most of the macro actions. Only a few of the macro actions have direct Access Basic equivalents. To execute a macro action, use the *DoCmd* statement, described below.

DoCmd Statement

Use a *DoCmd* statement to execute a macro action within a Microsoft Access Basic procedure.

Syntax:

```
DoCmd action [actionargument],...
```

Notes:

Some of the most common actions you'll use from Access Basic include ApplyFilter, Close, DoMenuItem, FindNext and FindRecord (for searching the recordset of the current form and immediately displaying the result), Hourglass, Maximize, Minimize, MoveSize, OpenForm, OpenQuery (to run a query that you don't need to modify), OpenReport, and ShowToolBar. Although you can run the Echo, GoToControl, GoToPage, RepaintObject, and Requery actions from Access Basic using a *DoCmd* statement, it's more efficient to use the new *Echo, SetFocus, GoToPage, Repaint,* and *Requery* methods.

See Also: Microsoft Access provides built-in constants for many of the macro action parameters. For further information, search for "Macro Action Constants" in Access Help.

Examples:

To open a form named Customer in Form view for data entry, enter

```
DoCmd OpenForm "Customer", A_NORMAL, , , A_ADD
```

To close a form named Supplier, enter

```
DoCmd Close A_FORM, "Supplier"
```

Actions with Microsoft Access Basic Equivalents

A few macro actions cannot be executed from a Microsoft Access Basic procedure. These actions, however, have equivalent statements in Access Basic, as shown in the following table:

Macro Action	Access Basic Equivalent
MsgBox	*MsgBox* statement or function
RunApp	*Shell* function
RunCode	*Call* subroutine or *Execute* function
SendKeys	*SendKeys* statement
SetValue	Variable assignment (=)

Actions You Cannot Execute in Microsoft Access Basic

You cannot execute the AddMenu, StopAllMacros, or StopMacro macro action from Microsoft Access Basic procedure.

Trapping Errors

One of the most powerful features of Microsoft Access Basic is the ability to trap all errors, analyze them, and take corrective action. To enable error trapping, use an *On Error* statement, as described below.

On Error Statement

Use an *On Error* statement to enable error trapping, establish the routine to handle error trapping, skip past any errors, or turn off error trapping.

Syntax:

```
On Error {GoTo lineID | Resume [Next] | GoTo 0}
```

Notes:

Use a *GoTo lineID* statement to establish a code block in your procedure that handles any error. The *lineID* can be a line number or a label. In your error handling statements, you can examine the built-in *Err* variable to determine the exact nature of the error. You can use the *Error* function to examine the text of the error message associated with the error. If you use line numbers with your statements, you can use the built-in *Erl* function to determine the line number of the statement that caused the error. Use a *Resume* statement, after taking corrective action, to retry execution of the statement that caused the error. Use a *Resume Next* statement to continue execution at the statement immediately following the statement that caused the error. You can also use an *Exit Function* or *Exit Sub* statement to reset the error condition and return to the calling procedure.

Use a *Resume Next* statement to trap errors but skip over any statement that causes an error. You can call the *Err* function in a statement immediately following the statement that you suspect might cause an error to see whether an error occurred. *Err* returns 0 if no error has occurred.

Use a *GoTo 0* statement to turn off error trapping for the current procedure. If an error occurs, Microsoft Access passes the error to the error routine in the calling procedure or opens an error dialog box if there is no previous error routine.

Examples:

To trap errors but continue execution with the next statement, enter

```
On Error Resume Next
```

To trap errors and execute the statements that follow the *MyError:* label when an error occurs, enter

```
On Error GoTo MyError:
```

To turn off error trapping in the current procedure, enter

```
On Error GoTo 0
```

A Complex Microsoft Access Basic Example

A good way to learn Microsoft Access Basic techniques is to study complex code already developed and tested by someone else. In the PROMPT sample database included on the companion disk that comes with this book, I created a function that dynamically creates a new table and then inserts into the table a complete list of all the error codes used by Microsoft Access and the text of the error message associated with each error code. You can find a partial list of the error codes in Microsoft Access Help, but the table provides the best way to see a list of all the error codes. You might find this table useful as you begin to create your own Access Basic routines and set error trapping in them.

The name of the function is *CreateErrTable()*, and you can find it in the *MyFunctions* module. You can see the function statements listed below. You can execute this function by running the *CreateErrTable* macro, which you can find in the PROMPT database.

NOTE: I've added line numbers to some of the lines in this listing to make it easy to follow along with the line-by-line explanations in the table following the code listing.

```
01 Function CreateErrTable ()
02 ' Declare variables used in this function
03 Dim dbMyDatabase As Database, tblErrTable As➥
 TableDef, fldMyField As Field
04 Dim rcdErrRecSet As Recordset, lngErrCode As Long,➥
 intMsgRtn As Integer
05 Dim varReturnVal As Variant

    ' Create Errors table with Error Code and Error String
    ' fields.
    ' Initialize the MyDatabase database variable to the
    ' current database
06   Set dbMyDatabase =➥
 DBEngine.Workspaces(0).Databases(0)
      ' Trap error if table doesn't exist
      ' Skip to next statement if an error occurs
```

```
On Error Resume Next
Set rcdErrRecSet =➥
dbMyDatabase.OpenRecordset("ErrTable")
Select Case Err   ' See whether an error was raised

  Case 0          ' No error--table must already exist
    On Error GoTo 0   ' Turn off error trapping
    intMsgRtn = MsgBox("ErrTable already exists.➥
Do you want to delete and rebuild all rows?", 52)
    If intMsgRtn = 6 Then
    ' Reply was YES--delete rows and rebuild
      ' Turn off SQL warning
      DoCmd SetWarnings False
      ' Run quick SQL to delete rows
      DoCmd RunSQL "Delete * From ErrTable;"
      ' Turn warnings back on
      DoCmd SetWarnings True
    Else                     ' Reply was NO--done
      rcdErrRecSet.Close     ' Close the table
      Exit Function          ' And exit
    End If

  Case 3011          ' Couldn't find table,
                     ' so build it
    On Error GoTo 0   ' Turn off error trapping
    ' Create a new table to contain the error rows
    Set tblErrTable =➥
dbMyDatabase.CreateTableDef("ErrTable")
    ' Create a field in ErrTable to contain the
    ' error code
    Set fldMyField =➥
tblErrTable.CreateField("ErrorCode", DB_LONG)
    ' Append the "ErrorCode" field to the fields
    ' collection in
    ' the new table definition
    tblErrTable.Fields.Append fldMyField
    ' Create a field in ErrTable for the error
    ' description
    Set fldMyField =➥
tblErrTable.CreateField("ErrorString", DB_TEXT)
```

(continued)

(continued)

```
        ' Append "ErrorString" field to the fields
        ' collection in
        ' the new table definition
        tblErrTable.Fields.Append fldMyField
        ' Append the new table to the TableDefs
        ' collection in
        ' the current database
        dbMyDatabase.TableDefs.Append tblErrTable
        ' Set text field width to 5" (7200 twips)
        ' (calls sub procedure)
        SetFieldProperty tblErrTable![ErrorString], "ColumnWidth", DB_INTEGER, 7200
        ' Set recordset to Errors Table recordset
        Set rcdErrRecSet = dbMyDatabase.OpenRecordset("ErrTable")

      Case Else
        ' Can't identify the error--write message and
        ' bail
        MsgBox "Unknown error in CreateErrTable " & Err & ", " & Error$(Err), 16
        Exit Function

    End Select

    'Initialize the progress meter on the status bar
    varReturnVal = SysCmd(SYSCMD_INITMETER, "Building Error Table", 32767)
    ' Turn on hourglass to show this might take a while
    DoCmd Hourglass True

    ' Loop through Microsoft Access error codes,
    ' skipping codes
    ' that generate "User-defined error"
    ' or "Reserved error" message
    For lngErrCode = 1 To 32767
      If Error(lngErrCode) <> "User-defined error" And Error(lngErrCode) <> "Reserved error" Then
        ' Add each error code and string to Errors
        ' table
```

```
39        rcdErrRecSet.AddNew
40        rcdErrRecSet("ErrorCode") = lngErrCode
41        rcdErrRecSet("ErrorString") = Error(lngErrCode)
42        rcdErrRecSet.Update
43      End If
      ' Update the status meter
44    varReturnVal = SysCmd(SYSCMD_UPDATEMETER,→
 lngErrCode)
      ' Process next error code
45    Next lngErrCode

      ' Close recordset
46    rcdErrRecSet.Close
      ' Turn off the hourglass--we've finished
47    DoCmd Hourglass False
      ' And reset the status bar
48    varReturnVal = SysCmd(SYSCMD_CLEARSTATUS)
      ' Select new table in the Database window
      ' to refresh the list
49    DoCmd SelectObject A_TABLE, "ErrTable", True
      ' Open a confirmation dialog box
50    MsgBox "Errors table created."
51 End Function
```

The following table lists the statement line numbers and explains the code on each line for the preceding Access Basic code example:

Line Number	Explanation
01	Declares the beginning of the function. The function has no arguments.
02	Notice that you can begin a comment anywhere on a statement line by preceding the comment with a single quotation mark. You can also create a comment statement using the *Rem* statement.
03	Declares local variables for a Database object, a TableDef object, and a Field object.
04	Declares local variables for a Recordset object, a long integer, and an integer.

(continued)

continued

Line Number	Explanation
05	Declares a variable of data type Variant that is used to accept the return value from the *SysCmd* function.
06	Initializes the Database object variable by setting it to the current database.
07	Enables error trapping, but executes the next statement if an error occurs.
08	Initializes the Recordset object variable by attempting to open the ErrTable table. If the table does not exist, this generates an error.
09	Calls the *Err* function to see whether an error occurred. The following *Case* statements check the particular values that interest us.
10	The first *Case* statement that tests for an *Err* value of 0, indicating no error occurred. If no error occurred, the table has opened successfully.
11	Turns off error trapping because we don't expect any more errors.
12	Uses the *MsgBox* function to ask whether you want to clear and rebuild all rows in the existing table. The value 52 asks for an exclamation-point Warning icon (48) and Yes/No buttons (4). The statement assigns the value returned by *MsgBox* so that we can test it on the next line.
13	If you click Yes, *MsgBox* returns the value *6*.
14	We're going to run an SQL statement to delete all the rows in the table, so turns off the system standard warnings to avoid an unnecessary message box.
15	Runs a simple SQL statement to delete all the rows in the target table.
16	Turns warnings back on.
17	The *Else* clause that goes with the *If* statement on line 13.
18	Table exists and you clicked the No button on line 12—closes the table.
19	Exits the function.
20	The *End If* statement that goes with the *If* statement on line 13.

(continued)

continued

Line Number	Explanation
21	The second *Case* statement. Error code 3011 is "object not found."
22	Again, we don't expect any more errors, so turns off error trapping.
23	Uses the *CreateTable* method on the database to start a new table definition. This is the same as selecting the Table tab in the Database window and clicking the New button.
24	Uses the *CreateField* method on the new table to create the first field object—a long integer named ErrorCode.
25	Appends the first new field to the Fields collection of the new Table object.
26	Uses the *CreateField* method to create the second field—a text field named ErrorString.
27	Appends the second new field to the Fields collection of the new Table object.
28	Saves the new table definition by appending it to the TableDefs collection of the Database object. If you were to halt the code at this point and repaint the Database window, you would find the new ErrTable listed.
29	Now that the table exists, calls another subroutine named *SetFieldProperty* in this module that creates the ColumnWidth property for the ErrorString field and sets it equal to 7200 twips (5 inches). This ensures that you can see most of the error text when you open the table in Datasheet view.
30	Opens a recordset by using the *OpenRecordset* method on the database table.
31	This *Case* statement handles all other errors.
32	We aren't prepared to handle any other errors, so shows a message box with the error number and error message.
33	Exits the function after an unknown error.
34	This *End Select* statement completes the *Select Case* statement on line 09.
35	We now have an open, empty table. Calls the *SysCmd* function to place some text on the status bar and initializes a progress meter. We know we'll be looking at 32,767 different error codes.

(continued)

continued

Line Number	Explanation
36	Turns the mouse pointer into an hourglass to indicate that this routine will take a few seconds.
37	Starts a *For* loop to check each error code from 1 through 32,767.
38	Lots of error codes are either "User Defined" or "Reserved." We don't want any of these, so don't add a row if the *Error* function for the current error code returns one of these two strings.
39	Uses the *AddNew* method to start a new row in the table.
40	Sets the ErrorCode field equal to the current error code.
41	Sets the ErrorString field equal to the text returned by the *Error* function for this code.
42	Uses the *Update* method to save the new row.
43	This *End If* statement completes the *If* statement on line 38.
44	After handling each error code, updates the progress meter on the status bar to show how far we've gotten.
45	This *Next* statement completes the *For* loop begun on line 37. Access increments *lngErrCode* by 1 and executes the *For* loop again until *lngErrCode* is greater than 32,767.
46	After looping through all possible error codes, closes the table.
47	Changes the mouse pointer back to normal.
48	Clears the status bar.
49	Puts the focus on the ErrTable table in the Database window.
50	Displays a message box confirming that we've finished.
51	End of the function.

You should now have a basic understanding of how to create functions and subroutines using Microsoft Access Basic. In the final two chapters, you'll use what you've learned to complete major parts of the Prompt Computer Solutions application.

22

Automating Your Application with Access Basic

Now that you know the fundamentals of using Microsoft Access Basic, it's time to put what you've learned into practice. In this chapter, you'll learn how to perform many of the automation tasks you saw in Chapter 20, but this time you'll use Access Basic in Form modules.

Reviewing the Task Flow in PROMPT

As you recall from Chapter 20, the flow of tasks within the Prompt Computer Solutions application is as shown in Figure 22-1.

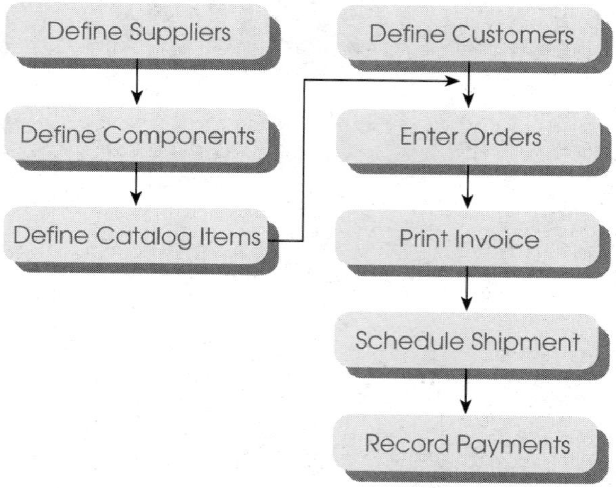

FIGURE 22-1. The task flow in the PROMPT application.

In Chapter 20, you learned how to automate the tasks for suppliers, components, and products in the catalog using macros. In this chapter, you'll create forms to handle customers, handle orders, and provide options to print invoices, and you'll automate them all using Access Basic.

Creating the Customers Form

In this section, you'll build a form to add and display customer information, one of four additional forms you need in order to complete the Prompt Computer Solutions application. The easiest way to create the Customers form is to go to the Database window in the PROMPT sample database and select the Customer table. (You can find the PROMPT database on the companion disk that is included with this book.) Then click the New Form button on the toolbar. When the New Form dialog box opens, click the Form Wizards button. Use the single-column Form Wizard to create a single-column form.

Add the fields shown in Figure 22-2, choose the Standard look for your form, and name your form *Customers*. (Be sure that the name ends with an *s*.) When the Form Wizard has finished, move some of the fields on the form to create a second column and size the controls so that they display all the information. Add an unbound object frame control to display the Prompt Computer Solutions, Inc., logo. (You can find the PRLOGO.BMP file on the companion disk.) Your result should look something like that shown in Figure 22-3.

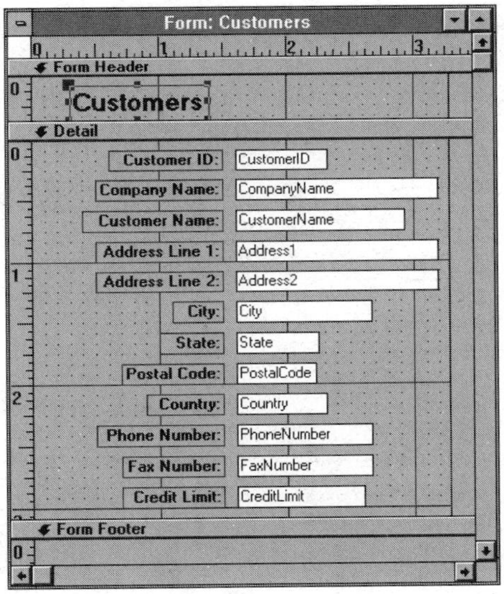

FIGURE 22-2. The fields on the single-column Customers form.

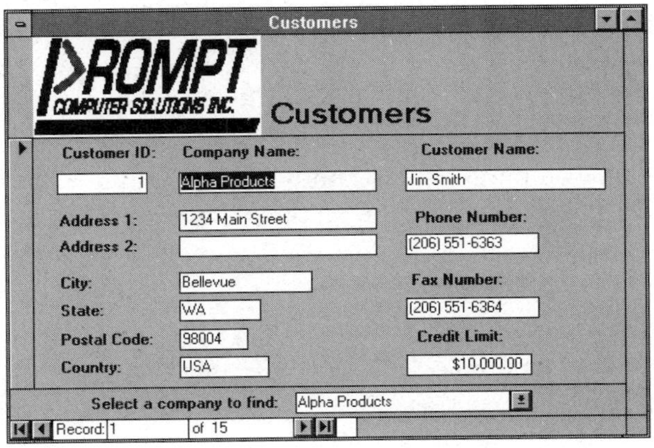

FIGURE 22-3. The finished Customers form in Form view.

At the bottom of the Customers form in Figure 22-3 is a combo box with the company name. The combo box wasn't created by the Form Wizard, of course, but you can create it yourself now. (A bit later you'll see how to create some Microsoft Access Basic code to use a value you choose in this combo box to "jump" to a new customer record.) The underlying query for this control is called *Company List*; the query contains company names in ascending alphabetic order. Figure 22-4 shows you the query, and you can find this query in the PROMPT database.

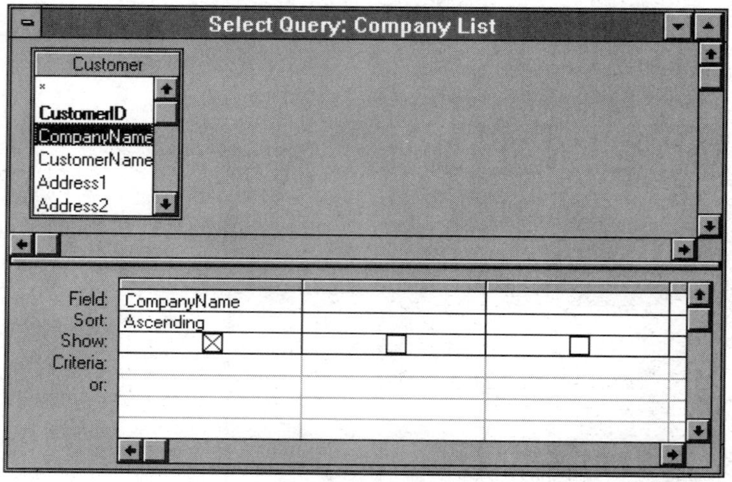

FIGURE 22-4.
The Company List query.

After you've created the query, open the Customers form in Design view and add the unbound combo box control. If you have the Control Wizards activated (by clicking the Control Wizard button in the toolbox), you can use the Combo Box Wizard to build the combo box. Choose the Company List query and tell the Wizard that you want to see the CompanyName field in the combo box and that you want Access to remember the value for later use instead of binding this combo box to a field in the Customer table. Open the property sheet for the control, set the Name property to CompanyPickList, and set the Limit To List property to Yes (to prevent the typing in of a nonexistent customer name). The property sheet is shown in Figure 22-5. You'll notice that the Combo Box Wizard placed the SQL text from your source query in the Row Source property. You could place the name of the query as the row source, but if you ever accidentally changed the query, this combo box might not work anymore.

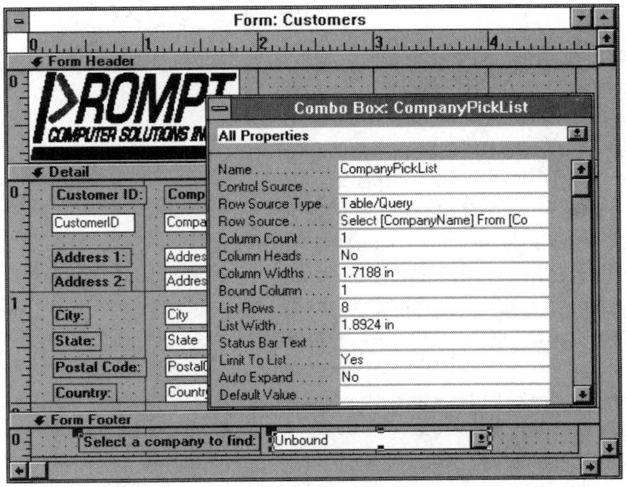

FIGURE 22-5.
The property sheet for the Company-PickList combo box.

Automating the Customers Form

You need to create three Access Basic procedures to begin automating the Customers form:

- When a row is about to be deleted, you should check for any outstanding orders for this customer. If orders exist, show a "custom" error message and cancel the deletion.
- Each time the form shows a new row, you should synchronize the CompanyPickList combo box so that it always displays the current company name.
- When you choose a different company name in the Company-PickList combo box, you need to use the *FindRecord* macro action to display the information for that company on the form.

To create some Access Basic code to handle checking for outstanding orders, open the Customers form in Design view, display the property sheet for the form, and click in the On Delete event property box. Click the Build button on the right side of the property box, and choose Code Builder in the Choose Builder dialog box. This opens the Form module and places you in the *Form_Delete* sub procedure. You can use the *DCount* function in an *If* statement to see whether matching order rows exist. If they do, use the *MsgBox* statement to display a custom message and then set the *Cancel* parameter to True to cancel the deletion. Your code should look something like this:

```
Sub Form_Delete (Cancel As Integer)
Dim strNewLine As String
' Check for outstanding orders for this customer
  If DCount("[OrderID]", "[Order]",→
 "[CustomerID]=Forms![Customers]![CustomerID]") <> 0 Then
    ' Orders exist - initialize the
    ' Carriage Return/Line Feed variable
    strNewLine = Chr$(13) & Chr$(10)
    ' Issue "custom" warning message
    MsgBox "Orders still exist for Customer " &→
 strNewLine & Me![CompanyName] & "." & strNewLine &→
 strNewLine & "Delete all orders for this customer"→
 & strNewLine & "before proceeding.", 48,→
 "Delete Customer - Action Required"
    ' Set Cancel parameter to True to stop the delete
    Cancel = True
  End If

End Sub
```

NOTE: You must enter all statements in Access Basic on one line in your procedure. Because of line length limitations in this book, statements or functions that accept long parameter strings must be displayed on multiple lines. When this happens, you'll see a continuation symbol → at the end of each line to indicate that you should enter the text as a single line in your function or procedure.

TIP: In a form or report module, you can use a shorthand notation to reference the form or report or controls on it. You can use *Me![CompanyName]* instead of a syntax such as *Forms![Customers]![CompanyName]*, You cannot, however, use the shorthand syntax in a parameter string passed to a function (such as *DCount*).

To synchronize the CompanyPickList control, you need a single line of code in the procedure for the Current event. Find the On Current property for the form in the property sheet, click the Build button next to the property box, and choose Code Builder in the Choose Builder dialog box. This opens up the form module and places you in the *Form_Current* procedure. Each time the form displays a different row, copy the value in the CompanyName control to CompanyPickList control as follows:

```
Sub Form_Current ()
  Me![CompanyPickList] = Me![CompanyName]
End Sub
```

If you switch to form view at this point, you'll see that each time you move to a new record, the CompanyPickList control shows the current company name. You can also move to a customer that has orders, select the row by clicking the row selector bar on the left, and press the Del key to try to delete the customer record. (If you're using the sample data from the PROMPT database, customer 2, Beta Consulting, has orders.) Your custom message, as shown in Figure 22-6, should display from your *Form_Delete* procedure.

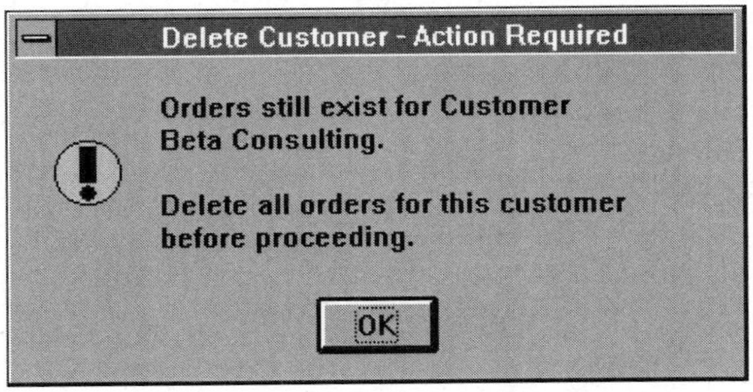

FIGURE 22-6.
The custom error message from your Access Basic On Delete event procedure.

Finally, you need a procedure attached to the After Update property of the CompanyPickList control. Each time you select a new company from the list, you want to run this procedure to move to that customer on the form. Do this by setting the focus on the CompanyName control and running the FindRecord macro action to match the new value in the CompanyPickList control. Select the CompanyPickList control while the Form window is in Design view, click the After Update property box in the property sheet, click the Build button on the right side of the property box, and choose Code Builder in the Choose Builder dialog box. This opens the Form module and places you in the *CompanyPickList_AfterUpdate* procedure. Use the *SetFocus* method to move the focus to the CompanyName control. (The FindRecord action acts on the control that has the focus.) Your code should look like this:

```
Sub CompanyPickList_AfterUpdate ()
  Me![CompanyName].SetFocus
  DoCmd FindRecord Me![CompanyPickList]
End Sub
```

NOTE: The *Form_AfterInsert* and *Form_AfterDelConfirm* procedures must requery the CompanyPickList control in order for the new customer to be displayed on the form. See the PROMPT sample database to view the code for these procedures.

Save the form and switch to Form view, open the combo box at the bottom of the form, and select a different customer name. The form should now show you the data from the record for that customer. We'll come back to this form later in the chapter to add a button to start a new order for the current customer, but first you need to build a form for entering orders.

Building the Orders Form

If you've followed along in the book to this point, you should feel comfortable with the techniques for building a complex form and subform based on queries that combine information from multiple tables. You built such a form to maintain catalog entries in Part 4 of this book, and you learned how to use macros to automate that form in Chapter 20. You'll need a similarly complex form to enter orders for Prompt Computer Solutions. This section shows you how to build the Orders form and teaches you a few new techniques you can use to automate forms with Microsoft Access Basic.

The PROMPT sample database contains an Order table containing summary information about each order (with entries such as Shipping Address and Discount) and an OrderItem table that contains an entry for each catalog item included in the order. Each order can have multiple items, so it makes sense, in designing an Orders form, to create a main form to hold the order summary information with an embedded subform for the order details.

The Order table contains the CustomerID field as a foreign key to link back to the customer information. Therefore, you can verify information from the Customer table at the same time that you create or review orders if you include the Customer table along with the Order table in the query you'll use for the Orders main form. The query should look something like the one shown in Figure 22-7, below, and Figure 22-8 on the next page. If you're building a new database for the Prompt Computer Solutions application, you can create this query by including the Order and Customer tables and the fields shown in the two figures. You'll find this query already defined in the PROMPT database. A bit later in this chapter, you'll see that you can take advantage of the ability to update nonkey fields on the "one" (Customer) side of the query to change address and phone contact information.

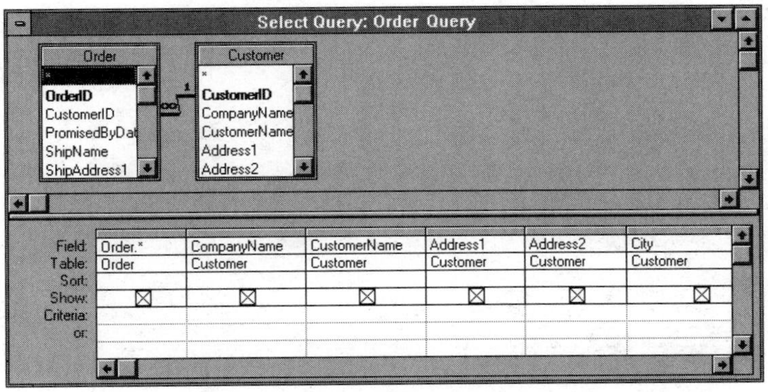

FIGURE 22-7.
Some of the fields in the QBE grid of the Order Query.

Using the Order Item Query that underlies the subform in the main Orders form, you'll be updating information in the OrderItem table. This table contains the OrderID (linked via properties in the subform control to OrderID in the Orders table), CatalogItemID, Quantity, and QuotedPrice fields that you'll want to update using the subform. The value in the CatalogItemID field isn't very informative by itself, but you'll show the Description field in a combo box on the subform to set the value in the CatalogItemID control. It's also a good idea to include the Catalog

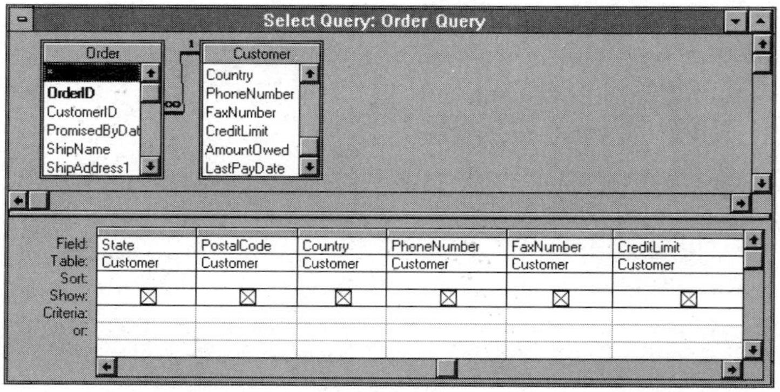

FIGURE 22-8. The rest of the fields in the QBE grid of the Order Query.

table and the Type table so that you can link the ItemTypeCode field to the TypeDescription field. This lets you see the related item type name when you add a catalog item to an order. Also, you'll need the OurCost and Price fields from the Catalog table to help decide on the actual price to charge the customer for this order, and you'll need the NumberIn-Stock field to show whether this system can be shipped to the customer right away. The resulting query should look something like that shown in Figure 22-9. You can find this query already built for you in the PROMPT database.

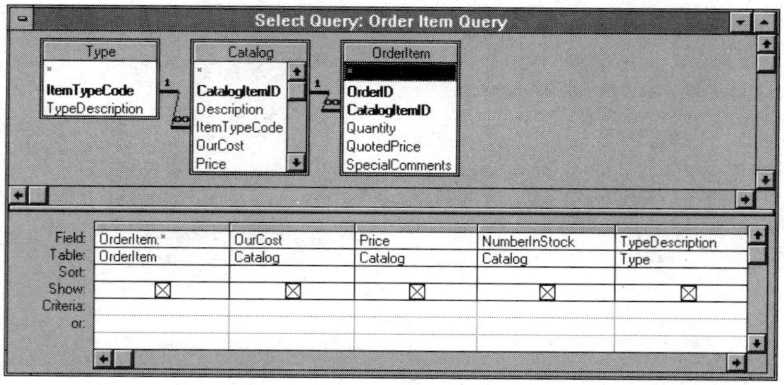

FIGURE 22-9. The Order Item Query on which the Order Details Subform is based.

After you've created the Order Query and the Order Item Query, you're ready to start building the main part of the Orders form. You can call the main form *Orders*, and you can call the subform *Order Details Subform*. Figure 22-10 shows you the completed form and subform. On the main form in the form header, include controls for the OrderID,

CustomerPO, and OrderDate fields from the Order table (by way of the Order Query). Set the Link Child Fields and Link Master Fields properties of the subform to OrderID.

NOTE: Later in this chapter, in the section titled "Triggering an Invoice," you'll see how to create an event procedure to print the related invoice using the command button you can see in this figure.

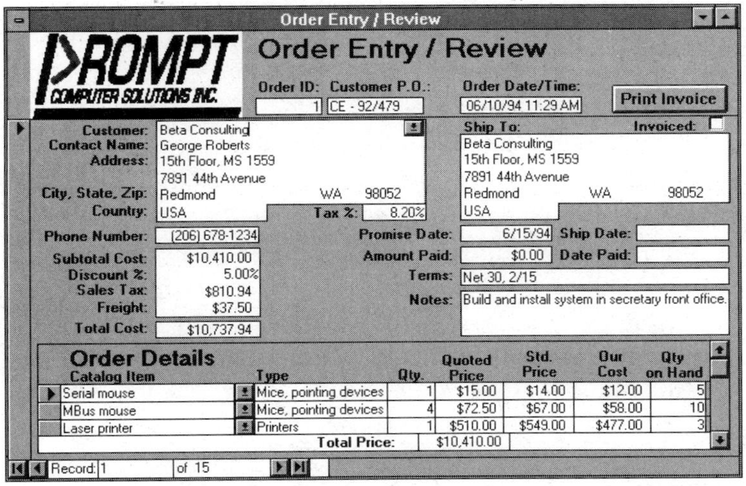

FIGURE 22-10.
The Orders form in Form view.

On the main form, in the detail section, there is a combo box bound to the CustomerID field of the Order table to show the related CompanyName from the Customer table. (See the next section, "Picking a Customer on the Orders Form," for details.) The ContactName, Address, City, State, Zip (PostalCode), Country, and PhoneNumber fields all come from the Customer table in the underlying query. Something that's not obvious from looking at the form is that there's a hidden control bound to the CompanyName field next to the Ship To label. You include this control to make it easy to fill in a default ship name using a bit of Access Basic code. (See the section "Automating Data Entry," later in this chapter, for details.)

The detail section of the main form contains code defined for events on many of the controls to help data entry and to calculate values. For example, when you're entering a new order and you select the first ShipTo field, a procedure automatically copies the name and address information for the chosen customer if you haven't already typed in the ship name. Also, whenever you change the state, sales tax percentage, discount, or freight amount, procedures automatically recalculate the total cost.

The subform is automated in several ways. The design for the Order Details Subform is similar to the Catalog List Subform you built in Chapter 15. You need a combo box to display catalog item descriptions, designed so that you can also update the CatalogItemID field in the OrderItem table by selecting a description. You should set the TypeDescription control's Enabled property to No and its Locked property to Yes so that no one will be able to change data in this field. Also, an event procedure for the subform sets the initial quoted price value to the catalog price, as explained later in this chapter in the section titled "Automating Data Entry."

You can also update the address, city, state, zip, and phone number fields in the Customer table via the source query for the main form. Because any change to customer information on this form also changes the same customer information for every other order for this customer, it would be nice if a warning let you know when this is about to happen—but you don't want to "cry wolf" on every change to every customer field on the form. Later in this chapter, the section titled "Handling Customer Updates" shows you how to create a practical warning.

A later section in this chapter, titled "Creating Custom Confirmation Messages," shows you how to intercept deletes on both the main form and the subforms and issue your own custom confirmation messages. And the section after that, titled "Triggering an Invoice," shows you how to link the Print Invoice command button to the Invoices report you created in Chapter 18.

Selecting a Customer on the Orders Form

In Chapter 13, you created a combo box on the Components form that was used for selecting a supplier ID. The CustomerID combo box on the Orders form works in much the same way. For the Row Source property of the combo box, enter an SQL query that selects from the Customer table the CustomerID field (to which you'll bind the combo box and thereby set the customer ID in the order) and the CompanyName field (to display comprehensible data in the combo box). You can see the property sheet for the combo box in Figure 22-11. Notice that the Column Count property is set to 2, and the Column Width settings are set to 0 inches and 2 inches. The 0 setting causes the first column, CustomerID, not to be displayed. Because the customer ID (to which the control is bound) is a number, you also need to set the Text Alignment property to Left to display the characters in the CompanyName field properly aligned.

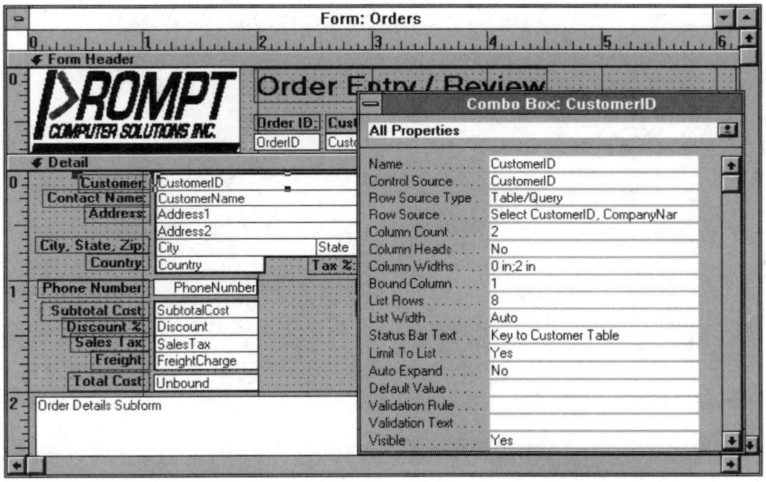

FIGURE 22-11.
The property sheet for the CustomerID combo box.

Selecting a Catalog Item on the Order Details Subform

You need a combo box on the Order Details Subform form to help you pick a product to include in the order. The PROMPT sample database contains only about 40 products, so selecting a product from a combo box works pretty well. If you create a longer list of products, you might want to consider a "select product" button on the subform. This button could activate another form that could classify products by type to make them easier to locate. You would need code in the "chooser" form to paste any selection back into the current row in the Order Details Subform.

Figure 22-12 on the next page shows you the Order Details Subform in Design view. You can also see the property sheet for the

CatalogItemID combo box. This combo box uses the first two fields from the Catalog table. The first is the CatalogItemID field from the OrderItem table that's bound to the value of the combo box. The second column is the Description field from the Catalog table, to make it easier to locate the product you want.

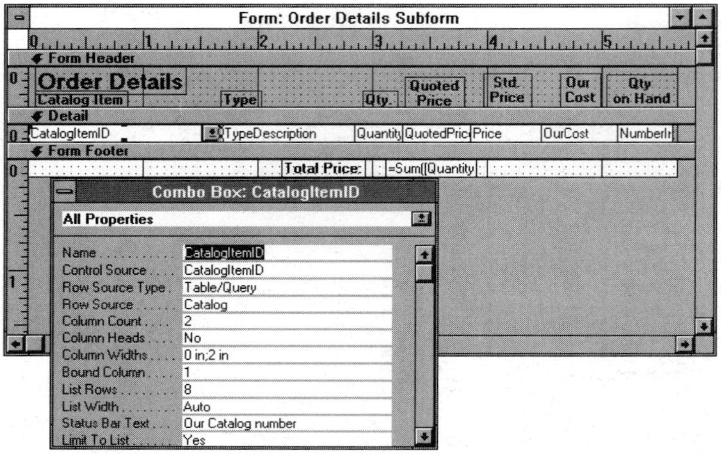

FIGURE 22-12. The Order Details Subform form in Design view and the property sheet for the CatalogItemID combo box.

Automating Data Entry

You can customize the Orders form to help make entering data simpler. The first opportunity to do so occurs on the main form. When you tab to the ShipName control, it would be nice if that information were filled in automatically from the customer data (when you haven't already typed in a new value). You can make this happen by setting the On Enter property of the ShipName control so that it triggers the *ShipName_Enter* procedure. Click the ShipName control, and then click the On Enter property box. Click the Build button and choose Code Builder. In the procedure, enter the following statements:

```
Sub ShipName_Enter ()
' If the ShipName not set when entering it, then
' help out by copying customer data

  If IsNull(Me![ShipName]) Or IsEmpty(Me![ShipName])→
 Or Me![ShipName] = "" Then
    Me![ShipName] = Me![CompanyName]
    Me![ShipAddress1] = Me![Address1]
    Me![ShipAddress2] = Me![Address2]
```

```
    Me![ShipCity] = Me![City]
    Me![ShipState] = Me![State]
    Me![ShipPostalCode] = Me![PostalCode]
    Me![ShipCountry] = Me![Country]
  End If

End Sub
```

The procedure copies the data only if you have not already typed information in the ShipName control. Notice that the CompanyName control is an "extra" text box with its Visible property set to No. Because you're already showing the company name in the CustomerID combo box, you don't need to show it again; however, this control makes it easy to reference the CompanyName control to copy its information to the ShipName control.

The second opportunity to make it easier to enter data is on the subform. Each time you select another catalog item on the subform, it would be handy if the initial quoted price were set to the normal price you charge for the item as reflected in the catalog. You could then adjust the price on the form if necessary to get the sale. Open the Order Details Subform in Design view. Click the CatalogItemID control, and then click the After Update property box. Click the Build button and choose Code Builder. In the procedure, enter the following statements:

```
Sub CatalogItemID_AfterUpdate ()
' Set the quoted price equal to the normal price
' when a new catalog item ID is picked

  Me![QuotedPrice] = Me![Price]

End Sub
```

Calculating Values

Several calculations occur on the Orders form and the Order Details Subform form. First, any time you add, change, or delete an order item, the cost of the order needs to be recalculated and copied to the SubtotalCost field in the Order table. In addition, the sales tax based on any new subtotal must be calculated and a new grand total displayed. If the total for the order exceeds the customer's credit limit, it would be a good idea to display a warning message.

To further complicate matters, any time a customer's state is changed—either because you picked a new customer ID or you changed the value in the State field—a new sales tax percentage might come into play, which affects the sales tax stored in the Order table as well as the grand total displayed on the form. Also, you need to recalculate the total cost if you change the discount or the freight charge.

To deal with these calculations, you need two functions and six event procedures:

- A *CalcTotal* function in a module that calculates a new sales tax, subtotal, and grand total any time you make a change in the subform or change the sales tax rate, discount, or freight charge on the main form. This function also verifies that the new order total doesn't exceed the customer's credit limit. You need to create this function in a module because it can be called from events on the Orders form or the Order Details Subform or the Customers form. (See the section titled "Linking Customers and Orders," later in this chapter.)
- A *SetTaxRate* function in a module that determines the new sales tax rate whenever you change the customer's state or the customer ID (which might also change the state).
- An event procedure for the After Update property of the CustomerID control on the Orders form to call the *SetTaxRate* function.
- An event procedure for the After Update property of the State control on the Orders form to call the *SetTaxRate* function.
- An event procedure for the On Current property of the Orders form to set the value of the unbound TotalCost control whenever you move to a new row.
- An *UpdateCost* procedure in the Order Details Subform module to calculate a new subtotal on the main form and call the *CalcTotal* function noted above.
- An event procedure for the After Update property of the Order Details Subform to run the *UpdateCost* procedure whenever you insert a new row or change the data in a row on the subform.

- An event procedure for the After Del Confirm property of the Order Details Subform to run the *UpdateCost* procedure whenever you delete a row on the subform.

To create the module to handle the functions that you'll call from several forms, click the Module tab in the Database window and then click the New button. Microsoft Access opens a module window and shows you the Declarations section. Your Declarations section should contain the following statements:

```
Option Compare Database    'Use database order for
                           'string comparisons
Option Explicit

' Declare a global variable that's true when we're
' in a new row on the Orders form
Global intNewOrderRow As Integer
```

You'll set the *intNewOrderRow* variable to True in event procedure for the On Current property of the Orders form to indicate a new order row. When you're entering a new order, you won't automatically force a save of the row in the *CalcTotal* function because you might decide not to save the new row at all. (See the following section.) When you're changing an existing order, you want to force a row save to be sure the subtotal always matches the sum of the totals from the OrderItem rows.

The *CalcTotal* Function

The first function you need is the *CalcTotal* function in this new module. Click the New Procedure button on the toolbar, and then enter the new function name. Microsoft Access creates an empty function procedure for you. Enter the following statements in the procedure:

```
Function CalcTotal () As Integer
' Calculates new sales tax, subtotal, and total cost
' on the Orders form and saves the current record
' whenever a new customer ID is picked, the state
' changes, the sales tax percent changes, the discount
' percent changes, or a row is updated or deleted
' in the Order Details subform.
```

(continued)

(continued)

```
' This function is called by procedures in both the
' form and subform modules and from an event procedure
' of the Customers form

' Use a form variable to make syntax easier
Dim frmO As Form

' Declare a new line variable for MsgBox
Dim strNewLine As String
  strNewLine = Chr$(13) & Chr$(10)

  Set frmO = Forms![Orders]

' Check for Null subtotal cost and zero it if Null
  If IsNull(frmO![SubtotalCost]) Then→
 frmO![SubtotalCost] = 0

' Check for Null discount and zero it if Null
  If IsNull(frmO![Discount]) Then frmO![Discount] = 0

' Check for Null Sales tax percent and zero it if Null
  If IsNull(frmO![SalesTaxPercent]) Then→
 frmO![SalesTaxPercent] = 0

' Check for Null freight charge and zero it if Null
  If IsNull(frmO![FreightCharge]) Then→
 frmO![FreightCharge] = 0

' Calculate new sales tax based on subtotal cost
'   (subtotal cost - discount) * tax percent
  frmO![SalesTax] = CCur(CLng((frmO![SubtotalCost] *→
 (1 - frmO![Discount])) * frmO![SalesTaxPercent] * 100)→
 / 100)
' .. and add up a new total cost
'   (subtotal cost - discount) + sales tax + freight
charge
  frmO![TotalCost] = CCur(CLng((frmO![SubtotalCost] *→
 (1 - frmO![Discount])) * 100) / 100) +→
 frmO![SalesTax] + frmO![FreightCharge]
```

```
' Check for total cost exceeding credit limit
  If frmO![TotalCost] > frmO![CreditLimit] Then
    MsgBox "WARNING!" & strNewLine & strNewLine &→
 "Total for this order exceeds" & strNewLine &→
 "limit amount of " & Format$(frmO![CreditLimit],→
 "Currency") & strNewLine & "for this customer.",→
 48, "Credit Limit Exceeded"
  End If

' Save only if not on a new row
  If Not intNewOrderRow Then
    ' If the form has unsaved data (is "dirty"),
   ' then save it.
    If frmO.Dirty Then DoCmd DoMenuItem A_FORMBAR,→
 A_FILE, A_SAVERECORD
    End If

  CalcTotal = True

End Function
```

Because the calculation of the discount involves multiplying a currency value by a floating-point value, the function multiplies the result by 100 and uses *CLng* to round the result to an even penny. The function then divides that result by 100 and uses the *CCur* function to create a fixed dollars-and-cents amount.

Near the bottom of the function, the statements test the *intNewOrderRow* variable that you'll set in the event procedure for the On Current property of the Orders form. If this is not a new order, and the order has changed, the function saves the current record by using a *DoCmd* statement to issue a DoMenuItem macro action. Sometimes, moving the focus from the subform to the outer form automatically saves the row. If this is the case, the Orders form's Dirty property won't be set. The function needs to check this property because you'll get an error if you try to save a row that doesn't have any changed data.

The *SetTaxRate* Function

The second function you need calculates a new tax rate based on the new value of the State control when you select a new customer or change the State field. Start a new function named *SetTaxRate*, and enter the following statements:

```
Function SetTaxRate () As Integer
Dim intReturn As Integer ' Dummy variable for function
                         ' call
Dim frmO As Form         ' Form variable to simplify
                         ' syntax

  Set frmO = Forms![Orders]

' set sales tax rate based on the state
  Select Case frmO!State
    Case "WA"
      frmO![SalesTaxPercent] = .082
    Case "AK"
      frmO![SalesTaxPercent] = .078
    Case "CA"
      frmO![SalesTaxPercent] = .085
    Case "ID"
      frmO![SalesTaxPercent] = .065
    Case Else
      frmO![SalesTaxPercent] = 0
  End Select

' Now call the common calc total function
  intReturn = CalcTotal()

  SetTaxRate = True

End Function
```

Note that the sales tax rates shown in the *SetTaxRate* function are not necessarily correct. You should consult each state's taxing authority for the correct rates. Also, this function tests only for the states that are valid for the Customer table in this application; if your application covers additional states, you might want to use a sales tax table to set the correct rates. At the end of the function, the function calls the *CalcTotal* function you created above to reset the totals based on the new sales tax amount.

Use the Compile Loaded Modules button on the toolbar to check your work. Save the module and name it *Orders*. If you're working in the PROMPT database, you'll find this module already defined.

> **TIP:** If you need to create functions that you can call from several forms in your application, it's a good idea to give the module a name that's related to the tasks its functions perform. Because this module works with the Orders form, it makes sense to give the module a similar name.

The CustomerID After Update Event Procedure

Now you're ready to begin creating additional event procedures for the Orders form to call the functions you've just created to automatically perform the calculations you need. Begin by opening the Orders form in Design view. Click the CustomerID control, and then click the After Update property box. Click the Build button, and choose Code Builder to open a procedure to handle this event. In the procedure, enter the following statements:

```
Sub CustomerID_AfterUpdate ()
' Set sales tax rate based on state when CustomerID
' changes

Dim intReturn As Integer ' Dummy variable for function
                         ' call

' Now call the common function to figure out tax rate
  intReturn = SetTaxRate()

End Sub
```

You've already written all the complicated code in the *SetTaxRate* and *CalcTotal* functions. You only need this bit of code to call those routines when the CustomerID changes.

The State After Update Event Procedure

You need an identical event procedure to handle updates to the State control. Click the State control, and then click the After Update event property. Click the Build button, and choose Code Builder to open a new subroutine to handle this event. In the new subroutine, enter the following statements:

```
Sub State_AfterUpdate ()
' Set sales tax rate based on new state

Dim intReturn As Integer ' Dummy variable for function
                         ' call

' Now call the common function to figure out tax rate
  intReturn = SetTaxRate()

End Sub
```

The Orders Form On Current Event Procedure

The last subroutine you need for the Orders form to handle data calculation needs to respond to the On Current event for the form. If you recall from Chapter 19, On Current occurs each time you move to a different row, including a new one. Choose Select Form from the Edit menu in Form Design view to see the form properties. Click the On Current event property. Click the build button, and then choose Code Builder to open a subroutine to handle this event. In the subroutine, enter the following statements:

```
Sub Form_Current ()
' On entry of new record
' If order ID is Null, then we're on a new record
  If IsNull(Me![OrderID]) Then
    Me![TotalCost] = 0
    intNewOrderRow = True
  Else
```

```
' .. set total cost
' Just in case there are any Nulls lurking around
    On Error Resume Next
    Me![TotalCost] = CCur(CLng((Me![SubtotalCost] *→
 (1 - Me![Discount])) * 100) / 100) + Me![SalesTax]→
 + Me![FreightCharge]
    intNewOrderRow = False
  End If

End Sub
```

You can tell when you're in a new row because the OrderID field will be Null. After you begin to type any data in the new row, Microsoft Access sets the value of the OrderID field, so you need to set some other variable—such as the global *intNewOrderRow* variable you created in the module—to "remember" that you're still in a new row. If this is a new row, the total will be 0. If it isn't a new row, the procedure sets the total cost using a formula similar to the one you created in the *CalcTotal* function.

You'll add a few additional statements to this procedure later to handle the warning message you want to issue when you attempt to change one of the customer fields. (See the section later in this chapter titled "Handling Customer Updates" for details.)

The Order Details Subform *UpdateCost* Procedure

You need to detect two events on the subform to update the subtotal cost on the main form: After Update and After Del Confirm. Because both events need to run the same code, you can create a common procedure that you can call from both event procedures.

Open the Order Details Subform in Design view, and then click the Code button on the toolbar. Microsoft Access displays a blank module window. Click the New Procedure button, choose the Sub option, and then enter *UpdateCost* in the Name text box and click OK. Microsoft Access displays an empty new sub procedure. Enter the following statements in your new procedure:

```
Sub UpdateCost ()
' Called by After Update and
' After Delete Confirm event procedures

Dim intReturn As Integer ' Dummy variable for function
                         ' call

' Calculate a new subtotal cost on the main form using
' DSum
  Forms![Orders]![SubtotalCost] =¬
  DSum("[Quantity]*[QuotedPrice]", "[OrderItem]",¬
  "[OrderID]=Forms![Orders]![OrderID]")

' Now, call the common calc total function.
  intReturn = CalcTotal()

End Sub
```

This procedure uses the *DSum* aggregate function to calculate the new subtotal directly from the OrderItem table. You might have noticed that there's an unbound control on the subform that also displays the subtotal by using the *Sum* function. If you're wondering why you can't just copy the value in this subtotal control value to the SubtotalCost field on the main form, it's because things happen asynchronously in Access. If you change something on the subform, the After Update or After Del Confirm event usually occurs before Access gets around to recalculating the value in the unbound control. If you copy the value in the unbound control, chances are good that it won't reflect the new total yet. Using *DSum* ensures that you always get the right answer. You can see that this procedure calls your *CalcTotal* function to finish the calculations after it has set a new subtotal.

The Order Details Subform Event Procedures

To complete all the automatic calculations, you need two simple procedures that respond to the After Update and After Del Confirm events of the Order Details Subform. With the subform in Design view, open the form properties, and click the After Update property box. Click the Build button and choose Code Builder. In the empty procedure, enter the following statements:

```
Sub Form_AfterUpdate ()
' Call the common UpdateCost procedure
  UpdateCost

End Sub
```

Likewise, click the After Del Confirm property box, click the Build button, and choose Code Builder. In the empty procedure, enter the following statements:

```
Sub Form_AfterDelConfirm (Status As Integer)
' Call the common UpdateCost procedure
  UpdateCost

End Sub
```

NOTE: To call a procedure, you need only enter the procedure name. If the procedure requires parameters, enter them following the name, separated by commas.

Handling Customer Updates

Although you can update any of the nonkey fields from the Customer table on the Orders form (provided you don't set the Locked property of the controls to Yes), you probably should display a warning if you try to change any of these fields. Why? Because any change to one of the customer fields also changes that field value for every other order for this customer. However, you don't want to issue the warning message for each and every change to a customer field on the form—and here's how to prevent that from happening.

You can create a module-level variable that you reset each time you move to a new row (in the On Current event procedure) but that you set once you issue a warning message for any single order. To do that, open the Orders form in Design view and then click the Code button. Microsoft Access shows you the empty Declarations section of the form module. Enter the following statements:

```
Option Explicit

' Declare module level variable
' to track customer field update warning
Dim intCustUpdate As Integer
```

Recall that the *Option Explicit* statement is a good way of asking Access to check that you've properly declared all your variable names. This helps catch any names you might enter incorrectly. As you might guess, you'll use the *intCustUpdate* variable to help you issue a warning only once for each order.

Changing the *Form_Current* Procedure

It would also be a good idea to lock all the customer fields when you're entering a new order row to keep you from trying to change customer data. If you really want to enter different address information, perhaps you should change the Customer row first (using the Customers form) before you create a new order. To both set the *intCustUpdate* variable and determine whether to lock customer fields, you need to add some lines to the *Form_Current* procedure you created above. Choose Form in the Object drop-down list box on the toolbar, and then choose Current in the Procedure drop-down list box to display this procedure again. Change the procedure so that it looks like the following example:

```
Sub Form_Current ()
' On entry of new record, set customer update warning to
' False
  intCustUpdate = False
' If the order ID is Null, then we're on a new record,
' so lock the customer fields
  If IsNull(Me![OrderID]) Then
    Me![CustomerName].Locked = True
    Me![Address1].Locked = True
    Me![Address2].Locked = True
    Me![City].Locked = True
    Me![State].Locked = True
    Me![PostalCode].Locked = True
    Me![Country].Locked = True
    Me![PhoneNumber].Locked = True
    ' .. and zero the total cost field (unbound)
    Me![TotalCost] = 0
```

```
        intNewOrderRow = True
        Else
    ' Otherwise, unlock all customer fields
        Me![CustomerName].Locked = False
        Me![Address1].Locked = False
        Me![Address2].Locked = False
        Me![City].Locked = False
        Me![State].Locked = False
        Me![PostalCode].Locked = False
        Me![Country].Locked = False
        Me![PhoneNumber].Locked = False
        ' .. and set total cost
    ' Just in case there are any Nulls lurking around
        On Error Resume Next
        Me![TotalCost] = CCur(CLng((Me![SubtotalCost] *¬
      (1 - Me![Discount])) * 100) / 100) + Me![SalesTax]¬
      + Me![FreightCharge]
        intNewOrderRow = False
      End If

    End Sub
```

The *CustUpdateCheck* and *CustWarn* Procedures

Now you need a procedure that you can call from the Before Update event procedure of all the customer controls. This procedure checks the *intCustUpdate* variable to see whether a warning has already been issued for the current Order row. If not, the procedure calls another procedure that uses the *MsgBox* function to verify that you want to make the change. If you answer Cancel, the procedure sets the *Cancel* parameter passed from the calling Before Update procedure to True to halt the update. It also uses a *SendKeys* statement to simulate a press of the Esc key to undo your change to the field. If you reply OK, the procedure lets the update proceed but sets the *intCustUpdate* variable so that you won't be bothered again on the current order.

With the Orders form module open, click the New Procedure button on the toolbar. Click the Sub type, and enter *CustUpdateCheck* as the name of the new subroutine. Microsoft Access shows you an empty new subroutine. Enter the following statements:

```
Sub CustUpdateCheck (Cancel As Integer)
Dim intAnswer As Integer    ' Place to receive answer from
                            ' MsgBox
  ' Check to see if we've already issued a warning on
  ' this order
  ' If so, then done
  If intCustUpdate Then Exit Sub
  ' Issue warning on customer field update
  CustWarn intAnswer
  ' Check the answer for a "cancel"
  If intAnswer = 2 Then
    Cancel = True
    SendKeys "{Esc}"
    Exit Sub
  End If
  ' Set warning issued for this order
  intCustUpdate = True

End Sub
```

You can see that the *CustUpdateCheck* procedure calls another procedure named *CustWarn* to issue the warning message. Start another new procedure, and enter the following statements:

```
Sub CustWarn (intReply As Integer)
' Common routine for issuing customer field update
' warning
Dim strNewLine As String
  strNewLine = Chr$(13) & Chr$(10)

  intReply = MsgBox("If you change address or phone→
 number" & strNewLine & "information for customer " &→
 Me![CompanyName] & strNewLine & "on this order, this→
 information changes on" & strNewLine & "all orders→
 for this customer.", 49, "Change customer info")

End Sub
```

The Customer Field Before Update Event Procedures

To complete the handling of customer field updates, you need to add a Before Update event procedure for the Address1, Address2, City, Country, CustomerName, PhoneNumber, and PostalCode controls. Choose each one of these in turn, click the Before Update property box, and add an event procedure for each that looks like this:

```
Sub Address1_BeforeUpdate (Cancel As Integer)
' Call common customer field update sub
  CustUpdateCheck Cancel

End Sub
```

Now, if you try to change any of the customer fields, you will see a warning—once for each order. If you cancel the change, your procedures will undo the change for you.

Creating Custom Confirmation Messages

Referential integrity protects the relationship between the data in the Order and OrderItem tables on the Orders form—that is, an OrderItem record cannot exist without being connected to an Order record. Also, Cascade has been set between the two tables so that Microsoft Access deletes matching OrderItem rows whenever you delete an Order row.

Although Access issues its own delete confirmation messages, it would be nicer to trap the delete events and display your own custom message. You can do that for both the Orders form and the Order Details Subform. For the Orders form, you need two event procedures.

Open the Orders form in Design view, and click the On Delete property box. Click the Build button and choose Code Builder to start a new procedure to handle this event. The following example shows you the code you need:

```
Sub Form_Delete (Cancel As Integer)
Dim intAnswer As Integer
Dim strNewLine As String

  ' Initialize new line string
  strNewLine = Chr$(13) & Chr$(10)

  ' Issue delete confirmation message and save result
  intAnswer = MsgBox("Are you sure you want to delete"→
 & strNewLine & "Order Number " & Me![OrderID] &→
 strNewLine & "for " & Me![CompanyName] & "?", 33,→
 "Delete Order")
```

(continued)

(continued)

```
' If answer was "Cancel" then set the cancel parameter to
' True
  If intAnswer = 2 Then Cancel = True

End Sub
```

Because you're handling the delete confirmation yourself, you also need a simple Before Del Confirm event procedure to stop Access from displaying its own confirmation dialog box. Click the Before Del Confirm property box for the form, click the Build button, and then choose Code Builder to start another procedure. Your statements should look like this:

```
Sub Form_BeforeDelConfirm (Cancel As Integer,→
 Response As Integer)

' Already trapping and confirming delete in Delete event,
'  so tell Access to continue without a confirmation
'  dialog box
  Response = DATA_ERRCONTINUE

End Sub
```

If you now try to delete an Order row, you'll see your custom dialog box. You can still cancel any delete. You can create two similar procedures to handle deletes on the Order Details Subform.

Triggering an Invoice

What if you're ready to ship an order and you need to print an invoice? In Chapter 18, "Advanced Report Design," you learned how to create the Invoices report. You can add a command button on the Orders form to format and print an invoice for the current order.

In the Orders table, a Yes/No field called Invoiced indicates whether you've previously printed the invoice for an order. You shouldn't need to print an invoice more than once. You should set the Enabled property of this field to No and the Locked property to Yes so that you can't set the field from the form. You'll set this field from a procedure instead. Notice the Print Invoice button on the Orders form in Figure 22-10. The On Click property for this button is set to trigger the *PrintIt_Click* procedure in the form module. Here is the *PrintIt_Click* procedure:

```
Sub PrintIt_Click ()
' On Click of the Print Invoice button
Dim strNewLine As String
Dim intAnswer As Integer

' First, check to see if invoice already printed
' If so, use MsgBox to verify a reprint

  If Me![Invoiced] Then
    strNewLine = Chr$(13) & Chr$(10)
    intAnswer = MsgBox("Do you want to print the¬
   invoice" & strNewLine & "for Order Number " &¬
   Me![OrderID] & " again?", 292, "Reprint Invoice")
    ' If answer is "No" then exit
    If intAnswer = 7 Then Exit Sub
  End If

' Turn on the hourglass to show this may take a moment
  DoCmd Hourglass True
' Set the invoice flag
  Me![Invoiced] = True
' and save the record
  DoCmd DoMenuItem A_FORMBAR, A_FILE, A_SAVERECORD
' Display the invoice in print preview
  DoCmd OpenReport "Invoice", A_PREVIEW, ,¬
 "[OrderID]=Forms![Orders]![OrderID]"
  DoCmd Hourglass False

End Sub
```

Linking Customers and Orders

The last little bit of magic you can create is linking the Customers form to the Orders form. It would be nice to use the Customers form to search for the customer for whom you want to enter a new order and then to click a command button to open the Orders form, ready to start a new order. The procedure for the command button should also copy the current customer ID from the Customers form to the Orders form.

To begin, open the Customers form in Design view and add a New Order command button, shown in Figure 22-13 on the next page. Click the On Click property box for the button, and start a new event procedure. Enter the statements shown here:

```
Sub NewOrder_Click ()
Dim intReturn As Integer  ' Variable for function call

' Open the Orders form in data entry mode
    DoCmd OpenForm "Orders", , , , A_ADD
' Set the customer ID
    Forms![Orders]![CustomerID] = Me![CustomerID]
' Call the common procedure to set the tax rate
    intReturn = SetTaxRate()

End Sub
```

Notice that the procedure also calls the *SetTaxRate* function that you created in the Order module to ensure that the tax rate matches the state for this customer.

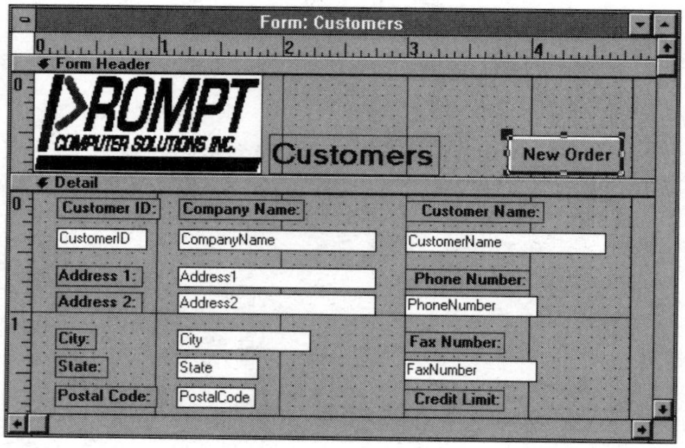

FIGURE 22-13. Adding a command button to open a new order for the current customer.

As you've seen in this chapter, Microsoft Access Basic is an incredibly powerful language with almost limitless possibilities. The tasks you can accomplish are only limited by your imagination. In the final chapter, you'll use some more Access Basic and macros to complete the linkage of all the tasks you've created in the Prompt Computer Solutions application.

23

The Finishing Touches

You're on the home stretch. You have just about all the forms you need for the tasks covered in this book. You need one additional form to make it easier to print groups of invoices. You also need a main "switchboard" form to get you started and provide the jumping-off place to all your tasks. A custom menu bar and a form menu that eliminate many of the design tools you won't need while running your application would be nice. Finally, you need one special macro that Microsoft Access will run every time you open your database. The *Autoexec* macro sets up your application environment and opens your main switchboard form.

Setting Up a Print Invoice Menu

You might find it convenient to print a group of invoices all at once. You can create a form that will let you print all outstanding invoices or only selected ones to complete your "Print Invoices" task.

You can see the Invoice Selector form in Design view, as shown in Figure 23-1. Using the option buttons on the form, you can print all uninvoiced orders or you can print a group of orders you select. When you choose the Print Selected Order option, a subform appears. The subform is shown in Design view in Figure 23-2.

The subform is a continuous form that displays the OrderID, CompanyName, and Invoiced fields, using a query called Order List that sorts the information in ascending order by company name and order ID. Set the Default Editing property of the subform to Read Only so that you can view and select rows but can't change the data. You could have used a combo box or a list box that displays only the CompanyName field to select an order to print, but because a company might have several outstanding orders, this form shows both the CompanyName and OrderID fields along with the Invoiced control. You could also add a filter to this subform to show orders for the current month only.

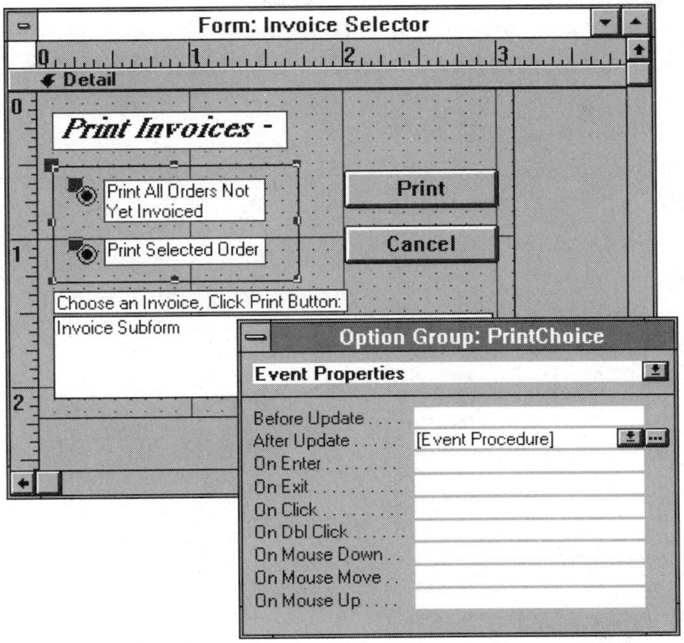

FIGURE 23-1. The Invoice Selector form in Design view.

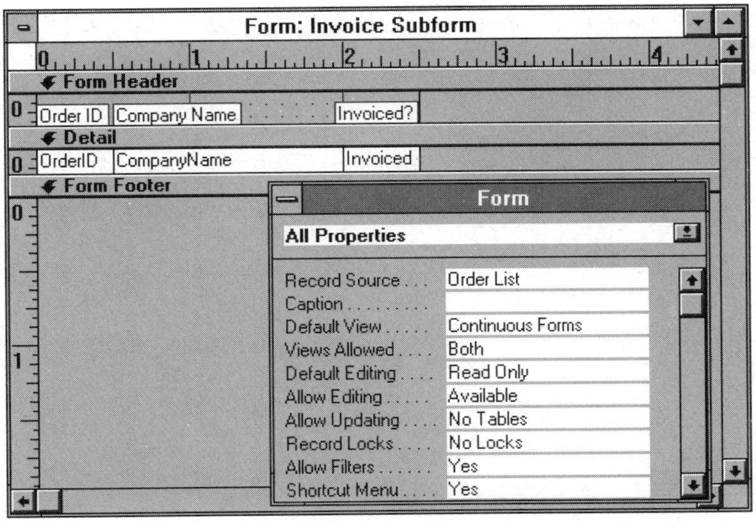

FIGURE 23-2. The Invoice Subform in Design view.

You need one procedure in a module (that you can call from both the main form and the subform), three event procedures on the main form, and a single event procedure on the subform to automate the Invoice Selector form. First, let's look at the procedure that prints the invoices. You can find the *PrintFromSelector* procedure in the Invoice Select module in the PROMPT sample database. Here are the statements for this procedure:

```
Sub PrintFromSelector ()
' Called from On Click of Print button,
'  on Invoice Selector, or from On DblClick of
'  OrderID field on Invoice Subform

Dim frmP As Form  ' Form variable to make syntax easier
Set frmP = Forms![Invoice Selector]

  ' If choice is print all, then ...
  If frmP![PrintChoice] = 1 Then
    ' See if there are any un-invoiced orders
    If DCount("[OrderID]", "[Order]",→
"[Invoiced]=No") = 0 Then
      ' No unprinted orders, so tell 'em and quit
      MsgBox "An Invoice has been printed for all→
orders.", 64, "All Orders Invoiced"
      Exit Sub
    End If
    ' Orders to print, so hide the print selector form
    frmP.Visible = False
    ' Open Invoice report for all unprinted orders in
    ' Print Preview
    DoCmd OpenReport "Invoice", A_PREVIEW, ,→
"[Invoiced]=False"
    ' Turn off SQL warnings
    DoCmd SetWarnings False
    ' Set all orders to "invoiced"
    DoCmd RunSQL "UPDATE DISTINCTROW [Order] SET→
[Order].Invoiced = True WHERE Invoiced = False;"
  Else  ' Choice is print selected order
    ' Hide the print selector form
    frmP.Visible = False
    ' Print the selected invoice
```

```
    DoCmd OpenReport "Invoice", A_PREVIEW, , "[OrderID]→
= Forms![Invoice Selector]![Invoice→
Subform].Form![OrderID]"
    ' Turn off SQL warnings
    DoCmd SetWarnings False
    ' Set selected order to "invoiced"
    DoCmd RunSQL "UPDATE DISTINCTROW [Order]→
SET [Order].Invoiced = True WHERE (([Order].[OrderID =→
Forms![Invoice Selector]![Invoice→
Subform].Form![OrderID]));"
    End If
  ' Turn SQL warnings back on
  DoCmd SetWarnings True
  ' Close myself
  DoCmd Close A_FORM, "Invoice Selector"
End Sub
```

As you'll see in a moment, this procedure is called from the Click event of the Print button on the Invoice Selector form and also from the DblClick event of the OrderID control on the Invoice Subform. The procedure first tests to see which option you've chosen in the PrintChoice option group. If you've asked for all uninvoiced orders to be printed, the procedure checks whether there are some to print. If there are none, the procedure displays a message and then exits. If some orders haven't had their invoices printed, the procedure runs an SQL update query to flag all these orders and then displays those order invoices in Print Preview.

Notice that the procedure hides the Invoice Selector form. This is necessary because the form is a dialog box. The form must still be open (but hidden) if you've chosen only one invoice to print. The OpenReport macro action must be able to refer to the order ID that you select. If you don't hide the form, however, it stays displayed on top of your report in Print Preview. After the report is open, the procedure closes the form to get it out of the way.

The first procedure you need for the Invoice Selector form is one to respond to changes to the PrintChoice option group. The option group has a default value of *1* (all invoices), and the subform control is hidden when the form first opens. The After Update event procedure checks the new value of the option group and hides/unhides the subform as appropriate. Here are the statements for this procedure:

```
Sub PrintChoice_AfterUpdate ()
  If Me![PrintChoice] = 1 Then
    Me![Invoice Subform].Visible = False
  Else
    Me![Invoice Subform].Visible = True
  End If
End Sub
```

The second procedure for the Invoice Selector form handles the Click event for the button labeled Print. As noted above, this procedure calls the *PrintFromSelector* procedure. The statements for the procedure are as follows:

```
Sub PrintIt_Click ()
' Call the common print procedure
  PrintFromSelector
End Sub
```

Finally, the Invoice Selector form has a procedure to handle the Click event for the button labeled Cancel. (The name of the button is GoAway.) This procedure simply closes the active form, as shown here:

```
Sub GoAway_Click ()
  DoCmd Close
End Sub
```

Last, but not least, a procedure for the Invoice Subform responds to a double-click on the OrderID control and calls the *PrintFromSelector* procedure. Here is the procedure:

```
Sub Order_ID_DblClick (Cancel As Integer)
' Call the common print procedure
  PrintFromSelector
End Sub
```

Defining the Main Menu

The last form that you need to build in order to link your application together is called the Main Menu. This is a simple form with a logo, a title, and six command buttons. The command buttons open the forms you've defined in the application. You can see the form in Design view in Figure 23-3.

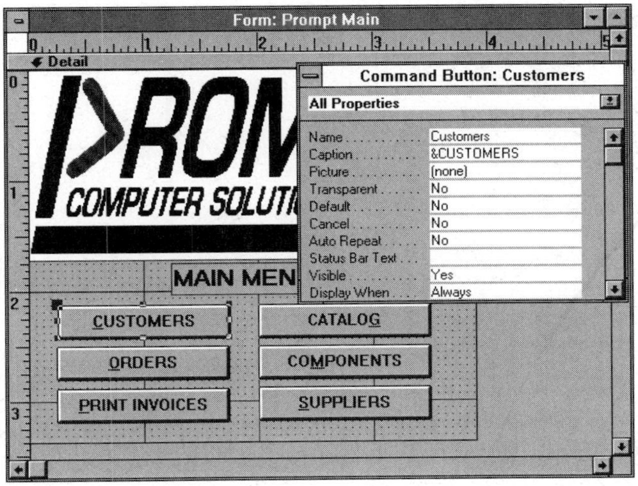

FIGURE 23-3.
The Main Menu form in Design view, showing the property sheet of a command button.

One feature worth mentioning here is the use of the special ampersand character (&) in the setting for each control's Caption property, to define an access key for the control. In the Caption property for the Customers command button, for example, the *&* character precedes the letter *C*. The letter *C* becomes the access key, which means that you can "push" the Customers button by pressing Alt-C as well as by using the more traditional methods of clicking with your mouse or tabbing to the control and pressing the Spacebar or the Enter key. You must be careful, however, not to choose a duplicate access key letter.

> **NOTE:** The access key for the Catalog command button in this example is *G*, to avoid conflict with the *C* access key for the Customers command button.

You can use an access key to make it simpler to select any control that has a caption. For command buttons, the caption is part of the control itself. For most other controls, you can find the caption in the attached label. For example, you could define access keys to select option or toggle buttons in an option group.

For each command button, you need a simple event procedure to handle the Click event and to open the appropriate form. Here is the procedure for the Customers button:

```
Sub Customers_Click ()
' Open the Customer form
  DoCmd OpenForm "Customer"
End Sub
```

After you've built a custom form toolbar and menu bar and also a macro to start the application, you'll need a procedure for the On Unload event of this form to put everything back. See the later section in this chapter titled "Using *Autoexec* to Start Your Application" for details.

NEW!

Designing a Custom Form Toolbar

After your application is running, you probably don't want or need some of the design features getting in the way. You might also want to provide some additional buttons to give you direct access to commands, such as Save Record and Find Next on your form toolbar. You can accomplish that by creating a custom toolbar in this application that you'll open for all forms.

Click in the Database window, choose Toolbars from the View menu, and click the New button in the Toolbars dialog box to create and open a new custom toolbar. Microsoft Access gives you an opportunity to give the toolbar a meaningful name. In the PROMPT sample database, this toolbar is named Prompt Form Toolbar.

After you have a new toolbar, you can click the Customize button in the Toolbars dialog box to add buttons to your toolbar and customize the spacing. As you learned in Chapter 14, "Customizing Forms," you can also change the button faces. Figure 23-4 shows you the custom toolbar from the PROMPT database. As you can see, the Design View and Datasheet View buttons aren't available. A Save Record button and a Find Next button have been added, the Cue Cards button is not available, and the Help button has been changed to open Microsoft Access help at the Contents screen instead of changing the mouse pointer to a question mark. A bit later, you'll see commands added to the macro that starts the application, to open this toolbar and close the built-in Form View toolbar.

FIGURE 23-4.
The custom Prompt Form Toolbar in the PROMPT sample database.

Creating a Custom Form Menu Bar

Because you've removed some of the application design buttons from the form toolbar, it would also be nice (and consistent) to replace the built-in menu bar with a custom menu bar. You could then set the Menu Bar property of your forms to point to this menu bar macro.

To define a custom menu bar, you must first create a menu bar macro that defines the menus you'll see on the menu bar itself. For each Menu, you need to add a line in the macro that executes an AddMenu macro action and set the Menu Name property of each to identify the name of the menu. Use the Menu Macro Name property to identify macros that define the commands on each menu.

Figure 23-5 shows you the macro that creates the custom form menu in the Prompt Computer Solutions application. You can see that the first line defines another macro for the File menu that adds commands to the menu. Notice the use of the ampersand (in *&File*) to denote the access key for this menu.

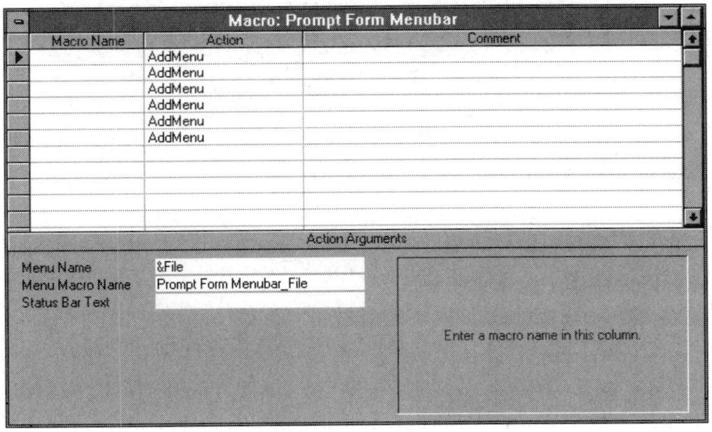

FIGURE 23-5.
The macro for the custom form menu bar in the Prompt Computer Solutions application.

Figure 23-6 shows you the macro that adds commands to the File menu on this custom menu bar. You list each command on the menu by using the Macro Name column. Note again that you can designate an access key by preceding it with the & character. You can ask Access to draw a line between sections of the menu by inserting a line with a minus sign in the Macro Name column. Each macro that adds menu commands can execute either another AddMenu macro action to add a submenu or a series of macro actions to define the actions that you want Microsoft Access to execute when you choose this menu command. In many cases, you'll use the DoMenuItem macro action to make a built-in menu bar command available through your custom menu bar. But you can also execute any other macro actions, including running another macro or running an Access Basic function.

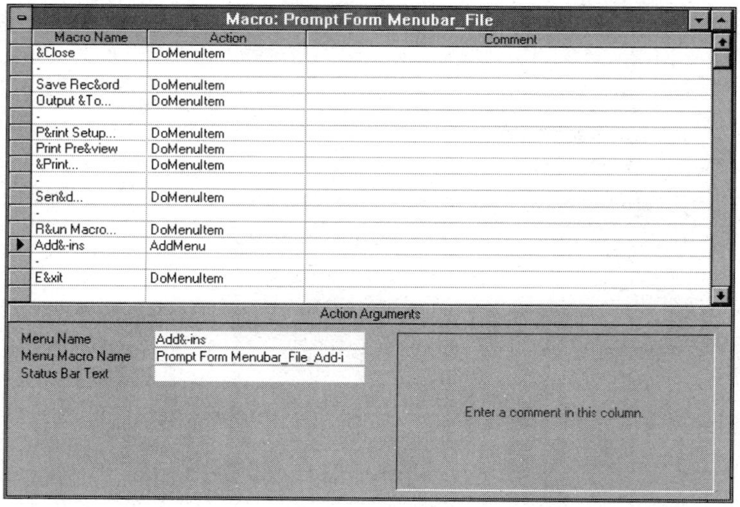

FIGURE 23-6. The macro that defines the commands on the File menu on the custom form menu bar in the Prompt Computer Solutions application.

NEW!

You can see that defining an entire set of menu macros could be quite laborious. This is especially tedious if you need to define different custom menu bars for different forms. Fortunately, version 2 of Access includes a special Wizard to help you build menu macros. Click in the Database window, choose Add-ins from the File menu, and then choose Menu Builder from the submenu. Access starts the Menu Builder and displays the first dialog box, shown in Figure 23-7.

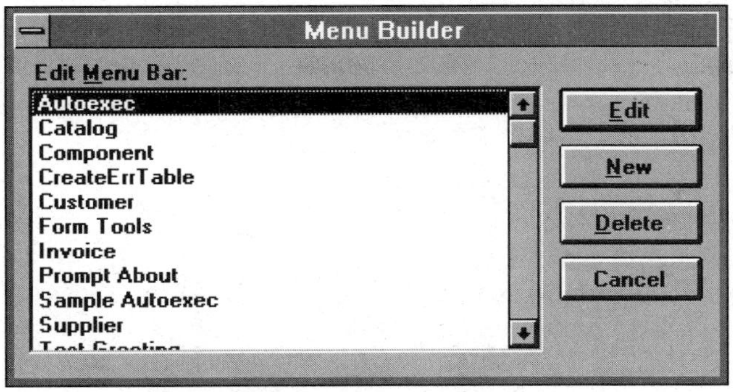

FIGURE 23-7. The first dialog box in the Menu Builder.

The dialog box shows you all available macros in your database. You can choose a macro that you know is a menu bar macro and click Edit to review and change the menu bar definition. You can select a macro and click Delete to delete that macro. If the macro you choose to delete is a menu bar macro, the Menu Builder also deletes any menu macros that add commands to the menu. Click the New button to start a new set of menu bar macros. The Menu Builder displays the dialog box shown in Figure 23-8.

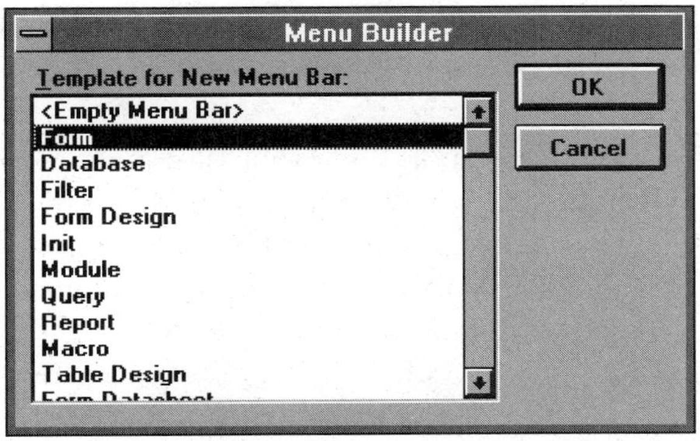

FIGURE 23-8. Choosing a template for a new set of menu bar macros.

You can either start a brand-new menu bar or choose one of the templates that completely mimic the built-in menu bars in Microsoft Access. Because you want a slightly modified menu for all the forms in this application, the Form menu bar is a good place to start. Select Form and click OK, and the Menu Builder shows you this menu bar template in the Menu Bar edit dialog box, as shown in Figure 23-9 on the next page.

FIGURE 23-9.
The Menu Bar edit dialog box.

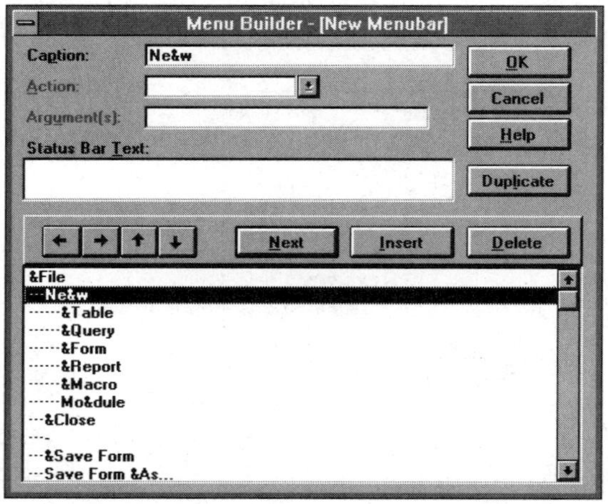

Within the Menu Bar edit dialog box, you can click each element of the menu definition in the lower list box and view the detailed definition in the controls above. If the element executes a macro action, you'll see that macro action and its arguments in the appropriate controls at the top of the dialog box. This Menu Builder supports the AddMenu, DoMenuItem, RunMacro, and RunCode macro actions. If you need to build a menu command that does something more complex, you can build a skeleton macro with the Menu Builder and then edit the resulting macro.

After you've selected an element in the lower list box, you can use the up and down arrow buttons to move the element in the list. You can use the left arrow button to promote an element to a higher level or the right arrow button to demote an element to a lower level. Use the Next button to move the highlight down one element at a time. You can move the highlight past the last element to define a new element at the end of the list. If you need to create an element in the middle of the list, select the element below where you want to insert a new element and then click the Insert button. If you need to remove an element, select the element and then click the Delete button.

In many "production" applications, you won't want the user opening objects in Design view or creating new objects, so you might want to remove all the New commands from the File menu. You probably don't need the Save Form and Save Form As commands. On the View menu, you might want to remove the Form Design, Toolbars, and Options commands. You might not need the Hide, Unhide, and Size To Fit Form commands on the Window menu. On this particular custom toolbar, I added a custom command to display an information dialog box from the Help menu. In Figure 23-10, you can see an element inserted below the About Microsoft Access element and a new element for the About PROMPT command. The menu command runs another macro that uses the MsgBox macro action to display some information about PROMPT in a dialog box.

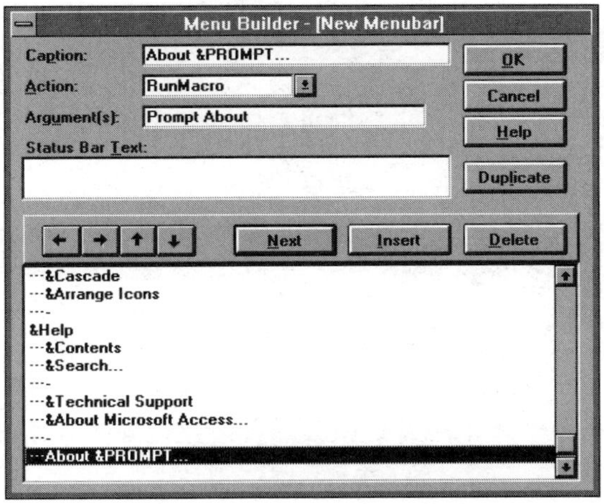

FIGURE 23-10. An addition to the Help menu on the custom form menu bar.

When you're done defining your new menu bar, click OK to save it. If it's a new menu bar, the Menu Builder asks you for a name for the menu bar macro. The Menu Builder created eleven new macros, shown in Figure 23-11 on the next page: one for the main menu bar and one for each menu. If you set the Menu Bar property of your forms to point to the menu bar macro (Prompt Form Menubar), you can see the new menu when you open the form, as shown in Figure 23-12 on the next page.

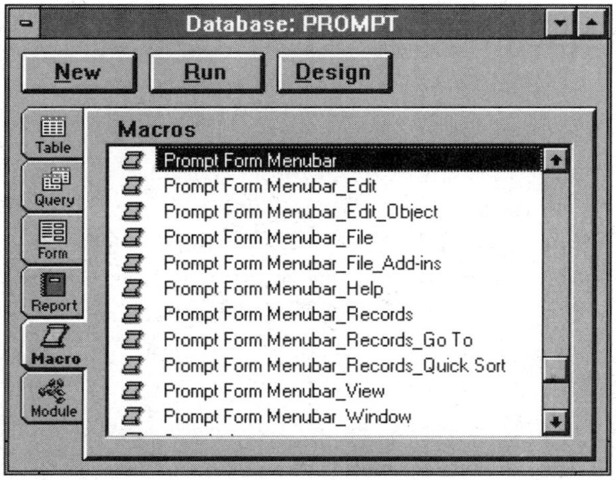

FIGURE 23-11. The list of menu macros built by the Menu Builder in the PROMPT sample database.

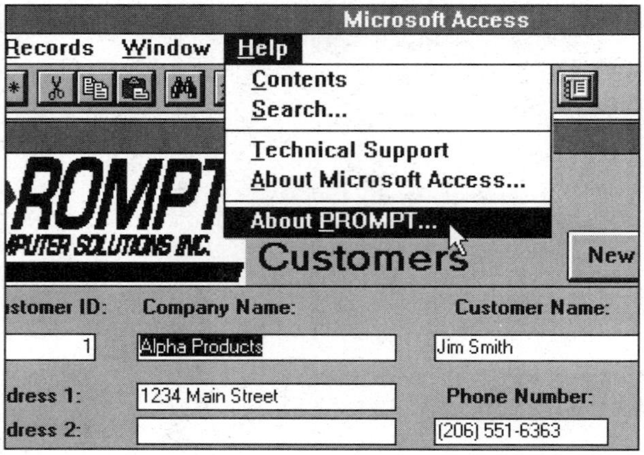

FIGURE 23-12. The new Help menu for the Customers form.

Using *Autoexec* to Start Your Application

At this point you have all the pieces you need to fully implement the first six tasks of the PROMPT sample database. But there's an additional Microsoft Access feature you might want to employ. You can create a macro in your database called *Autoexec,* and Access will run *Autoexec* each time the database is opened. An *Autoexec* macro for PROMPT, such as the one shown in Figure 23-13, can be used to automatically open the Main Menu form.

In Figure 23-13, you can see that there are seven macro actions in the PROMPT sample database *Autoexec* macro. The Echo macro action disables the display of intermediate steps.

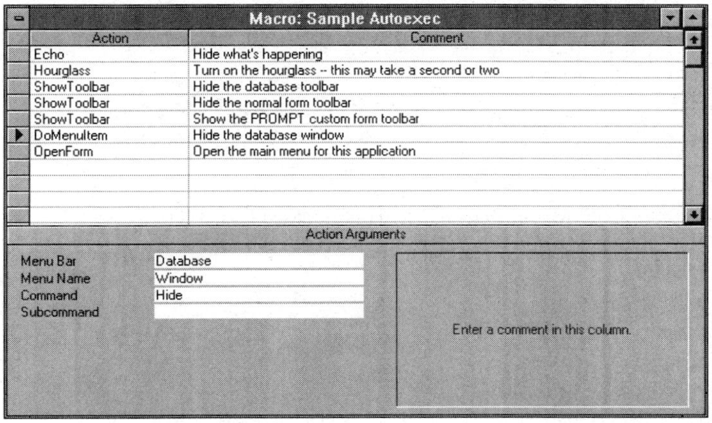

FIGURE 23-13.

An *Autoexec* macro for the PROMPT sample database that will automatically set the toolbars and open the Main Menu form.

When you use the Hourglass macro action to change the mouse pointer to an hourglass, you give the database user a visual cue that the actions that follow might take a few seconds. The Minimize macro action minimizes the Database window to an icon. The next two macro actions hide both the database toolbar and the built-in Form View toolbar. The third ShowToolbar macro action displays the custom form toolbar for this application. The DoMenuItem macro action hides the Database window, and the final macro action opens the Main Menu form in Form view.

Figure 23-14 on the next page shows the settings for the seven macro actions described above.

TIP: If you need to open a database without running its *Autoexec* macro, choose the Open command from the File menu, click the name of the database in the Open Database dialog box, and then press Shift-Enter.

Macro Action	Argument Box	Setting
Echo	Echo On	No
	Status Bar Text	(none)
Hourglass	Hourglass On	Yes
ShowToolbar	Toolbar Name	Database
	Show	No
ShowToolbar	Toolbar Name	Form View
	Show	No
ShowToolbar	Toolbar Name	Prompt Form Toolbar
	Show	Yes
DoMenuItem	Menu Bar	Database
	Menu Name	Window
	Command	Hide
	Subcommand	(none)
OpenForm	Form Name	Prompt Main
	View	Form
	Filter Name	(none)
	Where Condition	(none)
	Data Mode	Edit
	Window Mode	Normal

FIGURE 23-14.
The settings for the *Autoexec* macro.

Earlier, I mentioned that you might want to add another event procedure to the main form macro to put the toolbars back when you close the main form. Define the following Microsoft Access Basic statements in an event procedure to handle the Unload event for the main form:

```
Sub Form_Unload (Cancel As Integer)
' When you close the main form,
'  put everything back

  ' Hide the Prompt custom form toolbar
  DoCmd ShowToolbar "Prompt Form Toolbar", A_TOOLBAR_NO
```

```
    ' Show the normal form toolbar "where appropriate"
    DoCmd ShowToolbar "Form View", A_TOOLBAR_WHERE_APPROP
    ' Show the database toolbar
    DoCmd ShowToolbar "Database", A_TOOLBAR_WHERE_APPROP
    ' Unhide the database window by selecting
    ' something in it
    DoCmd SelectObject A_FORM, "Prompt Main", True

End Sub
```

If you take a look at the Open and Activate properties for the Invoice report, you'll find they call Access Basic procedures to temporarily hide the custom toolbar whenever the report has the focus. You'll also find that the Close and Deactivate properties call procedures to reshow the custom form toolbar when the report closes or loses the focus.

I hope you're as impressed as I am by the power and simplicity of Microsoft Access as an application development tool. As you've seen in this book, you can quickly learn to build complex applications for the Windows operating system. You can use the relational database in Access to store and manage your data locally or on a network, or you can access information in other popular database formats or in any server-hosted or mainframe-hosted database that supports the emerging Open Database Connectivity (ODBC) standard. You can get started with macros to become familiar with event-oriented programming and to prototype your application. With a little practice, you'll soon find yourself writing Access Basic event procedures like a pro.

Whether you use Microsoft Access to build your own personal applications or to create applications for others to use, I'm confident you'll find it one of the most powerful and easy-to-use products you've ever worked with.

PART 7

Appendixes

A

Installing Microsoft Access

To install Microsoft Access for a single user, you need a Microsoft Windows–compatible computer with the following configuration:

- An 80386 or higher microprocessor (80386-20 recommended as a minimum)
- At least 6 megabytes (MB) of RAM (8 MB or more recommended)
- A hard-disk drive with at least 19 MB of free space for a typical installation
- A high-density floppy-disk drive (either a 1.44 MB 3.5-inch or a 1.2 MB 5.25-inch drive)
- A mouse or other pointing device
- A VGA or higher display
- MS-DOS version 3.1 or later (version 6.0 or later recommended)
- Microsoft Windows version 3.1 or later

To run Microsoft Access as a server on a network, you need:

- Network software supporting named pipes such as Microsoft LAN Manager, Novell NetWare, or Banyan VINES
- A Microsoft Windows–compatible computer with at least 11 MB of free disk space for the Microsoft Access software, plus additional space for user databases
- User workstations configured as specified above for a single user

Before you run the Microsoft Access Setup program, be sure that no other applications are running on your computer, and then start the Windows operating system. If you're installing Access from floppy disks, place the first installation disk in your high-density floppy-disk drive, and choose the Run command from the File menu in Program Manager. Type *a:\setup* in the command line text box (where *a:* is the drive letter for your high-density floppy-disk drive), and press Enter. To install from a network drive, use File Manager to find the directory to which your system manager has copied the Microsoft Access setup files. Run SETUP.EXE in that directory. If you're installing Access from a Master License Pack, include an /L switch in the command line when you run Setup, as in *a:setup /L*. If you're installing from a network (without a

Master License Pack), include an /N switch in the command line when you run Setup, as in *a:setup /N*.

The Microsoft Access Setup program asks for your name and your company name and then lets you choose the directory in which you want the Access files installed. Setup then asks whether you want a Typical, Custom, or Laptop setup. A Typical setup installs all the Access options. A Custom setup lets you choose which Access options you'd like installed, including program files, Help files, Cue Cards, database drivers, Microsoft Graph, and the sample databases. A Laptop setup installs only the Access program files. A Typical setup requires 11 MB of hard-disk space; a Laptop installation requires 5 MB of hard-disk space. If you've installed network software on your computer, Setup gives you an opportunity to join existing workgroups.

Managing ODBC Connections

If you want to use Microsoft Access to connect to SQL databases that support the Open Database Connectivity (ODBC) standard, you must install the ODBC driver for that database and the Microsoft ODBC administrator. Microsoft Corporation provides the ODBC driver for Microsoft SQL Server with Access. You can find this driver and an ODBC installation program on the last installation disk or in the ODBC subdirectory on your network setup drive. To install the Microsoft SQL Server driver, run the separate ODBC Setup program from the ODBC floppy disk or subdirectory on your network setup drive.

After you complete ODBC Setup, you'll find a program group in File Manager called Microsoft ODBC. This program group contains the Microsoft ODBC Administrator icon. Double-click this icon to install or modify your ODBC Setup. When you do so, you'll see the Data Sources dialog box, shown in Figure A-1 on the next page.

To add new data sources, you must first define a logical name for each available ODBC server type. Select an available ODBC driver, and then click the Add button to see the Setup dialog box for the driver. Click the Options button to expand the dialog box, shown in Figure A-2 on the next page.

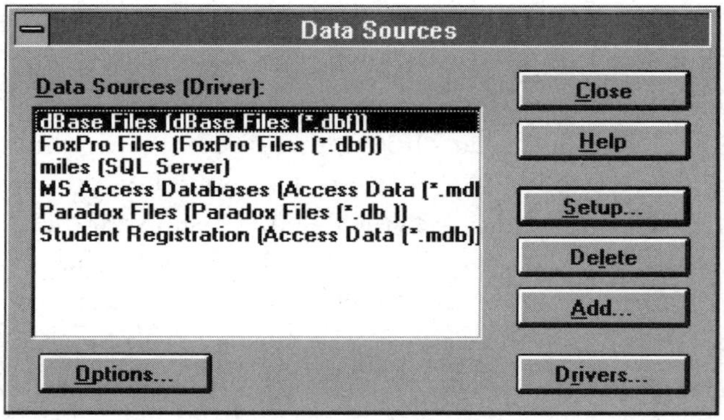

FIGURE A-1. The Data Sources dialog box.

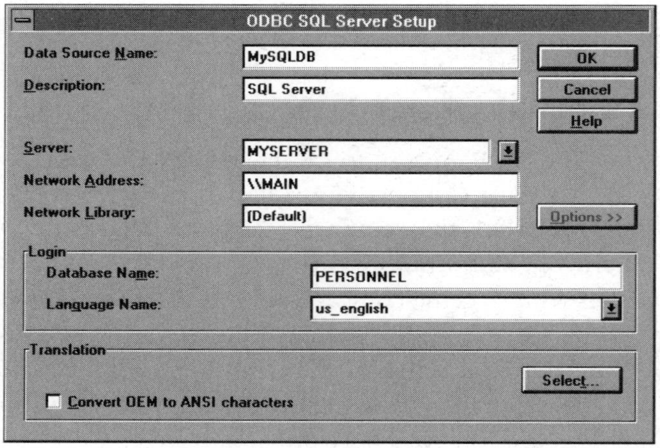

FIGURE A-2. The ODBC SQL Server Setup dialog box that configures the SQL driver.

Fill in the text boxes with the proper information, and click the OK button to return to the Data Sources dialog box. (See your network administrator to determine the Setup information.) When you've finished setting up your ODBC drivers, click the Close button in the Data Sources dialog box.

Within Microsoft Access, you'll use the data source name to attach to each SQL ODBC server. (For details, see Chapter 10, "Importing, Attaching, and Exporting Data.")

Converting from a Previous Release

Although version 2.0 of Microsoft Access can work with the data and tables in a database file created by version 1.0 or version 1.1, you cannot use version 2.0 to modify the forms, reports, queries, macros, or modules in an earlier-version database. You might be able to run your version 1.0 or version 1.1 database application using version 2.0, but your application could fail if it attempts to modify queries, forms, or reports as part of its normal execution.

You can easily convert a version 1.0 or version 1.1 database file to version 2.0. Start the Microsoft Access version 2.0 program, and choose Convert Database from the File menu. In the Database To Convert From dialog box, choose the version 1.0 or version 1.1 file that you want to convert. Access shows you the Database To Convert Into dialog box. You must specify a different file for your version 2.0 database because Access won't let you replace your version 1.x file directly.

Conversion Issues

Microsoft Access version 2.0 will report any objects or properties that it was unable to convert, by creating a table in your converted database called Convert Errors. The most common problems you're likely to encounter are field validation rules that reference another field, a Microsoft Access built-in function, or your own user-defined function. Because field and table validation rules are now enforced by the JET DBEngine, you cannot use functions to validate data. (See Chapter 21, "Microsoft Access Basic Fundamentals," for a discussion of the Microsoft Access version 2.0 architecture.) However, this now means that validation rules you define are always enforced, regardless of whether your data is being accessed from the Microsoft Access application environment or from another application environment, such as Visual Basic.

NEW!

Other changes in version 2.0 that might affect your application code or how your application runs include the following:

- The *User( )* built-in function is now called *CurrentUser( )*. Microsoft Access version 2.0 still attempts to support references to *User( )* within the proper context.

- Many objects and collections now support a Name property. You must be careful to use the correct syntax in code when referring to the Name property rather than to a Name object or a field in the object or the collection.
- Microsoft Access version 1.x allowed you to perform a Save Record menu command on a form even if the data in the form had not changed. Version 2.0 generates an error. Be sure to check the Dirty property of the form before using Save Record.
- Version 1.x supported a CancelEvent in the OnClose dialog box of a form. You must now use CancelEvent in the OnUnload dialog box. OnClose no longer supports a cancel. The conversion utility correctly changes OnClose to OnUnload in most cases.
- Version 1.x allowed you to specify the default value of a text field without double quotation marks. You must now enclose all text default values in double quotation marks. The conversion utility adds double quotation marks in most cases.
- Many more query fields are updatable in version 2.0. For example, if you do not want to allow certain fields on the "one" side of a query to be updatable in a form, you must set the form controls to Locked=Yes in version 2.0.
- In version 1.x, the Visible property of a control on a form mapped to the hidden property of that control in Datasheet view. Version 2.0 supports a separate ColumnHidden property for datasheets. If you want a column hidden in both Form view and Datasheet view, you must now set both properties to False.

B

Sample Database Schemas

This appendix contains two categories of information. First, it contains the table designs for the PROMPT sample database (a database for a company named Prompt Computer Solutions, Inc.). These are the tables you use to develop a full database application as you work through the chapters of this book. The whole database, with its tables and sample data, is also on the companion disk included with this book. (See "Using the Companion Disk" on page xxiv.)

The second category of information in this appendix is a series of four database schemas. These schemas contain the table designs that you can use as the foundation for the following types of databases:

- Music collection or music store database
- Cooking or restaurant database
- Bookstore database
- Human resources database

The Prompt Computer Solutions Database—PROMPT

This section contains the table designs for the PROMPT sample database application. The PROMPT database is used in the examples throughout this book. Before building these tables, you should be familiar with Chapter 5 ("Building Your Database in Microsoft Access") and Chapter 6 ("Modifying Your Database Design") of this book.

> **NOTE:** If you copy these tables and the data from the companion disk, please note that the companies, names, and data used in the PROMPT database are fictitious.

Figure B-1 depicts the PROMPT database schema. It shows the field lists for the 10 PROMPT tables. The names of the tables are shown in the title bars of the field lists. The relationships between the tables are shown in the table at the top of the facing page:

First Table	Relationship	Second Table
Customer	One-to-many	Order
Order	One-to-many, cascade	OrderItem
Catalog	One-to-many	OrderItem
Catalog	One-to-many, cascade	CatalogComponent
Component	One-to-many	CatalogComponent
Supplier	One-to-many	CatalogComponent
SalesRep	One-to-many	Order
Type	One-to-many	Catalog
Type	One-to-many	Component
Catalog	One-to-many	MonthlySales

Each table's fields are listed below the title bar. Some lists of fields are too long to be shown in their entirety. Notice that there are lines connecting the field lists. These lines show the relationships between the tables.

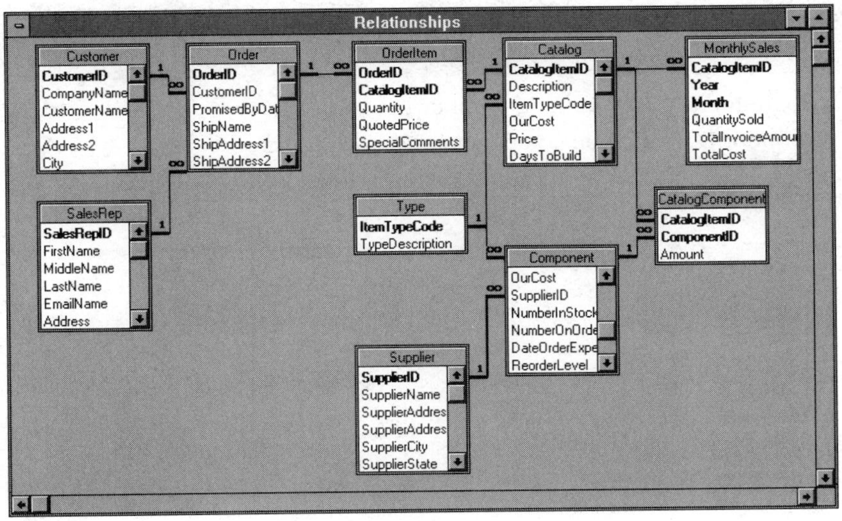

FIGURE B-1.
The PROMPT database schema.

Catalog Table

Field Name	Description	Type	Length	Primary Key
CatalogItemID	Our catalog number	Counter	4	✔
Description	Description of item	Text	50	
ItemTypeCode	Code for type of item	Text	3	
OurCost	Our cost for item	Currency	8	
Price	Normal selling price	Currency	8	
DaysToBuild	Days to build one of these (if constructed by Prompt)	Integer	2	
NumberInStock	Number on hand	Long Integer	4	
Diagram	Picture of item	OLE Object	0	
LongDescription	Extended description of item features	Memo	n/a	

CatalogComponent Table

Field Name	Description	Type	Length	Primary Key
CatalogItemID	Our catalog number	Long Integer	4	✔
ComponentID	Unique component ID	Long Integer	4	✔
Amount	Amount of this component in item	Integer	2	

Component Table

Field Name	Description	Type	Length	Primary Key
ComponentID	Unique component ID	Counter	4	✔
Description	Description of item	Text	50	
Manufacturer	Item manufacturer	Text	50	
Manufacturer-ItemCode	Manufacturer's catalog code	Text	20	
ItemTypeCode	Code for type of item	Text	3	
OurCost	Our cost for item	Currency	8	
SupplierID	ID of regular supplier of component	Long Integer	4	
NumberInStock	Number on hand	Long Integer	4	
NumberOnOrder	Number on order	Long Integer	4	
DateOrder-Expected	When next order will arrive	Date/Time	8	
ReorderLevel	Reorder when stock drops below this value	Long Integer	4	
Economic-OrderQty	Best amount to order at one time	Long Integer	4	
LongDescription	Extended description of item features	Memo	n/a	

Customer Table

Field Name	Description	Type	Length	Primary Key
CustomerID	Customer ID	Counter	4	✔
CompanyName	Customer company name	Text	30	
CustomerName	Name of company contact	Text	25	
Address1	Street address line 1	Text	30	
Address2	Street address line 2	Text	30	
City	City	Text	20	
State	State or province	Text	12	
PostalCode	Zip or postal zone code	Text	10	
Country	Country name	Text	6	
PhoneNumber	Phone number	Text	20	
FaxNumber	Fax machine number	Text	20	
CreditLimit	Maximum credit allowed	Currency	8	
AmountOwed	Total amount owed	Currency	8	
LastPayDate	Date of last payment	Date/Time	8	

MonthlySales Table

Field Name	Description	Type	Length	Primary Key
CatalogItemID	Our catalog number	Long Integer	4	✔
Year	Year of sale	Integer	2	✔
Month	Month of sale	Integer	2	✔
QuantitySold	Total sold in month	Long Integer	4	
TotalInvoice-Amount	Total invoiced for item	Currency	8	
TotalCost	Total cost for item	Currency	8	

Order Table

Field Name	Description	Type	Length	Primary Key
OrderID	Unique order ID	Counter	4	✔
CustomerID	Key to Customer table	Long Integer	4	
PromisedByDate	Date order was promised to be ready	Date/Time	8	
ShipName	Name of person or company to receive shipment	Text	50	
ShipAddress1	Street address only (no post-office box allowed)	Text	30	
ShipAddress2	Street address only (no post-office box allowed)	Text	30	
ShipCity	Shipping city	Text	50	
ShipState	Shipping state or province	Text	50	
ShipPostalCode	Shipping zip or postal code	Text	20	
ShipCountry	Shipping country	Text	50	
SalesRepID	ID of rep placing order	Long Integer	4	
OrderDate	Date order was placed	Date/Time	8	
ShipDate	Date order was shipped/installed	Date/Time	8	
SubtotalCost	Cost of items in the order	Currency	8	
Discount	Discount % on this order	Double	8	
SalesTaxPercent	Tax % for order	Double	8	
SalesTax	Total sales tax for order	Currency	8	
FreightCharge	Shipping charge for order	Currency	8	
CustomerPO	Customer purchase order number (if any)	Text	15	
Terms	Payment terms	Text	20	
Invoiced	Flag to indicate whether order has been invoiced	Yes/No	1	
AmountPaid	Amount paid to date	Currency	8	
DatePaid	Date of last payment	Date/Time	8	
Notes	Special notes about order	Memo	n/a	

OrderItem Table

Field Name	Description	Type	Length	Primary Key
OrderID	Unique order ID	Long Integer	4	✔
CatalogItemID	Our catalog number	Long Integer	4	✔
Quantity	Amount ordered	Integer	2	
QuotedPrice	Price quoted for order	Currency	8	
SpecialComments	Any special terms quoted to customer	Memo	n/a	

SalesRep Table

Field Name	Description	Type	Length	Primary Key
SalesRepID	Unique sales rep ID	Counter	4	✔
FirstName	Sales rep first name	Text	50	
MiddleName	Sales rep middle name/initial	Text	30	
LastName	Sales rep last name	Text	50	
EmailName	Sales rep electronic mail name	Text	50	
Address	Address	Text	255	
City	City	Text	50	
State	State	Text	50	
Zip	Zip	Text	20	
HomePhone	Home phone number	Text	30	
Pager	Pager/car phone number	Text	50	

Supplier Table

Field Name	Description	Type	Length	Primary Key
SupplierID	Unique supplier ID	Counter	4	✔
SupplierName	Supplier name	Text	50	
SupplierAddress1	Supplier address line 1	Text	50	
SupplierAddress2	Supplier address line 2	Text	50	
SupplierCity	Supplier city name	Text	50	
SupplierState	Supplier state code	Text	2	
SupplierPostal	Supplier postal or zip code	Text	10	
SupplierPhone	Supplier phone number	Text	11	
SupplierFax	Supplier fax number	Text	11	
OwedToSupplier	Amount currently owed to this supplier	Currency	8	
DatePaymentDue	Date of next payment	Date/Time	8	
PaymentAmount	Amount of next payment	Currency	8	

Type Table

Field Name	Description	Type	Length	Primary Key
ItemTypeCode	Item type code	Text	3	✔
TypeDescription	Description for class of items	Text	100	

Music Collection or Music Store Database

You can use the Music database for keeping track of your favorite recordings. It can also serve as the basis for an inventory database for a music store. The relationships between tables are shown in Figure B-2 on the next page.

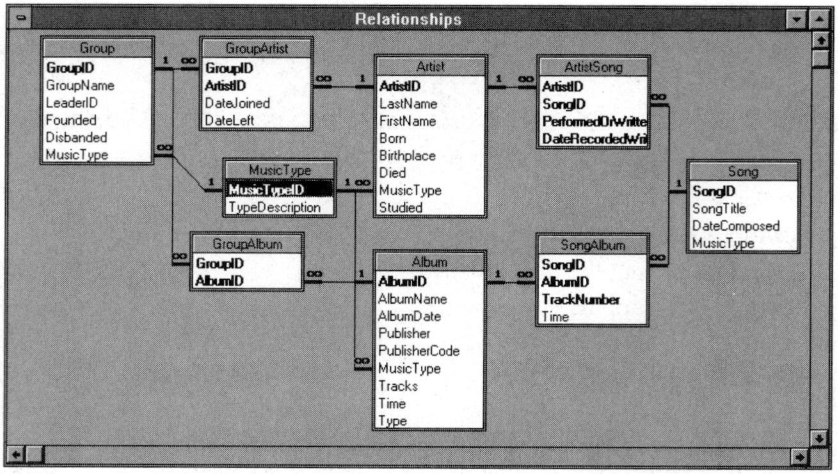

FIGURE B-2.
The Music database schema.

Album Table

Field Name	Description	Type	Length	Primary Key
AlbumID	Unique ID of album	Counter	4	✔
AlbumName	Name of album	Text	50	
AlbumDate	Date album was published	Date/Time	8	
Publisher	Name of album publisher	Text	50	
PublisherCode	Publisher's item number	Text	20	
MusicType	Main type of music on album	Long Integer	4	
Tracks	Number of tracks on album	Integer	2	
Time	Total running time in minutes	Double	8	
Type	Media type: C = CD, T = Tape, V = Vinyl disc	Text	1	

Artist Table

Field Name	Description	Type	Length	Primary Key
ArtistID	Unique ID of artist	Counter	4	✔
LastName	Artist's last name	Text	25	
FirstName	Artist's title, first name, etc.	Text	25	
Born	Artist's birth date	Date/Time	8	
Birthplace	Place artist was born	Text	50	
Died	Date artist died	Date/Time	8	
MusicType	Main type of music for artist	Long Integer	4	
Studied	Place where artist studied music	Text	50	

ArtistSong Table

Field Name	Description	Type	Length	Primary Key
ArtistID	Unique ID of artist	Long Integer	4	✔
SongID	Unique ID of song	Long Integer	4	✔
PerformedOr-Written	P = Artist performed this song; W = Artist wrote this song	Text	1	✔
DateRecorded-Written	Date artist recorded or wrote this song	Date/Time	8	✔

Group Table

Field Name	Description	Type	Length	Primary Key
GroupID	Unique ID of group	Counter	4	✔
GroupName	Name of group or orchestra	Text	50	
LeaderID	ID of lead artist (or conductor)	Long Integer	4	
Founded	Date group was founded	Date/Time	8	
Disbanded	Date group disbanded (or changed leader)	Date/Time	8	
MusicType	Main type of music produced by group	Long Integer	4	

GroupAlbum Table

Field Name	Description	Type	Length	Primary Key
GroupID	Unique ID of group	Long Integer	4	✔
AlbumID	Unique ID of album	Long Integer	4	✔

GroupArtist Table

Field Name	Description	Type	Length	Primary Key
GroupID	ID of group	Long Integer	4	✔
ArtistID	ID of artist	Long Integer	4	✔
DateJoined	Date artist joined the group	Date/Time	8	✔
DateLeft	Date artist left the group	Date/Time	8	

MusicType Table

Field Name	Description	Type	Length	Primary Key
MusicTypeID	Unique ID for music type	Counter	4	✔
TypeDescription	Description of music type	Text	30	

Song Table

Field Name	Description	Type	Length	Primary Key
SongID	Unique ID of song	Counter	4	✔
SongTitle	Name of song	Text	50	
DateComposed	Date song was written	Date/Time	8	
MusicType	Type of music of song	Long Integer	4	

SongAlbum Table

Field Name	Description	Type	Length	Primary Key
SongID	ID of song	Long Integer	4	✔
AlbumID	ID of album	Long Integer	4	✔
TrackNumber	Track number on album that contains song	Long Integer	4	✔
Time	Length of song on album in minutes	Double	8	

Cooking or Restaurant Database

You can use the Cooking or Restaurant database to keep a record of your favorite recipes or to keep records if you run a restaurant. The relationships between the tables are shown in Figure B-3.

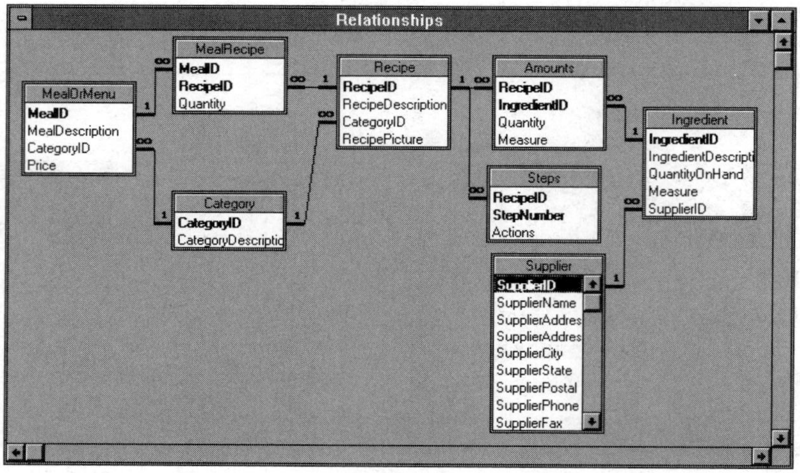

FIGURE B-3.
The Cooking or Restaurant database schema.

Amounts Table

Field Name	Description	Type	Length	Primary Key
RecipeID	ID of recipe that this amount applies to	Long Integer	4	✔
IngredientID	ID of ingredient	Long Integer	4	✔
Quantity	Amount of ingredient required for recipe	Double	8	
Measure	Measurement type (tbs., tsp., lb., cup, etc.)	Text	10	

Category Table

Field Name	Description	Type	Length	Primary Key
CategoryID	Unique ID of category	Counter	4	✔
Category-Description	Description: Breakfast, Brunch, Lunch, Dinner; Meat, Poultry, Seafood, Salad, Appetizer, etc.	Text	50	

Ingredient Table

Field Name	Description	Type	Length	Primary Key
IngredientID	Unique ID of ingredient	Counter	4	✔
Ingredient-Description	Description of ingredient	Text	50	
QuantityOnHand	Amount in stock	Double	8	
Measure	Normal measure (tbs., tsp., lb., cup, etc.)	Text	10	
SupplierID	ID of usual supplier of ingredient	Long Integer	4	

MealOrMenu Table

Field Name	Description	Type	Length	Primary Key
MealID	Unique ID of this meal	Counter	4	✔
MealDescription	Full description of meal	Memo	n/a	
CategoryID	Category of meal	Long Integer	4	
Price	Price of meal if a restaurant	Currency	8	

MealRecipe Table

Field Name	Description	Type	Length	Primary Key
MealID	Link to MealOrMenu table	Long Integer	4	✔
RecipeID	Link to Recipe table	Long Integer	4	✔
Quantity	Serving size of recipe in meal	Integer	2	

Recipe Table

Field Name	Description	Type	Length	Primary Key
RecipeID	Unique ID of recipe	Counter	4	✔
Recipe-Description	Description of recipe	Text	255	
CategoryID	Category of recipe	Long Integer	4	
RecipePicture	Picture of prepared dish	OLE Object	n/a	

Steps Table

Field Name	Description	Type	Length	Primary Key
RecipeID	Recipe that uses this step	Long Integer	4	✔
StepNumber	Step number in recipe	Long Integer	4	✔
Actions	Description of what to do	Memo	n/a	

Supplier Table

Field Name	Description	Type	Length	Primary Key
SupplierID	Unique ID for supplier	Counter	4	✔
SupplierName	Supplier name	Text	50	
SupplierAddress1	Supplier address line 1	Text	50	
SupplierAddress2	Supplier address line 2	Text	50	
SupplierCity	Supplier city name	Text	50	
SupplierState	Supplier state code	Text	2	
SupplierPostal	Supplier zip or postal code	Text	10	
SupplierPhone	Supplier phone number	Text	11	
SupplierFax	Supplier fax number	Text	11	
OwedToSupplier	Amount currently owed to supplier	Currency	8	
DatePaymentDue	Date of next payment	Date/Time	8	
PaymentAmount	Amount of next payment	Currency	8	

Bookstore Database

You can use the Bookstore database as the basis for a bookstore database application, or you can use it to save information about each book in your personal library. The relationships between the tables are shown in Figure B-4 on the next page.

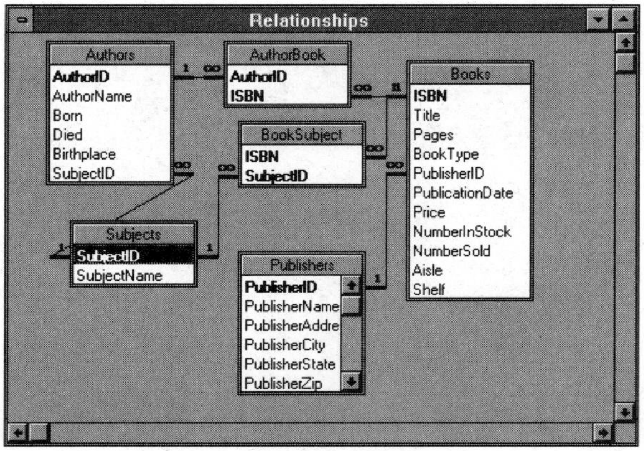

FIGURE B-4.

The Bookstore database schema.

AuthorBook Table

Field Name	Description	Type	Length	Primary Key
AuthorID	Link to Authors table	Long Integer	4	✔
ISBN	Link to Books table	Long Integer	4	✔

Authors Table

Field Name	Description	Type	Length	Primary Key
AuthorID	Unique ID of author	Long Integer	4	✔
AuthorName	Name of author	Text	50	
Born	Date author was born	Date/Time	8	
Died	Date author died	Date/Time	8	
Birthplace	Author's place of birth	Text	100	
SubjectID	Author's main subject specialty	Long Integer	4	

Books Table

Field Name	Description	Type	Length	Primary Key
ISBN	Unique ID of book	Long Integer	4	✔
Title	Title of book	Text	110	
Pages	Number of pages	Long Integer	4	
BookType	P = Paperback; H = Hardback; T = Trade paperback	Text	1	
PublisherID	ID of publisher	Long Integer	4	
PublicationDate	Date of first publication	Date/Time	8	
Price	Cover price	Currency	8	
NumberInStock	Number in inventory	Long Integer	4	
NumberSold	Number sold to date	Long Integer	4	
Aisle	Aisle ID in bookstore	Text	5	
Shelf	Shelf number	Integer	2	

BookSubject Table

Field Name	Description	Type	Length	Primary Key
ISBN	Link to Books table	Long Integer	4	✔
SubjectID	Link to Subjects table	Long Integer	4	✔

Publishers Table

Field Name	Description	Type	Length	Primary Key
PublisherID	ID of publisher	Counter	4	✔
PublisherName	Name of publisher	Text	50	
PublisherAddress	Street address	Text	50	
PublisherCity	City name	Text	30	
PublisherState	State	Text	2	
PublisherZip	Zip or postal code	Text	12	
PublisherPhone	Phone number	Text	12	

Subjects Table Definition

Field Name	Description	Type	Length	Primary Key
SubjectID	Unique ID of subject	Counter	4	✔
SubjectName	Description of subject area	Text	120	

Human Resources Database

You can use the Human Resources database to provide the skeleton for a human resources application. The relationships between the tables are shown in Figure B-5.

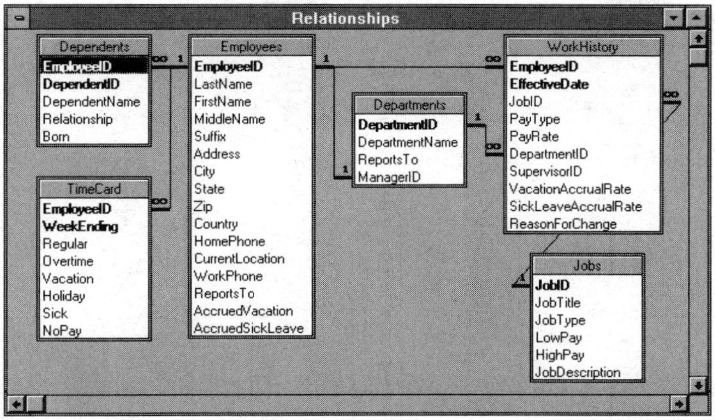

FIGURE B-5.

The Human Resources database schema.

Departments Table

Field Name	Description	Type	Length	Primary Key
DepartmentID	Unique ID of department	Counter	4	✔
DepartmentName	Name of department	Text	50	
ReportsTo	Self-link	Long Integer	4	
SupervisorID	Link to Employees table	Long Integer	4	

Dependents Table

Field Name	Description	Type	Length	Primary Key
EmployeeID	Link to Employees table	Long Integer	4	✔
DependentID	Unique ID of dependent	Double	8	✔
DependentName	Name of dependent	Text	50	
Relationship	Relationship of dependent	Text	50	
Born	Birth date of dependent	Date/Time	8	

Employees Table

Field Name	Description	Type	Length	Primary Key
EmployeeID	Unique ID of employee	Counter	4	✔
LastName	Employee last name	Text	25	
FirstName	Employee first name	Text	25	
MiddleName	Employee middle name	Text	25	
Suffix	Jr., Sr., III, Ph.D., etc.	Text	10	
Address	Street address	Text	40	
City	City name	Text	30	
State	State	Text	2	
Zip	Zip or postal code	Text	11	
Country	Country	Text	25	
HomePhone	Home phone number	Text	12	
CurrentLocation	Current location ID	Text	30	
WorkPhone	Work phone number	Text	12	
ReportsTo	Self-referencing key	Long Integer	4	
AccruedVacation	Number of hours of vacation available	Double	8	
AccruedSick-Leave	Number of hours of sick leave available	Double	8	

Jobs Table

Field Name	Description	Type	Length	Primary Key
JobID	Unique ID of job	Counter	4	✔
JobTitle	Title of job	Text	50	
JobType	E = Exempt; N = Nonexempt	Text	50	
LowPay	Bottom of normal pay range	Currency	8	
HighPay	Top of normal pay range	Currency	8	
JobDescription	Full description of job	Memo	n/a	

TimeCard Table

Field Name	Description	Type	Length	Primary Key
EmployeeID	Link to Employees table	Long Integer	4	✔
WeekEnding	Week ending date	Date/Time	8	✔
Regular	Regular hours	Double	8	
Overtime	Overtime hours	Double	8	
Vacation	Vacation hours	Double	8	
Holiday	Holiday hours	Double	8	
Sick	Sick leave hours	Double	8	
NoPay	Time off without pay	Double	8	

WorkHistory Table

Field Name	Description	Type	Length	Primary Key
EmployeeID	Link to Employees table	Long Integer	4	✔
EffectiveDate	Date position effective	Date/Time	8	✔
JobID	Link to Jobs table (0 = Termination record)	Long Integer	4	
PayType	H = Hourly; S = Salaried; T = Temp hourly	Text	1	
PayRate	H, T = Hourly pay; S = Monthly pay	Currency	8	
DepartmentID	ID of department where working	Long Integer	4	
SupervisorID	Link to Employees table	Long Integer	4	
Vacation-AccrualRate	Hours per pay period	Double	8	
SickLeave-AccrualRate	Hours per pay period	Double	8	
ReasonFor-Change	New hire, Raise, Promotion, Transfer, etc.	Text	25	

Index

Note: *Italicized* page numbers refer to figures.

Special Characters

A

D

F

G

H

K

L

M

O

P

R

S

T

U

V

W

X

Y

Z

Notes

Notes

John L. Viescas is an independent database consultant with more than 20 years of database design consulting experience. John has lectured at conferences and user group meetings around the world, including highly rated sessions of Microsoft Access at the Microsoft Tech*Ed conferences. He has also written numerous articles for magazines such as *Smart Access* and *Access Advisor*. He was recognized in 1993 and again in 1994 as a Most Valuable Professional by Microsoft Product Support Services. He graduated *cum laude* from the University of Texas at Dallas with a degree in business finance. He resides in Redmond, Washington, with his wife and one of their seven children.

The manuscript for this book was prepared and submitted to Microsoft Press in electronic form. Text files were prepared using Microsoft Word 2 for Windows. Pages were composed by Microsoft Press using PageMaker 5 for Windows, with text in Garamond and display type in Avant Garde Demi. Composed pages were delivered to the printer as electronic prepress files.

Cover Designer
Rebecca Geisler

Interior Graphic Designers
Kim Eggleston, Carolyn Davids, Lynne Faulk

Illustrator
Mark Monlux

Interior Electronic Artist
Lisa Sandburg

Principal Typographer
Jeannie McGivern

Principal Editorial Compositor
John Sugg

Principal Proofreader/Copy Editor
Deborah Long

Indexer
Shane-Armstrong Information Systems

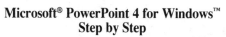

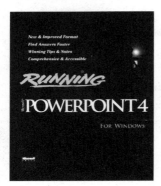

Desktop Companions

If you want quick answers to your questions, look no further than the handy new Field Guides from Microsoft Press. Field Guides are arranged by tasks and organized in easy-to-use, and easy-to-remember sections with rich cross-referencing for easy lookup. They include tips, procedures, hints for troubleshooting, definitions, and command descriptions. Look for the friendly guy in the pith helmet who leads you through from start to finish.

Field Guide to
Microsoft Access® for Windows™
Covers latest version
Stephen L. Nelson
208 pages, softcover 4¾ x 8 $9.95 ($12.95 Canada)
ISBN 1-55615-581-6
Available April 1994

Field Guide to
Microsoft® Excel 5 for Windows™
Stephen L. Nelson
208 pages, softcover 4¾ x 8 $9.95 ($12.95 Canada)
ISBN 1-55615-579-4

Field Guide to
Microsoft® Word 6 for Windows™
Stephen L. Nelson
208 pages, softcover 4¾ x 8 $9.95 ($12.95 Canada)
ISBN 1-55615-577-8

Field Guide to
Microsoft® Windows™ 3.1
Stephen L. Nelson
208 pages, softcover 4¾ x 8 $9.95 ($12.95 Canada)
ISBN 1-55615-640-5

Microsoft*Press*

Microsoft Press® books are available wherever quality books are sold and through CompuServe's Electronic Mall—GO MSP.
Call 1-800-MSPRESS for direct ordering information or for placing credit card orders.*
Please refer to BBK when placing your order. Prices subject to change.

*In Canada, contact Macmillan Canada, Attn: Microsoft Press Dept., 164 Commander Blvd., Agincourt, Ontario, Canada M1S 3C7, or call (416) 293-8464, ext. 340.
Outside the U.S. and Canada, write to International Sales, Microsoft Press, One Microsoft Way, Redmond, WA 98052-6399.

Building Forms with a Form Wizard

Forms allow you to customize how you view and work with your data. Even if you're a novice at form design, you can use a Form Wizard to create forms so that you can begin to work with your data.

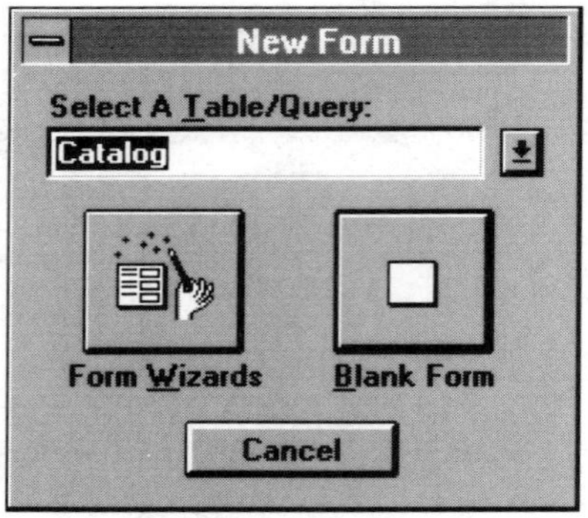

Step 1:

Choose the table or query that selects the data you want to display.

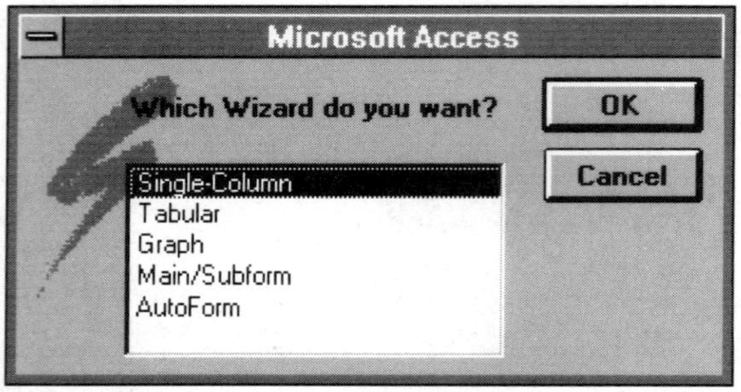

Step 2:

Select the type of form you need.

Step 3:

Select the fields you want on your form.

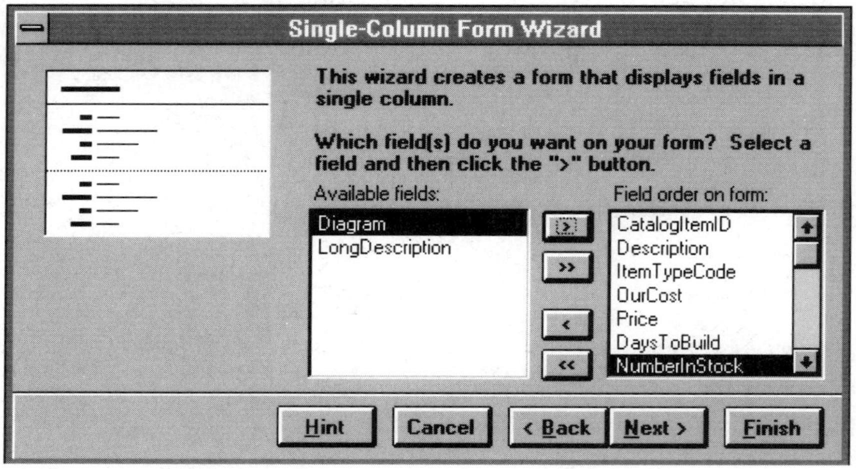

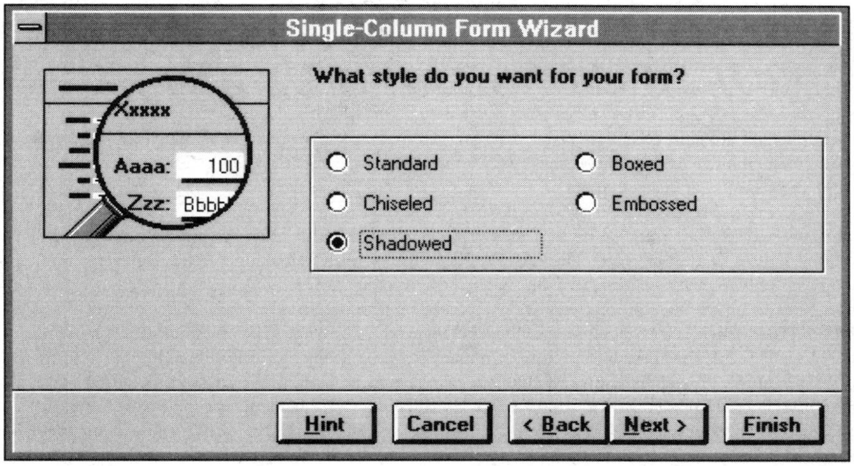

Step 4:
Select the "look" for your form.

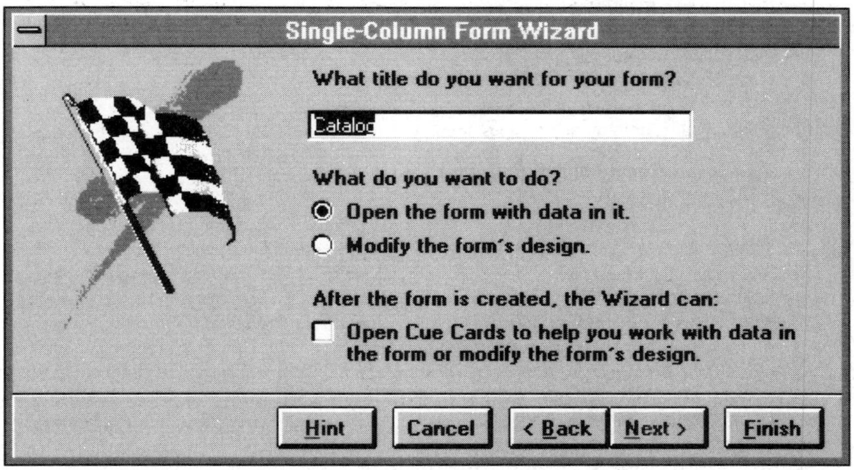

Step 5:
Give your form a name, and decide whether you want to make additional changes to the form.

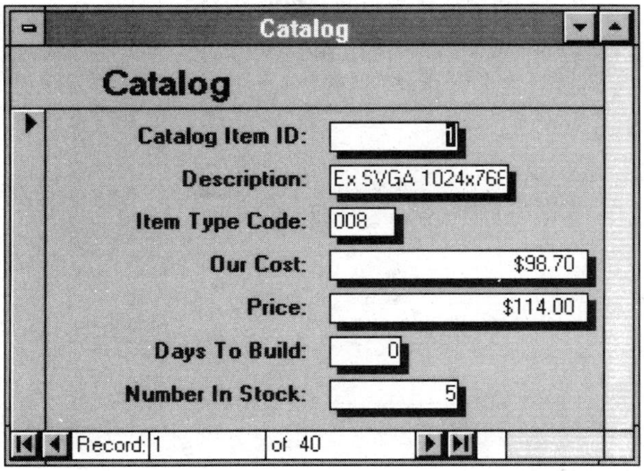

Step 6:
Presto! You can begin working with data on your new form.

IMPORTANT— READ CAREFULLY BEFORE OPENING SOFTWARE PACKET(S). By opening the sealed packet(s) containing the software, you indicate your acceptance of the following Microsoft License Agreement.

MICROSOFT LICENSE AGREEMENT

(Book Companion Disks)

This is a legal agreement between you (either an individual or an entity) and Microsoft Corporation. By opening the sealed software packet(s) you are agreeing to be bound by the terms of this agreement. If you do not agree to the terms of this agreement, promptly return the unopened software packet(s) and any accompanying written materials to the place you obtained them for a full refund.

MICROSOFT SOFTWARE LICENSE

1. GRANT OF LICENSE. Microsoft grants to you the right to use one copy of the Microsoft software program included with this book (the "SOFTWARE") on a single terminal connected to a single computer. The SOFTWARE is in "use" on a computer when it is loaded into the temporary memory (i.e., RAM) or installed into the permanent memory (e.g., hard disk, CD-ROM, or other storage device) of that computer. You may not network the SOFTWARE or otherwise use it on more than one computer or computer terminal at the same time.

2. COPYRIGHT. The SOFTWARE is owned by Microsoft or its suppliers and is protected by United States copyright laws and international treaty provisions. Therefore, you must treat the SOFTWARE like any other copyrighted material (e.g., a book or musical recording) except that you may either (a) make one copy of the SOFTWARE solely for backup or archival purposes, or (b) transfer the SOFTWARE to a single hard disk provided you keep the original solely for backup or archival purposes. You may not copy the written materials accompanying the SOFTWARE.

3. OTHER RESTRICTIONS. You may not rent or lease the SOFTWARE, but you may transfer the SOFTWARE and accompanying written materials on a permanent basis provided you retain no copies and the recipient agrees to the terms of this Agreement. You may not reverse engineer, decompile, or disassemble the SOFTWARE. If the SOFTWARE is an update or has been updated, any transfer must include the most recent update and all prior versions.

4. DUAL MEDIA SOFTWARE. If the SOFTWARE package contains both 3.5" and 5.25" disks, then you may use only the disks appropriate for your single-user computer. You may not use the other disks on another computer or loan, rent, lease, or transfer them to another user except as part of the permanent transfer (as provided above) of all SOFTWARE and written materials.

5. SAMPLE CODE. If the SOFTWARE includes Sample Code, then Microsoft grants you a royalty-free right to reproduce and distribute the sample code of the SOFTWARE provided that you: (a) distribute the sample code only in conjunction with and as a part of your software product; (b) do not use Microsoft's or its authors' names, logos, or trademarks to market your software product; (c) include the copyright notice that appears on the SOFTWARE on your product label and as a part of the sign-on message for your software product; and (d) agree to indemnify, hold harmless, and defend Microsoft and its authors from and against any claims or lawsuits, including attorneys' fees, that arise or result from the use or distribution of your software product.

DISCLAIMER OF WARRANTY

The SOFTWARE (including instructions for its use) is provided "AS IS" WITHOUT WARRANTY OF ANY KIND. MICROSOFT FURTHER DISCLAIMS ALL IMPLIED WARRANTIES INCLUDING WITHOUT LIMITATION ANY IMPLIED WARRANTIES OF MERCHANTABILITY OR OF FITNESS FOR A PARTICULAR PURPOSE. THE ENTIRE RISK ARISING OUT OF THE USE OR PERFORMANCE OF THE SOFTWARE AND DOCUMENTATION REMAINS WITH YOU.

IN NO EVENT SHALL MICROSOFT, ITS AUTHORS, OR ANYONE ELSE INVOLVED IN THE CREATION, PRODUCTION, OR DELIVERY OF THE SOFTWARE BE LIABLE FOR ANY DAMAGES WHATSOEVER (INCLUDING, WITHOUT LIMITATION, DAMAGES FOR LOSS OF BUSINESS PROFITS, BUSINESS INTERRUPTION, LOSS OF BUSINESS INFORMATION, OR OTHER PECUNIARY LOSS) ARISING OUT OF THE USE OF OR INABILITY TO USE THE SOFTWARE OR DOCUMENTATION, EVEN IF MICROSOFT HAS BEEN ADVISED OF THE POSSIBILITY OF SUCH DAMAGES. BECAUSE SOME STATES/COUNTRIES DO NOT ALLOW THE EXCLUSION OR LIMITATION OF LIABILITY FOR CONSEQUENTIAL OR INCIDENTAL DAMAGES, THE ABOVE LIMITATION MAY NOT APPLY TO YOU.

U.S. GOVERNMENT RESTRICTED RIGHTS

The SOFTWARE and documentation are provided with RESTRICTED RIGHTS. Use, duplication, or disclosure by the Government is subject to restrictions as set forth in subparagraph (c)(1)(ii) of The Rights in Technical Data and Computer Software clause at DFARS 252.227-7013 or subparagraphs (c)(1) and (2) of the Commercial Computer Software — Restricted Rights 48 CFR 52.227-19, as applicable. Manufacturer is Microsoft Corporation, One Microsoft Way, Redmond, WA 98052-6399.

If you acquired this product in the United States, this Agreement is governed by the laws of the State of Washington.

Should you have any questions concerning this Agreement, or if you desire to contact Microsoft Press for any reason, please write: Microsoft Press, One Microsoft Way, Redmond, WA 98052-6399.